AMERICAN
Zoom

AMERICAN
Zoom

Stock Car Racing— from the Dirt Tracks to Daytona

Peter Golenbock

Macmillan USA

Macmillan General Reference
A Simon & Schuster Macmillan Company
1633 Broadway
New York, NY 10019-6785

Library of Congress Cataloging-in-Publication Data

Golenbock, Peter, 1946–
    American zoom : stock car racing—from the dirt tracks to Daytona
/ Peter Golenbock—1st Paperback ed.
        p.   cm.
    Includes index.
    ISBN 0-02-032782-X (pbk.)
    1. Stock car racing—United States.   I. Title.
    GV1029.9.S74G65   1994
    796.7'2'0973—dc20   94-14944   CIP

Manufactured in the United States of America

First Paperback Edition 1994

10   9   8   7   6   5   4

To my boy,
Charles Eliot Golenbock

CONTENTS

ACKNOWLEDGMENTS

Before I began doing interviews for this book, I had an overriding concern. A few years earlier I wrote *Personal Fouls,* which caused the very popular (but Machiavellian) Jim Valvano to lose his job coaching basketball at North Carolina State. My concern was that loyaly to Valvano would run throughout the entire state, or that since *Personal Fouls* was an exposé, people in racing might fear I was writing an exposé about them and that, as a result of this concern, I would find myself writing about NASCAR without a helmet, a seat belt, or a ride.

Would anyone talk to me? It's a question I ask myself before every book. It's why starting any book is always an adventure. I was a stranger coming into NASCAR. Ahead of me loomed an unsettling uncertainty. Nothing was known.

A friend of mine from the sadly missed St. Petersburg Pelican senior baseball team, Charles Yancey, was starting a company making a suntan lotion called Sportique. It comes in a yellow and white tube, and Charles's idea was to put the design on Joe Gibbs's new race car for the '92 Daytona 500.

Charles was kind enough to give me the name of the man who was putting the deal together, Bill Averitt. Charles arranged for the three of us to have lunch, and we did.

Bill told me he had gone to North Carolina State. He searched my face for a reaction. I gulped. He then laughed. He said he had stopped caring about N.C. State basketball long ago. He said he felt what I had written was right.

Bill generously provided me with the list of his contacts in NASCAR. At the top of his list were Ed Carroll, the general manager of the Joe

Gibbs race team, whom he had been dealing with, and Bob Tomlinson, the general manager of the Bob Whitcomb race team, whom he had known since he was a kid.

By phone, I made arrangements to meet with Ed Carroll and Bob Tomlinson and flew to Charlotte, where it turns out almost every major race team is located. My original plan had been to spend time with three or four race teams as they prepared for the Daytona 500 of 1992. I figured that with the cooperation of Ed Carroll and Bob Tomlinson, I was halfway there.

I arrived at the office of Joe Gibbs racing, late, only to discover that Ed Carroll had not received permission to talk to me from Joe Gibbs. I would have to wait till he arranged approval.

It was an inauspicious start. But Carroll, who expressed enthusiasm about the project, advised me not to worry. The man to see in the interim, he said, was Tom Cotter.

Several times Carroll told me, ''Go see Tom Cotter,'' without telling me anything more about him. ''You *need* to see him.''

Experience has taught me that when someone gives you friendly advice, take it. I called the genial Tom Cotter and drove ten minutes from the Gibbs race shop on Harris Boulevard over to Cotter's office on Clark Street.

Tom Cotter, who runs his own public relations firm, had several years earlier been on the public relations staff of the Charlotte Motor Speedway. Tom, who embraced my project wholeheartedly, knew *everybody*.

He offered me access to his entire Rolodex file, which for a writer is two legs up in getting the job done. Then he offered to call the race teams for me. Who did I want to interview?

I wanted to hug him. Not having to cold-call sources was a first. Take my advice: If anyone in or out of racing needs a PR expert to help lead the way to happiness, call Tom Cotter. His intelligence, kindness, and enthusiasm will work magic.

Grateful, I told Tom I would start with his clients. He represented Junior Johnson's Maxwell House race team, and Tri-Star's Country Time Lemonade Drink team, as well as the Gwaltney Busch circuit team and the Mazda race team in IMSA.

I arranged to meet with Junior and then with George Bradshaw of the Country Time team. Tom called team owner Chuck Rider and set up a meeting with the Bahari race team. He arranged a meeting with Felix Sabates of SABCO, and then he called Richard Petty, who said the only time he had in his hectic schedule was that day at five at his condo by the speedway. Could I come then?

I was speechless. Ed Carroll could not have been wiser about going to see Tom Cotter. And so Richard Petty, The King, became the first interview for this book. I was pinching myself. It was like writing a book about the old New York Yankees and starting with Mickey Mantle. In baseball, the stars are always the hardest to pin down. For my first book, *Dynasty,* I had had to chase Mantle halfway across the continent before finally catching up with him.

But here was Richard Petty, *the* star, readily agreeing to let some stranger from some other world invade his home and ask him questions for an hour and a half. I've been around professional sports all my life, and I couldn't believe it.

Furthermore, when I asked Richard a hard question, he gave me an honest answer. I had done my homework, and he knew I was looking for history, not pablum. Like most of the men interviewed for this book, he seemed to hold back very little.

And so, my initial fears turned out to be baseless. What I discovered was that the men involved in racing had but one concern. As George Bradshaw, the owner of the Tri Star race team, said to me, "Promise me you're not writing another *Days of Thunder.*"

That movie, starring Tom Cruise, had misrepresented several aspects of racing, making it seem, for instance, that race cars are built in old barns and that cars can get smashed up during the Daytona 500 and still come back to win. Bradshaw understood that the moviemakers had taken license with reality in order to enhance the drama, but it bothered him deeply. He loved his sport, and he hated for Hollywood to somehow misrepresent it. I assured him that *American Zoom* would stick to racing history and that the quality of this book would hinge on the collective memories and anecdotes of the participants.

"If you can do that, racing will thank you," Bradshaw said.

It is I who have to do the thanking. I give thanks for having had the opportunity to get to know firsthand the beauty of North Carolina. The winding drive from Charlotte through the wooded mountains to Asheville was breathtaking. Charlotte is a great city, and nearby Lake Norman provides so much fun for so many people.

Thanks to the guys at the Sandwich Construction Company, a great place to eat and soak in the racing atmosphere, for their hospitality.

Thanks mostly to the racing community—the owners, crew chiefs, mechanics, and racers who shared their time and lives with me. I have never run across professional sportsmen so willing to take a break in incredibly busy schedules to sit and reminisce. I have never seen such dedication or love for one's livelihood. To a man, the subjects in this book embraced what I was attempting to do, and did more than their share to make sure I succeeded in my endeavor.

In addition to the members of the race teams, former car builders Smokey Yunick and Ralph Moody, and Humpy Wheeler, the brilliant Charlotte Motor Speedway czar, shared their lives with me, and I am grateful.

Chip Williams, Bill Seaborn, and Andy Hall of NASCAR, and Jim Foster and Donna Freismuth of the Daytona International Speedway gave their fullest cooperation, both in the research for the manuscript and with tickets and pit passes for the Daytona 500 extravaganza. This book would not have been what it is without their cooperation.

Later Donna and Russ Branham arranged for my four-year-old Charles to meet two of his favorite drivers, Davey Allison and Ernie Irvan. I have never seen the boy's eyes so wide. I never will forget, Ernie asked Charlie, "Do you drive a Ford or a Chevy?"

"A Saab," Charlie said. You had to be there.

Davey and Ernie signed photos for him, and he went home that day a fan for life. His dad had been sold long before.

And so there is an enormous amount of my gratitude to be spread around. It goes out to Pat Allison, Bill Averitt, George Bradshaw, Russ Branham, Ed and Anne Carroll, Cliff Champion, Derrike Cope, Tom and Pat Cotter, and the staff of Cotter Communications—Bob Boyles, Mel Poole, Renee Cobb, John Amon, and Suzanne Lipsiea—Dave Fuge, George Gardner, Andy Hall, Jeff Hammond, Bill Ingle, Jimmy Johnson, Junior Johnson, Dave Marcis, Banjo Matthews, Larry McClure, Larry McReynolds, Ralph Moody, Bud Moore, Andy Petree, Richard Petty, Shelton Pitman, Cliff and Adrienne Powers of Southern Pride Racing in St. Petersburg, Chuck Rider, Felix Sabates, Bill Seaborn, Jr., Kirk Shelmerdine, Bob Tomlinson, Michael Wallace, Michael Waltrip, Bob Whitcomb, Chip Williams, Wayne Williams and Rhea Law, Waddell Wilson, Leonard Wood, Charles Yancey, and Smokey Yunick.

Thanks also to Don Grassmann, for his friendship and his wonderful photos, copyeditor Tom Cherwin, and to Craig Butler and Greg King of WORKplace on Route 19 in St. Pete for saving me and my files after I stupidly shorted out my computer with thousands of hours of transcripts in it.

This book was the brainchild of Tony Seidel and Dave Weiner, and to them, thanks for proposing this idea to me. Thanks too to Macmillan's Rick Wolff, who had a broad enough perspective to realize how huge NASCAR's Winston Cup stock car racing is in America.

I hope this book is everything you three—Tony, David, and Rick—hoped it would be.

Finally, thanks to Neil Reshen, my business manager, and to my wonderful Rhonda B., who indulges my passions, even when they seem foolish or excessive, and to our junior racer, Charles Eliot Golenbock, known in racing circles as "The Chunkster." Look out, Ironhead.

This is a sport that has brought so much joy and sheer fun to our lives. Thank you all. It was an experience of a lifetime.

"Driving a race car is like dancing with a chain saw."
—Cale Yarborough

"The best way to make a small fortune in racing is to start with a big one."
—Junior Johnson

"Those boys playing football get their $2 or $3 million up front, and if they don't have a good day, they are not out anything. They still get paid on Monday. If we don't win, we don't get paid on Monday."
—Richard Petty

"Success [in race car driving] is like surfing: You're doing what you can to stay on the board, but you really aren't in control of anything."
—crew chief Kirk Shelmerdine

AMERICAN
Zoom

Introduction

Twin one-car-at-a-time tunnels lined with corrugated gray sheet metal allow cars to get in and out of the expansive infield and track at the Daytona International Speedway. The opening of The Tunnel, as it is called, looks small from the outside, but it has been the gateway to some of the most exciting stock car racing in history. Every driver who has ever competed here has driven through it.

The Tunnel is as meaningful to stock car fans as the Fenway Park wall or the Wrigley Field ivy are to baseball fans. Adding to the Tunnel's mystique is the phalanx of brusque guards checking entrance documents, the way the Russkies once did when they patrolled Checkpoint Charlie going from East to West Germany. Get through The Tunnel, and you arrive at racing's promised land.

The first time I came to the Daytona International Speedway no one was racing. I wanted to see, feel, and otherwise experience the majesty of the historic raceway without the participants or spectators, like going to Yellowstone Park in the winter when the crowds have gone. I drove up to the guardhouse and showed my credential to the pass inspector. Solemnly he nodded.

I put my car in first gear and slowly headed toward the dark, round opening in the high wall. As the car entered it became very quiet. I could hear the crunching of the tires on the damp asphalt. Above there were water stains on the ceiling. I was alone with my thoughts of all the great racers, living and dead—Fireball Roberts, Curtis Turner, Joe Weatherly, Richard Petty, David Pearson, Darrell Waltrip, Dale Earnhardt, and the rest—who have driven through this passageway on their way to destiny. I felt humbled and sentimental, the way I once had been as a ten-year-old walking the cavernous center field of Yankee Stadium, Mickey Mantle's

1

hallowed turf, touching the sacred monuments to Babe Ruth, Lou Gehrig, and Miller Huggins.

The Tunnel's pathway descended, and I headed down. The car ended its gentle descent and halfway through began heading back up. The bright sun reappeared at the other end of the cement cone. Once out, before me was a huge green and brown field, and beyond it a sizable freshwater lake. Behind the lake was a slim black ribbon, Daytona, which stretched for two and a half miles in a sort of oval. The straightaways were a mile long and the banking of the whole track was so steep that it was hard to walk up it wearing wing tips. A car has to be going 85 miles an hour just to keep from sliding back down the track!

When I saw the glory of the track for the first time, I exhaled. Many years ago I had driven a small German sports car of mine on the Maine Turnpike at 120 miles an hour. I remember the sensation of flying, except the car never left the ground. When President Nixon dropped the national speed limit to 55 miles an hour, my thrill-riding days were over.

I pondered the possibilities. "I bet I could go 160 here," I thought. Of course, to qualify for the Daytona 500, you have to be able to go 180. My thoughts didn't even come close to qualifying.

Looking at the immensity of Daytona, I was feeling much the way I did back in 1973 on the day when Ron Blomberg of the New York Yankees asked me to shag for him. I was in Yankee Stadium at noontime doing research for *Dynasty*, my book on the Yankees. Blomberg and Hal Lanier were taking batting practice, and they needed someone to catch the balls and throw them in.

I borrowed Blomberg's glove and went out to right field. Back then I had thought of myself as a better-than-average softball player. Blomberg hit twenty-five fly balls in my direction. Every one sailed over my head. I was forced to admit to myself that I didn't have the foot speed to catch his line drives. Embarrassed, I finally decided to stand with my back against the right field wall. Only then did I start catching them.

And when it came time to throw the balls in, it took me twelve bounces to get the ball from right field to second base. The pros did it on the fly.

That experience proved to me the huge difference in talent between the pros and the pros-in-their-own-minds. I reminded myself not to even think about thinking about competing on this track. I fought the urge. The reverie of drafting with Richard Petty was irresistible.

If the sport of baseball keeps popping up in this introduction, it's because the two sports are so similar. An Easterner, I grew up believing there was no team sport as exciting, interesting, or worthwhile to follow as baseball, that no team sport had the personalities and stars that baseball had, not football, not basketball, not hockey. Auto racing wasn't even a consideration.

A lot of Easterners still feel that way because of their abject ignorance about Winston Cup stock car racing, which is odd, since there are NASCAR tracks in the East, great Winston Cup venues such as Watkins Glen, the Poconos, Dover, and Loudon, NH.

But the newspapers of the East—the *New York Times,* the *Boston Globe,* the *Philadelphia Inquirer,* to name a few—pretty much ignore Winston Cup racing except to post the results in little type on the transactions page. Their sports editors are stick-and-ball guys, so Winston Cup racing gets less coverage than most team sports, despite the fact that the Goodyear Tire and Rubber Company in 1990 conducted a survey and discovered that a full 26 percent of Americans are race fans, including 14 million women.

For all my friends back East (or West) who aren't exposed to Winston Cup racing, you are missing out on something very special. Every race brings excitement, drama, danger, and heartbreak, as well as an exhilaration that goes with watching sleek, colorful cars rocket at top speeds for hundreds of miles, sometimes only inches apart.

I can't believe I would ever say this, but Winston Cup racing is every bit as great a sport and as much fun to follow as major league baseball. *American Zoom* is my attempt to prove this to you. Before I came to stock car racing, I felt that no other sport provided the lore, drama, and excitement of our national pastime. I have written many books on baseball, because baseball players tell wonderful, interesting stories and have a real passion for the game.

About twenty years ago I interviewed two of the Four Horsemen of Notre Dame for a proposed book on college football. I spent hours trying to find out what was special about their coach, Knute Rockne. All halfback-turned-federal-judge Don Miller could tell me was, "He was a great coach." So much for a book on football.

American Zoom is several books. It is an oral history, told by many of the greats and insiders in the sport of NASCAR racing, who talk about the cars and especially the people who have made racing history. Many of the contributors have competed in the Daytona 500, and they talk about those experiences as well as their highs and lows at NASCAR tracks across this country.

It is also an insider's book. If you want to know what racer Tim Richmond *really* was like, his general manager, Jimmy Johnson, tells you his memories of him. *American Zoom* will tell you about the characters of the sport—Roberts, Weatherly, Lund, and Turner; through the stars of the seventies—Richard Petty, David Pearson, the Allisons, Bobby and Donnie, and Cale Yarborough; down to current-day stars like Waltrip, Earnhardt, Davey Allison, and Ernie Irvan, as their owners, crew chiefs, and team members talk openly about their lives in racing.

I found stock car racing to have interpersonal relations very similar to those in major league baseball. In baseball, there are twenty-some-odd players and one manager. In stock car racing, there is one "player" and twenty-some-odd managers. The relationships needed to succeed are similar. In both sports, it helps greatly if there is teamwork and dedication and if everyone gets along. It doesn't always happen in either sport, and the differences among participants often change history.

Periodically someone will say to me, "Baseball is so boring." Usually if a man says this it is because he couldn't play it as a kid and still holds a grudge, and if it is a woman, it's probably because she wasn't encouraged to play as a youngster. If the person is arrogant about his disdain for baseball, I will then say, "Only boring people find baseball boring." It's not the best way to make new friends.

But I hold the same feeling toward people who feel that way about Winston Cup stock car racing. If baseball is chess with a bat, ball, and glove, stock car racing is chess on wheels. Once you get to know the men in and out of the cars, Sunday afternoons from February to November take on a different tone. Once understood, Winston Cup stock car racing is an utterly captivating sport, peopled by some of the most interesting, funny, warm, witty, disciplined, passionate, and talented participants in all of professional sport.

I have become addicted to the Winston Cup race circuit. I avidly read the weekly newspaper, the *Winston Cup Scene;* I talk on the phone to my racing friends; I collect racing memorabilia. And now that CBS, ESPN, and TNN televise every race, I know I can get my racing fix if I so desire.

I have discovered a whole new world.

The writer Jacques Barzun, in his book *God's Country and Mine,* once wrote, "Whoever wants to know the heart and mind of America had better learn baseball." Jacques, it turns out, was only half right. Any of the millions of Winston Cup racing fans can tell you why.

The Daytona 500 by STP

February 16, 1992

It's the largest picnic in the world. One hundred and fifty thousand race fans were making a pilgrimage to the huge oval in northeastern Florida's fun-and-sun city of Daytona Beach. They came from every state in the union, including Alaska and Hawaii. From arteries heading south out of Georgia and east and north from other parts of Florida, an endless string of motorcars, campers, and RVs exited Highways 4 and 95 and congregated in a vehicular tangle on State Road 92, the concrete pathway leading to the Daytona International Speedway.

The cars, trucks, RVs, and vans had begun arriving seven days before, and through the night before the race they kept coming, a continuous stream of mostly American vehicles that began to fill the entire infield area inside the mammoth track and spread out around the acres of parking space outside. Despite the throng and the inconvenience for those creeping slowly toward their destination, no horns tooted, no fists were raised in frustration. The slow-moving cortege toward the speedway was remarkably incident-free. Most of those who were coming had been there before. Two days after the big race, the race for the next year is sold out. Seats are as hard to get as tickets for a pro football game of one of the stellar NFL franchises like the New York Giants or Washington Redskins, where the only way you can get a seat is if you inherit one. Since these race fans knew prior to setting out what they were in for, no one was fazed by the ordeal of the expedition. They understood that there would be a long wait in traffic but that regardless of how long it took, it would be worth every minute of it.

And for those few who had never seen the track before, their first glimpse would be an eye-opener. One can read that the track is two and a half miles around, and intellectually one knows that is a long distance,

5

but even if you've been to the Rose Bowl or to the Kentucky Derby, the first vision of Daytona brings a whistle or some sort of exclamation, much like when you look across the Grand Canyon or Niagara Falls for the first time.

As your car creeps down State 92, from a distance you can glimpse the tall north stands. You keep going. The stands keep going. There is a dog track—and more stands. There is jai alai, and more stands. There is the tall Winston Tower, for the press and special guests, and more stands. And beyond, the stands keep going. The track is a tri-oval that is 2.5 miles around, and along the front straightaway for about a mile, there are tall stands. Every seat is sold out, and most tickets cost $85. Why were over a hundred thousand mature adults plunking down almost twice as much money as what they would have paid for the cost of the average Broadway play to watch a bunch of cars go around a track? Did they know something the Eastern stick-and-ball sports fan didn't?

From watching the milling crowd wandering slowly around the perimeter of the titanic speedway, anyone could see that the "good old boys" days of stock car racing were long past. These were no redneck, shotgun-toting hillbillies out for an afternoon of drinking and raising hell. Represented here was middle America, husbands and wives holding hands, strolling amid an upbeat carnival atmosphere. It was something like a middle-aged Woodstock, with the same conviviality and shared community, only instead of their love of rock and roll, it was the celebration of fast cars and American tradition.

Surprisingly, perhaps half of the fans were women, and these were not hangers-on attending just to be with their husbands or boyfriends, as one finds at many baseball, football, and basketball events. A lot of women sported the colors of their favorite drivers, and surprisingly their clothing did not always match that of their husband. A Darrell Waltrip fan decked out in Darrell attire walked hand in hand with a woman wearing Bill Elliott's likeness and colors. Another couple, a team arguing for Davey Allison on one T-shirt and Darrell Waltrip on the other, gamboled by.

These couples held hands, despite their differences, unashamedly expressing their freedom of choice. Only the Dale Earnhardt couples matched. Why was this? Perhaps Earnhardt men, emotional and rabid about their hero, refuse to allow their wives or girlfriends to root against him. Perhaps Earnhardt-type men are only attracted to Earnhardt-type women.

Watching the spectators mill about, it was clear that the Daytona 500 was not only a sporting event but also a celebration of American business. Fueled by the introduction of the myriad nonautomotive sponsors about ten years ago, the Daytona 500 has emerged as a high-profile reward for valued customers and has been a meeting place for corporate officials, friends, and associates. In addition to the die-hard race fans who could be immediately identified by the colorful signature apparel of their favorite driver, there were thousands of well-dressed middle-management types in slacks and sport shirts, and even a few in shirts and ties. Many were employees or executives of the hundreds of firms involved in the automotive world. Most brought their wives.

To entertain important guests, most major sponsors rented hospitality suites and reserved seats for their best buyers and customers. At $85 a ticket, the Daytona 500 was an attraction for people who had, not for those who were lacking. The days of the redneck fried-chicken-and-beer crowd were a distant memory.

Inside the huge track a large portion of the infield was filled with cars, trailers, and RVs. Even more vehicles could have been shoehorned inside, except that Bill France, Sr., had built the 44-acre Lake Lloyd. At Daytona, no venue goes untapped. Abu-Garcia, a maker of fishing equipment, and Evinrude, the boatmaker, were cosponsoring a fishing contest for drivers and other race officials. The lake was the perfect refuge for drivers beset by the crush of fans and media. Ned Jarrett, a former driver and now one of the race broadcasters, caught more fish than anyone, by far.

Under a blue and white tent a short walk from the lake, the dozens of companies under the Philip Morris umbrella were hosting a gala for a thousand or so of their best customers.

Philip Morris, once best known for its cigarettes of the same name, owns the companies that make Maxwell House coffee, Miller Beer, Country Time lemon drink, and Kraft Bull's-eye Barbecue Sauce, brands that can be found displayed prominently on NASCAR race cars. Philip Morris, like the most successful sponsors, realized long ago that to make an optimal impact from sponsoring a race team, it must spend as much to promote and advertise as the two to three million per car spent for the right to be known as Sterling Marlin's Maxwell House Coffee Ford or Bobby Hamilton's Country Time Oldsmobile, or Rusty Wallace's Miller Pontiac.

Thus, on Friday, Philip Morris flew in all these guests—top-level customers of grocery chains, presidents, vice presidents, wannabe vice presidents, aides to vice presidents, wives to vice presidents, employees, and customers—mostly from the South, but not all, put them up in area hotels and motels, and on Saturday kept them busy with golf and tennis tournaments, a trip to Universal Studios followed by a sit-down dinner where everyone was encouraged to talk shop and racing and feel good about their association with the sport.

It was Sunday morning, and the thousand guests were now milling under the huge tent in the middle of the infield. Most guests were munching on Entenmann's Danish and drinking Maxwell House coffee, while others were being shuttled in fifty-person shifts to the pit area to meet various drivers and mechanics and have their pictures taken in front of a race car. At the end of the day, Philip Morris would fly everyone home.

Maxwell House coffee was spending over $100,000 on its guests, but the goodwill alone had to be worth ten times that amount. If I were a supermarket store manager and Maxwell House took me to the Daytona 500, wined and dined me, and brought me to meet Junior Johnson and Sterling Marlin, you can bet that blue and white can of rich Colombian beans would get an eye-level prominence in my store. For just as the Daytona 500 is about racing, racing is about shelf space.

By ten o'clock in the morning, the spectators were beginning to fill the long expanse of seats along the west side of the arena. Each long section was named for a racing great killed in the line of duty. There was the Joe Weatherly section, the Fireball Roberts section, another section named for Sir Hugh Campbell, who had set land-speed records in the 1930s on the sands of the old Daytona beach course, and other sections named for land-speed daredevils DePalma, Segrave, Lockhart, and Keech, all dead, a subtle reminder of the danger and daring of racing fast cars.

An hour later there were still plenty of unfilled seats, not because the inhabitants weren't on hand—despite the terrible traffic, very, very few seats would be unoccupied for the 12:15 start—but because thousands of fans were outside taking in the experience of ''souvenir row,'' a three-block area not far from the southern end of the track, where dozens of individual trailers owned by the race teams were lined up to sell clothing, glassware, miniature die-cast cars, racing cards, posters, quirky souvenirs like life-size figures of some of the race drivers, and even Rusty Wallace roasted peanuts. How much money any one trailer takes in is anybody's guess, but it has been reported that memorabilia takes in two *billion* dollars a year.

It is estimated that in addition to shelling out for the ticket at Daytona, each fan in attendance will spend about $200 on mementos. After I spent fifteen minutes by one of Dale Earnhardt's trailers, I knew the estimate was too low. A steady queue of eager fans were waving their money toward the venders, vying for attention, snapping up Earnhardt souvenirs as though they were priceless treasures.

Racing card companies that have sprung up have made their founders virtually instant millionnaries. In 1988, a young man named Jim McCullough produced a 100-card set. He named them Maxx cards, after himself. First produced in Myrtle Beach, such a set today sells for $850. Other companies followed suit. Today there are Traks, Pro Set, and Redline Racing, and as collectors manfully strive to accumulate one of every card made, the amount of money spent on the hobby grows and grows and grows.

Each driver, I am told, gets $40,000 a year just for allowing a card company to print his picture. There is gold in them thar trailers, and on this day throngs of fans lined up to spend their cash as though it had no value. Such is the love of the sport by those who follow the carnival from town to town, thirty stops at seventeen different sites along the way from Daytona Beach to Sears Point, California, from Brooklyn, Michigan, to Phoenix, Arizona. The passion for racing is heartwarming and pure. It's not a gambler's passion; it's a kid's passion. I always felt that way about baseball—it gets in your blood and stays there. Winston Cup racing is just as infectious.

Daytona is stop number one on the NASCAR tour, the World Series and Super Bowl of stock car racing on opening day. For race fans, it is Christmas and New Year's Day in February.

The race was scheduled to begin at 12:15. That meant it would. It is one of Bill France and NASCAR's credos. Be on time. Start on time.

Along pit road the competing cars began to line up, their crews pushing the colorful American dream machines into position. The first two cars in the front row were there because during the week they had posted the fastest two marks in the time trials.

In the front row, shiny and beautiful, were Junior Johnson's two Fords—on the pole was the deep blue Maxwell House car with the number 22, and on the outside was the deep red number 11 Budweiser car.

The driver with the fastest time is called the pole sitter, and today it would be Sterling Marlin who had posted a winning one-lap time of 192.213 miles an hour. In other words, Marlin went around that two-and-a-half-mile distance in just under 47 seconds. Small planes can do that.

Bill Elliott, in his first appearance under the Junior Johnson banner, had been an eye blink slower at 192.090.

Most everyone predicted the Fords would have an advantage in horsepower, and the prediction had proved out: During the time trials the next four fastest cars also were Fords, driven by Mark Martin, Dorsey

Schroeder, Phil Parsons, and Davey Allison. Breaking the monopoly was the Goodwrench Chevy Lumina, driven by racing's bête noire, Dale Earnhardt.

The time trials determine only the first two places and the back spots at the end for cars that crashed or did poorly during the 125-mile qualifying races, so except for placing Marlin and Elliott in the front row, the times were but a gauge for who was running with horsepower. Two and a half miles was one test; five hundred miles would be something different.

Behind Junior Johnson's two cars, lined up two by two all the way down the tarmac, were the other forty cars. The positions of the cars in the next fifteen rows had been determined by the results of the twin 125-mile races held on Thursday.

Dale Earnhardt sat on the inside of the second row. He had won the first of the twin 125s, after spinning out Sterling Marlin and earning once again the admiration and enmity of the fans.

Earnhardt was a five-time driving champion. He had won again in 1991, but wasn't feeling very upbeat about it in that he knew he had won the title only because no one else did very well either. Earnhardt won but four races in '91, matching Harry Gant, but he had finished well enough in the other races to edge out Ricky Rudd and Davey Allison for the title.

Like Earnhardt himself, the Earnhardt fans were pleased but not ecstatic over the title. Like old-time New York Yankee fans, they had become used to domination by the black Chevy, not a stumbling to victory. As 1992 was about to get under way, the Earnhardt faithful held out hope and expectation that its hero would end his winless streak at this jinxed track and defeat the phalanx of Ford favorites, Davey Allison of Robert Yates racing, and Junior Johnson's two boys, Sterling Marlin and Awesome Bill Elliott, who in 1991 wasn't awesome—quitting his brothers to try to find the key to being awesome once again.

The Earnhardt haters, meanwhile, were eager to see Ironhead, as they derisively called the dour Earnhardt, fail once again at Daytona. Earnhardt is a villain to many, and he is disliked with the same passion pro wrestling fans exhibited toward the Iron Sheik, who during the hostage crisis used to stand in the ring and sing the Iranian national anthem. On several cars driving to the speedway, signs could be seen that read, "Anyone But Earnhardt." Wherever on the track Earnhardt might be, first or in the middle, everyone would be keeping a close eye on the 3 car.

Lined up beside Earnhardt in the second row was the blue-collar Morgan Shepherd, driving the red and white Citgo Ford for the legendary Wood brothers. In the third row were the blue and white Valvoline Ford driven by the tenacious Mark Martin and the black, yellow, and red Havoline Ford driven by glamour boy Davey Allison. Allison, critics knew, would be revving the engine with the most horsepower. The car's owner, Robert Yates, had been building engines for years, and his research and development for the Ford Motor Company gave him an edge over everyone.

The cavalcade of sleek cars stretched back in a burst of color. In row four the yellow and red Kodak Film Chevrolet driven by Ernie Irvan, the crasher, sat beside Ricky Rudd's orange, yellow, and white car with the Tide soap detergent logo festooned in front. Rudd, talented but cautious by nature, was driving a Chevrolet for Rick Hendrick, the owner of dozens of car dealerships across the south.

Behind them were drivers disappointed not to be closer to the front, marquee names like Harry Gant, Darrell Waltrip, Rusty Wallace, 1990 Daytona 500 winner Derrike Cope, Ken Schrader, and Michael Waltrip, Darrell's baby brother. Richard Petty, The King, sat in the sixteenth row, one row ahead of his son, Kyle, and Dale Jarrett, Ned's son, was in row eighteen.

Richard Petty's STP Pontiac, striped horizontally with baby blue across the top two-thirds, then a skinny stripe of white, then a wider stripe of red with the white number 43 on its sides, drew a significant share of attention. Richard Petty was the sentimental favorite, for this was to be The King's final year in racing, ending a career that began in 1958. Petty had won two hundred Winston Cup races, almost twice as many as the number two driver, David Pearson, but he hadn't won a race since the Firecracker 500 in 1984, when President Reagan had flown to Daytona to watch him do it.

Everyone, including The King himself, knew the time had come for him to hang it up. His 1992 Farewell Tour would give his legions of fans one more opportunity to salvage sweet memories from the past.

Also toward the back of the long line were cars driven by teams without the finances to compete as equals, veteran drivers unable to attract major sponsors, like Dave Marcis and Dick Trickle, as well as drivers without the experience to attract them, like Mike Potter, Kerry Teague, and Bob Schacht.

At the very end of the line were drivers who had not qualified well and then had crashed in the qualifying races. Decent finishes in the 1991 point standings for the driving championship had earned them their spots. In the very last row was Alan Kulwicki in his orange and white Hooters Ford and next to him was Waymond Lane "Hut" Stricklin in the Raybestos Chevrolet owned by the legendary Bobby Allison. Stricklin, a talented driver, is married to the daughter of former racer Donnie Allison. Donnie Allison is racer Bobby Allison's brother. Stricklin is Bobby Allison's driver. It's all in the family.

With about a half hour to go before the race, the ceremonies began. Overcast skies kept the temperatures in the low 70s. It was warm but not hot, shorts and shirtsleeves weather in sunny Florida. In the overcast sky two blimps advertising Goodyear and Shamu the killer whale from nearby Sea World floated lazily along with a news helicopter and two biplanes pulling advertising slogans.

The first order of business was the presentation of an award to members of the trucking community whose bravery had saved lives on America's highways. The award, the 1991 Goodyear Hero of the Year, went to Philip Houck, a driver for the P.A.M. Transport Company. Houck, from Tupelo, Oklahoma, had come upon a crash scene and, noticing a car on fire with three children locked inside, had smashed the windows with a pipe and pulled the children out seconds before the vehicle exploded into a fireball. For his heroism, Houck won a $20,000 savings bond.

Next to be introduced was Joe Gibbs, the owner of Car 18, Dale Jarrett's Interstate Batteries Oldsmobile. Gibbs, best known as coach of two Super Bowl champion Washington Redskin teams, had begun a race team, and the Daytona 500 was to be the car's first effort.

Said Gibbs over the loudspeaker, "I was a NASCAR fan forever. Now I'm part of it; I'm going to get a chance to live this dream."

Gibbs, a gracious man, received an enthusiastic ovation.

Next to be introduced were corporate executives from the racing fraternity. First came the suits from GM, followed by Ford, Unocal, R. J. Reynolds, Coors, Goodys, Outboard Marine, CBS-TV, and Mark III Vans, and then execs from various racing circuits around the country. The PA announcer then cited the Glad Bag company. "We have the cleanest facilities in history," he intoned. They did, too. You couldn't find even a hot dog wrapper anywhere on the grounds.

Behind where I was standing on pit road adjacent to Richard Petty's crew and equipment, I overheard a woman complaining about her personal automotive problems.

"I ought to put STP in my car. I have an oil leak," she said.

Replied the man she was talking to, "If anything will stop it, that stuff will." The STP executives sitting in the stands behind me would have been tickled. Here was a microcosm of what racing promotion is all about.

On the shortwave radio Sterling Marlin, the pole sitter, was facetiously asked by his crew chief Mike Beam what his pulse rate was. I could hear the conversation because for $340 I had bought a Uniden Bearcat scanner and was eavesdropping, along with thousands of other race fans. There was added pressure on Marlin in that his team stood to win a bonus of $182,400 from Unocal gasoline if he won the race. As the car's driver, he stood to take home as much as 50 percent of it.

In one of NASCAR's best promotions, Unocal, which supplies the gasoline for all NASCAR events, posts $7,600 into the pot before each race. If the pole sitter wins the race, he wins the money. If he doesn't, the next week another $7,600 is added to the pot. It had been twenty-three weeks since last April when Rusty Wallace won the Valleydale Meats 500 at Bristol and a $22,800 jackpot. If Sterling Marlin could finish first in the Daytona 500, he and owner Junior Johnson stood to split a combined purse of $326,000 and change.

In response to Beam's wondering about his blood pressure, Marlin, a driving addict who races go-carts and any kind of car under any kind of condition, laughed heartily.

As the ceremonies continued over the loudspeaker, a minister delivered the invocation.

"Thank you for the joy and pleasure we have in this great speedway. Thank you for seeing the flag of the United States fly. Thank you for letting us watch these great drivers drive. Amen."

In a matter of moments, the hopes, dreams, fears, and folly of the race teams would be realized. Though many were hoping victory would be theirs, only one car would cross that line first. The cars represented thousands of hours of work by dedicated crew members to make those engines as fast as they could be and to turn out bodies as sleek and aerodynamic as a car could get. Out there on a track many millions of dollars in sponsorship money was at stake, as team owners battled to keep the sponsors they had or to attract new ones, mechanics fought for their reputations, and drivers raced for the glory and riches that come from winning this illustrious race. Aside from the financial considerations, there was one other beguilement for the drivers sitting in their brightly painted cars that made this day special: To a man, what they loved to do more than anything else on earth—including eating, wenching, or fishing—was to drive that race car fast, and here they were at the most prestigious stock car race in the world, one of forty-two select drivers about to compete in racing's World Series at speeds approaching 200 miles an hour. To be a part of this made them feel vibrant, alive—feelings they never took for granted.

The attention of the public-address announcer turned toward The King,

Richard Petty. As grand marshal of this race, it was Petty's duty to say the magic incantation that starts every race: "Gentlemen, start your engines."

Sitting in his red, white, and Petty-blue Pontiac with the oval STP logo on the hood, Petty, the most revered figure on the track, who could never be anything but who he is—an original—barked over the PA system for all to hear, "Come on guys, crank 'em up. Let's crank them up and go."

Seconds later, once the red Pontiac pace car set off down pit road, crank them up they did as the forty-two competitors turned over their unmuffled engines and the sound of angry bees filled the huge arena.

LAP 2

Junior Johnson
The Bootleggers

The recently departed redneck, roughneck reputation attached to the sport of stock car racing used to be justly deserved. When the sport first began to organize itself in the late forties after the end of World War II, the leading drivers were mostly bootleggers, men who illegally ran whiskey from hidden stills to hundreds of markets across the Southeast. These men were the *real* Dukes of Hazzard, only there was nothing funny about their business. Driving at high speeds at night, often with the police in pursuit, was dangerous. The penalty for losing the race was jail and loss of livelihood.

The bootleggers had the fastest cars. They could go 95 in first gear, 115 in second. Few police cars could go faster than 95. The bootleggers' cars also had the best equipment: special springs and shocks for handling on the turns. Parts were imported from California, where the hot rod was king.

The local sheriffs were intent on catching bootleggers not so much because selling untaxed whiskey was illegal, but more because if the sheriff could catch his prey, he then could sell the car at auction and reap half the returns. Often, the bootlegger would buy back his own car, and the cat-and-mouse game would begin anew.

Sheriffs went to great lengths to corral the faster, better-handling cars. Some tried attaching a cowcatcherlike device to the bumper. It was like a large ice tongs. The trick was to catch a bootlegger with a full load going up a hill and clamp onto the car before he could get away. To combat the clamp, the bootleggers resorted to putting the bumpers on with coat hanger wire. The lawman would latch on, the bootlegger would floor it, and the fender would roll under the front wheels of the revenuer's car and get tangled. By the time the revenuer got the bumper free, the whiskey runner was long gone.

Junior Johnson

Other sheriffs relied on their marksmanship, shooting the radiator with a shotgun. Some bootleggers countered by installing a steel plate to protect the radiator. Others put the radiator in the trunk with air scoops that ran from the front to cool it.

To keep the law from catching them, the bootleggers had other tricks as well. They made "bootleg turns," spinning 180 degrees and driving off in the other direction; spilled oil on the roads; tried throwing up smoke screens; created roads where there were none; and devised a system of using a second car to block the sheriff while the car with the load got away. The old Burt Reynolds–Jackie Gleason *Smokey and the Bandit* movies weren't far off the mark. The kingpins also paid off the sheriffs to stay in business, something even the movies didn't talk about.

Tim Flock, an early stock car racing champion, came from a family of bootleggers. He recalled that the first race among the bootleggers was held in the mid-1930s in a cow pasture in the town of Stockbridge, Georgia, about fifteen miles outside Atlanta.

"We didn't have no tickets, no safety equipment, no fences, no nothing. Just a bunch of these bootleggers who'd been arguing all week about who had the fastest car would get together and prove it."

According to Flock, the participants formed a track by running around and around an oval about a half-mile round until the tires dug up enough dirt to make the course visible.

"These guys would run and bet against their own cars, betting who had the fastest car. That night they'd be hauling liquor in the same car. About fifty people saw this dust cloud and came up trying to see what was causing it." The next time, the crowd swelled to a hundred. Then it tripled. Before long, the cars were racing every Sunday. (According to Flock, the car owners would buy four tires from Sears & Roebuck on Saturday, race them on Sunday, and bring them back on Monday. "Naw, I don't know how they got wore out so fast.") By the 1940s, a crowd of five thousand at a stock car race was not uncommon.

Among the moonshiner haulers famed for their racing skills were such racers as Tim, Bob, and Fonty Flock, who worked for their uncle Peachtree Williams, one of the biggest bootleggers in the state of Georgia; Buddy Shuman, who once was shot in the neck while running moonshine; Wendell Scott, a black racer who was once arrested after swerving at high speeds to keep from hitting a bunch of drunks walking on the highway, then skidding off the road into a house; and the most famous of them all, Junior Johnson, who drove hundreds of sorties delivering moonshine. Johnson, dubbed "the Last American Hero" by author Tom Wolfe, was chased by the law often, but never was caught behind the wheel of a car.

Everything Junior Johnson did, he did on a legendary scale. Toward the sunset of his moonshining days, he was hauling product in 16-wheel semis. In 1956, after he had gained national attention for his racing exploits, he was trapped by the feds at his father's still. He was arrested and convicted, and spent two years in jail.

During a racing career that began in 1953 and ended in 1966, Junior won fifty races, eighth on the all-time list. Racer Dan Gurney remembers Junior as an intimidator, a driver who would never back off in the corners. "He reminded me of the bullies from my earlier days in school, where you didn't want to catch their eye," Gurney once said.

As a race car owner going into the 1992 season, his cars have won 131 races and more than $15 million in prize money. A sharp businessman who amassed a fortune in chicken farming and the leasing of road construction equipment, Johnson has been a mechanic, tactician, and problem solver of extraordinary ability. Each year his team is listed among the favorites.

Junior Johnson sat in a conference room in his racing complex in Ronda, North Carolina, not far from where he was born and raised. He leaned back, his hands clasped behind a shock of closely cropped white hair. Junior Johnson's memory goes back to the days before Bill France, Sr., organized NASCAR and made it into what it is today. Johnson, whose name is synonymous with the sport of stock car racing, was thinking about all the years that had passed and was looking for the words to explain just how much the sport and the world had changed in his sixty-one years.

Once Ronda, North Carolina, had been in the middle of nowhere, a tiny name on the map among other sleepy towns in a state known for tobacco and moonshine. Today, the town hasn't moved an inch, but it has become one of the centers of NASCAR racing, an attraction that yearly brings thousands of pilgrims from around the world to its doorstep. The man everyone comes to see: Junior Johnson, the former bootlegger who has seen so much. It is part of the genius of this surprisingly gentle and sensitive tough guy that though he finds it hard to believe just how much his world has changed over the years, he has been able to grow, change, and prosper along with it.

JUNIOR JOHNSON: "It isn't the same as it was in the thirties and forties. After the Depression came and the war was over with, the inflation in the country boomed and reached almighty highs and lows through the years, just growed beyond what anybody could have imagined it would be. There is no way you can imagine growing up in the thirties and thinking,

'In the nineties this is where we are going to be.' *Nobody* could ever imagine that.

"When I was a boy, most of the people were basically just living off the land. They were farming, getting their milk and butter from cows. They got eggs from their chickens. They raised hogs, raised grain and corn and flour. They had vegetable gardens. And from that, that's what they lived on. They made their clothes themselves, so life was very poor, but it was survival.

"Most of the people who had jobs worked at the Chatham Manufacturing Company, which made upholstery for automobiles in Detroit and for furniture factories. Back then, it was a humongous factory to all of us. Now, it's not much bigger than our racing complex. The company paid two or three dollars a week, five at the most. Nobody paid anything back then—a nickel, dime an hour.

"When I was a boy, the economic conditions didn't matter to me, because I wasn't trying to survive. My father was in the moonshine business. He was one of the few around in this community who had money and could do more than some of the other people could do who didn't have a way of making money. He was willing to gamble on being arrested for making moonshine in order to support his family in a more realistic fashion than some of the other people were.

"Making moonshine was a hand-me-down trade that came down through the generations. By the time one was too old to make it, another had already picked it up. It was important that the location of the still be kept secret, because the revenuers were out there looking for it. Sometimes the moonshiners put them underground, put them in buildings. They would be back in the woods where no one could see them or find them. There were a lot of ways to conceal them. It was a cat-and-mouse game. We knew their names, and they knew ours. And when Daddy needed someone to drive, way before I ever got my driver's license, three or four years before, I was hauling moonshine from here to Lexington, High Point, Greensboro, Thomasville, Winston-Salem, just about everywhere in the central location of the Piedmont, to Charlotte, Concord, Kannapolis, Hickory, all around, and on the road that became a cat-and-mouse game as well, and as a result, I learned how to make the motors fast and how to make the cars drive good, and it was a trade that I took right on to racing with me.

"It was an every-night affair that we had with the revenuers, the highway patrol, the ABC officers, and the alcohol and tobacco tax people. We had to outrun them just about every night, sometimes two or three times a night. It was hard, dangerous, scary work. That's just what it was.

"Basically away from both of their workplaces, the bootleggers and the revenuers were friends. Very rarely did you ever see one of them when they weren't friends. Sometimes they would block the roads, and the driver would try to get around them and they'd hit a car, but never with the intention of trying to hurt anyone. The bootleggers understood they were going to be chased and could be caught, and if it looked like they were going to be caught, they'd concede, and that was the end of it. As I said, it was hard, hard work, very dangerous work.

"In the early bootlegging days, most of the cars were '39 or '40 Fords, some earlier like '36 or '37. They were the best-driving, fastest cars at the time. And then, as time went along in the early fifties, the Cadillac motor division came out with an overhead valve engine that they used in ambulances, and what we would do was scan the junkyards or anywhere else where we could find a Cadillac ambulance that had been wrecked, and we would buy that motor and then modify it and put it into a '40 Ford, and then we had a tremendously fast automobile, and the only way they could catch a car like that was if it had trouble or if they caught us setting still, loading or unloading. On the road it was impossible to catch. Every once in a while a guy would bust a tire or wreck, and occasionally they would block a road and catch one, but if you didn't have any trouble, it was impossible to catch on the highway.

"I made as many as four runs a night. I did that from the time I was thirteen until I was in the mid-twenties, 365 days a year, seven or eight times a week, probably more than that.

"I knew everybody who was in the whiskey business. Before racing, I knew the Flock brothers. I knew Curtis Turner, Bob Smith, the Martin boys. Clay Earles, who owns the Martinsville Speedway, used to be in the whiskey business. I knew him before. The two guys who own the North Wilkesboro Speedway dabbled in the whiskey business.

"At a certain time, these drivers would get together, race, and re-schedule their whiskey hauling for the night. I participated in these races after I was sixteen.

"Right away, I figured out that the whiskey business was an asset to me, because I already knew about fast cars and how to make cars drive better, and what I had to do to handle that car. I had that experience because I learned it in the whiskey business.

"The first race I ever drove was at North Wilkesboro. The first *big* race I ran was a modified race at Darlington in 1953. That was the early stages of racing, before the switch from modified racing to the Winston Cup, or what back then was called Grand National racing. Modified racing has phased itself out, and now the only place you can see modified racing is in the state of Connecticut, up at Stafford Springs. Bill France, who owns the Daytona Speedway, was the one who favored stock car racing. He felt that the people could relate to the cars as to what they were driving. If you were driving a '51 Ford, and a '51 Ford was running on a racetrack, you could relate to it better than to a '34 Ford modified to run. France was the one who started NASCAR, and he had a lot to do with everybody's career in racing. I don't think a single soul in racing today—Glen Wood, Bud Moore, myself—wasn't helped by Bill France, Sr., and a big involvement came from him for them to be in racing.

"My first victory came at Hickory, North Carolina, in 1955. It was for B&M Motors, a motor company here in North Wilkesboro. A friend of mine, Jim Lowe, and I ran against the factory teams. It was a big feat for a rookie, a young guy who didn't know what he was doing, to show up and beat up on the big guys. It was a big victory for me. And in 1956 I got signed by the Ford Motor Company to a contract . . . when I got caught by the revenuers.

"I began driving Grand National races, but I didn't just jump into stock car racing and forget about my whiskey business, because that was where my bread and butter was coming from. If I won a Grand National race, the most I could win would be a thousand dollars. I could make $1,000 in one night running whiskey, so my business was more profitable for me than driving a stock car. A stock car was fun, something I enjoyed doing, competing against other competitors, so I tried to do them both, and I established myself in stock car racing, and my name was in the papers day in and day out all over the United States, and then I became a target for the revenuers to go after simply because if they could catch me, they had the big-name person they could use to play against the bootlegging business. They were trying to stop the business, and the bigger the person they could catch and punish, the more impact it would have on the people doing it.

"Well, they caught me at the still back here in the mountains, and so they sent me to prison for two years for it in 1956.

"They had my father's still staked out, and I walked into their trap. I wasn't involved in it other than he asked me to go out and build a fire for it, 'cause that morning he got up late. You had to be able to fire it up an hour before daylight so the fire would be hot and it wouldn't smoke. Nobody would know where your still was at if you couldn't find the smoke.

"But Daddy had gotten up late, and he hadn't had the time to get up to the still to build a fire, and I had just gotten in from driving a race in Pennsylvania. I had driven all night and just gotten home, and he asked me to build a fire in the still for him. He said he'd come on as quick as he'd get dressed.

"So, you know, I did what my father asked me to do regardless of the consequences. I can live with it. It was a freak thing that they caught me. 'Cause ordinarily they would not have caught me.

"When I got out I went back to racing. No one held it against you, because in the whiskey business you weren't trying to kill nobody, just trying to live and let live. The government was selling whiskey in liquor stores, so most people didn't look at it as against the law, but there was a law against it.

"If you made a gallon of whiskey, they made $11 in tax on it. You could make it for 75 cents to a dollar and sell it for $3 or $4, so you could triple your money. How did they expect you to pay $11 a gallon when you only sold it for $4 a gallon? It's the same way today if you beat the government out of taxes. It's what everyone was trying to do back then.

"The guys I was competing against back then were wild. Buddy Shuman was a very talented driver and mechanic and car builder. He was one of the top-notch people. He was wild, but Curtis Turner and Joe Weatherly and Fireball Roberts, Speedy Thompson, Slab Weidenhouse were wilder than he was, a lot wilder. I didn't really hang out with them because I was younger, and my business kept me tied up. I was busy doing my moonshining and very confined to what I did, and when I raced, I did it more for the pleasure than the money.

"Then around 1959, 1960, there came a time when the whiskey business was no longer attractive moneywise, unless you were in a humongous situation, and then it became too risky. You had to put up too much money and stood to lose too much to be profitable, and so long about that time I chose to give it up. I did come back from prison and dabble in the liquor business a couple of years after that, but once I decided to get out, I got out and stayed out. I concentrated on car racing, and in 1960 I won the Daytona 500."

LAP 3

Ralph Moody

The Wild, Wild West

Ralph Moody began racing in the 1930s. He grew up in Littleton, Massachusetts, twenty-five miles northwest of Boston, and as a youth began racing midgets and modified cars. Like Junior Johnson, he was partial to the Fords of the late thirties. Unlike Johnson, who stayed close to home because of his whiskey business, Moody was an itinerant. When winter came to New England, he migrated south, racing in Virginia, the Carolinas, Georgia, and Florida. He settled in the Charlotte area in 1956.

Moody became partners with Red Vogt, a legendary stock car driver and one of the most knowledgeable engine builders of his day. Together they ran the Ford race team for a former racer named Pete DePaolo.

Later Moody and Vogt agreed that they needed a businessman to help them out. They turned to a man named John Holman, who had been PR director for a road race in Mexico.

When Vogt couldn't get along with Holman, who was brash and crass and unyielding, the legendary driver left the business. A new concern began under the name Holman-Moody.

Quickly Holman-Moody, with the backing of the Ford Motor Company, became the premier car building firm in racing. At its peak in 1960, Holman-Moody built four hundred race cars. Holman was the businessman, Moody the mechanical brains of the operation.

Driving for Holman-Moody were many of the legendary drivers of the period—Curtis Turner, Joe Weatherly, Marvin Panch, Fireball Roberts, Fred Lorenzen, and David Pearson.

The stories told about these legendary racers reflect a period in America that today seems long gone. The Depression created a class of hungry, often fierce, competitive men who without formal educations dragged themselves up by their bootstraps and who, even after they attained

23

Ralph Moody (© International Speedway Corporation/ NASCAR)

success, never lost that hard inner drive. For Turner, Weatherly, Roberts, and Lund, early stars of racing, life was a never-ending string of parties and competitions that ended for each in tragic deaths. Isaac also died in his car, from a heart attack, they say, but more likely from carbon monoxide asphyxiation.

Curtis Turner, the quintessential party boy, had a saying: "If you feel bad enough before you start a race, nothing can happen to bother you." On the track he was a fearsome competitor who would think nothing of forcing you off the track if you were in his way. Curtis had a feel for how far he could push his race car. He could get his car completely sideways at 135 miles an hour and save it, where other drivers would lose control.

Off the track Turner loved women, V.O. and 7UP, and flying. When he threw a party at his 14-acre home, it might last a week. His rule was you had to get drunk. If you didn't, you didn't get invited again. At one shindig Joe Weatherly was seen using a fire extinguisher to serve drinks into flower vases. Young girls danced on tables. Guests lay on the floor passed out. Said Tim Flock, "Curtis was a party man."

Turner was a businessman who made, and then lost, millions. He sold timber, owned movie theaters, and with Bruton Smith built the Charlotte Motor Speedway, before it went broke. Humpy Wheeler has often said that the mistake Curtis made was to try to mix racing with business outside of racing. Others say Turner was too much of a rogue and a risk-taker to ever keep his money.

In 1961 Turner tried to organize the NASCAR drivers into joining the teamsters union. Turner wanted the drivers to receive 40 percent of each purse, and in return hoped teamster boss Jimmy Hoffa would help him save his failing track.

Turner had once teamed with NASCAR head Bill France in a Pan American road race, and he had saved their lives when he averted a plunge off a steep cliff by driving the car into the rocks on the other side of the road. But despite their shared past, France broke Turner's efforts, in part because he knew that hidden in the agenda of Turner and Hoffa was to introduce pari-mutuel betting to the world of NASCAR races, something France felt would ruin the integrity of his sport.

France threatened to close the tracks, find new drivers, and put any union drivers out of work, and Turner found himself isolated when the rest of the drivers disavowed his efforts. France banned him from racing for life, but after four years allowed him to return.

Turner, an expert pilot, often took businessmen up in his airplane to sell them timber. According to Tim Flock, he'd have them so scared they didn't want to look out the window. Said Flock, "He would fly over the worst timber in the world and say, 'There's some damn fine timber down there,' and they'd say, 'Okay, okay, can we go back down to the ground now?' and that's why he sold so much timber.''

A jokester, Turner had the habit of turning off one of the two engines in mid-flight and pretending he didn't know what was wrong. He would say to a passenger who had never flown before, ''Go ahead, you fly it.''

Turner died on a Sunday afternoon on October 5, 1970, when his Aerocommander crashed into a mountainside near Du Bois, Pennsylvania, twenty minutes after takeoff. His body was found a half block away in the woods. The passenger, golf pro Clarence King, was strapped in the cockpit seat. Speculation was that while Curtis was sleeping off a toot in the back, King had suffered a heart attack, and the plane had crashed.

Turner's sidekick was Little Joe Weatherly. They were the Don Quixote and Sancho Panza of stock car racing, drinking buddies, hell-raisers. Weatherly loved to play practical jokes. He had a stuffed mongoose in a box, and he'd pop it open and scare the unsuspecting. He wore one suit that was half gray and half red.

One time Weatherly had a lifelike rubber snake, which he threw one day at an unsuspecting Cale Yarborough, scaring him badly.

That night Yarborough caught a five-foot rattlesnake, removed its fangs, put it in a burlap bag, and took it to the track the next day. Little Joe sat in his race car. Yarborough pulled the snake out of the bag and dropped it on Weatherly's lap. Weatherly gave him a grin. And then the snake began hissing. Weatherly leaped out of the car white as a ghost, then red with anger. Weatherly went to his toolbox and pulled out a ball-peen hammer. Yarborough ran for his life and was lucky Weatherly didn't catch up to him.

''I knew he would have killed me if he had caught me,'' says Yarborough.

Because Weatherly was very superstitious, other drivers drove him crazy by throwing peanuts onto his seat before a race. He thought the color green brought him bad luck, so, of course, they were always bringing him something green.

Joe Weatherly died January 19, 1964, at the Riverside track. It was the fifth race of the season. He was trying to catch the eventual winner, Dan Gurney, but the brakes of his Mercury failed, and Joe went wide into the dangerous turn six and hit the wall on the left side. He wasn't going more than 85 miles an hour, but his head extended out the driver's window and his skull slapped against the concrete wall, killing him. His was the first death on a NASCAR track in seven years.

Glenn ''Fireball'' Roberts, perhaps the first superstar in stock car racing, died six weeks after a fiery crash at Charlotte on May 24, 1964, four months after Weatherly's fatal crash.

Roberts, who had won thirty-two races in a career that began in 1947, was talking of retirement at the time of his death. He had started young and was able to beat all comers until Fred Lorenzen challenged him and proved himself superior. On the day Roberts died, according to Lorenzen, Fireball didn't want to race. Weatherly's death still haunted him, and his desire to race was gone.

Banjo Matthews, then a driver and today one of the sport's most famous car body builders, remembers that Roberts was losing his skills. A couple times he had spun out on superspeedways during practice. Roberts, who had socked away a lot of money, talked to Matthews about retiring. He talked of going to work for a beer distributorship to do PR work. According to fellow driver and friend Neil Castles, he intended to become a radio broadcaster. He had been taking a course in public speaking.

The night before the accident, Roberts and Ned Jarrett sat poolside at a motel and talked. Roberts said his competitive edge was missing. He talked about quitting. The thrill was ebbing. His nerves were beginning to jangle.

The morning of Roberts's death, Banjo Matthews helped him put on his uniform. Roberts complained that the flame-retardant fiberglass in the uniform made him break out in a rash. As a result, he had cut his sleeves off. According to Matthews, Roberts told him he didn't feel up to racing.

"Glenn," said Matthews, "get your ass up and go get in your car and go home."

"I can't do that," said Roberts. Matthews wanted to know why.

"Because all these people are here to see me race," Roberts said. He said he also felt obligated to Ford and his sponsors.

During the race Junior Johnson hooked the rear of Ned Jarrett's car, spinning out both cars. Roberts came down the straightaway, swerved to avoid Johnson and Jarrett, and smashed into an opening in the concrete wall. After the car became airborne, it turned upside down and the fuel tank broke open, with the fuel cascading into the car. Back then there was no rubber bladder or fuel cell to prevent spilled gas. When the car came to a stop, the fuel began to pool around the car.

Suddenly, the lavender car with the white number 22 ignited. Fire raged. Roberts, strapped in the car, knew to hold his breath to keep the flames from searing his lungs. As the fierce conflagration burned all around Roberts, Ned Jarrett bravely sought to drag him out of the wreckage.

"My God, Ned," said Roberts, "help me. I'm on fire."

Jarrett finally did pull him out, burning his own hands, and once he got him out, he began tearing off Roberts's clothing. Roberts, still conscious, helped. After the rescue squad finished attending to Roberts, the racer was taken to Charlotte Memorial Hospital by helicopter. He was burned over 80 percent of his body.

For a while it looked like Roberts would make it, despite third-degree burns over 60 percent of his body. "He is a remarkable patient," announced his doctors, who after several weeks said he was improving. But after an operation to remove burned skin on June 30, his condition worsened. Pneumonia set in. He lapsed into a coma and never regained consciousness. Glenn "Fireball" Roberts died on July 2, 1964, of the burns, pneumonia, and blood poisoning.

After the funeral, a relative complained, "Want to hear about bad taste? Glenn gets burned to death, and the mortuary sends the family a smoked ham. That's the goddamn South for you."

Lee Petty, who won fifty-four Grand National (now Winston Cup) events, wasn't like the others. He had never been a bootlegger, and as a result wasn't part of the "in" group. Not that he cared. Petty was so much of a loner that if you went up to him and said hi, chances are he would not respond.

Lee Petty came from a farming background. During the Depression he sold biscuits and later had a small trucking business. He turned to racing and, like many before and after him, found out just how tough it was to be an independent owner-driver.

Petty, unlike most of the others, was a family man and too serious about winning races to party late into the night. He was a churlish despot who would do anything to win. One time in the mid-1950s, Petty put wing nuts and armor plating on the side of his Oldsmobile, so that anytime his car brushed against the side of another car, he'd shred the opponent's sheet metal. Charlton Heston's enemy had done that to him during the chariot race in *Ben-Hur;* Lee Petty did it for real.

One time during a race at High Point, Lee Petty came into the pits. His boy, Richard, a member of the pit crew, climbed up on the hood to wipe the mud off the windshield with a rag. The crew finished changing tires, and without saying a word to Richard, Lee Petty drove away, with a petrified Richard still upon the car, hanging on. Lee drove one entire lap before he returned to pit road to let Richard off. And after the race, he cussed the boy out. When Richard himself began to race, there were times when Lee bumped him and caused him to crash, so great was his desire to win.

Ralph Moody raced against them all, and once the racer from Massachusetts turned to building cars for a living, all the greats, including

Petty, Junior Johnson, Fireball Roberts, Marvin Panch, Freddy Lorenzen—anyone who drove a Ford—bought cars from Holman-Moody.

Before Ralph Moody and his partner John Holman split up in 1971, they built Holman-Moody into a juggernaut. Their facility was an awesome automobile warehouse, with race cars stored on shelves like books. They built racing boats, Indy cars, modified racers, and motor homes.

Today it is largely abandoned, an empty shell, but even in disrepair, its grandeur and splendor can be imagined. John Holman has died, and Ralph Moody lives in retirement in Charlotte, his home filled with dozens of tarnished trophies from the glory days of Holman-Moody. In his driveway sits one of his race cars, a Ford Talladega, which he says is so powerful he lets his son drive it on the street only on seven cylinders. Today he helps out the few young racers who seek him out. You wouldn't know it by looking at him, because Ralph Moody is mild-mannered and a gentleman, but he once was a fierce racer. After he quit driving and started building cars, his skills in making autos and working with people made him one of the legends of the sport, during an era when stock car racing was peopled by the rough and tumble.

RALPH MOODY: "The drivers back then were real country boys. They come from the woods. Ain't nothing going to hurt them, they figured. Tim Flock and his brothers would raise hell all the time. Tim would drive in a race with a monkey in his car. His brother Fonty at Darlington ran in shorts, a T-shirt, and sneakers.

"Junior Johnson was wild as hell. I can remember running against him at Wilkesboro. The track was dirt then, and one time I chased Junior, and he never made it through the number three corner, went off the hill—there never used to be a guardrail there—went over the bank, and disappeared, and after I came off the corner, he came back over the hill behind me, just came out of there still going!

"Most of them came from whiskey running. Curtis Turner was one of the biggest whiskey runners in the state of Virginia. Joe Weatherly was in that stuff too. That was a way of life. They used to trade booze for other things—for a long time it was all right, and then all of a sudden they made a law you couldn't do it anymore. It was the way the people lived. Hell, they ain't gonna stop them. It's like telling those people they can't grow chickens anymore.

"In the late fifties we had our race shop, and we worked on a lot of revenue cars that chased them cats, and we worked on a lot of whiskey runners' cars too. We'd hop up their cars, soup them up, improve their suspensions. We had fifteen guys who took care of them.

"Hell, a '40 Ford would go 150 miles an hour, and they'd run them as fast as they could go. We'd put in a big V-8 overhead valve engine and fix the suspensions so they'd handle. They'd some kind of run, boy.

"The revenuers couldn't catch them. Hell, no. Those guys grew up running those roads and knew where they were going, and the revenuers were trying to catch them in their home territory. Those guys would get out in the fields and play with them things, turn them around, go the other way, drive it through the weeds, the fields, anything it took to get away, and they knew every gate of every cow pasture.

"The only way they caught Junior, he was loading semitrailers to take them to Chicago and New York. That's how much he was hauling. He'd get semis up there and fill them up!

"I tried to keep Junior out of jail on that. We gave him a job. The judge said, 'If he's going to be running around racing, he'd better be in jail.'

"Junior made pretty damn good booze. It looked like clear water, was strong as hell, but it wasn't rotten. He did it right.

"Up into the 1970s, they were still making it. There was a racetrack in Alabama, and underneath the stands the police found a still. The guy running the track owned it. It's still illegal to make it and sell it without a federal tax, but people still make it for themselves.

"Back then the drivers were rough, boy. There was always some kind of fight going on. They'd wang-bang out there, but if someone figured it was a little bit out of line, if the guy figured you were too rough, there was a fight right then.

"One night Junior and Lee Petty, Richard's father, were running out here at the old Fairgrounds in Charlotte. The race was fifty laps, and after about three-quarters of it Junior was leading the race, and Petty couldn't pass him so he kept running into the left rear and banging on him, trying to spin him out, knock him out of the way, and finally old man Petty cut Junior's left rear tire down.

"Junior came around and came into the pits. Junior was driving for the Wood Brothers, and both brothers, Glen and Leonard, were there. I was standing there with them.

"Junior came in and said, 'Put a tire on it.' Glen said, 'Oh no, oh no, oh no.' I said, 'What do you mean, "Oh no"?' He said, 'We're in for it now.'

"They put a tire on it, and Junior went out there, and he sailed around there, and here came Lee Petty. Junior let Petty by and ran him down the end of the racetrack and never shut it down and ran him off the end of the big pigpen out there and over the wall. Petty went sailing clear out of the racetrack! The race was coming to an end, and Junior knocked him out just so Lee couldn't win it.

"I can remember another time when Tiny Lund and old man Petty got into it. This was at a little dirt track somewhere in North Carolina. The Pettys were mad at Tiny about something that happened during the race.

"There was a cement platform three feet high in the infield. The scorer was up there, and that was where everybody got paid. Old man Petty was standing up there with Petty's wife, and with their son, Richard. Richard wasn't racing then. He was young.

"Here came Tiny, and when he got there Petty's wife hauled off and knocked the bejesus out of Tiny with her pocketbook. Richard jumped on Tiny. The old man got into it, and Tiny got two of them by the head— Tiny was a great big guy, a good-natured guy. I never saw Tiny try to hurt anybody. Well, he was holding on to both of them while the old lady was banging him with a pocketbook, and Tiny was shouting, 'Moody, you son of a bitch, make her stop.' I told Tiny, 'Get out of here, and you won't get hit!'

"I remember one time we were up in Norfolk and Curtis Turner and Lee Petty got into it out on the track, just slam-bang, didn't knock either one of them out, but it certainly didn't get them anywhere, either.

"There was an old rail fence with a cow pasture behind it, and after the race was over, Turner was sitting on it. Old man Petty came over, and he had a newspaper in his hand, and he was slapping his leg with the thing. He said, 'You know, you screwed me up all night, and I ought to do something about it.' Turner said, 'Well, go ahead.'

"And whap! He hit Turner side the head and knocked him right off the fence. Old man Petty had a tire iron wrapped up in that newspaper!

"Old man Earnhardt, Dale's dad, was another one. He was pretty quiet, but if you gave him trouble, he'd get after it. He didn't take any crap from anybody either. It was kind of that way in those days. So much slam and bang was fine, but too much was too much.

"One night I was at Winston-Salem when Turner and one of the Myers brothers got into it, and afterwards one of the Myers boys came over to Turner with a wrench and said, 'You so and so, I'm going to kill you.' Turner was sitting over by the back of his truck. He reached in and came back with a pistol, and he said, 'You're going to do what?' The Myers boy said, 'I was just looking for a place to put this wrench!'

"Turner had a gun because he was always carrying a lot of money around with him from his lumber business. Curtis Turner was the wildest guy, as wild as you could ever find.

"Curtis had a doctor friend who lived in Charlotte, and the doctor friend bet him $500 he couldn't lead the race after the first lap. Curtis started sixth, and he knocked everybody off the racetrack to where he got to the end of the first lap and led it. Of course, it was the only lap he ran, because he tore up everything, including himself. But he won the $500.

"He was crazy as well. He and Joe Weatherly were buddies and would travel together, but on the track they were fierce competitors. At Darlington one time Weatherly passed him, and Curtis came back and knocked the crap out of him, got him out of shape, about tried to wreck him.

"Both of them drove for our team, and we didn't have any radios, and so I kept waving at him to quit that crap. When he came in to pit, I told him, 'Hey, you do that again, and the next pit stop, you pit the car yourself.' Curtis was running second. Weatherly was leading it.

"Curtis kept doing it, and when he came in, we just sat there, wouldn't pit him, so he couldn't go. In the pit he drove the car into a goddamn post. He was madder'n hell. The next day he came up to our shop and drove his Cadillac through our roll-up door. He was mad, boy. He was something else. Half of those guys were something else.

"Curtis was a character. He was a millionaire two or three times. He'd blow it and do something else and make it again. He was something else. Wild as hell. Hell, he owned just about every movie theater there was in Virginia for years. He sold timberland all over the country. He'd fly over the land and then sell it to them. Back then, everybody did something besides racing.

"Curtis had flown planes for a long time. He flew a jillion miles—God knows how far he flew. He never took any lessons. He just got in an airplane and flew it off.

"His first airplane he bought was a tri-pacer. He flew it to New York City and landed in the wrong place, and they about threw him in jail. When he came home, he ran out of gas and landed in someone's cow pasture.

"Turner didn't worry about anything at all. He had a doctor friend in a little town in South Carolina near Charleston, and he decided he would land in the downtown of this little town.

"People were coming out of church, and coming down he flew under the telephone wires, and as he landed he liked to have run over a police car, scared them to death, and he pulled that thing up and wiped out every light in the city! In an Aerocommander jet yet. He knew he was in trouble, so he flew just above the treetops to escape detection, but it didn't make any difference: When he landed, they were waiting for him.

"My wife saw him a short time later on a motor scooter. She said, 'What are you doing on that?' He said, 'Well, one reason I'm driving this, I don't even have a hunting license, never mind anything to fly or drive.'

"He was something else. And Joe Weatherly was just as bad.

"Curtis had an airplane, so Joe bought himself one. He never did know where he was going. He didn't know there were 360 degrees in a circle. He'd want to go somewhere, and his compass heading didn't mean anything—he didn't know how to figure out his instruments.

"He was flying guys up to Ohio for a business trip with Curtis. The weather was bad, and he lowered down, and all of a sudden a whole bunch of lights went by.

"One of the guys said, 'Goddamn, Joe, that was the Empire State Building.' Weatherly said, 'Hell no, we're in Ohio.'

"They made a loop and came back, and they like to run into the Empire State Building. He got clearance to land at one airport and ended up landing at a different one. I was always having to bail these guys out.

"One time Weatherly flew from Norfolk to Darlington, and he followed the railroad tracks all the way down there. The tracks ran right through the town of Darlington, and he followed them down. He saw the little airstrip in Darlington, went in, and landed. He then went over to the racetrack to go race.

"The race ended. He asked me, 'Where are you going?' I said, 'To Charlotte.' I had my airplane. He said, 'I want to go to Charlotte. When you take off, wait a little bit and I'll follow you.'

"I took off and circled around, and he came up and began following me. I could see him in the cockpit of his plane waving his arms about something.

"When I got to Charlotte, Joe was nowhere in sight. About an hour later he called up. He said, 'Is this you, Moody?' I said, 'Yeah, where are you?' He said, 'I thought you were going the wrong way. I'm in Spartanburg.' He was something.

"I used to go with him once in a while and fly his airplane. He got a new Apache, and he must have had it two or three months. We were scheduled to go test at Daytona. He said, 'How about going with me, just fly my airplane. It's got all kinds of radios, but half of them don't work. The guy showed me, but they never work.'

"I got in the plane and cranked it up. Whenever you get in a strange plane, you get out a checklist. I turned on the radios and dialed in. Joe said, 'Don't bother. It don't work.' I said, 'They're working.' He said,

'How the hell did you do that?' He didn't know there was a second switch for those radios. Joe just never did pay attention. He'd crank up and go. He didn't know how to make flight plans, so he'd just fly, wouldn't talk to anybody.

"It's a wonder they lived as long as they did."

LAP 4

Humpy Wheeler
You've Come a Long Way, Baby

The dining room high above the long stretch of asphalt track was mostly full. The napkins by the china were real cloth and the utensils had heft. The luncheon buffet featured a bounty of elegant foods, including baked chicken, Virginia ham, and freshly caught flounder. The vegetables were fresh, not frozen, the chocolate mousse rich and superb, the wine light and dry. The male customers wore suits, the women dresses or elegant pantsuits.

Outside the long plate-glass window, the mile-and-a-half paved oval of the Charlotte Motor Speedway sat bare and silent. The vista generated an expectation of excitement, even though no cars were in sight and the speedway's 118,000 seats lay empty. The track had been built for speed, and with imagination one could feel the sensation of barreling down the straightaway as fast as a car could go and turning left without lifting the pedal from the floorboard, with a train of determined competitors in hot pursuit. The thought was as breathtaking as the view.

While the diners chatted and ate, into the dining room walked an animated Howard "Humpy" Wheeler, the president and general manager of the Charlotte Motor Speedway.

Business has soared as stock car racing has enjoyed a boom, aided by the genius of Wheeler, the sharpest, wiliest, most innovative sports promoter in the world.

Bruton Smith gained control of the track in 1975 when he became majority shareholder. Though not even twenty years ago, this was before TV discovered NASCAR racing and before the megacorporations discovered the value of spending three million dollars a year to use racing to sell their products. Back then, a large investment in racing was a fool's gamble.

35

Humpy Wheeler

Along with driver-entrepreneur Curtis Turner, Smith, a successful car dealer, had gone bust the first time, when they didn't have enough money to finish building the speedway. They had tried to sell penny stock, but there weren't enough pennies, as banking institutions had turned their backs on the entire industry.

When Smith repurchased the speedway in '75, they immediately cleaned it up, planted grass, and made financial projections and a realistic budget. Their venture proved successful, and two years later Smith and Wheeler were able to borrow $2.2 million from the North Carolina National Bank to build a 10,000-seat addition, a press box, seventeen VIP suites, and an elevator, the first one at a racetrack in the United States.

In 1991 more than 800,000 visitors packed the speedway to watch stock cars and motorcycles speed around the track. In 1985, Wheeler conceived a ten-lap race for the previous year's winners, with a first prize of $200,000. The all-star race is called The Winston, and it has become a highlight of every season. Wheeler has instituted night racing for the 1992 edition of The Winston, a race he billed as "One Hot Night."

Wheeler is now financing a prototype for a mini-racer with roll bars and the same safety standards of the Winston Cup cars, for the cost of under $10,000. He wants the masses to race cheaply and safely.

The Charlotte Speedway today boasts 63 luxury VIP suites, a dining room that can seat 212 and is so crowded during race day that you can eat there only for an hour, and, overlooking the track, 52 custom-built condominiums, owned by such racing luminaries as Richard Petty, Felix Sabates, Chuck Rider, and Dale Earnhardt. The first 40 condos, built in May of 1984, were at the time a source of mirth, but when a second group of 12 were offered for sale in 1991, they sold out quickly—including the penthouse, which sold for $575,000. No one laughs at them anymore.

Entering the speedway dining room, Humpy Wheeler greeted, it seemed, just about every employee and guest by name. After sitting down, he pointed beyond the glass enclosure to the infield, where bulldozers were moving earth. A man constantly seeking ways to promote racing at the track, Wheeler indicated the layout of what would soon be a go-cart racetrack.

"Do you realize how many people drive go-carts in competition?" Wheeler asked. I didn't know. "A hundred thousand," he said. I could see that Wheeler's mind was envisioning every one of them paying him handsomely to compete on his track.

Wheeler, a hands-on manager who believes in attending to every detail, boasted that the chicken tasted as good as it did because he insisted on cooking it in canola, not vegetable, oil. After taking a few bites, he asked the waitress to seek out the chef and compliment him.

He is proud of the canola oil, just as he is proud of the success of his million-dollar baby, and proud of the grip that racing enjoys over the hearts, minds, and pocketbooks of so many Americans.

Humpy Wheeler's mom grew up in Bessemer City, North Carolina, a textile mill town about thirty-five miles west of Charlotte. She grew up in gentile poverty, and the last thing she wanted was for her son to become involved in anything that went back to the roots of the old South. (In the South, gentile poverty referred to poverty-stricken people who tried to work their way out of it, as opposed to those who chose to do nothing about their poverty.) She didn't want her son to live in a log cabin or listen to hillbilly music or chew tobacco, and she sure didn't want him involved in the redneck, roughneck world of stock car racing.

But Wheeler, like many intelligent, restless young Southerners of the postwar period, needed a challenge and excitement beyond the traditional farming or textile-mill life. The outlet he and others discovered was car racing. This was a sport the small-town Southerner could get involved in and use to make something of his life. From Birmingham, Alabama, through the Carolinas and up to Washington, D.C., red clay, the greatest natural track surface in the world, abounds, and in the two Carolinas alone more than two-hundred tracks sprung up for the three or four thousand drivers who came there to race their Ford flathead V-8s.

HUMPY WHEELER: "My mother, who is eighty-one now, recently brought a friend of hers who is eighty-five up to my home. Her friend is a widow whose husband was a very prominent textile executive. This lady remembers me primarily as a boy, even though at the time of her visit I was fifty-one years old. She remembered when I was operating old dirt racetracks in Gastonia and other places back when I was in my twenties, and so we were sitting around talking. She had never been to Charlotte Motor Speedway.

"She said, 'Well, Howard'—that's what my mother's bridge club called me—she said, 'I always thought you would amount to something more than somebody who ran an old racetrack.'

"Here was a lady in the present time who still had this terrible feeling about a rough, old thing called stock car racing. If I hadn't seen how racing has changed with my own eyes, I don't think I would have believed it myself.

"The good Lord directs some of us, and I consider it a privilege to have found out what I really wanted to do at an early age. I can remember it was

1947, and I was eight or nine years old growing up in Belmont, North Carolina, which is twelve miles west of Charlotte, a pretty boring place for a person who always liked color. It was the Bible Belt, and no one did anything on Sunday or you got shunned—no one was allowed to speak to you—so one of the things we used to do on Sundays was go down to Highway 29, which was the main route from Atlanta to Richmond, and I can remember vividly watching the race cars as they drove on their way to the old Charlotte Speedway, which was six miles down the road.

"And when I saw those race cars, I just had to find out what happened when they got cranked up on a racetrack, and so I would thumb over to the track. You could do that back in those days and not worry about getting killed, and I would go over there and get in free, because kids under twelve were always let in free if they were accompanied by an adult, so I'd just go up to some guy and say, 'Let me walk in with you,' and he would, and then I started selling Coca-Cola over there, and I was hooked. When I was a teenager, I made racing a business.

"When I was fifteen I raced old stock cars, '37 Ford coupes. Back then it didn't cost much money to race. All you had to do was take a stock '32, '34, or '37 Ford coupe, which you could buy for a couple hundred dollars, and rebuild the engine. We'd buy a World War II seat belt out of an F-6F fighter from a surplus store and take the lights out of the car, and put a Lincoln or Cadillac wheel and tires on, and you had a race car. Most of the time we didn't even put a roll bar in them.

"I accumulated enough money from working, bought a car, and I could even make money racing, because I didn't have more than $800 cash in the car, and you could win $200 if you won a race, so if you won four races, the car was paid off. And I won races.

"My stock car career was interrupted when I was lucky enough to get a football scholarship at the University of South Carolina. I sat on the bench and watched a lot of games, but I continued my racing, and I also helped the track promoters. You would follow a circuit. Thursday night it was the Columbia Speedway, Friday night at Asheville, and Saturday night at Greenville-Pickens or Hickory. I got to meet all the drivers.

"One of the most interesting was Ralph Earnhardt, Dale's father, who was a dear friend of mine. Ralph was a very stoic person. He was tall, thin, and always had a flattop or burr haircut. At the track he didn't have much to say, and he didn't work on his car when he arrived. When that car came off that trailer, he was ready to race.

"Ralph's style was interesting, because what he would do, usually he would run second and put incessant pressure on the front-runner, be inches away from him, particularly at tracks that were really hard to drive, like Columbia. You made one slip, and you were gone. And Ralph would generally win the race in the last couple laps, because the leader would make a mistake or because Ralph had been playing with him all night.

"Ralph would never have said this to anyone, of course, but the great drivers are like the great poker players: They don't continually show their hand. In other words, maybe Ralph could have lapped the field, but if he had done that, NASCAR would have been all over him, trying to find out what he had in the car that nobody else had. So a lot of times Ralph would barely beat people. And your smart drivers have known how to do that. I can remember in 1967 Richard Petty won twenty-seven races that year in a fantastic manner, and he had so much more car under him than anybody else did, but he never really showed his hand, except at North Wilkesboro when he had to make up a seven-lap deficit and came back to win the race.

"After I graduated college, the first thing I did was lease a racetrack and start promoting. I picked my first track because I knew it was going bust because it wasn't being operated right. I had been to so many races as a spectator and a driver, and also I had helped promoters publicize their races, so I knew instinctively which tracks were run good and which weren't, and over the next four years, I bet I promoted 130 races, starting in 1960, my senior year in college. I made a lot of money, and of course I lost it all, because I didn't know how to keep it. Warfare with other track promoters cost me a bundle, and one time I didn't have enough liability insurance when a couple of spectators got hurt. When you're twenty-two years old, you think you know everything.

"Operating dirt tracks in those days was a tough, dirty business, because there was a lot of money to be made, and the drivers were very, very tough people, very independent. Stock car racing was a rather violent sport, because there was a lot of crashing and banging around. The local drivers didn't like that I allowed outside drivers to compete at the track to improve competition and sell more tickets.

"I wouldn't let anybody get away with anything in those days. I kept a tough crew around me and a .38 in the glove compartment of my car. I didn't arm myself at the track because I thought that was a sissy way of doing things. I had been a boxer and a football player, and I thought I could take care of myself, and I did not want to show the drivers I was afraid of anything.

"And so one night I was shot at point blank with a .38. By a driver. I can't remember his name. He missed me.

"Also, some of the track operators, who were a lot older than I was, to put it mildly some of them were crooks and would do anything—and I'm talking about *anything*, including murder—to eliminate the competition.

"One time while I was operating a track over in Gastonia a competing track operator sent a guy over to get me. I don't know if he wanted to kill me or not, but he wanted to hurt me. The guy hit me in the back of the head with a Stillson wrench.

"Another time a competing promoter pistol-whipped my announcer, busted him up so badly we had to take him to the hospital.

"I don't want to overemphasize the tough atmosphere, because most of the time it wasn't, but it could turn ugly very, very badly in a short period of time.

"Racing back then mostly took place in the nonurban areas of the South. The communities where these tracks operated did not have a lot of law enforcement, and so people protected themselves. Someone had a farm, and there was a lot of stuff to steal on the farm, but it would be the last place a crook would go at night, because the farmer had a pretty good supply of armament, and the first time his dogs barked, he'd shoot first and ask questions later. So people wouldn't bother him. That was the kind of sense you had that spilled over to the tracks.

"It was not uncommon for fights to break out in the grandstands. When a driver spun another driver out, it got people in the grandstands riled up. As a promoter what you wanted to guard against—and I had to learn to do this instinctively—was letting the spectators get to the drivers. If that had ever happened, there would have been a riot.

"This happened a lot at high school football games in the South when spectators from the two sides would spill out onto the field, because there was nothing to keep them apart.

"But at the racetrack a promoter couldn't get insurance unless you had a wheel fence to protect the spectators from wheels that would fly off race cars, something that doesn't happen much today, and that wheel fence was what made it very hard for people to get onto the track surface, and so the fighting for the most part was limited to drivers fighting drivers and fans fighting fans.

"Fights in the stands were usually brief, and they didn't spread because people were having too good a time, and it was never with weapons. It was always fists. Taking a weapon out on another person wasn't considered fair play in the rural South in those days. If you had a difference with him, you hit him or slapped her. Women fought each other too.

And then it would be over, and you'd have to carry one of them to the hospital and the other one would be arrested. That solved the problem, because the offending party would be gone.

"It was the same way with the drivers. I can remember once at Lakewood Speedway at Atlanta, Curtis Turner got into it with Tiny Lund. Turner was a real character, probably one of the best pure race drivers the United States ever produced. From the seat-of-the-pants standpoint, the man could do things with a race car very few other people could do. But though he was this wild man on the track and could fly any kind of airplane and would, in any kind of weather, he was scared to death of drowning.

"So he wrecked Tiny, and it was Tiny's own car. Tiny wasn't driving for someone else, and there were no sponsors as we know them today back then.

"And Turner wrecked people all the time, but he had this amazing ability to get away with it, because he could become very charming to keep his teeth from getting knocked out.

"Turner came in after the race. Tiny was a huge man, about six-foot-five, 280 pounds, and when he got his Irish up, there was no sweet-talking him about anything. Tiny picked Turner up and took him over to the lake about a hundred feet away, and Tiny began to drown him. This is absolute fact. About the fifth dunk, Turner promised Tiny that he would buy him a new race car.

"I really thought the man was going to be drowned. I don't think Tiny would have actually drowned him, but you never know in the heat of the battle, and Curtis sure didn't know the answer to that question, and so he definitely did the right thing.

"I can remember one time at Bowman-Gray Stadium, a flat quarter-mile track in Winston-Salem, Bobby Allison had just come up after winning a lot of races in the lesser divisions, and Bobby had a little Chevelle he was racing, and Turner was driving for the Wood Brothers in one of Holman-Moody's powerful factory Fords.

"It was almost impossible to pass anybody at Bowman-Gray Stadium; it was like racing in a parking lot. Bobby should have won the race, but he couldn't get around Curtis. Curtis kept blocking him, and finally Bobby went into the corner, and Curtis let him go right in front of him, hit the brake, and then he hit Bobby and spun him out. Curtis then banked off Bobby's car and went on to win the race.

"The race over, Turner parked his car at the start-finish line. It was a big old '66 Ford, this Wood Brothers Ford, and suddenly everybody started to scatter, because down the track Bobby Allison has put his car in reverse and he's going wide open in this little Chevelle, and he slammed into Turner's car as hard as you could hit it. It was un-be-lievable! And Turner didn't know what to do. He wasn't about to fight. Turner wouldn't fight anybody.

"The rough-and-tumble nature of stock car racing permeated the sport up until about fifteen years ago. The sport didn't change until the corporations made their presence felt around 1972. In the period between 1960 and 1969, which was the real beginning of the superspeedway era, racing was fueled by Detroit and Akron tire money. And that all went away in 1969. The car companies got out of it. All of a sudden Junior Johnson and Bud Moore and the rest of the car owners were left with only the equipment. They had no sponsors, and for a few years they were able to run with the equipment they had. Racing during that period wasn't too interesting, because it was more 'I'm going to survive and finish and make some money.'

"But it seems like every time somebody gets out, some other entity comes in, and in this case it was R. J. Reynolds.

"R. J. Reynolds carries a big stick in North Carolina, and when they decided to get in it, the blue bloods and the bankers, who don't look down on the tobacco industry, said, 'This might have something to it. There might be some folks there.'

"And that's when the boys from the mountains were thrown in with executives and engineers, instead of promoters and each other, and when the sponsor system came in, when these companies had parties, those who didn't know how to dress learned, and the ladies got a chance to get involved a little bit more, and all of a sudden racing started growing up a bit socially, so we didn't have to stay in the garage or at the racetrack all the time. We could go over to the country club, even learn how to play golf. I can't remember anybody knowing how to play golf in racing before the mid-sixties.

"And when the automobile factories came back into racing, they tended to send some of their better people, because racing was such a challenge. For instance, if you're an engineer for a tire company, and the company really wanted to find out how good you were, they didn't send you to tractor-trailer tire development; that would take two years to figure out what you're going to do with truck tires. They'd send you down to the racetrack, and they'd find out in one day whether you could help that race team. And when the factory people came to town to live, they were MIT graduates, Stanford graduates, and they brought some sophistication, and then we started to travel to some better places.

"Instead of going on the northern tour back in the sixties and staying in their hotel rooms, we started traveling to New York City to find out what was going on. We were introduced to a lot of sophistication and brainpower, and that helped us feel a lot more at home with the money people of America, so if the president of a Fortune 500 company came down, we felt more at ease, and then the TV networks got involved, and they brought their people in, and so the society that permeated the culture of this little town of about five hundred people who are involved in Winston Cup racing started changing.

"Today that culture has been further intermixed by the influx of a lot of money. Until ten years ago nobody made any money in stock car racing. Compared to other professional athletes, drivers didn't make that much money. Owners didn't, promoters didn't. They were well off, but it wasn't the big money it is today. This whole culture has been fired with a tremendous amount of money made in a short period of time.

"At the same time there are tremendous pressures on everybody that didn't exist fifteen years ago, and there is an escalation of social skills required to survive that were not necessary fifteen years ago. The rural Southern culture is embedded in the culture of this little racing town, but each time a man like Felix Sabates, a Cuban émigré, or Bob Whitcomb, who is from New Hampshire, moves in, the culture changes, and it has been very interesting to watch.

"The fans are turned on to racing like never before. We are finding out you can't do things good enough for fans anymore. I think back to when Bruton Smith came up with the idea of building forty condominium units around the first turn. I thought he was crazy, didn't think they would sell.

" 'Add more seats,' I told Bruton.

"But Bruton wanted to use the money from the sale of the apartments for capital improvements: paving the track, fixing the drainage system. You may not make any money off fixing the drains, but if the fans get stuck in the mud, they won't come back. Also, it's hard to borrow money for capital improvements because they don't bring a monetary return. Bruton was looking to the future. He realized improvements had to be made.

" 'I think I'm right, and I want to try it,' Bruton replied.

"We announced the sale of the units. Four months later, we had sold exactly one—a racing fan from Kansas City who owned a chain of service stations bought one.

"We tried selling the condos to race team owners and big companies, even offering a three-year buy-back clause: If the purchaser was unhappy, he could get his purchase price back within three years. There were no takers.

"We were facing a real disaster. We told each other, 'We've always been able to overcome. We need to get creative.' I thought to myself, 'If they won't write about us, maybe they will laugh at us. Anything.'

"I decided to try to get the word of the sale of the racetrack condos on 'The Johnny Carson Show' as a joke. You know, have him say these crazy North Carolinians are building condos for the traffic in front of them running 190 miles an hour. I wrote to one of the show's researchers. We got nowhere.

"Then we tried the David Letterman show. Three weeks later we got a call from a member of his staff. 'Is there someone we can call to talk about it?'

"We had a guy, Evans Kaiser, who had a great phone voice and he was funny, and so David Letterman called Evans Kaiser, and they made a joke about it. You know Letterman. 'Are you going to let your kids walk across the street?' He carried on like that.

"Well, the next day the bit ended up in the *Charlotte Observer*, and for some strange reason it appeared in the *Wall Street Journal,* and then other newspapers started writing about our crazy idea, and in the next seven months, we sold twenty-eight units!

"We get a good short return on the condos, but we get a longer, better return on the suites. When we built them, we thought the suites for the corporate sponsors and the race teams were great. Each suite has sixty-six trackside seats, an area for a buffet, a TV. We thought our new office building was great. But we are learning that whatever we do, it isn't good enough for the public. The fans are screaming at us, telling us to make these facilities even *more* glamorous. Same thing in football and baseball. Look at Joe Robbie Stadium and see how it was built. Joe Robbie knew what those people wanted: glitz and glamour. At the same time you can't shut out the people who can't afford that. You don't want to appear that you are turning away from those people, 'cause they are still the driving force behind stock car racing, and they always will be.

"It's important that the costs are not so prohibitive that the good, young driver will be precluded from getting into racing. NASCAR started the Sportsman series to enable the young driver to get started. We wanted to make sure they could drive a race car that could be built for about the same amount of money as a good bass boat, about $18,000. It seemed all the young guys who want to go bass fishing can afford a bass boat, even if they live in a house trailer. We succeeded in doing that.

"In May we had our Sportsman race at the Speedway. We had eighty-two entries. One entrant came in a Cadillac hearse. He cut the body right behind the driver's seat, welded a plate and window in it, and made the back part a car carrier. I asked him what it cost. He said, 'I've done all this for about $2,000.' And I looked over at one of the trailers that had brought one of the Winston Cup cars. They had about $150,000 in that thing, and they both got here.

"New owners have come into Winston Cup racing and have overspent, because that's what they know will win them races. We will have to continue to try to get the cost down. Could this lead to major problems down the road? It could. It has the potential.

"As a result, a great deal of pressure will be put on the marginal tracks. At least twenty cities want to build superspeedways in this country, and three are ready to go—Dallas, the Quad Cities area of Illinois, one in Atlantic City. These people are talking about putting up a tremendous amount of prize money at an ultramodern facility. NASCAR is still trying to work with the tracks that brought them to the dance, but these tracks are being forced to raise purses and spectator services, and there is talk that it will be the short tracks like the one at North Wilkesboro that go out. The last track to go down was Nashville, not because they wanted to, but they were not financially able to keep up with the demand.

"I worry about the high cost to the fan. I worry about the rising costs of running a race team. The escalation of costs can kill a racing circuit. Critics say, 'Stock cars aren't sophisticated. They don't have computers on board.' We don't *want* computers on board, not when a Formula One car with a computer on board costs $3 million *a race*. The people in the grandstand don't care. They want to see Dale Earnhardt and Darrell Waltrip trading paint.

"I have one other worry. Part of the problem has been brought about by the sponsors. As Harry Gant says, 'The sponsors are scairt of the driver doing something to hurt their image.'

"That bothers me a little bit, 'cause I don't want to see a bunch of drivers in Brooks Brothers suits carrying attaché cases with their race helmets in their other bag. It makes it hard to sell tickets. You gotta keep the sawdust on the ground. That's what makes racing go.

"Also there is a tremendous peer pressure from the other competitors and from NASCAR to mold yourself into the same cookie cutter, 'cause then you are easier to handle. It takes a person with a very strong will to buck all that. Even a rebel like Tim Richmond found himself in a very uncomfortable situation most of the time. The driver who spins out another driver and then comes back around, he hears the entire grandstand wanting to tear his head off, booing him to death, and it's the most intimidating thing in racing, because collectively you have a big city booing you, and so there is all this pressure on the drivers to conform, to be nice. We are taught that 'nice' means not being different. And so to take one other degree of difficulty out of what they are doing, most of them will choose to get into a mold. It's a shell of protection, and as drivers, they become much less aggressive. They will argue the point, because no driver wants to admit he isn't aggressive, but I've seen it. And it can totally destroy a career. I've seen that happen too.

"I'm hoping that the longer the sponsors remain in the sport, the more comfortable they will feel with a driver who doesn't walk the same path everybody else does all the time.

"I hate sameness, boredom. I love color. I love excitement. It's one reason we invented The Winston, the all-star race. It comes down to a ten-lap shootout for $200,000. In '87, Dale Earnhardt, Geoff Bodine, and Bill Elliott got in a tangle on national television. After that tangle, Earnhardt and Elliott bumped each other during a caution. Earnhardt went on to win the race and the money.

"Who was at fault will never be settled, because it involved the three of them. They were all running to the same spot, and who knows whose fault it was, if anybody's. I knew things were going to get wild.

"When they gave the checkered flag, I hurried from the control tower right down to the flagstand, went under the wall, and ran over to the garage area. I knew I was going to get blamed for the ten-lap format, which produced this, which is exactly why we did it—not to produce this confrontation, but to have more pressure and competition. Well, it was a hell of a lot better to have them screaming and hollering at me than each other, and drivers and crew chiefs came over beating me and calling me all kinds of names. I had told myself, 'When you get to the garage, be a sponge. Whatever anyone says, don't do anything to incite it.' So the purpose was served.

"As soon as I walked into that garage area, it was chaos—cars coming in, drivers getting out, everyone hot. Ernie Elliott came over screaming and hollering, mad as a hornet. Geoff Bodine was mad, and he hollered about a bunch of things. There was a fight in the garage among several drivers. Kyle Petty was one of them. A few punches were thrown.

"I thought, 'Well, I am back at the Robin Wood Speedway on Saturday night.' ''

Smokey Yunick

LAP 5

Smokey Yunick
The Survivor

There aren't many of the NASCAR pioneers left. Most died prematurely from hard living or harder crashes. Among the early greats, Red Vogt has died, as have Tiny Lund, Fireball Roberts, Joe Weatherly, Curtis Turner, Fonty Flock, Marshall Teague, Buddy Shuman and Bobby Isaac.

Only a handful of the greats remain, including Tim Flock, Lee Petty, Ralph Moody, and a controversial owner-mechanic genius named Smokey Yunick. The owner of The Best Damn Garage in Town on Beach Street in Daytona Beach, Yunick is renowned for his innovative engine and chassis designs. His stock cars won three Southern 500s at Darlington, two Daytona 500s, and the Indianapolis 500 in 1960 with driver Jim Rathmann.

Yunick won forty-nine NASCAR races in the early fifties with Herb Thomas behind the wheel, and later won with drivers Paul Goldsmith and Fireball Roberts. His cars won at Daytona 500 in 1961 with Marvin Panch and again in 1962 with Roberts.

Yunick, always an independent and outspoken man, has created controversy throughout the years. His reputation has been that of a mechanic who would try anything to gain an edge, and as NASCAR tried to stop him, over the years his spats with the organization and its czar, Bill France, turned bitter.

Before the Daytona 500 of 1968, Smokey entered driver Gordon Johncock in a Chevrolet. NASCAR technicians looked the car over closely, removing the gas tank, draining it, and measuring its contents to determine whether it had a greater capacity than allowed under the rules.

The inspectors gave Yunick a list of nine items he had to change on the car for it to qualify for the race.

Yunick groused, "Better make it ten," and with a flair for the absurd left the empty gas tank lying where it was and drove the car back to his garage, leaving the NASCAR tech experts speechless!

Another time Yunick built a car that seemed legal, until the NASCAR officials measured it. Yunick knew that a smaller car with a regulation engine would run faster, because it made a smaller hole in the air, and he built a Chevelle that fit the regulations in every way, until someone noticed that the tires stuck out farther than on the other cars. It was discovered his car was smaller than the other cars because Yunick had built this car seven-eighth size, downsizing all aspects of the car to make it look proportionate! After that, NASCAR started to use templates for tech inspection. To race, the car had to fit the standardized metal plates. It's been that way ever since.

Smokey Yunick should be wined and dined as a national racing legend and treasure, but apparently he has forfeited his seat of honor at the table because of his continuous biting criticism of both Bill France and NASCAR. It's only human nature that men in power don't reward their critics.

Not that Yunick has reserved his admonishments for NASCAR. Yunick *never* engaged in politics and adamantly refused to sit back and take it when he felt someone was taking advantage of him. He is one of those principled, stubborn men with one standard—something is either right or it is wrong, and he will do or say what he feels is right, regardless of the consequences.

In 1959, for instance, as he was preparing to go to race at Indianapolis, Yunick told the mayor of Daytona Beach he was calling his car "The City of Daytona Beach" and asked whether his honor could arrange to get him a $5,000 fee, which was what he needed to pay the Indy entry fee, eat, and sleep during that week of Indy trials and racing.

The mayor liked the idea, and it was announced in the paper that the city was going to present Yunick with a check just before he left for the big race.

The day Smokey was supposed to leave, the mayor called to say he could have the money, but only if he changed the stenciling on the car from "The City of Daytona Beach" to "The Halifax Recreational Area," which was what the tourist area encompassing all the little towns around Daytona Beach was called.

It would have been easy for Yunick to repaint the name on the car and take the $5,000. He badly needed the money. But Yunick refused on principle. He told the mayor, "Nobody in the world is going to know what the Halifax Recreational Area is, and you'd just be throwing your money away. I'm not going to change it.''

Television, radio, and news reporters flocked to his garage for the ceremony at which the mayor would present him with the check. In private Yunick warned the mayor, "I told you I'm not going to change the name and take your money." The mayor said, "You'll embarrass me if you don't take it." Yunick agreed to accept it.

In front of The Best Damn Garage in Town, the mayor got up and gave a little speech, and the four thousand people in attendance clapped. The mayor handed over the check, and in front of everyone, Smokey Yunick tore the check into four pieces and threw the shards into the wind.

Smokey said, "I can't thank you, because you didn't do anything for me. I'm actually doing you a favor. No one would know where the Halifax Recreational Area is."

And with $600 in his pocket and the enmity of the powers that be, he left town, arriving at Indianapolis with one car, no spare engine, no spare parts, and no money to speak of. He still qualified for the race.

In the 1970s Yunick got out of both NASCAR and Indy racing for the same reason. It became too expensive to own a car without a corporate sponsor, and Yunick didn't want to have to depend on the largess of others to keep him running. He dropped out of NASCAR competition in 1970 and left Indy cars in 1975. He can still be found at his desk at The Best Damn Garage in Town, smoking his pipe, talking engines, cars, and racing history with anyone who asks—and many do—and you can read his colorful and informative columns in *Circle Track* magazine.

Smokey Yunick is, above all, a survivor. For four years during World War II he was a bomber pilot, and he survived because he figured out the best means of staying alive and pursued it. In life he has survived the rigors of hard living. Like Ralph Moody and many of the other competitors of his day, racing, and not the accumulation of money, was what Henry "Smokey" Yunick lived for. He is a living reminder that racing in the good old days was a hard and dangerous occupation.

SMOKEY YUNICK: "Actually, I don't know my real name. I think I know what my right age is. I operate off a birth certificate I bought for ten bucks from a priest in Philadelphia. At that time I was sixteen, and they said, 'Your name is Henry, Howard, or Gregory—take your pick.'

"The war had started, and I wanted to fly, so a real nice rich guy named Pitcairn, who I worked for, fixed me up with a birth certificate, because you couldn't do anything without it. I rode down on a motorcycle, and we decided my name was Henry, and we decided my birthday was May 25th, and I decided I was born in 1923, and that's what I used ever since.

"My dad died when I was young, so I didn't get to talk to him. We lived on a little farm in an area north of Philadelphia called Nishaminy. I did all the work on the farm, and all we had was one horse—plowed with it, cultivated with it; boy, that's a real job. We couldn't afford a tractor, but I got the idea that if I bought a one-driver rear end from a Ford Model T one-ton truck, and welded it to a 6-cylinder Dodge, a car with a fairly powerful engine in it, and cut the thing in half, I could make a tractor out of the two. That's how it got started. And I was intrigued with motorcycles, started playing around with them, racing them.

"I quit high school when I was a junior. I went a couple months into the eleventh grade, and then we had problems—it was bad times then so I had to get a job, because I had to support a mother and a sister, so I got a job working in a garage, $10 a week, and I worked in a machine shop for a guy named Pitcairn who invented the autogyro and the mail-wing-airplane, and all those old mail pilots were still there in his factory. Pitcairn told me, 'I'll teach you to weld and get you an Army-Navy certificate.'

"I had gotten the flying bug from listening to the pilots, and when the war started, I got that birth certificate, and then I flew for the Air Force for about four years through World War II.

"I started in Africa, went up into Europe, and from there went to China-Burma-India, from there to the Philippines and then to Okinawa, and then the war was over. I made the whole deal.

"When I went in, I couldn't wait to get over there. I went over as a B-17 pilot, and we were sent to a place called Marrakesh, on the Gold Coast of Africa, and I would say inside of ten minutes those German fighters cured me totally of ever wanting to have anything to do with the war. The rest of the time, I did it because I was told to, but I really didn't want any part of it, but in those days it wouldn't have run through your mind to say, 'This is stupid.' So I did what I did, but after some bombing missions, you learn how to fly where you have a little chance to survive.

"The best place to survive was to fly Carolina Charlie. If you looked up, we flew in a diamond, front and back, left and right. Carolina Charlie was the trailing plane. You had to fly very close to keep all the guns together. If I flew from the left side, I could see the copilot in that plane next to me as plain as day. Those vapor trails don't mean anything to you, but if you fly in formation, they drive you crazy. You get vertigo to where you can't believe it. If you flew up front, you had to overlap the other plane twenty feet above or below. That was their idea of the best way to survive, but unfortunately when you got into the flak, once they saw where One was, they knew where Two and Three were going to be.

"But tail-end Charlie was the best place, because you didn't have to watch the vapor trail because Charlie didn't overlap by half a wing like the others. And you could move. If you were the wing man, you had to sit there and take it.

"I came out of the war a first lieutenant. Those who flew up front or wing made colonels or brigadier generals. I probably was called a screwup, but I'd given up winning the war in the first ten minutes. I was just doing what I had to do in order to survive. I'm sure I was lucky, but I also helped my luck quite a bit. Some poor son of a bitch might have gone over there, might have been a hell of a good pilot, but if he got killed his first mission, that isn't going to do you much good. If some guy centered you with those 88s, why, you were done, or if a fighter happened to come through there and put about twenty-five rounds in the right place, why, down she went.

"Real early in the war I was just getting ready to go overseas, and I was stationed at a place called Dyersburg, Tennessee, about fifty miles from Memphis. I went to the state fair, got drunk, and the next morning I had to fly high-altitude formation and my appendix broke. The Air Force had a rule that you couldn't fly for a certain number of days after an operation, so I stayed in Dyersburg as a test pilot. That sounds great, but I was just an engineering check pilot. In other words, they overhauled the plane, and somebody had to fly it for eight hours and write down all these numbers. It was boring as hell.

"They didn't have radar then, so they didn't know where the hell we were when we flew, so I'd pick out places on the map I wanted to look at, and Daytona was one of them. I could get down here and back to Dyersburg in the amount of time necessary. It looked so good from the air that I decided if I ever got out of the Air Force, that's where I wanted to live. And that's how I came to Daytona. Also, I hate cold weather.

"When the war ended, everything happened. I came back and met a girl, and like a dumb son of a bitch wanted to get married, and we got married, and it was cold up in New Jersey, where I was working as a mechanic in a garage.

"I was working on trucks, and they had a huge garage door, and inside that huge door they had a little door, and the service manager was supposed to go in and out that little door, but that big door had an electric button, and every time he wanted to go in or out, he'd push the button, and the whole son of a bitch would go up, and he did that all day long, and my stall was right next to the door, and when he'd open that door the cold wind would really hit you.

"After a week or two, I asked the service manager, 'Couldn't you use the small door?' But he still kept doing it, and so one morning he did it two or three times, and I remember his name was Al something, Al Winters maybe, and I said, 'Al, I know it doesn't bother you, but it's really aggravating me. The next time you open that son of a bitch unnecessarily, I'm going.'

"About three minutes later he did it again. I got out from under that truck, loaded my stuff, and dragged it out the door and threw it in the back of my car.

"I lived in a house trailer I had just bought. This happened in the morning, and by two in the afternoon I had my house trailer hooked up, the tools loaded up, and when my wife came home about five o'clock, I said, 'I'm going to Florida.'

"My wife was a graduate nurse. She said, 'I don't want to go.' I said, 'Let me unload your stuff, because I'm not staying here another day.'

"She decided to go with me—too bad. I drove straight to Daytona, pulled into a trailer court, couldn't get a job for a week, so I started fixing cars there. Everybody had some kind of problem with his car or trailer. And that's how I got started. I did that for about six months, and then an old blacksmith downtown had more space than he needed, and he needed a little help, but he didn't want to hire anyone, so we made a deal: I'd help him in exchange for the space.

"I saved up $500 or $600 and made a down payment on this ground my shop is on here, borrowed some money, and built a garage, and I've been here ever since.

"I got involved in racing through a very good mechanic-driver here named Marshall Teague. Marshall worked as a machinist in a parts store called Motive Parts. I bought most of my parts there, so I got to know him. Marshall built nice race cars, but he'd get it 90 percent ready and he'd have to go to the race with the other 10 percent undone. He'd always run late, and somehow he got me to start helping him.

"The first Southern 500 at Darlington—the first 500-mile stock car race—took place in September 1950, and Marshall went up there with a Lincoln, and he was driving it, and I was running the pits. We fell out about halfway through.

"Even though Marshall had more than he could handle with his own car, in 1951 he decided he was going to run two cars. He had a deal with Hudson for a couple nickels. He drove one car, and Herb Thomas drove the other. Thomas wanted all the money, so Thomas divorced from

Teague, and in 1952 Hudson came to me, I guess on Marshall's recommendation, offered me $200 an engine—about a dollar an hour—to build engines for Herb Thomas.

"Herb Thomas was a dumb farmer who could really drive, was really a good driver. He was smart in the race. He knew how to pace himself, as compared to the rest of the guys he raced with. He was as good as they came, and they have never given him enough credit for his ability.

"But the poor son of a bitch was practically a sharecropper starving to death. The first three or four years I was around him, I never saw him in anything but longhandle overalls and high-topped farmer's shoes. Herb was a terrible-looking guy whose teeth were all rotten, and he wasn't that old, around thirty-two. But the poor guy had worked like a dog since he was ten, barely making ends meet, and then suddenly here he is in the papers every week.

"Herb never shared his winnings with me, and then when the season was over, he'd sell the car or give it to his brother to drive. Ah, it really wasn't important what he did with the car, but all I got was my $200 an engine. That was it. I didn't get anything for building the cars, got nothing out of the cars, got no prize money. Hudson led me to believe that after some time passed, I'd get really well paid, but the only thing they ever did for me was in 1954 they gave me a new Hudson Hornet.

"Why did I do it? Don't know. Just liked to race. I was quitting all the time, because my garage was busy. Herb was running thirty to forty times a year, and I had to leave Friday night and be back to open the garage Monday morning, and of course I would go dead tired because I built the race cars at night and I'd come back dead tired from the trip. Back in those days it was a little different—you built the engine, the chassis, the whole works, and usually the best you could hope for was one unpaid helper, some other idiot about as dumb as I was who liked racing enough to come down every night and help you.

"Most of the tracks we raced on back then were horse tracks, county-fair type, narrow tracks with tight corners and fence nails in them. They were dug out, with horrible dust, holes. They had no facilities. Even at Darlington, if you wanted to take a piss, you had to stand in line for an hour; there was one toilet. The starter stand was on top on the inside of the track, and down at the bottom was a one-holer toilet. The only drinking water available at Darlington was a spigot. There was one telephone. If you wanted to make call, you had to get in your car and go to a gas station.

"The tracks weren't well kept, because the promoters were poor. The promoter would make a little money one week, and then he'd have a race three months later and it would rain him out, or nobody would come, so he didn't have any money. We were running for nothing, and he couldn't fix the racetrack.

"I can remember the second Southern 500 in September 1951. Herb Thomas won it. It was the first long race on asphalt, and all the cars started blowing tires—there were 640 tires blown in that race.

"It wasn't long before everybody was out of tires. The fans all got drunk, and they were begging us to take their tires and wheels. All we had was a wire fence to keep them from the fans, and they would take the wheels and tires off their cars and pass them to us, and we took them and put them on the race cars. Then we'd blow them, and the rim would get bent, and there was this big pile of rims and tires.

"When the race was over, there were about five hundred cars sitting on Coca-Cola boxes with no tires or wheels. And these drunks were saying, 'I need my tars (tires) and wheels back.' But we had blown them all out. Finally, I got drunk, got in my car, and went home.

"It was so crazy back then. One driver who was especially fun to be around was Curtis Turner. With him, it was a never-ending party from one minute to the next, nothing but fun. Curtis was very generous, and one of the greatest natural talents that ever sat in a race car. He could really drive. But he drank too much, and when it came to race time, the poor son of a bitch was half drunk and half pooped out, so he made some mistakes. But he *was* a lot of fun. I ran with him all the time.

"I even took him to Indianapolis one year. I was teaching him how to run up there when we wrecked the car. Yup, I spent a lot of time with Curtis drinking, chasing women, racing, raising hell, teaching people how to turn around in the middle of the road at 60 miles an hour, putting cars in swimming pools. And there were the times we'd wreck the race car and go rent a Hertz and race it. I did that at West Memphis one time; did it at Riverside too. Frank Mundy did it several times. The rental agreements being what they were, there wasn't much they could say. You'd buy the insurance, which was $2, and bring that son of a bitch back looking like it had been hammered by a car crusher.

"Another of the top drivers was Tim Flock. Tim was one of the best. He'd play; he was a good player, but he wasn't nowhere near as wild a partier as Curtis. Tim drank and chased women and was a good race driver, damn near as good as Turner, but you didn't get as close to Tim as you did to Curtis. With Tim, you would meet him at the racetrack. He would never be down to help with the race car, and after we finished up at the track, we probably wouldn't see him that night. With Turner, he'd stay where we stayed. We'd all eat together and then party together. And every night was a wild-ass party, 'cause they wouldn't let us work on the car after dark.

"Buck Baker was of the caliber of Tim and Curtis, a wild son of a bitch, drunk as hell. I never got close to him. He had a nasty streak I didn't like. When he got drunk, he'd show off. He was bad about fighting, and when he got drunk he was a nasty son of a bitch. If Curtis got drunk, he just got funnier. Joe Weatherly was the same. But not Buck. But Buck *was* a real good driver.

"I never got close to Lee Petty either. There wasn't too many people who liked Lee Petty. Petty was a good driver. Herb Thomas and him tried to get along, but Lee was a two-faced dirty driver, and I would find it real hard for him to scrape up too many friends in racing today. He didn't start driving until he was thirty-nine. Lee had the same trouble Herb Thomas did. He was born very poor, had had a terrible struggle, started and did very well in race cars, worked like a dog, and was a pretty good driver, though he wasn't the caliber of Curtis or Tim by any means. But survival has much to do with speed, maybe more so, and Lee was a survivor.

"Fireball Roberts was another one who hung around my shop. He was born and raised in Daytona Beach. He had been a pitcher at the University of Florida, and they called him Fireball because he was a fastball pitcher, and apparently was a good one.

"Fireball was wild, drunk all the time, chased women all the time. He was wild like Curtis was, but Fireball had a nasty personality. He was a loner, like I was. He was interested in Fireball only, didn't care what anybody thought. I'm not saying that to knock him. That's the way he was. In my view, I figured anything was fair, except it was unfair to use somebody else to get where you wanted to go. In other words, I had license to do anything I could back up, but one of the rules was, 'Don't get where you're going stepping on top of people.' But it didn't make any difference to Fireball. He really didn't feel anything for anybody else. He wasn't a bad person, but there was no way you could like him like Turner or Weatherly.

"He was a very smart fellow, probably had a very high IQ. He knew quite a bit about the race car *and* the engine, but he would never help on the race car. He was very lazy. Herb Thomas wanted to learn, but never did, although Herb wasn't all that bad. He could have built his own engines and been halfway successful. His biggest drawback would have been dirty, sloppy work. Now Curtis knew nothing about engines, nothing about handling. You'd say 'How is it handling?' The car would be out to lunch, and he'd say, 'Great, perfect. Don't touch it.'

"But Fireball was a hell of a driver. Oh boy. There was a good possibility he was the best of them.

"Fireball was the first thinking driver. After practice, he would rate all the drivers for their abilities. Certain guys he would ride fender to fender with, run nose to tail lap after lap, Curtis and Joe, Tim and Fonty. But other ones, he'd say, 'I know I can pass him,' but maybe he would take three laps because he wouldn't ever go around the outside of him because the guy might lose it and hit him.

"Fireball was either racing or chasing women, and that was about it. Everything else was just something that happened.

"My wife hated racing. To her racers were bums, trash. Somebody asked her what her husband did, and the last thing in the world she'd say was a racer, 'cause that was terrible. She considered racers the lowest form of life on earth. And it wasn't just my wife who didn't like racers. Society classified racers as 'no-good bums.'

"Back in those days, we had a hell of a time staying in the Holiday Inn in Atlanta, the first Atlanta race in '60, because those people were convinced racers were bad people. A lot of places wouldn't allow us. I couldn't just go get a hotel or motel room. They would see that race car hanging on the end of your car, and they wouldn't let us in. We'd have to unhook it, leave the race car down the road, go get the room, go back and get the car, and even then it wasn't unusual for them to come back and tell us to leave. Within thirty minutes of bringing the race car in, the manager would be there to say, 'We don't rent rooms to racers. We'll refund your money. You'll have to leave.'

"What could we do about it? We'd have to leave.

"The change came very gradually. I can remember coming home from Darlington in '55, and there was a famous newscaster named Kaltenborn giving the nightly news, and at midnight he noted that Herb Thomas had won the Darlington 500 and said a few sentences about that, which shocked me, because the only way racers made the national news was if they got killed. Then it would be a headline on the front page, 'Racer Killed.'

"I can remember in '55 at Le Mans a Mercedes went into the crowd and killed eighty-eight fans. They were talking about banning car racing in America. President Eisenhower was all huffy, and everybody was hanging on the edge.

"It wasn't a concern to me. All I wanted to do was race. I didn't care about politics. Whether things were going good in the country or going bad, we never took it seriously. We never noticed, because we were so engrossed in racing. I never even knew what the prize money was on the entry blanks. I never paid any attention. In other words, there was nothing that could happen in my life to keep me from going to the race the next Sunday. Whatever happened in my family or personal situation or finances, somehow I would find the money to get there. Getting ready for the race: That was the number one priority.

"In 1954 we won the Southern 500 at Darlington with Herb driving. Darlington was the longest track we had, a high-banked, paved track. It was a place you could really race, so it was hands down the most important stock car race in the United States. Still, it was a chicken-shit facility run by a bunch of farmers. Why we took all the grief we did from Bill France and the people who ran Darlington and the rest of the tracks, I've never been able to figure out. I guess we just liked to race.

"I can remember going to Lincoln, Nebraska, a long way for a 100-miler that pays $500 to the winner. When I got there Ed Ott, the promoter, said to me, 'I'll tell you what. Your car is running pretty good. If you could run a dead heat with Dick Rathmann, I'll pay two first places.' He wanted the race to be exciting for the fans.

"We went to all the trouble to set it up. Herb and Rathmann were eyeing each other, doorway to doorway, to get a dead heat. The race ended, and he declared that Rathmann was the winner and paid him $500 and said we finished second and paid us $300.

"I said, 'Where is the other $200?' He said, 'You know I can't do that. That would be illegal.'

"The other thing that happened to you, if you ran pretty good, they worked on you during the inspection. If you had a fast car, they'd get rough on you. If there was someone else doing all the good work, they'd get on his ass. And often they would let the other guys do things, but I couldn't.

"And they *never* got off my ass. Of course, by this time I knew Bill France real well. You're working your ass off, and he's starting to get rich. I won three of his beach races. The first one I got $8,000, the last one I got $15,000. But Bill France had total control. It was a dictatorship. France got rich, and there was a whole bunch of us who started this thing who didn't live through it. A lot of them died early, and they didn't deserve to die, and Marshall Teague was one of them.

"Marshall died trying to get back in the good graces of NASCAR. France had a deal where the first guy who ran 180 miles an hour on the Daytona track, which would make it the fastest track in the world, would get $10,000.

"Teague killed himself trying to do that in a Zoomar special, which had the aerodynamics of a yellow pig. It was a beautiful-looking car for those days and times, but it was one you could fly. It belonged to a hell of a nice guy, Chapman Root, who never would have taken it out there if he thought it was going to kill Marshall. It ran 172, 173 miles an hour, and Marshall was trying to brave the rest of it out of the car.

"The morning he got killed he begged me to come out there and help him. I said, 'Marshall, you're crazy. That thing is wanting to fly. There ain't nothing you or I could do to it out there. If you really want to do this, bring the goddamn car over to the shop, get some money, and let's work on it about six months, and I think we can do it. But I don't want any part of killing you.'

"Two hours later he did it to himself. Marshall Teague had as much to do with NASCAR as Bill France did. The guy who *really* started NASCAR was Red Vogt. He got shit and shit on. The guy who put up the money for the first NASCAR charter was a guy named Raymond Parks, who they refused to put in the Hall of Fame at Darlington because he had a criminal record. I don't know how clean Raymond was, but I know he's a fine man now. But he was in the slot machine business, and so they kept him out of the Hall of Fame in Darlington. And it goes on and on and on.

"Back in those days, to prepare a car you had a rule book, and you had to use your imagination. They said it had to be a stock engine, and if it was my decision to move the crankshaft someplace in the block other than where they put it, there was no rule saying you couldn't. So it was the challenge of us versus the rule book. When it first came out, the rule book was quite skinny. As time passed, it became more and more elaborate.

"In '55, we ran that Packard the one race, switched to a Hudson for one race, then ran a Chevy. That year we won the Darlington race in that Chevy. At that time Maurie Rose got assigned here to help me make the Chevy run. I gave him the job, because he knew tires and knew the tire people.

"I said, 'This son of a bitch can't possibly win the race on speed. We're going to be inferior, and there ain't but one way we can beat 'em, and that would be tires.' I said, 'Go find me some 18-inch tires to fit this thing.'

"The rule book had said you couldn't have any tire rim over six or seven inches wide, but it didn't say anything about tread. So I got us a set of slicks and blew their asses off, and then they said, 'No slicks.'

"But there was another hooker in the rule book that didn't specify diameter, and after a couple of weeks Mauri called me from a junkyard in Akron and said, 'There aren't any 18s, Smokey, but I found some 16s that I think can do it.' Goodyear had made 200 Supersports, and Briggs Cunningham had bought twenty for Le Mans to see if he liked them better than the Dunlops. He didn't. The junkyard was going to burn what they had left if I didn't buy them, so I bought 174 of them for a buck apiece.

"We bolted them on, practiced, qualified, and went nonstop in the race without changing the tires and won the race with them. That was the first race Chevy ever won.

"I can remember before the race Carl Kiekhafer, who had a deal with Chrysler, wanted me to sell him some of my tires. Kiekhafer was the first one who organized the team concept. Chrysler had given him a substantial sum of money over three years, and he came down with an army of employees and three or four cars, and he was the first one to pay the drivers a salary.

"The standard deal was the driver got no expenses, no money, and half the prize money. Kiekhafer gave his drivers half the prize money *and* an annual salary, plus a bonus for winning the pole, a bonus for winning, and he was able to run three or four cars in each race so if Tim Flock fell out, Buck Baker was in a position to win.

"He was an important person in the history of this sport, but he wasn't well liked. He had a PR department that gave out a daily sheet—no more, no less. You didn't get to ask him a question.

"As I said, he tried to force me to sell him some tires. He got Bill France to come down and tell me I had to sell Kiekhafer the tires or I couldn't run them myself. But I had reason to know he wasn't going to do any such thing because France had been the instigator to get me to run Chevys. He wanted to hook GM. Darlington was a one-race deal, and I figured the last thing he would do was stop me from running.

"I wouldn't sell Kiekhafer the tires. I didn't like Kiekhafer at all, because we had had various run-ins. A matter of fact, for years we had a picture of Kiekhafer framed on the toilet seat in my garage.

"Kiekhafer didn't deal with me like he was my peer. He decided what he liked or didn't like, and he'd send representatives to NASCAR, and of course the Chrysler sponsorship was important to NASCAR, so they gave him some concessions they wouldn't have had he not been influential with Chrysler. But he didn't get my tires.

"The Daytona beach race was a little different from the other races, because it was the only long track we ran. We geared up for maximum speed. There was no fast way to get through the corners. You threw the car sideways and tried to keep from going over the bank. You used the transmission. You couldn't run in high gear and keep going so you put a little more clutch in than you normally would, because we had to use a lot of brakes. But the gear ratios were all set for speed.

"Before Darlington was built, the beach race at Daytona was the biggest thing we had, and it was easy to get to. It was a very special race. Bill France probably couldn't get a lot of money out of it because there was no way to keep the people out. The only weapon he had was to put up a bunch of signs around where the people were sneaking in saying, 'Watch out for the rattlesnakes.' He made sure you knew. The snakes were there, but he played it to the hilt, and so a lot of people did pay rather than chance it. But a lot of people did get through, and that's probably why he didn't pay any money, because he didn't take any money in.

"Herb Thomas never won the beach race. He would have won in 1954, but some guy put sand in our gas tank. A *lot* of sand.

"We made the mistake of not watching the car. Two or three hours before the race we took it down to the beach and parked it. We got away from it, weren't watching, and some son of a bitch put in around eight or ten pounds of sand.

"The race started, and we had a big lead, I know we would have won the race, but after ten laps it just quit running. When I got back to the shop and checked it out, everything was okay, except we couldn't get any fuel. We pulled the fuel tank out, cut it open, and that son of a bitch had about a half a bucket of sand in it. A fan for somebody else, I guess, someone who was pulling for another Hudson, must have done it.

"After the Hudson deal blew up—that's a long story—there was a guy who ran Packard named Jack Nance, who had been a hotshot appliance salesman from General Electric. He must have been a hell of a salesman, because Packard was in deep trouble, and they hired Jack to run it. One of Jack's ideas was a race program, so he called me and came down and talked to me and offered me a job, which was maybe $10,000 a year to race a Packard.

"I entered it in the Daytona beach race in 1955. Herb Thomas drove. Back then you had to run stock, and to make it run I increased the valve spring pressure, and in the pace lap the son of a bitch broke a valve spring, so it didn't go very far in the race, twenty-two laps, because it was a junk engine with junk parts. That Packard was a hopeless case.

"I told Jack, 'There ain't no way I can make that goddamn thing win. You pay good, but it's not worth it to me to go knowing I can't win. I can't change the rules, the parts aren't worth a damn, the car is too heavy, the transmission is no good, the rear end is no good, the suspension is too weak, nothing about the car can be fixed.'

"So I quit them. I figured the Buick had the potential to do it, and it's another long story, but I got ahold of one. Buick furnished me with a car and engine. I built it into a race car and built the engine. They were also supposed to pay me, but they had a chief engineer named Kelly, who apparently overstepped his bounds when he said he could come up with the money.

"We went with that Buick to Langhorne, which was a horse track, and sat on the pole and were leading the race, and with about five laps to go, we ran over a big spike from the fence and got a flat, and by the time we changed the tire, that was the end of that.

"I told Herb to bring the car back to my shop at Daytona, that Buick hadn't paid me and I wasn't going to run it anymore. Either they would keep their promise to pay, or I was going to sell the car. Herb said, 'Let's run it at the Charlotte Fairgrounds next week.' I said, 'No. It's going to need new axles, new spindles, change the gears, go through the engine. For what it pays, there ain't no way.'

"He said, 'I'll do it myself.'

"I said, 'Don't do that.'

"The car wasn't back by Friday. I called and couldn't get Herb on the phone. He went ahead and ran it at the Fairgrounds, an axle broke, it flipped three or four times, and he broke his leg. And I never did see that car again either.

"After that I had the Chevy deal. A long story, but I took the Chevy on a one-race deal with Herb as the driver. Twice Chevy begged me to take Herb.

"I decided we better test the car first, so I finished up a little quicker so we could run it at West Memphis, a mile-and-a-half, high-banked dirt track. That was Herb's first drive after his injury. That's when I made an amazing discovery: After the wreck, he wasn't the same driver.

"He wouldn't go fast. He was a totally different driver. I brought the car back here and rebuilt it. I was already committed. At the Darlington race, the game we were playing suited Herb's style, and we won.

"I figured he would straighten out. I built a '56 Buick for him to drive at the beach. We had a car that could easily have won the race, but the way I saw him driving at the beach worried me. He finished ninth, and the windshield was so sandblasted you couldn't even see through it. 'Cause Herb wouldn't get on past them.

"When the race was over, I told him, 'Herb, we're done. You're not going to drive for me anymore. We have a problem. I have never had anyone seriously hurt or killed, and I'm not going to start now. You're scared shitless.'

"Obviously, he didn't agree with that. By now I was running the Chevy program, and I said, 'If you want to keep going, I'll give you both cars. I'll give you the spare engines and parts, and I'll give you Ray Fox. He works for me, and we'll pay his salary and pay for a shop and pay you $2,500 a month.'

"Herb went on to win the championship in '56, but Keikhaefer then got Bill France to add a couple extra races at Hickory and Wilson, stretched the schedule so Buck Baker, who drove for Keikhaefer, could win the championship.

"The race at Hickory wasn't enough, and Baker wasn't going to be able to do it in the second race, until Herb went over a fence. Keikhaefer won the championship while Herb was laying in the hospital with his brains knocked out.

"After I sent Herb on his way, I got Paul Goldsmith off motorcycles and started racing with him. Goldsmith had won the race on the beach on a motorcycle, and he came up and told me he'd like to drive a stock car. He had never driven one before, but I thought, 'I can take this guy and make a hell of a driver out of him.' And it turned out I was right. He *was* a hell of a driver. Matter of fact, Paul Goldsmith had more natural talent than any driver I ever had anything to do with. He was good.

"Goldy was very, very quiet, a very likable guy. He'd work on the race car with you. He had good manners. Herb Thomas had the manners of a pig. Goldsmith was a very, very fast race driver, had extremely quick reflexes.

"We had a coiled rubber snake in a can. You'd take the top off, and this thing would come flying out to scare you. Goldy was the only guy who ever caught it! He caught the son of a bitch! He didn't know what was in the can. But he got it.

"It didn't take him any time at all; inside of three or four races, I'd say, he was as good as there was. Goldy should have won the Darlington race in '57, but that came to a bad ending.

"I was running two cars that day, Goldsmith and Curtis Turner. Goldsmith had the pole at 119.291 and Curtis qualified second. It was another one of those days when everything was right. Nobody could have done anything to stop us.

"Our big problem was that Goldy got with one bunch of gamblers and guaranteed them he would not lead the first lap. And then Turner got with another bunch of gamblers out of Atlanta and he guaranteed them *he* would not lead the first lap.

"They came off turn four, Goldy in front trying to slow down to make Turner go by him. They went across the start-finish line the first lap in the race with Goldy on the brakes, with all four tires smoking and Turner pushing him. Cotton Owens crossed the line first.

"We didn't get fifty miles into the race when Fonty Flock spun out going into three, and both Bobby Myers and Goldy smashed into him. There was nothing Goldy could do. Myers was killed and Fonty got hurt. That took care of Goldy, and then Curtis Turner took over, and Lee Petty ran into him in turn three, bent the car all up, sent him to the hospital, and after we put a new radiator in the car, we put Joe Weatherly in the car and finished way back in the race, and that really pissed me off, because the *Saturday Evening Post* was going to give me $25,000 for my life story *if* I won the Darlington race, which would have been four times.

"I was going to buy a new Apache airplane with the twenty-five grand. They had the check up there waiting for me. The plane was even sitting in the little dirt airport behind turn number three. And it all went to ashes.

"After the race I was trying to get out of the infield. I was driving a new '57 Ford. Goldy was in the hospital; Turner was in the hospital. I was hot and tired, pissed off about losing the airplane, and about half drunk when a guy in a brand-new DeSoto inched his way almost off the track to the gate, and he got in front of me where I couldn't go any more.

"I jumped out of my car and went over to him and said, 'Buddy, that's a damn nice-looking car.' He said, 'I just got it.' I said, 'I'm hot and I'm tired. I got to get to the hospital in a hurry. You have bad manners. If you want to keep this car looking pretty, you can back up a little bit. I'll talk to the guy behind me.'

"He said, 'Screw you.'

"A state trooper was standing there looking at the whole thing. I walked back to the guy in back of me and said, 'Back up a little bit.' He backed up five or six feet.

"I backed up and put that son of a bitch in low gear, and I flew forward, and I whapped that goddamned DeSoto, and car parts flew everywhere.

"That trooper came over and went over to the driver of the other car, and he said to him, 'What the hell are you doing pulling up in front of him? Look what you did to his car. Back her up now.' Then the trooper waved me on.

"The trooper said to me, 'I was watching that thing. It was a chicken-shit deal the way he cut you off. I'm glad you whapped him.'

"Goldy did win the Daytona beach race in 1958, in a Pontiac. I spent most of the time working on the engine, and the time spent on the suspension had to do with durability. A lot of time was also spent on brakes.

"This was a horsepower race, and we had the horsepower, and Goldsmith did a good job. If you didn't watch it, you could get in the sand and hit a place that was a six-inch drop before you'd hit the dirt, and if you hit that with the inside of your wheels, it could throw you into the boonies. So it was a very dangerous course. And that backstretch was very narrow. It was very hard to pass on the backstretch, but he had won the thing on a motorcycle, and he was real good. He beat Curtis Turner by five lengths after Curtis spun out in the surf on the backstretch. It was the last race ever held on the beach.

"In 1959 Bill France opened the Daytona Speedway. It added a lot of class to racing, and it got a lot of interest from more sponsors. It was very definitely a positive forward step.

"France was a wheeler-dealer. Ralph Richard was a county commissioner, and France got Ralph to agree with him about building a new speedway, and Ralph controlled the county commission so whatever he wanted to do, he did.

"But in all fairness to France, that was an impossible swamp when he started. It was a mess. The land wasn't being used for anything. That was anything but a nice piece of ground, a terrible place. You couldn't go in it. If you went out to the middle, you'd be up to your neck in mud.

"What France did was dig a lake to drain the water, and then he pumped and dug the mud out, took it out and let it dry, and used it to make the banks of the track.

"I was over with Bill France when I first saw the new track. He was trying to finance it by selling stock for a dollar a share, and he wasn't having any luck. I got busy and made about ten speeches at Rotary, Kiwanis, Elephants, Raccoons, all the clubs, urging the people to buy stock. That must have helped a little but it wasn't enough to do the trick. Once in a while I would look in and see how they were coming. But always they were short of money.

"Then he got the Union Oil Company to put up a million bucks, raised money here and there until he got it done. France gambled everything he had to build that track.

"And once France built the speedway, he started making money. You could sell a lot of tickets for that one. As it turned out, when he built the track, it was a hell of a smart move.

"The first race at the new speedway was won by Lee Petty. I didn't respect Lee because he was a dirty driver. Lee won by outlasting you, staying out of wrecks. Shoot, he won most of his races from three laps down. That first race at Daytona, NASCAR said Johnny Beauchamp won, and Lee just raised hell. I don't know what the truth was because I was drunk by then. If Lee had won, it was by a half inch. But nobody else would have put up that fuss. They'd have raised hell, maybe started a fight, but it would have been over. 'I'll get your ass next week.' Not Lee. He got lawyers, camped on the racetrack, wouldn't leave. And four days later he was awarded the victory.

"Junior Johnson won the next year. When Junior first came into racing, he came in on a nickel-and-dime budget, and you couldn't see what a good driver he was. It happened enough times that something would fall off that I dismissed him. Then he got better rides, and you could see he could drive. Junior went, something Lee couldn't do. And Junior wasn't a dirty driver. He was very talented, one of the best. He drove hard every inch of the way. You had to respect him.

"My cars won the Daytona 500 twice on that new speedway. And a couple times at the Fourth of July race. Marvin Panch won for me in 1961, and Fireball won in 1962.

"Marvin drove for me a couple years. Marvin was a real, real nice guy and a good driver, but not a super driver. For the Daytona 500 in 1961, I had a new car with Fireball, and a leftover one, a year old, and so I decided to fix up the old one and let Marvin drive it. They were running one-two all day, and then Fireball blew and Marvin won it.

"I let him drive it a couple of other places, and then at Darlington I didn't want to run two cars; it was too much work. I only ran Fireball, who was leading the Darlington race by two and a half laps, but Fireball had the flu, was nauseated, and had a cold, so we had to change him. It was one of those days when the race car was right, and there was no race to it. Fireball was just gone, but when he got sick, we put Marvin in, and he gave that whole lead up to a guy named Nelson Stacy. Son of a bitch if Stacy didn't run him down, pass him, and win the race. Boy, that pissed me off. I don't think I used Marvin anymore. Gave the guy a two-and-a-half-lap lead!

"Around that time Holman-Moody became powerful. Ralph Moody was a real good driver on short tracks, a real sharp chassis man, and not too bad on engines. Nice guy too. They don't come any nicer than Ralph.

"Ralph came from New England—he still has a strong New England accent—and came to Charlotte where he threw in with John Holman. Holman was a nice guy, but kind of an asshole, a crooked son of a bitch and a backstabber. He had every bad habit there was. Ralph took it straight up. You could trust Ralph, but not Holman. I had bad dealings with him all the time. He screwed me coming and going. It was no accident. We all knew how it was.

"I can remember one time leading a race at Langhorne. We were running superchargers, and I had the thing figured out to where it was no contest. Paul Goldsmith was driving for me.

"Holman made cars for Ford, and Ford had never won with a super-charger, and John said to me, 'Ford really wants to win this race. You've got to slow Paul down and maybe not blow up that engine.' Holman wanted to make it look like more of a race. I said, 'Oh, okay.'

"Fireball was driving for Holman and running second, and Fireball got within about fifteen yards of him, and I said to Holman, 'What the hell is going on, John?' He said, 'We're here to race, ain't we?' He had suckered me. I said, 'Oh, okay.'

"I went down and told Goldsmith to go, and he came off turn four the next lap, increasing his lead steadily, when he threw both rear treads off his rear tires into the grandstand. We had to put a new pair of tires on, and when the race was over, we lacked about 150 yards of catching Fireball.

"Holman came over and said, 'That's racing.'

"That was the kind of deals he'd do to you all the time. And I know he was screwing Ralph moneywise. Holman's biggest single problem was he was money-crazy. John wasn't good at anything. He was a junk dealer. He didn't know anything about chassis, engines, couldn't even drive.

"I'm not in NASCAR racing anymore. I got out in 1970. I used to be asked all the time to build cars, engines, but no more. I don't like what has happened to racing. I'm not knocking it, but the kind of racing I knew, I'd go home and build a race car and you go home and build a race car, and we'll unload our cars at Daytona, and then we'll walk down the track, and I'll pull my pants up, look around, and say, 'Sons o' bitches, let's have a race.'

"I want to race other mechanics with drivers. We weren't doing it for money, we were doing it because we wanted to race each other, to see who could build the fastest car. No more. That doesn't exist now. It's all done with dollars now. If you don't have three million dollars, there is no way you're going to be able to compete."

LAP 6

Big Bill France

The Visionary

On December 12, 1947, William Henry Getty France gathered racing promoters from around the Southeast for a meeting at the Ebony Bar atop the Streamline Inn in Daytona Beach. France had been promoting races there since the late thirties and saw the need to set up an organization of promoters, mechanics, and drivers to regulate the sport. France, who had two middle names because his parents hoped the Getty name would bring their son riches, had been into cars since high school, when he and a buddy named Hugh Ostermeyer built a canvas-covered race car with a Model T engine capable of running 90 miles an hour.

In his native Washington, D.C., he had worked in car garages and service stations, driven in sprint car races, won, and too often gotten burned by promoters who skipped out with the proceeds.

He remembered one race in 1930 in a town called Pikesville, Maryland, where a winning purse of $500 had been trumpeted. He finished fourth. When he went for his prize money, he was told the winners got $50 and he $10. France, angry, wanted to know why, when the purse was supposed to be $500. He was told that the larger purse had been announced as a ploy to impress the fans.

Acutely aware that unscrupulous promoters were tarnishing the image of the sport, Bill France believed that for the sport to grow, an association of racing promoters was needed. France wanted to see a set of rules that would keep the cars, and the competition, uniform. Another goal of his was to provide insurance for the drivers, and to inaugurate a point system so drivers could compete for a driving championship.

France had attempted to promote his beach race as a ''national championship,'' only to be told he could not do that unless he had rules, a point championship, and an organization that crossed more than one

Bill France (© International Speedway Corporation/NASCAR)

state line. The rebuff likely was the impetus for his call to organize, and yet, as far back as 1938, when France began promoting the race on the beach at Daytona, he had expressed his belief that the sport was in need of a set of rules to keep cars uniform and competition equal.

At the end of that 1938 beach race, the first racer to cross the finish line was driver Smokey Purser. After Purser received the checkered flag, he drove away from the beach and out of sight. The race's technical director, Ed Parkinson, became suspicious. He figured Purser was hiding something and went and tracked him down at a local gas station. Purser was caught trying to remove special high-compression cylinder heads for cars that ran at high altitudes. France disqualified him.

During the organizational meeting France expressed his feeling that the first and foremost goal should be equal competition. He sought to codify the rules to help reduce cheating. If this was to be "stock" car racing, each car mechanic had to know what he could or could not do. France knew it wouldn't be possible to catch everyone, but he knew he at least had to try to curb the most flagrant abusers.

As part of the new organization, France said, he wanted the sport to be able to list its champions, to memorialize their records and their earnings. As a promoter France was well aware of the importance of records and statistics, and he kept records of who led after each lap as a clever way of getting local merchants involved in his races.

Among the prizes France had awarded in the 1938 race on the beach at Daytona to lap leaders were a bottle of rum, $2.50 credit at a local men's clothing store, a box of fancy Hav-a-Tampa cigars, a case of Pennzoil motor oil, a pair of $5 sunglasses from Walgreen's, two cases of Blue Ribbon beer, and a $25 credit on any automobile in Dick Rose's used-car lot. This principle of sponsor involvement has never changed. The only difference today is the amount awarded by sponsors.

France made one other proposal, one that was to distance and distinguish his new organization from all other racing groups.

He told the other promoters, "We need to think about our image. If you race a junky-looking automobile—even if you take a new Cadillac, take the bumpers off, and let it get real dirty—then in people's minds it would still be a jalopy.

"We need to have races for the most modern automobiles available. Plain, ordinary working people have to be able to associate with the cars. Standard street stock cars are what we should be running."

France's farsighted reasoning bordered on genius. Back in 1947 he could not have foreseen the day when car manufacturers would pump millions of dollars into racing, but ultimately, that was the result of his thinking.

When in 1950 Joe Littlejohn drove his Olds 88 Rocket 98.840 miles an hour to win the pole in France's beach race, it gave a big boost to Olds 88 sales. No new cars were made during the war (nor was there any auto racing; Bill France built sub chasers), but once the war ended, the car manufacturers used racing to sell and promote their products, as Hudsons, Chevys, Chryslers, and Fords vied on the NASCAR circuit. The dealers' slogan became: "Win on Sunday, sell on Monday."

At that historic first meeting, Bill France was named president. When a name for the organization was requested, the first suggestion was NASCRA, the National Stock Car Racing Association. But a small group in Georgia already had that name, so driver-mechanic Red Vogt suggested an alternative: the National Association for Stock Car Automobile Racing. There was some concern that NASCAR sounded a lot like Nash Car, but Nash was a minor auto manufacturer, and the recommendation was seconded and passed.

The group needed money to incorporate. Louis Ossinsky, a Daytona Beach attorney who was a customer at Bill France's gas station, volunteered to do the work. The incorporation date was February 21, 1948. The group's headquarters was located at 88 Main Street.

In order to give this new organization some publicity and clout, France hired the world-famous endurance record driver, Erwin "Cannonball" Baker, to be NASCAR's commissioner of racing. Baker, who knew cars, was known to be fair, and his authority gave the new organization needed prestige.

The first "new car" race was held at the Charlotte Speedway on June 19, 1949. It called for two hundred laps over the three-quarter-mile dirt oval. Beside Fords, Oldsmobiles, Buicks, and Chryslers, there were Hudsons, Lincolns, a Mercury, and even a Kaiser.

Under the new rules set down by Bill France and NASCAR, the cars had to come off the showroom floor. There could be no tampering, no souping-up of the engines. For this season, the oldest a competing car could be was a 1946 model.

The Charlotte race, the first ever in the Grand National championship series, was won by Glenn Dunnaway in a '47 Ford owned by Hubert Westmoreland. After the race, inspectors discovered a wedge that had been placed to stiffen the rear springs of Dunnaway's car.

The car had been used during the week for bootlegging. The use of a wedge was typical of bootleggers' cars. But it was in violation of

NASCAR's rules, and Dunnaway was disqualified and the victory given to Jim Roper, who'd driven a '49 Lincoln. Roper was awarded the $2,000 first-place money.

The other drivers, who included Tim and Fonty Flock and Red Byron, knew that Dunnaway hadn't known about the wedge and chipped in part of their purses. Dunnaway went home richer than if he had won.

After the race, car owner Hubert Westmoreland sued, claiming his car was stock and demanding his prize money. In court, the lawyer for NASCAR, in discussing the illegal wedge, kept repeating over and over the term "bootlegger." NASCAR won the case.

The era during which most of the cars were owned by bootleggers had come to an end.

A new age, that of the superspeedway, was about to begin.

During a poker game in 1949, stock car race promoter Harold Brasington proposed that an asphalt track be built near his home in Darlington, South Carolina. Brasington had visited the Indianapolis Speedway, and he envisioned building a similar track for stock cars.

Brasington took a huge risk, and with an advance sale of $25,000 worth of tickets was able to complete construction. Brasington, who had competed in Bill France's beach races, originally gave the race sanction to the Central States Racing Association, but when he found himself short on drivers, he called Bill France and invited him to view the site. Impressed, France pledged his NASCAR drivers.

On September 4, 1950, Darlington International Raceway's first Southern 500 was staged, four hundred laps around a mile-and-a-quarter paved track, the first paved track built in America. Seventy-five cars competed. It took fifteen days to qualify the field. There were few hotels to accommodate the crowds, but nonetheless that first year thirty thousand fans flocked to see the race.

The favorites were Red Byron and Curtis Turner, but the winner was Johnny Mantz from Long Beach, California. Mantz had qualified 43rd, but he won because his car was light and because through his Indy racing he had connections with tire people in Dayton, Ohio, and was able to arrange to put heavy-duty truck tires similar to Indy-style tires on his car.

During the race Mantz changed tires three times; the cars using standard tires had to change tires as many as twenty-four times. Twenty-two cars had blowouts. Mantz averaged 76.26 miles an hour to win.

When he crossed the finish line, the second car, driven by Fireball Roberts, was nine laps back. The owners of Mantz's car: Hubert Westmoreland, Alvin Hawkins, and Bill France.

Bill France had been enamored of the superspeedway concept, and since 1949 he had tried to coerce the ruling political body of Daytona Beach to allow him to build a similar facility there. He felt that stock car racing needed a track that was wide *and* banked so cars could run in different grooves and pass in the turns. Indy car racing had been king up to that time, but France believed the Indy track to be wrong for stock car racing. It was too narrow. Around the turns the cars would have to run single file. And because it was flat, the wear on the cars would be too great.

Bill France's fate had been tied to Daytona Beach since 1934, when he, his wife, Annie, and his infant son Bill Junior headed south to escape the winter ice and cold of Washington, D.C., in his Hupmobile. They crossed the border from Georgia into Florida, and on a beautiful fall day stopped their car on the sands of Daytona Beach to go swimming. The beauty of the place charmed them. Annie and Bill, who was fed up with lying on his back under cars in the freezing cold and roaming the wintry capital to restart dead batteries, decided to end their journey. (Legend has it his car broke down in Daytona and so he stayed, but France always denied the story. "I was a mechanic," he said. "If it had been broken, I would have fixed it.")

They rented a little one-bedroom house for $15 a month furnished, and France got work, first as a house painter, and soon thereafter as a mechanic at J. Saxton Lloyd's Buick-Pontiac-Cadillac garage.

In March 1935, with France in attendance, Sir Malcolm Campbell drove his supercharged V-8 to a land-speed record of 276 miles an hour on the sands of Daytona Beach. The problem for Campbell and other land-speed racers was that though the Daytona Beach sand was wide, flat, firm, and long enough for most races, Campbell's incredible speed made racing there too dangerous. He needed a longer, flatter, smoother, less windy course.

Later that year, Campbell took his Bluebird to the beds of Utah's Bonneville Salt Flats and broke the record at 301 miles an hour. Daytona Beach was abandoned forever as the land-speed capital.

In an effort to resuscitate the city's racing reputation and a flagging economy, on March 8, 1936, Daytona city officials staged a 250-mile stock car race for all comers. The man in charge was a well-known racing promoter named Sig Haugdahl. He devised a combination beach-road race, with the backstretch and turns on the sand and the front straightaway on the paved street closest to the beach.

It was a handicap race, with the slower qualifiers leaving the line first. Twenty-seven drivers entered, including France, who drove a Ford owned by a man named Glen Brooks. France started tenth, leaving about eight minutes after the slowest Willys.

The initial race had some problems. The worst one was that if you drove too slowly, you got stuck in the sand, but if you went too fast, you risked turning over.

The heaviest cars got struck in the sand, and because speeds were slower than expected, the tide came in before the race was over. The north turn, at around two hundred miles, was completely blocked with stuck cars when the officials called it.

Since the race was prematurely shortened, it took several days for officials to figure out that Milt "Red" Marion had won. Bill France, who swore he passed Marion a couple of times, was awarded fifth place, twelve laps back. Marion won $1,700 in prize money and France received $375. At that time the minimum wage was $14.50 a week.

The other negative was that since there was no way to fence in the entire course, thousands of spectators watched the race without paying. The city fathers lost $22,000 on the promotion.

The next year, under the aegis of the Elks Club, the race was shortened to fifty miles to ensure that tides wouldn't be a factor. The crowd was so anemic that the winning driver was awarded a purse of $43. The Elks were dissuaded from promoting a race again.

The Chamber of Commerce thus needed to find a person or group to promote the race in 1938. It asked France, whose Pure Oil gas station on Main Street had become a headquarters for the local racers, if he knew anyone who might be interested in putting on the race.

France made a collect call to an Orange City hotel owner by the name of Ralph Hankinson. Hankinson had had some experience running fairground races. Because France felt the deal would benefit Hankinson, he called collect. Hankinson refused to accept the 15-cent call.

France had been racing a 1937 Ford coupe owned by a local restaurant owner named Charlie Reese on the weekends. Reese asked France if he would have an interest in taking on the promotion.

France foresaw that the race had a future if run right. He saw that when a motorcycle race was organized, fans flocked to see it. He figured the lack of success of the stock car event was a result of inadequate or inept promotion.

France told Reese, "I can get the cars and the drivers, but I don't have any money."

Replied Reese, "I'll put up the money and you can do the work." France agreed, and that first year sold five thousand tickets at 50 cents apiece. The next year they raised ticket prices to a dollar, and after donating 10 percent to the Bundles for Britain campaign, France and Reese split $2,000. The annual beach race at Daytona was saved.

After the war Florida boomed, as Northerners sought the same sun Bill France had discovered back in the early thirties. France knew that the wild growth of the beach community would one day doom the beach races.

In anticipation of the day when he would be barred from staging his beach race, he began lobbying politicos for a permanent facility if Daytona Beach wanted to keep motor sports from leaving town. France first broached his idea of building a paved track at Daytona in 1949.

A county Racing and Recreation District was formed, land was bought by the commission, and France got a ninety-nine-year lease from them. The chairman of the commission was Sax Lloyd, who owned the Buick-Pontiac-Cadillac dealership where France had worked when he arrived in Daytona Beach.

France sold three hundred thousand shares of stock at a dollar a share and then had to borrow $600,000 from oil millionaire Clint Murchison and his financial advisor, Howard Sluyter. France could have built a conventional track with the original money, but he was so convinced of his vision of a banked track that he refused to compromise. He went deep into personal debt to see the realization of his dream.

France started selling tickets and used a lot of the ticket money for construction costs. Ten years after the Daytona International Speedway opened, he paid off the original $600,000 loan.

When the Daytona International Speedway opened in 1959, the drivers marveled. Where Darlington was a fast mile-and-three-eighth track, Daytona was two and a half miles around, and with its long straightaways, breathtaking speeds of over 140 miles an hour were attainable.

When driver Lee Petty saw the huge track at Daytona for the first time, he realized that his world of short-track, dirt-track racing would soon be coming to an end.

"We knew stock car racing was never going to be the same again," he said.

Jim Foster, who today is president of the Daytona International Speedway, worked side by side with William France, Sr., from 1967 and marveled at the growth of the sport under his leadership. He saw both sides of the man, the toughness and the compassion. Bill France passed away on June 7, 1992, ten days after our meeting. Big Bill France had been a controversial figure; the autocratic way in which he ran NASCAR at times angered both car owners and drivers, who accused him of unfairness and self-interest. But if you look at the Big Picture, one thing is very clear: The vision of Bill France made NASCAR stock car racing the immensely popular sport it is today. The influence of Bill France on the sport will be felt as long as race cars run fast.

JIM FOSTER: "I can remember the first time I ever met Bill France, Sr. I grew up in Winston-Salem, North Carolina, and he was promoting races at Bowman-Gray Stadium. I lived on the south side of town near the stadium, and I had gone down and climbed under the fence to get into the race, and after I got through I looked up, and here was this great big, tall man standing there, and he took me by the arm and marched me to the gate, and he took me out the gate, and he said, 'Son, now come back in. This is the way you get into the race—through the gate.'

"He let me in free, and he told me anytime I wanted to come to the races, I could come, but I should see him and come through the gate. And several times after that I did. That's the sort of guy Bill Senior was, a very compassionate guy.

"I was in high school during the time of World War II, and with the war going on the *Winston-Salem Sentinel* was short on help, and I was the sports editor. I had been a reporter.

"I wrote a daily column as well as put out the afternoon paper. I went to work at 4 A.M., put out the paper, and missed my first two classes of school. But my teachers graded me on the columns I wrote.

"I went into the Navy at seventeen as a volunteer as soon as I got out of high school. I began on a deck force and ended up training myself to be a radioman, and that's what I was when I got out.

"I got into the war at the very tail end of the Okinawa invasion. I was on an ATF, a seagoing tug. The war was about over. We had dropped the bomb on Hiroshima, and we had the task of going in and pulling landing craft off the Okinawa beaches. The Japanese were still hid out in the caves up in the mountains. We got shot at a little bit, but nothing serious. After the war was over, we still had some suicide planes coming into Okinawa harbor trying to take out some of the ships.

"After that, my ATF was the first ship to enter Nagasaki harbor after the second atomic bomb. We were the lead ship in the occupation going in. We went in and cleared some wreckage so the ships with the troops could enter safely.

"I can remember as we entered the harbor, you could see a lot of people up in the hills running like they were leaving town. They didn't know what to expect, but we were there about two weeks, you could see them coming back, see clothes out on the lines as they were feeling more and more comfortable. We had a lot of young kids with burns and scars who came down to the ship and begged for food.

"We had been there a month when they finally allowed us to get off the ship. Trucks took us out where we could stretch our legs, and they drove us through Nagasaki, and the thing that impressed me was that here was the city, and here was the industrial zone, and zap, right there a line was drawn, because it went from the city to ashes—smokestacks standing up and everything else devastated for miles.

"After the war, I came back to the Winston-Salem newspapers, then decided I wanted to go to college on the GI Bill, and I got a scholarship as a news bureau director for Catawba College in Salisbury, North Carolina. I covered some races, football, other sports, and then I became sports editor of the *Salisbury Post*. In 1950 I covered the very first Southern 500 at Darlington.

"I remember Bill France had saved the race. The Central States Racing Association was going to put the race on, but it couldn't attract enough drivers, so Bill France went in and put that first race on. They didn't have a press box. They sent some tickets, and I sat in the grandstand. I remember it being the longest day in my life. Seventy-five cars started, and all the Oldsmobiles were burning out rear ends, the Nashes were breaking right front spindles, the Cadillacs were wearing out tires every ten laps.

"I went to the Greensboro paper as golf editor, covered a lot of NASCAR races during the seven years I was there, and then I went to Chrysler as their Southern news bureau director. I handled the publicity on their race teams in 1965 and '66, and I came to work for Bill Sr. in 1967. My title was assistant to the president and director of public relations. That was twenty-five years ago.

"When you think of Bill France, you think of this great big, strong man who's tough as nails. He didn't have the education a lot of people had, but he was smarter than anybody I ever met, hip-pocket smart. He had a great mind, a great memory, could remember someone's name after meeting him for the first time.

"He was the type of man, when he walked in the room, everybody turned their head and looked for some reason. He was big, about six-foot-five, but it was the way he carried himself, the air about him. He was very persuasive, and he had street smarts, and if anyone took him on and opposed him, he would do whatever was necessary to win. If you remember, when Curtis Turner led the players in trying to form a union, Bill banned Curtis Turner from racing for life, but then he came back and reinstated him four years later.

"I was in the office when Curtis came down to see him. Curtis said, 'Bill, I screwed up and I want to race. I have some years left here that I can race, and I'd like to race.' And Bill went over and put his arm around him and said, 'That's fine with me, Curtis. Let's do it.' And they went out and had drinks together and they were back friends again. And that's the kind of guy Bill Senior was.

"In this business it's hard to get close to drivers. Bill Senior was probably closer to Tiny Lund than any driver. Tiny Lund was a great big guy, and one of the nicest people you'd ever meet, and he'd always come by to see Bill, and they'd kid around and arm-wrestle, and when they had the drivers' strike at Talladega in '69, Tiny told them all to go to hell, and when Tiny died in a crash at Talladega, Bill really took it hard. He broke down in his office.

"Whenever people write about Bill France, Sr., they write about how he would take on General Motors or Ford or how he took on the drivers and the teamsters union when the drivers threatened to form a union, or how he stood up against them at Talladega in 1969 when they threatened a strike by going out and driving a car himself.

"The thing that most people miss is he is one of the most compassionate people too. He didn't like people to know that, but I had an office right next to his for many years, and anybody could walk in there and say he was an old race driver. 'I raced against you at Lancaster in the thirties, and I'm down-and-out a little bit.' And he'd reach in his pocket and peel some bills, and the man would leave.

"One time I said to Bill, 'Did you actually race against him?'

"He said, 'I'm not sure, but if he's down-and-out, I'm going to help him.' He was that type of person. He was also that way with his employees. At times he couldn't do a lot for them, but his dedicated employees he'd always take care of. They didn't have a retirement program, but when they were ready to leave and they got sick, he kept them on the payroll.

"Fonty Flock is a pretty good example of the way Bill is. Fonty was down on his luck, and he had cancer. Bill brought him down to Daytona, gave him a job, created a role where he was supposed to put together coupon books for race fans so they could get discounts in different cities. He also gave people high-speed rides around the track.

"Fonty—he was the guy who once raced with a monkey in his car— was quite a character. He spent most of his time at the dog track and at jai alai. But Bill took care of him, sent Fonty in his airplane for cancer treatments.

"Bill Senior had control over the sport, but a large part of what he did with his power was to make certain the competition stayed strong, that one make of car didn't have a big advantage over another. And he taught that to his son, Bill Junior. And I must say that Bill Junior is doing a better job of that than Bill Senior did. Bill Junior does it with finesse. Bill Junior will get the car owners and mechanics together and talk to them and explain to them, 'If we don't have good, competitive racing, you won't have a sponsor, and the fans won't come, so we have to be fair about it.' And it works. It worked for Bill Senior too.

"But with Bill Senior, if one brand of car was going out there and getting a four- or five-lap lead every race, then there is no race. It's like a bully beating a little guy every time he sees him every day, so Senior on the spur of the moment would say, 'You can't use that engine anymore.' Or 'You have to add so much weight,' or Zap, do this,' and it would create a furor in the sport. This still goes on today, but the owners and mechanics understand the reasoning behind these decisions better.

"Bill Senior built the Daytona Speedway. He was very proud of it. He first went to the city and asked the city to build it, and they turned it down. Either they didn't have the money or didn't want to invest, but he kept trying, and finally he and some friends, a lawyer and other businessmen, came up with the plan to get the Racing and Recreation Commission organized, which could get a lease with the city for the property.

"Once he did that, he sold stock at a dollar a share, but the money was never enough. He'd pay bills and then get to a point where work was going to stop because he was out of money, but somehow he'd always come up with some way to find it.

"He told me that one time he had to have $30,000 within a week or the dirt contractor was going to quit moving dirt. He tried to borrow it and couldn't. He had a friend with Coca-Cola whose name was Gerard. His job was to buy billboards in stadiums, and he traveled the area a lot and knew Bill. In fact, he stayed at Bill's home. So Bill called him up and said, 'I need $30,000 within the next four or five days. What I'll do, if you give me the $30,000, I'll sell you an ad in our souvenir programs every year for ten years for $3,000, and I'll give you exclusivity on product sales at the track.'

"Gerard went back to Atlanta to his bosses, and he called Bill up and said, 'I can't believe it. They turned me down on it. They think the money will be gone because they don't think you'll ever get the track built.'

"So that night Bill looked up to see who was the chairman of Pepsi-Cola, and it happened to be Don Kendall. He called Kendall and said, 'You don't know me, but my name is Bill France. I'm in Daytona Beach, and I'm building a racetrack.' Kendall said, 'Yeah, I've heard something about that.'

"Bill said, 'I need $30,000, and here's what I'll do,' and he offered Kendall the same deal he had offered Coke.

"Kendall said, 'Where do I send the check?' As a result, Pepsi has been with us since the very beginning. Coca-Cola has knocked on the door, and they still do every year, because we built Talladega and we serve Pepsi there, and we bought Darlington, which was a Coke track for all those years, and we switched it to Pepsi, and we bought Watkins Glen, which was a Coke track, and we switched that to Pepsi.

"And we had one year where Pepsi changed management up near Watkins Glen, and the new people canceled their advertising, didn't want the program ad, didn't want anything to do with racing. I went to Bill, and I said, 'Coca-Cola has told me that whenever Pepsi stubs its toe to call them.'

"Bill said, 'Well, I don't think we need to do that. I'd rather just go without 'em.' So we went a year without any money coming in from Pepsi. He ran their ad from the year before in all the programs and didn't charge them. And Pepsi came back the next year, stronger than ever.

"But that's the kind of loyalty Bill has. That's the kind of loyalty Bill and the France family has had to the small tracks like North Wilkesboro. The big speedways have wanted the North Wilkesboro dates, but Enoch Staley, who runs that track, has been with Bill since the beginning. And the Frances have never taken a date away from a racetrack and given it to somebody else, except from his own, which was Hillsboro. That's where Talladega got their dates. But he hasn't taken dates from North Wilkesboro or Martinsville, because they were there at the beginning, and he stood by them.

"It's the same way with the little decals on the cars, the contingency program. Those decals are worth a *lot* more than what those companies are paying, but they have been on those cars forever, and how are you going to tell a company, 'You are too small for us now'?

"In a lot of other racing associations, they go with whoever is the highest bidder. NASCAR has never done that. That's the Bill France philosophy: 'If you're with me and working with me and loyal to me and help me, I'm with you all the way.'

"And if you weren't loyal to Bill France, then Bill France wasn't going to be loyal to you. I know there are people out there who hold very bitter feelings for Mr. France, because of the empire that Bill France has built. Smokey Yunick is one of them. Smokey has probably told you, because he tells everybody that he's very bitter about Bill, because, to put it blunt, he couldn't get away with his cheating. If you remember one year the tech inspectors accused him of running extra gas somehow, and he got mad at Bill and drove his car away with the gas tank taken out of it.

"Only Smokey knows why he has been mad and has knocked NASCAR and has knocked the Speedway. He probably feels living here in Daytona Beach he should have some real special consideration, which he probably would have had if he had been a team player.

"But Mr. France had something that *none* of the others had, and that was vision. Bill France was a visionary. He saw where the sport was going to go, and he believed in it strongly, risked every penny he had. When he built his Speedway, he went deep in debt, and for years afterward was besieged by creditors. And when the others were selling their Daytona Speedway stock, he bought. And Daytona was a huge success, and he built the Talladega track, and he bought Darlington, and he bought Watkins Glen, and it's all because Bill France had this vision. Bill France was the one who took on the risk. It's the risk-takers who become wealthy. And mostly it's those who refused to take that risk who were left bitter and angry.

"For Bill France, building the Daytona Speedway was a dream. You know how dreamers are. I have a friend out in Arizona who dreams of putting up a big resort. He says it'll have casinos, and he wants me to invest in it. He's a dreamer. And it *may* be built. And I won't be disappointed at all that I'm not going to be part of it. Because I am *not* a dreamer. I won't take those chances.

"Without Bill France, there would have been no NASCAR, would have been no racing as we know it today.

"Bill France had foresight. He wanted the track to be for more than just stock car racing. He wanted motorcycles, sports cars, Indy cars, boats. The whole thing was a swampland, what they call wetlands in Florida—shrubs, trees—and he drained the swamp and made the 44-acre Lake Lloyd in the middle of the track. He did have a boat race, and a driver was killed in the very first one, and he decided it wasn't big enough, that once they got their speeds up if the throttle stuck, it was too dangerous, and he didn't hold any more. He was going to have Indy car racing, but Marshall Teague was killed in practice for that, so he didn't have that either.

"The man who assured that Bill France would succeed in finishing his racetrack was a man named Howard Sluyter. Without Howard Sluyter, he probably wouldn't have succeeded.

"Bill had met Clint Murchison, the Texas oil millionaire, along the way. Murchison was stymied in a city somewhere and couldn't go to where he was going, and Bill flew him to Fort Lauderdale in his plane and got to know him. The thing Clint did for Bill was to introduce him to his financial advisor, Howard Sluyter.

"Murchison told Bill, 'Get ahold of Howard. He'll help you.'" Howard was a big, tall guy like Bill, and they hit it off, and Howard put together the financial packaging to keep it going. Bill finished the track in time for the 1959 season.

"Bill was very proud of the track. He and his wife, Annie, had signed personal notes, and for many years the going was tough for them as they paid off the debts. Now that he has succeeded, no one remembers the huge risk he was taking. The weather was always a factor. At the time there was no television. A lot of people thought he was crazy.

"I attended the very first 500 at Daytona in '59. It was breathtaking, because it was so much bigger than anything that came before it. You think of Darlington, which is a mile and three-eighths, and then you come to Daytona and see this: a two-and-a-half-mile tri-oval. The asphalt was so black. Everything was fresh. And what was amazing, you could sit in the grandstand and actually see the entire racetrack, which is something nobody had built up until that time. At Indianapolis, you can't see a thing. The track is flat, there are buildings in the infield, a golf course. You can see only a little bit. At Daytona you can see it all, so it was spectacular, and the speeds—143 miles an hour; that was turning it on! Then when the race started, and the cars ran so close together and at such high speeds, it changed the whole nature of the sport.

"When I came to work for Bill, he was just thinking about building a track in Alabama. I went with him most of the trips as we negotiated.

"Alabama might seem in the middle of nowhere, but if you draw a 300-mile circle around Talladega—that is the distance race fans come from. They can drive down, see the race, and drive home in one day. There were 28 million people inside that circle.

"Originally someone had called him to look at some land in Anniston, Alabama, and he went to look and said it was no good. About six months later one of the men at that meeting called him back and said, 'I know a piece of land that's ideal for what you said you needed. It'll make an ideal place for a superspeedway. It's the Talladega Airport property.'

"So we went up, met with their industrial development board, and we built them a jet strip in exchange for the land, and Governor Wallace agreed to build an eight-mile, six-lane road connecting one interstate with another. Bill had been chairman of the Democrats for Wallace campaign in Florida, and Wallace carried Florida in a big way. Charlie Snyder was Wallace's campaign manager, and that's how we got to know Charlie

Snyder. And once we had access to Governor Wallace and once he saw the potential of what the track could do for the state of Alabama, it was easy for him to make a decision: 'Yeah, let's build those roads, because we need them to bring all these people to Alabama and get all this publicity for Alabama.'

"We built that track in 1969 and ran the first race in September of that year. Earlier that same year came another momentous event: The government banned tobacco advertising from radio and television and the tobacco companies needed an outlet to spend some promotional dollars.

"Junior Johnson and Ralph Seagraves from R. J. Reynolds were good old mountain buddies, and Junior and Ralph had talked about a car sponsorship, but Reynolds at the time did not want to put their name on a car, probably for the same reason the airlines gave, although we did have Piedmont Airlines on a car at one time. Most airlines said, 'We don't want to be involved with anything dangerous.' And I think Reynolds felt the same way.

"So Junior brought Ralph Seagraves to see Bill France, Sr., about how they could get involved, so when the Talladega track was being built, we worked out a program. In fact, I wrote out the proposal to them to sponsor the first Winston 500. At the time they were concerned the publicity would only benefit them in the South, so we got them to sponsor the Winston Western 500 at Riverside, California. And at the time I talked to them about the NASCAR point fund—the monetary prizes for the top drivers—and at first they said they weren't interested, but then the success and publicity they got out of their race promotions changed their minds, and the next year we started the Winston Grand National Championship. We wanted to make sure the partnership was going to work, and after several years we saw it was going to be a long-term partnership, so we went ahead and changed it to the Winston Cup.

"Before Reynolds became involved, most of the sponsors were automotive-related sponsors—Champion spark plugs, Goodyear, Firestone, Moog transmission companies, service stations. Once Winston came in and started using racing in their marketing and had almost instant success, then the beer companies got in, and as we progressed other consumer companies started getting involved.

"Most companies are very secretive about their studies of how much racing promotions help their sales, but for instance, Tom Chambers has publicly said that the sales of Goody's Headache Powders doubled in a two-year period, and he credited it to auto racing.

"The real phenomenon came along about 1984. About then we made it known that among the older race fans, 48 percent were women. I can remember I had invited the president of the Stokely-Van Camp division of Quaker Oats to see the 125s at Daytona. He had never seen a race before. We were walking around outside the track before the race, and he said, 'I can't believe these women.'

"I said, 'If you think these women are good-looking, you ought to see the ones over in the pits.'

"He said, 'That's *not* what I'm talking about. I just can't believe they are here in these numbers.'

"As a result, Gatorade came in as a sponsor, and they now sponsor the Gatorade Circle of Champions. And at the same time Procter & Gamble came in, Crisco, Tide, Hanes with panty hose, even candy bars, and that started what was a whole new deal bringing in store managers and presidents of chains to the races and entertaining them.

"The other factor that contributed to the growth of the sport with respect to sponsorship money was the start of our own radio network, the Motor Racing Network. Originally, we had a local Daytona radio station feeding out the 500, but they didn't want to do any other races, and we didn't have any control over them. I convinced Bill Senior that we should take it over ourselves and control it, and today we have over four hundred stations on our network. We hire the announcers, and if I walk into the booth and tell the announcer, 'Sometime in the next fifteen minutes, give a good plug for the race coming up in two weeks at Richmond,' by God, he better do it. So now the announcers can talk about the races coming up, and we didn't have that before. And when the announcers on the local radio refused to call it the 'STP Pontiac, Richard Petty's number 43,' we told our announcers to do it just that way, and that way car owners could go to a sponsor and say, 'If you sponsor us, I can guarantee you a minimum number of mentions on the network radio.' As a result, the network has done more to help racing than anything in the last twenty years.

"Bill France, Jr., is running NASCAR now, and his brother Jim, who is not in the forefront as much, is also very influential in the decision-making. The only difference, it's not as conservative as it used to be. Bill Senior was not conservative at all, but his wife, Annie B., was, and she looked after the purse strings, and she kept him from doing a lot of things he wanted to do, because they didn't have the money then. You might say she was as much responsible for the success as Bill was.

"She didn't want her picture taken. She didn't want any credit. She didn't want to be interviewed. It was tough to get her to do just about anything, but she was business manager, secretary, and treasurer of both NASCAR and the Speedway for many years.

"As a corporation, the Speedway now is a $47 million company. In 1992 the Daytona 500 took in between $10 million and $12 million. Racing continued to grow, and I'd like to think stock car racing might one day be as big as baseball and the other sports, but baseball and basketball have the benefit of all the colleges and the alumni, and the other roadblock we face is that a lot of the influential people in New York, Boston, and Chicago who are with newspapers and media were raised in ball sports, weren't raised in stock car racing, and therefore they print tennis or golf and not racing. In the South it's different, because we had all these little tracks, probably more racetracks than minor league parks.

"They'll cover the Daytona 500. We expect a total circulation of 77 million sitting in our press box for the '92 Daytona 500. The Daytona 500 is now on a par with the Kentucky Derby and the World Series. And it's all because of the vision of one very great man: Bill France, Sr."

LAP 7

Richard Petty
The King

The 1992 Daytona 500 by STP, with its built-in rivalries and its historic import of place, would take on an added significance in racing history. It would be the final Daytona 500 for Richard Petty, The King, the Babe Ruth of stock car racing. The winner of an incredible two hundred NASCAR-sponsored races, Richard Petty began driving in 1958, the year before his father won the initial Daytona 500 Superspeedway race.

After thirty-four years of racing, Richard Petty would enter his final year in the sport with seven driving championships, seven victories in the Daytona 500, and almost $7,500,000 in winnings.

Like a lot of rookies, Petty had an inaugural season that featured a string of crashes. He destroyed five cars in his first fifteen races. He got to continue because his father owned the cars.

He didn't win in '59, the year his father, Lee, won the driving championship, but in '60 he rose to second in the points standings, behind Rex White, while his dad finished sixth. That year Richard finished third in the Daytona 500, and on February 28, 1960, in his next race at Charlotte, won his first victory when his father, driving in relief of another driver, bashed challenger Rex White thirteen laps from the end and almost wrecked him. The prize money was $800. Richard Petty was twenty-two years old.

Richard won six races in 1962 and thirteen races in '63, and when Plymouth decided to enter racing big time in '64, it backed two teams owned by Petty and Ray Nichols of Highland, Indiana. The cars featured a 426-cubic-inch, hemispherical combustion engine, called the hemi, and the combination of Petty and the 400-horsepower hemi was overpowering.

In the qualifying heats at Daytona in '64, Paul Goldsmith, who drove

Richard Petty

the other Plymouth, set a course record of 174.910. Petty was second at 174.418. In the Daytona 500 Petty finished a full lap ahead of the second-place finisher, Jimmy Pardue, and set a new record for the 500-mile distance: 154.334 miles per hour.

The next year Bill France outlawed the hemi engine. Petty, angry, quit NASCAR and went to drive dragsters. When France relented later in the year, Petty returned, and in '66 he again won the Daytona 500. When Petty beat Buddy Baker at Daytona in 1971 they were members of the only two factory-sponsored teams.

Petty's battles with David Pearson and then with Bobby Allison kept race fans coming back to the track during a stagnant era before TV and the R. J. Reynolds sponsorship, when stock car racing was desperately searching for financial stability.

In all, Richard Petty won the Daytona 500 in 1964, 1966, 1971, 1973, 1974, 1979, and 1981. He piled up roughly one-third of the Daytona victories during the years in which he dominated NASCAR racing.

Perhaps the most famous Daytona 500 Richard Petty *didn't* win came in 1976, when he and David Pearson drove side by side toward the checkered flag. Coming out of turn two, Pearson shot his Mercury around Petty's Dodge. Pearson, in the lead, drifted high into turn three. Petty tried to duck down low, and as they came off turn four, they were door to door, inches apart. Then they collided. Out of control, Pearson hit the wall nose-first, clipping Petty's rear bumper. Both cars went skidding out of control.

Petty's Dodge stopped on the infield grass, a hundred yards from the finish line. His engine was dead. It could not be restarted. Pearson had come to a stop at the foot of pit road, perhaps fifty yards from the finish.

Pearson, showing uncanny presence of mind, kept his foot on the accelerator while in neutral, keeping the engine running, so that when he finally came to a stop, he put the car in gear and was able to limp from the infield grass onto the track and across the finish line. No other car was on the lead lap, so Petty was awarded second place even though he completed only 199 laps. That race is considered the most dramatic finish in superspeedway history.

After the race Petty was asked what he was thinking while the crash was taking place.

"Well," he said in his most endearing manner, "I wasn't exactly hollering, 'Hooray for me.' "

Three years later, Petty was the beneficiary of another renowned Daytona 500 crash, which occurred on the last lap when Cale Yarborough and

Donnie Allison tangled, wrecking each other and allowing Petty to roar across the finish line with the 1979 Daytona victory.

Because his last victory came in the Firecracker 500 at Daytona in 1984, a drought of eight years, racing fans do not expect victory from Richard Petty at the 1992 Daytona 500. They realize his days of running up front are over.

Nevertheless, because their love for him is universal and without reservation, any small triumph, such as a strong passing move or a top-ten finish, will be greeted with loving applause and adoration.

As Petty prepares for his final season, his time has become more valuable than ever. Despite a schedule that calls for him to be busy virtually every minute of the day, Richard Petty, who has prided himself on never having turned down a request for either an interview or an autograph, genially agreed to discuss his life in racing.

Petty, wearing his traditional western garb and sunglasses, arrived at the entranceway of the condo complex outside the Charlotte Motor Speedway. Though his home base is his racing complex in Level Cross, North Carolina, Petty purchased one of Bruton Smith's condos for those times when business calls for him to remain in Charlotte.

We rode the elevator to the fourth floor. He unlocked the door, and we entered. The rug was a white shag. Two comfortable couches opposed each other. It was dusk, and despite the fading light, the large picture window afforded a bird's-eye view of the racetrack. Bruton Smith's idea of selling condos overlooking the track may have seemed wacky and eccentric when first proposed, but sitting here with Richard Petty overlooking the track seemed perfectly natural—fitting, in fact.

Richard Petty cracked two cans of Pepsi, brought over a cup for his chewing tobacco, and sat comfortably while he talked about his life in racing.

"You know," he said with a smile, "there is no man on earth who has been interviewed more times than I have."

This was said not with braggadocio, but as a matter-of-fact statement.

"I believe that," I replied. I tried to think who else might have been in the running for such a distinction. Presidents come and go. Muhammand Ali? He retired a long time ago. Charles Lindbergh? Elvis? They had been recluses much of their lives. John Wayne? Clark Gable? Movie stars are kept from the press by agents and bodyguards.

Other famous American athletes, like Mickey Mantle, Willie Mays, and Hank Aaron, shunned the press whenever possible and signed autographs grudgingly. Few of the newcomers in any sport seem to embrace the media and the fans. Even Michael Jordan, as great a player as he is, seems uncomfortable in an uncontrolled interview situation.

Richard Petty, the winningest stock car driver of all time, decided early on that he owed the fans and the press, rather than the other way around. No matter how many wins he had, if a fan wanted an autograph, Richard Petty would oblige, repaying his legion of fans for their loyalty by allowing them easy access. Millions of Richard Petty autographs grace walls and scrapbooks all across America. He has been lionized for his success on the track, but it is for his obliging nature and down-home personality that Richard Petty shall always be regarded as The King.

RICHARD PETTY: "We grew up right beside where we live right now, in the house Mother and Daddy still live in, which is right beside Petty Enterprises. I was twelve years old before we had electricity in the house. All the roads were dirt, but we used to ride our bicycles and wagons.

"Daddy started racing when I was ten years old. We had a stable, cleaned the floors out, and put race cars in it, and he worked there a couple years, and then we moved back into the house I was born in. My grandmother and granddaddy died and we ended up with the house, and then we built a little reaper shed beside. It had a dirt floor for the first year and a tin roof and no sides. I finally put sides on it and some cement on the floor and we worked there until 1956, and then they built another little shop right behind that one, and in '57 we built some more on the other side, and in '58 did more, and from racing we just kept building buildings.

"When my daddy started out, there wasn't money to be made. We had a family-owned operation. We had one race car, and sometimes we were lucky and had a second, but there was not much work done on the cars. We used stock tires and stock wheels.

"The monetary deal is completely different than it used to be. Back then, at the end of the year, if you won $50,000, you went to the bank and deposited as much as $10,000 at the end of the year. Now you might win a million dollars in prize money, and you're lucky to take $10,000 to the bank.

"When we first started, I went to school, came home at night, and worked on the cars. We lived in the country, and all the other boys would milk the cows or plow the fields. I would go work on the race cars. I played sports, and when practice was over, I'd come home and work on the race cars and get up and go to school the next day, play a ball game, and come home and work on the race car.

"When I was in high school, I did all the engines. There was a lot of stock parts on the car, so there wasn't near the work as there is now. One man could do everything; he could build the motors, the rear ends, the transmissions, the body work, paint the car, tow it to the racetrack, pit it, do everything. Now everything has to be done by a specialist. It was professional to us at that time, but it was really a very young sport, and so it was very amateurish from today's standards.

"Where you used to have a motor man, now you have a specialist who does nothing but head work, another one who does nothing but block work, another who does nothing but cam work. It's just like in football, where today you just about have a coach for each position.

"When I was a boy, the basic team was Daddy. He worked on the cars, did all the work, towed the car to the racetrack, and drove it home after it was done with. In the summer my brother Maurice and myself and my mother, we would all go with him, and we'd pit the car, though most of the time we'd run 100-mile races, and you didn't have to make a pit stop. There were a few racetracks where we had to change tires, but usually each driver would take a man with him, and then they would all get together and pit one car, and then another car would come in, and they'd pit him, so everybody worked together trying to make it work, because nobody had a full crew.

"In the 1960s when they started the superspeedway era, you had to make professional pit stops, and then all of a sudden people started bringing three or four people, started getting trucks to tow the cars, that kind of new improvements came in, and it just kept growing.

"Back in the fifties, the factories got involved in racing. Then when it got to costing the car manufacturers too much money, they banned involvement in racing in '57, but by the early sixties they started slipping back in. Ford and Chrysler got going pretty strong again, and they stayed until 1970, and pulled out again, and they stayed out until about ten years ago. Today they don't have factory teams per se, but they give us certain experts to help out, and they let their cars use the wind tunnels.

"They want their cars to win, but every car is on its own. Everyone is an individual, and so today we go out for twenty-nine weeks, and every week we have to beat thirty-nine other cars. No one knows at the beginning of the year how much money they will make. We only get paid for what we do that particular day.

"These boys can get their $2 or $3 million up front for playing football, but if they have a bad day, they aren't out a penny. They still get paid on Monday. If we don't win, we don't get paid on Monday. The crews are the same way. They work on a percentage. The better they do, the more they make. The incentive is there.

"I tell you, when I was growing up, going to school, playing ball, working on the race car, my ambition was to be a good mechanic, to be able to build a race car and pit race cars. I never really thought much about driving until I got out of high school. All the time I was growing up and going across the country with Daddy, everyone said, 'Are you going to drive a race car?' I said, 'No.' It never bothered me I wasn't. I was working on the race car, still going to school, and playing football, baseball, and basketball.

"Then after I got out of school, I wasn't playing ball, and I decided I might want to drive one. As soon as I got out of high school, the only thing in front of me was racing. It was all race car, race car, race car, and so I thought, 'Maybe I want to drive.' I asked Daddy, and he told me to come back when I was twenty-one, that he would think about it, so I worked those four years, never asked him, never thought about driving.

"When Daddy said no, that was it, because Daddy was footing the whole bill. At that time there was no factory backing, no corporate sponsorships, no money sponsors. You might have 'Joe's Hamburger Joint' or 'Bill's Used Cars' on the side of the car, but that was about it as far as sponsorship. It wasn't a deal where I could go somewhere else and get a race car. I didn't have enough money to have one myself, so we had to operate on what we had to operate on, and when I got old enough to where I could start, I started driving in July of '58. My father had a good year that year because he won the championship, and when we came back in '59, I raced my first full season driving convertibles. That year my father came back and won the first Daytona race, won the championship that year, so as far as making money, we were as good as there was, and that helped me to get started.

"I came along during the best part of his career as far as making money, and it gave him the leeway to let me have a car. If he had had bad seasons and hadn't been winning races, and if there had been no money, I might still be working on cars.

"I said to Daddy, 'Can I try?' He said, 'Yeah, okay, there's a car. Go get it, fix it up, and take it to the race.' It was a '57 Oldsmobile convertible.

"I can remember that first year, the first race I ran, I finished sixth. The same night my father, brother Maurice, and another boy who worked for Daddy went to Asheville, North Carolina, to run a Grand National race, and me and Dale Inman and another boy went to Columbia, South Carolina, to run a convertible race.

"We went down, qualified thirteenth, and finished sixth in the race. I had never been on a racetrack with a helmet on and a seat belt hooked up until I went to Columbia. That was the first time I ever got in a race car and went tearing down into the corner to see how hard I could go. I felt comfortable with it. Man, we thought we were some work, and the next week we went to Bowman-Gray in Winston-Salem, and I spun out four or five times, and then we went to Toronto, Canada, for the first Grand National race that I ran, and I ran into the wall and beat the car all up. That was the first race that counts against my 1,150 starts. The first race I ran I was clean out of the country. We came back to Buffalo, ran another couple races on the Northern tour. I can remember back then there were no interstates. To get from one town to another, you had to stop at every light along the way.

"After the sixth-place finish in that first race, the rest of the races I didn't finish. I was having some problems, like driving into fences or running into cars or turning over. But I can remember running that first race and saying to myself, 'This is what I want to do.'

"And after we run some, then I got a little confidence in the deal.

"Still, I had to go through the crash stage of the initiation, and sometimes that got pretty bad, because you'd get running real good and then crash, and at that time if I crashed the car, I was the one who had to fix it. I had to do the bodywork, straighten the chassis, build the motor—whatever it was that had to be done, I had to do the work. It got pretty frustrating sometimes. But every once in a while I got a glimpse of doing real good, running well before I crashed, and that gave me the confidence to think, 'One of these days we're going to get it all together.'

"I learned to drive by driving. There is no school where someone can teach you on the blackboard. You have to get in that car and hit the walls and find out all about it for yourself. All that talking isn't going to do you a bit of good. Car racing isn't like football or baseball or basketball, where you have certain plays, certain ways to hold the bat or ball, or like in golf where there is a certain way to hold the golf club. There is no one way to hold the steering wheel. Each driver has a unique style, his own unique situation, how to do it, how to set the car, how he feels things, how he senses what's going to happen. All you can say is, 'Here are the fundamentals. there is corner number one, corner number two, corner number three, corner number four. Try to stay as low as you can through one and two, drift up the wall, and go back to three and four on the inside.' That's about it, man. All the rest of it you have to go out and gut-feel.

"You have to pay the price. I don't care who you are—somewhere along the line, you're going to have to pay it."

"I can remember going with Daddy to the first Daytona 500 in 1959. The race was held on Sunday, and Daddy and Johnny Beauchamp crossed the finish line together, and initially Bill France awarded the race to Beauchamp, but it was Wednesday night before they made their decision to give it to us.

"After the race was over that Sunday, Daddy was pretty much upset they didn't award him the race. He felt confident he had won it. So did we.

"We were going to head on back home. Then we thought, 'No, we better stay here in Daytona.' Even though they had awarded it to Beauchamp, it was still up in the air, and there was still a chance for us to get the win, and so we stayed.

"You got to remember, there is always a lot of politics, and at that time the factories had gotten out of racing in '57, and this was '59, and when we went to Daytona that year, there was a bunch of Thunderbirds— Beauchamp was in a Thunderbird—and we were in an Oldsmobile. It had been pretty well decided by everyone who was standing on the finish line that Daddy won the race, but Bill France, Sr., called that Beauchamp won, okay? We felt the reason was that France was trying to influence the factories to get back into racing. It wasn't that he was against Lee Petty. He was looking at it from a political standpoint. He said to himself, 'If Ford wins this race, I might have a chance of talking them into getting back into racing.'

"But the press, all the pictures anybody saw, showed that Daddy won the race. So France finally had to come back and say, 'After looking at all the evidence and talking to everybody, we're going to have to award the victory to Lee Petty.'

"France was the one who was calling the shots. It was his track, his race, but there were enough people who knew that Daddy won, so he finally figured, 'If I make Ford the winner, someone is going to come out with pictures, and they will show I made a mistake, and that's not going to be good.' So France went ahead and made Daddy the winner.

"If you've ever seen the photo, there are three cars in the picture. Joe Weatherly was in a Chevrolet on the outside. He was the first one to the line, but he was a lap behind. Daddy was in the middle, and his Olds-mobile clearly was in front of the Thunderbird. There was no question— Daddy won that race.

"I entered the Daytona 500 in '59 driving a convertible. The deal was, they had two circuits, one for hardtops, another for convertibles. Daddy

96

said, 'You're learning, so you go over to the convertible circuit, and you learn what's going on in it. I'll run in the Grand National circuit.' A lot of times we raced separately, but in some races they were mixed and we raced against each other.

"That race was my first superspeedway race. See, up until that time, Darlington was the only superspeedway before they built Daytona, and in '58 they wouldn't let me run at Darlington because I was just starting out, didn't have enough experience. But at the Daytona 500 in '59, they put the hardtops on the inside row and the convertibles on the outside row. After eight laps, my car blew an engine. I won $100 in prize money.

"I remember one race at the Lakewood Speedway in Atlanta that year when Daddy and I competed against each other. I was in a convertible, and he was in a hardtop. I was flagged the winner, but then he protested, and they found out they hadn't counted one of his laps, and he won the race. He was some kind of competitor. In fact, if you go back to that first Grand National race in Toronto, he was the one who crashed me. Cotton Owens and Daddy were racing for the lead, and Cotton slowed up to give me a chance to get out of the way, and Daddy just knocked the tar out of me, knocked me into the wall, tore the bumper off my car. He went on to win the race.

"Then in 1960 they didn't have convertibles anymore. I was still a rookie, and in the Daytona 500 I ran third and Daddy ran fourth. Me and him and Johnny Allen, a boy from Cleveland in a Chevrolet, ran the last part of the race together. Daddy's car's distributor was messed up. It would only turn so many rpms. I beat Daddy because his car would run just so fast.

"That year I came in second in the point standings to Rex White. Daddy came in sixth. I was still learning to drive, and then in '61, just when I was about ready to race for wins, Daddy got hurt bad in the second Daytona qualifying race when he and Johnny Beauchamp tangled and crashed. He was like I am now, on his downhill drag. He left before I ever got as good as he was.

"There wasn't any rivalry between Daddy and Beauchamp. As far as I know, they got along good. Beauchamp didn't run much on the NASCAR circuit because he was from Keokuk, Iowa, and came from the IMCA circuit. But in '61 it so happened that Daddy and Beauchamp got together at Daytona, and Beauchamp pushed him to the wall, and that ended Daddy's career. It ended Beauchamp's too. He started having blackout spells. That eliminated both of them.

"It was a freak deal that it happened to be the same two as were involved in that close finish in '59. It was strictly an accident. Banjo

Matthews spun coming down off three and four, and Daddy and Beauchamp were racing the last lap, and Daddy saw Matthews, and Beauchamp didn't, and they got hung up, and it was just one of those things. Just a racing accident. No one remembers, but in the first qualifying race that year, Junior Johnson and I got hung up, and my Plymouth went flying over the wall.

"By '64, Chrysler had developed the hemi engine. We just blowed them away. It was one of them no-contest deals. They throwed the flag, and we were gone. Know what I mean? We came back and got the checkered. That was about it. That was the first time I ever had a car that was as fast as anybody else's. Our cars had handled better than other cars, and so all of a sudden we got some horsepower, so man, it was trucking along.

"I had run good at Daytona before, ran a second and a third, and it's a track I really like. I had a lot of confidence in the car, a lot of confidence in myself, and when the car performed, it gave me that much more confidence to go on and do what I needed to do.

"In the 100-mile preliminary, I drove off and left everybody, but then in the 500 the thing ran out of gas on the last lap, and when I got to the start-finish line, Bobby Isaac and Jimmy Pardue went across at the same time, and I still think I won that race, but I wasn't running but 10 miles an hour and these other cats were running 170, and they gave me third.

"The hemi was the most powerful engine I ever had. That was built strictly for racing. Up to that time all we had was a stock engine. Chrysler was getting back into racing, and in '63 they began working on some heads and different things, like what Chevrolet and Ford were doing, and then they decided to get into racing the full route, so they built the hemi engine.

"We didn't get to run in 1965 because Bill France outlawed the hemi engine. He just said, 'You can't run it,' and then in the middle of '65, after Chrysler had put it in its Plymouth Belvedere, France said we could put it in a big car. We said, 'No, we're not going to mess with it.' So I went drag racing. And then sometime in July of that year, they said, 'Okay, you can run the thing,' so I came back and ran fourteen races that year, and the only superspeedway they let me run was Rockingham, because they said we couldn't run in anything over a mile. They wouldn't let me run Darlington or Charlotte or Daytona. And then in '66 they made us take the hemi and cut it down from 426 cubic inches to 405. We still blew them away.

"We went to Daytona in '66, and we were real fast. Dick Hutcherson probably had the second-best car. He had a Ford. We were the only ones competing for the fastest time.

"When the race started, we just blew them all away.

"In '71 at Daytona, Buddy Baker and I had the only two factory cars. We ran for Chrysler. I beat him by ten seconds. I beat Bobby Isaac in '73, beat Cale Yarborough in '74, but the Daytona 500 that got away occurred in 1976.

"That was the year NASCAR discovered extra fuel lines of nitrous oxide in a lot of the cars. When they took their gas away from them, they were nothing. Know what I mean? David Pearson and myself were the fastest cars. We drove off and lapped everybody.

"I was leading going up the backstretch, and David passed me and went into the corner, and when he did, he went in and moved up, and I went down under him and got beside him in the middle of the corner, and coming off the corner, just where the hump is, I thought I cleared him. I was going to move out and block him; only thing is, I hadn't cleared him. Missed by just about six inches. He caught my right rear. It wasn't his fault. It was my fault. He was stuck in there, but if he had lifted and let me in there, he definitely wasn't going to win. He had moved out as far as he could, and like I said, I didn't quite clear him, and he caught me on the side rear and sent me sideways.

"I got back onto the track and thought I had it straight, but I didn't. I went head-on into the wall. He went down through the infield and headed toward pit road, and there was a car coming down pit road that hit him and straightened him out, otherwise he would have hit the inside guard-rail. Instead, he came back across the track.

"I made it all except fifty or maybe a hundred yards, but I couldn't get the thing started up, so he won the race. But it *was* exciting.

"The press tried to make a big deal out of it, but we didn't make nothing out of it. David and I *never* had no trouble. We ran against each other probably more than anybody. We had run more firsts and seconds than anybody has ever run against each other. David was the best I ever ran with.

"If you don't have confidence in another driver, you will sit back and wait for him to make a mistake and then get by him or you will try to get by him as quickly as possible. You're not going to race with him any more than you have to. David and I had full confidence in ourselves and in each other, so if you drove the car in the corner beside him, you knew he wasn't going to intentionally knock the tar out of you or vice versa, so you could do some really fierce racing. You knew he had complete control of what he was doing, and you knew he felt the same about you, and so you could put on a heck of a race.

"Today you have a lot of drivers out there with really good cars but who don't have the experience to run these superspeedways. They have sponsors who are spending two or three million bucks, and so they feel obligated to do things they are not capable of doing. So then you get the conflict of cats driving over their heads. You have boys who have run four or five years and never been big winners, and instead of going out and saying, 'If we run in the first eight or ten, we'll make money,' they try to run faster, and so they crash and take out four or five cars.

"See, it used to be when you ran, there used to be a dozen drivers you could pretty well trust. Now there aren't but three or four.

"It's a different world what these drivers are facing. Used to be, everyone drove with the finesse of being able to handle that car, of being right on the edge and knowing where that edge is at. I don't think you will ever see drivers with the finesse of Bobby Allison, David Pearson, and Cale Yarborough. You'll see one or two, but not as a group.

"Today only two or three drivers out there can drive that way. The rest of them are driving on the edge, and there is no telling what's going to happen the next lap. These cats run that bare edge for five hundred miles. That doesn't make it right or wrong. It's just not the way we used to do it.

"If I was drafting Pearson on the racetrack and he went down into the corner and I followed him, if he made a right-hand turn, I would make a right-hand turn. I had that much confidence in what he was going to do. He wasn't doing it just for his health. I trusted him that much. There are only one or two right now where I'd do that. You don't need to know who. I have to drive against the others.

"David loved to drive the race car, but that's all he wanted to do with it. He wasn't interested in the PR part, wasn't interested in making anything out of it. All he loved was to drive the race car, and he was super. He could win on quarter-mile dirt tracks, quarter-mile asphalts, superspeedways, road courses—it didn't make any difference.

"See, some people are good on road courses and some are good on short tracks and he was good on everything. He was a winner. All he wanted to do was get in the race, drive in the race, kiss the queen, and go home. But he was not good from the PR standpoint. It didn't translate to the fans. As long as he was a winner, he was driving a Ford product, and the Ford people thought he was great. But when he went away, they let him go away, because he didn't have a personal contribution to make, didn't have a personal relationship with the fans. They were pulling for Pearson because he was driving a Ford product. They pulled for me because I was driving a Chrysler product. I just approached it differently. For me, racing was my total life. To him, driving a race car was only a portion of his life.

"I will never turn away a fan who wants an autograph. The deal is that no racetrack has ever paid me a penny. NASCAR has never paid me a penny. STP has never paid me a penny, and no car company has ever paid me a penny, in the sense that it is the fans who bought the products, bought the tickets, bought STP or Pontiac, and that money goes through those people and then comes to me. So without the fans, the tracks or NASCAR or STP or Pontiac wouldn't be here, and I wouldn't be here.

"The fans are the nucleus of racing. Without the fans, we wouldn't be sitting here in my living room overlooking the racetrack, because there would be no racetrack, there would be no Richard Petty. The fans are the root of the whole sport. I learned this from my father: The fans are the ones who pay for everything. If you don't have them on your side, the sponsors won't be interested in you, the tracks won't, nobody. I have been one of the fortunate few who have been able to succeed on both sides of the racetrack. I was lucky enough to be able to have good cars to win races and lucky enough to associate with great people on the outside. Some can do one or the other, but not many can do both. I've been blessed.

"Three years after losing that Daytona 500 to David, it was someone else's turn to crash on the last lap at Daytona and give me the victory. Early on in the race Cale Yarborough and the Allison brothers, Bobby and Donnie, got into it and spun off in turn number two. This put Cale two laps down, and he fought and made his laps up. Donnie had also gotten a couple of laps down, and he also made his laps up. Both Cale and Donnie were far superior to what I was. Cale and Donnie were twenty seconds ahead of us. They were done gone. We couldn't even see them on the racetrack, so we weren't interested in them.

"Fighting for third place was me, A. J. Foyt, and Darrell Waltrip. Of our three cars, A. J. Foyt really was the fastest. I kept dogging him and dogging him, and Darrell Waltrip was running with me and Foyt, even though he had a broken valve spring. His old car was running in the draft, keeping things going.

"On the last lap, the three of us were tied up with each other, trying to figure out how to finish in third place, when the blinker lights came on. When Foyt saw those lights, automatically he lifted. Normally that's what you do when the blinker lights come on. I never lifted. Well, Foyt soon realized what was going on, but that was enough to beat him.

"That left it up to me and Darrell, and Darrell's old car wasn't running too good. Not that I was in such good shape; I wasn't running on all eight cylinders.

"At that time we didn't have radios, so nobody could tell us what was going on. I still couldn't see anything because Cale and Donnie were so far ahead, there was no smoke, but by the time I came around to the backstretch and started going into the third corner, I looked over, and there were the two cars laying in the infield.

"The day before my son Kyle had won the ARCA race. He came around leading the race on the last lap, came off number four, and the boy who was running second started to go in on him. Kyle came off the corner and went all the way down on the inside to keep the boy from getting under him, just cut him off so he wouldn't have a place to go.

"When I came off the fourth corner, Darrell started to move down, so I decided to do the same thing Kyle had done, move down inside. In fact, Darrell kept going, down onto the flat—not that I run him down there. And I was able to beat Darrell to the line, and by the time we got back around to the crash, Cale and Donnie and Bobby were out there fighting.

"When we came off the number two corner after we took the checkered flag, I thought Darrell was going to come out of the car, he was so happy. He was jumping up and down and waving his arms, because he had never finished good at all. He had finished second with a fourth-place car, and we were both tickled. He pulled up beside me and was just jumping up and down.

"As I rounded the track for the victory lap, Cale and Donnie and Bobby were still fighting. I came back around and took the crew into the winner's circle. I didn't know until later how bad it got, that they really got on the floor, really got with it.

"The reporters asked me upstairs, 'What do you think about them crashing?' The '76 race was still on my mind. It hadn't been but three years. I knew how it felt. I had been there.

"I said, 'Them cats don't have any class.' They said, 'What do you mean?' I said, 'When me and Pearson did it, we did it over by the grandstand were everybody could see us. Cale and Donnie did it on the backstretch out of sight.'

"In 1981 I won Daytona for the last time. It was the year of the first downsized car. Bobby Allison had the fastest car all week long. He set on the pole and ran a great 125-mile race and he dominated the 500-mile race. I just trucked along, running third, fifth, eighth—just running with the crowd. Allison led, and then with twenty-five laps to go, he ran out of gas coming down the backstretch and had to come in. They had to gas his car, and they changed all four tires. So everyone else in contention followed suit.

"Dale Inman was the crew chief, and he left me out. He said, 'Run as far as you can.' So when everyone stopped, I was leading the race.

"We still needed gas. But our strategy had been to wait until everyone else showed what they were doing. Dale knew if we got gas and changed tires like everyone else, there was no way we could win the race; we'd still be fifth. So he kept me out there until everybody made a pit stop, and then after the last of our group of eight came in, he said, 'Come in.'

"When I came down pit road, Dale said, 'One tank of gas.' I hustled on down through there, got the gas, and when I went back out, I was still leading the race. In my mind, right there, that's what won it. I knew it was close on gas, and so did Dale, but the only chance we had to win this race was to do what we were doing.

"When I went back with twenty-five laps to go, I had a ten-second lead, my car was handling really good, I could run wide open. Once I went back out, I thought, 'The only way I'm going to win this race is to never lift this car no matter where the traffic is.' If I had to run close to the wall, it didn't make any difference. I'd catch cars side to side and still pass them. I never did lift.

"Allison couldn't do that, he had to be real careful, because his car wasn't handling quite as good as mine. He got within four or five seconds of me, but I ran just as fast as he did. And then coming off the fourth turn of the last lap, my car ran out of gas. I had been racing with Cale, drafting with him, trying to keep myself going, and it looked like I pulled over to let him go, and I did, because I couldn't go. But I still had enough to beat Bobby as I coasted across the start-finish line.

"Bobby had run out of gas and lost the race. I ran out of gas and won the race. It's the circumstances. I had a good car, not the fastest car, but we used the right strategy.

"Part of my success has to do with timing. When I came along, it was the perfect time, because just when I was starting out, racing was going from the old school of racing into the superspeedway era of today. I took the sport from the days of Fireball Roberts, Lee Petty, Junior Johnson, and Curtis Turner and spanned the time of the growth of NASCAR to the days of Dale Earnhardt, Darrell Waltrip, Davey Allison, and Kyle Petty. And NASCAR is going to grow from here without me, but it will never grow as much as it did during those thirty years that I was here. There isn't enough room for it to grow that far.

"So I was very fortunate. People ask me, 'Don't you wish you were coming along now?' because these cats are winning a million dollars a year. I say, 'No.' Because Richard Petty would not be the same force in racing if he had come along at any other time. This is a bad example, but it's like George Washington being there when they needed him, or Abraham Lincoln or Franklin Delano Roosevelt. Each was the man for the time. Like in golf, Arnold Palmer took the sport from a country club deal to the common man. He to me is Mr. Golf. And so I was put here at the right time in order to grow in that transition.

"I've just been lucky. That's all I can say. It wasn't that I set out to do a lot of the things that happened. There is no explanation for it. It just happened.

"I'm not as competitive now as I used to be. I used to enjoy the competition, the racing part of it, but I don't get a chance to race that much. I just enjoy driving the car. That's the way I approach it, so that means I'm not as competitive within myself. That means I lose that half-a-car length every lap, and first thing you know, I get behind.

"I'm comfortable with the speeds I'm running. I used to be comfortable running over and above what everyone else was driving. If some cat could drive this hard going into the corner, I could drive that hard. Now these cats drive to this point, and I back off. My capabilities are less.

"It used to be, no matter what anybody could do, I could do better. Or I felt like I could. In my mind I could, so I made it happen. Like what Dale Earnhardt is doing now. He has full confidence in himself, in the crew, full confidence in the car, and he's got full confidence the circumstances will be on his side.

"I've been through that. But lately, if there is a wreck, it runs into me or I run into it, so you lose confidence to go that extra step, and then you get behind.

"I've had some bad accidents, but I've been lucky in that I blacked out long enough not to remember the bad parts. I remember what led into it or the aftermath, but never when I hit the wall or got hurt bad. So the good Lord has that built into me. I don't ever have to wake up and feel all the pain that went with it.

"We won seven of the Daytona races. Daddy won one, and Pete Hamilton, who drove for us, won one, so Petty Enterprises has a pretty good record at Daytona. Two or three of those races I won, I shouldn't have won, but then there were two or three that I should have won that I didn't, so it balanced itself out.

"We'll get up for the Daytona 500 come February. We always have."

Junior Johnson

LAP 8

Junior Johnson

The Legend

It is mid-November. The 1991 NASCAR season has been over for barely a week. The entire industry has closed its road show, the floating motor carnival that moves from city to city across the nation much like the performers for Ringling Brothers. There are but four short months to prepare for 1992. NASCAR has issued its new specifications for all cars, and in race shops throughout the Piedmont of North Carolina within a 100-mile radius of Charlotte, a beacon of the New South where 80 percent of the shops are located, mechanics work fifteen-hour days preparing for the upcoming season.

In the Junior Johnson race shop in Ingle Hollow, North Carolina, the buzz of excitement concerns Johnson's newest acquisition, driver Bill Elliott. Elliott wowed the racing world in 1985 with eleven wins, including a $1,000,000 bonus from the R. J. Reynolds tobacco company for winning three of the Big Four events—the Daytona 500, Talladega's Winston 500, Charlotte's World 600 (which Darrell Waltrip won), and the Southern 500 at Darlington. Winner to date of almost $11 million in prize money, Elliott shocked the racing world after the 1991 season when he left his family-run team to accept a lucrative offer to drive for Johnson.

The news has stirred the racing industry, moreover, because it meant the continuation for Johnson of a two-car team, something he had vowed never again to attempt after a disastrous experiment in 1984 when Darrell Waltrip and Neil Bonnett drove for him. Waltrip, who resented any attention given to Bonnett that might have taken away from his own success, ended up acrimoniously leaving Johnson. The rift left Johnson with a bad feeling. He swore he would never try to service two drivers again. Never say never.

In 1991 Johnson returned to a two-car team with Geoff Bodine and

105

Sterling Marlin. This time, it was agreed both teams would share all their information. The year went smoothly. But Elliott is a driver with a lot of ego, like Waltrip. Elliott isn't likely to want to be anything but top dog.

Junior had been aware of the benefits of having a two-car team. One plus is that NASCAR only allows a car to test seven times during the season. If you have two cars, you can test twice as many times.

Another plus, Junior realized, is that if one car is running fast and the other slower, on the superspeedways the less-fast car can make up time by drafting with the faster car. Ricky Rudd and Ken Schrader, the two Hendrick Motorsports drivers, sometimes take advantage of their relationship in just that manner. The problem, of course, is that the two drivers have to want to cooperate. As competitive as most drivers are, getting them to cooperate isn't always easy or possible, even when they work for the same owner. In racing, you can't win if you can't get along.

For the 1992 season Bill Elliott was coming to Ingle Hollow to replace Geoff Bodine, who had been let go to make room for the redheaded racer from Dawsonville, Georgia, who was leaving his family and owner Harry Melling to drive for Junior Johnson.

Who could pass up the opportunity? During his twenty-six-year career as a car owner, Junior Johnson's teams have won six national championships and 131 races, and in fourteen of the last twenty years his drivers have finished first, second, or third in the point standings.

The 1992 season shapes up as another banner year for Johnson and his Thunderbirds. The experts predict great performances from the Ford engines. The one question mark concerns possible conflict between Elliott and Sterling Marlin. Like Darrell Waltrip before him, Bill Elliott is not the sort to play second fiddle to anyone. He is too fierce a competitor to give a break to anyone, including a teammate, so the question is: Will Sterling Marlin be amenable to playing second fiddle to the more flamboyant Elliott? That also remains to be seen.

As the 1992 season looms, experts, observers, and pundits all agree: With "Awesome" Bill Elliott and Sterling Marlin driving for him, it appears that one or both of Junior Johnson's race teams will contend for the driving championship, cooperation or no. Winners tend to keep winning. All his life it's been that way for Junior Johnson.

JUNIOR JOHNSON: "When I first started out as a driver, I would jump from owner to owner, always looking for a better car, a better race team, a better everything. My basic nature is a perfectionist, and I don't want anybody to tell me it can't be done, or there ain't no way of doing it. I don't like that. And that goes for my own crew and drivers.

"I was driving for Ray Fox in 1960 when I won the Daytona 500. I was such a big underdog, I had no chance at all to win that race. But in practice the Wednesday before, I had picked up something that was happening on the racetrack which would enable me to challenge the faster cars. I figured out about drafting, that if you rode directly behind one of the faster cars, the two of you could go faster than if you or he rode all by yourself.

"When Sunday came and the race started, I would stay with one of the fast cars until he went to the pits, and then I would simply pick up the next one that came by or was up front with me and stay with him until something happened to him, and then I would go to the next one. I hitched rides all day long from one car to another because my car could not run with a third of the cars in the field unless it had a draft.

"And basically, I chose to hitch rides with Pontiacs, because they were far superior to the Chevrolet I had. They had better horsepower and aerodynamics than I did, but with me drafting, I was just as good as they were. I drafted Fireball Roberts a long time, Jack Smith a long time, Cotton Owens, Banjo Matthews, Bobby Johns, and Paul Goldsmith. I hung with the Pontiacs all day long, and when it was all over, I was determined the winner simply because I had hitched rides and was at the front all day long.

"I got out of racing in 1966. When I left driving, I knew I had had all that I wanted, and I was done with that part. I was driving cars and owning the cars and working on the cars, and I had my farm and a grading business. I built roads for the state at that time, and I was involved in so many things I couldn't concentrate on doing everything. I had won a lot of races on all the big tracks, and when I'd win a race, I had already won it before, and there wasn't any excitement in it. There wasn't nothing there for me to get excited about, 'cause if I went to North Wilkesboro and won the race, I had already won it two or three times prior, maybe more than that, and I could see where the motivation I had to drive was gone. To get the checkered flag—well, what was that?

"When I went in to owning race cars, by that time they had built some humongous racetracks, and things were beginning to boom. The factories were getting into it, and it was just more interesting for me to work on cars and manage and run my business than it was to drive. I could have drove anytime I wanted to, I just didn't care nothing about it.

"I started my race team in 1966. I had four different drivers that year, and the next year I had three more. I was hunting for the kind of driver who basically had the same instincts I had. I've had four like that throughout my career: Lee Roy Yarbrough, Cale Yarborough, Bobby Allison, and Darrell Waltrip.

"Lee Roy had determination and a no-quit attitude. Nobody much liked Lee Roy because of his flamboyant ways, but he's right at the top of the list of the all-time great race drivers, and I've seen them all. He was flamboyant off the track and on it, and some owners, who put talent behind personality, didn't like him, but I think that's the wrong way to approach the race driver. Give me the talent, and I will live with his personality, and I've had that in several race drivers.

"In fact, I got along with Lee Roy probably the best of any race driver I ever had, 'cause he did his job, and I did mine, and his personality had nothing to do with what I hired him for. I hired him to do a job, and that was what I was looking for him to do. His personality was his business. It was none of mine.

"I've been criticized in my lifetime for things I've done. You can't worry about what other people say about you. I can remember during the Firecracker 400 in 1967 Cale Yarborough, who drove for the Wood Brothers, ran out of gas in front of my pit, and I poured a can of gas into his car. He went and won, and Lee Roy finished second, and later on NASCAR ruled that if you went by your pit, you could not back up, and nobody else could service you. You had to get a tow truck to push you back to the pits.

"Well, I'm not a person to destroy some driver just to win a race. That's not me. I like to win a race, but I like to beat the guy to win it. When Cale went by his pit, he was out of gas, and I was the gas man on our car at that time, and I seen him come down pit road, and I knew he was out of gas—he was coasting with the motor cut off—and I stepped out with a can of gas, he stopped, and I put it in. And away he went. I don't regret that. That's what anybody should have done. That was the right thing to do. You don't hurt somebody in that kind of position. I feel that Glen Wood and them boys would have done the same thing for me.

"Lee Roy sort of gets shortchanged when they talk about the great drivers. Toward the end of his career he was suffering with a mental illness—his sickness is something people don't know about or don't want to discuss. And that's sad.

"There are four or five versions of what happened to him. Some people say Lee Roy got bit by a spider and got some kind of disease. A lot of people speculate he got into drugs. He had had a tremendous bad wreck in Texas and a real bad wreck at Indianapolis, but Lee Roy raced on through the rest of the year after Texas, and as far as I could tell he was perfectly fine.

"He was forced to quit in 1977, and me and Lee Roy split at that point, and I wasn't around him much after that. I know he got sick and had trouble. They say Lee Roy tried to kill his mother.

"I went to visit him in the hospital, and it was very, very sad. He could remember everything from the 1970s and back, but nothing forward. He didn't even remember his racing career. Lee Roy kept getting worse and worse, until he died of a brain hemorrhage in the mid-eighties.

"In 1971, I was looking for $800,000 to sponsor my race team. I went to talk with R. J. Reynolds. I was the first person to talk to them. Reynolds had gotten cut off from television and radio and were looking for places to put their advertising dollars. I told them I was looking for $800,000. They told me they were looking to spend $300 or $400 million! That's the kind of money they had for TV, radio, magazines, and billboards. They had money coming out of their ears, so I suggested they talk to Bill France, Sr., and see what they could work out as far as sponsoring the sanctioning body, and that's what they did, and that was the greatest thing for racing that ever happened, and I don't care what anybody says. The Reynolds Tobacco Company sponsoring the Winston Cup is the best thing that ever happened to us. Reynolds made it possible for racing to survive.

"When Ford dropped out of racing in '71, I dropped out, and then in 1971 I was contacted by Richard Howard, who was promoting races for the Charlotte Motor Speedway, to build a car for the World 600. I did that, built a Chevrolet, and put Charlie Glotzbach in it. Charlie dominated that day until Speedy Thompson got in a wreck and put us out. Bobby Allison went on to win it.

"I ran Charlie in quite a few races the rest of that year, which proved to NASCAR that Chevrolet could race in NASCAR, and then in 1972, I worked out a relationship with Bobby Allison—he had the Coca-Cola sponsorship—and we won ten races, finished in the top five in twenty-five of the thirty-one races, and should have won the championship, but we had a problem at Talladega. Then Bobby wanted to run his own race team, so in 1973 I picked up Cale Yarborough. He stayed with me for eight years and had a tremendous career.

"By 1973, racing was beginning to change. I was seeing a lot of people beginning to ease into racing with a lot of money, big, rich people, big sponsors. Reynolds Tobacco Company was beginning to entice a lot of large corporations into it. Their advertising began to take hold. So many things were beginning to take hold.

"Cale was coming back from Indianapolis, where he had been with Gene White running Indy cars. We had run against Cale a lot when he was with Glen Wood, and when he went to Indy, Glen picked up David Pearson. So when Cale came back, he was the best choice for us, because as a competitor he was very, very tough when Lee Roy was driving for us. It was either Cale, Lee Roy, or Richard Petty who won the race, and most of the time it came down to Lee Roy or Cale, though Richard also won a lot of races during that time, so Cale was an asset to us. He was a very, very hard driver. The Woods and them boys ran only sixteen races when he ran for the championship, but they were very, very tough. They'd win half of the ones they ran, and we'd win about the rest of them, and Richard Petty would get what of them Wood boys and me didn't get.

"Cale was a very, very good pick for us. He was a great competitor, did a wonderful job with us. I've seen him drive cars I couldn't believe he could drive—wrecked up, patched up, tore up, no way a human being could drive something like that—but he was tough and strong, did not give up, had an attitude that was unbelievable.

"And when Cale decided he wanted to cut back on his racing activities, we went after Darrell Waltrip and had a great career with him. Darrell was like Lee Roy. I didn't care about his personality. His ability to drive a race car and his determination were what I was after. Everybody said me and him wouldn't get along, but I wasn't hiring his personality; I was hiring his talent.

"Darrell was the Dale Earnhardt of his time, very determined, had a lot of skills, was not scared of the race car. I'm not saying he's scared now, but he's a little careful compared to what he once was.

"In 1984, I decided to add a second car, and I hired Neil Bonnett in addition to Darrell. It's a problem when you've got a guy like Darrell that thinks the way he does. If he's working with a race team, he wants that race team to focus on Darrell Waltrip, and when he lost my personal attention to his car, then he wasn't satisfied. He wanted my time to be devoted solely to him. When I went to run two cars, that could not happen.

"And so he decided to go and drive for somebody else. It was a financial decision for him more than anything else, because at the same time I was starting to look for another driver to replace him. Darrell had reached his peak and was going down the other side. He started dropping off from winning twelve races a year for me to seven, six, four, two, three, and then two, and then I started looking around for a different driver because I felt like we had used Darrell up, and that's putting it exactly the way I felt about it. We needed young, fresh blood behind that steering wheel, a younger person with a lot more determination than Darrell had.

"First Terry Labonte was put in, and Terry is a good race driver and a great person, but he and the crew never did hit it off, so we went searching for another driver. We had a three-year contract with Terry, and both of us lived to the end of the contract and did our jobs. He did his, we did ours, and no regrets. It just wasn't what we were looking for, and then we went to Geoff Bodine and ran two years with him. The first year was fine, and the second was a disaster. He and the crew failed to communicate. And also, I brought on a second car the second year, which might have disturbed his attitude. He didn't want to be involved in a two-car team because already he had been involved with a three-car team over at Hendrick Motorsports, and so from that point on we started looking for another driver to put in the car.

"We have now found the driver we were looking for, Bill Elliott. He was with his brothers. Bill comes here by himself. And now I have Sterling Marlin and Bill, and they are going to do a great job for us. They will be two outstanding race teams. One of them should win the Daytona 500 come February. They will have the car and the equipment, and one of them should win—if they don't get involved in a wreck.''

LAP 9

Ralph Moody
The Car Builder

Loud, brash John Holman joined forces with quiet, tough Ralph Moody in 1956. Holman, from California, made sure parts came in on time, salaries were paid, orders for race cars got filled, and arrangements for shows and races were completed. Moody, a Yankee from Massachusetts, made sure the cars were built right and ran fast.

Holman-Moody became the racing laboratory for the Ford Motor Company. Drivers for Holman-Moody made up a Who's Who of racing's Hall of Fame, including Cale Yarborough, Junior Johnson, Bobby Isaac, Bobby Allison, Marvin Panch, Curtis Turner, Fireball Roberts, Joe Weatherly, Freddy Lorenzen, and David Pearson. One year Holman-Moody built, staffed, and provided pit crews for six Grand National race cars.

Moody, who was elected into the NASCAR Hall of Fame in 1970, was a carmaking innovator who invented many of today's safety features, including the fabricated cage construction, a device called a floater to keep the wheels from falling off, stronger spindle pins, and a bladder to protect the gas tank from leaking gas and catching on fire.

Because of Ralph Moody, the sport of stock car racing suffers few deaths, despite the horrific nature of its high-speed crashes. Unfortunately, it took the death of two of racing's heroes—Fireball Roberts when his gas tank leaked, caught on fire, and burned him over most of his body, and Joe Weatherly, who died when the left side of his car crashed into the wall, crushing his head against it—to get NASCAR's ruling body to adopt some of Moody's safety measures.

From the beginning, says Ralph Moody, he was plagued by destructive meddling both by his partner, John Holman, who he came to detest, and by the executives of the Ford Motor Company, who, Moody says, thought they knew more than he did about stock car racing. Turmoil seemed to rule at what was then the premier car-building facility.

Now retired and living in Charlotte, Ralph Moody doesn't mince words about his life in racing.

"A lot of people who worked for me said I was a miserable son of a bitch," Moody said. "I heard it a lot of times. Fred Lorenzen used to say that. 'Miserable son of a bitch,' he called me. I'd tell him, 'Yeah, but I win races.' "

RALPH MOODY: "When John Holman and I first started, we had help from the Ford people, but they weren't knowledgeable about what we wanted, didn't know what it took to make a race car work on a racetrack. I got to know a guy named Don Sullivan, a young man who was old man Henry Ford's right-hand man—Don Sullivan was the guy who was in on the design of the flathead Ford, the 302, a real smart guy.

"Well, all Ford had for us were street shocks, or you'd try to adapt truck shocks, or maybe we'd put in two sets of street shocks, but they weren't worth a crap. They were wrong, backwards, to run a race car, and so one Christmas—my wife was about to kill me—I was up to the factory trying to get the Monroe people to design us some shocks.

"Well, they came down with two sets, and they weren't exactly what we wanted, but they were a hell of a lot better than what we had. We got to Daytona and met with another group of shock makers, and they had shocks you could take apart, revalve and change them, and finally we got what we wanted, and so I had the shock people at Monroe look at them, and they got all mad at us. They said we didn't know what the hell we were talking about, said what I was doing wouldn't work. They were smart people and all, but we were doing things ass-backwards to what they had been doing all their life.

"Racing, of course, is a whole different setup. Finally, they made us some the way I wanted them. Even Bud Moore was complaining, 'Them goddamn shocks are no good.' Until he couldn't catch us, and then he had to have some too. After that, we were selling them by the truckload. It changed everybody's outlook on the thing.

"When I first started, cars ran with stock rear ends, and the axle would break. As a youngster, I ran midgets or sprint cars, and I would modify them by putting in a floater to keep the wheel from falling off, because with midgets, if you broke an axle, you'd break your damn head. Willy Thompson and I made a floater and put it in our car without telling Holman, and we didn't have that trouble like a lot of other cars.

"Finally I said to NASCAR, 'Let me show you something. We need to put this in the car so they don't keep wrecking and hurting people.' Oh boy, they had a fit about that. I said, 'Hell, it ain't gonna run any better; it's just a safety measure.'

"The same thing happened when I came up with the dry sump, like they got now. They didn't want us to run it.

"They wanted stock cars, but if you are running 100 miles an hour in a stock car and something happens, you get killed. You *have* to put safety equipment in it. I can remember when we took two Thunderbirds, one for Curtis Turner and one for Joe Weatherly at Darlington, and the rules said you had to have doors with hinges on them. You would close the door and put two slabs of iron bolts through it around the doorposts. Hell, you were always ripping those damn doors off. Guys were sitting with no protection, didn't have any sides, just a roof and a top. And they'd just squash the car. I kept saying I was going to install a roll bar, put the loop on top, side bars, brace bars, cross bars, and three high-door bars. We went to Darlington, and the NASCAR officials made us take it off. Afterward, we went to Atlanta, and Nelson Stacy got hit, a car broke right through, busted up his pelvis, legs, ribs, goddamn about ruined him. Then they decided, 'What did you do there? Let's look at that.'

"It was the same with the roll bars, which didn't become standard until 1958.

"The problem with the uni-construction cars was they just folded up. Uni-construction is just stamp metal set out there with an engine hung in it. If you stick the car into the wall, the engine comes back where you are. There was no strength or protection at all, so in 1963 I decided to make a fabricated chassis to provide the driver more safety. NASCAR wouldn't let me run it, and in '64 I made one that way and took it to Atlanta and tested it, ran the crap out of it, and it was strong. I ran the two-by-four rails down by the rocker panels and hooked the roll cage to it. And I hooked it to a changeover fabricated '64 Ford snout, which was a real rugged thing. It used to be a roll cage attached to a tin floor, and it wasn't safe.

"After a while they decided we could run it, and so we took Curtis Turner to Bristol in a Ford Torino, and in practice it outran everybody so bad Chrysler decided they'd go home. Chrysler was going to pack up and leave, so NASCAR wouldn't let it run.

"Finally, they let it run. Darel Dieringer slaughtered the wall up in Wilkesboro with Junior Johnson's car, and the engine came back into the car eighteen inches. Imagine if you hit one that hard at Daytona? That's when NASCAR decided, 'Yeah, go with the new frame.' It wasn't long afterwards that I was fabricating frames for everybody. It was safe. It didn't crumple up. That's why the cars are so tough now. The wrecks you see . . . look at the one Darrell Waltrip took at Daytona. You see him come down the backstretch, on the grass, wham—but it stayed together.

"But it took a lot of hassle and fight to get them to let me do that. And of course, it was a goddamn Yankee doing it. But the thing is, I grew up racing, since I was a boy helping to build sprint cars. I had a background people never realized I had. People didn't know I built cars for thirty years before I came to Charlotte. When I was a youngster I would race midgets every night of the week and Sunday afternoons, ran seven nights a week driving modifieds.

"My goal always was to put something in that car that didn't break. I remember when I first raced midgets, Model A Fords, Model T Fords, the front axles had very short spindle pins, and they'd break often, and so I kept looking for something that didn't fall off, didn't break. They are running the same chassis setup that I started around 1956. The stuff was pretty bullet-proof. But it took a long time to get some of this stuff permitted: safety nubs, the floaters, the front spindles, the roll bars.

"When we moved into the superspeedway era with Daytona in '59, you could run into trouble burning the bearings in the hubs, so we just fattened the hub up a little, made it a little bit larger, and today you very seldom see someone breaking a hub, spindle, steering linkage, or a rear end. That stuff just doesn't break anymore. Very seldom do you see a broken axle.

"I've never said anything about this, but the thing with Fireball Roberts never should have happened. We had the car fixed up in a way that it never should have squashed the gas tank. They said we couldn't run it that way. We had it fixed up at Darlington, and we had to change it, and at Charlotte Fireball hit the wall, and it squashed it, and he burned up. After that, they changed the rules and allowed the reinforcements so it didn't happen again, and you see some terrific wrecks, but very rarely is there a fire. Sterling Marlin had one at Bristol in 1991, but I cannot remember another going back for a long, long time. And one of the reasons Marlin caught on fire was that his crash came right after a pit stop, and the tank was full. Today they have brackets around the tank to reinforce it, and they also have a fuel cell, which they didn't have back then.

"NASCAR has done a hell of a job. It wanted to put on a show, but they didn't have people who were knowledgeable enough. They weren't sitting there thinking about trying to make something better. We did it, because if you did that, you could sell it and make a lot of money on it.

That was the thing. If you make something that's good, you're going to sell the hell out of it. Our improvements were why we grew so big.

"The only thing that stopped it, it got to the point where Holman and I couldn't get along, and I got the hell out of there.

"Holman was a funny guy. Very few people liked him. He could do a lot of things. He was a big help making the business run, but he had his way of doing things and the hell with everybody, whether it was right or wrong. You just couldn't contain the guy.

"Everything worked fine at first. I was racing in NASCAR, and then we raced in USAC a couple years so we could sell in that circuit. When I went up there, we blew those guys away! And we were running against the Indy drivers and the hotshots. We would outrun them with no strain. Bob Myers was one of my first customers. I sold him an engine, a set of springs, got him running, and the next thing you know, boy, we had orders for equipment, race cars, engines, suspensions, everything.

"We grew so big we moved near the Charlotte airport, bought the old barracks buildings. We had a marina in Florida where we made racing boats, had a shop in California where we were making desert buggies. All told, we must have employed more than six hundred people at our peak. In 1960 we built four hundred race cars from here to California, as fast as we could build them. We made them as fast as we could turn them out.

"Our cars were front-runners. If Holman-Moody built something, it ran up front.

"I remember when Richard Petty first started. Richard is a nice guy, a hell of a competitor. The big reason Richard ran so good and so much was that Chrysler and later STP were backing him, and most of the other guys couldn't afford to go to all the races. Hell, he used to run fifty, sixty races a year.

"Hell, before you went to the race, you might as well give it to Petty. 'Cause he'd go to all these short tracks and win most of them. Who was there? The only reason he wouldn't win was if he broke or got in a wreck. There were only two or three cars that could run with him. Today, there are sixteen cars that can win a race.

"It got so in 1968, I said to Ford, 'Why the hell don't you run at least one time for the championship?' 'Why?' they asked. I said, 'Wouldn't it be a feather in your hat to win the championship with a Ford?' We had David Pearson driving for us in 1968. They said, 'Go ahead and run for the championship.' So we ran for the championship and won it.

"They said, 'You think you're so hot? Do it again next year.' And the next year we won it again. And then Ford said, 'The hell with it.' They didn't care about winning all the damn races.

"And at that time Harry Hyde was running a car for Chrysler for Bobby Isaac. Petty was sucking hind tit when he had good competition. Not to take anything away from him—he won races too when there was competition, but not as consistently—and as the competition got stronger, his wins came further and further between.

"We lost David Pearson in 1970 when he got mad at everybody and quit. Halfway through the year before Ford had wanted me to quit running his team, and so Dick Hutcherson was running Pearson, and Pearson wasn't happy. Jesus Christ, I was trying to take care of four or five drivers because they all knew I had the knowledge to get in the race car and find out what was wrong and fix it. And Ford didn't want me driving any race car because they were afraid I would get hurt.

"Anyway, Hutch took over in the middle of '69, and it went fairly decent, but in '70 it just didn't work. We finished the season, and David was going to quit. Finally, the Ford people talked him into staying.

"At the first race at Darlington, Jake Elder was on the car, Hutch was running it, and the car wasn't working right. Hutch called me about it, and I said, 'It's Saturday. You called me the last minute. What the hell are you going to do?'

"Sunday morning they changed everything—the shocks, springs— tested it, and put it on the racetrack. David came in, and they hadn't told them what they had done. David jumped in the car, took off, they waved the green flag, and when he came off turn four, he skinned the car down the goddamn wall. Right then he knew something was wrong, so he came around slowly the next lap and put it in the pits.

"He said, 'The hell with you people,' and he quit. He couldn't trust them with what they were doing.

"When I had a pit crew working for me, they didn't do anything to that race car until the driver and I agreed on the chassis setup. No one turned a screw until the driver and myself knew what we were doing. The crew didn't do anything to the engine but what the engine man said. You don't send a driver out there blind.

"Some teams don't do that when the driver and crew chief don't get along. They sneak up on their driver and say, 'This will work. He won't know it.' And by and by, the driver finds out, and he doesn't trust his people anymore.

"Back in '68 we had Bobby Allison, and he won three out of five races, including Rockingham, and ran second in the other two, but Ford didn't like him. I tried and tried to get Bobby and Donnie on the team, but

Ford never would take them. Shoot, they didn't like Freddy Lorenzen when I got him. I had to bitch and fight about that. They didn't like Tiny Lund when I put him in Marvin Panch's car at Daytona in '61 when Panch got burned.

"They said, 'Pick a replacement.' I said, 'Tiny.' For a week they wouldn't put him in. They said, 'Pick somebody else.' I said, 'Hell, no, you pick someone else.' They finally agreed, and Tiny won the Daytona 500 that year.

"It was the same way with Cale Yarborough. All the guys I picked, Ford didn't want. Hell no. I put Cale in the car at Darlington. He was broke. I was feeding him. He didn't have any money because he kept crashing his car. I told him, 'Just ride around out there, don't race, so you can make some money.'

"Junior Johnson was driving at the time, and Cale was doing what I told him, and Junior lapped him. Well, Cale took out after his ass and passed Junior, and then he bounced off somebody and hit the wall and crashed, but boy, Cale could drive the wheels off it.

"After four or five rides, Ford finally said, 'We'll try him.' But I always had a hassle getting the people I wanted to drive.

"Like I said, I had trouble with Ford about hiring Freddy Lorenzen, and he was a great one. I can remember schooling Freddy for a week, telling him about Curtis Turner. Turner was tough as hell on a racetrack. I said, 'Turner is going to be leading the race. You can beat him if you listen to what I'm telling you.' I said, 'Turner is a guy who if you went outside will get you into the wall, shut you off.' I said, 'Freddy, act dumb. Toward the end of the race just try to keep passing him on the outside, the outside, the outside. He ain't gonna let you. At the last moment, jump down inside him, move his ass out of there, and go on.'

"On the white flag Freddy did just that and went on to win the race. After Freddy took the checkered flag, Turner was so hot he went down the backstretch and plowed right into him.

"Lorenzen wanted to beat Fireball so bad, because Fireball had a big name. Boy, Freddy got so he could beat his ass too. Oh yeah. I remember the race at Darlington in '64, Freddy and Fireball were running head to head. When they came in to pit, I checked each of their tires, whether they needed to change them or not, and when they both came in for the last pit stop, I said, 'Go. No tires.' And they were gone. Both had at least a lap on the field and they were really fighting each other, not banging one another because I would raise hell if they did that.

"They were running one-two out there, and the first thing I knew, John Holman came down to the pits and said, 'The Ford people said to pit

Lorenzen.' I said, 'You tell him.' So Holman went out and told Lorenzen, and Freddy ignored him. Holman said, 'How come he ain't coming
in?' I said, 'He ain't coming in unless I tell him.' So Holman got a pit
board and wrote down, 'Come in,' and Lorenzen ignored that too. I said,
'John, go and tell Fireball to pit.' He said, 'No, they want Freddy to pit.'
See, the Ford people wanted Fireball to win the race because he was
buddy-buddy with them pretty good. I told John, 'You go back and tell
them guys that I'm running this race. When this is over, I will do something else, but I'm going to finish the job today. Tell them that.'

"He came back a little bit later and said, 'They said you're fired.' I
said, 'Good.'

"So Lorenzen won the race, and Fireball was second—we won, one-
two, and John went up there to Victory Lane. I didn't even go. I said to
the crew, 'Leave the car set right there. Just get your clothes and go
home.' I sent them all home and left the car, the equipment, everything,
sitting there.

"The Ford people didn't go home to Detroit after the race. They had
a big meeting at the shop the next day in Charlotte. I said, 'How many
times have you told me, "Don't listen to anybody—when you start a
race, you run that team like you want to"?' I said, 'You gave me the
authority. You have it on paper, and don't come out there in the middle
of the goddamn race and tell me what to do. If I do wrong, then you can
raise hell later.'

"Sometimes their meddling would drive me crazy.

"I remember a race in Milwaukee. Whitey Gerkin was driving for us,
and he was leading the field by a lap. If we give him a shot of fuel, we
win the race. The Ford guys leaned over the fence and said to me, 'Don't
stop. Tell the guy to keep going. He doesn't need gas.'

"I said, 'You guys are always telling me what to do. You tell him.'
They did, and he ran out of gas, and we finished fifteenth.

"I told them, 'You took the race away. Pay the man.' And they paid
him the win money. And Holman, whether they were right or wrong,
always would say, 'Just do what they say.'

"See, John Holman was always sucking up to the Ford guys, because
he was afraid they would take the thing away from us. Our shop *was*
Ford. But I knew they wouldn't do that. They wanted to win races. I
remember in 1967 we had Mario Andretti in one of our cars. He ran the
first race of the season at Riverside and didn't do very good. But I knew
he could drive a race car. So we had a meeting one night in our hotel. The
Ford guys said, 'What do you think about him?' Holman said, 'He ain't

big enough. He can't drive one of the big cars.' I said, 'Let me have him, and we'll see whether he can drive a race car.'

"In fifteen days we built a new car for him, and we took that thing to Daytona. I wish somebody had a movie of that, because at the time drivers wouldn't run up high. You had to run those big cars fast to run them high. And I got him all tuned in to what to do.

"I drove his car, got it working, showed him where to run it. He poked his ass in that thing, and he was gone. He wasn't used to it, so he ran out of gas twice, got up top on a hill, and coasted in for gas. He was way behind, and he just blew them all away again. Twice he did that—ran like a bear, won the race. First shot he was ever there. Tell me he can't drive a race car.

"That day Holman and I had a big hassle. John was mad because I was always on the road with the cars fielded out of our shop. NASCAR only allows one owner on a car—the insurance coverage was on the person instead of a business—so when Andretti came, Lorenzen was under my name and so was Andretti, and Holman got mad. He went down and got NASCAR to take my name off Lorenzen's car and put his name on so he'd have a winner, because Lorenzen ran good at Daytona. Trouble is, Lorenzen came in second! Andretti won. Goddamn, Holman was mad.

"And what happened during the race, we only had a pickup pit crew for Andretti's car. Hell, the guy who was gas-lifting was sixty years old. We didn't have a pit crew worth a crap. We had other men on other cars, and as soon as something happened to them, I went and grabbed them up. John came over and told me I couldn't use them. The reason he did that, he wanted Lorenzen to win. I liked to kill him. I threw him out of the goddamn pits and got the Ford people to tell John to stay the hell out of the pits. Boy, John was some kind of mad.

"We had a lot of bad feelings between Holman and me, but no one else saw it. If somebody came in our place and bought an engine or a race car, nobody saw what was going on behind the scenes. And whoever bought our equipment got the best. It was as good as anything anywhere. I remember one year we were running Dick Hutcherson. We had sold Ned Jarrett his car, and he as much as said his equipment was inferior to Hutch's. I told Ned, 'You get the job done, and you'll win the championship. You get the same equipment we got.' I just wouldn't sell inferior crap. And Ned won the championship that year. I raced all my life, and I know how I would feel if somebody was doing that to me. That's why we had such a hell of a business. We sold equipment to plenty of guys who beat us. But if they didn't beat you once in a while, they ain't gonna buy any more.

"Holman and I finally split up in 1971. We were barking at each other about this, that, and the other thing. John was a hell of a promoter, but he made a lot of enemies. John could screw up my people more in just ten minutes, and then I couldn't get them to work for a week. Day after day, little irritating things. He'd buy parts we didn't need. He bought boats all over Florida, cost a fortune. He bought double-decker busses to make motor homes out of them. I would get so mad about stuff like that. I'd tell him, 'Don't do that,' but the board of directors let him get away with murder. I was so busy, I wasn't there to keep up with a lot of it.

"I remember one year he made a deal with Bobby Allison. If Bobby won, he got 50 percent of the purse; if he came in second, it was 40 percent. Well, that year Bobby won ten superspeedway races.

"After he won three or four of them, John said, 'Jesus, we're paying him too much money. We ought to pay him 30 percent.' I said, 'You made the contract with him. That's what you have to live with.' Well, every time Bobby won, John would complain. I said, 'Damn, John, you win a lot more for first than you do for second.' Bobby was making more money for us getting 50 percent than he would have if he was finishing fourth or fifth.

"At the end of 1971 I had collected almost $2 million in sponsorship checks. Holman didn't know it, but I had. I went and told him, 'I have a big chunk of money going into next year with Bobby.' He said, 'We aren't running Bobby Allison. We aren't running any goddamn race car. I'm going to work on trucks.'

"I whipped the checks out and showed him. He said, 'Well, that's different.' I grabbed them back and put them in my pocket. He said, 'What are you going to do?' I said, 'Give them back.' And I did.

"Why fight it? We had fought all of '71, and I had had enough. I wanted out of it. Not to be talking about the guy, because he's gone, but when we started, I never took a dime. Every dime I made went into the business. We'd go to Milwaukee and make $6,000, and I didn't take a penny. I was living on my own money. We were great friends then, *great* friends.

"And then when things really got going, there was a lot of money, and it got so my partner wanted to run the whole show, tell me what time to get up, what time to go to bed, and it just became too much. I don't want to tell off a lot of people about it, because it's long gone, but I don't really give a shit. That's the way it was.

"In '71 I was a partner and didn't want to be liable for anything that happened in the future, so I got a lawyer to tell me how to find a way out. It had become too much of a hassle, with lawsuits and stuff, and I wanted out of it. The lawyer told me the only way I could get out of it was to get voted out of the company, to get the people irritated enough to get me the hell out of there. But no matter what I did, it didn't happen.

"Finally, I went to the bookkeeper, one of Holman's buddies, and I told him, 'The only was they can get me out is to vote me out at a board meeting.' I said, 'They will *never* get me out. They will have to vote me out of this place.'

"The bookkeeper went and told Holman right away. And boy, that's what they did. I grabbed the first phone and called my lawyer. He said, 'Great.'

"I didn't take anything. I just walked out. Holman told people he wasn't going to give me anything, but he did. It took five years, but he did.

"I walked away and opened my own place. Waddell Wilson, Keith Russell, and a bunch of guys left Holman and came to work for me. And so Holman didn't have anybody to run the performance program any more. Who the hell would he hire? John gave Banjo Matthews some jigs and some drawings, and that's how he got started. He gave Hutcherson and Pagan some stuff, and they started building cars.

"Holman built a race car for Bobby Unser to go to Riverside, and it was a sled. Didn't come near to making the show.

"I ran my engine shop for seven years, had a good time with the business. We ran two or three different drivers. We had Janet Guthrie. That was fun. But it was seven days a week. So I decided to get the hell out.

"The things that run best are the old things I came up with twenty years ago. Harry Gant has an old car with the old suspension and front steer, and the struts and setup are like it's supposed to be, and that son of a bitch works. Harry just sets there and picks his nose most of the time. I went to Richmond and watched Harry, and hell, he was just sitting there grinning, his old car worked so good. Well, back in my day, my cars worked just that way.''

Waddell Wilson

LAP 10

Waddell Wilson

The Engine Builder

In racing the fans see the beautifully painted cars on the track. They know each car by heart—its number, the name of the sponsor, and the driver. Often they also know the owner of the car. But there are other behind-the-scenes toilers who work on cars who are integral to the success of a race team—the chassis and the engine builders.

In the beginning all the engine parts came from the factory. Today only the head comes from the factory, and every other part has to be tooled and sanded and shined and rubbed, to the point that a camshaft alone costs $1,200, pistons cost $700 a set, the engine parts total around $30,000.

Once the parts are accumulated and laid out, it is then the job of the engine builder to make sure the parts are strong, to make sure the engine runs fast and without stopping for as many as six hundred miles at a time. It is a pressurized profession. During any given race, one or more engines will blow. There are dozens of reasons why. But each time it happens, there is an engine builder running to his medicine cabinet for the Goody's powder. To build engines over a long period of time in NASCAR competition, you better have a strong constitution.

Waddell Wilson, who has been building engines for twenty-nine years, sat in the offices of Hendrick Motorsports complaining about an ulcerated stomach. One of the most highly respected engine builders in the sport, Wilson, who began building engines with Holman-Moody, oversees the engine-building program for the entire Hendrick operation. If something should go wrong with the engine for either Ricky Rudd's Lumina (sponsored by Tide) or Kenny Schrader's Lumina (sponsored by Kodiak chewing tobacco), the buck stops at the door of Waddell Wilson.

In 1991 Rudd battled Dale Earnhardt down to the wire to finish second in the race for the driving championship. I went to see Waddell Wilson in late November 1991, only weeks after he and the Tide team suffered what to them was the disappointment of finishing second to Earnhardt. Wilson's constitution was suffering from what he described as the worst pressure he had ever felt in a career that began in 1963.

The hardest pill to swallow came during a road race at Sears Point in June of the 1991 season. Ricky Rudd trailed Davey Allison nose-to-tail as they battled on the final lap. There's a hairpin turn just before the start-finish line that requires a driver to brake hard. With Allison in the lead and Rudd right behind him, the two cars came up on veteran driver Dave Marcis. Marcis moved to the outside to let them pass.

Davey went into the turn, hard. Ricky Rudd came up behind Allison and barely tapped him. Davey spun out, and Ricky went into the lead.

Rudd crossed the finish line first, but as he passed the line, Rudd received not the checkered flag, but the black flag. After reviewing the films, NASCAR did something it had never done before in the history of the sport: It stripped the apparent victor of his spoils and handed the trophy to Allison.

Dave Marcis, who had the best seat in the house, testified that Davey Allison had gone into that final turn so hard he would have spun out even if Rudd hadn't hit him. Nevertheless, NASCAR ruled that Rudd had deliberately spun out Allison and gave Davey the race, prompting the Chevrolet fans to charge that NASCAR decided the way it did as a result of pressure from Ford, which had been threatening to pull out of racing.

Adding insult to injury, after the race Davey Allison charged Rudd with causing him to spin out.

"NASCAR did the right thing; they deserved to be disqualified," Davey Allison said.

Whiner, said race fans, who harkened back to the first 1991 Bristol race, when Davey ran into the rear of Darrell Waltrip's car so hard he lifted the back end off the ground. NASCAR black-flagged Davey in that one, made him sit in the pits for a lap for rough driving. During a rain delay shortly thereafter, Davey started yelling and screaming at Darrell, saying he had had every right to bang him because of an earlier incident during which Waltrip had tapped the back of his car.

Replied Waltrip later, "That little kid, just because he's an Allison he thinks he can do anything he wants. He can't get away with this stuff."

Darrell was right and Davey wrong, and race fans knew it, so when NASCAR set a precedent by placing Rudd second in the Sears Point race and giving the victory to Allison, *everyone* was upset, because it was a race Allison didn't deserve to win. Rudd was doubly hurt, because he was attempting to catch Dale Earnhardt for the driving championship, and he needed every point he could get.

Feelings ran raw between the Allison camp and the Rudd team as they prepared for the second-to-last race at Phoenix. All season long Rudd had either led or was second in the points standings for the driving championship, but at Phoenix, Ricky had a bad run and Allison won the race, thereby overtaking Rudd for second place in the standings.

In the final race at Atlanta, Allison's car died when the battery gave out, and he lost four laps in the pits while his crew changed the battery. Rudd finished on the lead lap, with Allison two laps back, earning Rudd some vindication and enabling him to wrest back second place from his Havoline tormenter.

After the season, at the NASCAR awards ceremony on national TV in December, Ricky Rudd, in a surprise, presented Davey Allison with what he called a "crying towel." It was an antagonistic gesture made with a smile. A quick thinker, the surprised and angered Allison took the handkerchief and wiped Rudd's face with it. People in the audience of the Waldorf-Astoria in New York and on national television watched with amusement and fascination. It was a page more from professional wrestling than from racing.

Despite this clever rejoinder, observers silently applauded the normally placid Rudd for expressing his true feelings. It became Ricky Rudd's symbolic revenge. In what appears to be the closest thing to a feud in the racing world, everyone wondered how the bad feelings between Davey Allison and Ricky Rudd would manifest themselves in 1992.

Waddell Wilson, who supervised the building of Rudd's engines, refused to criticize NASCAR for taking away Rudd's win at Sears Point, but the existence of his ulcer spoke louder than his words.

"We were still able to win a million dollars," said Wilson, "and we completed the most laps, but I felt we had an awfully good shot at winning the championship. But things had to go right to have done it. When we went to Sears Point in the final race and ended up being penalized—they took the race away from us—that was *so* detrimental to the team. It devastated Ricky, really took the wind out of his sails. This had never happened before in the history of the sport. It got us off the track, just hurt us the rest of the season."

Talking about it, he had a pained look. To Waddell Wilson, a perfectionist all his life, second place is never ever good enough.

*   *   *

WADDELL WILSON: "I grew up in the mountains of North Carolina, in a little town called Bakersville. Back when I was in high school, I loved fast cars. I loved listening to the races on the radio. I loved pulling for the drivers close around me, Banjo Matthews and Junior Johnson and Ned Jarrett, and of course I admired drivers like Fireball Roberts, because they were so colorful.

"After I graduated from Nashville Auto and Diesel College, I lived in Miami for a couple of years. I built a race car and drove it myself and won some with it and loved it. It was a '37 Ford, and this was halfway through the 1959 season in a big Sportsman race, there was a guy running behind me, and he turned me around and flipped me, and I ended up with the car on its side. I remember there was a fuel line running down the left side of my leg and gas running on me, and I was about half knocked out, and someone came up to me and said, 'I smell gas.' I was afraid someone smoking a cigarette was going to set me on fire.

"They got me out, took me in an ambulance, and when I came to enough to know what was going on, I got out of the ambulance, because I wanted to find the guy who wrecked me, but I didn't. But that ended my racing, because I couldn't afford to fix the car.

"At that point I figured I'd rather work on them. I left Miami and went back to North Carolina, got married, and then came to Charlotte and got a job with Holman-Moody in 1963.

"When I asked for a job, I was told they didn't have any openings. I started out the door, and John Holman was coming in and met me and asked me what I was doing, and when I said I was looking for a job, he said, 'Step into my office.' So I did, and I could see he wasn't real interested until I told him I had graduated from Nashville Auto and Diesel College, and then he asked me when I could start to work.

"I said, 'I can be here in the morning.'

"In Miami I had worked on my own car engines, and was working at Cummings Statesville building engines, and then when I went back to North Carolina I worked at a Ford dealership building engines, and also drag engines. The Highway Patrol was having me tune their cars up.

"I really loved engines, loved to make them go fast, and it was something I could do, so they put me in the engine room, and I stayed at Holman-Moody for ten years. When I arrived, Holman-Moody had thirty employees. When I left ten years later, over two hundred people were working in the shop at Charlotte. That was *the* place. That place trained more people: Jake Elder, Dan Ford, Robert Yates, Jimmy Tucker, Larry Wallace, a lot more.

"We built engines for a lot of vehicles other than NASCAR—engines for boats, USAC, sprint car engines. One time I worked on a car that ran moonshine, though I never did get into running moonshine myself.

"Three or four months after I got there, I was told to go up to another building and work on a race car that was going to Daytona. I was underneath the car getting a set of tailpipes built for it. Ralph Moody was there, and John Holman came in, and then I saw one set of legs running after the other set of legs and then one of them sailing out the door, and it was John Holman going after Ralph Moody. I thought, 'This is a heck of a deal.' They had a lot of respect for each other, but they didn't get along very well, not at all.

"After I started working there, they put me on Fireball Roberts's car. I enjoyed working with Fireball. He was a quiet individual. I didn't go out at night and socialize with him. His life-style was so different from mine. Fireball would come in the morning and sit on the workbench and really wouldn't say much to anyone. I considered him a loner. He didn't socialize during the day when I was around.

"Fireball had a lot of ability, and he was very smart about a race car. At Daytona we'd be setting out on the pit wall, and new drivers would come along and ask him about drafting, and at that time it was something new to the sport, and Fireball was one of the first ones who got the hang of being able to draft, he knew how to slingshot, he could take a slower race car and was able to win with it. And everyone recognized that.

"He was a heck of a driver. I remember at Daytona in July it was a race between Fireball and his Ford and Junior Johnson and his Chevrolet. The two of them almost lapped the field, and when Junior fell out, Fireball won.

"We had a good season, and then in '64 Fred Lorenzen and Herb Nab came to me and wanted me to work on their car and build their engines. Wayne Mills and Herb Nab worked on the car, and so I figured I would because there was more harmony on their team than there was on Fireball's team, and in 1964 we had a heck of a season. Of the sixteen races we entered, we won eight of them.

"Richard Petty and his Plymouth had his hemi engine that year, and it really had a lot of horsepower, but Ford really had a good race program.

"We won at Bristol, Atlanta, North Wilkesboro, Martinsville, and then at Darlington Fred beat Fireball, giving Holman-Moody a one-two finish. The next race we entered was the World 600 at Charlotte, and that's when Fireball had his fatal crash. The crash happened on the backstretch. I remember seeing horrible black smoke coming from there, but I didn't know Fireball got stuck in the race car for a period of time before Ned Jarrett was able to get him out of the car. Fireball hung on for more than a month before he died.

"We were leading that race until Fred had to make four pit stops within the space of about ten laps—we had paper in the carburetor, then a flat tire, and then someone misplaced the gas cap. It cost us the race, but we came back and won three more races.

"Fred gave everything he had to racing. He was very hyper, but smart. I ran around a lot with Freddy and had a lot of respect for him. He didn't chase women or booze it up. We'd go out and eat together at night and talk about that race car. We'd go to breakfast the next morning, and all he'd want to talk about was that race car. He had a one-track mind—that race car.

"He was one of those drivers, if I changed the wedge and put half a round of bite in the car, changing the pressure on the right front or left front, changing the handling of the car, he could feel it. A lot of drivers can't even feel a round, never mind a half round.

"And Freddy had such a great feel for his car, and he knew its limits. People don't realize it, but he not only could drive it, but he was a mechanic as well. When we'd get back from a race Monday morning, he would be there with his work clothes on, working with us on the car. He knew what needed to be worked on, was real smart about it.

"Through '64 and in '65 Freddy made a lot of money. I noticed in the morning he would pick up the paper—he had started playing the stock market, and he did well. And in '65 he made a lot of appearances that took him away from the race car, and so he didn't win that many races in '65. That was frustrating to me because when he was around, things seemed to go smoother. At the same time, everyone else changed on the car at the end of '64. I was the only one left.

"We did win the Daytona 500 in '65. That was a heck of a day. I remember building the engine for the car and having problems with it and having to work on it one night all night—we found out late it had a cam bearing problem, and we had to take the engine back apart, change the cam bearings, and put it back together and go directly to Daytona.

"Back in those days we were asking a lot of these engines, and we were finding a lot of weak points in them, and that was one of them. The bearings are really not designed for this. We had to take the old bearings out, put new ones in, and hope they made it. Same kind of bearings made of the same material. You just hoped and prayed you ended up with a good set of cam bearings.

"The race came down to us and Marvin Panch, who drove for the Wood Brothers. Marvin was leading, and there was a threat of rain, and when it started sprinkling the caution flag came out. In the race to the start-finish line Freddie was able to pass Marvin in three and four, and in doing so Freddie knocked the fender in on the right side of the car near the tire. Then the rain set in, so they stopped the race.

"We were setting on the start-finish line, in front with a flat tire and a fender in on the tire. We were in trouble.

"But they called the race, and in 1965 we won the Daytona 500.

"That year we won both Charlotte races, the World 600 and the National 500, but in July practicing for the Firecracker 400, Freddie wrecked, and it hurt him. It cut him up, and it put us out of the race because it tore the race car up.

"In '66, when Ford and Chrysler pulled out of racing, his goal was to achieve a win at all superspeedways. The only one he lacked was Rockingham. In the fall race, I worked and worked to try and help him win that race.

"At the time, with downsized engines, you could run a smaller engine with less weight in the car, so we went with a 396. We had a lot of oiling problems. I knew it was a ring problem, so what I would do was build the engine, go to the racetrack with the car, practice with the engine, and then I would go back to Charlotte with the engine, take it apart, rebuild it, put it back on the dyno, and the next morning I'd be back down to Rockingham.

"The Saturday before the race I finally got the problem worked out, and Sunday morning we had a decal on it, 'Perfect Circle,' a company that made rings. Before the race a representative from Perfect Circle asked me if there were Perfect Circle rings in the race car.

"I said, 'There are a combination of rings. One ring is yours, but there are others.' He went and took the decal off the car.

"We went ahead and ran the race, and I remember Richard Petty was running real strong that day, and the way the pit stops were going, we were a half lap ahead of him most of the time, but then he had engine failure, and we ended up winning the race by two laps over Don White in a Dodge. That made Freddie Lorenzen a winner on all the superspeedways.

"In 1967 Lorenzen decided to retire. He returned later, but that was the end of the Holman-Moody relationship, and in the latter part of 1967, David Pearson came to drive our race car. Again, the rest of the team changed, and I was the only one who remained. I stayed on and built engines just as I had been doing. And in 1968 the Ford Motor Company pointed to us to run for the championship.

"At that time you had to run fifty-odd races. Not many competitors wanted to do that. Not the Wood Brothers. They wanted to run super-speedways and nothing else because there wasn't much money, only a couple thousand dollars for winning, on the short tracks.

"Running for the championship was for prestige, and Ford footed the bill. And when David Pearson came to drive the race car, boy, he had a feel for a race car, and he was a super individual. He could get a little pouty at times when things didn't go right, but boy, if you kept him in a good mood, you couldn't find a better driver. He would travel with us to and from the races, a lot of times go with us in the tow truck, and he was one of the boys.

"In 1968 and '69, we ran fifty-two races each year. I had to build a new engine for every race plus supervise the testing for other cars. I was building engines for A. J. Foyt, who was running in USAC races, run them in Milwaukee and all the places in the Midwest they ran. And I enjoyed doing it, because AJ was one man I certainly admired and still do. He was one of the most versatile drivers I've ever seen.

"Anyway, those two years I averaged working seventy hours a week, but I enjoyed it. There was not a lot of pressure, though at that time it was really hard on my wife and kids because I would be gone so much and she wasn't able to go to the races. I really admire her. If it hadn't been for her being behind me, I never would have been able to be successful.

"We were doing well because we had a super driver and a super team, and Ford Motor Company was backing us. Everything went smoothly, and we won the championship both years. The car we had to beat was Richard Petty's, because he was right there every week. And he won a lot of races both years, just like we did. And that meant a lot to us, to be able to pull that off against a team like Richard's. Bobby Isaac with Harry Hyde was the other strong challenger in '68. There were other teams, but usually it came down to David Pearson and Richard Petty.

"Think about Richard Petty and what he did. To win two hundred races, you have to run a lot of races, and that's how he did it. David Pearson won a lot of races for the same reason, and that's why no one will *ever* break Richard's record, because we don't run that many races any-more, and racing is too competitive now. Back then, especially on the short tracks, you had two or three cars that could win. Today, any one of ten cars can win it.

"I remember one night in '68 we were at a short track and David Pearson was driving, and we were running second to Richard. John Holman got aggravated with David because it didn't look to him that he was trying to catch Richard. John had a topcoat on and a hat with a little tassel on top, and he went out on pit road and started waving that hat, trying to get David's attention to go faster. And I kept noticing David kept going faster and faster, and each lap I thought he was going to wreck because he'd slide from wall to wall. David caught Richard, passed him, and won the race, but David was so mad when he came in, he came sliding into the pits, jumped out of the race car, and we never did see him after that. He won the race, but he won it because he was so furious.

"We won the championship for a second time in a row in '69, but in '70 Ford pulled out of racing, so we backed up and didn't run all the races.

"It really hurt when Ford pulled out. It devastated Holman-Moody, because they were relying so much on factory support. They had to lay off workers. We went ahead and ran the car in '70, and in '71 David drove the car until Darlington, and then he quit. He and John Holman weren't seeing eye to eye, so David left. He went to drive for the Wood Brothers.

"Bobby Allison came to drive the race car. At that time we were running Mercurys on the superspeedways and Fords on the short tracks. Bobby had run his car at Darlington, blew up his engines, and he was broke, and he came and asked Ralph Moody for a job, and Ralph hired him. We went to Talladega in '71 and ran second. Bobby's brother Donnie won the race.

"The next race was the World 600 at Charlotte, and Bobby beat Donny to win the race, and from then on we had it going, won race after race that year, eleven in all on superspeedways. We won both Charlotte races, both Michigan races, we won Riverside, won Dover, won the Southern 500 at Darlington. We won a lot of races against the likes of Richard Petty, Charlie Glotzbach, in Junior Johnson's Chevrolet. We weren't factory-backed, but they weren't either. We just won race after race. Bobby made it look easy.

"When he won the race at Dover, he got out of the car and said, 'Man, I didn't have to run this thing wide open, and we still won by two laps.' We had a good team and a heck of a pit crew and a good chassis and good engines, and we had it all put together, and it was an unbeatable combination at the time, one of the best I've ever been involved with.

"Dan Ford, Bill Holman, and myself were the three who took care of the race car. We lived that thing. I built the engines, and Dan and Bill took care of the race car, and at the track we worked together. We really got along good, and everything just worked fine.

"Bobby Allison was one of those drivers who had a lot of determination, had a heck of a feel for a race car. He came up the hard way. He knew race cars like the back of his hand, and he knew the driving styles of the other drivers. He could get as much out of a race car as anyone I've ever seen, because he had that burning desire to win races.

"He was also a great motivator of people. He'd give the team credit and he was a team player. He was one guy who had a lot of pride, and if someone said, 'This won't work,' or 'That won't work,' he'd kill himself to prove it would work. He was spirited. When everything was going well, you couldn't have been with a better person. When things went bad, Bobby could get aggravated real easy.

"If he felt NASCAR didn't call a ball a ball, then he would get aggravated with them and tell them. A lot of times he would say things that were detrimental to him, that would hurt him, and it held him back some. But he was one of the great racers of all time. He and Richard Petty had a lot of battles, and it was something to see those guys go at each other. One was about as good as the other. There was a lot of good racing out there.

"I never said anything to Bobby about his outspoken ways. I felt that was out of my field, something I really didn't need to be involved in. I felt at times it hurt him, but Bobby was a big boy, and if he felt it was right, you gotta do what you think is right.

"And at the end of the '71 season John Holman and Ralph Moody had their big fallout. I remember one Saturday afternoon I was working in the shop, and John was up in his office. His office was high up in the new building overlooking the complex. He was on the telephone, and Ralph came in and wasn't aware John was on the phone, and he fired up the race car.

"John came out of his office, came down to the ground floor, and he had this big forklift, which we called Big John, and he got that forklift and ran it up under the race car, and he drove that race car outside.

"Then he came back in and started to get after Ralph, and they ran through the office, and one of them ran through the screen door, tore the door off the hinges, and that was the end of it. John fired Ralph.

"In '72 Leonard Wood asked me to build engines for the Wood Brothers. Ford built engines for the Wood Brothers. All the engines were furnished out of Holman-Moody. AJ drove the car at the beginning of the season. They won Ontario and the Daytona 500. At the same time I was hoping John Holman would reconsider and run a race car again, because I loved racing.

"The Wood Brothers ran just the superspeedways and won a bunch of races between their two drivers, David Pearson and A. J. Foyt; had a heck of a season. David drove the last half of the season. All I did was build engines for their cars.

"At the end of the year I decided I didn't want to stay there any longer. Ralph Moody was gone, and everything was going downhill, and there was no factory backing, so I decided to leave. Ralph Moody and I opened up an engine shop. We built engines for Bobby Allison and Benny Parsons, and then in '73 we furnished engines for Benny, and I helped him that year, and he won the championship."

Leonard Wood

Leonard Wood

Kings of the Superspeedways

Look on the road map, and Stuart, Virginia, doesn't seem all that far from Interstate 77, a highway cutting through the western part of North Carolina that runs from the northern border of the state all the way out the bottom. From the highway it appears to be a short hop through Toast, North Carolina, to Mount Airy, and then a longer leg into Stuart, across the Carolina border.

The map deceives. It's fourteen miles from the highway to Mount Airy, and the rest of the trip the route winds beautifully through farmlands and countryside on the two-lane Route 103, until finally you make the final ascent up the asphalt road into the bosom of rural Stuart, the home of the famed Wood Brothers.

Competitors together in NASCAR since 1953, Glen and Leonard Wood have won ninety-five Winston Cup races, forty-three by David Pearson. Their cars have won four Daytona 500s with four different drivers: Tiny Lund, Cale Yarborough, A. J. Foyt, and Pearson. The 1963 victory by Lund, who took over from Marvin Panch after he helped rescue Panch from a burning sports car, and Pearson's heart-stopping win over Richard Petty on the final lap after the two crashed were two of the most famous 500s ever run. Other legendary drivers to race their car 21 include Speedy Thompson, Curtis Turner, and Buddy Baker.

Statistics attest to the competitiveness of the Wood Brothers' Ford-backed dynasty. Over their illustrious career, they have finished in the top ten 394 times out of 724 entries.

Once in Stuart, a one-motel town in the green hills of southern Virginia, it still isn't easy to find their shop. Ask anyone, and they'll give you these directions:

"Go down the hill, turn right at a concrete bridge, pass an auto parts store, and keep going until you find it."

It seems simple, until you try to do it. Street names are elusive. Everyone you ask seems polite, but less than forthcoming, so you accept the sketchy route and keep searching.

The problem: The shop *is* hard to find. I rode aimlessly for fifteen minutes before walking into an auto parts store close by the shop and discovering it to be my key landmark. I was lucky the shop was open at 7:55 in the morning.

Leonard Wood, Glen's younger brother and the spokesman for the team, met me at eight. Leonard, sixty-seven, was getting ready for Daytona, and he had a full day of work ahead. It was another reminder of the long hours put in by *everyone* involved in racing.

LEONARD WOOD: "Glen is nine years older than I am. He began in racing in 1950 when he and a partner paid $50 for a car. Our first car was number 50 because he paid $50 for it. I was his chief mechanic, and I've been his chief mechanic ever since.

"I can remember the first time we raced the car. Glen drove it, and he was involved in a little accident. A guy spun out in front of him and hooked his rear-end housing. It bent it, so we towed the car home.

"On the way home, the housing being bent caused the axle to break, and in those days the axle held the wheel on, and when it broke, it ran the wheel off, and when the car dropped, the gas spout was on that side, and it jerked the gas spout out. Sparks created from dragging it on the pavement set it afire, and it burned up right there in the middle of the road.

"We rebuilt it, put it back together again. Then he put the number 16 in it, after Bill Snowden from Florida, who had a real fast number 16.

"Before we entered Grand National racing, we raced in the Sportsman class, which is the same thing as modifieds, only the engine only had one carburetor. We ran in that quite a few years, and Glen was the North Carolina state champion in 1954. He was really quite good, smooth on asphalt. You have to be smooth to keep from burning your tires. In fact, in all my years in racing, the most fun I had was when Glen was driving. After that it became a business, but back when we started, we were having fun.

"We ran a few Grand National convertible races in '56, and then in '56 we started running hardtops. Through the years we ran modifieds, and on our convertibles we had number 22, but when we started racing against Fireball Roberts he was 22, and the hardtops had preference over the convertibles, and so Glen decided to put number 21 on it, and that's what we've had ever since.

"I was in the service from March 1957 through March 1959. Our first big win was at Bowman-Gray Stadium in April 1960, when we beat Rex White.

"Racing was a hard struggle back then. You didn't have any sponsors. A sponsor would paint the car for free in exchange for putting their name on the side of it. You had to make your own specialty pieces for the car, because it was far cheaper than buying them. And back then, you had to come up with your own ideas to try to beat the other guys. All the mechanics came up with their own tricks and secrets. Back then it was a lot more secretive. You didn't tell anybody *anything*.

"When you came up with something that made the car run faster, you didn't tell; you kept it to yourself. Back then, if someone had a camshaft better than yours, you'd worry to death trying to figure out what the guy was running. Even if the man *told* you what he had, you wouldn't believe him. In fact, if he told you he *didn't* have a particular camshaft, you'd believe he had it.

"Nowadays, you can go to any team in the garage area and they'll tell you pretty close to what they're running.

"We didn't run in all the races because of the expense. We only ran a select few. After we started in the Winston Cup division, we mostly ran the superspeedways. You could make more money than running on the short tracks.

"I can remember Glen won three races in a row at Bowman-Gray Stadium in a '58 Ford. In one race the Pettys, Lee and Richard, had the two pole positions, and Glen was third, and during the race Lee let Richard, who was just a boy, get in front of him so Glen couldn't pass him on the inside. Glen was all over Lee, so Lee then wanted to get by Richard, so when he went by him, Glen got him also, and they got about halfway through the race, and Glen caught Lee in traffic and passed him and went on to win the race.

"Lee and Richard drove pretty hard against each other. I knew Lee. He's sort of hard to explain. He was a *very* competitive person. I'm sure you've heard the story about Richard winning his first race. Lee had him disqualified. There was a discrepancy in the number of laps they ran, and Lee protested and was given the win. Lee was a business-type guy, more business than Richard.

"Junior Johnson was another driver we ran against. Junior joked with us more than Lee did. I can remember Glen was on the pole at the

Charlotte Fairgrounds, and Junior wanted to drive the car. Glen decided to drive it himself.

"They had watered the track before the start of the race, and it was wet, a complete mess. Glen went into the first turn, and his car never did turn at all. It just slid over the bank and messed the car up a little bit. So Glen told Junior he could drive it. Junior said, 'No, you done made a mess of it.'

"I can remember one night at Bowman-Gray Stadium, Junior put an old wild, scroungy chicken in Glen's car.

"Another strong competitor was Smokey Yunick. He's a very intelligent, smart mechanic. Smokey was all business. I remember in 1960 he sat on the pole at Charlotte—he was sitting on the pole a lot then, and I remember wishing that it sure would be nice if we could do that. Ironically, in later years we came back and won thirteen poles in a row. It was a dream come true.

"Smokey is still very intelligent. He was a great racing engineer, and still is. Smokey still could be very competitive if he wanted to get back into it. But he's an independent-type guy, and he's had enough of racing.

"Ralph Moody was a good race car engineer, and a great driver as well. He really knew how to drive. He taught a lot of his drivers how to get around the track. I know Fred Lorenzen couldn't get around Charlotte until Ralph showed him how. Ralph would beat Lorenzen a second a lap, because he knew how to back off at the right place and get back on the right place to come off the turn and run faster down the straightaway.

"If you come off the turn five miles an hour faster, you're going to run all the way down the straightaway faster. Ralph knew how to do that.

"We got started with Ford in 1956. Curtis Turner and Joe Weatherly were a big part of our getting hooked up with Ford. Back in '54 and '55 at Bowman-Gray Stadium, Curtis and Glen ran against each other every week. Curtis had driven our Sportsman cars. He won a race for us at Flat Rock, Michigan. Curtis was a spectacular driver. I don't party, so I never partied with him, but you hear stories about Curtis that wouldn't sound like they were true, but they were.

"I can remember coming to the racetrack one morning and finding Curtis asleep in the race car. He was sleeping it off. He woke up, rubbed his eyes, and said, 'Morning, boss. You ready to race?' Then he went out and won the race.

"Joe Weatherly was a good friend of Curtis's, and he became a good friend of ours too. In fact, Joe drove for us at the Charlotte Fairgrounds in May 1961 and won.

"But it was Curtis and Joe who put in a good word for us with Ford.

"In 1960 three superspeedways opened—Charlotte, Atlanta, and there was another one in California. The superspeedways were a scary place to go. It was high-speed, and it got on your nerves a lot worse than running short tracks. Like at Daytona, you'd run 170 miles an hour, and that was unreal.

"The drivers never talked about it, but you knew a lot of them really didn't like going that fast, because they knew the danger of something happening.

"That year Speedy Thompson drove for us, and he won two races in a row in October, at Charlotte and then at Richmond. The victory at Charlotte was our first superspeedway win.

"Speedy was a great driver. A lot of drivers drive the car too hard and slow themselves down, but I remember Speedy would back off going into the corner at Charlotte—which we thought wasn't the right way to do it, but it made the car come off the corner a lot faster, so he won the race.

"I remember a race in '61 when Nelson Stacy relieved for Speedy. Nelson was driving much harder than Speedy had been, but Nelson slowed down three miles an hour less than Speedy had been running. So Speedy knew the correct way around. He was a great driver. He was a very determined driver when it came to battling.

"When Speedy got into our car, he was thinking about retirement. He was getting to the point where he wasn't as racy as he was in his early years.

"In 1962, Freddie Lorenzen began driving for Holman-Moody. Freddie was a very competitive driver, the type of guy who if his car wasn't handling right, instead of staying out there, he'd come in, make a pit stop, adjust the car, and go back out. At that time nobody did that, because you didn't want to get behind, but if Freddie's car was loose or was pushing, he'd make pit stops to correct it, and eventually it would pay off. It might help a tenth of a second a lap, and pretty soon he'd be back to pass you.

"Freddie was a nervous-type guy, fidgety, but he tried to the bitter end, didn't give up for nothing. He'd try everything he could do.

"In 1963 Fred won over $120,000. Joe Weatherly was the champion that year, and behind him was Richard Petty. We knew Richard was going to be a good one after the Daytona 500 of 1962. His car was probably ten miles an hour slower than Fireball Roberts's, but Richard held on to him all day long, drafting on him, finished second, and that's when we realized he was going to make a good driver.

"We won the Daytona 500 in '63, when Tiny Lund drove for us. That was one of the most memorable races in history.

"We went down there with Marvin Panch as the driver. Back then, we would stay at Daytona three weeks before the race. Marvin practiced, and about the second week he was to drive a Maserati in a sports car race, and it had little, narrow tires, and he backed off in the corner and it broke loose and went sideways and wrecked and got upside down and caught fire. Tiny Lund and one of the guys from Firestone and three others were coming through the tunnel just as this happened, and they ran out to the car and picked it up and dragged Marvin out.

"Marvin got burned bad, and we needed a driver, so Tiny Lund took the car. From his hospital bed Marvin had asked us to let Tiny drive.

"Tiny was the strongest, quickest big man you've ever seen. He was a determined driver too. I remember we had a caution flag at thirty-six laps. Our strategy was to stretch our gas mileage so we could finish the race making one less pit stop than Lorenzen or Ned Jarrett, so after we pitted on the caution, we ran forty-two laps before stopping, and then the next time forty-two laps, and then forty-two again, so the last time we only had thirty-eight laps to go, and they had forty-four to go on fuel. So even though we were running in third place, we knew it was the same as our leading the race, because it was only a matter of time before they came down pit road for gas.

"Well, pretty soon, here they came. It was a very emotional victory for everybody, especially after Tiny took over for Marvin. It was a Cinderella story.

"In August 1965, Bill France reinstated Curtis Turner after suspending him for four years for trying to start a drivers' union. Curtis had driven our cars years and years back, and like I said, he had put in a good word with Ford for us, so we were always good friends, and so when France said he could come back, he told us he wanted to drive, and we put him in a car.

"Curtis was one of the greatest race drivers as far as being able to control a car in a slide after it got out of shape. He was just *the* best at that.

"At Charlotte in October, we ran Curtis, A. J. Foyt, and Marvin Panch, and Curtis finished third behind Lorenzen and Dick Hutcherson, two Holman-Moody cars.

"During the race, because of the way the seat brace was made, Curtis broke a rib, so for the Rockingham race I made him a brace to come around the back. It rested on his shoulder rather than his side, and at Rockingham he beat Cale Yarborough to win the race. Curtis never lost his driving skills.

"It was a show just to watch Curtis race, the way he would work traffic. There was just something about him that was just a show to watch.

"Cale had been driving for one of the Ford teams, and Ford was looking at him and grooming him, and in 1966 Ford wanted us to put him in our car in Darlington, and we finished second.

"Some drivers are very competitive, and others are not. Cale was *very* competitive. He was the type of driver he drove so hard that if you gave him the 'go' signal, he would slow down. He was already driving the limit, so if you asked him to go faster, anything beyond his limit would slow him down. Sometimes I would give him the 'easy' signal, and he would run faster.

"At the Daytona 500 in 1968, Cale was running great for the first thirty laps, but then the engine began skipping. He came in, and I jumped into the car and put in a new ignition box. I remember while I was inside the car, Cale told me, 'Man, this thing will fly.'

"When I got out, he took off. He was a lap down to Lee Roy Yarbrough, and he made that lap up. He cut a tire, got another lap down to Lee Roy, and he made that up. Cale and Lee Roy then raced side by side, one taking the lead and then the other.

"With four laps to go, Cale caught him, and the two staged a dogfight, but at the end Cale was in front. It was a very exciting day.

"Cale has always said part of the reason we won was because of the pit crew, but one of the reasons we were better than the other teams is that for years we had a jack that could raise the car in just three strokes. Back then, some jacks took fourteen strokes. But that was one more thing you didn't tell anyone. Then a cameraman took pictures of it, so now you can buy jack that will raise the car in two strokes, even one. Now, everybody knows everything.

"Cale drove for us through 1969, but then in 1970 Ford pulled out of racing and stayed out until 1981. During that period, they didn't even give us a fuel pump. In 1970, A. J. Foyt was sponsored by Purolator, and we needed the sponsorship money, so we put AJ in the car. AJ was a very famous driver, and an extremely great driver. He would have won the Daytona 500 in 1971 except that we ran out of gas. But he won at Ontario, California, and then he won Atlanta.

"AJ had his Indy program going, and so he left us after Atlanta to go back and get ready for Indy. We needed to run all year long, so we signed

Donnie Allison to finish out the year, and he gave us a big victory at Talladega over his brother Bobby and Buddy Baker.

"In 1972, AJ again started the season for us, and this time he won the Daytona 500. That year the Petty car and Junior Johnson's car ran well, but then Richard had engine trouble and so did Bobby Isaac and Bobby Allison, and it wasn't even close. Once Richard went out, there was no one left to challenge us. Foyt then won Ontario, and David Pearson took over, and David won six more races that year for us, for a total of eight superspeedway wins.

"Everyone was saying David was washed up, but he came along at the right time for us. He did a good job, and we let him know it. David was the type of person, you needed to kid him a lot, pick on him. We had a good relationship. We picked on Cale too. All the drivers like you to compliment them, make them feel important. It makes a difference. You don't need to put your drivers down. You put your driver down, he's not going to do his job. And if he does a good job, let him know it, it makes him feel good—though it was not a problem to compliment David, because he was so great. He did such a great job.

"In 1973 David won eleven of the eighteen races he entered. In the next two years he was competitive in almost every race we entered. We should have won the Daytona 500 in 1975, but Pearson got spun out on the backstretch on the final lap, and Benny Parsons won it when he crossed the finish line right before David did.

"David won ten races in 1976, including perhaps the most famous Daytona 500 of them all.

"I can remember that after the qualifying heats, several of the faster cars were disqualified because they were caught with a nitrous oxide fuel line, and another car was disqualified because it had a trick grille closure. You weren't supposed to close off the grille, couldn't stop it up, but this car had a trick flap to close it, and was disqualified.

"The car David was driving was a notchback, which wasn't the best qualifying car, but it always ran good in the race.

"I can remember David was trailing Richard Petty with only a few laps to go. I called in, and he said, 'I'm doing all I can.' Then in the final lap David passed Richard going down the back straightaway.

"David was the type of guy who always told you he couldn't do it, and then he'd try to do it. Some drivers tell you they can, and they can't. But David never, ever told us he could do it. He'd always say he couldn't.

"As David passed Richard, the two cars collided, and while David was spinning around on the grass, he called in on his radio, and he said, 'He hit me.' He hadn't even stopped spinning, and he said, 'He hit me.' How did he have the presence of mind while he was spinning to tell you the guy hit him?

"At the same time David never did take his foot off the gas. He was concentrating on keeping the engine running while he was spinning around so it wouldn't die.

"From the pit area I saw the crowd roar, and I knew something had happened. The first thing I saw was Richard's smashed-up car coming back from the wall, sliding toward the finish line, and it looked like he was going to slide right on by it. I didn't see us. We were spinning around on the inside into the grass.

"Richard stopped a hundred yards shy of the line, and his engine died.

"And David, with his engine still running, chugged on up through the infield on the grass, got back onto the racetrack, and crossed the line. Right before he crossed, Benny Parsons passed us, and I thought, 'Oh, my goodness,' remembering what had happened the year before, but I immediately learned that Benny was a lap down, that we had won.

"I can remember after the race somebody asked David if he was mad. He said, 'No, but I was getting ready to be if I didn't win the race.'

"David had been with us seven years, and all through the '76 season he made a lot of statements he wanted to quit as a driver. We thought that was what he wanted, and we hired Neil Bonnett to drive for us in '79. Neil was a good driver, but it was a big mistake for us to have let David go. We wished many times afterward we hadn't split up.

"David was a great one. David never went out hunting for publicity. The guy *never* got out of his car and threw his helmet. He never got mad, whether he lost or what. When he got out, he was the same guy whether he won or lost, didn't make a big scene, didn't ever make a lot of racket, and nobody writes about a guy who doesn't make a racket. What I'm trying to say, David didn't hunt publicity, didn't go out of his way to get it.

"Neil was only with us a little while, and then we hired Buddy Baker, who won the Firecracker 400 for us in '83. Baker was as good as anyone I've ever seen at Daytona and Talladega, but we didn't feel it was working out real good, and we decided we wanted a younger driver. This was when we started running all the races. We decided the point fund for teams that ran all the races had grown too much not to run them all, and so we hired Kyle Petty.

"We had been watching Kyle. He had run some good races at Dover, Pocono, and other tracks, and from the beginning he did a really good job for us. He would have won several races had he not had a cut tire or some other problem we had. He was the type of driver to save his car, to wait until the end.

"Kyle went to drive for SABCO, and we got Neil Bonnett back, and then of course in April of 1990 Neil got hurt at Darlington. He didn't have anywhere to go, and the crash was a bad one, and I can remember we took him to the field hospital, and he didn't know anybody. It was a bad experience.

"Dale Jarrett took over for Neil, and then Dale this year went to the new Joe Gibbs team to join his brother-in-law, Jimmy Makar, and we hired Morgan Shepherd.

"We'd been watching Morgan for years. More than any other race driver, I've seen him get in more cars he had no business running up front in and doing well. I know one time Cecil Gordon had a car at Bristol, and everyone was sure Morgan was a lap down, but they checked, and he wasn't a lap down, he was right up there with the leaders. At that time Cecil's car had not run that great, but Morgan took that car and ran good with it. There were times he relieved drivers and put the car on the pole. Morgan is a great competitor, and we are looking forward to some great runs with Morgan in '92.''

LAP 12

Bud Moore

The Old Guard

Travel south from Charlotte down Route 85 about an hour, cross the North Carolina border into Spartanburg, and get on Highway 585 going into town. At the third set of lights, make a left, and you'll see Beaumont Mills, a stark, imposing textile factory that looks like a penitentiary, with tall white turrets and a fence topped with barbed wire around the entire complex. Cross the railroad tracks, and on the right-hand side of the street is a low red-brick building with simple white lettering that reads "Bud Moore Engineering."

Unlike the trendy race shops built by some of the newcomers to the sport, such as Chuck Rider, Felix Sabates, or Joe Gibbs, Bud Moore's shop is a throwback to the olden days. There is no souvenir stand. No grand tours are offered. There are no frills, like a visitor waiting room, or a glass partition to keep the noise and the odor of gasoline from visitors. Unlike the new shops, which display the bright neatness of an operating room, this shop is dark and somber, and there are even a few tools lying on the floor by the cars. At Bud Moore's there is but one activity—men in smudged work clothes working on the red and white Motorcraft race cars.

Tall and imposing, Bud Moore, sixty-six, is quiet, usually serious, and very intense. He is a man to be reckoned with. While still a teenager fighting the Germans in World War II, Moore safely landed on Utah Beach during D day. Later he and his jeep driver captured a German headquarters by themselves. In subsequent battles, Moore was hit by machine gun fire and by a mortar shell. Before the end of the war, he had earned five Purple Hearts and two Bronze Stars. Though he survived, you can tell that he has not forgotten those he left behind.

On the track, too, Moore, like so many racing veterans, has experi-

Bud Moore

enced death. Two of his drivers were killed on the track, first Joe Weatherly in early '64 and then Weatherly's replacement, Billy Wade, just one year later. As with his Army experiences, Moore can talk about it with controlled emotions, but you can see he still feels the pain.

Standing beside one in the fleet of the bright red Motorcraft Fords waiting to be worked on, wearing a dark work shirt and jeans, Bud Moore seems as immutable as one of the figures on Mount Rushmore. It is as though he has always been there and always will be. He has been building engines and cars since 1946, founding his race team in 1961 and winning Winston Cup titles in 1962 and 1963 with the legendary Weatherly at the wheel. He was the first owner to put a two-way radio in a car. A traditionalist, he has refused to allow his drivers to wear a cool suit, the space-age clothing that pulls cool air into the racing helmet and lowers the body temperature of a driver while he's out on the track. Though temperatures reach 140 degrees inside that car, Moore insists his drivers endure the heat.

"I don't like the additional weight," has been his official excuse. But in private he will say, "Cool suits are for pansy asses."

Some competitors quietly whisper that Bud Moore's unwillingness to change with the times may be one reason he hasn't been as successful as he once was, but most say that's just wishful thinking, that on any given day Moore's car can win a race.

His supporters say Moore's fifty-nine victories and forty-one poles are testament to his success, especially given the fact that through the years Ford has been far more supportive of other factory-sponsored teams, first Holman-Moody and more recently the teams of Junior Johnson and Robert Yates. As a result, they say, in recent years Moore has lost some great driving talent—such as Dale Earnhardt, Ricky Rudd, and Kenny Schrader—to richer race teams. But through it all, Bud Moore continues to be competitive year after year. In 1990, Morgan Shepherd was sixth in the point standings, and he was twelfth in 1991.

As Bud Moore prepares for the 1992 season, Geoff Bodine, the Yankee from Chemung, New York, will be behind the wheel. Bodine, a well-spoken, hard-driving racer, made the PR mistake early in his career of feuding with Dale Earnhardt, and so has been far less popular than some of the Southern glamour boys, but none of that matters to Bud Moore. The high-strung Bodine can drive, and he is capable of winning races, and for Bud Moore, the rest is irrelevant.

BUD MOORE: "I grew up in Spartanburg on a farm. When I was a boy I learned the workings of farm machinery and worked on my dad's tractors and his Model T.

"When I was eighteen years old, I was drafted into the Army. After basic training at Camp Van Doren in Mississippi, I reported to Fort Dix, New Jersey, where I joined the 90th Infantry Division. When they sent the 90th overseas, we got on the *Capetown,* a British ship. There were seven thousand of us on that ship. It took fourteen days to go to Liverpool, because of the zigzag course, on account of the German submarines. I was in one compartment with three hundred other guys sleeping on hammocks and cots.

"We landed in Liverpool, and they sent us to another town called Knighton, in Wales. We were impounded there, couldn't go out on the town or anything. We didn't know what was going on until the end of April, when they told us we were going to have some maneuvers, that we were going down to have a dry run at an amphibious landing on the English coast.

"About the 1st of June they took us down, and we got on LCI-149, a landing craft. We got loaded at the dock and pulled out and went a little ways. The next morning we moved out a little further and finally got out into the English Channel. That's when I saw all the ships out there. It was the largest collection of ships imaginable.

"I told all my boys, 'This ain't no damn dry run, I can tell you this right now.'

"D day was supposed to be June 4, but the weather was bad and we sat anchored in the harbor a couple days. The night of June 4 we had a PT boat pull up beside the ship, and some officers got off, and they came on board and got everyone topside. They pulled down a great, big map, and they started explaining some of the stuff on it. They said we're going to land here, and there, and there. I said, 'Boys, I'm telling you right now, that's France. That's not England.'

"Our regiment had been selected to make the landing, and at five in the morning on June 6, we hit the beach.

"I was lucky, fortunate we didn't go to Omaha Beach. Omaha was the one that got the daylights kicked out of it. I was told later we lost ten thousand men at Omaha.

"We landed on Utah, which was right next to Omaha. I got off that beach just as fast as I could. Machine gun fire was everywhere, and we lost quite a few people, but nothing near like the deal at Omaha. Most of our platoon made it through. We had casualties, but they weren't severe. The first day we got in, got off the beach, and moved in maybe a half mile.

"It didn't get dark that night until eleven o'clock, and I can remember we were dug in. The shelling had stopped, and things had quieted down, and about one in the morning I started hearing rumblings. The moon was shining real bright, and all of a sudden we could see aircraft coming over. ''I thought, 'What in the world is this now?' It was the 101st and the 82nd Airborne dropping behind the lines.

''We pushed inward. We ran across where a lot of the glider pilots had crashed. The Germans had camouflaged trees so the pilots would think they were landing in empty fields, and the trees killed a lot of them, and some of them were hanging up in the trees. It was a heck of a sight to see.

''All in all, I had some kind of experience. It was something else to be in it, though I sure wouldn't want to go through it again.

''Before I really got hurt bad, I was on the front lines for eleven months and fourteen days. We fought all the way across France. I can remember sitting by a little window of a hotel on a street corner in Pierre when we bombed a ten-mile strip from St. Lo to Pierre to let General Patton's army go through. I watched all those planes come through and all those bombs falling. It was unbelievable.

''We cut the Cherbourg Peninsula off, and as Patton went through on his way to Paris, we made a swing and turned back, went below Paris, and headed toward Germany, and by the time we got stopped, we had already crossed the Siegfried Line and the Rhine River.

''Our reconnaissance caught a railroad trestle and bridge intact, and we had actually crossed into Germany when General Eisenhower pulled us back. I didn't know why, but we were out of fuel. We had outrun our supplies, and so they pulled us all the way back to Le Mans, France. Patton was right in one thing: If the supplies had kept up, the war would have been over quite a bit sooner and they'd have saved a lot more lives.

''Later on we made the Moselle River crossing. That's when all hell broke loose in Bastogne. The 101st and 82nd Airborne units were trapped up there, so we went to Bastogne.

''I never will forget the first time I saw General Patton. Late one evening he was standing on the courtyard steps, and he was holding a briefing. He said, 'We're in deep trouble in Bastogne. We're about ninety miles away. The weather is bad. They are kicking the hell out of the 101st and 82nd, got them surrounded, and they're killing them as fast as they can.'

''He said, 'We're going to leave here, and we're going up there and get them boys out and kill every son of a bitch we run into as we go.'

''And we did. We went to Bastogne, and I saw that man standing on the side of the road directing tank traffic, and he rode a tank with us to Bastogne. That's why everyone called him 'Blood and Guts.' I don't think there was a soldier under his command who wouldn't have gone to hell and back with him, because he didn't sit back ten miles away and tell everyone what they better be doing. He came up to see what the problem was, and you can admire a general with his capacity of leading people. He was a hell of a general is all I can say. He got me back home.

"On February 22, 1945, I got eat up by a machine gun. Then I was out about six weeks. Then in May, during a fight, I was hit by shrapnel.

"When I returned home after the war, my friend Joe Eubanks and I began in the used car business. Joe and I had gone to high school together, and he went in the Navy, and I went in the Army. We were real good friends, and when we were discharged in 1946, we began buying and selling used cars. We'd go up to Philadelphia and around Norfolk and up in that part of the country buying cars, and bring them back to Spartanburg to sell.

"And then we acquired a modified stock car, a '39 Ford, which we took in a trade on another car, and that's how I got started in racing.

"I said to Joe, 'Let's go to the track Saturday and race it.' Initially, I was going to drive it and Joe was to be the crew chief. We took it to the Ralston County Fairgrounds to try it out. I ran it a few laps around the racetrack, and I spun out and went through the fence. I was going into the corners too hard. I decided right then that driving wasn't for me. That's why I got into being a mechanic.

In the fall of '47, beside having some dealings in the used car business, I opened a garage for myself on the other side of town on York Street doing outside work and working on that race car.

"You didn't make much money back then. Purses went as high as $300 for a victory. I remember that Bill France used to pay me $50 appearance money. We entered as many as sixty races a year. We'd run Thursday night, Friday, Saturday, and Sunday.

"In 1949, running modifieds, Eddie Samples out of Atlanta had the most points, and he won a new 1949 Oldsmobile for being the champion, and we were second to him by only a few points.

"We ran Columbia, South Carolina, on Thursday night, we ran Charlotte on Friday night, and on Sunday we ran at Asheville, Atlanta, or Macon. I remember we won thirteen races in a row on Thursday night at Columbia, and Buddy Davenport, the promoter at Columbia, paid a bonus to anyone who could come down and outrun us.

"It was a hard life, doing all the traveling we did—or rather, thought we were doing, which was very little compared to now.

"Joe and I ran all the way through 1955, running modifieds. We ran for Joe Littlejohn, who had the South Carolina racing circuit, and when

Littlejohn didn't have a race on Sunday, we ran for Bill France for NASCAR.

"In '55 I ran some Fords with Eubanks in Grand National racing, but when the factories pulled out in the first part of '57, I went to work for Buck Baker and then Speedy Thompson, handling their cars. Speedy Thompson won at Darlington in '57, and Buck Baker won the driving championship in '57.

"In '58 I built a Chevrolet for Baker, and in '59 I built one for Jack Smith, and Smith won four races, and in 1960 he won the July race at Daytona, setting a world record of 146.842 miles an hour for 250 miles. That was one of the first races in which a driver and crew chief talked to each other on a two-way radio.

"Toward the end of 1960, I got a deal with Pontiac to run my own team. That's when I hired Joe Weatherly to drive for me in '61. Joe was available because Holman-Moody was changing things around. I talked to Weatherly, and the Pontiac people talked to him too, and in 1961 we won a lot of races, and in '62 we won the championship, and in '63 we again won the championship.

"Weatherly was in his prime then. Fireball Roberts was one of the best drivers back then, but Weatherly stood right along with him in that category.

"When it came time to crawl into that race car and go racing, Joe was all racing. But out of the car, Joe was sort of a clown. He loved to pull jokes on everybody. You'd be surprised at some of the stuff he pulled to have a big laugh. There was never a dull moment when Weatherly was around. He'd do anything.

"I never will forget, he used to have a little ol' box he called a mongoose. He'd say this mongoose was from China. It was in a box with screen wire over it. All it was was a foxtail. But Joe would get telling people how fast that thing was and how dangerous it was, and people would get down and look at him and get to poking around the box, get right over it, and just as they got to looking, Joe would push a button, and that damn foxtail would spring right into their chest, and damn, it was something.

"I can remember we were at Darlington for the Southern 500, and Lomis Colvin, the wife of the owner of the racetrack, was there with the wives of all the big Ford brass. There were five of them.

"And Joe saw them coming. He grabbed this little mongoose box, and he interrupted them, and he said, 'You have to see this.' And he set it on the ground.

"Joe gathered all the women around the box. They were all dressed in their nicest dresses. He began talking up something real good, poking the mongoose with a stick, telling them how dangerous it was. They were all bent over the box, looking at it, and just about the time he got them just right, he flipped that button, and that thing flew out, and there were five women scared to death. There were five wet spots on the pavement!

"This was less than an hour before the race, and Joe was laughing so hard, he was laying down on the ground.

"Those ladies were so embarrassed, I'm telling you. And about thirty minutes later Bob Colvin, the owner of the track, came down through the garage area, and he said, 'Where is that kinky-headed son of a bitch?' I said, 'Who are you talking about?' He said, 'You know who I'm talking about.' And I started laughing. He said, 'I'm going to kill that little son of a bitch.' Aw, that was the damnedest thing you have ever seen.

"In 1963 we won the championship, despite the challenge from Freddie Lorenzen. Freddie came from USAC, ran up North. He was a Yankee coming down South. Freddie was driving for Holman-Moody. Ralph Moody really liked Freddie. Freddie had good equipment, good cars, and a good crew behind him. And Freddie *was* a good race driver, and he did challenge us for the race championship that year. We won our share, and we wound up champion for the second year in a row.

"But then early the next season at Riverside, in the first major race of the season, Joe was killed.

"We had only run two or three laps of the race, and Joe had lost second gear in the transmission. There had been a big crash about lap 15, and the red flag came out. Back then, you could work on the car under the red flag; now if it comes out, you can't.

"I was just going to park the car, but Joe came in and said, 'Let's change the transmission.' I said, 'Joe, you're going to . . .' He said, 'Put a transmission in it.'

"We jacked it up, pulled the transmission out of the car, and put a new one in. After about fifteen or twenty minutes, we got him back out, and when the race resumed, we were only two laps down.

"Joe was really running the car hard, trying to make up the time we had lost, and he was running awfully good. But on lap 86, we lost a right front wheel cylinder going into turn five, and just as Joe made the left turn into turn six, a dangerous hairpin curve, he was going too fast, and the car got airborne going into six, and he hit the wall on the driver's side, hit his head against the wall, and was killed.

"Later on, we found out what happened. Back then we had drum brakes, and brake adjusters that automatically adjusted the brakes. Because Joe ran the car as hard as he did, it wore the brake pad down, and the adjuster adjusted itself so far out, it fell out, and that's why the cylinder failed.

"The driver who took Joe's ride was Billy Wade. He was driving a little bit for Cotton Owens, and he wanted to drive for us, so we hired him. Billy came from Texas. He was an awfully good driver. In '65 we also had Darel Dieringer. That year we went on the Northern Tour, and Billy won four races in a row, at Old Bridge, New Jersey; Bridgehampton, New York; Islip, New York; and Watkins Glen. He was the first driver in NASCAR history to win four races in a row. But in January 1965 Billy was in our car testing Daytona 500 tires for Goodyear when he was killed.

"Originally, Darel Dieringer was doing the tests to check the effectiveness of the tire shields, the tire within a tire we have now. The idea is that if the outer tire blows, you still have an inner tire to keep you on the track.

"Darel tested the tires by running over spikes at 100 miles an hour and 125. At high speeds he ran over that spike a couple times, and the tire didn't blow. He then went to 150 miles an hour, and when he hit that spike, the tire, which had been bruised, exploded. It blew off the wheel, and Darel crashed, hit the wall, tore the car up, and cracked some ribs.

"This was about the middle of the week. I was in my office in Spartanburg when I got a call from Florida. The car was wrecked, and Darel broke some ribs, but Goodyear still needed to finish the tests. The only thing we could do was get Wade's car ready and send it down.

"We were running ten-lap runs. We'd run all morning and gotten through eating lunch, and Billy went out again. He came around the ninth lap, going into the tenth and final lap, when going into turn one he blew a right front tire, the wall hit him, and we lost him.

"Darel's ribs got better in time for the Daytona 500, and in '65 he sat on the pole with a Mercury. Sure did. We ran the Mercurys the rest of the year, and we ran pretty good, won some races and then in '66 Darel won the Southern 500 at Darlington.

"In the late sixties I was running a limited schedule in NASCAR, because Ford wanted me to run the Mercury Cougars on the Trans Am circuit. I had Parnelli Jones, Ed Leslie, Peter Revson, and a bunch of others running for us. Ford wouldn't let me run NASCAR in '68. We missed the Trans Am championship by two points because of a dead battery in '67, and in '68 we won the Grand American series with Tiny Lund. Jacques Passino of Ford then asked me to take over the Mustang program for SSCA in '69, and that year we almost won the championship, and then in '70 we whooped the Camaros real good, won the championship.

"Then in '71 we started the season with the Mustangs again. I was even doing some drag engine work for Ford. Another thing I was doing was helping Ford work on the restrictor plate engines. NASCAR put the restrictor plate on the big 429s and the 426 hemis, and Ford called and wanted me to come down and use their dynometer facilities. They wanted to run a 429 on the dyno and see if I couldn't help them work out the problem with the restrictor plate.

"Ford brought one of Junior Johnson's engines. Junior, Banjo Matthews, Bradley Dennis, and four or five other engineers came in, and we put the thing on the dyno.

"When they put the restrictor plate on it, it was down to 465 horsepower. They said, 'This is where the problem is.' I said, 'Yeah, you got a problem.'

"We worked here in my shop eighteen hours a day for two weeks. They tried all kinds of cylinder heads, camshafts—you never saw anything like it. We worked and worked and worked, and we did everything we knew how. We had two machinists working day and night making pieces, doing this work, and after we got done we put it back on the dyno, and it was 465 when we started and 468 when we got done.

"One of the engineers said, 'NASCAR got us by the ass now.' I said, 'Well you are right.'

"In the meantime I said, 'Why don't you do one thing? I have a little 351 Cleveland engine sitting here that will pull 530 horsepower.' I had been working on it, a small-block engine. They said, 'There ain't no way.' I said, 'Get that big hog off o' there, and we'll lay it on there and see.'

"They took it off, and we grabbed the little 351 and stuck it on the dyno. They warmed it up. I said, 'Run it, Brad.' And it pulled 533 horsepower! They couldn't believe it. I said, 'Why do you want to fool with the big one when you can get rid of all that weight on the front wheels?'

"The problem, though, was parts and pieces. Ford would have had to make crankshafts and rods and other parts, and they couldn't do it in time for Daytona, so they stuck with the restrictor plate engine. Then at the end of '71 Ford pulled out all the support. They jerked the rug out from under everybody.

"In 1972 I returned to Winston Cup racing, and the next year we built a '72 Ford and we put a 351 Cleveland engine in it. We took it to Atlanta with David Pearson driving, and we qualified fifth, and we ran fourth, which showed that the little engine had a lot of possibilities. In February 1973 Bobby Isaac finished second in the Daytona 500 with the Cleveland. "Then all of a sudden we were getting outrun something fierce. I couldn't figure out why. But in October 1973 when we got to Charlotte, Bobby Allison protested the engines of Cale Yarborough and Richard Petty, and the tech inspectors found them with 484s and 494s, and I said, 'It was no wonder we were getting our ass outrun.'

"After then, that's when our small-block engine came to life. Junior Johnson had started work on a small-block Chevy engine, and Ford and Chevy have been running the small engine ever since.

"I hired Buddy Baker to drive for us in '74. When it comes to the major speedways like Daytona or Talladega, nobody outdrives Buddy Baker if he has a car under him.

"We won Talladega three times with Baker and finished second a couple times in the years he drove for me. I have a plaque where on May 7, 1976, we set a world record, 169.887. The driver was Buddy Baker.

"Then in 1978 Harry Ranier, the first big-wheel millionaire to come into NASCAR, got Waddell Wilson and a couple others to work for him and hired Buddy Baker away from me.

"In the meantime, Bobby Allison was loose. Bobby had just got hurt in a modified race up in Minnesota somewhere, and he was recuperating and didn't have a ride, so I hired him, and we went on to Daytona and won the '78 Daytona 500 over Cale Yarborough.

"Our car performed exceptionally well all day. We had good pit stops, and Bobby drove as good a race as he'd ever driven. It was just our day, and when it's your day and everything falls and clicks, you're bound to win.

"The next year in '79, Bobby drove for us in one of the most famous Daytona 500s. That was the race where Cale Yarborough and Donnie Allison crashed on the backstretch of the final lap, and then Bobby got out of his car, and the three started fighting on national television.

"I could see it coming. I was watching Cale and Donnie, and I was saying to myself, 'Somebody is *not* going to make it back.' Back then, you did whatever it was you had to do to win, and it just so happened that Cale and Donnie got to tangling one another, and neither one of them won it. Richard Petty snuck in and got it.

"And then Bobby drove over to where Cale and Donnie were fighting, and he stopped, crawled out of the car, and got in the fight with them. That was a brother-brother deal. It was really all uncalled for, but it happened that way, and I'll say this: That race was on national television all over the United States, and there were 20 to 30 million people watching that race—might have been 50 million—and here are the drivers getting out and slugging one another, and if you want to know the truth, that is one thing that brought racing to where it is now. It was the first live flag-to-flag Daytona 500 we had, and here were the two top contenders out fighting over it.

"I could just see all those people in their living rooms, saying, 'Boy, that's something,' and saying to themselves, 'We have got to see the next race to see what's going to happen.'

"Bobby drove for me through 1980, and at the end of the year he left to go drive for Harry Ranier. I would say Harry was offering him quite a bit, and number two, Bobby wanted to run a little better on the short tracks than the Ford ran. We were having a lot of problems with the Ford engines on the short tracks, and I think Bobby felt by running Chevrolet or Pontiac, he'd be better off, 'cause Bobby really loved the short track racing. That was one strike against us.

"Anyway, he left us, and then we hired Benny Parsons, and we won some races with Benny. We won the last NASCAR race at the Texas Speedway down in College Station. We had some awfully good runs with Benny Parsons, but going into 1982 Dale Earnhardt was coming up, and he was a hell of a driver, and I hired Dale. I felt he was one of the most upcoming drivers ever to come along. And I'd say if we had the knowledge we have right today, knowing about valve springs the way we know now, we'd have won ten or twelve races each year Dale Earnhardt drove for us. I know there never was a race we went to we didn't lead or were in position to win, but we had engine problems. Out of thirteen races in '82, we lost valve springs in eleven of them.

"Dale Earnhardt was one of the most determined young drivers I have ever encountered. He had the desire, the will, and the go-get-it about him to get it done. When he sat down behind that wheel, he had the talent and the driving ability to get that car around that racetrack. If the car didn't work, he would find one way or another to get that car around the racetrack. That's why he's been Winston Cup champion five times now.

"I think Dale would tell you I taught him a lot of things. After a race, we always discussed racing. He always wanted to be at the front. The biggest problem I had with Dale was trying to hold him back. Let me put it this way: Back then, we had a 300-mile engine because of the weak valve springs. I'd tell Dale, 'We have 500 miles to run. You have to take it easy, sit there, ride a little while, or we're not going to make it.' I'd keep calling him down all the time.

"I remember one time at Darlington we were leading the race. I told him, 'All right, Dale, you have to take it easy now. Slow her down a little bit.' And when he did, he started running three- or four-tenths a lap faster! I told him, 'That's telling you one thing: You're driving too hard.' And we won the race. Sure did. Like I said, if we had the knowledge then of how to maintain the valve springs, there isn't any doubt in my mind we would have won ten races a year with Dale Earnhardt in 1982 and '83.

"I'd say in my career since 1960, I changed valve springs on our race engine every Sunday morning. I'd say me and Leonard Wood changed more valve springs than anybody in the whole circuit, and it's all because of one little problem, the solution to which we stumbled on three years ago. All it was lacking was oil. But back in '83 the valve springs were a serious problem for us, and at the end of the year Dale went back to Richard Childress. Dale was learning. I hated to lose him.

"I tried to talk him out of it, but Richard Childress had a little bit more to offer than we did. GM was pushing it, and they offered him a lot. I talked to the Ford people and told them what GM was offering, but Ford wasn't quite in the deal enough to make a different deal, so we lost him. And we hired Ricky Rudd, who had been with Childress.

"I enjoyed working with Rudd. He was a real nice up-and-coming driver, and we had a lot of good years together. Ricky was the most pleasant boy we ever worked with. He did us a real good job. We won some good races, and he went off to Rick Hendrick. Hendrick needed a driver, and he offered a big deal to Rudd, first one thing and then another. When Rudd said something about going to drive for Hendrick, we had a deal we thought was going our way with Ken Schrader. Schrader came down to Spartanburg and we came to terms on everything, we shook hands on the deal, and I told Lee Morse at Ford that we better get a letter of intent and get everything on paper, and he said, 'Don't worry about it. Kenny Schrader drove for Ford, and we brought him over here.' He said, 'We'll get the contracts ready and get it done by the time we get over to Darlington next week.'

"So when the Thursday before the race Kenny told me he was going to drive for Hendrick, I was really stunned. Hendrick offered him the moon, I guess, so he hired him away from us, and we went with Brett Bodine. Now when I talk contract, I make sure it's signed before he leaves the room.

"Brett Bodine had just started in the Busch Grand National series. He only drove a couple relief races for Junior Johnson when one of his drivers got hurt. Right at that point we didn't have any alternative but to hire a young driver. We chose Brett because of all the other drivers we went over and looked at, we thought he was the best, and today I still think he was the best choice.

"I liked Brett, but I had to let him go at the end of the year because my sponsor wanted a driver with more visibility. Today a sponsor wants a name driver who runs at the front.

"We hired Morgan Shepherd. He was with us in '90 and '91, but that didn't work out. Morgan had run his own team in the past, and he wanted to make all the decisions, and there was discord. He left us and went to the Wood Brothers, so we hired Geoff Bodine after he left Junior Johnson.

"Geoff Bodine was the first Yankee to challenge in the South. When he and Earnhardt tangled, the fans didn't like that. But he has become more and more popular. He has his fans.

"Geoff is a real likable person, real high-strung. He likes to win races. We're looking forward to some good runs out of Geoff this year.

"We'll be competitive. We'll be there. They are going to hear from us."

LAP 13

Bob Tomlinson
He's Seen It All

When Bob Tomlinson was growing up in Kannapolis, North Carolina, his house was a short walk through the woods from that of racer Dale Earnhardt. Tomlinson, who in 1991 was hired by owner Bob Whitcomb to run Derrike Cope's sputtering race team, was part of a trio of kids who gave the five-time Winston Cup champion his first ride.

Tomlinson played football at the University of North Carolina and then briefly with the NFL's Washington Redskins. He was a vice president of Cannon Mills in Kannapolis, worked in public relations with CBS Sports and at the Charlotte Motor Speedway, and has managed race teams for such car owners as Cale Yarborough and Darrell Waltrip.

Tomlinson is serious about life and his job, but he is a man who sees the irony and humor too. When Tomlinson was hired to be general manager of the Whitcomb team, it was in disarray. Cope had won the Daytona 500 in 1990 and a second race, but in '91 his car wasn't competitive. As he strives to make the team competitive in '92, Tomlinson will have to summon as much of that sense of humor as he will be able to muster.

BOB TOMLINSON: "I knew Fireball Roberts, Curtis Turner, Joe Weatherly. At that time we called them characters. *Every* driver was a character. We had drivers who, on Sunday morning, we had to pick them up and set them in the race car because they still were sobering up, and they'd win races. It was the old breed, hard like a lumberjack, like Buck Baker. Buck on too many occasions hadn't sobered up race morning. They helped him in the car and sat him in the car, and he sobered up sweating it out when the race was going on.

"Or I can remember when Herb Thomas won the Southern 500, drove

Bob Tomlinson

the car into the garage, put the headlights on, and drove it back to Bethel.

"Bobby Isaac was a down-home country boy with no education. He couldn't read or write. In fact, one of his wives was a schoolteacher who tried her best to teach him how to read and write. Isaac was in his own world when he was in a race car. Nobody could tell him what to do. In that race car, he had total control, but once he stepped out of that car and had to deal with the public, he felt like he was a second-class citizen. You had a lot of superstars back in the fifties and sixties who could not have cut it nowadays because of the necessity of PR and dealing with the public.

"Joe Weatherly had a big scar that ran down his face. When he was a kid he got cut up. Someone said he got hit with a hoe. I mean, talk about rough. Joe was a happy-go-lucky guy, and he'd go out Friday night and party and go fishing on Saturday, and drive Sundays. Joe Weatherly was a smart individual, but he stayed with his kind. He wouldn't mix with someone in the executive lounge. He would hang around the group that would throw bottles, like Curtis Turner. Curtis was a pioneer who was blackballed by NASCAR for four years because he tried to unionize the drivers.

"Curtis could deal with the big-money people. He was in the lumber business, and when Curtis came to the track, he would wear a sport coat, a high-dollar shirt on a pair of beltless pants. Curtis's appearance was a step above—sort of like Roger Penske coming to Winston Cup ten years ago. Roger presented his image back then when not too many others were doing that. So Curtis could have adapted. Joe Weatherly couldn't have. Bobby Isaac couldn't have. Fireball Roberts couldn't have, because Fireball felt at home wearing a T-shirt and a pair of jeans.

"Up until 1974, not too many people in racing would even wear a tie to the NASCAR banquet. Early on, the banquet was held at the Plaza in Daytona Beach, and one guy might have on a tux, and another a tie, and another might wear a T-shirt. Up to a few years ago I never saw Junior Johnson in a tie. I think the first time I ever saw a picture of him in a tie was at the NASCAR banquet in New York when Darrell Waltrip won the championship in 1985. Before then, never.

"So this sport has turned around to where the owners and drivers now think about how they look, how they act, and the image they project.

"Before that, they were like the majority of the people who were sitting in the stands—pump jockeys who worked at service stations or dealerships, guys from the textile mills who would bring their six-packs and drink until they fell down. That was their relaxation.

"Now the image has shifted to where the rednecks no longer can afford the high-dollar tickets, so they have moved down to what we call the 'beer and chicken bone' sections, the first six rows. We call it that because everyone throws their cans and chicken bones down to the front.

"I can remember ten or fifteen years ago when you had to have a lot of police in the stands to keep control. In recent years, it's nothing to see fifty thousand people and four or five policemen. They don't have hardly any trouble at all anymore.

"The middle-class to high-class people are the ones who are now going to the races. The banks are coming in, buying blocks of four hundred, five hundred seats, and the guy who is playing golf on Saturday is now sitting in the stands and watching the race.

"There is a second group, the infield group, that never wants to sit in the stands. This is a gypsy, Arab, migrating group. Each week they are picking up their tents and going somewhere else. They pay top dollar. It costs $50 a day just to bring your motor home in, plus another $150 for two tickets. If you bring your motor home to Daytona and stay the week, it's $500 to park that motor home. That's just for the site.

"I never think what the man in the stands is paying until an old college buddy calls and says, 'Can you get me two tickets?' As a friend and human being, I'm going to buy them for him, and then the man behind the counter says, 'Ninety dollars,' and I say, 'What?' I'm still thinking back twelve years ago when it was $35 for two. Time passes as you get older, and you don't think about it.

"In 1964, Fireball Roberts crashed over here at Charlotte and burned up and died, and Joe Weatherly crashed at Riverside and got killed. Weatherly went into that big sweeping turn and went right into the wall on the driver's side, and his head hit the wall and it killed him. When Junior Johnson was told, 'Joe Weatherly just got killed in the turn. His head came out the window and hit the wall,' Junior thought they were kidding. Junior said, 'Knowing Joe it probably broke the wall.'

"Fireball and Joe were the last of the real big heroes of that period besides Freddie Lorenzen. Fireball and Freddie were real close friends, and right after Fireball died, Fred retired. Because he had stayed day in and day out with Fireball in the hospital while Fireball was trying to recover from these burns, and it affected Fred Lorenzen. Fred was the Golden Boy, like Rick Flair in wrestling. He presented a good image, but with the equipment Freddie had from Holman-Moody, Fred should have won a lot more races.

"After the characters came David Pearson, and of course, Richard Petty. Richard Petty was *the* guy, along with David Pearson. They were the top. Each weekend they were competing against each other. One drove a Mercury and the other at the time drove a Pontiac. Pearson was Ford and Petty was General Motors. Before that, Petty drove Chryslers for years. He was the last of the Chrysler-product drivers before they got out of racing.

"The greatest of them all was Richard Petty. When the manufacturers got out in the early seventies, he carried the sport until R. J. Reynolds came in and put it where it is today. The respect Richard Petty has generated with his peers is nothing like I've seen in any other sport.

"When they say he's The King, he's The King. Dale Earnhardt might win eight or nine championships, and he might be The Prince, but he'll never be The King.

"Richard's daddy, Lee, was a great racer, but he was not accepted by the other racers, because he wasn't a bootlegger. He says he was, but he only says that because he wanted to be one of the boys with Junior Johnson and Curtis Turner and all the rest of them, 'cause at the time the true racers were the ones who were drinking and hauling the moon. Lee ran a service station, and he worked on all the local tractors between Greensboro, the big city, and Randleman, which is where they are from. Lee was a great race driver, but he didn't have the personality that Richard Petty has. I know Richard's mother and Lee, and I can't tell you where Richard's personality comes from. Momma Petty runs the whole show, and Lee Petty plays golf, and Lee is a nice guy, but he certainly isn't outgoing like Richard, who always talks, is friendly, never snubbed anybody.

"Years ago, before he won his 150th race, I watched Richard sit and sign autographs for two hours to every person left and shake his hand. You could tell it was getting numb, but that's what made him.

"One time I went with Richard and Lynda, his wife, to Gene's Steakhouse. Everything was paid for. All we had to do was eat. They brought out huge steaks. But people kept coming over to him, asking him to sign things, talking to him, and he took it all in stride. I finished my steak, Lynda finished hers, and Richard was still talking to people. On the way back to the motel, we pulled into McDonald's and got something for him to eat, and he never complained.

"For years I was a Paul Newman fan. I enjoyed going to his movies. Then one year we were at Daytona, and I was walking behind Newman, and it was late in the day, and there was a lady standing with three kids, and the oldest one was probably seven. No one else was around. She asked him for an autograph, and he said, 'I don't give autographs.' It was very rude. It changed my opinion of him completely.

"When you're as big as Richard Petty, people want to touch you, and he has given them every opportunity, unlike a lot of others.

"The reason Pearson disappeared from racing was that Pearson never liked to be around the public. Pearson might know you for twenty years, but he might know your name or might not. He may not take the time to learn your name or try to be friendly.

"Petty will remember your name and tell you the first time he saw or talked with you. He's always got time to talk to you. He's never treated anyone any better or any less. He's one of a kind.

"Pearson, as soon as the race was over, he wanted to get back home. On many occasions he would not accept prizes or show up at appearances when he was supposed to. Pearson felt confident when he was in the car, but he didn't have that same confidence out in the public. It was like his education wasn't there to generate the image he thought he should have, and so he backed away.

"David has invested his money very wisely, a pretty wealthy man. He has warehouses, property, and lives comfortably.

"During the late sixties and into the seventies, NASCAR had a hard time finding a good image other than Richard Petty.

"I mean, talk about rough, look at A. J. Foyt. I've seen AJ clean the lounge out at Daytona. A few years back AJ got in trouble hitting an official of CART when he was racing Indy cars. Cale asked him, 'AJ, what are you doing getting in all that trouble? You're supposed to get smarter as you get older.'

"AJ said, 'When I was young, I didn't know what they were thinking, so I would hit them. Now I *know* what they are thinking, so I don't waste any time—I just knock their pins off.'

"Bobby Allison was a good representative of the sport, but Bobby Allison was so eat up with racing he would run anything—if you asked him to race a go-cart, he would. Ask his wife, Judy. His whole life was racing. Allison was the only driver who would criticize NASCAR and wouldn't make headlines the next day. When others were critical, it would be big headlines. When Bobby bitched, nobody ever got on him about it. He's the only one who ever brought charges against NASCAR after one of their decisions and ended up settling for money. Allison could criticize and still get along. He was the only one.

"It's too bad Bobby got hurt, because he'd be driving right now, and he'd be just as competitive as anyone. Unfortunately, in 1988 he got in a wreck on the first lap at Pocono that was life-threatening. He got T-boned in the door, and he got a severe blow to the head, and had a fractured hip and multiple injuries. He has lost a little of his ability to react quickly, and sometimes his speech gets a little bad, and so the doctors told him it would be better for him not to get back in the car. Every once in a while he still takes a practice lap. Because I really believe that man could have driven a car until he was sixty or seventy years old, because he was another smart one. He was a charger, but he learned over the years the main thing is to stay in the lead lap, wait for a caution to come out, catch a break, and as a result you'll be right back up front, and you'll win the race.

"The other driver who had a positive image was Cale Yarborough. There are two reasons for that. First of all, Cale was a down-home South Carolina farmer who became a success. He was a local high school athlete, married the local girl, and the Southern fans related to all of this. The other thing is, he's a small man in height and has very strong convictions, and he is seen as the underdog who has to fight the uphill battle.

"Plus Cale never gave up. If he was six laps down, he'd battle your butt off, and you had to beat him. And if you wanted to get rough with him, he would tear your bumpers off. So he was a tough, manhandling, driving SOB, that's what he was.

"When I first went with Cale, I was on the radio, and through the turns I'd hear a sound something like, "Hmmmmmhmmmm hmmmm-hmmmmm.' After about three races, I finally figured out that when Cale was going through the turns and he didn't want to yell when he got a little loose, he would hum, and that's what I was hearing.

"And when Cale came on the radio and said he was getting loose, you'd better get him in, because that meant he was driving to the point where the car was completely out of whack. You'd better change a tire, do something, because he would drive that car until he hit the wall if you didn't. He had that much confidence in his driving ability. He had no fear, like Dale Earnhardt.

"See, when he was coming up Cale wanted to drive Winston Cup, so he went to work at Holman-Moody, and they gave him a job sweeping floors and later gave him the opportunity to drive. So after sweeping the floor, after getting off work, he and Slick Owens, who worked in the parts department, would go to the ABC store and get something to drink. Cale would sit on the back of Slick's motorcycle holding the whiskey, and they'd go down the road that way.

"One day a car was taking up a portion of their lane, and Slick swerved over to the other side of the road, and the motorcycle went into a bank, and Slick went one way and Cale went over his head. Slick said, 'The only thing I remember was those bottles hitting together.' Slick got up, and he said he could hear Cale saying, 'If he broke my liquor, I'll whip that SOB's ass.'

"They would do things like that—Cale, Curtis Turner, Joe Weatherly. They enjoyed driving the car, enjoyed partying, enjoyed whatever they did and the hell with tomorrow. It's a bygone era, because they didn't have the pressure of the owner, the sponsor, the manufacturer. People accepted them that way.

"Cale enjoyed thrills, sensations. He liked to skydive, wrestle an alligator, do crazy things. Now he's a little older, a little smarter.

"But in his heyday Cale got in confrontations with Bobby Allison, Donnie Allison, Pearson, every one of them.

"I was at the Daytona 500 in 1979 when he and the Allisons fought after the race. Going into the backstretch, Donnie Allison knew he couldn't beat Cale. Donnie was leading and Cale was going to pass him. Two other times Cale had done it the same way. The previous Daytona 500 that Cale won, he passed a guy on the backstretch and came around and took the checkered flag. So on this day Cale cut to the inside on the white flag lap, and Donnie Allison *knew* that Cale was going to pass him and was going to win the race, and so Donnie came down and on purpose tried to take Cale right off the asphalt and put him into the grass. Which he did. Cale hit the grass, and Donnie was up on the asphalt, but Cale shot right back up the track, and into the turn they crashed and came back down the track together.

"There is one question I can ask anybody, and nobody can answer it: Where was Bobby Allison running at the time?

"Everyone remembers that Bobby got into that fight, but where was Bobby running? I can tell you, Bobby wasn't even in contention.

"Okay, so Donnie and Cale crashed and then Richard Petty came around and won the race.

"Bobby came around to see how Donnie was, and they were out there fighting, so Bobby got out of his car and went over there, and Bobby joined in. The two Allisons were fighting against Yarborough, and in fact it was two firemen who broke it up.

"CBS had spent a bundle of money to televise the race live, and they had no idea this was going to happen. In fact, a camera had to go back and replay Richard winning the race, because they were showing the fight going on in the turn and not the checkered flag.

"What I remember more about it than anything else was that they sent a car around to get Cale, Bobby, and Donnie, to bring them back to the garage area real quick, because they were going to lock the press out. They didn't want bad publicity.

"Somehow the coordination got off. First of all, I wouldn't put three guys who were fighting in the backseat of a car. And so they brought them all the way around to the garage area, and they locked the doors in the garage area, and they wouldn't let in the press. But the press was standing outside, and here comes the car with all the fighters right into where the press were standing! It was like bringing them around and saying, 'Here they are, men.' So it didn't work out the way they planned.

"What was funny, two years later they had a roast in Charlotte for Cale Yarborough. Two of the guys on the panel were Bobby and Donnie Allison. Bobby got up and presented Cale with a set of boxing gloves. He said, 'I don't want to take anything away from his ability, but he could use some lessons.'

"But ever since that race, Cale has never cared much for Bobby. To Cale, first of all, what Donnie did, keeping him from passing like that, was a no-no. Second of all, the fight wasn't fair, two against one. Cale told me he felt Bobby had embarrassed him when Bobby got out of the car and went at him. That shouldn't have been. That was like a street fight. Cale felt we are too high class a people to do stuff like that. It embarrassed Cale to be seen fighting like that because his image means so much to him. Cale always made sure he had a clean image, and that's what people remember about him.

"A sad moment for Cale was when he announced his retirement three races from the end in 1988. NASCAR had him make one tour of the track, and they announced this was to be Cale's last race, but it didn't give the guy justice.

"And then the next season when Daytona rolled around, he had won more Daytona races than anybody else, counting the 500 and the Firecracker 400, and he had to walk in and see somebody else driving that car. You talk about a guy with ants in his pants. He'd go to that fence and hang on and just stare.

"I went over to talk to him, and I said, 'It's tough, isn't it.' 'Yup, pretty tough.'

"About six months later he talked to me about it, and his feelings were that when he got out of that race car, he was nothing. In other words, the praise, the glory was with the race car, not with himself, and he couldn't bear to face the world and be an average Joe—which he's not, but in his mind he was. It's like being a superstar in football, and all of a sudden your career ends, and you're not involved in the game anymore, and it's rough.

"You have conquered the mountain, and when you get to the top and look around, you don't have anyplace higher to go, so what's next?

"And there is something else that sticks out in my mind when you talk about drivers. First of all, it was saddening to people who had been racing a long time when David Pearson kept driving that car long after he should have gotten out. Another generation of drivers had come along who was making fun of him because he wasn't keeping up with the pack. So that took off a lot of the glory David once had. He should have retired and got out. He shouldn't have stayed in there.

"The next thing is, you are never going to stain the image of Richard Petty. I'm glad he has announced that 1992 will be his final year, though I wish he'd retire now. See, the drivers out there look after him. It's like my driver, Derrike Cope, he'll say on the radio, 'Okay, wait a minute. I'm getting around Richard. I'll catch up to the pack. Just give me a little time to get around Richard.' They look after him. In other words, they respect him, and they are not going to do anything to discredit him. But Richard has taken some terrible blows the last two years. He's hit a lot of walls, and after a while this adds up.

"I can remember when Richard had his big crash at Daytona. His car was tumbling over and over and was disintegrating as it went, and finally it came to rest, and then he received one last blow from Brett Bodine, which spun him all around, and when the medics got to him, he had lost his eyesight, which is common.

"They carried him by ambulance and took him into the field hospital. Now Richard had always made the statement, 'When it stops being fun, I'm going to get out of racing.' So he was laying there, looking up, and they had a big light above him, and slowly his eyes were getting adjusted, the light was coming back and images were appearing. Finally, he could see his wife, Lynda, looking into his face.

"She looked down at him and said, 'Well, are you having fun yet?' And she walked out of the room. Richard laughs every time he tells that story.

"If you've ever had a chance to see Richard's chest, it looks like a road map, with scars and lines. His stomach has been operated on, because he's the only guy I have ever seen who smokes a cigar, chews tobacco, and takes Goody's aspirin powder at the same time. Now that's not good for your stomach. He wonders where half his stomach has gone.

"Two things you have to understand about Richard Petty. He can hear standing beside a race car with it running, but if you go into the truck, he's deaf. You have to talk loud. He has hearing aids in both ears. And the next thing is, Richard wears sunglasses all the time. Why? He doesn't like his eyes. He says, 'My eyes sink into the back of my head.'

"Let me tell you how Richard Petty is. Whether he is at his house or at the race shop or in a motel, he is Richard Petty. My wife and daughter and I were supposed to pick up Lynda and take her somewhere, and we were a little late. We pulled up, and my wife and I went up and knocked on the door, and Richard opened the door in his Jockey shorts and his boots. Richard said, 'Lynda told me to tell you to go ahead.' I said, 'Okay, Richard,' and I closed the door and left.

"My wife said, 'I never thought I'd see Richard Petty in his underwear.'

"Along with Petty and Pearson, there were a handful of others the fans would come and pull for: Cale Yarborough, Bobby Allison, Donnie Allison—until Darrell Waltrip came along.

"Darrell came into the sport from Nashville. The local track he was running was Owensboro, Kentucky. Waltrip's wife, Stevie, has a dad who is a very wealthy man. He's into natural gas. He put up some money for Darrell, other people put up money, and he came in under the sponsorship of Terminal Transport, the 95 car. He ran for Rookie of the Year, and he didn't win it. The next year he ran with Bud Moore, and then he went to DiGard, where he had a rocky relationship with the Gardner brothers. I was with DiGard when Darrell drove car 88, sponsored by Gatorade.

"The relationship was rocky because Darrell was very cocky. He ran his mouth a lot. Bill Gardner was a man who thought of himself as a billionaire, though he was on the lower end of millionaire, and Bill Gardner thought everything should be Bill Gardner and not Darrell Waltrip or anybody else on the team. And Di, who was DiProspero, a man who put up part of the money, got in an automobile accident and was paralyzed from the neck down, and so Bill Gardner put his brother Jim in charge of the team, and Jim drank a lot, and despite all this and Darrell running his mouth, Darrell still won a lot of races.

"Darrell was cocky. He opened his mouth and would say something against these Gods like Petty, Pearson, Cale, and the Allisons. And he backed up what he said. It was sort of like paying admission to see Babe Ruth hit a home run and the pitcher would keep striking him out. You start booing the pitcher. And so the fans turned against Darrell because he would win races and say things like, 'It isn't that hard. You just have to drive your butt off, but you *can* win races.'

"I remember when Bobby Allison fixed Darrell at North Wilkesboro in 1979. Darrell was beating on the back of Bobby's bumper to get out of the way, and Bobby got mad, let off, and put Darrell into the wall.

"Before Bobby wrecked him, Darrell's crew chief had come on the radio and told him, 'Don't beat on Allison anymore. Let off the thing. You don't need to do that.' And Darrell said, 'He'll take it. There ain't nothing he can do about it.' And about that time Allison let off, let him go underneath him, and just put him right into the wall.

"These drivers will tell you if a guy can beat on my back bumper, he can pass me. So don't hit me in the back. It's one thing a driver cannot stand. Somebody, somewhere down the line, is going to pay for it. And so Bobby took care of Darrell. Bobby said to himself, 'I've taken it and that's all.'

"And Darrell wasn't the kind of person to listen to his crew chief. That's what I mean about Darrell being cocky. But when he first came up, Darrell took on the establishment, and so the press and the fans started jumping on him, calling him 'Jaws' and other names. Other new drivers like Dale Earnhardt and Ricky Rudd knew they could win races, but they didn't feel they had the equipment to do it, but Darrell Waltrip was the one who succeeded in breaking the monopoly of the establishment drivers, and so all at once it went from six or seven competitive teams to twelve and fifteen, and now it's to where twenty of forty cars might end up the winner.

"A lot more people now respect Waltrip than used to. He created this new door for the others, although he was cocky. People booed him, threw things at him, couldn't stand him, but he opened the door up for the Earnhardts, the Rudds, the Schraders, and the new guys who came in, so it was good for the sport.

"Now the racer everyone wants to beat is Dale Earnhardt. I know Dale because my ex-brother-in-law was married to Dale's sister. I was raised with Dale Earnhardt.

"I remember when his arm was as big around as a pencil, when he skipped school and his daddy would get on him. He doesn't have that much education, seventh or eighth grade.

"Dale and I grew up in Kannapolis, North Carolina. Dale lived right through the woods from my house. His daddy drove too. His daddy, Ralph, was one of the few people who ran dirt track racing and made over $100,000 a year. He built the car, drove the car, and he built the engines. He was a one-man operation. He died in his kitchen when he was forty-four years old. He had hardening of the arteries and a massive heart attack. When Ralph Earnhardt died, Dale was nineteen.

"One year before Ralph died, the doctors told him to get out of the race car, and he got someone else to drive for him. His condition was more

severe than he let know. See, Ralph Earnhardt, Dale's daddy, hated doctors. It had really had to be bad for him to go to the doctor.

"You find out when you talk to these drivers, two things they hate are doctors and funeral homes. Doctors equate to hospitals. They don't want to accept the fact that something might be wrong with them, and if that's so, they might not drive the next weekend. And some of these guys have the attitude it's not macho to go, and they are tough.

"Ralph Earnhardt was a tough, tough individual. He was hardheaded. What hurt Ralph Earnhardt more than anything else, he was a hardheaded individual and he was too independent. And you might say that means the same thing.

"Ralph was offered rides to drive what was then Grand National and now is Winston Cup, to drive for different owners, and if he wanted to do it, he'd do it, and if he didn't, he didn't. For a while he built motors for Pontiac, which Fireball Roberts and all them others were using and winning races, and this was in the early sixties when they told him they would pay him $2,000 a month to sit in his shop and build engines for them. He said, 'Hell, I want to race, I don't want to build engines.' And Ralph told them to get lost.

"I remember when Bobby Isaac used to visit Ralph Earnhardt. They were the best of friends. See, Isaac didn't believe in banks. He'd walk around with a huge wad of money, perhaps $10,000, and he didn't mind pulling it out and showing it to you and saying, 'I had a good payday this weekend.'

"You can tell when people came from the mountains of North Carolina because they didn't believe in chairs, and Bobby would come over to Ralph's garage, and they'd go over and squat in a corner with their butt inches from the ground and talk for three or four hours, and if you did that for five minutes, somebody would have to pull you up. But if you went over to Ralph's shop, Bobby Isaac, Ralph, Ned Jarrett would all squat down and talk for hours that way.

"Isaac would tell Ralph, 'You ought to get back on the circuit. You don't need to be driving these dirt tracks anymore.' Ralph would say, 'Look at the money I've made,' and he'd pull out *his* money. And maybe Dale would come by, because I can remember one time Bobby Isaac gave him a jacket with a stripe running down it that had 'Bobby Isaac' on it and a little bumblebee, meaning a Dodge Charger, and Dale was so proud of that jacket he wore it until the strings were coming off of it.

"And then one day I remember Bobby Isaac was driving at Talladega for Bud Moore. In the middle of the race, Bobby climbed out of the car, and Bud said, 'What's wrong?' He said, 'Somebody riding in that car with me told me to get out of it.' Bobby went to the garage. Bud went over and looked in the car. He walked over to Bobby and said, 'I don't see a damn soul in there.' But that was the end of Bobby's superspeedway career. He refused to run them anymore.

"Ralph Earnhardt's name doesn't show up in the list of Winston Cup race winners, but he won hundreds of track victories no one ever kept records on. On the local tracks around Charlotte, Ralph would win Thursday, Friday, Saturday, *and* Sunday. People would call him from as far away as California asking for his advice. *Stock Car Racing Magazine* called him 'Mr. Dirt Track.' Ralph would tell Dale, 'There is only one lap you want to lead, and that's the last lap.'

"I've seen Ralph take Dale over to the side and get all over him because he lapped the field twice. Ralph said, 'Those people in the stands up there want to think that the second-place guy has an opportunity to beat you. If you start winning by two laps . . . I've learned my lessons.' Because one year Hickory racetrack banned him because he won all the races there. They told him they didn't want him back because he was killing attendance. Nobody will pay to see one driver win all the time.

"So Ralph told Dale, 'Never pull away and leave them too far behind. Pass the guy on the last lap and win the race. And *always* let the fans think the second-place guy can beat you.' Ralph was pretty smart about that.

"There are two things that help Dale but hurt Dale. The first one was that his daddy was so independent that you could stand there for forty-five minutes right beside him, and he would talk to you when he felt like talking to you. No matter what you said, you weren't going to get him to talk to you until he was ready to talk. So I think Dale learned from him that he didn't want to have a personality like that. He felt he should be a little more forward, because Dale would get so frustrated, he might ask his daddy for a dollar to go off with his friends, and his daddy might wait fifteen minutes before he answered him.

"I think too that Dale learned his daddy never made a rash decision. When Ralph decided something, it was thought out and logical. And his daddy always talked about racing and drew a lot of the tracks in the dirt with his finger and explained things to Dale that he uses today. I've heard Ralph say, first of all, 'You establish your territory.' That one little phrase is the way Dale Earnhardt drives. He establishes his territory. It's *his* territory, and you're not going to take it away from him.

"Dale has the God-given talent his father had. His father could make moves and make it look like the person wrecked by himself. I've seen it so many times where Dale creates a situation, and the man in front of him

Racing pioneer
Junior Johnson.
(© International
Speedway Corpora-
tion/NASCAR)

each road race, 1950. Curtis Turner, driving a Nash, is closely followed by Herb Thomas,
·iving a Plymouth. (© International Speedway Corporation/NASCAR)

The legendary
Curtis Turner
sitting in for
Ray Daniels.
(© INTERNATIONAL
SPEEDWAY
CORPORATION/
NASCAR)

Joe Weatherly and his well-oiled machine. (© INTERNATIONAL SPEEDWAY CORPORATION/NASCAR)

oe Weatherly distances himself from the
ack during a 1956 convertible beach race.
© INTERNATIONAL SPEEDWAY CORPORATION/NASCAR)

ee Petty, father of Richard and grandfather
f Kyle. (© INTERNATIONAL SPEEDWAY CORPORATION/
ASCAR)

Tiny Lund.
(© International
Speedway Corporation/
NASCAR)

Fireball Roberts.
(© International Speedway
Corporation/NASCAR)

Fireball Roberts, #22, keeps #527, Lem Svajian, from passing in a 1957 beach race.
(© INTERNATIONAL SPEEDWAY CORPORATION/NASCAR)

The popularity of stock car racing was evident back in the 1950s. Note the crowd gathered at this race as Jim Russell protects his lead against Joe Lee Johnson.
(© INTERNATIONAL SPEEDWAY CORPORATION/NASCAR)

The 1959 Daytona 500. In a photo finish, Joe Weatherly edges out Lee Petty, #42, and Joe Lee Johnson, #73, for the victory. (© INTERNATIONAL SPEEDWAY CORPORATION/NASCAR)

Richard Petty in the driver's seat of his victorious Plymouth on the infield at the 1964 Daytona 500. (© INTERNATIONAL SPEEDWAY CORPORATION/NASCAR)

(Left to right) Pete Hamilton, Lee Roy Yarbrough, Richard Petty, and Cale Yarborough are all smiles before a race. (© International Speedway Corporation/NASCAR)

The brothers from Hueytown, Bobby *(left)* and Donnie Allison. (© International Speedway Corporation/NASCAR)

Cale Yarborough poses with victory trophy after winning the 1983 Daytona.
(© International Speedway Corporation/ NASCAR)

Darrell Waltrip's pit crew puts new tires on the Tide car, helping him to the 1989 Daytona crown. (© International Speedway Corporation/NASCAR)

or behind him wrecks, and it would look like Dale had nothing to do with it.

"There are two or three things I've learned over the years. First of all, with the car designs we have now, on the superspeedways you can drive in a way that you play with the airflow of the other cars. You can actually turn another car sideways with the way you drive. But you have to know how to do it. And Dale Earnhardt is a master of that. Earnhardt can touch a car and never look like he touched it. See, a driver drives with the feel of his hands, and he knows how far that rear end is loose, how far it's going to come out from under him, all by the feel of his hands, and Earnhardt drives on the ragged edge all the time, and he enjoys it, where most of the other drivers won't even get to the ragged edge. I've watched Dale drive so long I can tell a lot of times from the pits whether Dale is going all out or not, whether he's going on that fine line, if someone gets close to him, whether he has 10 percent more or 15 percent, that the guy may think he's going to pass Earnhardt, but he's going to have a hell of a time, 'cause Earnhardt hasn't reached the ragged edge yet. And there is no such thing in Earnhardt's vocabulary that he can't do something in a race car. He can do *anything* he wants to with that race car.

"Richard Petty will tell you that Earnhardt is a cross between Fireball Roberts and Darrell Waltrip. Fireball was pedal to the metal, led a lot of races and blew up a lot. Buddy Baker was the same way. Earnhardt is pedal to metal, but he can drive a car and save it. He can get the best out of that car and still finish the race with it.

"With Darrell, the race will be three-quarters over, and all at once you wonder, 'How the hell did Darrell get leading this race?' And it was because Darrell would not go a lap down, he'd save his car, and then when it came time to push the button, he'd go to the front. Fireball would push the button at the start of the race and hope to hell he was there at the end.

"One thing about Fireball, he didn't have power steering. He didn't have a lot of things the drivers today have. I don't know how many drivers could drive five hundred miles in a 1970 car and finish. Earnhardt would be one of the few. Because it took a hell of a man to drive five hundred miles with no power steering and without the luxury they have now.

"If I compared anybody with Dale Earnhardt, it would be Cale Yarborough. Cale could get the best out of a car, drive the hell out of it, and still finish the race. But Cale Yarborough used brute strength and manhandled the car. Earnhardt has learned how to finesse the car. He's going to let it drift up the track and save it to go on in instead of jerking it right down there and holding it and going around through. It's like a conversation back and forth between the motor and Earnhardt. Everyone can tell you that Earnhardt is worth 30 or 40 horsepower, because he is going to ride that car around the edge, and he's going to make the car look good, and the motor men look good, because in the past other teams have hired his motor men, and after they leave him to take the big bucks, they're nothing, because not everybody is an Earnhardt.

"And he has two abilities you have to have in this sport. First of all, he can leave the race at the track when he gets in his van and drives away. The race is over, it's history, and he can leave that, totally remove himself from it.

"And the other thing, Dale never looks to tomorrow. He plans that day, lives that day, and then when tomorrow comes, he lives that. As a result, his fear factor is so superior to any of the other drivers out there. Like I said, his attitude is, 'Whatever happens, happens.' I'm not saying he's Presbyterian-like predestined, but when a driver goes into a turn, subconsciously he may think he's pushing the pedal when really he's lifting it, because his foot is shaking—that's the subconscious fear factor. And it's where Earnhardt and Geoff Bodine have it over the others. Dale has no fear. If you have a screen of smoke in front of you and you don't know what's on the other side, if you have ten people, three will step through it and seven won't. The fear factor is what controls. For a race car driver, the fear factor will mean miles an hour plus or minus.

"And because of his attitude about life, Dale doesn't feel any pressure. The pressure doesn't get to him like it does a guy who wonders and worries about the Sunday race on Friday. Dale takes each day as it comes, adapts to it and goes on, and it's a good philosophy if you can do it.

"A lot of drivers worry, and it takes all the fun out of it. Dale is still having fun. And with this sport changing so much, with the stakes climbing so high, it's hard to have fun. Today the driver has the pressure of the owner on you, the pressure of the sponsor, and the pressure of the car manufacturer on you. They are all putting out dollars and they expect you to perform. You might get congratulations from the owner and the sponsor, and the manufacturer may still want to know why you didn't do better. It used to be you'd get through at the track and go back to the motel for a swim or dinner, but now there are corporate meetings. You have to put your coats and ties on and go to dinner with the sponsor. So your time is not yours anymore. You gotta create an image. Even Dale has learned to play the game. He may not be the greatest speaker in the world, but he has come a long, long way from when he first started out.

"I was one of the group to put him in the first car he ever drove. It was David Oliver, Ray Oliver, and myself—my brother-in-law and father-in-law before I got a divorce. This was '74, '75, '76, '77. David works for the Hendrick team. Ray is retired now. Dale drives for Richard Childress. We were all in racing, teamed together for several years. We drove on dirt tracks Friday and Saturday nights.

"It used to scare me to death when he drove my car because he would drive it till he spun it out, and then he would know how far he could go. You could do that on dirt, because you'd just spin around, but then when we raced on asphalt, he would do it there too, where you were liable to tear the car up. But he had to learn. He'd still spin them after that, but he learned the point where he would have to cut the front end to come around.

"In 1978 Humpy Wheeler gave Dale a chance to drive an Osterlund car in the World Service Life 300. Dale had always ran good at Charlotte. Something might happen during a pit stop to cost us a lap because we didn't have the personnel, but if you look at the records, Dale always finished in the top ten with his own equipment.

"When Humpy got Dale his ride, he ran door handle to door handle with Bobby Allison and Allison just did beat him out. The fans were standing on their feet for fifteen to twenty laps, as this young guy was running Allison for everything he could do. Rod Osterlund signed Dale to a contract, and he won Rookie of the Year, which gave him the opportunity to compete until he finally won the championship. He was at the top of the tower and he had to project an image for the whole sport, and he wasn't ready for it, and he went and hid, because he could not go and talk at the big dinners. He could not meet presidents of these companies and know what to say. His self-esteem wasn't there, and he just wasn't prepared for it. It took Dale five or six years, going to school and doing things to clean up his act, so if you compare him now to what he was ten years ago, there is no comparison. He has mastered the skills needed to be a star in this business. I told a writer from *Car and Driver* magazine, 'If Earnhardt doesn't have a high school diploma, in stock car racing he has a master's degree.'

"But Dale got where he got because he was in the right place at the right time, because there are a lot of drivers out there on the short tracks with the talent, but they will never get the chance to race Winston Cup.

"I've seen a lot of drivers who got the chance but didn't have the talent. I've seen a lot who I thought would make it, but they didn't have the financial means and had to go back home. I've seen a lot of owners come in here who had money and left with none. I've seen a lot come in and stay in the sport and use their head, and they still have their money. I've seen it all."

Ed Carroll

Ed Carroll

The Newcomers

It isn't easy to start a Winston Cup race team. Unless you are a multimillionaire, you have one of those chicken-and-egg problems. You need an experienced driver and crew chief in order to attract a sponsor that will pay you to finance the team, or you need a $3 million sponsor in order to attract an experienced driver and crew chief. Either way, it's a tall order for someone new to the scene.

It is rare for someone to walk into Winston Cup racing and become competitive right away. Joe Gibbs, the Hall of Fame–quality coach of the Washington Redskins in the NFL, hopes to be one of the exceptions.

Gibbs drag-raced when he was a teen, and for years had secretly harbored a desire to own a Winston Cup race team. Gibbs acquired the backing of NFL Properties, which figures to benefit from the exposure in racing.

To get started, Gibbs, who is a born-again Christian, sought the advice of the highly respected Rick Hendrick and of NASCAR's chaplain, Max Helton.

Helton suggested that Gibbs contact Tom and Norm Miller, owners of Interstate Batteries. The Millers, who are also committed Christians, had sponsored fourteen races during the 1991 season with driver Stanley Smith. Helton knew they wanted to get into racing full-time and suggested a Joe Gibbs–Interstate Batteries tie-in.

Around the same time Gibbs was talking with the Miller brothers, he was also talking with Dale Jarrett, son of race-car-driver-turned-announcer Ned Jarrett. Papa Jarrett won fifty races, tied with Junior Johnson for eighth place on the all-time-winners' list. In 1961 and again in 1965 Ned had won the racing championship. Two years later a bad back ended his driving career and he turned to broadcasting, where he is a mainstay of NASCAR's TV and radio team.

Going into the 1992 season, son Dale had one win to his credit, a victory at Michigan in August 1991 for the Wood Brothers. A driver since 1984, Jarrett, thirty-six, is considered an up-and-coming talent. Like the other key members of the team, Dale Jarrett is a born-again Christian.

Gibbs recruited as crew chief Dale Jarrett's brother-in-law, Jimmy Makar, who had been a chassis specialist and crew chief for Roger Penske's Miller Draft race team that features Rusty Wallace.

Makar should have a calmer time of it working with Jarrett than he did with Rusty Wallace, who is much more hyper behind the wheel than the soft-spoken Jarrett. Rusty, who cusses like a sailor during a race, would come on the radio and say, "Jimmy, this car ain't worth a damn." Jimmy would reply, "Well, just park the damn thing. I don't care. Bring it in and park it."

Wallace was made part owner of the Penske team in '91, empowering him to be even more of a tyrant. During a race at Richmond he announced on the radio, "This car ain't worth a damn. I'm going to fire every one of you." Jimmy Makar won't have to worry about singed ears with the mild-mannered Dale Jarrett behind the wheel.

To run his team's business affairs Gibbs hired another devout Christian, Ed Carroll.

Carroll had begun in stock car racing as a representative of STP, the gasoline additive. For six years he worked closely with STP's most famous representative, Richard Petty, accompanying Petty to many of his promotional functions. Carroll loved working with Petty, but tired of living out of a suitcase. Moreover, he yearned for a stronger Christian fellowship in his professional relationships. When Carroll's close friend, Max Helton, told him about the team of Christians Gibbs was forming under the Interstate Batteries sponsorship, Carroll asked the chaplain if there might be an executive position for him. Carroll was hired to be general manager as the Gibbs team was readying itself to begin the 1992 season.

Carroll, no stranger to racing, realizes that it isn't easy to start a race team and immediately become successful. Though aware his Chevrolet Lumina would be at a horsepower disadvantage to the Ford Thunderbirds once the 1992 season got under way, Ed Carroll had confidence in the talent of his driver and crew and had faith that his team possessed the stuff to be competitive.

ED CARROLL: "People ask me, 'How can you be a Christian and go into racing?' I said to one man, 'Why would you say something like that?' He said, 'I remember as a kid the race cars had pictures of devils painted on them.' It clicked. As a kid you bought 'Hot Wheels' cars, and flames were painted on the hood of the cars. And that's what he was talking about. But, of course, racing has nothing whatsoever to do with the devil.

"To me, Winston Cup racing is a mission field, like going to Zaire. People need to know there is a different way to live and that someone cares about you personally.

"There are a lot more Christians in racing than anyone realizes. They are ministered to by an organization called MRO—Motor Racing Outreach—run by Max Helton, NASCAR's chaplain.

"Max had been the one to introduce Joe Gibbs to Tom and Norm Miller, the owners of Interstate Batteries. Tom and Norm met with Joe and gave Joe a sponsorship to form our race team. Then right before The Winston at the Charlotte Motor Speedway earlier this year, I had lunch with Max Helton. Max and I are very close, get along real well, respect each other's opinions, and Max began asking me a lot of questions about drivers, crew chiefs, who would I recommend? He told me Joe Gibbs was starting his team.

"I had worked for Ralph Salvino at STP for six years. Ralph, who was known as the Godfather of racing, started the STP racing program back in '69. Ralph was the one who got STP involved in NASCAR racing. He was a real good guy, was everyone's friend, but after STP was bought by First Brands in '88, Ralph tired of the corporate politics, and he retired. After he left I became disenchanted, and I was looking for something else to do.

"And so I told Max Helton, 'If they need a general manager, I'd be really interested in talking to him.' Six weeks later I hadn't heard anything and thought it was a dead issue, but at 11:30 at night, Joe Gibbs called me and said he was coming to town the next week and wanted to get together and talk about the job, and we did, and I got the job.

"The way the pieces of the puzzle fit together, the first thing you have to do is hire a driver, because if you get a viable driver then you get a sponsorship. The second step is to hire a crew chief and the third person is the general manager to oversee the operation.

"He had hired Dale Jarrett to drive. Dale's brother-in-law is Jimmy Makar, who had been working over at Roger Penske's for about five years. Roger Penske owns 51 percent and last year Roger gave Rusty Wallace and Don Miller the opportunity to own the rest.

"In that operation Jimmy was the crew chief, but because Rusty was the driver and became the owner, Rusty had a lot more input than most drivers. Rusty wanted things done in a certain way. And not that Jimmy was unhappy there, but Jimmy was looking for an opportunity, and over here with Joe Gibbs, Jimmy saw an opportunity to start from the ground floor and put together a team the way he wanted to do it, and he took it.

"We're running Chevrolet Luminas this year because of Joe Gibbs's relationship with Jimmy Johnson at Hendrick Motorsports. Jimmy, who runs the Hendrick race teams, helped lead Joe through the whole process of getting a team going, and in that process arranged to lease to Gibbs Chevrolet engines from Hendrick. Once Gibbs did that, Rick Hendrick was able to arrange a Chevrolet deal for Joe.

"I began in racing helping Richard Petty with his promotions. I consider myself privileged to have been associated with such a fine gentleman.

"When Richard Petty began driving, he would go to a race like at Richmond, and what his people would do was call ahead and set up a program with a local Richmond Plymouth dealer for him to come in for two hours, sit and sign autographs, and the Plymouth dealer could use that to draw people into his showroom, and they would pay him $500. They would bring the race car over, put it on display. Back then they had a little enclosed truck where they carried the toolboxes and parts, and the car would be on a flat, open trailer behind the truck. They'd take the car to the dealership, and the fans could look at the car and go inside the dealership for autographs. Two and three thousand people would line up at a Plymouth dealership. That would pay for the team's gas and hotel bills at Richmond. It was an easy way for them to help make expenses.

"Once they started that, they realized the fans really enjoyed it and how important it was to them, and it continually evolved. In November 1972, Richard signed with STP, and it was part of his contract he would do personal appearances, and he would get money for his racing program.

"It still works. I was with Richard two years ago in Washington, D.C., at a dealership in Silver Springs, on the D.C. line. You might figure, 'This isn't going to work.' But there was a steady stream of people all afternoon. People were lined up out the door!

"All the drivers are forced to sign autographs, but Richard not only signs them—when anyone comes up in line, Richard smiles at him, talks to him, makes him feel like he personally cares about him. You watch the other drivers signing autograph, like Dale Earnhardt—Dale doesn't feel comfortable with the public. Dale will sign it and hand it back, but he doesn't talk or even look up. Richard will take the time. You can have your picture taken with him. He goes out of his way to do that, and that has endeared him to race fans. It's one reason STP keeps putting money into his operation even though he hasn't won races in many years.

''The drivers today are basically divided into two camps. There are the drivers like Richard who are doubly blessed because they are successful on the track and also have talents for PR and the ability to talk to the press. Richard has always been open, made a point of being accessible and being open to the public.

''Dale Earnhardt is a real character, a throwback to the old days, like Curtis Turner. Dale's done it by hard driving. He's made a lot of enemies along the way, and a lot of fans.

''Dale races hard and in doing so sometimes bumps somebody. They spin out, and all the Bill Elliott fans are mad at you, all the Sterling Marlin fans. But that only lasts a short period, and people forget that. The thing about Earnhardt, he is such an incredible talent, he can put the car where nobody else can put it. He can drive it where nobody else can drive it. He can take a bad car and carry it where other drivers couldn't. But Dale is not that great at PR. He is not comfortable in front of a camera, kind of embarrassed and shy about it, doesn't know how to handle the popularity. That doesn't mean he can't. He does, but it doesn't come natural to him like it does to Richard Petty.

''There are other drivers who are great at PR. Take a Chad Little, who is very articulate, good-looking. Dale Jarrett, our driver, is very good at interviews. They haven't reached their peak as drivers yet. Darrell Waltrip has always been very good in front of the camera, though he has always tended to speak his mind.

''For instance, if another car ran into Richard, Richard would say, 'I lost it in the corner and crashed the car.' Richard told me a long time ago, if you have a wreck, even if you don't think it's your fault, the best thing you can say is, 'I screwed up; I'm sorry,' and ask everyone's forgiveness, and the thing goes away.

''Darrell will say, 'Yeah, that so-and-so ran into me and took me out.' And because Darrell had been so outspoken, he's had his ups and downs. As recent as five years ago, when Darrell's name was announced, the fans booed him. See, Darrell was good, but he never made any bones about it. He would tell people he was good, and they didn't like that. It was his attitude. He'd say, 'We didn't win today. We had the best car. We have the best team. We should have won today.' The fans just didn't like it.

''Another driver who's been hurt because he can't say he's sorry is Ernie Irvan. There was a real bad crash at Talladega in '91. Seventeen cars piled up.

''Ernie started up front. It was a restart, and for whatever reason his car didn't come up to speed like everyone else's, and he started falling back.

"There were two lines of cars, and he somehow got in the middle between them and was falling back, because everyone had the draft except him.

"Kyle Petty was on his right, and as Irvan fell back and moved up the track, he hit Kyle's rear quarter panel, which then turned Kyle's car down in front of the traffic, and once the car hit, it turned the other way, and then Mark Martin hit him, and it was a mess. Ernie wiped out the first five cars in the race.

"Ernie said, 'I was in the middle, and Kyle came down on me. It was Kyle's fault.'

"I've watched the tape over and over and over, and it just didn't appear that way to me, or to anybody else. For three months the press hounded Ernie Irvan. Anytime he was close to an accident . . . They had a wreck at Pocono. Because of what happened at Talladega, whether Pocono was his fault or not, he got blamed. 'There goes Ernie Irvan again. He's still doing it.'

"By the time the circuit got back to Talladega, NASCAR sat him down and said, 'You *will* apologize to the other drivers.' So they held a press conference—it was really the drivers' meeting, but they had cameras there—and he said, 'I have been driving over my head. I apologize.'

"What has helped Earnhardt, even though he's had all these on-the-track incidents, is that people tend to forget them quickly, because Dale is very humble, almost embarrassed about winning. Dale wants to win, but he doesn't like to stand in front of the cameras and talk about it. So the fans have been forgiving of some of the incidents.

"It's hard to compare drivers from one era to another, because the cars are different, the tracks have been resurfaced, the banks have been made higher, but in terms of driving ability I would rank Dale Earnhardt with the best four or five that have been.

"There are two classes of competitors out there: There are the racers, and there are the drivers. There are not that many racers, about 30 percent. The rest are just riding around. They think they are racing, but they are doing the best they can.

"I would put Ricky Rudd and Mark Martin in the category of racer. Bill Elliott is a racer. Dale Jarrett is becoming one. Dale Earnhardt. Richard Petty has been a racer in his day. The racers tend to win consistently. Darrell Waltrip is a racer. Kyle Petty is on the verge, or he may end up just a driver. He was really climbing, his stock looking strong, until he had a bad wreck at Talladega last year. It was an extremely painful experience for him. He got back in the car at the end of the year, long before the doctors thought he would, but I didn't see the fire that was there before he got in the wreck. Hopefully, it will come back.

"Richard hasn't won since 1984. He won two races by July that year. He won Dover and he won the Firecracker 400. In '84 and '85 Richard was driving for Mike Curb, and Robert Yates, who now owns the Davey Allison team, was the engine builder for the DiGard racing team at the time, and DiGard was selling engines on the side to Richard Petty. Bobby Allison drove for DiGard, and after the Firecracker race Allison, who hadn't won a race all year, told Robert Yates, 'I'm not going to drive anymore if you're going to sell engines to Richard.' So they quit selling engines to Richard.

"The rest of the year, Richard didn't win another race. They had an in-house engine program that was terrible. They used to joke that the space shuttle blew up because it had an engine by Curb Motorsports. In '85 Richard didn't finish many races because his engines kept blowing up.

"In '86 he went back to Level Cross and rejuvenated his Petty Enterprises team. He hired back a lot of the old people who had been working there. Prior to '84, Richard's brother, Maurice, had been his crew chief. Dale Inman had been there as well. Maurice went and did his own thing, so he wasn't with the team. Dale Inman came back, and Richard paid him real, real big money to come back, but it was kind of like the time had passed him by. The technology had changed, and they started experimenting with different kinds of suspensions and frames. For so many years they had a big advantage with horsepower—they had the Chrysler factory behind them—and back then they were able to try some off-the-wall things that worked. It wasn't that way any longer, though.

"I remember in '89 they built a car for Daytona, and the way they set up the suspension, when you went into a curve and let up off the gas, the anti-dive picked the front of the car *up*, the opposite of what normally happened to a suspension. I'm no engineer, but it didn't make any sense to me. It was a screwy setup that once had worked on one of the Plymouths in the early sixties. They decided, 'We need an advantage. Let's try this.'

"They got away from basics, tried to do too many things, and it was terrible.

"This year they are returning to the Laughlin chassis, which is what they should have been using all along. Jimmy Makar, who is our crew chief, has a philosophy that I also subscribe to: If you take what you know works and do the very best you can with it, you're going to be fine.

"But when you start going and doing weird things, it gets very difficult.

"The other thing that happened to Richard was that NASCAR instituted the carburetor restrictor plate in 1987. That came about because of an accident that Bobby Allison had at Talladega. He was doing about 210 miles an hour and he was in the middle of the dogleg on the front stretch. The car got a little loose, and he started to come around sideways, and once the car does that, it has the profile of an airplane wing. It's flat on the bottom and makes the air come over the top, so the only thing the car can do is fly. Very quickly Bobby's car got up in the air, and it tore down a lot of catch fence. A couple of spectators were hurt, none seriously, but it was a dangerous situation. If the car had gotten up in the stands, it could have killed hundreds of people.

"Rather than build stronger fences or higher walls, NASCAR decided to cut down the speed of the cars. Their solution was to cut down on horsepower. They could have mandated a taller rear spoiler, which would have created more downforce on the car and created more drag, which would have slowed the speeds and given better traction. I would have recommended that. They opted for lower horsepower.

"There are four barrels in a carburetor, and each one of the holes is almost two inches in diameter. To slow the cars down at Daytona, NASCAR made each car install a plate directly under the carburetor with four holes seven-eighths of an inch in diameter to let in the air. The plate takes a good 200 horsepower out of the motor.

"Richard's in-house engine program never got a handle on the restrictor plate problem. There are still a lot of teams that haven't. And that has really hurt Richard.

"And then there was a lot of bad luck. Back in '88 there was a tire war between Goodyear and Hoosier. On the surface you'd think, 'Great, you're going to get better tires,' but it was the worst thing that ever happened to racing. A lot of people got hurt. Richard suffered tremendously because his setup never was exactly right, and he would wear out the tires faster than anyone else. If they had stayed with Goodyear tires, they would have run and been fine. But so many times he was beat up so badly.

"I've never seen anyone in my life who can function with the amount of pain and injuries Richard can function with. Around 1976, he had a bleeding ulcer and needed an operation. Richard never told anybody about it. It hit him about halfway through the season, but he finished the season, and as soon as the season was over, he went into the hospital and had half his stomach removed. Richard used to be a real stocky guy. Now he is thin and slender, and has been since the operation.

"Richard has never had Novocain when he goes to the dentist's office. He figures if he gets Novocain to kill the pain, he won't know what the pain is and therefore might not remember to brush his teeth. He told me, 'If I can feel the pain, I'll be that much more dutiful in brushing my teeth.'

"One year at Pocono Richard broke his neck. He went to the hospital and had X rays and they told him, 'You broke your neck *again*.' He said, 'What do you mean, again?'

"Richard was in the middle of a string of 513 consecutive starts, a phenomenal record. The next weekend he went to Talladega, started the race, and got out at the first caution. He didn't want to wreck with a broken neck.

"I can remember the last bad wreck Richard was in. It was at the Daytona 500 in 1988. That was the first year they had the new Pontiac bodies, the Grand Prix. The aerodynamics were completely different from the old 2 + 2 Grand Prix. The car was a lot smaller. At the same time they put in a brand-new chassis with a three-link suspension. Richard was the first Winston Cup driver to try it.

"I don't know whether it was the combination of the chassis setup and the lack of downforce, but every time Richard would come out of turn four, the car would get real loose. And the thing that made it even worse was when a car came up behind him and got real close, that car would take the air off his rear spoiler. Instead of the air coming down the spoiler and down to the ground and pushing the car down, it would come to the spoiler and jump over the next car.

"Phil Barkdoll was right behind Richard, and I don't know whether he actually tapped Richard or was so close the car lost the air on its spoiler, but Richard's car went out from under him, and once it started to go sideways, it got air under it and began to fly.

"NASCAR mandated the mesh on the driver's side window after Richard got hurt at Darlington in 1970. He hit the wall, and the wall seemed to explode. The car went up in the air so high it tore down a telephone wire that ran across the track twenty feet above it. When the car finally came to a stop, it was upside down, and Richard's head and arm were hanging out the window. He could have been killed, but his worst injury was a dislocated shoulder. And it was captured so perfectly on film, everyone said, 'We need to do something about that. What can we do?' They came up with the safety window net.

"There are bars inside the car bracing the frame of the car now called Petty Bars, because Richard's fabrication shop was the first one to come up with that style of bracing. And once he did it, everyone saw a safety advantage and they did it too.

"If you go to Petty's Museum in Level Crossing, they have their 1970 Plymouth Superbird on display. Look at the roll bar and notice how minimally braced it is. If you want to see some older cars, Richard Childress has some old race cars at his museum in Welcome. Junior Johnson's '63 Chevy has a bucket seat and a bar around the seat. Once you got in it, you shut the door and then bolted it. How far we have come!

"It's incredible—you can go to a race, and Richard will start twenty-fifth. The first ten or twenty laps everyone watches the leaders, and by that time everyone has begun to look through the field to see what is happening, and if Richard is having a good run, all of a sudden you will hear the fans get excited. You can hear the heightening rush.

"Back in '88 the Charlotte Motor Speedway held a tribute to Richard Petty, a prerace show. They had two hundred sky divers land, and each one had the race date and place he had won stapled to their shirt. They had Governor Jim Martin, all kinds of dignitaries, and they ran them all across the stage and introduced them, and Bill Dollar, who is a local DJ on WSOC radio, had a script he read, and what happened was the most amazing thing I had ever seen.

"I hate going to the races because of the noise. My hearing is not what it used to be, and Richard has the same problem. He wears hearing aids in both ears. It's an occupational hazard. Even during prerace ceremonies there is still a lot of noise, because there are thousands of people milling around, talking. Bill Dollar began reading his script introducing the politicians, who then got up and said something about Richard. Jim Martin came forward. And when Martin began to speak, it struck me: 'I can't believe it—this place is quiet.' Every single person was sitting and listening to what Martin was saying. No politician anywhere can command that kind of respect. Most speakers get heckled, or ignored. Not this afternoon. The fans were honoring Richard, and so throughout the entire ceremony they sat quietly and listened.

"When '60 Minutes' was doing a piece on Richard Petty, we put a second seat in Richard's car and a window net on the passenger side and hooked up a radio in his helmet so Diane Sawyer could sit next to him and talk to him while he drove around the Charlotte Motor Speedway. They put three cameras in the car.

"In a piece that didn't run because she jumped to ABC soon after the taping, Diane Sawyer went around the track with Richard, and she was screaming, 'You are nuts. You are crazy. Nobody in their right mind would do this. I've been skydiving. I've been all over the world, but,' she said, 'nothing compares to this.'

"Richard said, 'Does that mean you don't want to do it anymore?'

"She said, 'No, I love it. Let's go again.' She was ecstatic.

"Before she got there, they needed somebody to test out the cameras, and I volunteered. I've been going to the races all my life. One of my very first memories is going to the races with my father. I have always been a race fan. I've done some drag racing, boat racing, raced motorcycles, been involved with NASCAR racing for ten years, so I felt that I had a pretty good idea of what it would be like to ride with Richard in that car.

"Every race fan tries to imagine it, and they say, 'I could do that. It would take a few laps to get up to speed, but I could do that.'

"I went out with Richard, and I'll tell you, in my wildest dreams I could never have come close to that. It's an incredible experience. At Charlotte it takes thirty-four seconds to go around the track. That thirty-four seconds seems like about ten. You're in the straightaway, you're in the turn, you're in the straightaway, you're in the turn. Everything happens so fast.

"You go down to the first turn, and all you can see is the track in front of you, and it looks like a wall, because it's curved up, and you're barreling down there and you think, 'We're not going to make the turn. We're going to go up over the wall and into the stands.' You start the turn and you realize it's turning, but you can't believe the tires will ever hold. You think, 'We're going to spin out. We're going to crash. I'm going to die.'

"Then once you realize the tires *will* hold, you think, 'The A-frame, the ball joints, the steering can't withstand this kind of g-forces.' But it does, and it's a real, real rush.

"We did about twelve laps, and Richard just sat there laughing, having a good time. Then it hit me. I thought to myself, 'Not only does he do this for six hundred miles, but he has to do it with forty-two other cars around him!'

"It was one of the great experiences of my lifetime.

"Going into the 1992 season, the way I see it, one of the disadvantages we are going have is that right now Chevy has a serious horsepower disadvantage versus the Ford Thunderbird.

"Back when Ford came out with the new Thunderbird in '83, NASCAR wanted more teams to use Fords. Ford had fallen by the wayside, there were only a couple Fords running, the rest were GM cars because of aerodynamics, and so NASCAR gave the Fords some advantages, let them run an inch lower than the Chevrolet Monte Carlos. The Fords had a lower rear spoiler.

"And so there were a lot of new Ford teams. Kyle Petty ran a Ford, also Buddy Baker. Bill Elliott ran away from everyone in a Ford, and halfway through the season NASCAR said, 'We'll raise the Fords a half inch and drop the Chevys a half inch,' and that will make up the difference. Because NASCAR's goal is to try to make everybody as equal as possible. They don't want Ford to win all the time, and they don't want Chevy to win all the time.

"At that point the Fords were a lot better aerodynamically, and then in 1986 the Chevrolet came out with the Monte Carlo SS Aerocoupe, which had the fastback rear window, and immediately it was a lot better than it had been, though still not as good as the Ford. And about '87, Ford came out with a new body style, which was even better than the old one, and this one ran in '87 and '88, and in '89 Ford improved itself even more, and that year Chevy came out with its Lumina, and as soon as the Luminas hit the track, everyone saw it far more aerodynamically sound than the Monte Carlo had been. Rumors were that Chevrolet had spent something like $4 million developing the Luminas for racing. I know that Richard Childress and Rick Hendrick did a lot of research and development on the car. They were testing the bodies for months before they actually raced them.

"Midway through the '89 racing season, everyone could see that the Ford was still a little superior aerodynamically to the Lumina, but not nearly as much as it had been.

"In '89 the Ford Thunderbird came out with a new body style—that year the Ford team could still run the '88's, but for the 1990 season everyone realized the new Thunderbird was too wide and too flat on the hood and as a result at high speeds the car didn't have a lot of downforce in the rear, was too loose, and was a bear to drive. It was, and is, a bad design. And so in '90 the Ford teams were saddled with it, and it hurt them. Those Thunderbirds just did not handle as well as the Luminas do.

"This is only a problem on the superspeedways, Daytona and Talladega. As far as the shorter tracks, like Charlotte, the aerodynamics don't come into play nearly as much.

"The Ford advantage for this year came about because Robert Yates, who owns Davey Allison's team, developed a new head to be used on the Ford cars. They put it on Davey's car, and they let him run it at Daytona last July, and the car ran like Jack the Bear. It was really fast. NASCAR didn't exactly give him approval for the new head, but rather looked the other way—the official line from NASCAR is otherwise, but everybody knows NASCAR wants Ford to win a manufacturer's championship. Chevrolet has won nine straight championships.

"Last year Chevrolet had the best-integrated teams. If you looked through the teams and compared them, you'd say a lot more GM teams were more cohesive than the Ford teams. For GM, Dale Earnhardt and his team have been together for a while. Ernie Irvan has a good driver, good crew chief, good engine builder, good chassis guy. For Ford, last year the Davey Allison team hired Larry McReynolds from King Racing to be crew chief. They had had a fast car, but it didn't handle right. It was a mess. After they hired McReynolds, they had an immediate improvement. They ran that new head through the rest of the year, and so did other Ford cars, and you could watch as each one of the Ford teams got it—Jack Roush and Mark Martin, and then the Wood Brothers with Dale Jarrett. At the beginning of the season Davey Allison was the only one who qualified well, and a couple weeks later Mark Martin was markedly improved, and then it was Dale Jarrett. For half a season Alan Kulwicki couldn't run a lick, and when he got the head, boom, he was up there sitting on the pole.

''Ford's improvement involved the design by Robert Yates and the work done by a fellow with an awful lot of computer expertise by the name of Sam Conway. The head porter had been the guy who takes a brand-new set of heads and sits there with a head grinder and grinds the head—smooths it out, making the air that goes through it the most free-flowing and efficient. The rougher it is, the more turbulence. The head porter must smooth it up and take out the bends and create the most efficient curves. It's real complicated.

''The head and the intake manifold determine how much air and fuel can go through the engine. An internal-combustion engine is nothing more than an air pump. You pump air in, and it goes out. The rushing air mixes with the fuel in the carburetor. The more air and fuel you can put in there, the more horsepower you're going to make.

''For years the head porter has been a key guy, but now there are digitized computerized milling machines that can mill on a five-axis radius. You can take your best port in a head, and a computer can read it and duplicate that port from one head to another. And this will give you a phenomenal increase in horsepower.

''At the end of the season NASCAR said, 'The new head is officially approved.' Well, they had been running all year long. So there is a concerted effort to be sure that Ford wins. NASCAR has done everything to see that that happens.

''I know a guy who has been working with Robert Yates developing the head, and he's seen engines on the dyno at 725 horsepower—that's an incredible amount of horsepower, when you figure it's 358 cubic inches, they run a single four-barrel carburetor, and it burns gasoline from the pump. No exotic racing fuel. No fuel injection. Incredible! What Ford is accomplishing with its engine is absolutely phenomenal.

"Right now, the Fords are at 725 horsepower, and the Chevrolet is at 685 with the new 18-degree head, which the Chevys have to run halfway through the '92 season, a different design, so we'll see. It will be three or four months before Chevy really gets that head developed. They think they can get up to 700 horsepower, which will still leave us 25 horsepower short of Ford if Davey doesn't pick up some more someplace.

"I've been in racing long enough to know that advantages aren't forever. NASCAR always sees to that."

LAP 15

Dave Marcis

Racing on a Shoestring

There is a disappearing cadre of old-timers—longtime independent owner-operators struggling to stay in the stock car racing business, drivers of junkyard specials who manage to break even just by finishing. Three who survive are Dave Marcis, Jimmy Means, and James Hylton, racers who once were competitive but who no longer can run up front as sponsors overlook them while pouring more and more money into the coffers of their competitors.

Compounding their difficult position is the fact that these independents have long labored under the disadvantage of having to compete with little money, and as a result of their years of back-in-the-pack finishes—owing to inferior parts or a small labor force—sponsors are wary of their ever being able to run up front again. It is a vicious cycle that many believe will soon lead to their extinction.

Unlike Joe Gibbs, whose stature as an NFL coaching superstar enabled him to enter NASCAR racing and attract a multimillion-dollar sponsor right away, Dave Marcis, Jimmy Means, James Hylton, and J. D. McDuffie struggled for years without attracting major sponsorship. Means had Alka-Seltzer for a little while and Marcis had Big Apple Markets, but compared to the major teams, the money was small.

Means, called The Last Guy, is an optimist. "You never know," he says, "maybe one day I'll get a lucky break."

One independent who didn't survive running used parts at high speeds was the cigar-smoking J. D. McDuffie, a lovable, sweet man who couldn't walk away from the smell of the gas and the roar of the track. McDuffie got by on secondhand parts and once-run tires, until the race at Watkins Glen in August 1991 when his used parts failed, his car flipped, and he was killed.

Dave Marcis

The accident occurred on only the fourth lap of the race. When McDuffie's car lost a tire and his brakes, McDuffie careened into Jimmy Means and the cars went out of control.

McDuffie and Means both skidded low on the grass, with Means on the outside. Means could slow himself because he had four tires and brakes. But JD was at the mercy of fate, and he hit the tire wall, flipped, and landed on top of a guardrail, which went through the roof of the car and struck his head.

Jimmy Means, his car coming to rest not far from JD, could see that his friend was not moving. He rushed to the car. Blood was everywhere. Frantically, Means signaled for an ambulance, but it was too late.

Going into 1992, Jimmy Means sought to induce someone to drive for him. But even that would not be easy, because the drivers were suspicious of just how limited a budget Means has.

Independents in Winston Cup racing are going the way of the covered wagon and the propeller plane.

During a time when Hendrick Motorsports ponders spending $500,000 for a computer to port heads, Dave Marcis doesn't know where he's going to get the money to buy tires.

As the 1992 season approached, Dave Marcis, fifty-one, was worried. Racing had been his entire life, and the escalating costs of running a team were threatening to put him out of business if he isn't able to attract a sponsor. It was November, three months before the 1992 Daytona 500, and he hadn't had even a nibble.

As corporate image becomes more and more important in a sport that no longer is the domain of carousers and roughnecks, corporations are looking for the *Gentleman's Quarterly* look: young, sexy, and handsome driver/spokesmen like Michael Waltrip, Kyle Petty, Rusty Wallace, and Ricky Rudd.

And so the grizzled veterans are being passed over by Corporate America.

"All I want is a chance," said Marcis. "I can be a spokesman as well as any one of the other drivers."

For his entire career, with only a few years as exceptions, Dave Marcis has competed on a shoestring. But if the economics continue as they seem to be going, it appears the time is coming soon when the unsponsored independent drivers, the colorful underdogs of racing, will no longer be able to afford to compete. The sport will be much the poorer for it.

DAVE MARCIS: "I was seven or eight when I first became interested in auto racing. I read the hot rod magazines. My dad had a garage and wrecking yard, so I was around automobiles. He had a surplus of cars, so I got monkeying and tinkering with cars at a pretty early age. My brother and I would get cars he bought for the wrecking yard, and we would tear around in the field with them, bang them up or roll them over and crash them.

"We were on a farm near Wausau, Wisconsin, and there was a lane where cattle walked between two fields to go out to the pasture and graze, and I would estimate that distance as about a half mile, and we would run them cars up there, and there was a rock pile off the end of that lane in that field, and we would run them cars up that lane wide over and get in that field and turn them sideways and slide them up against the rock pile and roll them over. This was around 1954, when I was fourteen.

"There were a lot of dirt tracks—Schofield; the Fairgrounds; I can't remember some of the names of the little places around there—and I would attend those events on the weekends. I'd ride my bicycle as far as twenty miles to get there and climb up a big pine tree out in the woods outside the track and watch the event, because I didn't have any money to get in. And then I'd pedal back home after the races.

"I began driving in Wausau in 1958. Racing had left the area, and some of the people who had been involved in it wanted to get it going again, and they put an ad in the newspaper telling anyone who was interested to show up at the local bowling alley and tavern. I went, and at that meeting they discussed renting one of the racetracks, Red Mountain. They were trying to form a club to come up with the money to rent the track and get a PA system.

"If you joined right there, one of the advantages was to get a low number, and so I joined right there. The cost was $90, which was a lot of money at that time. I gave them fifteen bucks that night, and I made the commitment to join and pay them off.

"I got a '49 Ford and took off the front fenders. I didn't know much about cars at the time, and I was afraid to cut any of the electrical wiring in case the car wouldn't run, so I pulled all the wires loose and tied them into a big glob just hanging there. I put a roll bar in it, took the gas tank off, and put a five-gallon pail up in the back window, which was dangerous as hell. Back then we didn't know. And we started racing.

"That first race another fellow and I got together, and he rolled over into a pond that was there, and I rolled onto the outside of the racetrack. We took our mess home and fixed it up and brought it back the next week and just kept trying each week.

"One good thing about it was the majority of us had no experience. Most everyone started on the same rung.

"I looked in them hot rod magazines, and they would cover the events being run in the South, and I would always try to find out the size of the tracks and how fast the cars were running, in order to compare how I was doing. As near as I could tell, based on the times in the magazines, I felt I could be fairly competitive, and then in 1964 a friend and myself went down to Daytona, a last-minute deal.

"He had a gas station, and I had a tavern. He closed his gas station one night and came into the tavern. I said to him, 'Let's go to Daytona.' He said, 'Let's go. When do you want to leave?' I said, 'Right now.' I closed the tavern at one o'clock. He called his wife, and she came and got his receipts from the cash register and took them home, and he and I left from the tavern and drove to Daytona.

"We didn't have any money in our pocket hardly and didn't stay in any motels. We slept in the car. We watched the race. I remember Richard Petty was leading the whole race. That's when they first came with the Chrysler hemi, and he was really dominant. He just blew everybody away.

"I really got the bug then. I came back home to try to figure out what I could do to get down here and race.

"I bought a car. It was an ex–Fred Lorenzen car built for Ford Motor Company by Holman-Moody. The car was passed down to Iggy Katona, who ran it in ARCA, and for $2,000 I bought it from a fellow from Kentucky named Alvin Perry. Charlie Glotzbach had been driving it for him.

"I worked on that car for a couple of months, cleaning it up and taking all the paint off and stripping it and repainting it. It was Labor Day Weekend. I took it to the Minnesota State Fair for an IMCA race, my first time on a half-mile track—paved, three hundred laps. I finished second on Saturday, and on Sunday I entered the North Star 500, a 500-lapper, and finished third. I won more money that weekend than I had paid for the car.

"I next tried a USAC race in Milwaukee, and the engine blew up. I had no money to fix another engine, so the car sat around the rest of the summer. That fall I borrowed an engine from Ernie Tuff of Rushford, Minnesota, and I went to the Charlotte Speedway with it, myself and Dick Trickle.

"I called Norris Friel, who was a NASCAR inspector, and told him about the car and asked him if it would be eligible for competition, and he said he knew the car, said it was a good car and it would pass inspection and there would be no problem.

"Well, when I got to Charlotte it was a different deal. He found so many things wrong with the car that there was no way I could ever get it fixed up in time for the race.

"Trickle was wanting to do it, but I didn't think we could get it done, so we didn't. We had to go back to see Richard Howard, who was the promoter at that time of the Charlotte Motor Speedway, and he gave me $150 for gas to get back home.

"NASCAR was having a Sportsman race that fall at Atlanta, and I thought if we could get the work done, we'd go there.

"We were the first car to the racetrack at Atlanta, and they still picked us apart pretty bad. We spent two days working on the car. Pete Keller was the chief inspector there, and he kept us working on the car until Friday afternoon, about one hour before the end of qualifying.

"We got on the racetrack with maybe fifteen minutes to practice, and I had to qualify.

"I said to Tiny Lund, 'I have never been around a racetrack like this. I have to try to qualify. What do I need to do? Can you give me any pointers?'

"He said, 'There is a bad bump between one and two. Just drive the car in the corner until you hit that bump with the front wheels and then back off the throttle, and when you get to it with the rear wheels, get back in it. You can drive the car that deep without getting in trouble.'

"Well, I made her to the bump, and when I hit her, I got out of shape, and I gathered it all back up and about tore the wall down, but I made it. I qualified. I started about thirty-third, and I ran the whole race and finished. That was an accomplishment.

"After that, I decided to switch to Chevrolets. I wasn't that high on Fords. I was always a Chevrolet man, so a friend of mine, Larry Wehrs, from Wehrs Chevrolet Sales in Bangor, Wisconsin, bought a Chevrolet Chevelle from Don Beiderman, who was racing in Canada at the time, for me to race. We had to go to Henley Gray's place in Rome, Georgia, to get it.

"Larry was one of the first sponsors I had. When we made the deal I was supposed to pay him back from my winnings, but every time I tried to give him some money, he would never take it. He'd say, 'Let's order some better parts so we can run better.'

"We had also bought a new '68 Chevrolet that we were going to build into a race car. It had a 427 in it, but the car didn't arrive in time for the Daytona 500, so when the new car finally arrived, we took the engine out of it and put it into the Chevelle and took it to Daytona and entered the ARCA race, which was shorter and less competitive and didn't take as much money to get into as the Daytona 500.

"Just going to Daytona and driving through the tunnel and looking at the racetrack—I was used to going on a quarter-mile track, and when I saw it, my first thoughts were, 'Holy man, what the hell am I doing here?' But once I got on it and got going, it was all right and comfortable.

"We finished ninth, which was quite a thrill.

"After the ARCA show at Daytona in '67, I ran four or five more races in the South, and in '68 I ran seven races and ran quite well in some of them. I finished twentieth in the Daytona 500 that year. Then in '69 I came down here to North Carolina to race full-time. I moved to Arden, in the mountains near Asheville. Cecil Gordon and Bill Seifert, who were racing NASCAR at the time, knew of a shop up here I could rent. They knew a couple boys who helped me in the pits, and one of them boys had an aunt that had a place where a trailer house could be parked. I had been living in a trailer house in Wisconsin.

"We paid $60 a month for the shop and we went and talked to this fellow's aunt about parking the house trailer there, and it turned out she wanted someone there so she could feel safer, and it all fell into place.

"I started the 1969 season running Chevys. In my first race, in Montgomery, I finished tenth, then at Daytona in the qualifier finished twenty-first, but in the 500 finished seventeenth.

"I've kept my ledgers over the years, so I can tell you exactly what everything cost, and how much I won. Let's see, the entry fee and pit passes at Daytona in 1969 were $120. The motor bill was $268.94. I sent a telegram Western Union for $5.76. The gas and oil to get to Daytona and back was $225.74. Food was $321. Parts was $169, tolls $12. It cost $25 to letter the car. I paid Goodyear $156.80 for four tires, minus a $60 credit for four casings I turned in. We bought five more tires from Firestone—I don't know why, I guess they were available—paid $155.63 plus tax of $38.91 for a total of $194.54.

"In February 1969 I won $500 in the ARCA 300 and $2,045 in the Daytona 500. In the 125-mile qualifier I won $215 for a total winnings of $2,760. We were on our way. That year we earned $30,899.11 and made a profit running against factory cars. It's nothing like that anymore.

"I had decided to switch to Chrysler products for the 1969 season, and it turned out Tom Ingram, who had an engine shop in Asheville, had experience on Chrysler hemi engines, and that fell into place, too. I was going to be running Chrysler Corporation cars because the gentleman who was sponsoring me at the time, Milt Lunda, made a deal to buy out the race team of A. J. King Enterprises of Sevierville, Tennessee, buy his cars, trucks, and all the extra engines, and King had been running Dodges.

"The second race in that Dodge was at Bristol, where I finished sixth.

I was running against the name drivers—Richard Petty, David Pearson, Lee Roy Yarbrough, Cale Yarborough, Tiny Lund, Pete Hamilton, Bobby Allison—and holding my own.

"Richard Petty was my idol before I came to North Carolina, because I was reading about him in my hot rod magazines. He was superior, did a good job, but his equipment made him superior too, and the amount of money he had to work with. I may have been able to have been as superior at that time had I had all that equipment and money too. I think we did real well for what we had.

"What separated Richard Petty from everyone else was money. He had all of Chrysler's expertise behind him, always had new parts for every race. The Pettys had a good fleet of race cars, a lot of help, a lot of money, and the Chrysler Corporation. Bobby Allison was Chrysler. David Pearson had Ford Motor Company. Lee Roy Yarbrough was Ford, Cale was Ford. There was no Chevrolet competition at the time. Anybody who had a Chevrolet at that time was an individual, did it on his own, like I was with my Dodge. We were running our car on our own budget, with no factory support.

"At that time I didn't try to get factory support because I didn't know anybody, didn't really know who to talk to. I was a one-man, really a two-man show, and I didn't have a lot of time to talk to people about things like that. I guess I didn't know what was going on around me in the rest of the world. I was at the racetrack, at the shop, at the racetrack, on the road, and that was it—work, work, work, work, work. That's all there was.

"Once I started racing, I was competitive. In 1970 I finished in the top five seven times and the top ten fifteen times. I finished ninth in the point standings. From the beginning, to this day, my philosophy has always been to run my equipment as hard as it could run, whether it was capable or not, whether it was going to break down because I overran it or not. I just tried to finish as best I could. I always tried to get in front. Even when I finished seventh or fifth or second, I wasn't happy. I was always trying to do better.

"I never considered saving the car by driving more cautiously. I probably should have done that on more occasions, and maybe I would have ended up making more money, but if I had done that I would not have the reputation I have of getting the most out of what I have to work with, of not stroking. Plenty of drivers had the reputation of just being strokers, just start and finish, no matter where. I came to race.

"In 1971 at Talladega, Bobby Isaac was driving for Harry Hyde in the K&K Insurance Dodge. Bobby had a kidney problem and ended up in the hospital. It was questionable whether Bobby would get out of the hospital in time for the race, and Harry Hyde needed someone in the race car, so a few days before the race he asked me if I would take the car out for a couple laps of practice in case I had to drive it.

"I did, and Sunday morning, Harry said, 'Bobby isn't going to make it. You need to drive.' I put Bill Seifert in my car and drove Harry Hyde's car.

"I led a whole big bunch of the race, and with six laps remaining was in the lead, a substantial lead, and coming off the fourth turn the car burned a bearing, blew an engine, and caught fire, and we slid down the whole front straightaway and ended up way down in the first turn and lost the race. Had that not happened, I feel certain we would have won the race, because we had been leading for quite some time.

"The oil pressure had been fluctuating, and before our last pit stop, I told them over the radio about the fluctuating oil pressure, but when we pitted, we didn't add oil. Had we done that, maybe we would have won the race. I don't know.

"It would have been my first big win, so that kind of bothered me, but it was only a one-race deal. It's part of racing. You have to go back home and get to work on your own stuff.

"Jump ahead to 1974. Buddy Baker replaced Bobby Isaac in the K&K Dodge, and for whatever reason in '74, Nord Krauskopf, who owned the car, decided to run a restricted schedule and Buddy wanted to run all the races, so Harry Hyde called me and asked me to run the car at Charlotte and Rockingham, two fall races, with the understanding they were evaluating whether they were going to get in full-time or get out of the business, with the possibility of my driving for them in '75.

"I put Dick Trickle in my car. I was having a very successful year, but the advantage for me driving for K&K was that I had a chance to make some real money. It was taking everything I earned to race the next week. We were short-staffed, ran the engines two and three races, and I didn't have any money. It was an opportunity to get in a race car where all I had to do was concentrate on driving.

"I was in Wisconsin at Christmas 1974 when his crew chief, Harry Hyde, called me. He said, 'We're going to race, and Nord wants you to drive the car next year.' So I drove for K&K in 1975 and 1976.

"In 1975 I finished second in the points standings to Richard Petty. In thirty races, I won Martinsville, and I had sixteen top five finishes. In '76 I was sixth with three wins and sixteen top-ten finishes.

"Those were memorable years. At Martinsville, in the fall of '75, we qualified right up front, and we were very competitive all day long. We didn't luck into it; we earned it. We led the last forty laps and won the event. In '76 we won Talladega in August and Atlanta in November, two 500-mile races.

"At Talladega it didn't appear to me we were fast enough to win the pole. At that time we had a very minimum amount of rear spoiler, which could have been a half-inch high on the deck of that '74 Dodge. I told Harry Hyde, 'If you take that off, we can win the pole.' He said, 'You can't drive the car without it.' I said, 'I think I can. The hardest thing at Talladega is getting through the tri-oval. It's wide enough that if I get against the wall of the fourth turn and cut across on an angle and get to the apron in the middle of the tri-oval, I can end up at the wall at the flagstand. I think I can make it.'

"He said, 'I'm telling you, Dave Marcis, you can't drive the race car without the goddamn spoiler on it,' and I said, 'I'm telling you we're not going to win the pole if we don't do it. And I want to sit on the pole.'

"It was lunch-break time then, and he went away from lunch, and when he came back, I guess he had been thinking about it, and he came up to me and said, 'I'll tell you something, Dave Marcis.' I said, 'What's that?' He said, 'You know when Columbus took off, he didn't know where he was going to land either? If you want to take the spoiler off the race car, I'll do it.' He threw his hands up in the air and said, 'I'll do it, but I'm telling you, I don't think you can drive the car that way.'

"The car felt good in the first and second turns. I saw 100 rpms more on the tachometer down the backstretch than I had in practice. If your car is really going good on the entrance to the third turn at Talladega, you gain rpms, and I gained another 50 rpms, and I said to myself, 'Hell, I'll win this damn pole. I just got to get through the tri-oval.' And I quit worrying about it and put my concentration on what I was going to be doing in that tri-oval, and I got right against the wall coming up out of the late exit of the fourth turn and just cut her on the angle across that tri-oval and hit the apron about halfway through there, and the car bounced up a little bit, but I held on and just barely made the pole. Just barely. David Pearson was behind me.

"I never had any differences with David Pearson in my whole racing career. We raced hard together, side by side, in those days when I was competitive. We were always good friends.

"David was a little quiet. He never said a lot to many people. He was always polite, friendly, a good guy to race against. He would never get you in a bad position. If you were racing him and you came up in traffic and he had the chance to cut you short, hang you out, get you in a dangerous situation, in most cases he would back off or give you the hole and pass you back the next lap. He had the car to do that.

"My other win in '76 was at Atlanta. All day I raced David Pearson, who was pretty dominant there.

"In the fall of '76 Nord Krauskopf sold the K&K team to Jim Stacy. I didn't even know it was happening. Then bango, it happened. Nord just said it was too much of a hassle, fighting with NASCAR all the time. Stacy and Neil Bonnett were big buddies, and so Neil got in the car and I was out. I was back on my own.

"In '77 I drove some races for Roger Penske. That worked very well, but Roger ran a limited number of races, and I wanted to run them all. I ran twelve shows for Roger, and Roger let me use the car to run the other shows myself. My people worked on the car for those races, and Roger even helped me with the tires, and he gave me all the prize money. Roger Penske treated me better than anyone since I've been in racing. When I went to work for him, I was on salary, got paid commission and expenses, and it was the best I was ever treated. It's just he didn't run all the events. Being based where he was way up in Pennsylvania, he wasn't geared to run all the NASCAR races and be competitive. His main goal always was to be competitive, and he just didn't feel we were ready.

"In the fall after the '77 season Rod Osterlund bought out the equipment from Penske, through me. Roger was getting out of NASCAR racing, and I had first opportunity to buy the car and equipment if I could come up with someone to put up the money. Another team had offered him more money, but Penske was the type of person who kept his word, and I arranged for Osterlund to buy him out, and I drove.

"It seemed a good venture when it started. He offered me a flat fee of $6,500 a month to drive for him, a total of about $40,000, but in 1978 I finished fifth in the driver standings, just ahead of Richard Petty, finished in the top ten twenty-four races out of thirty, and won $200,000. I should have gotten 50 percent of that, so I really didn't get a fair shake. But at the time it was okay, because I felt we were building the team and getting it going, and I was looking forward to the '79 season. But it didn't turn out that way.

"What it boiled down to was: Roland Wolodyka was a key person working for Osterlund who unbeknownst to me wanted to get rid of me and my crew chief, Dewey Livengood, who was doing an excellent job, was very devoted. Dewey drove from High Point to Charlotte every day of the week, and he was the one who was due the credit for that car being as competitive as it was.

"But on a Tuesday night before the October Rockingham race, out of the clear blue, for no reason whatsoever, Roland fired Dewey.

"Osterlund had always told me that we didn't have any problems because a problem was only a phone call away to get it straightened out, so I called him, and he wouldn't accept my phone call. I kept trying to call him, and this went on for several days, and I never did get him. If you have a reason, you should be able to tell somebody the reason. And when they won't even accept my phone calls, and I was the driver, obviously they had no reason. As far as I was concerned, it was a dirty deal, and they didn't want to talk about it.

"I went to Rockingham and ran the race, and he showed up and wasn't very friendly, didn't even speak to me.

"I felt very bad that they fired Dewey. I didn't have a problem with their firing him, but not the way they did it and not when they did it. There were only three races remaining on the schedule, and they could have kept him around to the end of the year and taken care of him properly for the work he had put in that year. If they had not had him back the next year, that would have been their business. But to call a man on Tuesday night to tell him he was fired without him even being aware something was wrong, and considering we were in a position to win the championship—we were second in points at that time with three races remaining.

"I didn't have any enthusiasm after that. So the next race we went to Atlanta, and after we qualified that day, I made up my mind I was going to quit. I went over to the pressroom and called the press together and told them I was quitting. And everybody was shocked, because it was such a good year.

"I didn't think firing Dewey was right, and still don't, and that's why I quit.

"I ran Atlanta. Could have won the race, should have, and would have won the race if I had been driving for them the next year. I had the best car there, I led a bunch of the race, led right up to the very end, led the white flap lap, and I, uh, just didn't have my heart in it. I just didn't feel like I needed to win the race for Osterlund or put him on the NASCAR winner's circle. I knew I was leaving him, and I didn't do my best on that last lap. Richard Petty beat me to the start-finish line by two inches.

"And then they ended up giving the race to Donnie Allison, whom Richard and I both thought was a lap down. And that wasn't announced until the next day, so I actually ended up third. So I thought Richard had won and I was second, but anyway, I had a bad taste in my mouth for them treating Dewey the way they did, I didn't think it was right, because

Dewey was a super employee and an honest person, and it hurt me as bad as it did Dewey for what they did to him. Because I don't believe in doing things that way. I've always been honest and outspoken, but I say what I think, and so it costs me. I've just never been a good politician at playing politics with these rides. So in '79 I was back on my own. Osterlund got Dale Earnhardt in his car and was successful, until everything fell apart. He was out of the sport and tried to come back into the sport two years ago and didn't make it. He tried hiring me back last fall. He offered me $150,000 to come to work for him. But I'm not interested. I don't think what he did to Dewey was right.

"Dewey went to work for me after that, built engines for my Dodge, crew-chiefed for me, and even though we were on a limited budget, we were successful. Then around 1982 Dewey went to work for Billy Hagan, and has been with him ever since. He's been their head engine builder, and the middle of the '91 season he was promoted to crew chief. Terry Labonte is his driver.

"Since I left Osterlund, it's been a tough, rough road. In the mid-eighties the cost of running a race team began to spiral up, and it's just kept getting worse since. Part of the problem is they pass a rule like the restrictor plate rule, which is a good rule, but then they let you work on the intake manifolds to overcome it. And that's costly. If you're going to have a rule to slow the cars, why not enforce it and keep them slowed down? Why let car owners spend hundreds of thousands of dollars to try to beat the rule? An intake manifold should be stock, nothing done to it, and the restrictor plate should sit on top of it. Period. But that's not how it is, and so the teams with money spend hundreds of thousands of dollars looking for more horsepower that way.

"This has been very costly to small teams, and now the economy is in bad shape, and teams are losing sponsors. NASCAR has got to do something to reduce the costs. I've told Billy France, Les Richter, Dick Beaty, Bill Gazaway, they are all welcome to come here and look at my books and I could show them what it costs, month by month, to stay in business.

"For me, I have a pretty good supply of race cars, so my big expense is engines. I have a payroll of four or five people, lights, insurance, and you're not going to stay in business for much less than $15,000 to $20,000 per month, and that's not talking the race months like May, June, and July when you're going to double that figure. By the same token, plenty of teams tell you they spend $50,000 to $60,000 a race. We can get by on $25,000.

"In order to survive, I can't afford to overinflate my payroll. My people don't make what they could at other teams, but when we have a good month, I give them a bonus. I try to be fair about that. I try to treat my people right.

"Last year we had a pretty rough year. We had problems with thirteen engines. We had five or six wrecks that tore up the race car. We finished twenty-ninth in the driver point standings, thirty-second in owner points standings. We're in rough shape at this moment.

"The purses are way too small. The minimum purse for last place in any event today should be $10,000, and it's around $2,000. Two thousand dollars will not buy enough tires to get you qualified hardly. The tires now cost $1,000 a set, and you must have a set to practice on and one to qualify on. And then there are the motel, food, and gas expenses.

"As far as attracting a sponsor, how do you talk someone into giving you two million dollars, or one million? It's based on the ability of the driver to be a good spokesman and the success of the team, the likelihood of it remaining competitive. It's getting to the point where you don't have to be a good racer anymore as long as you're a good spokesman or a good politician. I still maintain it takes racers to put on a good show and be competitive that puts people in the stands.

"As for our record, it's been up and down, no consistency, and it's hard to get someone to commit millions of dollars for an inconsistent team.

"We have seven race cars and a nice shop, and it's all owned and paid for. In the fall of '65 I bought a trailer home, and I moved it from Wisconsin to North Carolina in '69, and we lived in that trailer home until November 1990, when we finally built a house for ourselves. But before we could get a house, my wife and I both realized the need for a shop for the race team, because if we didn't have a respectable place of business, it was going to be very hard to get a sponsor. So you can see we're not going to use a sponsor's money to set ourselves up in business. Sponsors should look at people who are involved in the racing business for a living and who have been at it and established, not to set up new teams.

"In 1990 Mike Miller, from the Big Apple Markets, came to me at Daytona and said he wanted to help us, and it started as a one-race venture, and then another race, and he said, 'What would it take to do this all year?' I came up with a figure of $400,000 to do a season. We *can* get by on that, but it's rough.

"They sponsored us the last two years, but going into the 1992 season, Mike said Big Apple only wanted to be an associate sponsor. We have sent out some proposals, and NASCAR is trying to help me. And I appreciate what they are trying to do for me. I mean, over the years there have been times when I have not spoken good about them, but anything I have ever said has been the truth, and they know it, and I know it, and everybody knows it. You're supposed to be up-front and straightforward and tell the truth. That's my philosophy. I am trying to get NASCAR to change and make it better for everyone in the sport. I praise them for getting racing to where it's at today. It's just they have to find ways to keep the costs down, and I think they are taking steps to do that.

"Having a smaller, leaner budget means we don't get to test as much as other teams. We can't afford to spend $20,000 on an experimental engine. We have to spend the money on a piece I *know* will run. We don't have the opportunity to go into a wind tunnel and test our bodies, so I know we're hurting there. We need more people. We have four and need six or seven. All these areas add up, especially on race day, though I still run the car as hard as it will go and hope my guys can make a great pit stop when I get there.

"Right now I'm preparing for the 1992 Daytona 500. I have allotted money in my budget to go to Daytona, with or without a sponsor. It's been rough.

"Last year at Daytona we started as a provisional starter at the back of the field. We were running great in the race. After one of the restarts early in the race, we were running fourth or fifth, and on the restart I missed a shift. I wanted to go from second gear to third, but somehow got the transmission into low and overrevved the engine and floated all the valves and spun down through the infield grass.

"We were running good. We were very competitive. I'll tell you what—if that hadn't happened, we were looking for a top five."

LAP 16

Waddell Wilson

Breaking the 200-MPH Barrier

Ever since getting his first job with Holman-Moody as an engine builder in 1963, Waddell Wilson has earned a reputation for being tops in his field. Cars he built for Holman-Moody won Daytona 500s for Fireball Roberts and Fred Lorenzen, and David Pearson won two driving championships driving cars with Wilson-made engines.

In 1975 Benny Parsons won the Daytona 500 with an engine built by Wilson for L. G. DeWitt. Three years later Harry Ranier hired Wilson and elevated him to crew chief status. Wilson was crew chief for such Ranier drivers as Buddy Baker, Bobby Allison, Benny Parsons, and Cale Yarborough, who knew that with the demanding, hardworking Wilson at the helm the car would run fast and long.

When Buddy Baker won the Daytona 500 in 1980, he told reporters, "No one could touch me. Waddell Wilson is the true reason that race car won today."

In 1982, when Wilson and Parsons were reunited on the Ranier team, Parsons became the first driver to break 200 miles an hour during a qualifying heat, a feat accomplished at Talladega.

Said Benny after his run, "I had heard jet planes fly over and make a sonic boom. As I was going around, I was waiting for the boom. It just didn't come."

Cale Yarborough became the first driver to qualify at over 200 miles an hour at Daytona, a feat accomplished in Wilson's car in 1984. Cale also went on to win the Daytona 500 that year. It was Waddell Wilson's fourth Daytona 500 victory.

Rick Hendrick, a man with the reputation for hiring the best, hired Waddell Wilson in 1987. Hendrick united Wilson and close friend Darrell Waltrip to form what observers labeled the Dream Team. But in racing, as in any team sport, putting two stars together doesn't guarantee success. A disastrous relationship followed. Waltrip went off to start his own team, and Wilson became crew chief for Ricky Rudd.

Today Wilson is head of research and development for the Hendrick racing machine. One of the legends of the sport, Waddell Wilson has built winning race cars for close to thirty years. So long as Wilson builds engines for Rick Hendrick, their cars will always be competitive.

WADDELL WILSON: "At the end of '74 I was working for L. G. DeWitt, a self-made millionaire, building engines for Benny Parsons full-time. LG was common and nice. You talk about a fairy tale come true, this was one:

"At the end of '74, the race team was broke. LG went to Daytona and borrowed money from Bill France—LG had money, but he wanted the team to stand on its own feet.

"We took everything we had left—cars, engines, used parts—and I was able to build an engine with used pieces, and then LG had someone in California get him a set of pistons with which to build a second engine. I told him, 'These pistons are for drag racing, and I don't think they will work in this engine, but I'd be willing to give it a try.'

"We went to Daytona with the first engine I built, and we practiced it, qualified, and then after we got through practicing and qualifying, we figured we'd take that engine out and put in the other one to run the 125 miles, saving the first engine for the 500.

"We put that second engine in, and it didn't even make two laps before the pistons seized up. We had to take it out and put the old engine in. It was all we had.

"The small-block engines had come in in '74, and so we had only a year's experience with them. They were still very fragile, and we were having trouble with the cylinder head, just numerous problems with the engines.

"Before we started the '75 Daytona 500, I tuned the engine as best I knew how, making sure the valves were adjusted just right, that everything was as good as I could possibly make it, in order to try to put a Band-Aid on the engine to where it would hopefully make it.

"At the end of the race Benny, David Pearson, and Ramo Stott were running in the lead lap. I just knew Pearson was going to win the race, from working with him and knowing how good he was. David was driving the Wood Brothers Mercury.

"But with two and a half laps to go, Pearson and Cale Yarborough came together in one and two, sending Pearson spinning. That put us in the lead, and we won the race.

"I would have bet my life we never would have won that race, but we did! We won the Daytona 500!

"And I remember that Benny couldn't believe it. Benny called it 'the biggest day of my life.' L. G. DeWitt was hysterical, beside himself, that we had pulled it off.

"In '75, '76, and '77 we had good seasons with Benny, who was one of the smooth drivers. He was one of the best people you could ever work with. He was probably too nice for his own good.

In '78 I left LG because the commute was killing me. His shop was in Rockingham, and the first year I lived down there but I didn't like it so I moved back to Lake Norman, north of Charlotte, and it was a two-hour one-way trip.

"In the middle of '77 I told Mr. DeWitt, 'I can't take this trip any longer. Back and forth every day is more than I can take.' That morning he sat down on a box of pistons and two hours later talked me out of quitting. I told him, 'At the end of the season I'm going to leave you, but until then, I'll give it all I have.' That was a handshake. And that's all you needed back then.

"At the end of the season we ran Ontario, and he went too, and on the plane he talked to me all the way out there and all the way back, but I wouldn't give in. He wanted to get me an airplane so I could fly back and forth each day, but I was thinking of the weather and the expense, and I didn't want to put him to that. It was too much.

"In 1978 I went to work for Harry Ranier, a coal miner out of Kentucky. Harry was an incredible man to work for. Whatever he told you he would do, he'd double that. He was so good to his people. He always took care of them. He worried about his people, and that was why he was so successful with his race team.

"Herb Nab was the crew chief, Lenny Pond the driver. That year we sat on five poles. At Talladega amid rumors Harry Ranier was going to replace Lenny in the car, we qualified fourth in an Oldsmobile, and with five laps to go, Lenny took the lead and beat Donnie Allison. That day we averaged 174.700 miles an hour, a record for a superspeedway.

"At the end of '78 Harry hired Buddy Baker to drive the car. At the same time Harry made me the crew chief. It was not a job I was looking for. I was content building engines and taking care of that aspect of it. When he called and told me, that was the last thing I dreamed he'd put me doing.

"At Daytona in '79, Buddy sat on the pole after setting a track record of 198.049. We won the Busch race. We won the 125. In the 500 we had an ignition problem early in the race and fell out.

"That year we sat on the pole at the Texas World Speedway, ran third, and won at Michigan, Martinsville, and Talladega.

"In '80 we went back to Daytona. The winter before I worked night and day, seven days a week on that engine. I took it apart five times. As for the body, at the end of '79 we lost the Charlotte race because the crew put the sheet metal on the car too high, messed up the race car. I told the guys I didn't need them anymore, and I had one man, Bob Sweetack, help me that winter with the car. I had him fix the car the way I wanted.

"At that time to fix it the way I wanted it, the cost was $10,000, which was a lot of money then.

"I remember when we went to Daytona in '80, I had the bill, but I didn't tell Harry Ranier that I spent $10,000 on that race car. I was scared he would fire me. That was another reason I made sure the car would run good.

"We sat on the pole, won the 125-miler, and at the Daytona 500 it came down to the latter part of the race. We needed a can of gas, and the way I had it calculated, we needed a *full* can of gas.

"I knew Bobby Allison was in Bud Moore's Mercury. Bobby was so good at Daytona and Talladega. I had worked with him in the past, and I knew how good he was, and there were a couple other cars still running with us—but we were leading the pack.

"When I told Buddy to pit, he came in. I knew how hyper Buddy Baker was, how badly he wanted to win that Daytona 500. When he came down pit road to get the gas, I reached into the window net when the car stopped and grabbed ahold of Baker, because I knew he would leave early if I didn't.

"I told the crew, 'Signal when you get the can. We need a *full* can of gas.'

"Well, sure enough, before I ever told him to go, I could see him putting that car in first gear, with me holding onto his uniform as hard as I could.

"With me still holding on, he dropped the clutch on the car. I was barely able to get my arm out of the window when he started coming toward me along with the gas man and the gas can. I let the gas can go and caught the gas man, so he wouldn't hurt himself.

"At that point I didn't think we had enough gas to finish the race, so on the radio I told Baker to take it easy and try to save gas.

"When we came out of the pits, we had a 6-second lead. I started clocking the cars. No one was drafting with him, and he still was gaining a full second a lap on the other cars. He was that much faster.

"He got up to a twelve-second lead, and I could not slow him down. Buddy would not listen. He wanted to get it over with so bad, wanted to get to that checkered flag. I knew what he was thinking.

"It came down to the last couple of laps over a caution flag. I was still afraid he might run out of gas, and I told him, 'Don't run on the banks. Get on the flat and keep the fuel in the pickup.'

"And Buddy was able to win the race in a record time of 177.602, a time that stands to this day. It was a highlight of my life. That was a great race.

"Everyone was talking about our car, because it was so fast. Bill France complained to me that I was stinking up the show, that we didn't need to be running so fast, and they made us change the front of the car a little bit, because we were coming up on some of the slower cars so fast they didn't see Buddy coming.

"I remember in the 125 race on Thursday, Baker pitted on the green, and we lost the lead to Cale Yarborough. On the radio Junior Johnson said to Cale, 'Here comes Baker. Whenever he comes by you, latch on him.' Later on Cale told me, 'By the time Junior told me that, Buddy was already past and gone.' Cale came on the radio and told Junior, 'Catch him? He's already gone.'

"We had an easy time in Daytona.

"This was 1980, and no one had ever won $100,000 in a race. The purse that year was $102,000. When the race was over, I was standing in the winner's circle with Harry Ranier, and I said, 'Harry, I know you've won a lot of money these last couple weeks, but I want you to know I have already spent $10,000 of your money.'

"He didn't care, he was so happy. But he wouldn't have been so happy if we had wrecked.

"Buddy was a guy who loved to drive a race car. He didn't know a lot about a race car as far as the chassis, the engine, what to do with it, but he was so much fun to be around. He's one of my favorite people. We would get up in the morning and go to the racetrack, and everything the crew did, he did, except the night before the race he'd go to his room and get room service and he wouldn't come out of that room until the next day. He'd stay in and rest.

"The only thing about Baker, when it came time for qualifying, if someone told him the track was wet or torn up, they could talk him out of running a good lap. Other people knew this, and they would really work on Buddy to aggravate him to keep him from running good. They would tell him everything they thought would upset him.

"At first when I was working with him, I wasn't aware of this. Later I began to notice we would be running good, and then something would happen. Everybody has his faults, and that was one of Baker's, but still, he was so much fun to be around, and I remember after we won that Daytona race in 1980, that was the highlight of his life because he had been trying, he said, for nineteen years to win that race. I was so happy we were able to pull it off for him.

"NASCAR kept trying to slow us down. At Talladega, they said our car wouldn't fit the templates, said our car was illegal. But when they put the template on, it did fit, and then they said we had the rear end offset, so I said, 'Okay, line the rear end up. Tel us where you want it, and that's where we'll put it.' And they did. And what was funny, we ran an even faster lap with it the way they wanted it!

"In the race Dale Earnhardt was driving the 2 car. The race was three-fourths over, and at the time, the left-side tires were running out as fast as the right-side tires, so our tire man kept telling me, 'There is no way we can make it unless we change all four tires.'

"Well, the 2 car was in the pit right next to ours, and they came in and changed two tires on the left. We came in, and I changed four tires. I was afraid not to, because I wasn't going to take a chance with a man's life. When Buddy went back on the track, Earnhardt had such a lead on us that Buddy couldn't see him.

"There were thirty laps to go, and we were twenty seconds behind, and I tried to talk to Buddy, and he said, 'I . . . can't . . . hear . . . you,' because he was so mad. He had been leading the race when he pitted and now he was way behind.

"Buddy started catching Earnhardt a second a lap. I said, 'Man, I can't believe this.' And on some laps it was more than that.

"With ten laps to go, Buddy was getting close. The crowd became involved; everyone was standing up cheering for Buddy to catch Earnhardt.

"With two laps to go, Buddy caught Dale and passed him right before the start-finish line and won the race.

"Meanwhile, everybody was saying Buddy couldn't win on the short tracks, and we went to Martinsville and won with him there.

"I had a lot of good times with Baker. I enjoyed working with him. He was never this good again, why I don't know.

"In '81, Bobby Allison came with us. We won the first race of the season at Riverside, a road race. The second race back then was Daytona.

"During the off-season we decided to run a Pontiac Le Mans on the superspeedways. We had tested an Oldsmobile, but it wasn't any good at all. We came back to our shop at Charlotte, and Bobby and I decided to build a Le Mans because it had a sloped back and we figured it would have the best aerodynamics.

"We weren't getting factory help, so we could choose any car we wanted, so we chose a Le Mans. We went over to NASCAR and asked them to give us a sheet on the rules and specifications, and they did, and it was okay by the rules.

"Mike Laughlin did the chassis, and we went to Talladega to test and we ran real fast down there. I figured other people would build one, too, but no one did. NASCAR didn't even have templates for the car!

"When we got to Daytona, all of our competitors were against us because they didn't want us running the Le Mans. NASCAR also hated the idea we were down there with that Pontiac Le Mans, although they couldn't say anything because it was okay by the rule book. They made the rules, we didn't.

"And then Bobby went out and sat on the pole with the car at 194.624. He won the 125 race, and we were leading in the 500 to the last pit stop, but Richard Petty was getting better fuel mileage than we were. He came in and got one can of gas, and we had to get two, and Petty just did beat us. That really hurt, because I wanted to win the 500 so badly for Bobby. We had won Riverside. We wanted to win *all* the races.

"In mid-June 1981 Bobby led by 357 points for the championship before a race at Riverside. Right before they started the engines, I told Bobby, 'Please don't blow up the engine. It's a really hot day.' I felt there was going to be a lot of engine trouble, and we didn't run long before we blew up the engine.

"From there on, we kept losing points, week after week. Darrell Waltrip caught us and went ahead, and it came down to the last race of the season back at Riverside in California. We still had a chance to win if we won and Darrell fell out of the race.

"For that last race, I put a rev limiter in the car so it would only turn so many rpms and then the device would shut off the engine. I told Bobby that I had put it in. I was afraid the engine would blow up like it did the last time. I wanted to save the engine.

"It came down to the latter part of the race. We were leading Joe Ruttman, who was driving a super race that day. There was a caution with thirty laps to go, and Bobby came in and we put four tires on his car, and at the same time I reached in and cut the wire to the rev limiter.

"I told Bobby, 'You've got it all now. The rev limiter is off, and you have four brand-new tires.'

"Bobby outran Joe Ruttman the last ten laps to win the race. Darrell ran a safe race, and he finished sixth, which gave him the championship.

"Benny Parsons came back with us in 1982. Our goal was to break 200 miles an hour qualifying. No one had ever done it before. When we tested at Talladega, we were able to do that, and at the Winston 500 at Talladega, we sat on the pole at 200.176.

"Darrell Waltrip had the car we had to beat, and though Benny led into the latter part of the race, he felt he was in the wrong position, that he would rather run second behind Darrell and pass him right at the end. And so he let Darrell pass him, and it cost him the race.

"See, in the latter part of the race there was a caution. There were four cars in the lead lap, and I knew it would be the last pit stop. Benny was leading, and I asked Benny if he wanted to pit, and when he went around the first time he said no, and the second time he said yes, and so we changed tires and put some gas in the car. I knew he wanted to be off the lead so he could slingshot by, and this pit stop would give him the chance to go wherever he wanted to go.

"They gave him the green, and he moved into second place, and then as he went into turn one, he took the lead. I didn't discuss it with him on the radio, because I knew we were being monitored by the other crews. I was letting him do what he wanted to do. The speed was good with us leading, so I figured that was fine.

"And it came down to the last lap. Four cars were running in a single file led by Benny. Darrell Waltrip was running second, and behind him Terry Labonte third, and behind him Kyle Petty was running fourth. Kyle's crew had told him to pull down low on Darrell and see if he couldn't beat him down the backstretch to beat him out for second. They had pretty much given us the race.

"But when Benny came off turn two, instead of holding his position, he came down to the inside of the racetrack, and the string of three cars flew right on by him. He was able to come back on Kyle Petty, and we finished third.

"I never saw Benny so hysterical in my whole life. I felt sorry for Benny, because it was a big letdown, it really bothered him. Benny realized later he should have stayed in front. I hated it for Benny, because I really liked Benny.

"During the '82 season Cale Yarborough came to me two or three times while he was driving for Junior. He said he didn't want to run full schedule anymore, didn't want to run for the championship. Since we were running a limited schedule, he wanted to know if he could drive for us.

"When he first came to me, I thought he was kidding, but he wasn't, and when I told Harry Ranier that Cale wanted to drive the race car, we all got together and hired Cale for the '83 season.

"At Daytona we had the Le Mans that qualified at 200 miles an hour and a new Chevy Monte Carlo, which was a lot faster than the Le Mans. AJ tested one car and Cale the other, and in the wind tunnel the computer figured that the Monte Carlo should qualify at Daytona at 203 miles an hour.

"We held the Daytona qualifying record at 198, and we had our hearts set on breaking 200 miles an hour, just like we had at Talladega. Well, during the week of practice the car wasn't running any faster than anyone else's, and I really couldn't understand what was wrong, because the car should have been going a lot faster. I worked and worked and worked and worked, but it didn't seem to go any faster. But I had never worked with Cale before, and what I didn't know was that Cale was sandbagging!

"Saturday afternoon he said, 'We're okay. Don't worry about it.' Well, I was worried sick about that car. I had been used to working with Buddy Baker and Bobby Allison, and those guys told you exactly what the car was doing the first or second lap around the track. It was unreal how fast they went out and ran.

"Anyway, when it came time to qualify, Cale let it out. On the first lap qualifying, we did break 200 miles an hour. At that time you ran two laps if you wanted to, and they took the best of the two. Cale was going around on his second lap, and when he got in turn four, the car went airborne and he wrecked it. We weren't able to fix the car, so we had to scratch our time. We had sat on the pole in '79, '80, '81, and '82 with Baker, Baker again, Allison, and Benny, and if we could have gotten the Monte Carlo fixed, we would have been on the pole with Cale. That would have meant five years in a row, but we just couldn't fix up the car.

"I had my son Greg bring the backup car, the Pontiac Le Mans, from the shop—we didn't even have it with us—and we qualified at 195 miles an hour.

"We started the 1983 Daytona 500, and the car handled well, but I could tell it was a struggle. The Le Mans didn't run as well as that Chevrolet would have, by no means.

"We ran up front all day, but we weren't able to be as dominant as we had been with Baker or Bobby. Coming down toward the end of the race, Cale was running second, and he said the engine was running hot. What had happened, the Pontiac had picked up a bunch of debris off the racetrack, and it stopped up the radiator. I was afraid we had busted a head, because we had been having a lot of head trouble. Fortunately, it wasn't that. The radiator was just stopped up and running hot.

"I told Cale, 'Just breathe it as much as you can. Don't run the car right directly behind the car in front of you. Get as much air in the radiator as you can.' There were twenty laps to go. But it stayed together the rest of the day.

"It came down to the last lap, and Cale slingshotted by and won by several car lengths over Bill Elliott, Buddy Baker, and Joe Ruttman.

"In '84 we still wanted to break the 200-mile-an-hour barrier at Daytona, and that year we went back with the Chevrolet Monte Carlo, and Cale sat on the pole at 201.848 miles an hour. Then we won the 125, and we won the 500 when Cale passed Darrell Waltrip going away on the final lap.

"Cale never wanted to be first on the last lap; he always wanted to be second. He felt he could win better from there. The only way Darrell could have stopped him was if he had wrecked him, and if you do that, you wreck yourself too.

"Harry Ranier and Chevrolet were a very successful race team, but here's what upset everything in '84: Right before the Daytona 500, Chevrolet threw a dinner, and they didn't invite Harry Ranier—none of us got invited—and it really upset him. During the season Lee Morse of Ford had called me and asked me if we would be interested in running Fords. I don't think Lee was ever aware that Harry had been snubbed by Chevrolet. I said, 'I'll have to talk to Harry and Cale and I'll get back with you.'

"I went to Harry and told him, and Harry said, 'Give me his number.' I knew the instant he found out Ford was interested that it was a done deal. And it was.

"We went ahead and switched to Ford, and it was a horrible experience. Ford had a Windsor engine that they hadn't raced yet, and they wanted us to run that during a time when the rest of the Ford teams were running Cleveland engines. It was a long, hard winter, because we had to put a lot of hours in on that engine. The boys still talk about the amount of hours we had to put into it.

"In 1985 we went to Talladega and Daytona to test and had a pretty good test in the wind tunnel, but for the first time in years we didn't sit on the pole. We qualified second.

"We started the Busch race at Daytona and were leading it when the engine overheated. I asked Ford to take apart one of the engines, and see why the water wasn't circulating through the engine. Well, they wanted *me* to do it, and I had to do it in the back of our truck at Daytona. I was going by they discoloration of the block, the head cylinders, and the head gaskets, and here I was, drilling holes, not knowing how many holes to drill or what size, but I went ahead anyway.

"We came back and won the 125 race, and then in the 500 we were leading the race and came in for a pit stop after about sixty laps and dropped a valve in the engine because it was overheating, and that put us out.

"I came back to the shop and did some more extensive research on the cooling of the engine, and we finally got that worked out. I then discovered there was no nickel in the block, and we had an oiling problem with the distributor, and I had to redo the distributor to get it fixed, and then there was the problem with the oiling system—I had to do the engineering work and race at the same time, and it was very difficult for me.

"I remember the second race at Talladega in '85; it came down to the end—Cale was leading, and Neil Bonnett was running behind us. Cale wanted to run second, but I told him, 'No, stay in front. You are over a half a second quicker than he is.' And that was the first time I remember Cale staying in front at the end, and we were able to win that race.

"At Darlington we were leading when the power steering broke, and we ended up running second. Then we came to Charlotte, and we had unscheduled pit stops twice because of tires, got a lap down both times, and we still ended up winning the race. So we won two races even though we had to do all the engineering work. We could have won more if it had gone smoother.

"That year Bill Elliott was way ahead of everybody. They had everything clicking, had a good crew. They couldn't do anything wrong. And they had a lot of luck, of course. We should have won the Darlington race, but then we had the steering problem, allowing him to win.

"At the end of '86, I left Harry Ranier. I had a better offer from Rick Hendrick, and it gave me the opportunity to work with Darrell Waltrip, who was one of my closest friends in racing.

"When Darrell first started racing, he got some engines from Holman-Moody. I worked there, and I'd help him when he was at the shop. Darrell was a real likable person, and because he was a rookie I tried to get him whatever help I could. He was very appreciative, and we developed a close relationship.

"When Hendrick hired me and Darrell, we were called the Dream Team, but it just didn't end up being a good marriage. I hated that, because I wanted it to work so badly. I don't want to say anything detrimental about him, but we had internal things going on that destroyed the relationship. It hurt me a lot deeper than a lot of people thought. Feelings were hurt. Darrell blamed me, and I blamed him, but fortunately Stevie, his wife, figured out what really created the problems, what started it upside down, and I don't know if there was anything we could have done about it, the internal problems with personnel . . . it was just a bad deal, period.

"I can't say that much against Darrell because we're back friends again and Stevie and my wife Barbara are friends, and I'm glad it's worked out to where we are friends again, though I'm not saying we'll ever work together again.

"The next year I worked with Geoff Bodine, and I enjoyed working with Geoff. He and Kathy are two nice people. Geoff was hyper, had a lot of talent. One problem we had was that Geoff was carrying on a feud with Dale Earnhardt. I remember I told Rick Hendrick, 'We need to do something about this, because this is creating a lot of extra work for us, these guys tearing up these race cars. It's killing us.' Every week we were fixing wrecks, and we weren't looking forward to going to the racetrack and getting knocked out or knocking out someone.

"I guess Geoff felt Dale was out to get him, and Dale . . . I don't know. It was a bad situation. Both of them wanted to win bad, and neither would give an inch. And the result was, they ended up tearing up the race cars.

"Bill France resolved it. I don't know what he said, but whatever it was, they took heed and that was the end of it. I was glad it stopped. That was no fun. None at all.

"Bodine is a good driver, capable of winning races. We won Watkins Glen and Pocono and sat on several poles that year. Geoff is kind of a loner. He doesn't go around and socialize like some of them do. His history is the first year he does a good job and then he gets aggravated because he can't do better the second year. And then he goes somewhere else. He's very much a perfectionist. That's me; I'm a perfectionist too. And so he went over to Junior's, and Ricky Rudd came in and drove the car for us the last couple years.

"Ricky Rudd is one of those drivers who wins championships, who finishes races because he's a conservative driver. He really takes care of the race car. He's not a charger like an Earnhardt, but he doesn't wreck the race car. That's a big plus, and that contributed to us running second in the points in '91.

"At Hendrick Motorsports my job is to do the R&D for both Ricky's car and Ken Schrader's car. I've been working on cars for twenty-nine years, night and day most of the time, seven days a week, and in this job

I don't have to go to the races, don't have to work nearly as many hours as I used to. When I first began, my wife had to stay home with the children, but the last several years she has been able to travel with me. She has gotten to enjoy it, to see things I had seen and had talked to her about.

"I am looking forward to the 1992 Daytona 500. It never ends up the way it's predicted, because every year something always changes from the year before. Dale Earnhardt will be tough because of his crew, and so will Jack Roush's team with Mark Martin. They will do better in '92 than they did last year. The two Hendrick cars will do well. It'll be interesting to see how Junior's cars will run. Bill Elliott and Junior together will be interesting. Bill has a lot of talent.

"Over at Hendrick, we're just going to work as hard as we can in any area we feel needs work to be done. You test, go to the wind tunnel, evaluate everything, and ask, 'Where are we weak? What do we work on?' And that's what you work on, and work on and work on."

Andy Petree

LAP 17

Andy Petree

The Local Boy

Winning chemistry, as in most sports, is elusive in stock car racing. It's often impossible to understand why a talented team of dedicated racers has trouble winning races. And when a team does win, it's just as difficult to explain exactly what went right, considering that all the elements from a losing effort the week before may have remained exactly the same. An Australian Formula One Racer, Alan Jones, after a study of Winston Cup racing, called it "bloody black magic." Perhaps he was right.

In 1991 Harry Gant, one of the elder statesmen in Winston Cup racing, won an incredible four races in a row—Darlington, Richmond, Dover, and Martinsville. He would have won a fifth in a row at North Wilkesboro if his brakes hadn't failed toward the end of the race. He finished second.

Gant's crew chief, Andy Petree, was as close to the action as anyone. He was the alchemist in charge when Gant and his Skoal Bandit team experienced its streak. But when it was over, he was at a loss as to how to recapture the magic. The elusiveness of victory is one of the elements of stock car racing that makes it so fascinating.

Petree grew up in the Newton-Conover area, about 50 miles north and west of Charlotte, but only 7 miles from the Hickory Speedway, a short track where a lot of top drivers like Harry Gant and Dale Earnhardt started their careers.

When Andy was eleven, his uncle, who was a Chevy dealer, took him to the track for the first time. His father loved the stick and ball sports and wasn't interested in racing.

Petree arrived at the parking lot of the track, got out of the car, and for the first time heard the roar of the race cars.

"It got to me just like vise grips," Petree remembered. That second, before he ever saw the cars, he knew that stock car racing would be his life. It was love at first hearing. He thought, "I can't believe this has been going on in my backyard and I didn't know about it."

From then on he dreamed about racing, fantasizing both about being a driver and working on cars. He would get his mother to drive him to the track. He could get in free if he was with an adult, so she'd drop him off, he'd walk in with another family, watch the race, call his mother on a pay phone, and she'd come and pick him up. He didn't have anyone as interested in racing as he was.

"It got a hold on me," said Petree.

One of the top drivers at the Hickory Speedway, John Settlemyre, worked for Petree's uncle and grandfather at their Chevy store. Settlemyre was a local hero who won five track championships. He agreed to let Petree work for him as a volunteer. Settlemyre had to; he worked for the kid's uncle. And as a result, Andy Petree got his foot in the door and began his climb toward becoming a crew chief for Harry Gant.

ANDY PETREE: "I pestered John Settlemyre until he took me to his shop. I was intrigued by the cars, and I asked so many questions of the people working on them—'How does that work? What does it do?' 'It's a piece of the rear end.' 'What does it do? Tell me.' 'They call it a ratchet.' 'What does a ratchet do?'

"And I would make them explain everything fully, up to the point where they couldn't stand to see me coming. 'Cause I'd ask question after question after question. I was just so hungry to learn everything about race cars.

"I got to be about sixteen. I was going to school and making money on the side driving a tank wagon for my dad's Gulf distributorship. On my sixteenth birthday, I was driving a 24,000-pound truck filled with gasoline. You can't do that anymore, but I did then.

"As soon as I got a little money, the first thing I was going to do was build a race car. Naturally, I was going to drive it. So I enticed one of my best friends, Jimmy Newsom, into going in with me. We split the $5,000 cost and built the car. That was *a lot* of money back then. We borrowed half of it, and once we started whenever I had a question I would call John or call Tommy Houston, who was a late-model Sportsman driver on Settlemyre's level, and I bet I called Tommy a thousand times to ask his advice.

"I got the best education in racing building that car. Money couldn't buy it. John may have lost patience with me, but I never lost my persistence. John *had* to help me, because he worked for my uncle and grandfather. Tommy always was patient. I probably don't give him enough credit for what he did for me.

"Anyway, we built that car, and we were ready to go racing, except we didn't have a motor and we had run out of money. We had underestimated the cost quite a bit.

"I said to Jimmy Newsom, 'I don't know what we're going to do. We'll have to let it sit until we can get a motor.' I was still planning on being the driver. But about that time a mutual friend named Dale Jarrett showed up at the garage one day. His dad is Ned Jarrett. Dale was a golfer and a baseball player, was a great athlete, had never shown any interest in racing up to then. He had his dad with him.

"Dale said, 'I'm really wanting to get into racing. What would it take to drive this car you guys have built?'

"I said, 'We really haven't gotten it finished. We need a motor, but that's not really why we've built it. We were kind of wanting to drive it ourselves.'

"Dale said, 'I really want to drive. That's what I want to do with my life.'

"I thought, 'This guy isn't serious. He's getting his daddy to help him with a little fun project.' I didn't take him seriously. But later Dale came back and said, 'I'll buy you a motor if you let me drive the car.'

"So we finally said okay. And I really didn't want to do it. I wanted to drive the car. But I figured, 'It can sit here, or we can race it.'

"So we started racing the car, and that set my career, by accident.

"The first race at Hickory was uneventful. We started the race fairly far back and finished ninth. Dale had the Jarrett name, but no one knew him. And he showed some talent. That night I could see, 'Yeah, this guy can make it.' What I questioned was his dedication, because he was a ballplayer. He knew nothing about a race car, nothing. Seriously, he didn't know a nut from a bolt.

"As it turned out, Dale Jarrett was *very* dedicated. Even though I was only seventeen, I had a solid background because I had started so young, and he started asking me the same questions I had been asking, and he started learning, and he learned every piece of that car. Today, Dale could build his own race car from the ground up. It's important for a driver to know how everything works. Not all drivers do, but most of the good ones do.

"Very quickly Jimmy Newsom discovered we were losing money,

actually a lot of money. It was costing everything we were making to run, and as a result Jimmy got disinterested real quick, and Dale and I bought him out. We took over his debts.

"We ran for three years, never won a race. We came close, but the important thing was Dale was learning, I was learning. We were running Class C on asphalt, and I had to make spring and weight decisions similar to Winston Cup cars. The education I got from running that car was ten times more than what I paid for it.

"By this time I interested my dad, and he gave me a little money. Ned was giving Dale a little. Back then my dad didn't have much money, and Ned was between careers, and I don't think he had much either. But they helped us as much as they could and encouraged us. Basically, Ned kind of stood back and said, 'We'll see if the boy wants to do it badly enough.'

"The dedication has to be within or you're not going to make it in this sport. People think Kyle Petty has been given a golden opportunity, which he has, but he still couldn't have made anything of it without the dedication.

"The education was the most important aspect of that part of my career. We spent what I consider a lot of money—we were spending *all* our money, every penny. I wasn't going to the malt shop or the ball games, didn't do any of those things normal kids did back then, but at the same time it was keeping me out of trouble.

"Back then people looked at racing as a redneck sport. I don't think they do today; maybe at that level. And when I graduated from high school and it was time for me to go to college, we sold the car and basically got out of debt.

"My mother and father wanted me to go to college. We didn't have a lot of money. They asked, 'What are you going to do with your life?' I didn't want to tell them. I thought they might laugh at me. I *knew* what I wanted to do. No doubt: I wanted to drive a race car for a living.

"My mom asked me, and I told her the truth. I said, 'I'm going to make a living racing, driving or working on them, one way or another.' My mother just lost it. She said, 'You're crazy. You better straighten up and start thinking about your life. You're not going to make a living doing that.'

"There were four kids in our family. She worked for my dad, and it was a struggling business, and actually it finally went under about that time. She didn't have any knowledge of racing. All she knew was I was working on what she considered to be junk cars. And here I'm telling her I'm going to make a living doing that. She said, 'You're living in a dreamworld.'

"I said, 'Maybe so, but that's what I'm going to do.'

"She said, 'Your father and I have been thinking. You're mechanically inclined. Go to Nashville Auto and Diesel College and learn the industry while working on cars. And it's an accredited college.'

"They talked me into going. I finished the automotive phase, the first six months, and I saw the diesel mechanics, and I thought, 'It might pay good, but I *don't* want to work on trucks for a living.' So I packed my stuff and went home. During the whole time I was there, all I thought about was stock car racing.

"I came back home, and Jimmy Newsom put me to work in his tire store, and I worked part-time on a couple race cars, including Dale Jarrett's. In the past it had *cost* me money to work on the race car, and now I was getting to do it for free, so to me that was like making money! Seriously, that's how I felt about it, and I did that for a while. I didn't have to spend the money on the car, and so I could get started with my life. I got my own apartment. I got married, and she got pregnant.

"For six months I got a job running a service station for a local doctor, but it didn't make any money, and he sold it, and I was out of a job. I had bought a house, and the baby was on the way, and I had no job.

"Finally, I told Dale, 'Your dad has lot of connections in Winston Cup racing. I need a job right now, and that's what I want to do. See if he can help me.'

"I didn't think anything would happen, but he told Junior Johnson, 'I know one of the best tire changers around if you need to hire one.' And it so happened Junior needed one. The fact was, I had changed tires maybe five or six times in three Sportsman races, because the races weren't very long. I had picked it up, but I didn't know if I could do it on the big-league level. Ned went way out on a limb to do that for me, but in May 1981, Junior gave me a job.

"When I arrived, Tim Brewer, Harold Elliott, and Jeff Hammond were there, and Darrell Waltrip was the driver. This was *big-time* racing.

"Right away Junior put me to work changing tires. I'll tell you, I was so nervous. I rode on the truck out to Texas, and all the way out I couldn't sleep or eat.

"We got to Texas and qualified ninth. Darrell Waltrip was our driver, and he started coming through the field, and all of a sudden early in the race under the green here he comes through the pits. I thought, 'Oh God, here goes.' I got my wrench. And then when he came by I noticed water running out of his exhaust pipe. The motor had blown up.

"It was almost a relief. I didn't have to do it.

"The next week we went to Riverside and sat on the pole. The race started. Jeff Hammond was the jack man at that time, but he had just gotten married and was on his honeymoon, so Junior came out of retirement to jack the car. I was out there with The Legend jacking the car, and I've never changed a tire in my life on a Winston Cup car, and we're leading the race, and we have a caution, and—I was scared to death!

"I don't know if Junior noticed how nervous I was. I was trying like hell to hide it. And I didn't realize I had been hired on a contingency basis. I thought I had a job.

"During the day Darrell made four or five stops and somehow I didn't trip over myself. The next week we went to Michigan, and I had a couple of good stops, and Junior went ahead and hired me.

"I worked there for about a month. Junior was paying me full-time, but I was just a tire changer on the pit crew; I wasn't working on the cars. I had a job in the shop, but they weren't letting me do anything. I was a gofer, but I wanted to work on the cars. I wanted to be involved in car building, preparing it, but there were so many people at Junior's place. I saw all he wanted me for was to be a tire changer and that the only reason he had given me a full-time job was because I needed one.

"I didn't feel I was contributing, because I didn't have that much experience and because he wouldn't let me learn and work on the cars. I finally went to Junior and said, 'Look, I appreciate your giving me a job, but you really don't need me. I'm going to find something else to do.'

"He said, 'I still need a tire changer.' I said, 'I will be more than glad to do that on the weekends. And that way I won't feel I'm taking your money and not giving you anything in return.'

"The next year he gave my job to one of his other guys. I got demoted to taking off the left-side lug nuts.

"I went to Daytona in 1982. I was looking for something else. I met Johnny Hayes, who was with U.S. Tobacco. Johnny is a vice president of U.S. Tobacco now, but then he headed up their motor sport division in this area. He had a deal with Phil Parsons running a Busch car, and he needed somebody to change tires. The Busch series runs on Saturdays, the day before the Winston Cup races.

"Johnny asked me, 'Would you change tires for us on Saturday?' 'Sure.' So I worked for Johnny on Saturday and Junior on Sunday, and I got to know Johnny and Phil Parsons, and I told them, 'I'd like to get in with you two and work on this car.'

"I worked on the car at night for nothing, like I had with Dale Jarrett, and after the Daytona 500, I thanked Junior and left. I probably did him a favor by quitting and giving one of his guys the chance.

"Toward the end of the season Benny Parsons, who is a great driver, lost his ride with Harry Ranier. He was out of a job. Johnny told us, 'I can arrange for Benny to run four or five Winston Cup races for us.'

"So I just happened to be lucky enough to be there. We had put together this little Bush team, and just like that, I went from Busch to Winston Cup. But only part-time.

"Johnny Hayes bought the car from Travis Carter, who was then doing cars for Harry Gant. Travis was also sponsored by Skoal. We took the car they prepared and raced it. We got motors from Herman Almond.

"We ran five races and did well, finished fifth in four of them. It really turned out well, and in '83 Johnny said, 'Let's build a building, run fifteen races, half the schedule, hire four or five crewmen, and do this with Benny as the driver.' It wasn't a bad deal. We had a good sponsor, Copenhagen chewing tobacco.

"Leo Jackson, who today owns the Harry Gant car, built the engines. Today his company, Precision Products Performance Center, machines the blocks. He also makes wrist pins and other motor parts.

"Johnny made Leo the man over everyone on the crew, and they also hired a crew chief, Cliff Champion. It was the four of us, and in '83 we had decent success, had four top-five finishes, finished second twice. I was building the tail pipes, the suspension parts, the rear ends, and doing the mechanic work. There were only four of us, so we had to share the responsibilities and build the cars.

"Cliff had the experience, and he taught us. He led us. The bulk of what I learned about Winston Cup cars I learned from Cliff. I learned the basics, how to grind the frame without hurting it. You mount bumper brackets on. They don't bolt on. You have to weld them on, and when you cut it off, he taught me that you don't grind past the parent material, because then you hurt the frame. You just grind to it. He taught me little things like that. But very important things.

"I thought we had had good success for a new team, and U.S. Tobacco did too, because they renewed us in '84. That year we won a race.

"With Junior we had won eight races, but I wasn't involved in it, I was just changing tires. I never felt part of the team. But when Benny Parsons won at Atlanta in '84, I was one of the main players. I can't tell you what that felt like. For my whole life that was what I wanted to do, and now I did it.

"There was no strategy to our winning at Atlanta. We just outran everybody, whipped them, beat them. Benny had to pass Cale Yarborough and Dale Earnhardt with twenty laps to go to win the race, and he did.

"Benny was an excellent driver, but no one talks about him because though he's won twenty-one races, he only won one or two a year, and you don't get that much recognition winning one or two races a year.

"I think Benny had as much talent as anyone who ever drove. He was an excellent driver, was very good with the press, very personable, just a good guy.

"We ran the fifteen superspeedway races with Benny in '85 and again in '86. And in the other fifteen Benny polished his broadcasting career. He was a spokesman for U.S. Tobacco. So he had the opportunity to do that too. He left us in 1987 when Tim Richmond got sick and he accepted an offer from Rick Hendrick.

"I didn't blame Benny one bit for taking the Hendrick job. The car had won seven races the year before. He *had* to take it. But that left us without a driver. Phil Parsons was also driving a car for the same team, and so we made it a one-car team and ran all thirty races with Phil in '87. We didn't win a race, but in '88 we won at Talladega.

"In '88 Leo Jackson and me and the guys who had worked on Benny's car prepared for the fifteen superspeedway races, and Richard Jackson and the guys who had prepared Phil's car got those cars ready for the short track races. It was one team, but it was like two teams. It's never happened before, and it probably won't happen again. We had decent success. In '88 we finished seventh in the points, but noses got out of joint. When you have people with the talent it takes to work on these cars, they tend to be competitive not only as a team but with each other. There is always bitching and bellyaching, and I'm sure I did my share. I was Leo's crew chief, and I would say, 'I hope our car is better than what Richard's bunch can build.' That was healthy. Some were rubbing against each other a little, though.

"And then Richard and Leo, who are great friends, decided to each have his own team. They also separated their business, with Richard winding up with the industrial side of their machine business and Leo winding up with the racing end of it.

"Leo needed a driver, and at that time Harry Gant was getting ready to leave U.S. Tobacco. He was talking about quitting Travis Carter and Hal Needham. Their team had fallen apart, hadn't done any good, and they finished way down in the points, and Harry felt he needed to move on. Leo figured we were already with U.S. Tobacco, and he talked to them. He said, 'I'll form another team if I can get Harry to drive for me. Would you all sponsor it?' And they said yes.

"Leo hired Harry Gant for '89. He also moved his team, which had been in Denver, North Carolina, 100 miles from his home, to Asheville, where he lived. The only person on our team willing to move was me. I didn't want to move; I didn't want to be transplanted. But I had and have the highest amount of respect for Leo Jackson. He's one of the smartest men in the sport, and Harry Gant was and is one of the best drivers in the sport. I wasn't an established crew chief, and he was giving me an opportunity to be crew chief for a top driver, and that was appealing. I felt it was a good career move.

"I saw an opportunity, and so I moved. I felt, 'We can build a car he can win in.'

"The other guys on the team felt the same way I did, but they didn't feel strongly enough to move their families away from home. In North Carolina roots are very important. For a year I was homesick. Three years later, I'm still homesick. A hundred miles isn't very far, but when you have friends and family and people you are used to seeing every day, moving is hard. I was thirty when I moved, and I had lived there all my life.

"In '89 Harry won the fifth race we were together, at Darlington. We were very inexperienced, but the guys in the motor room had an excellent motor, and Harry gets around Darlington better than any of them, and we won. That was a good driver's win.

"Harry Gant is a genuine nice guy, though he is a little shy. Harry was thirty-three before he ever ran his first Winston Cup race. He had been racing a late-model Sportsman on the Busch circuit and had won a lot of races. He's got a lot of talent, and he finally got his break at forty. If he had started earlier, he would have won a lot of championships.

"The thing about Harry, he is the toughest human being who ever lived to drive a race car. The heat doesn't seem to bother him. He has tremendous endurance. All these younger drivers seem to have trouble with these long, hot races. They wear cool suits. Harry has never used one. And I have never seen him winded when he gets out of the car.

"Harry is shy, and never looks for the limelight. He has found something he can make a pretty good living at, and that's why he does it. He probably still considers it a part-time job.

"Harry is a working kind of person—does carpentry work, owns his own steak house in Taylorsville, North Carolina. Before he raced he was a carpenter, building houses with his dad and brother. He does all of his own work, builds stuff for his kids.

"He's a country boy who has lived in Taylorsville all his life, lives in the same house he built, long before he ever drove a race car. He has built on to that house perhaps fifteen times.

"Harry has a good work ethic, shies away from the publicity, does a lot of personal appearances for Skoal smokeless tobacco. He's been their spokesman for ten years.

"With Harry behind the wheel in 1989 we finished second three times, and we finished seventh in the points. That was a very good year, but living in Asheville was very hard on my wife. It's been a long, hard road for us. A year after we moved here, we were separated for six or eight months. The first year my wife had worked for the team as a secretary, and then she quit, and shortly thereafter we were separated. She moved back to Denver. The year 1990 was very, very hard for me.

"We had our worst season that year. We won at Pocono, but our season was a downer. We didn't finish as many races as we should have, had engine problems, wrecked, and for some races we flat out weren't competitive, and I have to say that not all of it was because of my personal problems, but I have to think a lot of it was. My mind wasn't on it. My heart wasn't in it. My wife left, and I was destroyed. I can't tell you how bad it was.

"And then she returned home to me, and my life basically straightened out, and in '91 we had a great season, so it does go hand in hand. She's home now and we're a big happy family. I have two boys, and we're all happy now, but it was so very tough.

"And I'm thankful that Leo and the guys stuck with me. They were my family and helped me through that part, and I made some great friends through that.

"Before the 1991 season, we started getting more technical support from Oldsmobile and General Motors, and I felt we were going to be greatly improved from the year before. For the first time, we had access to their wind tunnel, which is very important. The shape of the car is everything. The shape determines the speed, the drag on the superspeedways, and the downforce. The wind tunnel is very sophisticated, tells you everything the wind and air is doing to the race car. Without it, you're not going to be very competitive.

"Our other advantage was the help of the GM engineers. They had an engineer named Terry Satchel, a chassis man, and we met him in Detroit for the wind tunnel tests.

"The test was helpful, but the relationship I developed with Terry was what made our season.

"Terry is a racer, very smart and very thorough as far as problem solving, and he showed me how to identify problems. He's an engineer, and I don't have an engineering background. I learned a tremendous amount from him. He taught me a lot about how to do my job. Problem solving is everything. That's my only job. And he showed me how to do it better.

"Before the '91 season began, we *knew* we had potential. We were starting to identify our problems, and knowing those problems, we were working on them and we were chipping away.

"We went to Daytona to start the season, and we qualified third behind Davey Allison and Ernie Irvan, but we were only a tenth of a second behind them.

"We finished sixth in the qualifying race and started the 500 in the eleventh position, and in the Daytona 500 we were going to finish in the top ten, but with ten laps to go, we got in a wreck. Harry desperately tried to finish, but he couldn't. Something happened to the front suspension, and he couldn't steer it. We sent him back out, but he couldn't go around, and we had to quit after 190 laps. We haven't had a good Daytona 500 with Harry since we started. I hope that will change this year.

"We went to Richmond after that, finished third; went to Rockingham, finished third; won Talladega on pit strategy when we stretched the fuel mileage, almost ran out of gas, and had one less pit stop than the other cars.

"Harry ran out of gas the last lap, and Rick Mast was behind Harry. Harry and Rick both are sponsored by Skoal, and it looked like Rick was pushing Harry across the finish line, but that's not what happened. What happened, Harry sputtered once, and Rick ran into him, and that's the way NASCAR ruled it.

"Darrell Waltrip, who finished second, was pissing and moaning, but his spoiler was down below the legal minimum, and fortunately we knew it, and we used that as part of our defense in talking with NASCAR after the race.

"A couple hours after the race they held a press conference and declared Harry the winner, said it was a bump and not a push, and they let Darrell's second place stand because they didn't check his spoiler when they should have. There was a lot of controversy, but that win felt good. It was the biggest race we had ever won with Harry.

"As for our race team, our bond was growing stronger. We were in there together digging. This is the best group of people I've ever been involved with. They're dedicated, talented, and easy to get along with. This team had *no* problems, and that had a lot of do with our success.

"As crew chief, I have one philosophy—to be everyone's friend. I like to be one of the guys, but at the same time I have to be the boss too. I like to treat them like I wanted to be treated when I was doing their job.

"In the middle of the season we suffered a lull. In mid-June we went to Pocono. We were the dominant car—until there was a rain delay. When we went back out, we didn't run well.

"This is a good opportunity to talk about problem solving. We just didn't run well the second half of that race, and we couldn't figure out why. In the past we'd say, 'We didn't run good. Let's load it up and shoot it again.' But we had a problem, and we hadn't identified what the problem was. The problem was that we hadn't identified the problem. We needed to know why the car didn't run well in that race.

"We started tracking it down, and we found that the ball joints, which hold the suspension where it's supposed to be, were bent. Thinking back, I recall that the same thing had happened back in April at Martinsville. At the same time, I told myself that Harry must have hit something. But Harry hadn't said a word about hitting anything, and at Martinsville, we had run great the first half, had faded badly, and finished fifth.

"When the same thing happened at Pocono, I specifically asked Harry whether he had hit anything, and he said he hadn't touched anything all day long. But the ball joints were bent. We started to look at everything on the car. What else is bent? We found that the trailing arms on the rear suspension also were bent.

"We bought stronger ball joints. We went to Daytona in July, then to Pocono again, and we broke a strut rod on the front suspension. Broke it! Another piece of suspension.

"We went back and redesigned the strut rod. We put a brace in the place where it broke. Aside from that, we had run good. If things held up, we would win races. We went to Talladega and broke a rod in the engine, which is just one of those things. It was the only engine failure we had all year.

"We didn't run well at Watkins Glen either. Then in late August we had a chance at winning Michigan and finished sixth when I made the wrong call. We had a set of tires that were old, had been sitting around our shop for six months, but the stagger was good on them. At the time we were running bias-ply tires, and the stagger—the differential in sizes from the outside to the inside—varies. The stagger on these tires was good.

"I had another brand-new set, but the stagger was no good on these. Which set of tires should I choose? I made the call. I picked the old ones. They were bad. Wrong call.

"At Bristol, one of Harry's best tracks, we had a chance to win but had a flat tire and finally wrecked, but we were one of the faster cars.

"I was looking forward to going to Darlington on September 1. I felt we had gotten all of our problems fixed.

"We went to Darlington and we won the race. We went to Richmond, and we won. We won at Dover. We went to Martinsville, and we won. As luck had it, we won four in a row! We had the team to do it all along, and luck had it that we did.

"Every week Harry's confidence level was rising. It was, 'Yeah, I can beat these guys week in and week out. I've got a car that can hold up.'

"As a team, the pressure on us was mounting. After we won at Darlington and Richmond, it became an obsession to win three in a row. We were getting more intense.

"We had been planning to take the Bristol car to Richmond after Darlington, but we ran so well at Darlington we made the decision to take the Darlington car instead. Darlington is a big track, and we were taking this car to a short track. Even Harry didn't agree with that. But we had something that was working, and Leo Jackson and I decided to run this car *and* this motor *every* race until it got beat.

"After we won Darlington, it was, 'Let's rebuild it.' It was the best motor we had. So we went to Richmond with that same car, and we won the race, and we ran the same car and motor at Dover and won the race, and took them again to Martinsville, and won the race.

"And if we should get on a roll again, we'll do it again the same way, and I'll tell you why. When you're winning, a lot of times you don't know why. In fact, most times you don't. You know you're doing all the right things, but you can't go out and duplicate it in another car. So when you have something that's working that well, you say, 'Let's just run it. Tee it up and do it again.'

"We went to Wilkesboro. We had had a definite plan to run a different car at Wilkesboro, but we stuck to our agreement. We went with the same car. And at Wilkesboro we won the pole, which we hadn't done in three years. So now we had a chance to win the Unocal bonus money—if the pole winner wins the race, it gets a chunk of money from Unocal. In this case, the bonus money was $150,000—if we won the race.

"The pressure had mounted. It was a stair step of pressure on the whole team, especially on me. Now we were getting afraid to lose. We had won four races in four weeks. We didn't want to lose that feeling.

"The $150,000 bonus was hanging out there. It was harder on us physically, because it's so much easier to come from behind and win. It's harder to lead all the way, and we had been doing that not only in this race, but four weeks in a row. It was really getting tough.

"All day long it looked for all the world like we were going to win it. No way we weren't going to win. And a brake line went. The one little thing in five weeks—the car had operated flawlessly for five weeks.

"Before the race one brake line didn't get tightened, and all through the race every time Harry hit the brake pedal, it dropped a tiny drop of fluid. Drop, drop, drop. All day the car was running flawlessly, and with ten laps to go—no brakes. And Harry had Dale Earnhardt right behind him.

"Harry finished second, and how he did that with no brakes was a miracle. But it killed us to lose that race. It *killed* us. Not only the bonus. We had a chance to set a modern-day record for winning five races in a row, a record we had tied with Bobby Allison and Darrell Waltrip. It killed our streak, and that Monday morning, it was like going to a funeral. And we had finished second! It was weird.

"Everybody learned a good lesson from it: Just because you're on top, you still have to make it happen. You have to do your job. There was no finger pointing afterward. It was just something that got overlooked. The fellow whose responsibility it was was the same guy who was part of winning four races in a row. He's one of our family, our crew members.

"This *is* a family; that's why this team is so special. The guy who did it took it very hard. He apologized without my even saying anything.

"I told him, 'You've done a lot for us, and I'm not going to jump on you. You know what happened. I'm not going to point a finger. You were part of all those wins, and we won it as a team, and we'll lose it as a team.'

"We finished fourth for the Winston Cup driving championship in '91, and though Harry has not had a good time of it in the Daytona 500, we are looking forward to this one coming up. We need good luck, we've been in the wind tunnel with a new car, and our motor department has found some added power. I'm optimistic.

"As for our competition, Dale Earnhardt has never won the Daytona 500, and he wants it worst than *any* of them, and the favorite has to be Dale, unless it turns out the Fords have a distinct advantage in horsepower.

"Still, in the end it's going to be who wants it the worst, who will take the biggest chance. You always have big wrecks at Daytona because somebody is taking a big chance. Even Earnhardt got caught in a wreck last year. He wants it bad. He's going to be the one to beat—if he doesn't get in a wreck.''

LAP 18

Larry McReynolds

The Conciliator

The start of the 1991 season brought disappointment and anger to the Robert Yates racing team during a time when the experts were extolling the speed of its engines, the handling of its car, and the skill of its driver, Davey Allison, son of racing legend Bobby Allison. The season started with a run-in at the Daytona 500 with Dale Earnhardt. With three laps to go Allison wrecked when Earnhardt took air off his spoiler and sent him spinning, and he had to settle for fifteenth place.

After the race Allison, whose outspoken criticism of his opponents has been viewed as "whining" by some fans and other drivers, announced that he no longer would be intimidated by the black-clothed driver from Kannapolis.

In the next three races the 28 Havoline car was so far out of contention that Allison's state of mind was irrelevant. In the fourth race, at Atlanta, Allison finished fortieth.

Team chemistry was bad. Part of the problem was Davey Allison, who was bullheaded. He argued with his crew chief—stern, gruff Jake Elder—and fought with his crew members over the fact that the car wasn't running better. Davey's father, Bobby, tried to lecture Davey on the importance of getting along with his crew, but the youngster refused to listen.

At the Coca-Cola 600 at Charlotte, Allison was leading. The caution flag came out, and when his competitors went in for tires, his crew told him 'Stay out there. You don't need tires.' But Allison didn't trust his crew, and he insisted he needed fresh tires, and because of the friction, he wrongly came in and lost the race.

Afterward Bobby Allison was so angry with his son he could barely speak to him. Davey asked Ralph Moody, who was in the pit, "What do you think?"

Larry McReynolds

Moody told him, "You're stupid as hell is what I think. Listen to your pit crew."

Robert Yates decided he had to do something to keep the team competitive. He fired Elder, and hired Larry McReynolds, a hardworking, tough-but-gentle soul with a soothing effect on all around him.

Even with McReynolds at the helm, Davey still had outbursts of temper, a character trait he inherited from dad Bobby. At Bristol, Davey was accused of giving Darrell Waltrip the finger, and then at Talladega in late July, in an attempt to catch Earnhardt, he desperately sought to enroll a drafting partner from among his fellow Ford drivers. None would come forward to cooperate, and Earnhardt won the race. Afterward a furious, out-of-control Davey Allison punched a wall and broke his hand.

McReynolds, in his mild manner, told Allison that if he wanted to win, he had to do it Larry's way. Concentrate on driving, the new crew chief told him. Tired of feeling frustrated, Allison consented, and in 1991 Davey Allison became a star.

Winning five races in 1991 under McReynolds's leadership made Allison's bursts of childishness incidental. The other drivers made fun of Allison's tendency to complain when things went wrong, but at the same time they were having to eat his dust.

Once McReynolds took over, Davey Allison and the Robert Yates team went on to win at Charlotte, Sears Point, Michigan, Rockingham, and Phoenix, and at the end of the year Allison was third in points in the standings for the driving championship.

In 1992, everyone says, *this* will be the team to beat, Dale or no Dale. It is the soothing confidence brought to the team by Larry McReynolds that has made this possible.

LARRY MCREYNOLDS: "I grew up in Birmingham, Alabama, and I became involved in cars on a part-time basis in the mid-seventies when I was fourteen or fifteen. I didn't have a hot rod street car. Those things didn't flip my switch. I had a little ole '71 Pinto I puttered around in, but I never had a hankering for dirt track racing. I've only been to a dirt track race once in my life. And I left halfway through it because of the mess that was going on.

"What infatuated me was asphalt, round track racing. I've never had a hankering to drive, just wanted to work on the cars and learn all I could about the building and handling of them, especially the chassis. Maybe it sounds like I have a one-track mind, 'cause I've never really got that involved with the motor side of racing. I've been fortunate to work with teams that had their own existing engine program.

"It isn't like skins and shirts, but there are two separate departments, the engine department and the race car department, and my interest is in the building and maintenance and upkeep of the car itself.

"As a boy, I used to watch a lot of races at the Birmingham International Raceway, ironically the same place Davey Allison got his start. My Aunt Noreen is the one who got me my start. She was the only one in my family who enjoyed watching racing, and one day she got the wild hair that she wanted to drive a hobby division car at Birmingham, so her husband, Butch, who was a good mechanic, but not a race mechanic, told her, 'Get yourself a sponsor, and we'll build the car.' In a short period of time she lined up a sponsor. She gathered a few thousand dollars to build an old hobby car that you drove out of a junkyard, so her husband and I built it—I'd have to say he built it. I was a helper and handyman.

"I was halfway through high school. I didn't have any experience, but I was eager and young, and I thought I could do anything if somebody gave me a chance. So we built this little old car. There wasn't a lot to doing it. You had to gut the inside, take out the windows. We got it ready to race in a week, with my uncle doing 90 percent of the work.

"I can't say that we did well. Aunt Noreen, who was ten years older than I, more like brother and sister than aunt and nephew, was really a street hot-rodder. On the street she would race her '64 Chevelle with a 454 engine in it, and she'd get in trouble all the time for speeding and drag racing.

"But she had had no track experience. We built the car and ran half a season.

"At the same time after school I worked in a salvage yard in Birmingham in the afternoons part-time. I'd work there and then at night work on Noreen's hobby car.

"I went along for a year doing this, learning more and more. And the salvage yard I worked for sponsored a late-model Sportsman car, which was the highest division that ran at Birmingham, about two divisions higher than my aunt was driving. My aunt was doing okay, but we weren't running that good—I can't say we had the best car in the world or all the money to spend on it, and maybe she lacked experience. But I knew the guy who owned the car sponsored by the salvage yard, a guy named Bobby Jones, and one Saturday the sponsor of the car, the owner of the junkyard, Charles Finley, asked me if I wanted to go to Nashville to watch his car run that night.

"We went, and before I knew it I was helping them on the car. 'Hand me this. Do this.' And that night Jones told me, 'If you ever want to do something besides help your aunt, give me a call. I'd love to have you help us.'

"Again, for free, a part-time hobby job, but that fired me up. I was sixteen years old, and this guy wanted me to help him, and after a few weeks I called him, and I said, 'I'd really like to help you on your car.'

"So I started helping him.

"My aunt was really mad at me. She didn't understand why I was doing it. We didn't speak for almost two years, because she felt I ran off and left her high and dry.

"I graduated high school, and I had moved up at the salvage yard to where I was working behind the parts counter, and once I graduated I worked there full-time all day long, and the more involved I got with the salvage yard, the more involved I became with the race team.

"We were starting to run a lot of places all over the country. In 1978 we won a lot of races with a driver named Dave Mader III. We won the Snowball Derby in Pensacola, a real prestigious race. In 1979 Mike Alexander started driving the car. We were doing well, but it was still a part-time, nighttime job for me.

"I was learning a lot about life and racing. I saw that nobody is going to hand you anything; you have to work hard for anything and everything you get. I didn't come from a real rich family. Parents didn't require me to go out and work when I was in high school, but I did it on my own, and I'll always treasure doing that. I learned there is nothing wrong with having fun, but the quicker you grow up, the better off in life you're going to be. I don't want my kids to grow up too fast, don't want them working in the afternoons after school, but for me at that time racing was in my bloodstream. If I wasn't at the junkyard, I was in that race car. And many nights I'd leave the salvage yard at five o'clock in the afternoon, run through a McDonald's drive-through, and go work on that race car all night long and quit just in time to go home and shower and change clothes. It was nothing to do that two nights a week. And on the weekends, we were racing all over the country. I can remember one weekend we ran Birmingham on Friday night, Nashville on Saturday night, and Richmond Sunday, and I had to be back at work at eight on Monday morning.

"The fella who owned the salvage yard had stopped sponsoring the car, and he wasn't working as closely with me as he had when he was sponsoring it. In fact, he did not want me working on the car, because I'd come into work tired and worn out. I had worked my way down to about 155 pounds, stayed sick all the time, and would take diet pills to stay awake and be able to drive, and finally in mid-1979 I decided, 'If I keep doing this, I won't live to be twenty-five.'

"Now I am the type of person, either I'm going to do something 100 percent, or I'm not going to do it at all. In other words, if you ask me to clean up my office, and I make up my mind to do it, I won't just vacuum the floor and dust the furniture, I will straighten the papers and the boxes and wipe the walls down. That's the way I am about anything I do.

"So I wasn't just going to work on that race car when I felt like it. Either I was going to work on it, or I was going to get away from it. And about that time, I was asking myself what I wanted to do with my life. I really didn't have a girl in my life, and I had never really dated; I never had time.

"I was flipping through a NASCAR newsletter. They run classifieds in the back, and lo and behold, there was a Winston Cup team, Rogers Racing, starting up in Greenville, South Carolina, hunting some help.

"I called them, talked to them, a shot in the dark, figuring I would never hear from them again, figured they got two hundred and fifty phone calls. I told them I didn't have a lot of experience, but that I wanted to get into racing full-time, I was single, and moving was no problem.

"Three weeks later they asked if I wanted to come work on a trial basis. They said they were coming to Birmingham in the summer of 1980 to run a race there. Don Sprouse, a local racer in Greenville, was going to drive their car and run for Rookie of the Year in '81.

"Labor Day of '80 they came to Birmingham. Well, the previous week I had worked on Mike Alexander's car, and we were running the same race. I had worked on his car all night long the night before the race, and when the Rogers team finally pulled through the gate, I left Alexander's car and walked down to this car and started to work on it. I was a nut-and-bolt person, a general mechanic. I packed wheel bearings, changed springs.

"After the race, I went back to Greenville with the Rogers team, and after working with them for about four weeks, they said, 'If you want to go to work full-time, you are more than hired.' I didn't hesitate. I went back to Birmingham, packed a Jartran trailer behind the car I was driving, and brought what little bit I had to Greenville—scared to death, I might add. I was twenty-one years old, scared real bad, but felt I had to do it.

"In '80 we ran two Winston Cup races, Richmond and Martinsville, got ready for winter, worked hard and got ready for 1981.

"We went to Riverside, which back then was the first race of the season, and we did not make the show. If you don't think that's disheartening . . . going all the way out to California and not getting to race and then having to load up and make the long haul back.

"The next race was the Daytona 500. I had only been there as a spectator. All during the years before I worked on race cars, Bobby Jones and I would go to Daytona in February for Speed Week, so I had seen it.

"We wrecked in the 125-miler, but fortunately we had run fast enough to make the 500, but halfway through the race Don Sprouse gave out, did not have the stamina to run five hundred miles, and if you can't do it at Daytona, chances are you aren't going to do it anywhere. Don was an older man. He and the car owner were close friends, and they had a dream they were going to do this together. When Don got out of the car, Kyle Petty drove relief for us, and he ran pretty decent for us, and we finished twentieth.

"We went to Richmond, qualified well there, and again, the same deal: Don gave out about two-thirds through the race.

"By that time Bob Rogers, the car owner, put friendship aside. He didn't have a sponsor and was spending a lot of money, though racing wasn't nearly as expensive as it is today. He had three employees and was renting engines from a guy in Asheville.

"After Richmond, Bob called the three of us together and said, 'What are we going to do? We can't operate this way.' We all knew that back at Riverside. But I was pretty young. I had been to five Winston Cup races. I'm going to make a decision to boost a driver? So I kept quiet.

"The crew chief, Raymond Kelly, wasn't bashful. He said, 'You gotta do something. We can't race this way.' So ironically—and I can tell you I had absolutely nothing to do with it—they hired Mike Alexander, who I had worked with when I left Birmingham.

"With Little Mike we had some pretty decent runs through the summer. We skipped Texas in June and Riverside because of some engine trouble and the cost of going there, but we made all the other races. Like me, Little Mike was real young, not nearly ready for Winston Cup racing, not even close, and he knows that today, and he tore up a lot of race cars.

"At the same time Bob Rogers's large fortune was turning into a small one.

"We finished dead last at Richmond in mid-September 1981, didn't complete a lap because of wiring problems, and with seven races to go, Bob and Mike parted company, and Bob hired Tim Richmond. Tim Richmond had left D. K. Ulrich and had been driving for Kenny Childers, and they had parted ways.

"Bob Rogers called Tim up, offered him some money to drive the car, and with Tim we ran really, really good. And by this juncture Bob Rogers had stopped getting our motors from his guy in Asheville and began renting motors from DiGard's engine builder, Robert Yates.

"In the fall Charlotte race, we were racing second with forty laps to go. Bobby Allison was leading, and we didn't have to pit, and he did, so we could have won the race. And we broke a crankshaft.

"We ran real good at Riverside—Tim was a great road racer—until Tim broke a shifter. We finished twentieth.

"I loved the way Tim drove a car. Tim Richmond—no doubt in my mind—was the closest thing to Dale Earnhardt, if not better. Jumping forward, and I'm not saying this because he's our driver, Davey Allison is right there with them too.

"But you could put Tim Richmond in a covered wagon, and if it would steer to the left, he would get the most out of it. And there is only a handful of drivers you can put in that category—Richmond, Dale, Davey Allison, and Cale Yarborough. And I think Ernie Irvan is right there with them. They milk the most they can out of a race car. It doesn't have to be a perfect setup for them to race good.

"So 1981 ended, and Bob Rogers's money was getting pretty low to go another year of racing without a sponsor. Tim Richmond knew this. He realized we wouldn't run the full circuit without a sponsor, so Tim went off and put together a deal with Harry Hyde and J. D. Stacy out of Kentucky.

"Here we were a race team with no sponsor, low on funds, no driver. So what were we going to do?

"Tom Sneva, and Indy racer, was hunting a part-time Winston Cup ride. He didn't want to run the full circuit. He had Simoniz as his sponsor, and Simoniz signed a twelve-race deal to carry us through the Charlotte race in May.

"We wanted to run the full circuit, so we got Sneva to run his races and got Donnie Allison to run the fill-in races with Simoniz on the car.

"We didn't run well with Sneva, didn't run well at Daytona or at Atlanta. I can't put all the blame on the drivers who left Rogers. The transmission went out at Daytona, and then the rear end went at Atlanta, so maybe we didn't have the best equipment and engines in the world. We were inexperienced and didn't have all the funds in the world to work with.

"So Sneva left, but Rogers's contract with Simoniz didn't say he had to be the driver, and at that time Neil Bonnett wanted to run all the races, but he was driving for the Wood Brothers, and they refused to run all the races, so Rogers was asked if he would run the races the Wood Brothers wouldn't.

"And so what we did, we ran Donnie Allison at all the superspeedways with Simoniz on the car and ran Neil Bonnett in a red, white, and blue car with no sponsor on the short tracks. We did that because if you are on a shoestring budget, you want to run all the races, because if you don't, your purse is much less because you don't get the show-up money for running all the races. So it pays to run all the races, especially if you're trying to find every dime you can.

"After about three races, Neil decided this wasn't what he wanted to do. We ran Donnie Allison in the World 600, finished way back when he had engine failure. Simoniz pulled away, Neil pulled away. So Bob Rogers said, 'I have to end this. I can't go any further without sponsorship.'

"He let the other two employees go. I had been with him a month shy of two years, and he kept me on and paid me for as long as I wanted a job. He wanted me to clean up, wax, and shine his racing equipment for an auction.

"In early July of '82, two months after he shut the doors, he held the auction. Mark Martin and his mother came to it. His mother was the business manager of the race team. That year he ran the full circuit and was named Rookie of the Year, more or less out of his own pocket.

"I didn't know Mark that well, but he and his mom bought a couple motors and a car, and while they were there, they asked, 'Larry, what are you going to do?' I told them I had a job until I found something. They asked, 'Would you like to work for us?' I said I would talk to them.

"A week or so later I went up and talked to Mark's mom. Their shop was at the Charlotte Speedway, where Darrell Waltrip is now. I went up there, and they hired me. Rogers let me go with his blessings. I moved to Charlotte and went to work for Mark.

"I went to work as his crew chief, which at the time I didn't realize they were hiring me for. I only had a year and a half experience under my belt. We ran the last half of the '82 season with me carrying the title of crew chief, which I was not ready for, and I shouldn't have had that job.

"They had had the support of Apache stoves, but the deal was going away, and their money was low, and it was known that at the end of the year they would shut their doors, and Mark was going to take a ride with J. D. Stacy for '83.

"Sure enough that happened, so I went job hunting during the winter. Meanwhile, I met my wife working for Mark. She was dating a member of Mark's crew. We three had become close friends, and right before the racing season ended, they split up, and she and I became closer friends—

that's all we were, friends—but the next thing I knew, by Christmastime we were dating.

"During my job hunt, I talked to Richard Childress, an independent owner, who offered me a job as a crew member. I talked to the Pettys. Richard Petty offered me a job, but the pay wasn't very good considering I would have had to commute from Greensboro to Charlotte. I was to work as a crew member on the 42 car, which Kyle was going to drive.

"There was also a new team being formed by Raymond Beadle called Blue Max. Raymond Beadle was a drag racer who had the Old Milwaukee sponsorship and wanted to go Winston Cup racing as a car owner. Raymond had raced smart. He was a multiple-car owner—had a sprint car, a drag car, and now a Winston Cup car. He drove the drag car, Sammy Swindell drove his sprint car, and Tim Richmond was going to drive his Winston Cup car.

"He had bought out all of M. C. Anderson's equipment. Tim Brewer was the crew chief, Harold Elliott was hired to be his chief engine builder, and when he hired Tim Richmond, whom I remained good friends with, to be the driver, Richmond recommended me to him.

"I went to work for Blue Max the first of December 1982, strictly as a mechanic. I even drove the truck. It was the first major race team I worked for. We had a lot of people, and we worked hard that winter.

"Tim was a pretty flamboyant person. I was around him a lot. He would go out with a lot of different women, lived a pretty outgoing life-style. Tim died of AIDS, but I can honestly say Tim wasn't a homosexual, and he didn't do drugs. I can form that opinion being around him as much as I was.

"The first four races of the '83 season we ran okay. Then we went to Darlington, and we sat on the pole. If you can sit on the pole, it's a big plus, means a lot psychologically, and it's worth some money.

"Darlington was one of those tracks Tim got around very well. Not a lot of drivers can get around Darlington well. Davey Allison can, Harry Gant, and obviously David Pearson did. It's a tricky racetrack. It's not symmetrical. Corners one and two are normal, but three and four are like three different corners with a straightaway in between the last two. It's an egg-shaped racetrack, and your car has to handle well, and your driver has to know how to get around there, because it's a one-groove racetrack.

"We sat on the pole, set a new track record: 157.818 miles an hour. Everyone on our team was all pumped up, but our race team was one of those that had a real pretty cover on it, like a book, but it was terrible on the inside. There were a lot of internal problems. We had paychecks that bounced. We would go weeks and not get paid. When we went to Daytona the first race, we hadn't been paid in three weeks. We got to Darlington, and they wouldn't mount us any tires because the tire bill hadn't been paid. Tim Brewer had to pay them some cash money to pacify them enough to where they would mount us some tires so we could qualify.

"The other problem was all the high-powered people who were hired had a power struggle. Crew members had been crew chiefs, and there was a lot of backstabbing.

"We started Darlington, took the green flag, went down the backstretch, and blew up, and that started another round of finger pointing.

"We came home from Darlington. At this point my girlfriend and I had fallen in love and were talking about getting married. I told her, 'Life is too short to go through this. It's one big turmoil, from the minute you walk through the door to the time you go home.'

"At the same time, Bob Rogers called me. He said, 'I want to go back into racing, but I want to do it a little smarter this time. I want to go Busch Grand National racing,' which is one division lower than Winston Cup. 'I can get Butch Lindley to drive.' At that juncture, he had won two or three Busch National championships and had won maybe four hundred races.

"I would have had to move back to Greenville if I had taken his offer. And at this point Winston Cup racing was important to me, though racing and being competitive was what mattered most. Also, I asked Linda to marry me.

"We moved to Greenville. She got a job as a dental assistant. We started with zero. Rogers had sold everything, and I and the two other guys worked like Trojans trying to get this team going. Before a race at Hampton, Virginia, we worked four straight days and nights to get a car ready. I slept the entire trip from Greenville to Hampton.

"We sat on the outside pole with Tommy Ellis on the pole. They ran fifty laps side by side, and about sixty laps into the race a car with an oil leak came from pit road and hit Tommy Ellis's left door, and Tommy hit us, and the last I saw our brand-new race car was going out of the racetrack on its roof!

"Even before that I sensed that Bob Rogers didn't have the money to do this deal again, and the Tuesday after Hampton, he said, 'Larry, I'm going to close the doors.' And this time he didn't say, 'I'm going to pay you two weeks' severance.' He said, 'This is it, the last day for everybody and everything.' And he locked the doors.

"Here I was, twenty-three years old, engaged to be married—we weren't scheduled to be married until October—and I'm in Greenville, South Carolina, again without a job. I was about to pack it up and go back to Birmingham and start over. If Linda wanted to come, fine; if she didn't, I'm sorry.

"But there was that little bit in my bloodstream that wouldn't let me quite do it. Linda was working, and that's what we were living off.

"A guy by the name of Bobby Hawkins owned a big tool company in Greenville. He owned the Winston Cup team David Pearson was driving for, but the team was operating out of David's shop and the employees worked for David. This was their deal, and their sponsor was Chattanooga Chew, which went with David.

"Bobby Hawkins called me and wanted to know if I wanted to go to work. I said, 'Absolutely. I got to go back to work, and I'd like to go back to work racing.'

"I went to work at David's, even though my paycheck came from Bobby. Me and one other boy in the shop were the only ones who didn't have the last name Pearson. David had his three boys working there—Larry, Eddie, and Ricky—plus me and this other boy. Me and Ricky Pearson were employed by Bobby to work on the Winston Cup car. David's other two boys and this other boy were employed by David to work on Larry's Sportsman car.

"We were only running ten Winston Cup races. David had no desire to run the full circuit.

"I'll always treasure being able to work with David Pearson. He was a super-nice person. He was a gentleman and a good businessman, and he did everything right. It was comforting to walk into that racetrack knowing you had the experience of a David Pearson sitting in that race car.

"We ran ten races in '83 and '84, a pretty good deal for me. For a guy who just got married, I didn't have to work late at night. We never worked weekends that we weren't racing. And I was making between $25,000 and $30,000. I had no complaints and probably would have done that the rest of my life if other things had not changed and come along.

"At the end of '84 Bobby Hawkins and David kind of got stagnant with each other. Bobby wanted to do more, to be more competitive; the other wanted less. They parted company. David went to drive for Hoss Ellington and took his Chattanooga Chew sponsorship.

"Ricky Pearson was *not* going to leave his dad—so I was the only employee of Bobby Hawkins, and the two of us had to move a truck, trailer, some cars, motors, and equipment to a shop Bobby had in Traveler's Rest, South Carolina, a suburb of Greenville.

"Bobby said, 'You've got a job indefinitely. Get our stuff in order. I don't know what we're going to do yet.' A short time later, he said,

'What do you think about building a short track Winston Cup car, and we'll try to get Butch Lindley to drive it?'

"I said, 'You've got my vote.' We talked to Butch, and he agreed. If you ask twenty people with racing experience who was the best Busch Grand National driver that ever was, eighteen would say, 'Butch Lindley.' Butch was smooth, won a lot of races, but he insisted upon being competitive, even if it was driving a go-cart. He didn't want to be a middle-pack burner or a back marker.

"We built a brand-new short track car, and we were going to run it at North Wilkesboro in April of 1985. Butch was still running a lot of short tracks all over the Southeast in a little Camaro. The week before Darlington Butch was going to run a short track race in his Camaro at Bradenton, Florida. On Friday morning Butch came by the shop. He had to leave to drive to Bradenton.

"I said, 'See ya Monday. We'll be ready.' Wilkesboro opened the following Friday.

"On Sunday morning about five o'clock the phone rang. During the race at Bradenton Saturday night Butch had broken a trailing arm, which holds the rear end in the car, and the car had spun the wrong way and he hit the wall on the driver's side. Butch hit his head against the wall, and he was in a coma. And he was in that coma for five years until he died in June of 1990.

"Out of respect for Butch, we didn't go to North Wilkesboro, but there where three of us working on that car full-time. It was our job, our livelihood, so the three of us and Bobby sat down to discuss what we were going to do. Bobby said, 'We gotta continue. Butch would want us to.'

"We called Morgan Shepherd, who didn't have a full-time ride. In my mind he was a good short track driver, a good driver period.

"The next race was Martinsville, and Morgan loves Martinsville. We qualified third. About ninety laps into the race we were running second, but coming off turn four the car blew a right tire, spun around, and hit the inside wall, wiping that race car out. I mean, it was reduced to nothing!

"We drove that thing back home. It was the only car we had; we had sold the old Pearson cars. And it was tore up. I never saw a car tore up so bad. It was killed.

"The short tracks are not good paying races, so Bobby and I decided to build a speedway car for Charlotte and Michigan, so during the summer we started all over again, working like a Trojan, with Bobby financing us out of his pocket.

"Bobby owns a company called the Carolina Tool Company. His trucks have a motor hoist and an engine stand in the back. He has them all over the country selling motor hoists, jack stands, band saws, engine stands.

"We decided that when we could go racing and do it right, that's when we would go. If we weren't ready financially or competitively, we wouldn't do it.

"We built a new speedway car, and Morgan agreed to drive it wherever and whenever we were ready.

"On September 1 we ran at Darlington and burned a piston, and then we ran real good at Charlotte and equalized a tire and ended up finishing seventh. Not bad. We were happy. We were a team out of Traveler's Rest with three guys, and we ran in the top five most of the day.

"My future? I didn't know. I was just racing as it came to me.

"In late October 1985 Kenny Bernstein, the drag racer, wanted to do what Raymond Beadle had done. Kenny acquired the Quaker State sponsorship, and they had wanted Joe Ruttman to be the driver. Kenny had a driver, the sponsorship, but he had no racing team.

"R. J. Reynolds was real close to Kenny through drag racing, and they knew of the Bobby Hawkins situation. RJR and NASCAR will work hard to form a team if they can help push it along, and so they drew together Bobby Hawkins and Kenny Bernstein.

"We were going to form a partnership called King Hawkins Racing, but it didn't take two weeks to realize that Kenny Bernstein and Bobby Hawkins, who are both super-good people, just weren't on the same song sheet. Their business techniques clashed. Bobby is going to work hard, make money, but he's going to have fun too. Kenny is all business—a, b, c, d. So right before the last race of the year, after the deal was done, Kenny offered to buy Bobby Hawkins out. Kenny offered a substantial amount of money, and Bobby said, 'Sold.'

"We went and ran our last race of the year at Atlanta. It was the same red, white, and blue car with number 16 on it, but Kenny Bernstein owned it, and we ran like a ra-ped ape down at Atlanta, ran second or third all day, and with twenty laps to go we equalized a tire, got a lap down, and finished fifth.

"During this whole deal in '85, I was the per se crew chief. There weren't but three of us, but I answered to Bobby and made the calls in the pits. By this point, I had seen a lot, and though I still hadn't done it for a full-fledged Winston Cup team, I felt I was ready.

"When Kenny came in, he designated me crew chief and hired six more full-time employees. Morgan Shepherd really wanted to drive this

Quaker State car the next year, but Kenny had already signed a deal with Joe Ruttman.

"Joe Ruttman is a super nice guy. He never blamed anybody but himself for anything. The hardest person on himself was himself.

"In 1986 we went racing for a full season, running Buicks. For a beginning team, I'm proud to say in the first ten races we ran really good. We ran real good at Daytona and got in a horrendous crash with Harry Gant and a bunch of others. We ran second at Richmond, the second race. We ran second at Martinsville, led at Dover, but we had a lot of motor failures in those first ten races, at Darlington, Rockingham, Charlotte, Dover.

"When an engine fails, 95 percent of the time it's somebody fault, whether the manufacturer that made the part or the mechanic who worked on it. If you burn a piston, that's a tuning failure. If you break a rod or valve spring, maybe you twisted it too tight, turning it too many rpms. It's always someone's fault, though you don't always play the finger-pointing game. But there is one thing you have to be careful of: Our sponsor was Quaker State, and it's bad to blow engines with an oil sponsorship.

"We went to Riverside, California, and four laps into the race we blowed the bottom out of the engine when we broke a rod.

"We had been renting motors from a guy in Asheville. Kenny said, 'I gotta do something different on motors.'

"At that point Robert Yates wasn't working on a race team. He had an engine racing company at the speedway, and the same shops I was in in '82 with Mark Martin. So we started renting motors from Robert Yates, and that was better, but about two-thirds of the way through 1986 Joe started having business problems with Kenny Bernstein, so you didn't have to be real smart to know Ruttman wouldn't be driving in '87, even though we had had some good races in '86, ran in the top five several times, and for a beginning team all in all it was pretty satisfying.

"Kenny wanted Morgan Shepherd. He had been impressed with the way he had run the year before. If our year with Ruttman was a four out of ten, with Morgan it was a five or six. We sat on the pole at Martinsville, but still there was something missing. I can't say Kenny and Morgan got along that good.

"Kenny is the kind of guy who will tell you what's on his mind, whether you want to hear it or not. He'll tell me, 'The car isn't handling very well.' He'd tell Morgan, 'I don't think you're driving it very well.' He'll tell the motor department, 'We don't have enough power.'

"I also have to say that Morgan changed some from '85. That year, when we were doing pretty much what we wanted, Morgan was easy to work with, easy to get along with, but in '87 he was under contract and harder to get along with, harder to please.

"At the same time Kenny Bernstein and Ricky Rudd were real good friends, because Kenny had driven a Motorcraft drag car and Ricky was driving a Motorcraft Winston Cup car for Bud Moore.

"Kenny and Ricky started talking in July of '87. You could see the handwriting that Morgan Shepherd wasn't going to drive our car more than one year. Sure enough, late in '87, Kenny hired Ricky Rudd to drive the Quaker State car for two years.

"Kenny Bernstein also brought in Ron Armstrong from California to be our engine builder in '88.

"Robert Yates had to leave us at the end of '86 when he was hired to run Harry Ranier's engine program. Kenny then hired Eddie Lanier, who today is Richard Childress's head engine builder, but in '87 we were lacking in horsepower.

"In 1988 with Ron and Ricky Rudd we had a really good year—but we also had a really bad year. Ricky won at Watkins Glen in August. In eight years of Winston Cup racing, it was my first win. It took about two weeks to sink in. It was the best feeling in the world to be crew chief and know you accomplished it.

"We sat on two poles that year with Ricky, at Martinsville and at Riverside, the last race they ever ran there, and we set a new track record. Nobody can ever take the track record away from the 26 car of Ricky Rudd.

"Ricky was a super-good person to work with. He's a smart race car driver. He can tell you what the car is doing, but he can't help you fix it.

"The bad part was he kept blowing up engines. During the last half of '88, from the 1st of September covering the last twelve races, we were leading four or five of them with less than thirty laps to go, led Martins-ville with forty to go, led Phoenix with thirteen to go, and we blew an engine each time.

"Ron Armstrong was a super-smart, super-dedicated worker, but it was like when they threw me in as crew chief in '82. It wasn't fair to the man to bring him in after doing some engine work on the West Coast and throwing him into Winston Cup competition for thirty races. We lost twenty-one engines between practice and testing and twelve in races.

"When you have an oil sponsorship, as we did with Quaker State, you can't blow that many motors. What were we going to do?

"Lou LaRosa, who was Richard Childress's chief engine builder, had left RCR [Richard Childress Racing]. He was available, but to get him, Lou said we had to move from Greenville to Charlotte. Lou would not move to us.

Kenny and I put our heads together. He said, 'Moving to Charlotte might not be all bad. That's where the nucleus of Winston Cup racing is. We can pull good help; we'd be close to a lot of the racetracks. It has to be a plus.'

"The winter of '88–'89 we moved the entire race team to Charlotte. My wife and I had been happy in Greenville. She was four months pregnant. She had supported me in anything and everything I've done, so I told her we would stay in Greenville, and I would commute the 101 miles each way. But after five months I couldn't do it anymore, and we moved too.

"Kenny built a brand-new shop in Charlotte; Lou LaRosa was our engine builder, Ricky Rudd our driver for '89. Everything looked good. In '89 we had exactly two engine failures. We won a race, at Sears Point, beating out Rusty Wallace in a close one. Ricky finished eighth in championship points.

"But though the engines didn't blow up, we didn't have much horsepower either. Some races we spotted Davey Allison and the 28 car as much as 100 horsepower. Lou LaRosa, who twice was Engine Builder of the Year, was one of those types of guys who never thought his engines had any problems. I would show him straightaway speeds, but his answer always was, 'I ain't got no weak motors.'

"By the middle of '89, Lou and Kenny Bernstein were not seeing eye to eye. And Ricky got fed up, and he said, 'I'll tell you what. I'm going to go drive for Rick Hendrick.'

"Between '89 and '90, drivers were pretty scarce. A lot of them were in the middle of their contracts, so Kenny let the race team vote on who it wanted. Brett Bodine, who had succeeded Ricky Rudd at Bud Moore's shop, was our choice; Quaker State liked it, and he hired Brett, who only had two years of Winston Cup experience.

"With Brett we ran a lot better than I thought we would. When we hired Brett, we set several goals. We wanted to win a race, and we wanted to finish in the top ten in points. We won the seventh race of the year at North Wilkesboro, and in the fall we sat on the pole at Charlotte, and we finished two positions shy of tenth in the standings.

"On the engine side, Lou LaRosa was still doing the motors. The motors were still suffering on the power side, and in July Kenny Bernstein told him 'You go home. I'll pay you what the rest of your contract calls for.' It would have been so much better if Lou had taken input, but he had his own plan, and that's the way it was going to be, come hell or high water.

"And when Lou left, Kenny let some of the guys in the shop run the engine program, and it was amazing how much better we started running. It takes a lot of horsepower to sit on the pole at Charlotte.

"After '90, I shook Kenny Bernstein's hand and agreed to stay with him two more years. Brett re-upped for two more years. Quaker State was going into their second year on their contract. We were all pretty excited.

"We went to Daytona in '91, and we had as bad a Daytona as you could ever have. We ran terrible in the time trials, crashed in the 125s, and crashed in the 500 because of all those goofy pit rules they had come up with. We had a flat tire and couldn't change it under the caution without giving up a lap, and when they restarted the race, it blew, and we hit the wall.

"We went to Richmond, had a good run going, but with fifteen laps to go, Hut Stricklin cut Brett off and we knocked the wall down again. After running decently at Rockingham, we went to Atlanta and sat on the outside pole. In the race, we finished a disappointing fifteenth. Once again, we didn't have the power we needed. It was like we had lost something. We had finished '90 so well, and our performance in '91 was way below our expectations.

"If you remember that Atlanta race, there was a rain delay after forty laps, and when it resumed, we ran terribly. The car was loose, the motor wouldn't run—Brett Bodine screamed and yelled all day about the motor not running.

"Two weeks before, at the Rockingham race, Robert Yates, who owned the 28 car driven by Davey Allison, approached me. He said, 'Larry, won't you think about coming over with us?'

"It wasn't the first time he had asked me. The first time was at Phoenix in 1989, and I thought about it and thought about it and thought about it, and when you are with a team as long as I had been, since the middle of '83, I'm the type of guy who likes to stick with the deal. I don't believe in job-hopping.

"I turned Robert down. I liked Robert's engine program, liked Davey, but against my better judgment, I just couldn't get my heart to go along with it. I had watched our team grow from two guys building an old car to get ready to go to North Wilkesboro with Butch Lindley to a major-sponsored race team, and with Kenny I was crew chief and general manager, and so I stayed.

"Robert approached me again before the '90 season. We sat in a

Waffle House north of Charlotte, sat from eight at night until one in the morning drinking coffee. Robert was offering me a good program. He wanted me to come. Davey wanted me to come. Davey and I had never worked together, but we were friends all the way back to Birmingham; but I was looking forward to the '91 season with Brett, because of the things we had done. We had sat on the outside pole at Atlanta, for instance.

"And then Robert asked me again at Rockingham in March of 1991. Robert told me they were doing okay but that Jake Elder, his crew chief, was cussing, raising cain, couldn't get along with anybody, and he wanted me to replace him. I told him, 'I haven't shut the door on it, but right now I'm here where I'm at.'

"After that terrible experience at Atlanta, where our car didn't run and Brett was screaming the whole race long how the motor wouldn't run, on the ride home my wife and I didn't say five words to each other. I said to her, 'I can't believe I let that 28-car deal slip through my fingers again. I ought to be over there working right now.'

"She said, 'All you have to do is call Robert.'

"I said, 'No, Jake is there. I'm not going to change jobs in the middle of the season.' If you remember, I did that once when I left Blue Max, and I was left with a wife-to-be and no job.

"We got home about ten o'clock. I was unloading the van. We had barely walked in the door, and the phone rang. I said, 'Linda, if that's for me, tell them I'm out feeding the dog, or asleep, or something.'

"She came to the door and said, 'Telephone.' I said, 'Linda, I told you . . .'

"She said, 'You just might want to take this phone call.' It was Robert Yates. He said, 'Larry, I'm going to make a change, one way or the other. I'm going to offer you this deal one more time.'

"I said, 'Robert, I want to talk to you in the morning at seven o'clock.'

"The one good thing about the offer he was making me, it was *not* for more money. It was a carbon copy of what I was getting with Kenny Bernstein, and I was glad. I wanted to come over for the right reasons, not the dollar reasons.

"We met in the morning, and we laid a program out about what we were going to do, and I accepted it, and I went and told Kenny I was leaving, because I knew the way Kenny operated. In racing it's best to end it and go away. And Kenny and I parted friends, even though Kenny didn't accept my decision. Being a businessman, deep down inside he knew why I was making this change. He knew if it was him, he would have done the same thing.

"So in April '91, I came over to Robert Yates Racing. I knew it was going to be good when I came over, but I never quite dreamed it would be as good as it's been.

"Here's the difference between Kenny and Robert, and I'm not saying this to put Kenny down or pump Robert up: Kenny has a drag-racing team he drives for with a Budweiser sponsorship that does really well. He has an Indy car, which at the time was backed by Mack Tools and now Quaker State. He has a Winston Cup team. His real money-maker is a sports marketing company in Indianapolis that does sports marketing and PR work for Quaker State, Buick, and Goodyear. He has a racing computer company called King Racing Components that markets a racing computer. He has so many irons in the fire, is going in so many different directions, he has no time for any one thing.

"Kenny and I would talk to each other every day of the year, Christmas day included, New Year's Day. Kenny couldn't be there, but he was a big communicator. I would find myself standing in phone booths in a two-minute conversation trying to explain to Kenny what happened at a race.

"Robert Yates is a hands-on car owner. He knows the ups and downs of Winston Cup racing. He's been at it for twenty-five years, and you don't ever have to explain anything.

"Robert is with you every single day of the week, eating, sleeping, breathing with you. He gets up at five o'clock with you, he leaves the racetrack at quitting time. He's in when you come in the door. He's here when you go home. Kenny can't be that way. He can't. He has too much going on.

"It was the toughest decision I ever made in my life. Making the decision to ask my wife to marry me wasn't nearly as tough as leaving Kenny and going with Robert Yates. Even now, when I see that 26 car go by, I think of myself with them, because I had been there that long.

"I came over to the Robert Yates team four races into the season. A week after I came we went to Darlington and tested for two days, and about halfway through the first day I knew we had the capability of running really good, that we had horsepower I never had had before.

"That night I called my wife and I said, 'I hate to make a premeditated call or make a rash judgment, but Linda, there is no doubt in my mind I made the best move in my life.'

"The other plus in making the change has been my chance to work with Davey Allison. This is no reflection on Brett or any other driver I ever worked with, but Davey is a very experienced driver, and he's very aggressive, and that means a lot. He runs every lap like it's the last one.

"Davey is also the calmest race car driver I ever worked with. Away from the race car, I never heard Ricky Rudd raise his voice to me—or to anybody else, for that matter—but when he buckled that helmet on, it was like a Dr. Jekyll and Mr. Hyde. He'd scream and yell and cuss for three hours all during the race, and then after the race he'd get out of that car and hug your neck. He was an excellent race car driver, but he'd scream and yell and cuss you for everything you were worth. The ignition switch would go off, and click, it was like turning off a character switch. But Davey Allison—I have never talked to anybody on the radio as cool and as calm, even when we're running bad.

"In May of 1991 we won the World 600 at Charlotte. That's six hundred miles, a tough race to win. It's tough to be there at the end, much less win it.

"With about thirty laps to go, you get that empty feeling, 'Something will happen any minute. The engine will blow, the gear will tear up, we'll blow a tire.' You get that way, because at the World 600, you have to run a hundred miles more than any other race, so you get that feeling.

"We had a nine-or-ten-second lead, and nothing could stop us from winning, unless . . .

"Davey and I weren't saying a lot on the radio. Every five or ten laps I was keeping him posted about the second-place car and about how many laps remained. He came on the radio, and he said, 'Larry, you aren't going to believe what's happening.' My heart went up to my throat. I said to myself, 'Well, here it is.'

" 'What happened?' I asked. He said, 'There's an Earnhardt fan hanging through the backstretch, and every time I go past him, he flips me off.'

"I said, 'Man, what are you doing that to me for?' I just knew he was going to say, 'We lost a cylinder, or the motor is tightening up, or something just fell off or went through the windshield.' And here he was, talking just like he was on a Sunday drive.

"At Dover the next week we ran terribly. We only had three bad races the whole year, and that was one of them. We were getting lapped every fifty laps, the car wouldn't turn right, and about four hundred laps into the race Davey came on the radio and said, 'Larry.' I said, 'Yeah.' He said, 'You got some doughnuts in them pits?' Krispy Kremes is an associate sponsor. I said, 'Yeah, why?' He said, 'Man, we ain't got a chance of doing much good today. I'm just trying to ride the thing out, but at the next caution, have Robert hand me a couple. I'm about to starve to death.'

"And that helps, him being so calm and cool and collected on the radio. So what I'm saying is Davey is the same person not only when we're winning and running good but also when we run terrible.

"And when you have a driver like that, it keeps the crew members pumped up, and they don't get discouraged. When you have a driver out there screaming and yelling and telling you how bad the car is, the crewmen finally say, 'Why am I working seventy hours next week for this cat? He's going to walk away after the race and not know we exist until the next Thursday.' With Davey, we have fellowship and unity, and it's that unity which will win races for us and hopefully win us the championship in 1992.

"The other good things about working for this 28 car is that if you went and asked anyone on the circuit who has the most horsepower, 100 percent would say, 'The number 28 car.'

"In the past I always questioned whether our driver was capable to win or whether we would have enough horsepower. But I can say in the twenty-five races I've been here, because of what I know about Robert Yates's engines and about Davey, those questions have never once entered my mind. In the last forty-eight races, we've had exactly one engine failure. We broke a crankshaft at Dover, and we aren't so sure we didn't do that in Saturday practice. When you have that kind of durability, that kind of power, and your driver is doing the job, and if we as the crew do our job, we should have a terrific season.

"I've heard people say many times, 'Larry did this, Larry did that.' Well, that's nice and makes me feel good, but I didn't come over here and wave a wand and say, 'Okay, all these cars are going to be good.' They had a good race team when I came here. The faces are identical to when I walked in the door. They just had no one to give them direction, to set a plan for them, to tell them, 'This is the car we're going to run in this race, this is the car we're going to run in the next race, and here is a list of what I want done to them.'

"They had nobody to pat them on the back when they did good, as well as tell them what they did wrong. They had a guy who screamed and yelled at them eight of the nine hours of the day, and to me it was like I walked into a house where there were nine children who had been beaten —good kids, beautiful kids, but they had been beat on for a couple years. They just needed someone to come in and say, 'Okay, you're a good worker. You can do it. I'm not going to scream at you. I'll tell you what you did wrong, but I'm not going to scream and hammer at you.' And that's all this team missed. They had all the ingredients, had the driver, had the power plant and the pit crew to change tires on Sunday.

"What tears teams apart are egos and people who think the team is on one level and they are up above them. I wouldn't ask my guys to do anything I wouldn't do myself. I wouldn't ask them to work any hours I wouldn't work myself. And hopefully, that will continue to make me a successful crew chief. The best quarterback or football coach is nothing without the people who support him. It's no different in car racing, and right now we have a nucleus that's tight. We're getting ready for Daytona in 1992. You'd have to say if anyone is favored, it has to be Dale Earnhardt and Richard Childress, which is another team that has the same faces year after year, or it has to be Davey Allison and Robert Yates. We'll be ready. If anyone wants to win the Daytona 500, to do it they're going to have to run faster than us.''

Kirk Shelmerdine

LAP 19

Kirk Shelmerdine

The Seer

To reach the tiny town of Welcome, North Carolina, located about 18 miles southwest from Winston-Salem, you drive north on Route 52 from suburban Lexington. Welcome, like many tiny Southern towns, used to be an isolated community of mill workers and farmers. Driving along, one passes mobile-home sites, barbecue joints with pictures of pink pigs on the road signs, and, as a reminder of the town's farming history, one old red barn stands forlornly, its roof sagging precariously in the middle.

Just before the town line, a new highway slashes through the thick pines. Isolation for Welcome, as it is for much of the Old South, is disappearing as new arteries bring more traffic and population growth and as the Yankees leave the Northeast and the Midwest Rust Belt and invade the South.

The Welcome Church of God is white clapboard and brick, and has a simple white steeple. The sign for the church is the first indication you are in the town. On the right is Amvets Post 760, and on the left is the school. At the first traffic light, one of only three in town, you make a right turn onto Industrial Drive. After crossing the tracks you arrive at the RCR complex. RCR stands for Richard Childress Racing. Richard Childress, who began as a struggling independent, today is a major force in stock car racing. His driver, Dale Earnhardt, has won the driving championship four of the last six seasons.

In front of the modern brick and glass complex, the American and North Carolina flags fly, along with a white flag with red letters that reads: "1990 Winston Cup champions." A naked pole next to it awaits the banner celebrating 1991.

If there is a legendary driver in NASCAR today, it is Dale Earnhardt. He has a legion of fans. Even more root against him. When he is on the track, *everyone* keeps track of his progress, wherever he might be running. In 1991 Dale Earnhardt won the driving championship despite having a subpar year. He didn't dominate, but he won just enough to deprive the fans of other leading drivers like Davey Allison, Ricky Rudd, Harry Gant, Bill Elliott, and Darrell Waltrip the chance to gloat. For many, going to a race to watch Dale Earnhardt *lose* is as satisfying as watching their favorite win.

If Richard Petty is The King, Dale Earnhardt is The Black Knight.

As I enter the shop, I can hear Mick Jagger and the Rolling Stones singing "Jumpin' Jack Flash" on the stereo system that blasts throughout the high-ceilinged building. It seems only fitting for the Bad Boys of Rock 'n Roll to be strutting their stuff in Dale Earnhardt's workplace.

In a large room, there are two rows of black Chevrolet Luminas. Half sit on red pyramidal chocks, the tires above the floor. The lighting in the large room is indirect, phosphorescent. Despite the work going on to the cars, it is so quiet you can hear the whir of the Very Fine fruit juice machine.

Banners festoon the light gray walls. One signifies Dale Earnhardt's victory in the Winston Cup Series in 1991. Another is for 1990. Another is for 1987. There are also banners for his victories in The Winston in 1987 and in 1990.

To the left is the engine room. In an adjacent room is a dyno machine. There are also rooms for parts and parts assembly.

To the right of all these rooms is the fabrication room. Adjacent but separate is the body shop. I am told the paint facilities are antiquated. The new machinery is on the way. With the new equipment, the wait for the paint to dry will be cut in half. Also in the works: another engine shop that will be devoted solely to research and development of his Chevrolet cars.

Richard Childress has constructed a juggernaut, and his facilities reflect that. But, according to competitors, the element that makes the team great isn't top equipment or money, though they are requirements to be a top team. Rather, what elevates the RCR team above so many of the others is the closeness of the race team, the lack of turnover among the crew, and the farsightedness of the operation. Childress and his general manager and crew chief, Kirk Shelmerdine, are always planning way ahead, working on new ideas for cars for the future.

Shelmerdine, who joined Childress back when the owner was just another struggling independent driver, has been an important member of the race team, a moderating influence when emotions begin to run wild. He has witnessed the transformation of RCR from also-ran to top gun.

Though he would never think of himself in these terms, the quiet-spoken, modest Shelmerdine is a deep-thinking philosopher who always has one foot firmly on the ground, the other striding into the future.

KIRK SHELMERDINE: "I was born in the Philadelphia area. My father was a salesman who worked in the computer field most of his career. We moved around quite a bit in the Northeast, but the Philadelphia area is where I spent most of my time growing up.

"Since I was a kid, I was intrigued with cars. When I was about ten, instead of cutting the grass, I was taking the lawn mower engine apart just to see what was in there. I could take it apart and put it back together without too many pieces left over. When I got a little older, I had go-carts to play with. My dad had no interest in it, still doesn't, but he knew I liked it and wanted it, and so he fixed up a soapbox car made out of wood with wheels and a motor and rope steering, and I went up and down the driveway.

"Once I got older, I had racing go-carts and motorcycles and dirt bikes. I was good at go-cart racing, considering what I knew, which was nothing. I managed not to hurt myself and not to go broke, which was pretty good. The guys who won had parents who spent their retirement money on their kids' equipment. I didn't do anything but put gas in it and fix whatever broke. It wasn't any way to try to win anything, but it was a good way to gain experience and have a lot of fun.

"When I was sixteen, I started thinking about driving a race car. Back then, stock car racing wasn't on TV much, and in the Philly area, everyone drag-raced, and that's what I did. We had a place in Philadelphia near the river underneath the Walt Whitman Bridge.

"We rode down there one night, and there were hot rods on both sides of the street for miles, with people racing in between. I couldn't believe it. The last couple years in high school, I was there every Friday and Saturday night.

"I never got beat. Of course, I picked who I raced, and that helped. I had a Chevelle with a big motor in it. We would race with five or six of us riding in the car. I doubt if we ever got over 100 miles an hour. By the time you got into fourth gear, you could tell if you won or not. That was a lot of fun, and we must have been doing something right to live through that.

"One of the places we had lived while I was a young teenager was Dover, Delaware. There was a stock car track there, and twice a year NASCAR ran Grand National races. I had a friend whose father was Jack Whitby, and he drove the pace car, and he was friends with the owners, and great friends with Tiny Lund, who was the first real race car driver I ever met.

"Meeting Tiny was a rude awakening. Tiny wasn't just heavy, he was real tall, a huge person, and you couldn't imagine him crawling in and out of the race car window. He and Whitby were buddies, and he'd be over there for dinner whenever he'd come to town. I remember that Tiny was different from the adults I was used to, from his appearance and the way he talked. I had never talked to anyone with a Southern accent before. The way I was brought up, you wore a jacket and necktie if you went to somebody's house for dinner. Tiny was wearing average casual clothes. It was a culture shock for me, though later it was easy getting used to.

"When I was seventeen, we left Dover and moved back to the Phila-delphia area, and that's where I finished high school. I was accepted into an extension campus of Penn State within five or six miles of my home. As far as I was concerned, it was going to be four more years of high school, and I just couldn't see it.

"I told my parents, 'I don't want to go to college. I want to do something else.'

"Right then my dad surprised me. I figured I'd never get by with that. It had been a pretty difficult time for my parents and me. My parents had two sons, and they assumed both of them were going to college and would become doctors and lawyers. And here I was, saying I didn't want to do it.

"He said, 'Whatever the hell it is you want to do, be the damn best at it you can. Even if you want to play poker, be the best poker player you can be.' He said, 'If you want to go somewhere and get a job racing cars, do it.'

"I wasn't ready for him saying that. But that's just what I ended up doing. I called Mr. Whitby—I had worked for him part-time and we got to be pretty good friends. He was a General Motors car dealer. I worked for him training hunting dogs to go out and get the ducks and bring them back. I was a bird boy, a fun job, and we'd go out on Saturdays, and I'd get a little spending money. Anyway, he knew a little bit about racing, and I went down and told him what I wanted to do. I asked, 'What's the best way to go about it?'

"He got me a job with James Hylton, who nobody has heard of nowadays, but this was 1976, and at that time James was one of the top independent racers, an independent being a guy who owns his own car and works on it himself and drives it and builds his own engines and doesn't really have any employees.

"So Mr. Whitby got me a job with James Hylton, doing anything, and less than a week before classes started, I packed all my things in my car and moved to Inman, South Carolina, outside of Spartanburg, and to stock car racing.

"When I arrived, I had no experience, especially as far as race cars. I started as a gofer. I swept the floor or got a wrench or a part, and since I was the only guy there, I soon got to where if there was work on the car or the engine to be done, I began helping with it, and pretty soon I was putting engines in and out and helping to put them together, and in a matter of a couple years I learned how to work on race cars, anything mechanical as far as bolting something on and off the cars, taking them completely apart and putting them back together again.

"I could do it all, because I started with James, rather than with a big team like Junior Johnson or the Pettys, where if I had gone to work for them, being an eighteen-year-old kid with no experience, they'd have had me cutting the grass and painting the fence and washing the trucks. Although I had to do that with James—he didn't have anyone else there—and I learned everything there was to learn, including chassis building, how the setup works, the springs, the shocks, everything. He built his own engines, so I had a lot of experience in a short time assembling them and starting them up and tuning them up and putting them in and out of the car. And I welded and painted and did bodywork—everything that comes with a race car. I had firsthand experience, and I got a lot of it in a short time.

"We had as good success on the track as you could expect. In the real early seventies James had won a couple races, and by this time it was carrying him. He was still getting a little sponsorship money here and there because of his past successes and because his car still looked as good as anybody else's car, but he couldn't afford to run them hard.

"In 1977 we finished seventh in the points. There were a lot of bigger teams that finished below us. But back then independent drivers finished well in the points. There were three or four then. Today, the independents can't afford to run well. It's a vicious cycle. You can't run well enough to win enough prize money to run well. It's a tough situation.

"The second year I was there, I became crew chief. I was also the truck driver, the parts washer, or whatever title I chose. I was the only employee, so I chose 'crew chief.'

"James had a trailer, and when I say 'trailer,' I mean a one-axle camper that you pull behind a car. It sat on his lot and had electricity and plumbing. He let me live there for free, and I got $50 a week spending money. I didn't really have any overhead: I lived there, and on the road we stayed in the hotels.

"I had pretty much given up my life to racing, but in my view what I was giving up was nothing but college, which was four more years of school, which I hated ever since kindergarten. I did rather well at school, but I hated every minute of it. So it wasn't much of a choice for me. I could go race or I could go sit in school. As far as I was concerned, it wasn't even a decision.

"I was with James Hylton three and a half seasons. He had a lot of part-time helpers in addition to me. The pit crew was all weekend guys who had other jobs during the week, and then Friday night they'd go to the race and work on the car Saturday and race Sunday.

"Some guys fished or played golf on the weekends. These guys went with James and were his pit crew. It was their hobby. They lived in a little town in South Carolina where there isn't a lot to do, and being part of a big-time race team was attractive to them. It was like a town team.

"We almost won a race in 1979 at Martinsville. In those days you had three or four tires you could choose from, and every once in a while the off-brand tires were faster, especially on the short tracks. I remember J. D. McDuffie, who was killed this year, one time sat on a pole at Dover because of his tires. All the independent drivers bought them because they wore longer, got more miles for your money, and because they were stickier, they ran faster. And at Martinsville, ole James was lapping the field, and we were down to the last hundred laps, and there were only two or three cars running with us, and I remember the radio announcer came over to me, and I didn't know what to say. I said, 'We're doing pretty good or you wouldn't be here.' I was scared to death.

"Then his old engine blew up, and we didn't finish too hot.

"At the end of my third full year, I decided I had the potential to do more than what we were doing. I wasn't making a whole lot more money than when I had started, but now I was twenty-two and I knew we were always going to be an also-run, and I wanted to work on cars that could win.

"I had been working from when we got up in the morning until midnight every day. We'd get up, work all morning, go somewhere and eat lunch, come back and work all afternoon, go somewhere and eat dinner, come back and work all night, and fall asleep. I did that for three and a half years.

"The other consideration was when I left home I wanted to be a race car driver. My plan when I left home in 1976 was to be a Winston Cup champion by 1980, and here it was 1979, and I wasn't any closer to it. I had started to build a Baby Grand car, a four-cylinder stock car, but I didn't have any money to finish it, and I didn't have any time because I was spending every minute working on James's car.

"I had become buddies with Gary Nelson, who was chief mechanic on Darrell Waltrip's car at DiGard. DiGard was on top, was winning a lot of races, was running for the championship, and they had a big sponsor in Gatorade. Gary was about my age, a young mechanic at DiGard, I had gotten to know him pretty well, and he got me a job there. It paid a little better, and I didn't have to work so many hours.

" 'This is a gravy job,' I thought. We won a lot of races. Part of what I did was change tires at pit stops, and at the shop I was a staff member, a mechanic, a helper.

"When I left James Hylton, he was upset. He made like he was mad at me, but I know he understood. And it was hard for me to tell him I was leaving, 'cause he had looked after me, brought me up as far as racing goes. We were together almost every waking moment for all that time. And he knew he wasn't going to get somebody else to work like I did for that kind of money, spend the umpteen hours a day on his car.

"DiGard was a whole other ball game, the big time. But I ended up working there only nine months.

"The place was completely nuts. Bill and Jim Gardner, two brothers, ran it. Bill owned the business, but he lived in New Hampshire and was never there. Jim ran the show. They were wealthy, but were race fans, not like Junior Johnson or Richard Childress, who knew every detail of the car. The Gardners liked racing and wanted to do it, but they really didn't know much about it, and looking back, I can only think the whole racing deal was a tax write-off for their other businesses. They had a hobby instead of paying all that money to the government. That's what we all thought, anyway. And that's the way we thought we were being treated.

"Jim was an all-right guy, was fun to be around, but we all thought racing was not the biggest priority in his life.

"Robert Yates was in charge of the engine room. He had two or three guys in there. Noah Brown assembled engines. James Harper was a machinist. Robert Gee was the body man. He's a real famous bodybuilder in Charlotte. Dan Ford was one of the top mechanics on the circuit. Buddy Parrott was the crew chief. A lot of people went through DiGard who are still in racing.

"A lot of the trouble came because Robert Yates had a lot of trouble with the owners getting equipment. Even back then engines were ridiculously expensive, and he would need parts and wouldn't get them.

"That wasn't the worst of it. Everybody there was nuts, and you never knew the next day whether you were going to have a job or not. They had a public relations guy who tried to rally everybody and give them speeches and tell them how great everything was, when we all knew it was pretty screwy. Darrell was having a contract dispute with the owners. They had a bitter fight about him getting out of his contract, which was for ten years. Yates was fighting with them, and Parrott got fired.

"And just when I got in there and got to know what I was supposed to do every day, Gary Nelson quit and went back to California.

"Every now and then we'd still win races, but things just weren't going well—at least what I was hearing was that things weren't going well. As far as I was concerned, everything was fine, but the other workers were all complaining, and things were festering, and everyone knew everything upstairs was crazy.

"Darrell would be saying in the papers how bad everything was, and the way it sounded to us was we could be out of a job tomorrow without any warning. Every day I went in there and had to ask someone what I was supposed to do. I never had a real assignment.

"So Gary left. Buddy Parrott was fired. Yates was fighting with the owners. The whole thing was in an uproar, and after eight months of this, I began thinking, 'If big-time teams operate this way, I'm not sure I want to be part of this.'

"I began to doubt whether I had made the right move five years prior, wondering if racing was the right thing to do. Here I was on the top team in all racing, and they were screwy.

"When they hired Jack Elder as crew chief, I decided to quit. It was the middle of the 1980 season. I worked on the pit crew two or more races. The last race I worked was the Firecracker at Daytona in July, and we blew up every motor we had. We finished thirty-first.

"Here I was, living in Charlotte, out of work. I had a small apartment, had half a race car down in South Carolina in a storage building, some parts, and that was about all.

"I went home long enough to convince myself that what I didn't want was to return home. I came back to Charlotte, and for four months I didn't do anything, just moped around, thought a lot, drank beer, and watched TV. I wanted to race my car, but I didn't have the money to do it. I had no place to work on it. I had a little money for rent, but no income. I was getting to the point where I had to spend my rolls of change. I *had* to do something.

"When I was working for James, Richard Childress had been after me to go work for him, 'cause I guess he noticed I could hustle when I had to and could work on a car. Off and on informally, Richard mentioned it—didn't bug me, just planted the seed. He's kind of that way. Richard won't force anything.

"I had worked for a big-time team, saw how they did things, and that gave me credentials, and I called Richard Childress up one day and said, 'I have a race car, and I want to be able to stick it somewhere and work on it at night and maybe race it once or twice, but I need a job too. Can you put up with that?'

"He said, 'Sure.' So that's what I did.

"At that time Richard wasn't doing an awful lot better than James Hylton. He had a little more polish. It seemed to be James had been in it ten years and was getting sick of it. Richard hadn't been in it that long and was still going uphill. He had two or three cars, two guys full-time, and he had more sparkle in his operation, *and* he was the only independent of the bunch that had a sponsor. He had Kansas Jack, which is a company that makes hydraulic automotive equipment, and he had CRC Chemicals, a Pennsylvania company that makes spray oil, glass cleaner, and automotive-type chemicals. CRC was his main sponsor. It wasn't a *big* sponsor, but the other guys didn't have any sponsor.

"I came up to his shop in Winston-Salem. He had just doubled the size of his building, and we were standing next to this jig, which is a giant table on which you construct cars from the ground up. He said, 'Look, I'm going to start building cars myself. I never like what I get when I buy them.'

"All this sounded interesting, something different from what I was used to. Here was a guy with plans to get *bigger,* where the other teams I worked for were on the way down the tubes.

"When I first went to work for Richard, most of the time I spent building engines. I could fit rings and bearings and torque the bolts. I knew the drill. In fact, he let me put one together one time he was going to sell. It had too many miles on it and he wasn't planning on racing it, and he let me put it together. When I got done, it sat on the floor forever, and before it was over, we ran the hell out of that damn thing. Because times were getting tough for him too. You couldn't get the money you needed to run well, and you couldn't run well enough to make any money, and the next year we ended up having to run that old motor.

"It was the start: Richard was driving the car himself. He was the owner, and he built the engines himself, a lot like James. He had a couple mechanics, and when I went to work for him, I didn't go on the road. I wanted a day job so I could work on my car at night and weekends.

"The other guys would get through working at nine at night and load everything in the truck and take off for Alabama or somewhere, and I remember standing there thinking, 'Jesus, how in the hell did I ever do that?' And, 'Boy, I'm not going to ever do it again.'

"I finally did get to race my car a half-dozen times. Like my go-carts, it was just junk, and I sold it and bought a house nearby. As far as investing in racing, it was the best thing I ever did. I got $3,000 for it, bought a house, fixed it up, painted it, rented it, and sold it and bought the house I live in now.

"In October of 1980 Richard had a falling-out with his crew chief, Dennis Connor. I don't know what it was over, but all of a sudden Richard was without a crew chief, and he said to me, 'You know how to do this. Will you look after the team until I can find someone else?' Because the other full-time mechanic who was there was a helper, not a crew-chief type guy.

"I had been eight months without having to go on the road, was rested up, so I said, 'Yes. Sure I'll do it.' So far, he hasn't found anybody else.

"By the end of 1980 Richard was out of money. The sponsorship was nice, but he couldn't keep up financially. Things weren't going too hot, and we were scraping the bottom of the barrel. The cost of the tires, the hotel costs, were skyrocketing. When we came to town the hotels doubled all the rates. They always have, always do. Costs were going up more than the return. Richard knew we were in trouble.

"In the winter between the 1980 and 1981 seasons the rules changed as the cars went from the big old giant model cars to the downsized cars. In '78 a Chevy Monte Carlo was a great big old huge thing. In '79 it was a tiny little shitbox. It got better in '82, but in the interim years, when Detroit was under pressure from the government for lightweight cars and emission standards and small engines and better gas mileage, the street cars in 1980 and 1981 were little tiny boxes, and because NASCAR has to keep up with the times, they downsized their cars too.

"This made it harder for Richard, because we couldn't use our old cars. They downsized the wheelbase, and we couldn't use the frame or anything. Fortunately, we had the capacity to build our own cars, and we did that, and we did some work for customers cutting down cars for income.

"Riverside, California, used to be the first race of the season. It was held in late January, and the Daytona 500 was the second race. The new rules from one year to the next took effect with the Daytona race, so you could still run what you had the year before at Riverside. This was because Riverside was also the last race of the previous season, so a lot of teams left their old cars out there until January and ran it.

"Richard had his big road race car from 1980, and he said, 'What the hell; I don't have to save it for anything.' And he bought new tires, a new engine, we put the best we could into that car, and Richard Childress damn near won the race. He finished fourth, between Dale Earnhardt and Richard Petty. Bobby Allison won it.

"That was the best I had ever seen him run, ever, even before I was working with him. He led most of the race, and then his clutch got hot and he couldn't shift gears well. He may have run her a little too hard early in the race. But I was really impressed, and it looked good for me, because I was acting crew chief. It felt good to see the car do well.

"That was the last hurrah for the big cars, so now we were building little cars. We cut down ours and cut down some for customers, and Richard was still out of money.

"He had considered hiring a young driver for Daytona. There are guys out there with a whole lot more money than brains, drivers with sponsorship money to spend at Daytona, and he was looking to try to get some of that money.

"We went to Daytona to test in mid-December, and we hired Greg Sacks to drive. He's a modified driver from New York State. He had some sponsorship money. He and Richard took turns testing the car, and we tried to get fancier and fancier trying to go fast, and Sacks lost it in turns three and four. Nobody knew how the little cars were going to act, and they were way different aerodynamically from the big cars. Back then nobody knew anything about wind tunnels. In traffic especially or if the car flipped sideways, these little cars had so much lift in them, they'd pick up off the ground, and nobody knew why.

"So I watched as Sacks turned sideways, no big deal, but the windward side of the car picked up and it turned over backwards. I can't tell you how many cars flipped during Speed Weeks. One guy was driving along and the front end picked up and flipped him over backwards going 180. And this happened to Sacks. He was higher than the Goodyear tower in the infield. He came crashing down pit road spiraling like a football, parts flying everywhere. There was not one piece of anything on that car that was any good. Sacks's helmet came rolling down pit road. We didn't know if his head was in it or not. Richard and I looked at each other.

"He said, 'I ain't going over there. Are you going over there?' I shook my head.

"It was the only new car we had, and not one bolt on it was any good anymore. The engine broke; that's how hard it crashed. Sacks hit his head pretty good and went to the hospital.

"So here we were going back up the road Christmastime with nothing on the trailer but a pile of junk. Why we even hauled it home I don't know. Now Childress was in real trouble.

"We started the '81 season just doing what we could. With Sacks hurt, Richard went back to driving, and we made it to August, and on Saturday before the Talladega race in early August, Richard said to me, 'I'm quitting driving. Dale Earnhardt is going to drive our car next week. What do you think?' I said, 'What the hell. We're not going to finish out the year the way we are.'

"Dale had been the Rookie of the Year in '79, and in '80 he was Winston Cup champion. At the start of '81 Dale was driving for Rod Osterlund, he had the best car out there, had Wrangler blue jeans as his sponsor, was *the* hot dog. And the week before Talladega, they are on top of the world, and Osterlund decided his team was never going to be worth more than it was at that moment, and he sold it to J. D. Stacy, a coal miner from Kentucky who liked big cigars and racehorses.

"And Earnhardt didn't like that one bit. Osterlund had the best people and the best equipment, stuff to build cars and money to operate, the nicest trucks, best shop, and here he sells it all to someone who is not established in racing. Nobody ever heard of J. D. Stacy, and Dale was afraid it wasn't going to be a top team anymore.

"Also Stacy told him, 'There are other drivers out there. I'm going to pay you this amount. You can drive if you want, or I'll get somebody else to drive. I don't give a damn. I don't care who you are.'

"Earnhardt didn't like the situation at all. Dale's contract with the owner may have gone out the window, but he still had a contract with Wrangler and while this was happening, Richard was thinking. He knew Earnhardt was going to go somewhere. Richard had no future if he didn't do something drastic. Also, we were running Pontiacs, and Dale was driving a Pontiac, and that would make the transition easier.

"On Saturday night before the Talladega race in early August 1981, Richard and Dale met with Junior Johnson and Phil Holmer of Goodyear at the hotel. Richard and Junior were pretty good buddies back through the years, and Junior was guiding him a little bit. I think Junior figured ultimately he was going to get Earnhardt as a driver. He had Darrell Waltrip at the time, and he was thinking, 'If Waltrip goes somewhere else, I gotta have a backup in the wings.' So it was in his best interest to get Earnhardt in with Childress.

"The thing that put it over the edge was the tire deal to let Richard use A. J. Foyt's tire allotment, because AJ had blown up in all his other races and still had his tires left, and Phil Holmer of Goodyear let Richard have them.

"So Richard drove his final race at Talladega and dropped out halfway through with engine trouble. Dale drove his last race for Stacy. He only made it a third of the way through before his engine went out.

"The next week at Michigan our car was blue and yellow with number 3 and Wrangler on it and Dale Earnhardt the driver. We began well, finishing ninth. We had a big-time sponsor and a hot-dog driver and we added three or four people who had been working with Dale for Osterlund, including Steve Blackwell, Roger Ligon, and Doug Richert. The truck driver, Rick Peters, also came over.

"But we still had the old junk cars to run. We had money now, so we bought some good motor pieces and bought new tires every week and we finished out the season. With what we had, we did okay, but we didn't win any races, didn't win any poles, didn't qualify too well a lot of the time. We got by.

"We thought we were going to win Bristol. After twenty-five laps of the 500-lap race, we *knew* we were going to win. But Bristol had a tiny, narrow pit road with an Armco fence between it and the racetrack, and back then, you drove fast in and out of the pits. Dale was coming in fast, and Mike Potter in an also-ran car was coming out fast and pulled out in front of him, and blammo, Dale hit the car and the inside of the metal Armco wall, where all the poles are, and just tore the car up. Everyone was furious. And that was the way the year went. We didn't do too hot.

"At the end of the season Richard told Dale, 'I can't offer you the car you need. I don't have a winning car to offer you right now. I wouldn't be doing you and your sponsor right to try to force you to stay. I'm just being honest. My cards are on the table. My team isn't the calibre you need right now.'

"Dale was a young guy, not even thirty, kind of raw, and he welcomed guidance. In one of the best things Richard ever did in terms of his relationship with Dale, Richard said, 'Go get yourself a ride with one of the top teams.'

"So that's what he did. He took off and took Wrangler with him, and in 1982 and 1983 he went and drove for Bud Moore.

"Richard was convinced he needed to quit driving and hire a name driver to attract money. He had had a taste of success and liked it.

"Richard did two things. He worked out a deal with Piedmont Airlines here in Winston-Salem to be his sponsor. The airline business was doing real well since deregulation, and what better team than one right there in Winston-Salem? Piedmont was localized in the Southeast, and they wanted to be national, buying slots on the West Coast, and racing was part of their plan.

"Richard also hired Ricky Rudd, a pretty decent young race driver, an up-and-comer, a good-looking kid. Ricky had been driving for DiGard before they shorted out and died. The situation there hadn't been any better for him than it was for me.

"When Rudd started out, he was driving his family-owned car. His family had a bit of money, and they had a one-car operation, going to whatever races they could.

"So Richard suggested Ricky Rudd, and Piedmont liked him, and we had a deal for '82.

"Beginning the winter before the '82 season and continuing for two years, we did more development work with chassis than we've done in the ten years since. Development work is trying new ideas. Even today, most teams buy a chassis from a car builder, put it together, and go run it. Back then we were building our own cars, and by '82 we had three cars and were starting to tamper with the design and the suspension geometry. Every week we would cut something off the front end and arrange it differently, or we would put roll bars in different shapes or cut them out, brace up the chassis, cut them, and weld them. Every week something was a little different, and we worked a lot of long hours, because we were looking for a chassis design that was uniquely our own. You still had to stay within the rules—all the parts still had to be out of the junkyard, every Pontiac had to look like every other Pontiac, but we wanted our own. A lot of times what you try doesn't work, but the goal is to make the car perform better, drive better, go faster.

"Ultimately, I'd like to have our car physically be better than all the other cars. NASCAR doesn't want that, and the other race teams don't want that, but that's one thing I would like to accomplish here. And it's hard to do that kind of long-term ongoing project and race at the same time. It's tough, because I have to split my time and attention. Each week we go with the best we have, but it's not near as good as it could be. I've got reams of design work and drawings for improvements. Some day we will try them all, but we have to race in the meantime.

"And Ricky Rudd really has a knack for that kind of innovation. Ricky is sensitive to the way the car feels and drives. He's different from Dale in that regard. Dale doesn't care about the details. He wants to go faster than the other guy, and he'll make the car do it. At that point Rudd was nearly the racer Dale was. Ricky didn't know much about drafting and running the car on high-speed tracks, getting in there and banging with other drivers and really driving the car faster and harder than it was capable of going, which is Dale's ace in the hole. Rudd would rather work with the car and do the details. We always thought that his problem was he wanted to do that during the race instead of just race. We still say that about him.

"But we made a lot of headway on the cars with Ricky in there that, looking back, we wouldn't have done had Dale stayed in the car. Because Dale's knack is not the tiny details, it's going out and racing and getting in front of the other guy.

"We didn't win any races in '82, but we won two poles, which the sponsor thought was pretty neat. We didn't win, but we were upscale. We finished better than we started out. We were respectable, decent, led some races, ran good in some, blew up some motors, and crashed some, but that's growing pains, and what interested me most, our car at the end of the year was in a lot better shape than at the beginning.

"In 1983 we switched from Pontiacs to Chevrolet. The factories had been out of racing since the seventies, but a lot of the guys who had worked in racing liked it and were still indirectly involved, especially the Chevrolet guys, because Chevy always was more performance-oriented than Pontiac or Buick. Chevy makes performance-type vehicles. Chevy never really went away, they just weren't sponsoring racing heavily anymore.

"In the early eighties, they started to become interested again, and whoever was in power at Chevy then decided that cars that win races still sell better than cars that don't. And Ford was starting to get revved up again about stock cars. Win on Sunday, sell on Monday.

"The factories like to outdo each other, whether it's gas mileage or winning races. They are competitive. So Chevy was after Richard Childress to switch. Richard was close to Junior Johnson, and Junior had always been a Chevy man, and Richard talked to the people from Chevrolet. They were coming out with a new car in a couple years, the Monte Carlo, and we liked the looks of that, and they made it more attractive for us to run a Chevy than a Pontiac, so that's what we did.

"And so in 1983 we started running a Monte Carlo. The first race of '83, the Daytona 500, we sat on the pole at 198.864 miles an hour. We did it by default.

"The cars were still unrestricted then. Just to show how far the cars have come, with the restrictor plates we are going faster than that now with half the horsepower.

"Anyway, we had the fastest time, and Cale Yarborough went out. He was driving Waddell Wilson's car, the 28 car, and the first lap he ran, he ran 200 miles an hour, and the second lap he went through turns three and four, got sideways, and the car flipped over just like Sacks did with us three years earlier. It flipped down the front stretch and was wiped out.

Cale was okay, but we got the pole. In the 500 we fell out when a camshaft broke.

"The next week we were fastest at Richmond, and the engine blew. At Rockingham, we got the pole and finished sixth, so we had some pretty good stuff running.

"We won our first race at Riverside in June, and Chevy liked that. Here was a new team switching to Chevy from another make. It was Ricky's first Winston Cup win after more than 150 starts. Richard Childress had never won a race. I don't think any of us who worked on that car had. I had been to Victory Lane several times with DiGard, but as far as having any responsibility for the car, this was a first for me, too.

"It was a blast. At that point we didn't realize what a big thing it was. We didn't know it was the beginning of something. But we were proud of ourselves. It was fun. The sense of accomplishment doing it is hard to describe. This was 1983. I had started in 1976, so in six years it was going from knowing which way to bolt on a carburetor to being the crew chief of a car that won a Winston Cup race. That's a long time, but it isn't a long time if you think about how much water went under the bridge in those six years.

"I didn't think about it at the time, but looking back, it was pretty outstanding. At the time it was, 'We won. Great. Let's party.' Because in those days we didn't worry about the future. All I knew was that there weren't any baseball games in L.A. that weekend, and so Riverside was the biggest sporting event in L.A. that weekend, and we won it. So we were on top of the world.

"Richard and I flew Piedmont home. A trucking company was an associate sponsor, and he provided us with an 18-wheeler and a driver, so we didn't have to drive the truck back and forth to the races anymore. We were climbing the steps.

"When we flew back from California, there was a big reception for us at the airport in Greensboro. All the people from the shop and their wives were there. It was a big day.

"We won another race that season at Martinsville in September, easily beating Bobby Allison and Darrell Waltrip. Martinsville was the closest track to our shop in Winston-Salem, so that was neat. The Piedmont people were there in force. They were happy.

"With three poles and two wins, '83 was another respectable season. There were a lot of teams with a lot more equipment than we had who didn't win two races, didn't win any poles, weren't doing nearly as well as we were.

"During 1982 and '83 Dale drove for Bud Moore. He kept Wrangler as his sponsor. When he left Richard to drive for Bud, he switched to a Ford, and they won one race in '82 and two more the next year. They were a top team, and we still weren't, but they didn't do a hell of a lot better than we did.

"In '83 our contract was up with Piedmont. And Dale's contract was up with Bud Moore. For one thing, Dale didn't like driving a Ford. He never did. He didn't like it when he started, but he needed a job and a good car.

"Dale got along with Bud. Bud has been around a long time, and Dale learned from Bud. But Dale didn't like driving a Ford, and they blew up a lot of motors. Dale was young and rough around the edges, and in the two years, they must have wrecked a dozen times.

"Dale is kind of funny. If the car is not fast enough, he's going to drive it as fast as the leaders are going. If you don't give him enough car, he'll crash trying to keep up with the other guys. The kind of driver he is, he's going to the front, and if he blows the motor up or if he wrecks the car, his attitude is you need a better motor or a better car. So his success with Bud wasn't as good as they hoped.

"Dale wanted to be in a Chevy. And Dale and Richard Childress still had a relationship, and Wrangler liked Richard okay. They both had a lot of respect for Richard telling Dale to go on because his team wasn't up to snuff. But after two years, we were in a lot better shape than before. Our cars were pretty damn good by then.

"And so Ricky Rudd was odd man out. He didn't choose to leave, but that was the way it was going to be, because Dale and Wrangler were coming back.

"Ricky Rudd ended up going to Bud. We switched drivers, and we also switched seats. The seats are custom-made for each driver. When you hire a new driver, you have to buy him new seats. We just switched seats with Bud, and that worked out pretty good, because our seats were in a lot raggier condition than his were. Bud didn't like that too much.

"And so in 1984 we were back with Dale and Wrangler again. Piedmont had been a good sponsor, but Wrangler had bigger dollars and had been an established winner in racing. It wasn't a million dollars yet, but it was comparable to any other team of the day. We were three or four notches better as a team than we were in '81.

"We had an okay season in '84. We ran at the top of the field most of the time, but we still had too much engine trouble to be in the points race. If you don't finish the races, you can't win it. Period. All the championships, the engines were the reason. All the championships we didn't win, the engines were the reason. You have to run better than the competition, and that is a team effort. That is one of Richard Childress's strong points. Most of his time he spends working on cars or in the engine room. When he was a driver, he built engines. If you have to put one reason mechanically why we've won as many championships as we have, having a solid motor program is it. The driver, of course, is a constant, and Dale is a great one. The only thing that's different is the car. Not finishing is what keeps drivers from winning championships, and in 1984 we won two races, finished in the top ten twenty-two times, and finished fourth behind Terry Labonte.

"In '85, we won four races, but we fell out of too many races to be competitive for the championship. In '86, though, we got our ducks in a row in the engine room and the whole time were making headway with the chassis. In '86 and '87 we had the best-handling car at just about every racetrack we went to. In '86 we finished every race and damn high in every race and we beat out Darrell Waltrip for the championship. In '87, we won it again.

"It was a tribute to our design efforts over the eight years prior to that. Since then the car dimensions have changed, and we can't use that design anymore from those years, and things have gotten harder. Now we're running this little round car, a Chevy Lumina, more aerodynamic, more modern-looking, but the hood clearance is less, and so there's a lot less room for the engine than there was.

"Also, back then our car was built to run on bias-ply tires, and we didn't slow down as much as some of the other cars. Today, everyone runs on radials, and so we've lost that advantage. We changed in '86, only six years, but the technology has come a long way since then. Hopefully, by the end of this decade, we'll be in as good a shape as we were by the end of the last one.

"After winning the championship in '86 and '87, we again won it back-to-back in '90 and in '91—though we're never satisfied. In fact, we had a mediocre car at best in '91. The thing wasn't driving well, wasn't handling well, the engine wasn't running well. Dale couldn't get off the corners at all.

"It's always, 'We did pretty good this year. Let's see about next year.' As far as having arrived, we just do what we can do. As Chocolate Meyers said to me the other day, 'It's a wonder we can ever get to a race, let alone win one.' Because racing is always a compromise. Even the car is a compromise, between speed and power and handling. We compromise our lives for our jobs.

"We have a rogue reputation, the Dirty Dozen, in large part because of Dale. We've always been a ragtag bunch of guys, not the most polished, hair-combed, fingernails-clean. As far as being shipshape and shirt-tucked-in, we're about as far from a troop of Marines as you can get. Things are crazy a lot, but it works. And racing dictates that things be crazy a lot. It may seem disorganized, but it's not. It's really very intricate the way everything works. The output of the team is what is impressive about us, more than looks or anything else.

"Whenever I get interviewed, they ask, 'What is the reason for your success? What's the formula?' There really is no formula. It's far from that. The chance mixing of people is as responsible for it as anything else. The mix of people is what makes us different from other teams. Everyone has the same stuff to work with. We just happened on a thing that clicks. We're going to do what we can to keep it working, even though we don't really know why. Sometimes even we wonder how we do it. Each of us realizes you could start over and throw everything in and mix it up again and it wouldn't work.

"Things have gone well, and hopefully they will continue to go well, but when they stop going well, I don't know if there's much we can do about it. It's circumstances, a little luck, and a whole lot of hard work that has made things the way they are.

"We are looking forward to the Daytona 500 in 1992. We have run well in just about every 500 as far back as '82. We won in July a couple of times, but the biggie has always gotten away from us. Bad luck, mostly. In 1990, we had a 40-second lead, which is almost a lap, and you don't usually do that at the speedways because of drafting. But in '88, when they started making us run with restrictor plates, we really concentrated on that a whole lot. A lot of other teams were saying what a pain in the ass it was, that no matter what you do you aren't going to go any faster with the plate, and they didn't want to delve into it and see what they could do with it. Other teams tried to make leaks to give them extra horsepower, and most of them got caught. We spent all our time making the damn thing run without any leaks. We never gave it a second thought.

"Richard spent many hours working on it. He said, 'We have to have this plate; let's make the air go through the hole as best we can.' We tried everything you can think of. We fooled with compression ratios, valve timing, endless combinations that have to do with how the engine pumps the air.

"And so we were the fastest car on the track at Daytona in '90, and that day we hit on the best combination, which enabled us to run away with it, until the end. We had a flat tire on the backstretch of the last lap and should have crashed. The thing was flat, the tire had come apart, and Dale slid up the track, and four cars got by us before Dale got to the start-finish line. I don't know how he finished with the tire gone, with nothing but a wheel on the right rear. Just from sheer determination, I guess. We were so disappointed. If we win that race the next ten times, you can never get that one back. But Dale really did take it well, especially in public. He didn't kick the wheel and stomp around and throw things and say bad words. He said, 'We ran awful good, as good as anyone could ask for, ran over something and had a flat at the end.' There wasn't much anyone could do about it. You know, there *is* luck involved.

"We finished fifth last year, and we're building a new car for Daytona that's supposed to be faster than the other one. There are ideas and elements incorporated into the new car that are two and three years old.

"We've been working on the car since May, and what's frustrating, there is a car laying on my desk that is already twice as good as the one we're working on, but it's going to take us five years to build it. That's the kind of thing that keeps you going. Racing gets under your skin and really is like alcoholism. It's a drug. You have to really be careful in your priorities, because you get going so fast and get caught up in the moment, the life is *so* fast, and you tend to do things wrong and not look past the hood. If another car is going faster than you for two or three weeks in a row, heaven forbid, you start looking at what he has and easily can lose sight of your own direction. You end up zigzagging around, bouncing off bumpers like a pinball machine, and pretty soon you're out of money and you've gone nuts. The tough part about concentrating on the long term is not to worry about the other people. You have to do your own thing, and it's hard, because if you don't win races and are constantly lagging behind, then you might lose your sponsorship, and the driver is going to start looking elsewhere. You have to keep up, but in order to stay on top five years from now, you have to know why you're on top and have to follow your planned course. It's hard to keep thirty people looking that way, and it's discouraging when you don't run good.

"Last year, the 28 car with Davey Allison outran us much of the second half of the year. We know the calibre of our team versus the calibre of their team, and we know the calibre of our driver compared to the calibre of their driver, and to get outrun by them is pretty discouraging.

"But you have to look at the reasons why things are happening, why you're successful when you are and why you aren't when you aren't, and not let all the spectacle and excitement of it catch you up.

"You run at a full panic every day all year long. And to keep the amount of panic to a minimum is tough. That's one of the things the other guys say I do for Richard—keep him idled back a little bit, because

Richard Childress wants to be light-years ahead of where we are now too. But you have to go at a certain pace, or else you're going to skyrocket and fizzle. If you want to stay on an even keel, you have to structure things that way. You can shoot straight up as high as you want, but sooner or later you'll come down.

"Because of our even-keel philosophy, we have a race team that has stayed together. You can't have a group remain a group unless everyone participates in keeping it a group. Each guy has to do what he can to keep things together. We know we're successful, and we all know we can't do it on our own off somewhere else. The reason we have done so well is each of the guys. And Richard looks out for us. He had one of the first profit-sharing plans, with incentives to stay for a long period. There will be a nest egg when we get too old to change tires. He has a bonus kitty, an incentive bonus plan, and a big chunk of money for winning the championship.

"You have to have a vision, and it has to be correct. Again, luck and circumstances have a lot to do with it. Success is like surfing: You're doing what you can to stay on the board, but you really aren't in control of anything. And the more you think you're in control, the more you're going to wipe out. You have to realize that all you can do is hang on as best you can. You don't have any control over anything else.

"And when you get to the beach, you have to decide then whether you want to swim back out or not. That's a few chapters in the future. I'm anxious to see how things go the next ten years. I know about the last ten; the next ten will be different. No one knows how it will end, but it *will* end.

"When you're Jesse James, the top gunfighter, another guy comes by with a gun and wants to be the top gunfighter, and the only way he's going to be him is to shoot the guy who is."

Cliff Champion

LAP 20

Cliff Champion

Out of the Loop

In any business, one builds a career one step at a time. The higher, more successful the climb up the ladder, the more precarious the steps become toward the top. So it is in racing. Make one blunder, offend one wrong person, and you can find yourself unemployed, because the racing community is so small and gossip spreads so quickly. Once you get a reputation of being someone whom the game has passed by, or worse, once you are tagged "uncompetitive," employment evaporates with surprising suddenness.

Cliff Champion was at the top. An expert mechanic, Champion had worked for several of the top teams in the game, including Harry Ranier, DiGard, and J. D. Stacy, and then in 1983 he was hired by Johnny Hayes of U.S. Tobacco to be the team's crew chief. There he made an enemy—his driver, Benny Parsons. Why? To this day Champion doesn't know. But Champion was fired in 1985, and he blames Parsons.

Champion's career might have been saved, but he made a serious blunder that sent his career spinning into oblivion. He was crew chief for Alan Kulwicki, who today is the most successful owner-driver in the game. But at the time Kulwicki was an independent with little money and no track record, and Champion felt he ought to be running an outfit with more money and a better chance of winning. After a minor disagreement with Kulwicki, Champion impulsively quit.

When he couldn't find work over the next five months, he became desperate and accepted work as a crew chief for a series of poorly run or underfinanced race teams. His cars stopped being competitive, and when Chad Little fired him in 1991 because he could no longer afford to pay him, Cliff Champion found himself out of the loop. Teams know he is looking for work, but teams with crew chiefs looking for mechanics won't hire him because they feel he will become resentful, and those teams looking for crew chiefs refuse to consider him because the impression lingers that "he has lost it."

Cliff Champion wants badly to get back into the sport he loves. But he is at loss to figure out what he can do to return.

CLIFF CHAMPION: "I grew up in Virginia Beach, and as a six-year-old kid I wanted and got a tool kit, and I carried it everywhere. I would take my brother's watch apart and see what made it tick, and at about thirteen my father bought an old Ford station wagon for his fence-construction company, and the motor went bad on it. He bought a toolbox, and he got me out of school a week before Christmas and let me change it.

"I was good at it. It came natural to me. He had mechanics who worked to keep his equipment up, but I said, 'I can do that,' so he said, 'Do it.' And I did. We got a factory-rebuilt engine and put it in.

"My dad was always running into customers who had a deal, and he had a friend in business who had an old go-cart his kid ran once or twice and didn't want, so he bought it for me. It had a 2- or 3-horsepower engine.

"He also owned a large lawn mower, like what the city used, with big bicycle wheels in the back and little bitty wheels in the front, and the thing had a 5-horsepower Yazoo engine, so I made a wooden stand that I could roll the lawn mower on, and I would unbolt the engine and put it on my go-cart. All week long I ran the motor on the go-cart, and come time to cut the grass, I'd roll it up there, unbolt it, and put it back on the lawn mower.

"Somewhere along the line, he came home one day and had a midget race car he had gotten from somebody. It didn't have a motor. I tinkered with that a while, and then my sister dated a guy who messed with hot rods, had a little Chevelle. I hung around with him and started working on cars, and he introduced me to guys who were drag racers.

"We would go to the local drive-in, where everybody would hang out in the back row and arrange the races, and we'd go out and race.

"One night when I was fifteen—I was just getting my driver's license—I went with a guy who owned a funny car to the car dealership where he was working on it at night. He was expecting a short-block motor back from the machine shop, and it came in about eleven at night, and he started putting it together. He asked for some help, so I stayed, and we worked on that motor all night long, putting it in the car and getting it running.

"I didn't call my parents, and I showed up at about eight Sunday morning, walked in the door after staying up all night working on the car, and my parents' first words were 'Where have you been?' 'I've been working on this car.' 'Well, you're going to bed.' 'No, I'm going to the drag race. I worked on the thing all night long, and I'm not going to miss out going to the racetrack with it.'

"I started traveling with the guy up and down the East Coast, nights and weekends, while I was going to school.

"I never got to my junior year. I knew all along I wanted to do something automotive. I was into drag racing, enjoyed it, it was interesting, but I could see then there wasn't any money in it. I was doing it as a hobby. I took racing magazines to school and read them. I didn't do any homework. I was one of the worst students there was. I was skipping school, messing with cars, so I dropped out in the tenth grade, and when I did, I got a job working in a Chevrolet dealership in new-car prep. And then I quit there and went to work for Ricky Rudd's dad.

"Ricky's dad had an old cinder-block shop where he rebuilt total wrecks. People would come by and say, 'I'd like to buy a part off that car.' And the next think we knew, he was selling more parts than we were rebuilding totals. So his daddy went and bought an old wrecker truck, and I started driving it. He'd go to sales and buy the cars, and I'd haul them back in.

"When Al Jr., Ricky's brother, graduated, the two of us started a rebuilding business by ourselves. We did it in his dad's garage while his dad let us spend his money and looked the other way. We cleaned out one side of his shop, built workbenches, fixed everything up for us. He didn't charge us any rent.

"I built a couple V-8 Vegas for myself and played with those on the street. I liked to mess around with things, but I never had any money.

One day Al Jr. said something about wanting to go to a stock car race. I had seen one before, didn't really care for them. They were boring to me. He wanted to go, and he insisted, and I said, 'If we can get into the pits and the garage and see what's going on, I'll go, but I'm not going to sit in the stands.'

"He suggested I call my cousin, Bill Champion, who used to race the number 10 Ford back then. Bill said he'd get us into the garage area.

"Bill was a second cousin, about my father's age, and I was a young kid. The only time I saw him was at a family reunion. He was a racer, but I didn't pay any attention to stock car racing. Until I went to that race, I didn't know anything about it.

"Bill got us into the garage at the July race at Daytona in 1974. It was my twenty-first birthday. The Daytona Speedway didn't impress me a whole lot, because I didn't know there were tracks that were smaller. It was like getting on a jet to fly for the first time. 'What's the big deal about a jet?'

"While the cars were practicing, the cars would come in, and the mechanics would tune them, adjust the valves, and I watched them, and I noticed that the guy who was adjusting the valves was doing it wrong. The valve and the camshaft have to be in a certain relationship to get the adjustment right on the valve. The valve has to be in a completely closed position to adjust the lash in it, and this mechanic was turning the motor so it was partially open. So when he turned the engine over, it had a lot of slot in it.

"I mentioned it to my cousin, so he told me to go ahead and do it, so I fixed that up for him, and later on in practice they went to take the car out, and there is a part of the steering—the older cars used to have a rubber biscuit just like a street car does between the steering and the steering box to absorb the shock from the bumps on the road, and when Bill went to back out, this rubber biscuit broke. The guys working there kind of stood there, so I said to Bill, 'Do you have one?' He said, 'Yeah, I have one in my truck,' and I ran over and got it and replaced it real quick. And the other guys were still standing there.

"At the race at Daytona, Bill's motor blew after one lap. He had a split cylinder wall, and when we got back to the shop, the first thing my cousin said was, 'We got to get the motor ready to go to the racetrack. You know anything about motors?'

"I said, 'I built street motors before.' I had read books, built a motor for a boat and a couple of old cars, but I had never done any real precision engine building.

"We got back to the motel at night, and he offered me a job. He was an independent, and an independent will pick up cheap help whenever he can, and I seemed willing. He offered me $100 a week plus 10 percent of what the car made.

"I was twenty-one, single. What the heck! I wasn't doing anything else. It looked like fun, so I decided to try it. And it was a lot more work than I thought it would be. But I had gotten married at nineteen, and I was going through a divorce, and that was the best thing that happened to me, working day and night. I worked until four in the morning. I loved it. This was therapy for me, kept my mind off things.

"And I remember one week we won $6,000, and he gave me $600, and God, back then it seemed like so much money. But the most important thing, Bill taught me the basics of stock cars. When I started, I knew nothing about a stock car. I didn't even know how to take a rear axle in and out, or a gear, or anything. So I worked for him about a year, and he taught me everything about cars.

"We ran Atlanta, and the engine blew up early. At Pocono we over-heated. At Talladega the engine blew up. At Michigan the engine blew up. At Darlington we overheated. At Dover the transmission failed. At North Wilkesboro we overheated, then Randy Hutchison drove at Martinsville and we overheated.

"We finished a race, finally, at Rockingham, fifty-six laps back of David Pearson.

"In 1975 Walter Ballard drove for us at Richmond, only to have the engine blow up, but then Bill got talked into letting Ricky Rudd drive for him. Ricky had driven go-carts and motorcycles, and his dad had been a racer years ago and had owned some of the cars Fireball Roberts and those guys drove. Joe Weatherly lived in Norfolk across the street from my cousin Bill, and when Ricky's dad had visions of Ricky being a driver, his dad was able to talk Bill Champion into giving him a chance.

"The first time Ricky got into a race car to drive in a Winston Cup race was at Rockingham in March 1975. Ricky finished eleventh, though he was fifty-six laps behind Cale Yarborough at the end. Ricky showed natural talent right away, though back then the attrition rate was pretty high, and there were only two or three teams that had first-class equipment and could run up front.

"Bill Champion is a real nice guy, but hardheaded, and he didn't have a very big budget, and when he would put used parts into the engine, we would have disputes. One time when Ricky was driving, we dropped a valve in the engine. In the race before the engine had blown up, and instead of putting in a racing valve, he put in a stock valve because that's all he could get, and at Atlanta Ricky had a pretty run going, and the part failed, and they had a few words and parted company, and it wasn't long after that that Bill and I parted ways too.

"I left Bill and went to work for James Hylton. Like a lot of guys, he taught me a lot about race cars. He taught me how to prepare them and how to be meticulous and what it took to make them run.

"I worked from eight in the morning until twelve or one every single day. I shared an eight-foot-long trailer with Ramo Stott, who was from Iowa. I remember one night we knocked off at ten o'clock at night, finished early, and Ramo and I had a night off and didn't know what to do with all this free time.

"We were on the town, going for it. We took a shower, went to town, and the only restaurant that was open that late was Shoney's! So we ate dinner there, came back, sat around and talked until two in the morning, because that's what our bodies were used to, and went to bed.

"I worked for James about a year, and then at the end of the 1976 season the Rudds wanted to buy a car of their own. They bought an old car from my cousin Bill, and I came home and helped teach them how to build a suspension, how to take the car apart and put it back together again, how to set the bearings so you don't burn them up, how much grease to put on them—a lot of little things you have to learn to build a stock car.

"We went to Daytona with the car to run a Sportsman race, but the car wasn't ready to qualify. It looked like it was going to rain, and we were sitting on the line, and we had to decide whether to take our shot or not. If it rained and we didn't run, we wouldn't qualify. So we went, and we weren't fast enough to make the race, and then it rained, and we couldn't try to qualify again.

"I talked to Richard Childress at the racetrack, and he told me to come up and talk to him about working for him. This was 1975, and Richard was driving the car at the time and he had a major sponsor, Kansas Jack, and he was expanding a little, and so he hired me as the crew chief, only nobody called you that. Someone had to be in charge and run things, and that's what I did.

"I only worked for Richard about six months, didn't get close to him, never got to know him that well. I know I developed a great respect for him. He was a very good businessman. He didn't let his emotions run his race team. He knew the dollar and he watched and he ran accordingly. And he was a nice-looking man, presentable to the sponsors, and that also helped get him where he is today.

"The last race of the '75 season, Richard went to Riverside. We were trying to build a new car, and I stayed back with a few other guys to build it. We had hired a new guy, a real young guy, and he and I were having a lot of friction in the shop, and in the meantime, Ricky Rudd and his family had bought a brand-new race car from Robert Gee. Richard Howard of the Charlotte Motor Speedway paid to have the car built, because Howard wanted Charlie Glotzbach to run in his race, and Charlie ran it for three or four races, and then Bobby Isaac drove it, and I guess Richard Howard figured it was a losing proposition, so they sold the car to Ricky and his family, and at the same time I was having trouble with that guy at Childress's, it was a headache, so Ricky called me to help him.

"When Richard got back from Riverside, I said, 'Look, this guy and

I aren't getting along, you all can have it,' so I left and went back to Virginia and helped Ricky get ready for the 1976 season.

"At the time I was the only one on the team with any experience. At first Raymond Fox, Jr., who sold them the car, was building the engines. We went to Daytona in February with the car, cracked the head in practice, ran in the 125, and with six laps to go blew a motor.

"We came back home, built us another fresh motor, and went to Rockingham. As we went by the green flag to qualify, the crankshaft broke.

"I went to Raymond Fox's shop with some motor parts and watched him build the engine. I came back home to Mr. Rudd and told him, 'These guys aren't doing right by you.' He told me to go back down there, so Al Rudd, Jr., and I drove back down there and loaded up all the motor parts and came back home, and I poured the parts out on the floor and started building the engines myself after that. I had to keep the car up too, and it was too much for me to do, and after a while I got so run-down that I walked out.

"Two days later I came back and told them I couldn't do both jobs. Al Jr. was a real good mechanic, but he had never built racing engines before. I wrote everything down on a piece of paper, handed it to him, and said, 'If you have any questions, ask me. I'm going to fix the car.'

"So he built the engines, and I kept up the car.

"And in 1977 Ricky Rudd was good enough to win Rookie of the Year against Sam Summers, who had M. C. Anderson as his car owner and David Ifft as his crew chief. Summers had big people and a lot of money.

"Ricky is a very competitive person. A lot of people think he's stuck-up, but in truth Ricky is real shy, a down-to-earth person. He doesn't even consider what he does real special, so why make a big deal out of it? He's just an average guy. He'll do anything for charity or kids and doesn't mind signing autographs, and when he gets autograph requests, he insists on signing every one of them.

"One of the reasons you don't see much of Ricky outside of racing is he doesn't live the high life, doesn't run around—a regular family man who has his wife go with him to all the races.

"He's private, not stuck-up. A lot of drivers run the short tracks for money. Ricky values his time alone, so even if he's offered $5,000 to run a race, he'll turn it down to spend time with his wife.

"It came down to the very last race of the year at Ontario Motor

Speedway. We had to beat Summers to win it, and on the twenty-sixth lap Sam blew an engine, we finished eighth in the race, which Neil Bonnett won, and Ricky was Rookie of the Year.

"Ricky and his brother were typical brothers. They had regular brother fights. Ricky was always complaining the car didn't have enough horsepower, and his brother was always saying, 'You can't drive the thing,' and so finally at the end of the season, his brother said, 'The car ain't got enough power? I ain't building motors for you. I quit.'

"So I said, 'Shoot, then I ain't gonna work on the car anymore either. Work on it yourself.'

"And in 1979 Ricky was offered a ride in the Trucksmore car by Junie Donlavey. Al Rudd, Jr., and I went back to rebuilding totals, and we rebuilt two or three that winter, when I went to work for Grant Adcox out of Tennessee, who got killed at Atlanta a couple years ago.

"Grant's dad, Herb, who owned a Chevrolet dealership, was pretty well off. I know he ran a progressive dealership, because when I went to work there, on the wall was a photo of his dad on the cover of *Time* magazine in an article about car dealerships.

"Grant called me up and asked me to help him get a car ready to go to Daytona. He had kept it down at Holman-Moody, and he had the body style changed from the older, bigger cars to the '77 Olds. He said it was ready to go, that all he needed was to put a motor in it.

"I had to go to Tennessee, but I was still single and all he wanted to run was Daytona, and after that I planned on going back and rebuilding totals with Al.

"I got to Tennessee, and it was more work than it was supposed to be. We ended up working on the car round the clock for three days nonstop, no sleep. We got done, loaded at eight at night, and set off for Daytona, a ten-hour drive.

"Grant Adcox had left the day before with his dad, and so this friend of Ricky's who I had brought with me gave me a couple yellow jackets, which is a mild form of speed. I got about thirty miles to a truck stop, and I was so tired I pulled in and slept a half hour, and then the yellow jackets took effect, and I got up and drove the rest of the way.

"We got to Daytona. Grant's father said to me, 'You have three days. All you have to do is put the motor in it.' We were renting motors from Waddell Wilson. We could have done that, but that's not the kind of person I am.

"The first thing I did when we got there, I jacked the car up and I could see the right front wheel was turning way out, and I fixed that and continued to work on the car, and with Buddy Baker qualifying for the pole at 196 miles an hour, we qualified fourth, which was outstanding—unheard of.

"The first thing NASCAR did was impound our car. They wanted us to take out all the aluminum work to make sure we weren't cheating. We took three or four panels off, and I told Bill Gazaway, the chief inspector, 'We just have a good motor. We got it from Waddell.' Gazaway checked with Waddell, and then he knew why we qualified good, and we quit taking the car apart, and they accepted it.

"The mistake we made was that the car was supposed to be prepared by Holman-Moody, where they changed the roll bar to fit the body style and they put a new housing in it. They were supposed to have packed the bearings, ready to go, something we didn't have time to check.

"We were running sixth in the race, and a little more than halfway through, the car locked up a wheel bearing. When we got back home and checked, we found the bearing wasn't packed all the way like it should have been.

"That was one of the best runs of Grant's career. When we got back home to Tennessee, he was happy the way things went and wanted me to stay. What the heck—I got an apartment and stayed the whole year. At the end of '79 money was tightening up and it was a bad time for car dealerships, and so they decided to get out of it for a while.

"Grant talked to Waddell, and Waddell told him to have me come see him. Just before Christmas 1979, Waddell gave me a job as a general mechanic for the Harry Ranier team. Buddy Baker was driving the car. That got me into big-time racing. I was with an established team. I wasn't with independents anymore. This was a real team—people had actual jobs, fabricators, machinists, not just two or three guys doing everything.

"I have always liked Waddell. I would love to work for Waddell again. I don't know a single bad trait he has. He's a perfectionist, and I enjoyed working for him. He was brought up in the Holman-Moody days when they punched the time clock, he went by the book, and I can remember we had a guy who worked there, and one morning unpredictably it snowed. We all lived within five miles to the shop except this one guy, who lived twenty miles away.

"When we woke up that morning, there were six inches of snow on the ground. We all got up and left early and got there by 7:30 except this one guy, who arrived at 7:33.

"Waddell was standing at the door, met him there, and told him if it happened again, he was gone. That shows how much of a perfectionist he is. He wants things done right. He was the one who taught me about aerodynamics. He was the first one who started using it.

"I was just one of the peons on the team. I was a newcomer. I didn't even get to know Buddy. He said hi, but he didn't know me, and I never got to know him. I worked there for about six months that year, so I never had any time to deal with him.

"We went to test at Daytona, and even though I was nobody, just coming in from a little team, when Waddell got through with some of the things he wanted to test, he turned to the rest of the crew and said, 'Do you have anything you'd like to test?' I came up with a couple of ideas, and he tested them. It impressed me that after asking, he had paid attention to what I said and even tried it.

"And we won Daytona in 1980. It was my first Winston Cup victory. It was the first time I had ever been with a team that had ever won a race.

"We also won at Talladega that year. I'll never forget, we went to push the car down to Victory Lane, and I was right at the driver's window, holding onto the windshield at the front fender, and Waddell was right in front of me. He had a hold on the steering wheel. There were a line of guys down the side of the car, and we made the turn into Victory Circle, and it turns from pavement to sand, and Waddell stumbled in the sand, his foot caught and he went down, and I was the man right behind him, and it looked like one of those centipedes, because everyone on the team walked right over him, the line bumping up as they walked right over him. It never bothered him. He got up and ran to Victory Circle.

"I was beginning to get known, and halfway through the year at Wilkesboro, some of the guys from DiGard came to me and said they needed a chief mechanic.

"When I was first working on the Rudds' car, we kept it at Robert Gee's shop, and DiGard kept its car there, and Nick Ollila, who works at Roger Penske's now, watched me work on our car, and he came over to me and said, 'You're going to be somebody.' I told him, 'I just do what I do.'

"I was making $15,000 working for Waddell, and even though I was just one of the guys in the Ranier shop, DiGard was offering a $3,000 raise and the chief mechanic's job.

"Waddell offered to match that, but I felt with Waddell, he was the boss and was always going to be the boss, and there was no room for advancement. DiGard wanted me as chief mechanic. I went over to DiGard. Darrell Waltrip drove the car.

"DiGard was run by businessmen, and I don't want to sound prejudiced, but they were Yankee businessmen out of Connecticut. They were big businessmen who didn't care about people; people meant nothing to them. It was money, all business. I saw them hire and fire people left and right who didn't mean anything to them.

"Darrell won some races when I was there. We had a bad year with motors, blew up seventeen times that year. There were hard feelings in the motor room, and between the motor room and the chassis room.

"I enjoyed working at DiGard. I was a little higher up than at Ranier, and I learned a lot about running a team.

"Buddy Parrott was the crew chief. Buddy is a very outspoken person. I like Buddy. He's a good friend of mine, but he speaks his mind. He's a man. He'll fight at the drop of a hat—he did back then, anyway.

"At the track we had some trouble with the motors, things he felt the motor room was supposed to take care of. One time we blew a motor in practice and went to put in another one, and the replacement motor wasn't ready. It had a leak in the water pump, and as a result on race morning we had to change the water pump, change the gaskets, and that morning we had to glue on a new valve cover gasket, which you don't do in racing because the glue doesn't have enough time to dry.

"The race started, and we were running up front in the top two or three, and a little way into the race, they black-flagged us because the oil valve cover was leaking. The glue never had time to dry.

"When Darrell brought the car in, Buddy took that valve cover off and flung it. It went flying through the pits, across the fence, and when we got back to the shop, he complained to the Gardners about the motor room, and Buddy must have forgotten that Robert Yates, who was in charge of the motor room, had an interest in the team. Some of the equipment belonged to Robert, the motor room was his, and Yates was close to the Gardners. He was what we called an 'honorary Gardner.' Gary Nelson was the other 'honorary Gardner.'

"There was an awards banquet about that time, a dinner in Charlotte, and everybody went, and rumors were flying that Buddy was going to get fired and they were going to bring in Jake Elder.

"Paul Sullivan was running the team for the Gardners. At that dinner Buddy went to Paul and said, 'At this dinner several people asked me if I still had a job. Do I, or are you going to hire Jake?'

"Paul said, 'You have a job. We're not going to hire Jake. Those rumors are unfounded.'

"The next morning they stopped Buddy in the parking lot. They told him he was fired.

"In the shop Dan Ford and I were working under the hood of a car, and Buddy came walking by us. He turned to us and said, 'I hope you like your new crew chief.' We looked at each other like 'huh?'

"Buddy walked back to the motor room, and the next thing I knew Noah Brown came out yelling, 'Somebody help me. Pull these guys apart.' We went running over. Robert Yates came out of the motor room, his shirt ripped, the side of his face all red. Buddy had gone in there and just decked him. Buddy must have hit him pretty good.

"Buddy wasn't the kind of guy to take it lying down. He felt he got screwed on the deal and had to do something. It didn't help him none and I'm sure it hurt him. But he let them know he didn't care for it.

"And Buddy walked out the door. They brought in Jake Elder, and things went along pretty good, and then at the end of the season Darrell left.

"All season long Darrell was complaining, bitching, doing whatever he could to get out of his contract. Darrell is a very talented driver, and a smart guy. He was under contract and felt if he complained enough, caught so much bad press, because he was calling the Gardners stinkers, which they were, that he could get out of his contract.

"He complained he hadn't gotten paid in a long time. You're supposed to get paid every thirty days, but they held his money. The Gardners were so tight with money. There was never any money there at that shop. At times motor parts would come in at the airport, and we couldn't get them because there wasn't any money in the bank; they had to get money wired.

"They had a real smart comptroller, Wayne Stembler, who is with Hendrick now, a very smart guy.

"I can remember two or three times we were getting ready to leave the shop for a race. We were supposed to leave town at noon. We had the car ready to go. They were supposed to give you per diem checks to leave town with, and he would hand us the checks, but we couldn't cash them until two o'clock. We would have to wait around until then for the money to be transferred into the checking account.

"One day the crew went to lunch, and we stopped at a local hardware store down the street from our shop. We were told not to make any more DiGard purchases at the hardware store. We were told, 'He's bad business. Don't go in there anymore.'

"But we still went in for our personal needs. We had our uniforms on, and the owner of the hardware store said, 'What's the name of the guy who handles your money?' We told him. He said, 'You tell that little son of a bitch that I'm coming up after lunch. He owes me $175. He hasn't paid the bill. You tell him I'm either leaving with $175 or $175 worth of his ass. One or the other.'

"We said, 'Great. We'll tell him.'

"We went back and we said, 'Wayne, you have a problem, pal. This guy is coming to see you right after lunch. He either wants your money or your ass.'

"The guy showed up after lunch, just as he said he would. And he walked out with a check in his hand. I watched as he folded it up, put it in his pocket, and walked out the door.

"In the middle of the season the people from J. D. Stacy's came to me and offered me a job. Doug Richert had quit and went to work for Junior Johnson, and they wanted someone to fill his position. Dale Inman, who was the crew chief, had left Richard Petty for all kinds of money, and he couldn't turn it down, even though he was driving an hour and a half each day from Randleman.

"When they first asked me I told them, 'No, I'm happy where I'm at.'

"But then I was back at the DiGard shop, and we had a guy who was a real good machinist, and his daughter had polio. He had to do therapy with her all the time, he was a real family man, working on the rescue squad—one of the best machinists around. He had been part of the pit crew, and he told them he couldn't go to the races anymore because he had to stay home with his daughter. They told him they were cutting back on part-time help and that he *had* to.

"He said, 'I'm sorry. I can't.'

"The next morning I saw him and another boy loading his toolbox in the back of a pickup truck. He was wearing cutoff jeans, and I figured it was his day off.

"I said, 'Hey, what you all doing?'

"He said, 'They fired me. They called me at home last night about eight and told me to come and pick up my toolbox.'

" 'No notice?'

" 'No.'

"I didn't like that. To me the Gardners were ruthless. When they fired you, they wanted you gone so you couldn't steal anything. When I left Waddell, I gave him two weeks' notice, and I worked just as hard during those two weeks as I did before then.

"To me, and I'm probably naive, I believe you should treat people the way you want to be treated.

"When they fired the mechanic with the sick daughter, I helped get the car ready to go to Nashville. It was loaded on the truck, and we went to the bathroom to wash our hands.

"They said, 'We'll meet at the shop at 7:30 tomorrow morning.' I said, 'I ain't going. I quit. That's it for me.' I left and went over to J. D. Stacy's to work.

"Stacy, who owned three cars, was aboveboard with all of us. The bills were paid at the shop, and our paychecks were there every week. We had top-line equipment, and as far as we were concerned, everything was fine, until the end of the season, when we heard we were going to have to tighten up a little next year.

"Tim Richmond was our driver in '82 after Joe Ruttman quit unexpectedly after the March Rockingham race. Tim had driven for D. K. Ulrich and a couple of independent teams, and Stacy was the kind of guy who would give someone like that a chance. We really didn't know how it was going to work out with Tim, but Tim did very well.

"The first race Tim drove for us was at Darlington. Tim was leading when a tire went flat, and he should have finished fourth, not fifth, but he was ahead of the leaders when they took the checkered flag, and in the mirror he saw the flag waving, and instead of coming all the way around and taking the checkered flag himself, he pulled into the pits, and by the time we got to him, it was too late.

"Tim was young and very talented. He made naive mistakes, not stupid mistakes because of nontalent. It was learning-process mistakes—he drove too hard, didn't always use his head, but he ran good and showed he had a feel for the car. He couldn't tell you what the car was doing, but he always gave it his best effort.

"Tim had a funny way of talking about the car, because before he came to NASCAR, he had driven Indy cars. He had been Rookie of the Year in Indy cars.

"His dad had owned some Indy cars, and it drained the money, became too expensive, and Tim had a name and they could see NASCAR racing was a cheaper way to go.

"Tim won two races and had seven top five finishes in 1982, but at the end of the year we knew we were in trouble at Stacy's. Many a night I would go over to his house and talk with him and his dad about getting something going. We were going to go somewhere together, but we just never could get anything going.

"The second-to-last race of the season we were at Atlanta. I walked over to the Skoal Bandit truck to get a sandwich, and Johnny Hayes was there, and he said, 'Cliff, we just hired your girlfriend.' I didn't know what he was talking about. He said, 'We hired Terry, your girlfriend.'

"Gary Brooks was on our team, and I said, 'Terry is Gary's girlfriend.' He said, 'We just gave her a job.' I knew Stacy was going to go away soon, and I said, 'Good—how about getting one for me while you're at it.'

"He gave me a number, and it turned out he was starting Johnny Hayes Racing. He said, 'We need somebody to come in and run the team.'

"Johnny worked for U.S. Tobacco, was a race fan. I told him, 'I'll work for $30,000.' He said, 'Why don't we make it $32,000.'

"He said he wanted to run a limited schedule, that he was building a shop in Denver, which isn't far from Charlotte. This was the first of December. He said, 'It'll be a month before we're ready for you, but we'll start you Monday.'

"I had a month before we were to go to Daytona to test. They had a little bitty office, and I'd go there and start ordering things for the team. I ordered radios and equipment for the shop.

"All they owned was a step van and a little trailer like you see at a local speedway. And they had bought a car from Leo Jackson. They also owned six or seven gears. That was it.

"I went down to Sears in Charlotte and started ordering. We didn't have heat so I ordered kerosene heaters. I walked around and said to the saleslady, 'I'll take two of those and one of those and one of those,' and I was buying left and right because I had to outfit a shop overnight.

"After a week I went to Johnny and said, 'How much money can I spend? What do you want me to buy?' He said, 'Buy what you need. Treat it like it was your own money. I'll leave it up to you.'

"We went to Daytona with Benny Parsons in '83. After eight laps the engine broke when a push rod went bad. That year we ran sixteen races and finished in the top five four times.

"Benny, who came from Detroit, was always a serious-type racer. He was down-to-earth, didn't cut up like some of other drivers, didn't drink or run around. Benny was married with kids, and he came down to North Carolina to make a go of it, and that's what he did. There are no stories to tell about Benny.

"On the track Benny was a conservative driver. In the beginning he ran with his own money, and he couldn't afford to go out full bore. We won Atlanta twice, the first time in the Atlanta Invitational, and later that year he won the regular race.

"It was the first time I had been turned loose in making decisions for the team, and it was a learning process for me. Leo Jackson had been hired to make the decisions at the track. Leo and Benny were close, and they would decide what to do with the chassis. My responsibility was preparing the car at the shop.

"Leo Jackson is a real smart man. I don't know anyone smarter than Leo Jackson, or anyone more honest. I enjoyed working for Johnny Hayes and Leo Jackson, more than anybody ever, and I learned so much from those two people.

"When I got to Hayes Racing, Benny and I never saw eye to eye. I didn't have a problem with him, but from day one, Benny never cared for me. I don't know why. He seemed to hold a grudge. I could lean in the window to talk to him, but Benny would make a point of waiting until Leo got there to tell him what was wrong.

"One time Benny asked me to call for a part for his cool suit helmet. I called, but the person I called wasn't in. Cool suits had come in about six months earlier. They had raced without them for twenty years.

"Benny said, 'How about my cool suit?' I said, 'I called and the guy wasn't there.'

"Later Benny told me, 'Boy, are you lucky. I called about the cool suit and spoke to a secretary, and I found out the guy you say you called just happened to not be there that day. You lucked out on that one.' Like I had been lying to him.

"And there was the time we were racing at Michigan. You can feel when a wheel is loose on the car, you can feel the vibration, and usually from the feel of the steering wheel, you can tell if it's a front or rear tire. Benny called on the radio and said he had a loose wheel. He said, 'The right front is loose,' and I changed it.

"When Benny came down pit road, I jumped down there, and when he left, I called on the radio and told him the wheel was *not* loose. I told him that because I wanted him to be careful when he got back on the track. I didn't want him out there thinking we had fixed it, have him go down the first turn and hurt himself.

"So on the radio I said, 'Benny, the wheel wasn't loose.' And he cussed me out. 'Don't argue with me. I said the wheel was loose.' I shut up right there.

"It hurt my feelings, but those weren't the worst times. Benny sold auto parts, including oil pumps for a firm that was having a company picnic. Benny was going to be spokesman at the picnic, and he wanted to bring a show car.

"U.S. Tobacco said fine, but they needed someone to take it to the picnic. It was the weekend of the Bristol race, and everyone else wanted to go to the race, so I volunteered, even though I had the weekend off. I was doing Benny a favor.

"My girlfriend and I rode up to the picnic, unloaded the car. People milled around the car, asking Benny questions about it.

" 'How do you get the lug nuts off and change the tire so fast?' he was asked. I squatted down, showing the people the procedure, while Benny explained how the stud doesn't have any threads on the end of it, and when you put the nut on, it slides over the end. And then he said, 'They tighten it with a gun.' And then he said, in front of my girlfriend and all these people, 'At least that's how he's supposed to do it, but sometimes they don't,' and he looked straight at me when he said it.

"And that pissed me off. I had driven all the way as a favor to him, and he slammed me right in front of everybody.

"One day at the end of the '85 season during the winter, I was told Tex Powell was going to be team manager. Back when Benny had his own team, he had worked with Tex.

"I had an office with all my books and files, and I had a car from Oldsmobile. You had to turn it in every 3,500 miles.

"We were working along, and Tex showed up and he was working too, and I went to lunch, and when I came back the cabinets in my office were gone, and my paperwork was sitting in the middle of the floor. I asked one of my secretaries, 'What happened to my cabinets?' She said, 'They told us to move them up front.'

"I stacked the papers in the corner. Later that afternoon Johnny Hayes came in. I was working on the trunk of the car with one of the guys, and he said to me, 'When you get ready to turn that car in to get a new one, don't bother. Just give the keys to Tex and let him get a new car.'

"I knew something was going on, but I didn't understand it. I gave the keys to Tex.

"The next morning I came in and I walked into my office, and Tex was sitting at the desk, his feet propped up. It startled me. He said, 'Can I help you?' I said, 'No, I guess not.'

"I went back to work, and when Johnny Hayes showed up, I said, 'What's going on? Am I fired?'

"He said, 'I don't really know. No, you're not fired.' I said, 'What's going on?' He said, 'I really don't know what to tell you.' I said, 'Should I leave?' He said, 'That would be the best thing. I really don't know what's going on.'

"I asked Leo, 'Have I done anything wrong? Are you unhappy with what I've done?' He said, 'No, I am absolutely happy with your work. I think you've done a fine job. I have no complaints whatsoever. It's not me who's pushing you out.'

"I asked Johnny Hayes, and he said, 'It's not me.'

"It had to be Benny, but I didn't have a close enough relationship with him to ask him. And if I had asked him, it wouldn't have done any good.

"And after I got fired, even though no one would tell me why, it was like I had been blackballed. Before then, I was on the uphill climb. Everyone was calling me, trying to hire me away. But after I was fired from that job, people stopped calling. I couldn't beg, borrow, or steal a job.

"I went to talk to Humpy Wheeler. He said he didn't have any idea what was going on, but he said I ought to talk with Alan Kulwicki. He said, 'He's just coming into racing. The boy has talent. He's going to be somebody.'

"And in December 1985 Alan hired me. I was going back to work for an independent. Alan couldn't pay me as much as I was making, and there were only three of us working in the shop, but it was a job.

"Alan was very intense. He's a man who knows where he wants to go, and he makes wise business decisions to get there. Some guys will over-spend. He won't. He knows his limitations, accepts them, and works within them. He's very smart that way.

"Alan treated me fine. I didn't have any problems with him, but for me it was hard working in that situation. I had gotten spoiled working for the big teams, and it was hard driving all night in a pickup truck and getting back on the road and sleeping five to a room and going back to the old ways of doing things.

"One day in March we had a blowup. He said something, and I said something smart-alecky, and he said, 'Maybe you need to be someplace else.' I said, 'Maybe you're right. As a matter of fact, to be honest, you *are* right. I'll see you.'

"I walked outside, and he came back out and said, 'We both got out of hand.' I said, 'It was bound to happen sooner or later. I don't see where it's going to work. Let's part company still friends.''

"I should never had done that. I should have stuck it out. I didn't have problems with him, except that one time, but job offers had come easy—I got the job with Alan quickly—and I was figuring a *big* team could use me and I'd get another job, no problem.

"I sat out for five months without a dime coming in. I called and called, and I begged, and nothing. I finally took a job with Cale Yarborough. Cale was unhappy with Jake Elder, fired him, and he hired me to be his crew chief.

"I had known Jake when we were at DiGard. You can't help but like Jake, but he's one of those people, when something goes good, he self-destructs. I remember at DiGard we had a real close relationship, and he gave me a nice Christmas present, and we got along great, and then all of a sudden he came in one day and said, 'You're working against me. You've worked against me the whole time.'

"It was like he felt the whole shop was against him, had become his enemy and it was like that at Cale's too. He came in, the team started to do real well, and after some time it became worse and worse and worse.

"But Jake knows the cars. He doesn't have book learning, but he's an amazing guy.

"I took his spot at Cale's. Cale was the owner and driver, ran a limited eighteen-race schedule. I still admire Cale. He's still one of my heroes. Cale is a very good businessman, serious about the dollar. Cale wants to win. He's a fierce competitor. He won't let anything get in the way, other than money.

"But what I learned about Cale is, he will come in and can tell you absolutely nothing about the car. He could not help you get the car to handle. When I was with Darrell Waltrip, Darrell would say, 'The car is too loose. I need more right front spring.' Or 'The rear springs feel too stiff. Soften them up a little bit.'

"With Cale, we put the stopwatch on the car, and if there was a problem, we would try something, and if the car ran faster, it worked, and if it didn't . . . You were just guessing, and it was very frustrating for me.

"We did have some good runs. We went to Dover, and the car was flying in practice on Saturday. There were maybe forty-five minutes of practice left, and Michael Waltrip blew an engine and crashed right in front of us, and we totaled our car.

"Immediately we broke out the spare car, and it had a motor completely ready to go. At the most we had to replace the air cleaner and fan. We unloaded the car, took the springs off the crashed car, put them right in, and we got in ten minutes of practice.

"The next day we started last, because we started the backup car, and we ended up running twelfth before we broke a header and dropped out of the race.

"Cale was there *only* to win. He wasn't running for points. If he's going to finish tenth, why bother? You aren't going to make enough money to pay for the tires, and he stood a chance of hurting himself or crashing the car. That's why drivers who run a partial schedule, if they get behind, they just park the car.

"We ran good at Michigan when we broke a brake caliper. Our biggest downfall as a team was the death of my right-hand man, Tracy Reaves. Tracy wanted to be a driver, and Cale gave him a car and motor to drive in an ARCA race twice a year, and he drove at Talladega and got killed.

"We were standing there watching, and all the guys were close friends, had goofed around, played together, and when he got killed, it tore the whole team apart. It never was the same.

"I was with Cale a year. The team manager walked into the shop one day, and I knew—because you can tell. The team was not winning. He said, 'I need to talk to you.' I could tell by the tone in his voice. I said, 'It can't be that bad,' and I laughed, because I knew what it was.

"He said, 'Cale is coming down. I hate to do this, but we're going to have to make some changes.'

"I said, 'Don't worry about it. It's not your fault. I know we haven't been running good.'

"I took a job with Mike Curb. He had been a California politician who once had big money and had owned Richard Petty's team. Sunoco was his sponsor, and Brad Noffsinger the driver, and Brad asked me if I wanted to work for Mike Curb.

"I took the job without even looking at the shop, and when I walked in, I saw the building was run-down and they had no equipment. Everything looked like it was twenty years old, was worn out. And they were out of money.

"We ran really good the first Pocono race of 1988. Brad wrecked in practice. I said, 'Get the spare car. We're going to get it ready.' The other crew members looked at me like I was crazy. They had never been serious about Winston Cup racing. We had to change everything to get it ready to go, and after we got done, he finished nineteenth. For a driver starting out, that was a good finish.

"We went to Talladega, and that's when I knew we were in trouble. We needed two spacers to go behind the wheel, at a cost of $8 each, and the team manager came over and said, 'Do you have any on the spare car?' I said, 'Yeah, but we're going to have to unload it and take the wheels off.' He said, 'Go ahead and do it.' I said, 'We're talking about $16. I'm not going to unload the car off the truck for $16.'

"He said, 'We ain't got the money.' Curb was taking all the money from the sponsorship and putting it into politics. Anytime he ran a campaign, he had no money to run the team.

"I quit, and I went to work for Larry McClure part-time, until Phil Barkdoll hired me for two seasons to help him run a limited schedule. They ran six races a year.

"It was easy. The money was there, no one else was calling. Nothing opened up. *Nothing.* If you're only running a partial schedule, people forget about you. You're just a face. I was seeing young people coming along who didn't have half my experience getting jobs, and I didn't. I resigned myself to the fact I was either doing something wrong or I was an asshole. Something wasn't working right, whether it was my attitude or personality, or I don't know what.

"I crew-chiefed a couple of races for Richard Jackson, but U.S. Tobacco wanted Bob Johnson, and over the winter of 1990–91, I went to work for Chad Little, who was an independent. Chad said he had money, but he didn't.

"We went to Daytona, ran pretty good, and we got back home and went to Richmond, and I got deathly sick. I went to the bathroom, collapsed on the floor, had IVs stuck in me. While Chad ran the Richmond race, I was in the infield hospital.

"He ran well, the best he had ever done, finished sixteenth, and when we came home, Chad came to me and said, 'I made a big mistake when I figured the budget. We're going to run out of money three-quarters of the way through the season if we don't cut back on something.'

"We went to a couple more races. We were one of the fastest cars at North Wilkesboro, and in practice one of the fastest at Bristol. Qualifying, we had a tire go flat. We took a provisional to get into the race, and when the race started, Chad went right to the front. We ran in the top five all day long, crashed, but finished fourteenth.

"We got home, worked on the car all day Monday to fix it, and about six in the afternoon Chad said, 'Look, I hate to do this, but we're running low on money. We have to let you go. You did a great job for us, but you're the highest-paid man here. We won't run as good without you, but we don't have any choice. It's either that or run out of money three-quarters of the way through the season.

"As soon as that happened, Leo Jackson called me to build a car for him. 'That's all I can use you for. Do that.' And I did, and it got to be summer of '91, and I built a lift for my wife's wave runner on Lake Norman, where we live. One of my neighbors liked it and asked me to build him one. So I did.

"I got the lift perfected, and I've been selling them all summer long.

"Leo told me to leave my toolbox at his shop and to come back when it gets cold. I said I would. Leo pays me as good as he possibly can. I can pay my bills, but barely, because I had adjusted my life-style to a higher salary. I'll manage.

"I'm waiting for another offer in racing, but I don't see one coming. I am not going to work for an independent. I won't work for someone who doesn't have any money. I love racing, but I won't take a job no matter what. I'm not like Richard Petty; if I can't go and run competitively, I won't go. Some people go crazy if they can't go the racetrack. It doesn't drive me crazy. I miss my friends. I miss working on the machinery. I enjoy going to Leo's and working on the cars. It may sound like I have bitterness, but I don't really."

LAP 21

Tim Richmond

The Racer Who Died of AIDS

The ghost of Tim Richmond, one of the most flamboyant racers to ever drive a stock car, haunts the sprawling Hendrick Motorsports complex off Morehead Road, not far from the Charlotte Motor Speedway. Richmond's feathered western hat sits atop one of his tall trophies in a glass case close by the reception desk. Photos of Tim cover the office walls. In 1986 Tim Richmond dominated the sport, winning an incredible seven races during the second half of the season, but during the winter he was bedridden with what doctors said was double pneumonia. Richmond seemed to have recovered after five months of bedrest, and returned to racing in the middle of the '87 season, but after several races the other drivers noticed that something was seriously wrong with Tim. At the track he looked terrible, seemed logy or perhaps was drunk. There were whispers he was sedating himself with drugs.

At Michigan he had to be dragged from his trailer in a seemingly drugged state, driven to his race car in a golf cart, and placed in his car before the race.

When the other drivers saw that, they were so concerned they protested his presence in the race car. After the race, opposing drivers demanded that NASCAR ban him from racing, and when NASCAR tested him for drugs and he tested positive, it did so. But Richmond argued it was a prescription drug, and sued.

There was a court hearing to decide whether NASCAR had the right to keep him from driving, but when the judge ordered that his medical records be produced, Richmond dropped the fight. He never raced again.

Richmond dropped from sight to return to the Cleveland area. He checked into a hospital in Fort Lauderdale, never to recover. On August

7, 1989, Tim Richmond died of acquired immune deficiency syndrome. He was thirty-two years old.

Jimmy Johnson was general manager when Rick Hendrick hired Tim Richmond to drive for the Hendrick Motorsports team in 1986. Their fortunes were tied together early in Johnson's stewardship. The compassionate Johnson still considers Tim Richmond a personal "hero," and though Richmond has been dead for several years now, Jimmy Johnson finds it hard not to mull what might have been had the carefree spirit with the love-the-one-you're-with attitude not caught the dreaded AIDS disease and died so young.

JIMMY JOHNSON: "In July 1983 I was working as an accountant for a Ford dealership, and a friend asked if I wanted to work for a new Toyota store in Fayetteville, which is my home, and I told him, 'No way.' 'Imports' was a bad word. He said, 'Would you be interested in going to work for Rick Hendrick?' I said, 'That's a different story.'

"I knew about Rick Hendrick from a mutual friend, Jody Honeycutt. I knew he was very interested in boat racing. I also knew Rick had bought City Chevrolet and made a lot of people take notice, because he was very young and had become very successful.

"When I had an opportunity to go to work for Rick, I decided to pursue it. I met Rick, and he hired me to work at the new Fayetteville Toyota store. He said, 'Work there for me three years, and you'll have your own store, I promise.'

"I was only there a year and a half, and the store was extremely successful. We were selling everything we could get our hands on. Rick assembled a strong sales force, we were young and innovative, and we had a good product, and I was good at keeping the costs down. We got Rick's investment back in six months!

"In November 1985 he asked me to move to Florida. He said, 'I'm starting a new store, and I need you to help run it.' Without hesitation, I agreed. My then-girlfriend, Pris, now my wife, lived in Frostproof, which is south of Orlando in the orange groves. The new store was in a Tampa suburb, Hudson, so I moved there with a group of managers, and Rick built the most beautiful Chevrolet store I had ever seen.

"We opened up October 13. In the middle of November, Rick said, 'I want you to move back to Charlotte.'

"I was living on the beach in Tampa in a fabulous condo, paying only $400 a month. I was five minutes from work. I said, 'Man, this better be good, boss.' He said, 'I want you to help me in the racing operation.' I said, 'Give me five minutes, and I'll be packed.'

"My biggest worry was telling Pris I was moving to Charlotte. It was a shock, but things worked out, and we were married a year later.

"When I moved to Charlotte, Rick's problem at the time was he was trying to run his race team out of a shoe box. He had a very, very qualified, hardworking guy named Dillard Hatfield who was the office manager of City Chevrolet and also handling the account for his race team. Dillard had his hands full.

"I came in December 1985. My initial job was to straighten out the accounting system. We had no computer. There was no formal accounting done. Accounts payables were in arrears. It took me a while to get it all straightened out. Rick gave me 100 percent control over the money side of the operation.

"Rick Hendrick is a racer who happens to be in the automobile business. He has driven drag boats 170 miles an hour. He hired a driver who set the world speed record, 222 miles an hour on the water. And then Rick's best friend, Jimmy Wright, got killed in the boat, and his heart was no longer in it. He came to Charlotte looking for Harry Hyde, because he heard that Harry had a place where he could store his boats.

"Harry Hyde figured Rick was interested in racing and had some money, and Harry said, 'If you give me a chance, I'll build you a Winston Cup car that's capable of winning a race.' That got Rick's attention.

"We had Geoff Bodine driving and Harry Hyde as crew chief, and we were adding a second team. Tim Richmond came to work with Harry, and Gary Nelson came aboard to work with Geoff.

"When I arrived we only had one shop, which we were renting from Harry. We didn't have a shop for Gary, so we had to rent one and buy equipment. We bought all four of [car owner] Billy Hagan's Monte Carlos. We bought Raymond Beadle's shop and leased back half of it to Raymond and Rusty Wallace, who beat us for the championship.

"I had a rental trailer that was beside Harry Hyde's own race shop, a room where I had a bookkeeper. I had to throw used race tires on top of the roof to keep it from vibrating when we ran the dynometer so I could talk on the telephone.

"I thought I knew a lot about racing, because I had been around it all my life, but I found out I was a green rookie. I had been to every dirt rack, every NASCAR track around Fayetteville, but when I became involved in big-time racing, I realized that 99 percent of the spectators and race fans didn't know anything about it, and I was one of them.

"I was accustomed to the two-stall garages in the back of the house where you had your dirt track racer and your trailer and you hooked it behind the truck and took off Friday night and came back Sunday night. And I really thought that was the way NASCAR was. I didn't realize you need seventy-five or eighty-five employees, many of them with master's and doctorate degrees, and a $10 million facility. I didn't realize how much money it takes. Our budget is about $40,000 a day, every day for 365 days a year. That's a lot of money. It takes a lot of money to run our operation.

"We have twenty race cars. We only race half of them. Each team has five cars that they race, and the rest are backup cars, and in addition there are four or five show cars.

"And so when I came to Charlotte in December of 1985, I was scared to death, and Harry Hyde took me under his wing.

"Harry and I didn't always agree. Harry is one of the smartest men in racing I've ever known, a master of organizing people. He was the most prepared person I've ever worked with in racing. He used to get a kick out of walking people through his shop, and he'd say, 'Here is my Daytona car. The engine is in it. Here is my Atlanta car. The engine is in it. Here's my Richmond car. The engine's in it. Here's my Rockingham car. The engine's in it.'

"Putting the engine in was the last thing you'd do. If the engine was in it, the car was ready to go racing.

"Harry started work at eight and finished at five. He worked his men extremely hard, but they knew at five o'clock they could get off. It wasn't midnighters or all-nighters, which is commonplace in today's racing.

"Harry spent a lot of time educating a real rookie. He probably thought, 'Why is Rick sending this punk to tell me how to run my operation?' But I didn't abuse the authority I had either. I knew I had to earn the respect of the driver and crew chief, and I did that by listening and keeping my mouth shut and not having ego attacks. I don't have that problem. My paycheck comes on payday like everyone else's.

"When I came in, I told everyone, 'Hey, my background is accounting.' And from the first day I arrived I remembered something told to me by Al Hendrickson, who was a big wheel with Southeast Toyota. He was giving a speech to the businessmen in the audience, and referring to the governor on the car that keeps you from running too fast, he advised, 'Be a governor, don't be a brake.'

"When he said that, I thought to myself, 'What is he telling you? Don't let them run too fast, but don't hold down the operation.' And I apply that every day. When someone walks in this door and says, 'I want to spend a half-million dollars,' and that's not uncommon, I must make the determination, 'Will that make us run faster?' And that's exactly what

I ask. Every decision I make, that's the determining factor. If the answer is yes, there is no way I can say no.

"Working under me was hard for Harry, real hard, and it was hard for Gary, because neither was accustomed to that. But I never interfered. One thing neither Rick nor I ever do is tell a crew chief what setups to run, what cars to run. That is their responsibility. They live by their decisions.

"That first year the highs and lows came real close together. The low came in an IMSA 24-hour race at Daytona. Wally Dallenbach, Jr., was the driver. We had a very very fast car, a fast driver, an excellent crew. We sat on the pole.

"I had rented two motor homes, parked them in the paddock area, one for eating and drinking and one for sleeping, and my wife and I went out and bought $500 worth of fruits, ice drinks, any kind of food you wanted. It was an hour before the start of the race, and as I was walking into the motor home with bags of groceries under my arm, one of the team members walked up and said, 'The engine just blew up.' We were running an inferior cast-iron block, because our budget was a fourth of Porsche's, and the block had cracked.

"We couldn't even start the race. That was devastating.

"Two weeks from then, in mid-February 1986, was the Daytona 500. Geoff Bodine was our driver. We had to beat Dale Earnhardt, and we were racing him hard. I don't know if we could have outrun him in the end, but we were very competitive. I remember being in the pits and being so nervous, I could barely watch.

"I turned my head away, and I heard people cheering, and I turned back and with three laps of go, Earnhardt was heading for the pits. I had seen him flash by, and I thought, 'Dale's out of gas. Can we make it?' And it was the longest three laps I ever spent in racing.

"We won the race, and it was the greatest thing that ever happened to me. Back then Rick Hendrick used to call me a bean counter. I would reply, 'Since I've been with you, you've had a lot of beans to count.' That day Geoff Bodine's win brought us $198,000.

"We partied late, late, late, and at five the next morning back at the racetrack, myself and three or four other guys cleaned up the race car and waxed it to be on 'Good Morning America.' I thought to myself, 'We're on "Good Morning America." ' '

"Geoff won another race at Dover. Our other driver, Tim Richmond, won seven races, had a phenomenal year. Between the two cars, we sat on sixteen poles that year!

"I remember the first time I met Tim Richmond. Rick Hendrick asked me to take a new car, a company car, to Tim at his summer residence in Fort Lauderdale. He was staying at Bahia Mar on an absolutely beautiful houseboat. When I pulled up to the houseboat in a Z-28 Camaro, there was Tim sitting on the deck eating crab's legs and drinking beer.

"Shortly after our introduction, I told Tim, 'I have a plane to catch. We have to take off.' I had no idea where the airport was, so I threw the keys to Tim, and we headed for the airport.

"It was around lunchtime, and we took off down a six-lane highway, running as fast as we could run in heavy, heavy, heavy traffic. I had never met this guy in my life, and I was petrified.

"Tim decided I needed a little excitement in my life. Without a word, Tim threw it in low gear, and with tires smoking jumped over the curb, headed in the other direction, and stopped in front of a coffee shop. He said, 'You want some coffee?' I said, 'I sure don't.' He said, 'Come on. We're going to get some coffee anyway.'

"We went inside. It was a topless coffee shop, which I had never heard of. We stayed there a few minutes and had our cup of coffee. I said, 'I really need to go.'

"We made it to the airport. I was half out of the car, shaking hands with Tim, telling him, 'It was nice meeting you; I look forward to racing with you in 1986,' when a cab that had pulled in behind us began tooting his horn. It made Tim mad.

"The cabbie tooted again, and when he did, Tim threw the car in reverse, floored it, and just knocked the heck out of the car. He scared the cabdriver to death.

"The cabdriver took off out of the airport wide open as fast as he could run. With me half hanging out of the car, Tim threw it in gear and chased off after him!

"Fortunately for the cabdriver, he was able to escape, and after we came around again, I was able to safely get out of the car and make my plane.

"Tim convinced me right there we were going to have a successful year, because I knew that anybody who could drive a street car like that wouldn't have *any* problem with a race car.

"And I turned out to be right, but the first half of the year I earned my money, because I had to literally stand between Tim and Harry Hyde to keep them from killing each other. I thought, 'What have I gotten myself into?' Because Tim was high-strung, and Harry was high-strung, and the two did not hit it off.

"Tim was complaining the car wasn't handling, and Harry complained that Tim wasn't driving properly. And during races they screamed bloody murder at each other. It was rough, really rough. On Monday Tim would come by or call, and he'd bad-mouth Harry, and Harry would bad-mouth Tim.

"Tim had driven for Raymond Beadle with some degree of success. He had wrecked a lot of cars, but Rick Hendrick got him because he liked his flamboyant style, loved his arrogance. Tim was like Muhammad Ali. He bragged a lot, was very boastful, but if you can back it up, it's not bragging, and that's how Tim was. He would say, 'Let me get at it, and I'll show you how to win races.'

"Well, we weren't winning, and it was frustrating him.

"And then we got to Charlotte. It was the end of May. We made it to Charlotte in spite of ourselves, and all of a sudden Harry, in his words, was 'able to catch up with Tim.' That had been the problem. Tim was better than we were. Tim had a terminology that was foreign to us and to Harry. In a practice or test session, Tim would come in and tell Harry, 'The car is rolling over in the turn.' Or he'd say, 'The car is hunting down the straightaway,' or 'The car is looking up at the fence.' Tim had his own clichés, and Harry didn't really know what Tim was talking about. Tim knew what was wrong, he just couldn't express it in a way Harry could understand.

"We came to Charlotte and ran second to Dale Earnhardt. Cale Yarborough was the force at the time, and we outran Cale, who finished third. Cale was trying to pass us for second and couldn't, and all of a sudden, without any forewarning, Harry and Tim seemed to mesh. What it was, Harry just figured Tim out. He figured out what he wanted, and when he did, if something didn't happen to the race car, we were unbeatable.

"We ran second at Talladega, and then we went out and won Daytona the Fourth of July, won Darlington, won Richmond, won Riverside, won both Pocono races. In the last half of the year we won seven races and were a force.

"I can remember the time trials at Riverside. Darrell Waltrip had the fastest time up to when it was our turn. Tim took off, and as he came down through the esses, he was totally out of control. He got through the right-hander and then the left-hander, and as he came to the main straightaway, I was wondering if he was ever going to get off the gas, because I knew the next turn at nine was very dangerous, that more people had gotten hurt there than at any place at any track in NASCAR.

"Tim was going so fast he couldn't get the car stopped with his brakes, so he threw the car into third gear—he had the old Chrysler transmission that Harry Hyde believed in rather than the fancy road racers that didn't need a clutch, and so when Tim threw it into third gear and dumped the clutch, he zinged the tach and we bent two valves, so we were running on seven cylinders, and you could even hear the car skipping badly as it went through nine, off nine, and down the front straightaway. But he put it on the pole.

"That afternoon we were ready to run our last practice session before we were to go racing. The big question was, 'What do we do about engines?' Harry Hyde and Randy Dorton, the engine builder, were discussing this, because the engine we qualified in was now junk. We had a Bingham and Reviss engine on the truck that had a lot of mileage on it but a lot of horsepower. We also had a brand-new engine that was a little down in horsepower.

"Our question to Tim was, 'What do you want us to do?' Tim's comment was, 'Aw, hell, put the little one in there, and I'll just drive harder.'

"And he won the race. And I remember after the race standing with Tim and Mary Frann, who played Bob Newhart's wife on 'Newhart,' a real good-looking girl. Tim was dating her, and he had a limo pick her up and bring her to the track. She was beautiful.

"The same year we were in the inaugural Watkins Glen race, and Geoff Bodine was running first, and Tim was running second. Geoff is a phenomenal road course driver, but so was Tim.

"I was spotting for Tim on the radio, standing on the back straightaway on the ESPN tower, so I had a great view of the whole backside of the racetrack.

"Because the radios weren't as good as they are now, Tim would call me, and I would relay what he said to Harry. The race was about half over, and Tim said, 'Find out from Harry how far behind I am.' I knew, and I said, 'You are twenty seconds behind.' He said, 'When there are twenty laps to go, call me and tell me, because I will go to the front and win the race.'

"I thought, 'Here he is twenty seconds behind, and he thinks he can make up a second a lap.'

"As fate happened, a caution flag came out, everyone pitted, and when Geoff and Tim came back out they were nose-to-tail, and Geoff knew his hands were full with Tim. They sailed down the straightaway in the first turn, and everyone turned right but Geoff, who went right off through the first turn. Tim eased to the win.

"If you look at a tape of the race, you'll see that Tim almost wrecked when he came off the last turn heading toward the checkered flag. He threw his left arm out the window and was steering one-handed, and when he came off the turn heading for the start-finish line at Watkins Glen, he almost lost it. The car went off the racetrack because he was waving to the fans. Tim was just being Tim.

"Once Tim began winning races, Harry Hyde and Tim Richmond became like father-son. Harry Hyde loved Tim Richmond; Tim Richmond loved Harry Hyde. That's what winning can do. It's why successful teams stay together and unsuccessful ones don't.

"In 1986 Tim finished third in the driving championship behind Earnhardt and Darrell Waltrip. When I went to the NASCAR banquet in December, Tim looked sick. He told me he was sick, was feeling bad. I thought he had a bad cold. It was the last time I saw Tim for months, because shortly after the first of the year in 1987, Tim went into the hospital. We were shocked. We only knew what the doctors told us, which was that he had double pneumonia. We knew nothing else.

"He was in Cleveland, near his home. Rick Hendrick flew up several times and saw him, and we stayed in close contact with Al and Evelyn, his mom and dad, two wonderful people. They told us he was at the point of death. We were petrified we'd lose him.

"Drivers like Tim Richmond don't come along every day. People like Tim Richmond don't come along every day. He was a motivator. He would take the crew out to dinner. We partied together. We won together. Just look at the photos on the walls of this office: Here is his Pocono win, and see that smile and that cockiness. We just bred cockiness. We were all feeling our oats because of Tim, and to think he might not be with us, it was devastating.

"I can remember one Busch race when Tim was far and away the best car, and we were leading, and Dale Earnhardt was running second, and Tim let Dale get up beside him. Tim was on the inside, Dale the outside, and then Tim would let Dale on the inside and he'd get on the outside, and he did it for show.

"We were hollering at Tim on the radio, 'Are you crazy?' Because Earnhardt is a very, very talented driver, the best. But we had him beat, and Tim knew it, and so Tim got beside him for ten laps, and he keyed the mike on the radio, and he said, 'Guys, don't worry. He's gonna hit the wall. You watch, he's gonna hit the wall.' Because Dale had to drive beyond the edge to keep up with Tim.

"And sure enough, we came off the second turn, and Tim was on the inside this time, and Dale slipped up and hit the wall. And we went on and won the race.

"I wouldn't say those two were close friends, but they had a tremendous amount of respect for each other. Tim talked a lot about Dale.

ckR

"I enjoyed watching those two race. The public, the fans, I, have been cheated because we didn't get to see them race each other but for a short period of time. It would have been the greatest rivalry since the Yankees and the Dodgers.

"Tim had been sick five months, and he returned to the racing circuit in mid-June at Pocono. Before the race I remember Tim unzipped his jacket and pulled it around his waist and put his cool suit on, and all the women in the stands went wild, and while he was doing that Dale walked by on his way to his car, and Dale said something to Tim, and Tim said, 'Yeah, buddy, let's go racing. Let's get it on.'

"Tim won the race, and then he won the next week at Riverside. At Michigan the next week Tim felt weak. He looked terrible. He finished fourth when Dale won it. At Watkins Glen, Tim appeared weak. He looked terrible. The race was rained out, and he felt better the next day and finished tenth.

"Tim drove his last race at Michigan, where engine failure put us out of the race early.

"Tim returned to Cleveland, and I didn't have any conversations with Tim after that. He went into a hospital in Fort Lauderdale and never came home.

"When he was at the point of death, we found out he had AIDS, so it was a blessing Tim died, something we looked forward to, because we knew how sick he was and what his family must have been going through. We're still very close to the Richmond family, and I can tell you their suffering is not over. It never will be.

"And for everyone to talk about him the way they did because he died of AIDS was very, very hard for me to take—the rumors about Tim and drugs, dirty needles, or he was gay. We all knew better than that. I never ever saw Tim Richmond do drugs. Dr. Jerry Punch told me that Tim Richmond was scared to death of needles. That's one thing Tim and I had in common. I hate them too.

"Tim got AIDS like Magic Johnson did. He was good-looking and lived a very glamorous playboy life-style. There wasn't a red-blooded male in the world who at the time wouldn't have traded places with him. But Tim loved hookers more than he loved the girl next door. He just had this thing for hookers, and that's how he caught AIDS, and there is no reprieve. Once you get it, it's just a matter of time.

"He was so dynamic, and when he zipped off his uniform to tease the crowds so he could put on his cool suit before the race, they would go wild, absolutely wild, and he ate it up.

"There has never been anybody like him."

Jimmy Johnson

The Organization

Jimmy Johnson, the general manager for the Hendrick Motorsports race team, was in a quandary. A manufacturing company wanted him to spend half a million dollars on a machine that by use of computer would take a perfectly tooled head on an engine and make it possible to duplicate the configuration on every other head. The machine could smooth out one set of heads a day, a job that usually takes five weeks to do by hand.

For Johnson, the machine would be a race team's dream come true. But there was a problem: If Johnson went ahead and spent the half-million dollars, the possibility existed that NASCAR might a year later make the new machine redundant by mandating that the car factories tool the heads ready-made for racing before giving them to their race teams, saving each race team thousands of dollars in labor costs.

Johnson called NASCAR and asked what the rule makers intended to do, but NASCAR remained noncommittal. If he bought the equipment, he was told, it would be at his own risk.

Johnson, who has carte blanche to spend any amount to increase the speed of the cars of his two drivers, Kenny Schrader and Ricky Rudd, had to decide whether to risk spending half a million dollars of Rick Hendrick's money on a machine he might not need a year later. Johnson was leaning toward gambling on it.

According to Johnson, what makes Rick Hendrick a special man to work for is Johnson's certainty that whatever he does, if he does it for the ultimate reason—*Will it help the team to run faster?*—Hendrick will back him. And since Hendrick has a seemingly limitless amount of money to spend on his cars, Johnson has the advantage of being able to spend whatever money he deems worth it to spend in order to go faster. His is one of only a handful of teams—RCR, SABCO, Bahari, and Junior

Jimmy Johnson

Johnson are others—who because of their backing by either Ford or Chevrolet, plus the wealth of their owner, can spend on demand. In a game where money translates into speed if it is spent right, it's an important advantage.

Like Rick Hendrick, Jimmy Johnson brings to the race team a personable quality and an understanding of human behavior, enabling him to motivate his teams to work hard toward the common goal: winning races.

His two drivers, Ricky Rudd and Ken Schrader, both are top-echelon drivers capable of winning races. If the Hendrick team has one weakness, it may be its fervent desire to be viewed as "nice guys." Hendrick, despite his wealth, wants badly to be liked by his racing associates and to be portrayed favorably in the press. So does Jimmy Johnson. Rudd, in his orange, white, and black Tide car, has always been viewed as a "good guy." Schrader, who will race sprint cars, go-carts, or anything else on wheels, has the reputation of being a man who can't get enough of racing. The whole package is very appealing to a sponsor. If Rick Hendrick suddenly announced he wanted to run six race cars, he'd immediately have sponsors lining up to finance them.

Rick Hendrick owns car dealerships up and down the East Coast. He has loyal sponsors who spend millions to finance the running of his cars. He has a squeaky-clean PR image. What he doesn't have is a racing championship.

Image doesn't win championships, and over the past years Hendrick's teams have been outrun by racing's mustachioed Black Bart, knave Dale Earnhardt. It seems ironic Rick Hendrick hasn't had a dominating racer since roguish Tim Richmond died in 1988.

Even after Ricky Rudd finished second in points in '91, no one at Hendrick seemed particularly happy about it or satisfied. It will be interesting to see what Rick Hendrick and Jimmy Johnson do in 1992 in their bid to give themselves the one thing money apparently just can't buy.

JIMMY JOHNSON: "We knew Tim Richmond wasn't going to start the 1987 season with us, and so we hired Benny Parsons. Benny drove the full season, and when Tim came back in the middle of the season, he raced a second car. Benny's car was number 25. Tim had 35.

"Through all our problems that year, Harry Hyde was able to prepare two cars, and he did it very successfully. After the season, we knew Tim was not coming back, and Benny was at a point where his broadcasting career was important to him, and we looked to get another driver, and at the top of the list was Kenny Schrader.

"We knew nothing about Kenny, other than we didn't see any down-

side. In 1987 he drove Junie Donlavey car and outran Bill Elliott in one
of the 125-mile qualifying races at Daytona, and that was darn impressive.

"I called Kenny Schrader's house, left word on his recorder to call me,
and thirty minutes later I walked back into our shop on Old State's
Road—the old Raymond Beadle operation where Waddell Wilson built
Geoff Bodine's car; we were leasing half of it to Team III—and there was
Kenny Schrader.

"I said, 'You got a minute?' He didn't even know I had called his
house. I said, 'Word has it you signed with Bud Moore. If so, congratulations. If not, I want to talk to you.'

"He said, 'Bud and I have talked, but Bud doesn't have a sponsor lined
up yet, and he doesn't want to make a deal until he does.'

"After Kenny and I talked for a while, we rode over to Rick Hendrick's office. Kenny said, 'I want to go home and talk to my wife. I want
to think about it.'

"Understand, it's not the money that entices a potential driver, it's the
potential. If a driver went to a brand-new team for $1 million a year, but
the team had no chassis or engine program, he'd be a fool. We had a lot
more to offer Kenny Schrader than just good income. He had seen what
Harry and Tim Richmond could do together. We had run good with
Benny Parsons. He felt he could go somewhere with us, but he wanted a
little time to think it over.

"I said, 'I will meet you in Darlington.'

"Before I left, I prepared and signed a one-page memorandum of
understanding of everything we had discussed the night before. I arrived
at Darlington the next day and asked him, 'What do you think?' He said,
'The garage closes at five o'clock. I will meet you at the first service
station after you pull out of the track and make a left.'

"We met. He said, 'I have something to do first. Before I sign that
contract, I have to make a phone call to Red Baron Pizza,' who was his
sponsor with Junie Donlavey. Kenny called and apologized for what he
was about to do, came back, and signed the memorandum to drive for us
in 1988.

"Kenny Schrader is a top-notch person. People love him, sponsors
love him, the crew loves him. He is a down-to-earth, fun-loving racer
with tons and tons and tons of potential.

"Shortly after we signed him, John Andretti, who is a friend of mine,
called and said, 'Jimmy, I want to tell you something: You hired a guy who
is wonderful.' For the life of me I couldn't figure out who he was talking
about, and I asked him who he meant. John said, 'Kenny Schrader.'" I

hadn't realized the two knew each other. John said, 'I raced him many, many, many times in sprints and midgets, and if you outrun Kenny Schrader, you win the race.'

"It made me feel really good that John felt Kenny Schrader was going to be a star someday. And that marriage has worked perfectly. Kenny has finished in the top ten for the driving championship all four years he's driven for us, but he hasn't won a lot of races because fate hasn't begun to shine on Kenny the way it did on Tim.

"We had the dominant car at Daytona two years in a row. In '89 we started dead last, because he wrecked in the 125s after sitting on the pole and had to take out a backup car. In the Daytona 500, after thirty laps Kenny was running second to Earnhardt. He caught up to Earnhardt and was getting ready to pass him when a caution came out. Then something happened in a pit stop that put us way behind, and again Kenny worked his way back to where he was on Earnhardt's bumper, only to blow an engine. We did that two years in a row.

"This year we played with the field at Pocono. Kenny led the first forty laps. We came in to make a pit stop and we got out of sync, and Kenny was back to twelfth place. In a matter of time he was back at the front, but Ernie Irvan spun Hut Stricklin out, and the wreck took Ricky and Darrell and Dale and Kenny. The Chevrolets were decimated. And it was a Chevrolet that caused the wreck.

"We should have won at Rockingham this year. We were leading the race, had a 30-second lead with Kyle Petty running second, and there was a caution flag, which allowed the field to close back up. Kyle had fresher tires than we did, and he caught us and won the race. We had been in the right place at the right time to win the race, but fate took it away from us.

"Kenny did win one of the most exciting races NASCAR's ever had, at Talladega in July of 1988. There were ten cars dicing for the lead on the last lap, and Kenny went around all of them and won the race. That was an unbelievable moment for me, and for Kenny and Harry.

"That year we were running three cars: Kenny, Geoff Bodine, and Darrell Waltrip. At the end of the year Harry Hyde quit. He probably felt he wasn't getting enough attention, and he was probably right in that a three-car team is not the hot tip; two cars is. Three is better than one, worse than two. And Harry saw that, and Harry elected to go out on his own, and he went with the Stavola Brothers and Bobby Hillin. We still stay in close contact with Harry. He's still one of our favorite people and a close friend of the family.

"When Harry left, we made Richard Broome crew chief. Let me tell you about Rick Hendrick, and you'll understand why Richard was given the job. Rick Hendrick is the most loyal employer I have ever heard of or worked for. If you work hard for him, are loyal to him, the sky is the limit, and it doesn't matter whether you are washing cars in his dealership or whether you are changing tires on his race car, you will move up in the company.

"Several years ago Jerry Potter of *USA Today* asked me, 'What is Rick Hendrick's key to success?' Before I had a chance to answer, Jerry said, 'Surrounds himself with good people.' I said, 'Yeah,' but then quickly I said, 'Nah, that's bull.' I said, 'Rick Hendrick doesn't solicit the best sales manager or best service manager. He promotes from within. Rick's key to success in the automobile business is he is very fair with his people, but the main thing is he can take an ordinary race car driver, crew chief, technician, salesman, and get that person to give him 110 percent. There is no magic to it. And Rick Hendrick works harder than any of us.'

"Richard Broome had been with Rick back in his boat racing days. He had built the 3,000-horsepower drag boat engines. Richard had also been crew chief for Geoff Bodine's Sportsman car that Rick owned with Robert Gee, and wherever that car went, it was a threat to win. So we selected Richard to be crew chief.

"In 1991 Kenny won Atlanta and Dover. Kenny finished ninth, one place better than '90, but with a little better luck, we could be saying, 'We won five races and killed them and finished third in the points.'

"As for our other car, the 5 car, when I came on in '86, Gary Nelson was crew chief. That year Geoff Bodine won two races, and the next year we went winless.

"There were problems that year, not for lack of effort, but because the chemistry between the driver and crew chief went sour. Gary Nelson was a workaholic, the best strategizer on Sunday I've ever seen.

"I second-guessed Gary a lot to myself during a race when he would make a decision. I would say, 'Boy, that was stupid. Why did he do that?' But he was always right, and I was always wrong.

"Geoff Bodine also had confidence in Gary's Sunday calls, but Geoff didn't like the setup, and if a driver doesn't feel good about it, he can't go out and drive the race car to the best of his ability. You have to make the car fit the driver. And if it doesn't, you can forget it.

"The driver is the factor you can't measure. You can have the perfect setup for the car, but if the driver doesn't feel good about it, or if he and the crew chief are fighting, you are going to run in the back of the pack.

"The thing about Geoff, he has the ability to set up the car. A Kenny Schrader will say, 'The car is loose, but I don't know how to fix it.' Geoff says, 'Gary, the car is loose. Go down twenty-five pounds of spring and

put such and such springs in.' Geoff was a master at that. When he made
a correction, it seemed to help.

"In 1986 we had some engine problems with Geoff's car, not with
Tim's, and his car fell out due to wrecks or engine failures nineteen times
out of thirty races. And we still finished second in total laps to Earnhardt.
If Geoff was still in the race, he was at the front. That first year with Geoff
and Gary Nelson, we were competitive, but the next year was a disaster.

"We didn't win a race in '87, and that really turned things upside
down. All you have to do for the driver and crew chief to get along is to
win. If you don't win, the marriage goes sour, and it did.

"A part in the car broke at the Watkins Glen race, and we put Geoff
into the wall pretty hard at the spot J. D. McDuffie was killed. Geoff was
running 150 miles an hour, and he hit the wall straight on. That car
stopped on a dime—150 miles an hour to zero in ten feet.

"Geoff was shook up, not seriously hurt but pretty shook up, and he
got pretty upset about it. We all understood. It was his life in that car.
That was the low point.

"Chevrolet wanted to do some research and development, and R&D
was Gary's strong point, and so we put him in charge of that and brought
Waddell Wilson over from Darrell Waltrip's car. And that's a whole
other story.

"Darrell and Waddell were as close as two people could possibly be,
like blood brothers. Waddell had been crew chief for Cale Yarborough,
and Darrell was driving for Junior Johnson, and we went out and hired
Darrell and Waddell, and we thought this was going to be a marriage
made in heaven. The press wrote: 'Dream Team.'

"Rick figured, 'Since we're doing so well with two teams, why not a
third?' Geoff and Tim had set on sixteen poles in twenty-nine races, so
the Dream Team started.

"We raced at Daytona the first race of the '87 season, and we didn't
make it back from there when these two best friends were wondering,
'Did I make the right decision?' Waddell would tell Darrell, 'You're not
Cale Yarborough,' and Darrell would say to Waddell, 'And you're not
Junior Johnson.'

"And all of a sudden the two were not getting along. And I can
understand that. My best friend lives in the Outer Banks, and we fish
together every Thanksgiving, but if we worked together, and he questioned my judgment, I would take it personally. If Darrell said, 'Waddell,
this setup stinks,' now all of a sudden his best friend is saying this, and
Waddell was taking it personally, and it was no longer something he
could fluff off.

"And Darrell is the kind of person who calls a spade a spade. If he thinks something, he says it. Darrell Waltrip will not talk behind your back. He'll tell you just how he feels, and I admire him for that. And he bluntly told Waddell, 'That's not what I want to do,' and Waddell would say, 'That's not what's going to make you run faster.' So one thing led to another. And you can imagine the frustration when you run like dogs, and it was really a downhill battle. The only race where we didn't have a problem was Daytona. That was the *only* race. Then Rick said, 'It's time to make some changes.'

"We had a problem with Gary and we had a problem with Darrell and Waddell, so Gary went to run our research and development chassis program, and we made Jeff Hammond crew chief for Darrell and moved Waddell over to Bodine.

"The Waddell-Bodine team started out real good. We won a couple races that year, including Pocono. And then the second year, for whatever reasons, didn't go well. It seems that during the first year of a team, things go good, and the second year, no. Again, if you're not winning, and you think you should be, the marriage falls apart.

"So after Geoff's second year we let his contract expire, and Geoff went on to Junior. And this was awfully hard for Rick Hendrick, because Rick started out in racing with Geoff. Geoff had brought us into Winston Cup racing, brought Rick into racing prominence, but Rick felt, 'We gotta get better. We don't want to run through another crew chief.' With Geoff we went through Harry Hyde, went through Gary Nelson, went through Waddell Wilson, so the feeling was, 'Let's try something different.' And that's not a slap in the face at Bodine, because Geoff and Rick are still very close. To this day Geoff is an extremely talented driver. The next year he won three races with Junior.

"We looked at a lot of drivers. Ricky Rudd fit our image—squeaky-clean, aggressive. Ricky started out driving for Richard Childress and won races. He went with Bud Moore when Earnhardt moved back over to Childress, and he won races for Bud Moore. Ricky went with Kenny Bernstein and won races with Kenny.

"Each time Ricky felt he was elevating his status, which is why 99 percent of the time it's the drivers who make the change, not the team owner. And it's not the money, it's the ability to win, and so Ricky felt a move from Bernstein, who is a friend of mine, to Hendrick with Waddell Wilson, a phenomenal crew chief with a great reputation, was a step in the right direction, and so he came with us.

"And in 1991 Ricky finished second in the points to Dale Earnhardt.

"We had a real shot at Earnhardt. We were at Charlotte, and there was a wreck in front of Ricky, and Ricky got way down off the racetrack to miss the wreck, and he slowed to about 40 miles an hour, and Derrike Cope smashed into him. And then fifteen laps later Earnhardt blew up. So we had a chance to pick up eighty or ninety points on Earnhardt, and instead we lost ten or fifteen points. That really took the wind out of our sails.

"And though we won two races, we only got paid for one because NASCAR took the Sears Point victory away from us.

"We were sitting on the pole, so we also would have won the Unocal bonus, which Hendrick Motorsports has never won. That was a loss of about $60,000.

"But we are *not* knocking what NASCAR did. NASCAR did what they thought was right, and we have to live by their rules. Other team owners, like Junior, are quick to criticize NASCAR. My feeling is if I criticized NASCAR it would be like if I criticized Rick Hendrick. You could say to me, 'Wait a minute, Jimmy, he's the one who's successful. He didn't get there being stupid.' And NASCAR didn't get where it is by being stupid, so even though it hurt us deeply when they took the race away from us, we look at it, 'If someone spun *us* out on the last lap . . .' And NASCAR felt that's what we did. We feel we didn't, but if we had an intention of going in and ramming Davey Allison and spinning him out, we got what was coming to us. But Davey was already spun out. Even Dave Marcis told NASCAR, 'The 28 car was already spun out when Ricky hit him. You are making a wrong decision.' But NASCAR had already made the decision. It was made instantly, because NASCAR was looking for something like that to set an example, after what Rusty Wallace did to Darrell Waltrip late in The Winston.

"So the black flag came out, and the checkered was given to Davey—the first time this happened in the history of NASCAR—and it was Davey who sat in Victory Lane.

"As much as we disliked the decision, we tried to put ourselves in Bill France's position, and he did what he had to do. Fans are always writing, saying, 'I'm a Chevy fan, and NASCAR is giving Davey Allison everything,' or 'I'm a Ford fan, and you're giving Earnhardt all the advantages.' But the fan really is uneducated about the real facts. NASCAR doesn't play favorites. That's the worst thing it could do. Their success is predicated on close-running competition, and their goal is to that end, and most of the time, their decisions are the right ones.

"Parity is the key. In 1985 Bill Elliott ran away with the competition, won some races lapping the competition, and NASCAR came in and ordered some modifications to his Thunderbird and slowed him down.

"I heard Richard Petty make the statement to Bill Elliott, 'You got what you asked for.'

"Richard said, 'I could have done that back in the sixties if I had wanted to. I could have lapped them four or five times like you're doing, but I was smart. I ran the last hundred laps of the race and won by two feet and went home with my check in my pocket. But you went out there wide open, blew everybody away, and NASCAR isn't interested in seeing that.'

"Bill Elliott was saying in effect, 'I'm the country boy from Dawsonville who you guys have kicked sand in my face. Now, I'm going to show you.' And it jumped up and bit him.

"NASCAR's success is built on parity, and every single decision it makes is parity first and safety second. You can bet, regardless of what they tell you is the reason for a decision, parity is the real reason.

"But finishing second to Earnhardt isn't bad. But it isn't where we want to be. At the awards banquet, we want his position in front of the stage.

"As we speak, we are preparing for the '92 Daytona 500. We are working hard on some new chassis designs, and on our engine side we're trying some new things, but we are limited with what we can do. In 1989 we spent half a million dollars trying to beat the system, and we beat it. Darrell Waltrip won and Kenny Schrader finished second, and we were dominant, but NASCAR made some changes that negated what we were doing, so it's no longer practical for us to go in that direction. At the present we are making a fixture that NASCAR has allowed us to put inside our intake to try to help us find some horsepower. When you're down to 420 horsepower and you're going to run speeds of 196 miles an hour, and NASCAR orders us to raise the air dam height and Chevy wants us to run a new 18-degree cylinder head—we're going to have a $700,000 inventory of cylinder heads that is going to be boat anchors in July—we wonder how fast we're going to run.

"We want to win the championship in '92, and that's where our efforts are going to be, so we have not put as much emphasis on Daytona this year as we have in the past. We will give 1,000 percent effort to winning that race, do whatever it takes to win at Daytona, but when Daytona is over, we go back to reality, which is you have to run well at all fifteen tracks, in all twenty-nine races, to win a championship.

"In 1991, if you averaged a sixth- or seventh-place finish in every race, you won the championship. But we're not strokers. You don't go out and win a championship by not losing it. Earnhardt, Rusty Wallace,

Bill Elliott won championships running as hard every lap as they could. If we said, 'Let's just finish sixth and win a championship,' Rick Hendrick would fire us all.

"We're looking to find as much horsepower as we can and to work hard on the fixture inside the intake. And if the Fords have a horsepower advantage, we feel NASCAR is going to make the competition come back to us rather than make us try to get up there to them. And, of course, as always, we pray for luck. We ask, 'Please keep us away from the bad.'

"The team that's going to be hardest to beat at Daytona is Robert Yates's team with Davey Allison. They're going to be tough because Robert has the Ford Motor Company behind him. Ford tends to spend a lot of money on racing, and it's made Robert a wealthy man and very successful. And Davey is a fine driver.

"I can remember in 1986 Tim Richmond was running in one of the 125-mile qualifying races at Daytona, and about the fourth lap he called on the radio and said, 'We have a vibration.' Harry Hyde said, 'Ride it out and hope for a caution flag.'

"Bam. A tire blew. Tim hit the wall hard. His right leg hit the transmission hump and the gearshift so hard it bent the transmission hump *and* the gearshift.

"Tim jumped out of the race car and hobbled across the racetrack and ended up in the hospital with a badly sprained knee. We didn't know if Tim would be able to drive.

"Up walked a kid named Davey Allison. Everyone knew who he was because he had had some limited success in ARCA racing. Harry Hyde talked me into putting Davey into the car as a standby in case Tim wouldn't be able to race.

"Harry Hyde, who is an extremely good judge of ability in race car drivers, said, 'Let me tell you one thing: You better get that Davey Allison, because he is a hell of a race car driver.' Boy, was Harry right.

"Davey never drove, because Tim was able to drive the 500, but even back then Harry Hyde had him pegged. And when Larry McReynolds came over from King Racing and replaced Jake Elder midway through the season, all of a sudden the team had chemistry, and they became a force.

"It's going to be interesting to see what's going to happen to Robert and Davey. Larry McReynolds and Davey will be going into their second year. I don't wish them any bad luck, but anytime one of the competition goes away, you have a better chance of winning.

"Look at our track record our second year; look at anybody's. Look at Tim Brewer and Geoff Bodine—second year awful. Geoff Bodine and

Harry Hyde—second year awful. Geoff Bodine and Gary Nelson—second year awful. Geoff Bodine and Waddell Wilson—second year awful. We didn't even get to the second year with Waddell and Darrell.

"When Robert Yates went out and hired Jake Elder, they went to Watkins Glen and right out of the box were a terror. Davey and Jake were buddy-buddy for five or six races when they were running up front, and then all of a sudden, it went haywire. Why, Lord knows. If I knew how to keep the second year from going haywire, I'd be worth a lot of money.

"The other team we're going to have to watch is Richard Childress's with Dale Earnhardt. Dale is the best. He can get the most out of the least.

"I've watched him now for years. I was a Dale Earnhardt fan when he first started driving, because he was driving Fords with Bud Moore, and I was working in a Ford store. I used to watch him come to the Fayetteville Speedway on asphalt, and the local boys blew the doors off him. He didn't dare mess with the local boys. But no more.

"Earnhardt can take a car that isn't perfect, maybe it's a little loose or pushing, and he can make more out of that car than any other driver out there. Sometimes I think if Earnhardt had our motor, God, the race would have been over thirty minutes ago. The guy is that good.

"You wonder why a new owner doesn't just offer Earnhardt $5 million to drive for him. I'm sure that's happened. But Earnhardt wouldn't do it. If Hendrick Motorsports goes out and develops a 700-plus-horsepower engine, and we've got a crew chief and a fleet of cars that goes out and kicks his butt, then we can call Dale up and say, 'Hey, you want to race for us when your contract is up?' And he would probably say, 'Yeah.'

"Drivers are loyal—to a point. As long as they are running good, they're loyal. But you have to put yourself in their place, and that's what I try to do. When we're negotiating, I ask myself, 'What does Rudd want?' And I always keep coming back to the fact that how you run today is what you're going to get paid tomorrow. If I can't put a good car up under Ricky, there is not enough money to keep him happy. When that driver sees his future going away, it doesn't mater how much money he's making.

"And from the other direction, if I don't put a good car on the track, when I go back and ask for more money the sponsor is going to say, 'Damn, what did you do for me this past year?' As you can see, the pressure to win is unbelievable.

"Part of the pressure the drivers and crew chiefs feel is that Hendrick Motorsports has had some degree of success, and we put a lot of pressure on ourselves to go out and win.

"This year we finished second in the points to Dale Earnhardt, and we were disappointed. There are eighty more competitors in NASCAR who would give their right arm to be where we were. But we were not happy with second place.

"Yeah, we have a great facility and great sponsors, but . . . second place will never be good enough."

Jeff Hammond (*l*) and Darrell Waltrip (*r*)

LAP 23

Jeff Hammond
What Makes Darrell Run

Darrell Waltrip began racing in 1972. He drove and won for Junior Johnson and later for Rick Hendrick, winning the driving championship in 1981, 1982, and 1985. Going into the 1992 season, Waltrip had recorded 81 Winston Cup victories, fifth on the all-time list behind Richard Petty (200), David Pearson (105), Bobby Allison (84), and Cale Yarborough (83). It is Darrell Waltrip who bridges the generation between the era of Bobby Allison and Cale Yarborough and today. Darrell Waltrip was the first of the driver-spokesmen, the new breed of driver suited both for winning races and attracting sponsors. It was Darrell Waltrip who led racing into its modern era.

As renowned as Waltrip has become for his driving ability, he is equally known for his volatility and his ego. He fought with the Gardner brothers all during his successful run with DiGard. He won with Junior Johnson, but left him when he felt he wasn't getting enough of Junior's attention. Then he went to drive for Rick Hendrick, where he joined with his best friend, Waddell Wilson. Very soon, it was clear the two hardheads couldn't get along. The squabbling was ugly, and Waltrip and Wilson parted company at the end of the year.

In 1989 Darrell hired Jeff Hammond, who had been a crew chief for Junior Johnson since he was twenty-two years old in 1982. Darrell knew him as a kid with a good head on his shoulders, one who, when chaos reigned, kept calm. Darrell had worked well with Hammond, and when the Dream Team broke up, he reached out for him.

In their very first race after their reunion, Darrell won the Daytona 500 of 1989, in part because of Hammond's sound strategy. Since then, Hammond and Darrell have become like brothers. One knows instinctively what the other is thinking, and their trust in each other is total.

The year 1992 marked the second year Darrell Waltrip owned his own team. In '91 Waltrip won two races, at North Wilkesboro and Pocono. In both races he beat Dale Earnhardt to the line for the victory.

Because Waltrip is both owner and driver, he won't get fired as a driver. The one important relationship in which Waltrip needs calm is with his crew chief. With Hammond in charge, once the race begins all Waltrip has to concern himself with is steering the car. Hammond, he knows, will take care of the rest.

JEFF HAMMOND: "I grew up in Charlotte, not very far from the Charlotte Motor Speedway. One Sunday morning when I was twelve, I was sleeping in late, and my uncle came over, actually got me out of bed, and said, 'Hey, boy, you want to go get a race car?' At that time, I had heard the cars run at Charlotte. When the wind blew good on a Sunday, I could hear them running.

"My uncle, Brad Tadlock, was thirty-three. Brad had always loved racing. He knew a lot of guys who worked for the old Holman-Moody. He had gone to a lot of races close by, and he just decided he wanted to drive a dirt car. Off we went, down to South Carolina, where we picked up a 6-cylinder 1956 Ford.

"We got the race car and brought it back home, and from that point on, every afternoon after I did my homework, I'd go over and tinker with the car—cleaning it, painting the wheels, doing little knickknack stuff—and before long he was calling me Smokey, after Smokey Yunick, because I liked to tinker with the car so much, even though I really didn't know what I was doing.

"My dad, my youngest brother, and I started going with him Friday nights to Monroe and Saturday nights to Lancaster. The first year out, he won a couple races. We had a lot of fun chasing after it that year.

"My dad really liked what was going on as far as the kids, and he said, 'Why don't we build our own cars?' Daddy had been a mechanic from way back when. When he was in the Navy and Air Force, he worked on helicopters. He met my mother while he was a mechanic down at Thomas Cadillac-Oldsmobile in Charlotte. He was a line mechanic for a long time, so he knew cars. He knew what needed to be done, and he could do it.

"We took the garage and got her all fixed up, bought us a welder and a tubing bender and a few odds and ends, and we went to the local junkyard and cut the body away from a 1965 Falcon, and we built our own race car.

"Dad wanted to teach us how to become mechanics, and he felt this was a good way to do it. We built the motor right there in the shop, and dad taught me how to lap valves and grind heads. At age thirteen I learned how to build an engine.

"He went out and hired us a driver, Gene Mandry, a heavy-equipment operator who my dad knew from doing some construction work. Gene had always had a love of cars, had a lot of souped-up cars on the road, liked to drive fast, so Dad said, 'See if you can drive fast on a racetrack.'

"That first year Gene won six heat races, two main events, and finished fifth in the points. Everybody was impressed with the effort we put forth that year. Matter of fact, we finished one position behind my uncle.

"Through high school I played football. On Fridays when we played football I always told the girl I dated, 'If we win, we go out. If we lose, I'm going to the racetrack.' I had a love for football and a love for racing, and I didn't have much of a relationship with my girlfriend. I spent many Friday nights at the racetrack. Through the summer months, we raced, working for my dad on the race car.

"Through him I got an appreciation of what it took to run a race team. Dad would take so much of my pay and use it to pay expenses. If we had engine problems or needed tires, I contributed as though I was an owner. It gave me a real good sense of responsibility and an appreciation for what he was doing for us and the values of what we were contributing to.

"During the next few years we changed drivers three times and started running at faster tracks, at the Charlotte Fairgrounds and Concord. As a result, we got the opportunity to run against a young Dale Earnhardt when he first started driving dirt cars. I was also very fortunate to be able to watch his daddy, Ralph, running against some of the greats, like Larry Wallace, Slick Poston, Stick Elliott, and Little Bud Moore.

"Ralph was the kind of driver, if you raced him clean, he'd race you clean. But if you lay on him or beat on him, you better be prepared for one wild ride. He always expected fair treatment, but if someone did him wrong, he made darn sure he paid him back double. And it's how he taught Dale to race. Good, hard, clean racing is fine, but if a man wants to do you dirty, double him three times over and make sure he doesn't forget it. Make him know not to mess with you.

"Back then, in '73, Ralph drove a Chevrolet. Most everyone ran General Motors engines. The Fords were not that strong. Larry Wallace was a cam grinder for Holman-Moody, and he and another gentleman built a Ford engine, and he had *the* fastest Ford, and I can remember on several occasions going to the Metrolina track and watching Ralph and Larry stage side-to-side, 25-lap runs. They'd start out in front, or near the front, and for twenty-five laps literally run door handle to door handle and never, ever beat on each other. You'd see a little tire smoke every now and then, but it was just some of the most fantastic side-by-side dirt track racing you'd ever want to see. It looked like two ballerinas out there, a ballet-type deal going on it was so pretty to watch.

"Ralph had the ability to race you side by side, inside or outside. It didn't make any difference. He didn't have to spin you out to win a race, but he could. Nine times out of ten he wouldn't.

"Dale would do a lot of the same things. I remember this one particular race he was running semi-modifieds against a racer named Gary Galloway. At that time Gary was top dog at Metrolina, and he and the guy he drove for, Buck Tucker, won a lot of races. Buck and Gary were featured in *Stock Car Racing Magazine* because they won twenty-some feature races in a row.

"I remember Dale had been racing Gary hard that night, and he could *not* get by him. He leaned on him. He beat on him. And finally Dale came off four trying to get by him, and he got Gary sideways, got into him real hard, but he could *not* get him spun out. Gary was on the gas and would not let Dale turn him around.

"I will never forget: Dale Earnhardt chucked his car into third gear, got a ton of bite up off the corner and turned him around, finally got him spun, beat him back to the start-finish line, and won the race. But it was so funny to watch—one of them wouldn't go around, and the other one was determined to get him around. It was almost comical the way they were shoving each other around, like two big old bulls rooting, trying to say who was boss hog that night.

"I knew Dale pretty well. Dale was a lot of fun to race against because he had a cockiness about him. He was full of himself, but there was a funness about him. He enjoyed driving race cars, had a good time doing it.

"Later in years, after Dale made it to the big time, we spent some time together at his lake house on weekends, waterskiing and tubing. We'd put two inner tubes behind the ski boat, I'd get on one, he'd get on the other, and we'd try to knock each other off. It didn't make any difference if we were skiing double or if we were just coming down the interstate, Dale was competitive.

"I remember one time racing him home on I-77. I was driving a little Pontiac Sunbird, and he was driving a pickup truck. My wife was in the passenger seat, and she became very upset when Dale shoved me. She was scared to death he was going to wreck us. Seriously. That's just Dale Earnhardt's nature.

"When I graduated high school, my main goal was to play professional football. In high school I was an outside linebacker and a tight end. At North Mecklenburg High School I made the prep all-American team and went to East Carolina College to play under coach Pat Dye, a super coach. I still have the playbook he gave us with his philosophies as far as football and life.

"During practice I ran a pass play, a wide-out. I caught the ball and was trying to get by the defender when he hit me on the inside of my left knee, and I tore all the cartilage and stretched the ligaments.

"I quit college. If I couldn't play football, I couldn't see any sense of staying there, spending money, wasting my time at school. So I came on back home and began doing construction work for my dad and building race cars at night for my uncle.

"While working on my uncle's dirt car, I began buying parts from Tiger Tom Pistone, who introduced me to a lot of people in racing, including Tony Bettenhausen, Jr., who was racing stock cars, Dick May, Walter Ballard, and Frank Warren, independent racers living in the Charlotte area who didn't have big sponsors and a lot of times needed help on the weekends.

"The first one who hired me was a guy named Carl Adams, out of California. I went to a couple races with him. We went to Darlington and wound up blowing a motor. After him I helped Frank Ward, who drove the Native Tan Dodge. Frank was an intense individual, and after a couple races I went to helping Walter Ballard, whose house and shop weren't too far from my parents, so it was real easy for me to commute over there after work.

"I stayed the longest with Walter, helped him for about a year and a half. I learned what to look for, how to check a car over for race preparation, how to change tires, a lot of little fundamental things, how to put in a gear and take it out properly, how not to lose the drive shaft. I learned to pack wheel bearings properly. I had been taught by my dad, but this reinforced it as to what it takes to make a Winston Cup car survive five hundred miles. I learned how to set up a pit, how to glue the lug nuts on the wheels. I washed the car, loaded the truck, learned how to get the car through inspection. These are the things you learn from the independent guys, because they don't have a lot of people, so everybody does everything.

"My dad was real good about letting me off early on Fridays, and I would drive to the racetracks and be there at night and help on Saturdays, attend the race Sunday, and then come back home and work for him on Monday. And a couple of drivers, Walter Ballard included, tried to hire me full-time.

"One thing I remember my dad telling me was, 'Just be patient, and you will get yourself a *good* job. Wait till you get a chance to go with a big team.'

"And through working over at Walter's, I was befriended by a gentleman named Herb Nab who was chief mechanic over at Junior Johnson's. Walter bought a lot of used race parts from Junior. We did a lot of business with Junior—bought race cars, engines, a lot of parts.

"Herb was one of the top mechanics in Winston Cup racing at the time. One time he came down to help Walter set up his car. I met him down there, and we got to talking, and from time to time I saw him at the racetrack.

"I was at Darlington in 1976, and Herb came over and wanted to know if I wanted to go to work for them. Junior had just had a guy quit. I never will forget it. I went home real excited. I got home real late that night from the race—it was about ten o'clock—and Dad was already in bed because he had to go to work the next morning.

"I went in and said, 'Dad, you aren't going to believe this. I need to have tomorrow off. I need to go to Junior Johnson's. They offered me a job.'

"Just like that, Dad said, 'I told you.' He knew one day it was going to happen, and it did.

"I drove to Junior's that morning. I got there about 8:15. I walked in the door, and Herb and a couple other guys were working on the car for the next race. Herb said, 'Boy, you know how to get a motor out of a car?'

" 'Yeah.'

"He said, 'Here's the toolbox. Help them get the motor out of this car.'

"We worked until lunchtime. I said, 'Herb, what's going on? What are we going to do?'

"He said, 'If you want a job, you got it.' He said, 'Can you weld?' I said, 'Yeah.' He said, 'Help me weld this frame up.' And that was it. I went up front after lunch and signed a couple of forms on social security and insurance, and from that day on I've been in Winston Cup racing.

"For me, going to work for Junior was like coming out of never-never land right into a fantasy world. It was a dream come true. At Junior's, I learned to be a body man. I cleaned blocks, got motors on the dyno, helped in every way; and also when you worked for Junior, you learned to work in the chicken house, take care of the chicken trucks, the cows, the tractors. Junior is a very farm-oriented person. He wasn't bashful

Darrell Waltrip at Victory Lane in 1989.
(© INTERNATIONAL SPEEDWAY CORPORATION/NASCAR)

The 1990 Daytona 500 winner Derrike Cope
(center) shows his trophy to the crowd.
(© INTERNATIONAL SPEEDWAY CORPORATION/NASCAR)

Dale Earnhardt and Morgan Shepherd are chauffeured to the track at Daytona. (© 1992 DON GRASSMAN)

Cars and crew await the start of the 1992 Daytona as the National Anthem is played. (© 1992 DON GRASSMAN)

Kyle Petty gives a pre-race interview. (© 1992 DON GRASSMAN)

Ernie Irvan contemplates his strategy. (© 1992 DON GRASSMAN)

Richard Petty receives more honors before the start of his final Daytona 500 in 1992. (© 1992 DON GRASSMAN)

Pit crews hard at work making last minute tune-ups. (© 1992 DON GRASSMAN)

A heartbroken Kyle Petty walks across the infield after being eliminated from the 1992
Daytona. (© 1992 DON GRASSMAN)

The unsung heroes: Harry Gant's pit crew is poetry in motion as they change the tires and fill
the gas tank. (© 1992 DON GRASSMAN)

Every racer's fear: another crash at Daytona forces cars and drivers out of the race. (© 1992
DON GRASSMAN)

A few of the hundreds of thousands who attend the Daytona 500 every year. (© 1992
DON GRASSMAN)

Dale Earnhardt's battered Goodwrench Chevrolet shows the wear and tear of this grueling 500-mile race. (© 1992 DON GRASSMAN)

The crew of the Haviland/Texaco Ford celebrate their victory. (© 1992 DON GRASSMAN)

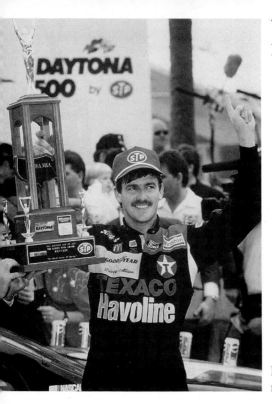

Winner of the 1992 Daytona 500, Davey Allison, raises his arms in triumph on victory lane. (© 1992 DON GRASSMAN)

Fans mill about the infield, basking after the race. (© 1992 DON GRASSMAN)

about walking into the shop and saying, 'Come on, let's help move some cows.' It was like being part of a big family.

"I watched Junior and learned from him. He had philosophies. One was, 'If it's not broke, don't fix it.' Another was, 'Try not to make a lot of waves.' His aim was to try to put the people together and let them work their own problems out if it was at all possible.

"Junior was not a heavy-handed boss man. He was laid-back, easy-going. He'd tell you how he wanted things done, and he expected you to do it. And he wasn't a frills type of guy. He believed in basics, not using tricks. Those are the things I learned from him, that you have to put together a car that will run five hundred miles and stay under your driver.

"I also learned that at the end of a race if you can take a chance and win, you take that chance, whether it be fuel or tires. Also, you always try to run a man out of gas. Always try to go farther than the guy you're racing. You do that by making sure your carburetor is tuned properly, by not pulling more gear than you have to, and by making your driver draft. That's where Junior's had his success, beating people that way.

"When I started our driver was Cale Yarborough. Cale is a mechanic's, and especially a chief mechanic's, dream. We called him 'Just-get-it-close Cale.' He was real easy to please. He'd tell Herb, 'Just get it close, and I'll make up the difference.'

"He had the physical tenacity to take a car that wasn't handling that well and run with the best of them, and a lot of times beat them. And that's the reason Junior loved him so much. He was Junior's kind of racer. It didn't make any difference what the situation came down to, he got in there and thrashed it hard. When he drove, he drove his guts out. He was the kind of guy who always kept after it, was always charging.

"Cale would go out front, stay out front, lead all the laps he could lead, win the pole, win a race, and if he didn't win, he'd run in the top five. And he wouldn't complain about the car a lot, and that's what Junior loved. Junior wanted someone to take his car, put it up front, and say, 'Everything's great.' And Cale won the driving championship three years in a row, in 1976, '77, and '78, and you couldn't ask for anything more than that.

"I always had a lot of fun with Cale. He didn't believe in drinking a lot when he was racing, but once we got through the season, he'd drink some beers and he'd tell stories about the things he used to do when he was growing up.

"He had a pet bear cub, Suzie. Junior gave it to him. He was flying alone with the bear, when it got out of its box. It had eaten through it.

While Cale was trying to land, he was holding the box upside down to keep the bear from getting loose.

"Another friend gave Cale a lion cub. Cale raised Leo from the time it was a baby, along with his dog. The way Cale tells it, Leo thought he *was* a dog. Cale even took him in the car with him, but when Leo got to weighing five hundred pounds, then it wasn't so funny when Leo jumped on you to say hello. Cale ended up giving Leo to the Spartanburg zoo.

"Off the track Cale was a comical individual, and on the track very serious, take-no-prisoners. He could drive the wheels off of it.

"One of Cale's most exciting races was one he didn't win. As far as strategy and a never-say-die attitude, the Daytona 500 of 1979 was one of the most exciting and memorable races ever.

"We had had a lot of problems down there, blown engines, but we finally got the car hooked up and were running really, really well. That year we had a lot of rain at Daytona, and early on the strongest cars were Bobby Allison in Bud Moore's car, Donnie Allison in Hoss Ellington's car, and Cale in our car.

"Early in the race we were going into turn one and two, and somehow Bobby and Donnie got together, and Cale was right in there with them. The three spun out and went down through the infield, and there was mud and water everywhere.

"Cale got stuck in the infield mud and couldn't get the car out, but fortunately we didn't really hurt anything. They finally got him out and brought him around to the pit, and we had to get the mud out from under the car and get the car cleaned up to where he could go ahead. We lost three laps.

"Donnie and Bobby hadn't had those problems—especially Donnie, who came through pretty good. And I remember Cale and Donnie had the two fastest cars on the track, and they hooked up and ran all day like that.

"The rule at the time was if there was a caution flag, you could race at full speed to the start-finish line and then you had to slow down and maintain position, so our strategy was to be in a position to take advantage of a caution flag. Cale would draft Donnie. Cale, not overusing the car, was deliberately running behind Donnie. He knew he could pass him, and whenever the caution flag came out, Junior would get on the radio and say, 'The caution flag is out. Beat him back.' And Cale would pull out and pass Donnie and beat him to the start-finish line and regain a lap.

"We were able to keep our cool. Junior kept Cale in the right position, and we were able to make up all our laps, one lap at a time. What I learned from that race was not to get excited, that you have five hundred miles to race, and you have to stay focused at all times.

"Junior *never* got excited, didn't blow up, didn't say, 'Man, we're three laps down. Let's quit.' And because of Cale's driving ability and Junior's ability to do what he does best—call a race—we got back into the race and had a real good chance of winning. In fact, we should have won that race.

"We had a really fast car, and Donnie had a really fast car, and Junior recognized that we couldn't really break away from Donnie without another car to help draft by him. For the last fifty laps, Donnie and Cale pulled away from the rest of the field.

"Going into the white flag lap, Donnie and Cale were running one and two, and a half lap behind, out of sight, were Richard Petty followed by Darrell Waltrip. Bobby Allison was with them, a lap behind the leaders.

"We went through one and two, and like every other time coming off two, Cale started to make his move on Donnie down the back straightaway. Well, Donnie moved over on him, moved over on him, kept pushing him farther toward the edge of the track. Sure enough, by the time they got in front of turn three, there was no place to go. Cale wouldn't let off the gas, and neither would Donnie. This was the Daytona 500, and neither one of them was going to give an inch. The two of them wound up wrecking. They had a big crash in turn three.

"In the pits we didn't know what had happened. We didn't know they had wrecked, and the next thing I knew, someone came over and said, 'They're in turn three fighting, Cale and Bobby and Donnie.'

"From my dirt track experience, when people start fighting, you go and help your driver. I looked at Junior, and he did not say, 'Go get them boys,' or anything like that. It was, 'You all ought to settle down.' He was very upset about not winning the race, but he was very calm and cool about the deal.

"I did what Junior did. Junior didn't do anything. He was the general. If he said, 'Charge,' we charge. He didn't.

"I remember one or two guys went off running, and Junior didn't like that, 'cause it was a done deal, and there was no sense getting all excited about it. Junior didn't like what happened, but he had never gone looking for trouble. He's always been real good about letting things take care of themselves.

"Richard Petty won that Daytona 500. He was always the major competitor back then.

"When I grew up, I was awestruck with Richard Petty. I'm like any kid. He was The King. Richard Petty is not known for this, but he was a crafty racer. He had the ability to take a race car and do some things a lot of drivers couldn't do. He knew when to run and when not to run. He was as much like David Pearson as anyone I've ever seen. You'd see him lay back, and when it came time to race, he'd race.

"I got to know him and saw how smart he could be and how good Dale Inman was and Maurice Petty. They made a really good trio, a combination that was hard to beat, because they were always being very creative.

"Junior told me that. He'd say, 'They are creative, and you have to be more creative if you're going to race against them.'

"And part of why they had to be creative was that they were stuck in Randleman, in the middle of nowhere, just as Ronda, where Junior is, is in the middle of nowhere, and Stuart, Virginia, where the Wood Brothers with David Pearson were, is too.

"All these teams were very creative, always thinking about how to get the edge on somebody. And you had three of the best drivers—Cale, Richard, and David—all who knew how to slingshot, to work against one another, to race each other hard wheel to wheel. It was very exciting to watch.

"I became Junior's crew chief after the '81 season. I was twenty-two years old. I was very fortunate, because I always had that safety net, where if I stumbled the least little bit, Junior was there to help me. And with the team we had, I was afforded an honor to be in that position, but at the same time I always felt very secure, because I had Junior right there to turn back to, especially early on.

"When I had to make a decision for pit stops and strategy, he would let me make a statement, and he'd either yes or no it, and that way I was getting an education what to do and what not to do.

"In 1986, Darrell was unhappy. Junior had a two-car team. Each had been very successful. And they started disagreeing a lot, and when that happens, it tends to carry over to the team. Junior felt he was right, and so did Darrell, and they reached a point where they felt they had done as much for each other as they possibly could.

"Sometimes it's a disagreement over the cars, over the program, the overall team structure, money reasons. Sponsorship situations. There are a lot of things owners and drivers can disagree on.

"And then Darrell got an offer to go to Rick Hendrick and work with Waddell Wilson, and when that happens, you have to make up your mind, 'Is this what I want to do?' Junior has to decide, 'Is this man worth this much money? Do I want to pay this much for his abilities?'

"Sometimes when you work with someone a long time, you have to part company, because you get stale and you start getting argumentative.

"While we were still with Junior, Darrell approached me at Talladega in late July and asked me if I would be interested in going to work for Waddell and Hendrick the next year. At that time I remember telling Darrell that I didn't think it would work, and I didn't think I could work for Waddell, so at that point I elected not to do the deal.

"Darrell and Waddell were really good friends. They had known each other a long time, used to go out and eat a lot when he drove for Junior, and at different times had talked about working together, and it was a situation where Rick Hendrick wanted Waddell and had the opportunity to get Darrell, and they decided to form a third team and pick up Tide as the sponsor. Even then, I didn't think it was going to work. I just couldn't see where he and Waddell would get along that well. I don't know why, but I didn't feel they'd mesh.

"And I turned out to be right. Their friendship was damaged. They are friends again, but not like they were at one time.

"They were called the Dream Team, but they didn't do what they thought they were going to do. They stumbled. And then Darrell wasn't happy with his situation at Hendrick, and I wasn't happy with my situation at Junior's, and we mutually agreed that we'd like to get back together again.

"Terry Labonte was driving for Junior in 1988. Junior was dismantling the team Neil Bonnett had had a couple years previously, so he had a lot of excess personnel. One of the guys he had was Tim Brewer. He wanted Tim doing the short track program and me doing the superspeedway program, and it was a confusing and conflicting deal. It was awkward for both of us and for the driver, because he was dealing with two different people.

"I was uncomfortable, and this was when Darrell offered me the chance to go with him. I didn't feel I was in a position to say, 'Junior, it's him or me,' didn't think it was the thing to do, so I decided in the best interest of the team and of me, it was best for me to move on.

"I went and told Junior I appreciated everything he did for me but that I felt it was time for me to leave.

"He said, 'I hope you're doing the right thing,' and that was the end of it. Junior is not a man of a lot of words, and he'd be quick to tell you he doesn't like it when somebody leaves him. He feels he puts a lot into a person, and he had given me a lot. How do you turn around and pay a man back for what he's given you? It was one of the harder things I've ever had to do. But I did it.

"When I left Junior, I went to work for Darrell Waltrip at Hendrick Motorsports. We won our first race together right out of the box, the Daytona 500 of 1989.

"One of the biggest lessons I had learned from Junior is that you always want to make sure you got all you could out of your fuel cells, to run as far as you possibly could on your gas. You do that by staying on top of what your fuel mileage is during practice and by knowing the limitations on your pickups. And, most important, whenever you get in position where winning a race can be done on a gamble, you go for it.

"You never want to gamble in the early part of a race, because if you lose the gamble, you get way behind. It's when the gamble is worth the gains, that's when you go for it. At the beginning of the race, if you're unsure whether there's gas left, you come in. If it's at the end of the race, you stay out, and that was one lesson I learned from Junior that stayed with me that enabled Darrell and me to win the Daytona 500 in 1989.

"We were working for Hendrick Motorsports. Tide was the sponsor. The year before we had been to Daytona with that car, and it had been incredibly fast, but we blew up before the end. We came back in '89 with the same car, and the car was running good, but it wasn't up to where it had been the year before. The car's name was Betty. Darrell named her that a year or so earlier when we first built the car. The song 'Betty Bein' Bad' was out, and this car had always been fast on the speedways, and so he called her that. And that year we qualified on the outside pole, and Ken Schrader was on the pole.

"Kenny Schrader had the fastest car. Schrader and Dale Earnhardt pretty much ran away from us. We just couldn't keep up with them. They had us outhorsepowered, outhandled, and we realized this about halfway through the race. We realized we didn't have the car to beat Schrader outright, so we rolled ourselves into another mode of running a strategy race, trying to make fewer pit stops than anyone else.

"That day we had a lot of green flag stops, so we put ourselves in a position where we had to stretch our gas mileage. We were about five-eighths of a lap behind, and so the first time we ran three or four laps further than Kenny did on the tank of gas, and the next time one or two laps, and by the end of the race we had him to where we didn't have to stop, and he did. Schrader had a good half a racetrack ahead of us, but he had to come in.

"After we made our final stop, Darrell went back out, and I called him on the phone. I told him, 'We're going to be close on gas. You need to draft everybody you can. Be conservative. You're going to be okay, because they have one more stop.'

"That's when Darrell began to draft everything he could find. If he could find a sea gull coming into the back straightaway, he got behind it.

"Kenny finally pitted, and when he returned he was a full straightaway behind us, but he was closing. Darrell was drafting, and Kenny was coming, and I kept telling Darrell, 'Don't worry about Kenny. Kenny can't catch you.' But as we got down to a couple laps to go, Darrell said, 'The fuel light is coming on. The fuel pressure is dropping.'

"I said, 'Shake it. Don't get excited. Be easy,' because the car sometimes will have little pockets of fuel, and it'll be close to the pickup, and if you shake the car around, rock it back and forth, the car will pick up whatever is inside the fuel cell.

"I kept saying, 'Shake it around. Shake it around. Keep shaking it. Wiggle the car around, try to shake up all the fuel you can,' and he did that, and he said, 'It's up, it's up,' and then, 'We're out of gas, we're out of gas.'

" 'You gotta keep going, man.'

"We were committed then. If we stopped, we lost. We had to run it until it quit.

"I was hollering at him, 'Shake it up, keep after it and draft,' and he would get down the back straightaway and say, 'It's running out, it's running out—no, it's picking up.' Back and forth. For three laps we hollered at each other.

"We took the white flag, and he hollered one more time, 'I know we're out this time.' I said, 'You've got to go. Just keep going.' And sure enough, we made it all the way back around until I finally saw him come off turn four and head for the checkered flag. The amount of gas left in that son of a gun wouldn't have hit the bottom of your cup.

"With the help of what I learned from Junior, that was one of those times when your cards have been dealt, and if you want to win the hand, you have to raise the ante a little bit, and it went our way.

"And after the race, I was so proud of Darrell, because he was able to do the job he did. It was a good feeling to be able to contribute—it was our communication that contributed to our pulling it off.

"I do what I'm asked to do as best as I can, but in this business I realize it's a team effort with everybody, starting with myself and the driver, but it takes all the guys being there and giving their input and support, 'cause if the engine crew hadn't built the engine as well as they did, if the pit crew didn't do their job, if Stevie Waltrip hadn't figured the fuel mileage as accurately as she did, all the things combined, then the situation with three laps to go never would have developed. We all work hand in hand, so closely it isn't even funny.

"I have been with Darrell eleven years, which is unheard of. It's my job to handle Darrell's moods. If we wreck and the car can be fixed, it's my job to pump the driver up and keep the crew motivated, and to come up with a plan to fix it. Fix the car and keep going, that's my job.

"And if everything is going really well, then I want to calm him down to where he doesn't overextend himself. If he's leading the race, I want to tell him where he is in relationship to second place, and if they are gaining on him he has to be told how many laps are left, to tell him he's got a good-looking line, to reassure him that everything he's doing is right.

"Most of the time when I'm needed, Darrell is in a situation that's scaring him and he needs to fix something, and that's what he's looking for.

"You are there to come up with something, to let him know you understand the problem and that you are aware of the circumstances, and that you have the people and necessary tools to make the car better.

"Whatever is going on, you work it out, and then you tell the driver the extent of your progress. He's there by himself. The driver is in a world of his own, isolated for three and a half to four hours. He is totally concentrating on trying to drive the race car, and his only connection to the outside world as far as what's going on around him is the guy at the other end of the radio—in our case, me.

"Whatever is going on, you work it out, and you keep telling him that. He's looking for somebody to take care of the problems he can't, and that's what myself and the rest of the crew is there for, to reassure him that, 'Hey, you are not there by yourself.'

"Darrell is a man who has been up, been down, been hurt, been ridiculed, been revered. He's had it all done to him at one time or another. But the one thing I am positive about is he *loves* racing, loves winning.

"He has always stayed focused. He has long-range plans. 'One of these days I'm going to own my own team and have my own drivers.' During all the time I've known him, he has been a great speaker about the sport, been a very positive ambassador. He has helped me overcome a lot of my fears as far as dealing with the public. When I grew up, I did not enjoy getting up in front of a group of people and talking. I'm not a polished public speaker, have never taken courses, but through watching him and seeing how he handles it, I feel I have learned. I really enjoy being around people who I can learn from, and there are so many of them in the sport—Junior, Benny Parsons, Ned Jarrett, and Darrell. I ask myself, 'What makes this guy tick? What makes him successful?'

"I can remember at the beginning of Darrell's career, I was working

for Cale in Junior's car, and Darrell was driving for DiGard. At Darlington, Cale and Darrell got together, and they wrecked, spun out each
other. After the race Darrell made a comment in the newspaper, and one
of the former flagmen told Cale that 'all Darrell has is jaws,' and Cale
made the statement about Darrell's being really quick to comment about
a lot of things, calling him 'Jaws.' Young drivers were supposed to keep
their mouths shut. And Darrell was not the typical redneck. He could sit
with reporters and chew the other drivers up with his clever remarks and
quick statements, but at the same time he could take it to them at the
racetrack, being on their back bumpers, and the combination of the two,
beating them on Sunday and beating them up again on Monday in the
newspapers, brought out some resentment to a certain degree. It was
something they weren't used to.

"Junior and Cale were running for Holly Farms that year, and so they
called Junior 'the Chicken Racer' and Cale 'the Chicken Driver,' and
when the circuit moved on to Charlotte, Humpy Wheeler, who did the
promotions at Charlotte, drove his car through the middle of pit road with
a big shark they caught on the Outer Banks—with a chicken stuffed down
its mouth. Humpy added more fuel to the fire, and so the nickname 'Jaws'
stuck with Darrell for a while.

"It didn't sit well with Darrell. It bothered him for a long time. It was
not something that was quick to leave. It took a long time.

"Another time at Charlotte, we had a wreck and the crowd was on
Darrell pretty hard, and he made the comment in the papers, 'I'll meet
you in the K mart parking lot.' That followed us for several years.

"But with maturity, it all turned around, he's gone full turn. He has
learned when to speak and how to speak, and he has twice been named
Most Popular Driver, an award Darrell does not take lightly. He's as
proud of that as he is of any of his three championships. It's very important for anybody, myself included, to feel like you've been liked in
your life by somebody other than your wife and your dog.

"The big turnaround for Darrell came at Charlotte in 1989. Darrell was
leading the last segment of The Winston with only a few laps to go, and
Rusty Wallace spun us out. Rusty made the mistake of saying, 'I never
touched him,' even though it was pretty clear after viewing the photo-
graphs that he *did* touch him.

"Darrell got out of the car, went up to reporters, and took five or six
really deep breaths. He than calmly made a statement about the circumstances of what happened. He said, 'The man *did* hit me, and I hope he
chokes on the $200,000.'

"If it had happened at the start of his career, he'd have run his mouth off long before he calmed down. It would have looked redneckish, and his emotions would have painted him in a bad light. But the manner and way he handled the situation told people, 'Hey, this man is serious about racing, but at the same time he can be composed.' And the events brought to light a greater evil, which was Rusty Wallace. Rusty took a lot of flak, and it was Rusty who became the 'new bad guy,' while Darrell became the family man with the little girl and the dog.

"And more important, Darrell has mellowed to the point where he appreciates the people who support him. He understands what the people mean to him, and especially since 1989, he has radiated that more than ever before, and the fans recognize it.

"If you knew him before and you see him now, it's like seeing two different people. He no longer comes across as the young, brash individual who has no concern for any man, woman, or child. Now this man is very well respected as a family man who understands the people who work for him and around him. People now feel a sincerity in his voice when he's talking to people and signing autographs. It's a different perception.

"As we aim toward the Daytona 500 of 1992, recently our car has had two bad crashes, at the Firecracker 400 and one at the Daytona 500. Our focus is to get on the track, run all day, and finish in the top ten.

"We know our Chevrolet is down on horsepower to the Fords. We are going to concentrate on aerodynamics and on our pit strategy, because it looks like having Darrell in the right place at the right time is going to be critical. And if we're in the same situation we were in in 1991 with ten laps to go, this year we will win the race.

"Darrell left Hendrick Motorsports to go out on his own at the end of the 1990 season, and I joined him, and in 1991, we came very close to pulling off an upset win in the Daytona 500.

"We were a little bit off as far as power, but as soon as we saw that Ernie Irvan and Davey Allison were getting away from us, we automatically went into another mode, running our race, conserving fuel mileage, not really worrying what they were doing, stretching it two, three, four laps per fuel cell, so we were once again going to need one less pit stop than either of them. We were looking to be at an even better position than when we won in '89.

"With ten laps to go, Richard Petty crashed and created a caution, and we still felt we had a chance to win, but then Rusty Wallace wrecked and ran across the front of us and took us out with him. We were a brand-new team in 1991, and we legitimately had a chance to win that race.

"This year, we'll even be better."

LAP 24

Alan Kulwicki

The Independent Thinker

Alan Kulwicki has always been a maverick. Bright, well-spoken, and as intense as the noon sun in July at Daytona, Kulwicki is known in racing circles as a guy who does things a little differently. It was a reputation that was whispered about when he first came into Winston Cup racing in 1985.

There is a story that was probably spread by one of his former crew members from back in Milwaukee, when he drove stock cars in the USAC circuit.

According to the story, his crew was working late, went out for pizza, and returned to the shop around midnight to find all the lights in the shop on and the doors locked.

They walked to the side of the building and peered into the window. Alan was sitting in a chair, staring straight ahead and holding a disconnected steering wheel, turning it every once in a while. His crew members could hear a tape recording of his last short track race blaring throughout the shop over the PA system—almost as loud, it seemed, as the actual race.

Kulwicki, his crew members could see, was redriving that race in his mind.

Then there was the day at Phoenix in 1989. Kulwicki won the race, but as he came down toward the pit road to turn into Victory Lane, his joy was so great, he decided to mark the occasion by doing something most memorable. He turned the car around and drove the track clockwise—a no-no—until he found Victory Lane. Kulwicki called it his Polish Victory Lap. NASCAR told him his performance was creative, but strongly advised him not to do it again.

Alan Kulwicki's fame in the NASCAR community grew in 1991, not

Alan Kulwicki

because of any race he won, but because when the influential and powerful Junior Johnson called him and offered him $1 million a year guaranteed to drive for his race team, Kulwicki, a struggling, independent (in more ways than one) owner-driver, turned him down.

Kulwicki had gotten $2.5 million from Zerex antifreeze in 1990, built himself a modern shop, and won a race and four poles on a tighter budget than many less-successful teams. Zerex paid the money because it didn't want Motorcraft to lure him away. The problem was that $2.5 million was a budget breaker that prevented Zerex from spending much money on off-the-track promotions. By year's end Zerex had changed advertising agencies and had decided to put most of its advertising budget into TV commercials. You remember the commercial: A lady comes out of an airport, her car is covered with snow, she starts it and drives away, safe because of Zerex antifreeze. The one who was frozen out by the ad was Alan Kulwicki. Zerex dropped Alan as a sponsor.

That's when Junior called Alan with the million-dollar deal to drive for him.

While Kulwicki was mulling the offer, Jimmy Johnson of Hendrick Motorsports met him at the Speedway Club at Charlotte and told him, "Alan, you talk good. You have an education. You're a college graduate. You don't look stupid. Take the job."

Kulwicki shook his head. He told the Hendrick GM, "I just don't feel good about it. I can't see going to work for Junior. I want to be my own boss."

Later Junior Johnson called again to ask if he wanted to drive for him. Kulwicki told him, "No, I have a sponsor lined up."

Junior asked him, "Who do you think you have?" Kulwicki told him, "Maxwell House." Junior said, "Son, you need to listen to me. You *don't* have that sponsorship." Alan said, "Yes I do." Junior said, "No, you gotta believe me. You don't have that sponsorship tied up."

"Yes I do," said Kulwicki. They hung up. The next week Junior Johnson announced that Maxwell House coffee was sponsoring *his* second car. Alan Kulwicki was really out in the cold now.

Neither Junior Johnson nor anyone else could believe Kulwicki had turned down this opportunity. Everyone in the racing community was aware Kulwicki was having trouble attracting a major sponsor. Sure Alan was a major driving talent, but his bluntness made him a risk for the majority of sponsors, who prefer the easy glibness of a Darrell Waltrip, Ricky Rudd, or Rusty Wallace. With Alan, who was hard to control, no one was quite sure what he would say when asked a controversial question. And here he was, without a sponsor, turning down a guaranteed $1 million a year just because he wanted to remain independent.

Commented longtime car owner Bud Moore on Kulwicki: "Can you name me one owner-driver who has ever been successful? I can't. Darrell Waltrip has the personality to do it, but he hasn't done it yet."

When word got out that Kulwicki had turned him down, Junior Johnson told the racing press, "Alan has won three races in five years, and should have won twenty. He's a one-man operation because that's the way he wants it. I quit driving because I knew I couldn't continue to drive *and* build a winning team. If I didn't know what it was like, I wouldn't say you can't do it."

Most people were convinced Junior knew what he was talking about; "Kulwicki's crazy," is what everybody, and I mean *everybody,* said about Alan Kulwicki. But there was another strain of strong feeling running through the racing community: admiration that Kulwicki had stood firm for what he believed in and would not be bought.

Kulwicki started the 1991 season at the Daytona 500 with his car painted the white, brown, and black camouflage colors of the United States Army. Three races into the season he got a one-shot deal with Hooters restaurants. By the end of the year Hooters, which promises *big* breasts for lunch with your hamburger, fries, and Coke, had spent about $750,000 in sponsorship money. It wasn't much, but it was enough to keep Kulwicki competitive. And a funny thing happened. The firm's original intention was simply to attract more customers to its restaurants, but because of its connection to racing, Hooters began selling franchises at a feverish clip.

Hooters is now a major sponsor, and Kulwicki will be a strong contender for the racing championship in 1992.

Alan Kulwicki now owns a big, modern building, has a big, happy sponsor, and appears to have a big, limitless future. And who knows whether the strong-willed Junior Johnson and the volatile, headstrong Alan Kulwicki might not have killed each other with tire irons before the season ended.

When Kulwicki first arrived in North Carolina from Wisconsin, pulling his car on an open trailer and intending to begin his own race team, experienced observers thought, "You could have done this back in 1958, but in 1985, never."

He has shown the entire racing world it *could* be done. We may never know whether he might have won more races driving for Junior Johnson. Maybe so. And maybe not. But this much is certain: It will be one of the more interesting subplots in racing for 1992.

*   *   *

ALAN KULWICKI: "I was born and raised in Milwaukee. My dad built race car engines. I was brought up around racing, went to my first race when I was about six years old. For ten years I never missed a race, until I started racing go-carts, when I finally had to choose between watching and racing myself.

"I don't know how my dad got interested in cars. He was a mechanic. A lot of guys who are good in the mechanical field who work on cars end up working on fast cars. My dad got hooked up with Norm Nelson, who was on a Chrysler-backed team at the time. He raced on the USAC circuit, which raced in the Midwest while NASCAR raced more in the South. In the sixties they were on a par, and then through good management NASCAR grew into what it is today, and through bad management USAC fell by the wayside as far as stock car racing was concerned.

"I played football and basketball in grade school, and my first year in high school I started racing go-carts. I was thirteen or fourteen, and when it came time to decide whether to go to training camp for football or go race go-carts, I chose racing, and I've been doing it ever since.

"I started racing before I ever had my driver's license. I'd be out there racing kids my age, and their dads would be out there tuning the engines trying to make the cars run faster, and my dad was usually racing with the stock cars. I wasn't competing with the other kids, but with their dads. If I would go out there and beat them, it would be frustrating to them. Sometimes the fathers wanted to win worse than the kids.

"I was dying to race. And I could see with some of those other kids, it was their dads who wanted them to do it. Maybe they didn't have as strong a desire to win as I did.

"To pay for my own racing, I built engines for other competitors in other classes, rebuilt engines to pay for my own go-cart. I made ends meet, and eventually when I moved into NASCAR, where the odds of making it are slim, for all those years I had learned how to make ends meet, how to survive, and it came in handy.

"I knew I wanted to race professionally, but my dad didn't want me to. He wanted me to go to college, get an education, and be an engineer or a doctor—anything but a race car driver, because it's a tough business and the odds of making it are slim. Being involved in the sport all those years, he could see that. It's not the most practical thing in the world to come out of high school and say, 'I want to be a race car driver,' because you don't know if you even have the ability, and if you spend years trying to find out and five years down the road discover you really don't have what it takes, then what do you do? You have forsaken your chance to go to college.

"When I got out of high school, I had just started racing stock cars at a local short track. I went on to college at the University of Wisconsin at Milwaukee and raced on the short tracks as a hobby, got my bachelor's degree in mechanical engineering, and then I worked for the Bear Wheel Alignment division of Applied Power Incorporated in Milwaukee.

"I took a local job rather than pursuing the best job farther away because I still wanted to race. I worked there for two years.

"The first thing I did was adapt their wheel alignment system into a system they use on the Indy cars at the Bear garage at Gasoline Alley at Indy. They used my system to bump-steer the cars and align them. I did that for six months, and that was pretty neat, because at least I was connected with racing and I got to go around and check out the Indy cars.

"After that I was involved in regular production working full-time as an engineer, and I got bored and it was time to leave. I was still racing as a hobby and going to school at night toward my master's degree. At that time I was an idealistic person, trying to do everything. But I knew my heart wasn't in engineering, it was in racing, and in 1980 I went racing full-time.

"I was never personally wealthy, never had a lot of money, but I took it one step at a time. Whatever level I was at, my goal was to do as best as I could and progress to the next level. If I had planned and budgeted everything I did, a lot of times I would have said, 'I can't do that. It's impossible. I'll run out of money in less than a month; I'd better not do it.' But sometimes you take a gamble on blind faith, and you find a way as you go.

"In 1980 I began running USAC and some local short track races, and in '81 I started running ASA. USAC was the United States Auto Club, more like what NASCAR is today. ASA was the American Speed Association, which ran sophisticated short track cars on the highest level. They were lighter, had fiberglass bodies and coil-over suspensions, and I did that through 1985.

"When you race on local short tracks, you go back to the same tracks two or three times a week, and you at least get to be good through repetition, if nothing else. With ASA, we traveled quite a bit, and once you start doing that, every track is different and you learn how to adapt, how to start running bigger, faster tracks, to run speedways.

"A lot of it I did by the seat of my pants, and all along, there have been people who helped me out. When I was racing go-carts, I met Jim Braun. He was trying to groom his son Jeff to be a professional race car driver, and his brother helped him too, and I got to be friends with them, and the very first race I ran, Jim Braun was my partner. I put up $1,000 and did all the work, and he put up $2,500, and we were equal partners. I worked my way up from there.

"I wouldn't say I was a protégé, but he took me under his wing and tried to teach me some things about how to grow up, how to succeed in business, about the sport. It wasn't a great deal of money for him, he could afford to lose it, but it was an interesting venture. His son Jeff never did become a professional driver.

"He got out, and then his wife was a partner for a year, and then in 1982 we got together again and started my ASA team, and we almost won the championship. Jeff came to work for the team in '83 and we ran another season, and then we went our separate ways, and that was the last time I ever drove for somebody else full-time.

"After we went our separate ways, I realized I had to have a significant sponsor. I looked hard and long, and finally ended up getting Hardee's restaurants to sponsor me. That was when they were sponsoring Cale Yarborough in NASCAR. I was their Midwest representative in 1984 and 1985.

"To get a sponsor, you have to convince them there is a benefit in it for them. You are selling them something, and what you are selling is advertising. They are paying X number of dollars to have their name on the car, because they think the exposure is going to benefit them, just like any other form of advertising.

"I had started at the bottom with sponsors. My initial sponsor was $250 a year paid by a Chevrolet dealership in Wisconsin. After paying to paint the name two or three times during the year, I didn't net $200. But I had a sponsor. And then the next sponsor was a radio station, the biggest rock station in Wisconsin at the time, and I went as far as I could with them, and the next breakthrough was Hardee's, and part of that deal in '85 was that I had to run five Grand National races, and so I ran the entire ASA circuit for them *and* five Winston Cup races, hitting a few markets like Richmond and Dover that Cale Yarborough didn't run because he wasn't running a full schedule. That was my introduction to NASCAR racing.

"I had studied the people who made it and those who didn't. 'Why did they make it? Why did they fail? What do I have to do to make this my home?' I had been planning to move to NASCAR for four or five years.

"There was a short track racer named Dave Watson who almost made it to NASCAR and didn't quite. When I was in ASA, I looked up to Mark Martin a lot. He looked like he was going to make it big, and then he stumbled and fell and had to go back and start over again, and eventually he did make it. I looked up to Rusty Wallace. We all raced against each other in ASA, but Mark and Rusty were a year or two ahead of me.

"I was one of the top five drivers in ASA. I've never really excelled or dominated at any level in the sport, because anytime I got to be pretty good at that level, I'd move to the next level. I didn't want to stay driving ASA for five years and win the championship. It was, 'Okay, I know I can do this. What's next?'

"To fulfill my agreement with Hardee's to run the five Winston Cup races, Bill Terry, a businessman from Greenville, South Carolina, built a brand-new car and we bought two engines from Prototype Engineering, the place from which I had been buying my short track engines. I gave him my Hardee's sponsorship money, and we were going to run five races.

"So I had a brand-new car, which was a good car, when I went to Richmond in September 1985, my first Winston Cup race. Richmond was a track similar to what I had run the majority of my career, and I was running really well, but when I went out to qualify, I drove the car way too deep into the third turn and crashed it.

"They came pretty close to loading it up and going home. To this day I don't know what would have happened if they had done that. But they decided to stay and fix it, and we started the race, and I finished it, ran nineteenth, and we went on and ran the next race at Dover and finished twenty-first. I didn't crash that car seriously after that.

"I was trying to make an impression, trying hard, maybe a bit too hard, but we ran well in the remaining races, good enough to attract offers of a couple of rides and a couple of sponsors.

"I said to myself, 'Now is the time to make this move,' and I sold all my ASA equipment. I gave notice on my apartment, and I made plans to move South. This was late October. I said, 'This is it. It's time to go.'

"I sold my equipment, so I had nothing to turn back to. Sometimes, the easier it is to turn back, the greater the odds that you *will* turn back.

"I was loading my stuff into the trailer I was going to use. It was half full of shop equipment. The welder was in the front, and the bed was hanging between the tire racks. The file cabinet was in back, and all of this was sitting in the truck when a week before I was to leave, the truck had an electrical short, and the truck and everything in it was destroyed. I was lucky it didn't burn the whole building down and everything next to it.

"I thought, 'Is somebody trying to tell me something? Maybe I shouldn't be doing this.'

"I was planning to leave, to move out of my apartment, they were having a going-away party for me, but not one of the rides or the sponsorships materialized. It was time to go, and I had no place to go.

"Bill Terry had always said, 'If these other deals don't come through, come on down and we'll go as far as we can.' I figured I would go down South and run.

"Bill Terry ran race cars as a hobby. He had money, but not by NASCAR standards. When he said 'as far as we can,' I took that to mean a third to a half of the '86 season if I didn't find a sponsor. My belief was I had that to fall back on, and I said to myself, 'I'll take that gamble.'

"When I got down there, I learned that 'as far as we can' meant one race. We were going to the Daytona 500, and if we made that race, that was to be it. Quincy's was sponsoring us for that one race.

"We went to Daytona and missed making the race on the last turn of the last lap. My qualifying time wasn't good enough, and so I had to finish at least fifteenth in the qualifying race. I was running fifteenth with only a couple hundred yards to go when Lake Speed and Dick Trickle drafted on by.

"We still owed Quincy's a race, so we went on to Richmond. I went out and qualified sixth fastest, and there were six cars left to qualify, and it started raining. And it never stopped raining and because they didn't finish the qualifying runs, they made up the field by points and entry postmarks. Because we didn't make the race at Daytona, we didn't have any points, and Bill Terry was late sending the entry in, so we went from sixth-fastest qualifying to not making the show.

"Then we went on to Rockingham. We *still* owed Quincy's a race. We made the Rockingham race and finished fifteenth. I was the highest-finishing rookie, and after that I decided to buy the car from Bill. Quincy's gave me $200,000 to run twenty races, and I moved to Charlotte, leased part of a shop, hired two guys, and ran my own team with two employees the rest of the year.

"There were a number of reasons for my decision. Without running Bill down, he was not a professional racer. He wasn't willing to spend his own money. He wanted to do it as a hobby, and this was a rough road ahead. It was going to be my career. And when we got to Richmond and the entry had been sent in late, that's when I decided I was better off with my career in my own hands. And in 1986, I ran twenty-three races on about $200,000 and won the Rookie of the Year title.

"Running all those races on $200,000 was the most efficient thing I had ever done. If I had to duplicate that again, I don't know if I could. It was a tough deal, but obstacles are things you see when you take your eyes off the goal. I was swimming for my life, and I just went and did it. Money was real tight, but actually, it was a fun year, as much fun as I've ever had, because I was living my dream. Anything I did was better than what was expected of me. I was traveling to all these new tracks, and every city, every motel, every restaurant was someplace new, and as tough as the financial pressure was, in a lot of other ways it was exciting. Today, with bigger sponsors, the financial pressure isn't as tough, but there is pressure to win and produce, so the pressure is just different.

"Before coming to the NASCAR circuit, I had been racing stock cars for twelve years, so I wasn't in for any big surprises that first year. It wasn't easy, but it was pretty much what I expected. I had been around it enough to know by then.

"When I came in, I tried to come in humble and respect everyone who was there, and in turn they respected me. Everyone was fair to me. Everyone said, 'You can't do this because you're not a good old boy from the South,' but because of the way I approached it, no one picked on me just because I wasn't from the South. And today the sport has grown so much that if prejudice existed before, it has pretty much broken down.

"In 1987 I was able to attract Zerex anti-freeze as a sponsor, and they stayed with me for four years. During that period I built a new shop, got a new semitrailer, and was constantly building and growing. Every penny I earned went back into racing. Until a year ago, I lived in a one-bedroom apartment.

"At the end of the '90 season, Zerex informed me they were getting out of racing due to changes in conditions in the marketplace. They got out because they wanted to spend their advertising dollar differently, not because they weren't satisfied with the race program. I was notified late in the year, and all the new deals that had come along—Western Auto, Pennzoil—were already taken, so I didn't have a sponsor.

"In 1991 I went to Daytona with the Army car with the camouflage. R. J. Reynolds paid the expenses of five cars during Operation Desert Storm, one for each branch of the armed services, as a show of support for the troops over there. I drove the Army car, and then I ran a couple races with a white generic car with 'AK' on the hood, and when I went to Atlanta and won the pole, it was the first time in twelve years an unsponsored car had won the pole at a NASCAR race.

"That day the car that Hooters had sponsored didn't make the race for the second or third time in a row, and it happened that Atlanta is where their corporate headquarters is. The race was on network TV, and it was a good market area for them, and they came to me and asked if I was interested in their sponsoring my car for that one race.

"I was a little leery of it at first. I was negotiating with a cereal company, and a toothpaste maker was also interested, and I wondered, 'If I take on Hooters for one race, will the cereal or toothpaste company see me as not clean-cut or wholesome enough, and then after one race Hooters will go on down the road, and I'll be left standing there without a sponsor?'

"So I was a little hesitant to do it. But the bottom line was, I needed the $20,000 to survive, to keep going. So I took the deal, and I led part of the Atlanta race on network TV, and finished eighth. Hooters got a lot of exposure, and they decided to stay with me for three more races, and after that they were either going to stay with me the rest of the season, or get out.

"They stayed, and that's when we painted the car orange and white and got uniforms. It wasn't tremendous money, but enough to keep us from falling by the wayside. Last year there were owners who had a lot more money than I did who never did find a sponsor. The Gulf War had everyone thinking pessimistically, and then when the war happened, sports marketing was not a hot item.

"At the end of the 1991 season, we signed a three-year agreement for Hooters to be my main sponsor.

"I met Bob Brooks, the president of Hooters. I figured he was going to be a forty-year-old businessman with a mustache and big gold chains around his neck, driving a Corvette. He turned out to be the opposite of that, a clean-cut, straightforward businessman. Hooters has a sports bar atmosphere. There is nothing wrong with the way the waitresses dress. They wear shorts and T-shirts or tank tops. It's not a topless restaurant. And everything Hooters has done with the girls at the tracks has been in good taste. I am honored to have Hooters as a sponsor.

"Having a sponsor doesn't affect the way you run. I don't drive more or less conservatively because I do or do not have a sponsor. I run the car as hard as I can and fix it later if I have to.

"Winning, or not winning, is what affects you. That's what gets you the sponsor, and then once you sign the sponsor, you can ask yourself, 'How many cars can you build? How many engines? How many people can you hire?'

"You cannot buy success in this sport, and you can never guarantee it, because all of the top teams have budgets of $2 million or more, so even if you have a couple million dollars in sponsorship, that does not guarantee you'll be successful, because there are forty cars out there, and twenty of them can win.

"What the money guarantees is that you will be competitive, or it should. If you're not, it's your fault. The limiting factor becomes lack of knowledge or ability, and people will use money as an excuse, and I have never done that in my career. Other people will say, 'If I had Bill Elliott's money, I could do what he does.' I never said that. I did the best I could with what I had and focused on getting better and better. Bill Elliott didn't have the kind of backing he does now when he started out either. He got it because he was good, because he performed. Bill now drives for Junior Johnson. It was the deal Junior offered me, but I turned him down. And if anybody would have ever told me I was going to turn down an offer to drive for Junior Johnson, especially for that kind of money, I would have said, 'He's crazy. Take him away.'

"When I came down here, my whole net worth probably wasn't $50,000. Hell, I can spend that much a week right now keeping this going. Initially I ran my own car because I *had* to, because nobody was offering me a ride, and once I got past the Rookie of the Year stage, I started getting some offers, but then I had Zerex as a sponsor, and the offers to drive were fair, and then our team got a little better and the offers got a little better, but they were never better than what I felt I could do on my own.

"When Junior made his offer to me, I seriously considered it. Had he made it a year earlier, I'm sure I would have taken it. But we had started running well. He saw we could run up front. We weren't big winners, but we had potential. I was on the verge, and with Zerex as the sponsor I was making pretty good money running my own team, and when Junior made me his offer, it was like, 'How much money does it take to be happy?' I read somewhere, and I've always said, 'Work to *become,* not to acquire.' If you ever become what you set out to become, you will acquire everything you need or want in the process, so money wasn't the main concern. I figured I could make pretty good money and be happy running my own team. If I drove for him, maybe I'd be happy and maybe I wouldn't.

"In the end, I don't have any second thoughts about it. I don't regret that. The offer came back once or twice after that, and whether I did the right thing or not, the jury is still out. Time will tell. In three of the last four years I've won a race, which is enough to prove it isn't a fluke, though I haven't won as much as I'd like to win. I'm not the Winston Cup champion. I'm not Dale Earnhardt. At least yet.

"If I decide I'm not a good enough owner to win the championship, I could sign with a Junior or a Hendrick. I don't foresee that right now. If I sign with Hooters three more years, I'm far enough into my career that I will probably continue this way.

"I haven't won as many races as I'd've liked to the last three years, but Junior hasn't either. For all the money and all the cars he has, they haven't won more races or more poles. We both could have done better. This year Junior will have a two-car team with Bill Elliott and Sterling Marlin.

"I was thinking about driving for Junior, really thinking about it, and then he started that two-car team, and I decided I didn't want to do that. I'm either really smart or really dumb. Either I passed up a bunch of money or I'm way ahead of the game, because a lot of the guys who have driven for other people, like Darrell Waltrip when he drove for Hendrick or Junior, have won races, won championships, but you notice Darrell is happiest back on his own, running his own team.

"Rusty Wallace ran for somebody else, won the championship, and he wants to be his own owner, at least part owner. And whether this is right or wrong depends on who I have working for me. If you have the right people working for you, it's not as hard to manage.

"Junior was telling me, 'We'll let you do whatever you want, let you set up the car however you want it set up.' Well, if I can set it up the way I want it set up, the car is going to run the same whether you own it or I own it. If you know how to make it run better, or if you have better people who can make it run better, then maybe I'd win more races in your car. But if you want me to drive it because you think I can drive it good and that I know how to set it up, then I can set it up the same way whether you own it or whether I own it.

"And I'm not being smart or cocky. I respect Junior for all he has done in racing. But I have seen drivers bounce from team to team to team. Look at all the experienced drivers Junior has had before he offered me that ride, and he hadn't been satisfied with any of them. He wasn't really satisfied with the guy he chose instead of me. He's down the road, and now Junior's on to the next one. If I get my team to the level I want it maybe this will give me the most stability in the long run. Time will tell. The jury is still out. In the meantime, we'll just be competitors and go race against each other and see what happens.

"I have factory support from the Ford Motor Company, and even Ford wanted me to go and drive for Junior a couple years, because they thought that together maybe we could be more successful than apart. Ford wants to see its cars win races. They thought that might be the best way for that to happen. We've been successful, but not as successful as I would like, but we haven't reached our ultimate potential as yet.

"I think we're on the verge of getting there as a team. I've learned a lot of things. I think I know how to get there eventually. Maybe we can do it in 1992. Maybe it's going to take another year. The farther I go into this business, the more I realize you have to plan ahead. We are way ahead of where we were last year, but we are still not planning as far down the road as Richard Childress.

"We're building a Daytona car, working hard to get that finished. Last May the chassis builder for Childress was showing his chassis to other people, trying to sell them. Childress was taking delivery of it at the end of May. They may have started working on that car in July. We started ours the end of November. When you start the Daytona 500, that car doesn't know when it was built. As long as you've done it right and on the line, that's all that counts. But the earlier you build it and the more time you take with it, the more you test it, the greater the odds you are going to get it right.

"Last year we didn't even build any new cars. So this year we are way ahead of last year, but I still see more progress. We're in the growing stages.

"I have been an inspiration to the short track racers around the country, because there are thousands of guys out there who would love to be doing this. I mean, I am living my dream, and there are thousands of guys still dreaming about it. They are saying, 'He did it, and maybe there is still that 2 percent chance I can do it too.'

"The other thing, I stood up for what I believed in, in being my own man, my own person. I am proud to have promoted the idea that going for the most money is not always the best route, that what will make you the happiest is.

"We'll see if I'm right. Time will tell."

Bill Ingle

The Taskmaster

Sometimes a team doesn't win races, and no one is quite sure why. This is particularly true of Bahari Racing, owned by Chuck Rider and Lowrance Harry. Chuck Rider, who most often speaks for his team, is one of the nicest, finest individuals you would ever want to meet. He wears a perpetual smile, and when he wears his bright yellow sports jacket, his aura seems to glow. If you talk with him for five minutes, you consider him a friend.

Chuck Rider is owner of Automotive Electric Associates, an outfit that distributes auto parts to mechanics and jobbers. Founded in 1926 in Charlotte, AEA serves the Carolinas, Virginia, and Georgia with five warehouse locations, 350 employees, and 750 jobbers. AEA handles 285 lines of auto products and over 165 parts numbers.

Among its products, AEA distributes Briggs & Stratton engines and All Pro Auto Parts. All Pro boasts over thirty huge warehouses east of the Mississippi; its stores blanket the East Coast. Rider and Lowrance Harry *own* 160 of these All Pro retail outlets.

For his driver, Rider has chosen a man as personable as he is. Michael Waltrip is a PR man's dream. The tallest driver in NASCAR at six-foot-five, Michael is a good-looking guy who, like his older brother Darrell, speaks assuredly and well. Michael and Chuck Rider can be seen in the national commercials for Pennzoil, their sponsor.

When he started in Winston Cup racing, Michael had the advantage of his last name. He lived with Kyle Petty in Charlotte while building a Darlington Dash series car at Petty Enterprises in Level Cross. Michael's commute to his shop was ninety miles round-trip, and one afternoon Lynda Petty asked him if he wanted to move into the Petty home and live in Kyle's old room. He moved in in February 1985, and

Bill Ingle

lived there until November. He was twenty-one, sixteen years younger than Darrell.

By day Michael worked with the fabricators doing aluminum work, and at night he would sit with Richard Petty until one, two in the morning eating popcorn, watching TV, and talking about what Michael should be doing: finding a way to get into Winston Cup racing.

While Michael was living there, a Maine native named Dick Bahre who was living in Statesville, North Carolina, asked the young man to drive for him in the Coca-Cola World 600 in Charlotte. The catch: Michael had to scrape up $10,000 to do it. Humpy Wheeler told him, "If you make the race, I'll help you."

Michael raised a little more than the $10,000, and he qualified twenty-second for the race. After four hundred miles he had transmission problems and fell out, but he was on his way.

In '86, Waltrip and Dick Bahre got a small sponsorship from Hawaiian Punch, and Michael was runner-up for Rookie of the Year to Alan Kulwicki. His best finish was eleventh. That year he finished in the top twenty in points.

The next year Waltrip and Bahre ran ten Winston Cup races. Their financial condition bordered on desperation. They were working on several deals to get a sponsor, but none materialized.

Michael finished tenth at Martinsville in late April 1987, and then qualified thirty-seventh for the Charlotte 600 in a yellow car. Bahre had painted it yellow in an attempt to attract Century 21 as a sponsor.

The color is important, because trying to qualify for the same race were Chuck Rider and Lowrance Harry, whose yellow car failed to qualify. Rider and Harry had as a sponsor their company, All Pro Auto Parts. They didn't have a car. Rider and Harry were committed to running in the race, and on Friday before the Coca-Cola World 600, they struck a deal to sponsor Waltrip and Bahre.

Waltrip finished eleventh, despite a fender bender. A little more than a month later, Rider and Harry bought into the team.

Chuck Rider began to rebuild the race team. He bought some new cars, started an engine shop, built a fabrication shop, and then constructed a building as large as an airplane hangar, stuffing it with car after car of yellow Pennzoil racing machines—almost thirty in all, one for each track—plus Busch cars, backup cars, and show cars. It was, and is, a breathtaking display of putting one's money where one's mouth is; twenty-five full-time employees work on the cars.

Waltrip, meanwhile, continued his education. He had a lot to learn. Before driving Winston Cup, he had driven 4-cylinder, 2,300-pound compact cars. He admits, "I probably started with as little experience as anybody ever had."

In '88, he would run well one week, terribly the next. The car didn't even qualify at Daytona, and to keep the sponsor—Country Time lemonade drink—happy, Rider and Harry rented the competing Evinrude car, added the Country Time decals, and ran it in the race.

"That's what really made the statement to Michael, to Country Time, to each one of the members of the team, that we had the commitment and determination to compete," says Chuck Rider.

Michael finished twenty-first in the '88 Daytona 500. At Pocono he finished second. In '89 he had a couple of finishes in the top five, and in '90 he had five.

Meanwhile, Rider kept getting better and better deals from sponsors. He had been running a car with both Country Time and Maxwell House on it, and when Pennzoil offered him more money and a better deal, he saw that a marriage between him and his All Pro shops and Pennzoil was one made in financial heaven. Pennzoil sought a greater market share in its competition with Quaker State, Valvoline, Exxon, and Citgo, and Chuck Rider, through his race program, gave it to them.

Chuck Rider told the Pennzoil executives, "We promise you will not find anyone better to sell your oil."

Michael Waltrip goes to a half-dozen regional meetings around the country, meeting the people who sell Pennzoil and letting them know he's going to help them sell their product. His TV, radio, and print ads have been extensive.

Pennzoil's sales have grown, and so have All Pro's. All that's missing is a Bahari Racing victory.

In 1991 at Atlanta, Michael Waltrip was leading the race. In the team members' minds, they had arrived. But because they had to make one extra pit stop, Kenny Schrader, Bill Elliott, Dale Earnhardt, and Morgan Shepherd were able to pass Michael, and he finished fifth.

"I feel like we can be the best," says Michael Waltrip, "and that day at the racetrack made a lot of people realize we can be."

The next week at Darlington, Michael should have won, but a pit crew member changing the right front tire had a problem with his air wrench, and it cost the team the race. He finished third to Ricky Rudd and Davey Allison.

Waltrip finished fifteenth in the point standings in '91. He has yet to win a race. Experts say he, along with Sterling Marlin, are the two best drivers on the Winston Cup scene never to have won.

When picking crew members, the big question Chuck Rider and

Michael Waltrip ask each other is, "Can he get along with everybody?" Bill Ingle joined the team as a crew member at the end of the 1989 season. He had been a member of the crew for Junior Johnson and then for Alan Kulwicki.

When Mike Beam left Bahari to go to work for Bill Elliott, Ingle was named Bahari's crew chief. Ingle, who is hardworking and extremely competitive, is a team player who understands what Chuck Rider wants: victory with harmony and a touch of class. Until Michael Waltrip wins his first Winston Cup race, no one at Bahari—neither Chuck Rider, Michael Waltrip, nor Bill Ingle—will feel vindicated. Until then, experts will look at the bright yellow car with the numeral 30 and shake their heads as if to say, "See, money can't buy *everything*."

BILL INGLE: "I grew up in the Mooresville area, near Charlotte, and I have been involved with cars and motors since childhood. My uncles, Leroy and Larry Ingle, were mechanics. They did some drag racing, and they built dirt cars when I was a teenager, and I went with them when they went to the races. We had a driver by the name of Haywood Plotter, who was taught to drive by Ralph Earnhardt, Dale's dad.

"Haywood and Ralph had been real good friends. He told me how exciting it was to drive against Ralph, 'cause he was just so good, like it was second nature to him. He said it was remarkable to watch the man go.

"When I was ten, I could pull an engine apart and put it together. This may seem minor, but I also learned how to glance at a tool and know the size of it without having to read the number to know the wrench size. It's a talent you pick up from handling the tools. You look and grab the one you want, without having to take the time to look. The other thing I learned was to be able to go under a car and take every tool needed, rather than having to keep going under and out, under and out, or asking for this tool or that tool. I learned all those things.

"When I was thirteen I began working part-time helping out at the dirt tracks—maintaining the cars, building them, getting the parts and pieces it takes to make them go. I worked long hours at night building engines and welding chassis pieces. I would read the hot rod magazines, read articles by Smokey Yunick and Junior Johnson, and then in 1982, when I was twenty-six, I was asked to help work on Junior's cars.

"I had a friend named Jeff Stutts who was working for Junior. They were having electrical problems with the race car. I had begun learning automotive electronics at sixteen and picked it right up, and so my friend told Junior, 'You call Bill, and he'll fix it.'

"They called me, and I went up to Junior's shop, looked at their car, and helped them sort it out. They had a lot of resistors under the dash where they didn't need them. The Buick people had done a whole bunch of wiring in the cars that didn't need to be, so I just kind of simplified it, got it down to basics, and made it all work, and showed them it would work. The crew chief at that time was Jeff Hammond, and he asked Jeff Stutts, 'Does he like racing?' 'Well, yeah.' 'Why don't you bring him around?' So I started working part-time helping them. I helped them prepare the car and do the maintenance and went to the racetracks.

"I didn't become a full-time member, because I had my own automobile electrical business. I rebuilt alternators and starters of street cars. The biggest part of my business was fleet truck firms. Race cars were just a hobby, and so I would leave my business Wednesday, Thursday, or Friday and go to the track weekends.

"I worked for Junior full-time starting in '87, and then I left the next year. What I remember about Junior is he is a very intelligent man and very quiet. I doubt that man says two hundred words every weekend at the racetrack. I would have really enjoyed working for Junior full-time with his cars, but at his age and because of his other businesses, there was no way he could work full-time at his race shop. But the times he would come around, I was usually the first guy there in the morning, 'cause that is part of my work ethic and always has been, and Junior would come down with his dogs, and we'd talk about the things we were going to do to the race cars. Or he would say, 'You got any ideas?' and if I had an idea, I would say, 'Junior, what do you think about this?' He's got so much experience, and he'd say, 'Let me tell you why that won't work.'

"I can remember we were trying all sorts of things to make our Daytona car go faster—do things to the restrictor plate, different gearing, different transmissions. He'd say, 'You can try it if you want to, but it's probably not going to work,' and it never did. Junior just had a tremendous amount of knowledge.

"It was a lot of fun back then. All the guys kidded, cut up. You worked long hours, but you didn't feel the pressure. NASCAR hadn't gotten to the business point it's at now. There weren't the dollars in it there are now. When I first got to Junior's in '86, he was just ending his relationship with Mountain Dew and had switched over to Pepsi and the Pepsi Challenger that was driven by Darrell Waltrip.

"Neil Bonnett joined Junior in '84, and I was with Neil's car. And in '86 there weren't but four or five other competitors you had to worry about every week. The field was full, but you had only Petty, Dale Earnhardt with Bud Moore in the Wrangler car, Kyle Petty in the Wood Brothers, Bill Elliott, and at that time Harry Gant, who was running with

Hal Needham. Travis Carter was the crew chief and they were tough for a while, but they kind of fell off toward the end.

"Back then Junior won the biggest share of the races and sat on the most poles. It wasn't anything for Junior to sit on a minimum of six poles and win eleven to thirteen races a year. His cars were dominant, and I would say a big part of it was his knowledge and experience. He trained a lot of people. He helped me gain a lot of knowledge I have. I had had the basics from dirt track and short track racing, but the vast majority of my knowledge came from working up there with Junior Johnson.

"Junior liked people who were hard workers and dedicated to what he was trying to accomplish, and I guess I fit that mold, because anything I've ever done—and this may sound like I'm patting myself on the back, but anything I've done, I give 100 percent to whoever I've helped.

"Everyone is loyal to Junior, because he's good to you. He is a fair man. But once you get on the bad side of him, he is finished with you. There is no more.

"I can remember him telling me that one day. He was giving me some of his knowledge. He said, 'If you have a problem with the people in the garage area, try to avoid anything confrontational. If they do something you don't like, and they become your enemy, just ignore them as you pass them by. Just pretend they don't exist.' And if you watch the man in the garage area, which I do, there were times when another guy and I would walk up to him, and he would speak to me and ignore the other person. That would let me know he didn't care for the other person. 'Cause if he doesn't care for you, he won't even acknowledge you're in the world. He'll just pass you right on by.

"Junior Johnson is a fascinating man. The people can say what they want, but he is a very smart man. I gained a lot of knowledge from working up there, just keeping my mouth shut and listening to what he had to say.

"In 1986 Junior was running two teams, one with Neil Bonnett in the 12 car, the other with Darrell Waltrip in the 11 car. There was friction between the two teams. I would say the friction came more from the 11 side back to the 12 side than the other way around. They felt they were being shortchanged on certain parts, or something like that, and it just wasn't the case. I felt Junior was a fair and honest man and gave both of them equal-quality pieces to work with. At the time my feeling was, 'I work for Junior Johnson, not for any one car.' Whatever needed to be done, on either car, I was willing to do it. There were times when our car was finished, and I would go to the upper shop to try to help get their car loaded or whatever needed to be done. Not everybody felt that way.

"And at the time Darrell was tough on crew members. He was the type of guy who took all the credit himself, but at the end of that year he left Junior and went with Rick Hendrick, where he and Waddell Wilson formed what was supposedly the Dream Team, and that year humbled Darrell in a lot of ways. He's where he spreads the credit out a little more now.

"You can't just throw a group of people together, and I don't care if they're all good, there has to be synergy, it all has to click, and you have to put the right people and the right pieces together to make the thing work, and they were convinced it was going to work, and it didn't—Darrell and Waddell didn't click, and that made the team not click, and then Darrell got back on his own and brought Jeff Hammond down from Junior's and hired him to help get things sorted out in the shop, but still he wasn't able to dominate the way he was able to at Junior's, because he didn't have what Junior had. And right about that time the big money started coming into the sport, and more and more teams became competitive.

"In 1986, Tim Richmond was a wildcat. He was tough and hard to beat, and if the guy hadn't gotten messed up, he would be Dale Earnhardt's biggest competitor right now. It would have been tough for Dale Earnhardt to have done what he did if he had had to race Tim Richmond every week, and I think even Dale would admit that. 'Cause the guy was a super race car driver. He knew no fear. Guys like Earnhardt and Rusty Wallace like to work on their cars. Tim Richmond didn't know very much at all mechanically about his cars. All he knew was, sit down, put the straps on, the helmet on, and go wide open. And he could keep it under control, and he could drive it out of control. He was a superstar.

"At the time I noticed Tim's weight changes. I saw him get little and then I saw him get big again. He was a partier, wild, lived on the wild side of life, and you really didn't know what was going on. And I really didn't want to know.

"In the middle of the 1987 season I quit at Junior's. I didn't have another job when I left, but if you're good and determined and you're willing to work, you can get a job in this business. But you have to be willing to work, something I've always been willing to do. If it was seven days a week, twenty hours a day, I did it. So I was confident there would be a job opening somewhere. I had jacked, changed tires, gassed the car, so I knew I could get a position somewhere on a pit crew.

"What made me move on—I'll be honest and say it—Tim Brewer, the crew chief, was never hard on me, but he was pretty hard on some of the other guys. I would see some of the people who were really trying hard, working hard and putting out, and he was hard on them, and it just didn't set right with me. A lot of times he came down on them when they didn't do anything wrong. He would carry personal problems from other areas into the job place. I understand he isn't like that anymore, that Junior has molded him, filed him down since those years, but back then he was really high-strung, temperamental. I didn't feel he was being fair to some of his crew, and I was feeling some mental strain, and you can have just as good a time without the mental strain, and so I felt it was time to move on.

"I can be as tough as any man out there, and I can also be as fair as any man, and it wouldn't bother me if you asked every one of my crewmen how fair I am and also how stern I am, because I believe you have to have their respect, but you also have to be fair with them too, because they are human beings, and it's a tough sport. It requires a lot of dedication, a lot of sacrifice, especially when the guys start getting older, start getting married and have children, and that family starts sacrificing, and it becomes tough on the guy to go home. If a person is having trouble in the shop and it goes on for a little while, if you look at the depth of the problem, it's usually the home. You sit down and try to talk to him and try to work the thing out to help him get the problem solved at home. If I can leave him home for a couple of weeks, keep him away from the racetrack so he can do a couple things with his family, or if I can find a way to bring his family with him for a couple of weeks, often I can get it worked out.

"Alan Kulwicki had been talking to me a good bit. He would call me on occasions and want to know different things. Why he picked me out of a group of people, I don't know, but when I left Junior's, he called me pretty frequently about coming to work for him, so I decided, 'Here's a guy trying to get started, and he seems to have the driving ability.' . . . I saw him struggling, trying to get his own deal going, he had a couple cars, so I decided in the middle of the '87 season to go to work for him and try to help him out.

"When I went to work for Alan, I discovered he could be a really weird person. He was new to the Winston Cup scene, and I had been around, and he seemed real receptive to trying to learn and gain as much knowledge as I had, but Alan just wasn't self-assured, and he was unable to make a decision. I'm the type of person, I make a decision, and I stick with it, right or wrong. If it's wrong, life goes on and I work it out. If it's right, I'll take it and go on. But Alan was so unassured of himself. He is a real good race car driver; he has that ability to drive the car—but when it came to managing people and getting the race team together, he was his own worst enemy.

"Today financially Alan seems to be in great shape. If he's only in racing for the financial gain, he's doing what he needs to do. But he had the opportunity to go to Junior's and drive, and in my opinion, if he wanted to be known as a great race driver, that's where he should have gone, taken off the burden of managing, of handling other people, laid that on Junior and just concentrated on driving the race car. 'Cause Junior would have given him what he needed to win. So as far as history goes, Alan hurt himself.

"I worked with Alan through the end of '87. He didn't have the money, didn't have the sponsors, and I had been offered some jobs elsewhere. Jeff Hammond left Junior's to join Darrell Waltrip at Hendrick, and Jeff asked me if I wanted to join them, and so I went to work for Rick Hendrick on Darrell's car in 1988.

"Hendrick is a fine gentleman. He owns thirty-one car dealerships, and he had been very successful in racing. The only thing about Rick—unlike Chuck Rider, who's here every day seeing what goes on, Rick had managers to look after the race teams for him. That's okay, because that's why you hire managers, but I felt if he had been there more personally, he'd have had a better hands-on feel. But what do you do? If I could have worked for Rick Hendrick himself directly, chances are I would probably still be there. But I didn't see eye to eye with some of the people he had there in management, so better opportunities arose. See, when you are working for someone and you can't do things your way, the only thing you can do is suck it up or stick it out until another opportunity arises where you *can* do things your way, and that's when you make a change. A lot of people don't want to be in a position of responsibility. I thrive on it. I enjoy it. I have a lot of gray hairs and am missing some hairs for my age, but I don't mind responsibilities.

"And at Hendrick, we were doing things, creating a lot of unnecessary work to be done. Things just weren't organized at that particular time, and so I walked away, because I'm an organized person, and when you see things going on and say, 'If you had only done this . . .' or 'If you had prepared yourself for this . . .'

"I would see things happening, and I had the desire to be in charge, and that made me more critical of what was going on. And after the '88 season, I quit Darrell and went back to Alan Kulwicki.

"Kulwicki came to me and said, 'Look, I've changed. I'll be better. I have some money now, and I'll pay you better, give you what you want, and we can really do well.''

"And Alan and I really did work together good at the racetrack. I don't know if he would admit it, but I helped him a lot, gave him a sense of confidence, and he helped me too in some ways. I gave him the sense of confidence that he could do it, right, wrong, or indifferent, and he did it. He sat on poles in places where he had never qualified any better than fifteenth or twentieth.

"We would have conversations where we'd say, 'This is really working out good, and we're really running good together.' But still, his way of working with people just didn't sit right with me, and I went through ten months of it through October of 1989. What bothered me most was he expected from people what he wouldn't do himself. I'm the crew chief here at Bahari, and right now I am sitting here dirty, and I don't *have* to do that, but I will do anything in the shop that needs to be done, and the other twenty-two men know it, and therefore I have their respect. If I say, 'Will you do this for me?' they do it, because they know if they don't, I will.

"Alan was a person who wasn't willing to do what he expected of others, or if he would do it, he couldn't do it as well as they were doing it. And he was very critical of them, never gave them any pats on the back. His men just stayed down all the time. Since he's been in business he's had two hundred people work for him. There are a lot of people going in and out those doors, and a lot of good people who didn't stay very long.

"I left the 1st of October in 1989 and came to work for Bahari Racing. I didn't know much about them. Just by seeing the cars at the track, I knew it was a young team. They hadn't the major bucks. The two owners, Chuck Rider and Lowrance Harry, had pretty much done everything out of pocket to get started.

"At Charlotte in October, Chuck had walked up to me and asked me if I would be interested in joining his organization as crew chief and head fabricator. This was one of several opportunities offered to me, and I said I would talk to him, and after the race I came down to his shop, looked the facilities over; they only had four or five cars and most of those were destroyed, pretty rough, you might say. But Chuck convinced me to take the job.

"It didn't take long for me to appreciate Chuck and Lo. I've never worked for anyone with the understanding that those two people have. They have such a high tolerance level, I don't see how they can do it.

When things go wrong, they get positive, more positive, pat you on the back and say, 'Don't worry about it. These things are going to happen.' I'm harder on myself than they are on me, because I want to see this team win *for* them and *because* of them. They deserve it.

"When I began at Bahari, Michael Waltrip was the driver, and I didn't know what to expect from him. And he, I'm sure, didn't know what to expect from me. All he knew was what his brother Darrell and others in racing could tell him about me. He seemed to have confidence that I could help him get the job done.

"I observed the team beginning with North Wilkesboro in October 1989. I noticed the team needed some work, some polishing of the crew members. We needed to get organized, to be prepared for things to happen. We also needed better cars and equipment, and Chuck and Lo were ready to step up and do that. They said, 'Whatever you need, we will supply in order to get the job done.' And we began. . . .

"It takes a period of time for a driver and crew chief to work together and understand each other. The crew chief has to know what the driver is looking for in a car, and the driver has to be able to relate back to the crew chief what he's feeling and needs. In 1990, we had some pretty good runs and finished the season in good shape. Five times we finished in the top five. Our best finish was third in the Mello Yello 500 at Charlotte.

"A cylinder was messed up and we finished thirty-eighth, but we went on to finish fifth at Atlanta, losing to Ken Schrader, who made one less pit stop than we did. Three weeks later we dominated at Darlington, finishing third to Ricky Rudd and Davey Allison. Most important, we showed everyone we could run up front, and that gained us some respect through the garage.

"You can tell when you become a contender. Before then, other crew chiefs and team members would walk by and never speak to you or never come around your car and talk to you. They only visit the big boys, and now all of a sudden, they began coming around and looking and talking and asking and trying to figure out what we were doing. And then other people began paying us compliments for the way the Bahari cars were beginning to look, noticing things had become more professional, and that made the whole team feel good. For the most part these have been the same crew members since the inception. They just needed some guidance. I had gained a lot of knowledge through the years working with other people, and I applied it here.

"I wouldn't say it's been the smoothest-running machine all the time. We've had hard times, but we've sat down, talked things out, and kept going. Chuck Rider's calm ways have been an important factor, and so has my maturity. Chuck has helped me mature, and I will give him that credit. Now I look at things with a different perspective. He has shown me different ways of working out problems rather than by just being hard-nosed. When I first came here, he referred to me as 'the drill sergeant.' In the past two years he has softened me, mellowed me. I can now say, 'Let it go. It's not that serious. Let it run its course, and we'll get back on the track.'

"I've learned that getting along with the driver, being able to communicate, is more important than the weight of a spring. You keep coming back to that word: communication. It's what it takes to make a Winston Cup team go. I guess a marriage is the same way, isn't it?

"Looking forward to 1992, I would say Ford's cylinder heads give them a horsepower advantage. GM has a new cylinder head, but at this time it hasn't shown anyone anything good, but it's like any new piece: You have to work on it, and you'll see where the gains are. We have to use it starting in July, so we have seven months of research and development to make that piece better than the piece we have.

"One of the biggest things that keeps me going, it's a total team effort. I am only as good as the people working under me and with me. I never say they work *for* me. When we finally win, we're *all* going to win. When we lose, we *all* lose. We'll learn from our mistakes and try to prevent them from happening again. Some things are unpreventable, but if there is a way to prevent it, that's what we work on.

"I don't know how to express it enough: I couldn't do my job without the other guys on the team. Neither could the driver. Neither could the owner. And we couldn't do it without a good owner and a good driver. I'll wash your back, you wash mine. It's got to be a full circle. I'm proud to say there is no backstabbing on our team. No one is jockeying for position. This is very rare in racing, and it all comes from our owner, Chuck Rider. He's one of the best there is."

George Bradshaw

LAP 26

George Bradshaw

Luck Finds a Way

Chuck Rider, co-owner of Bahari Racing, owns more than a hundred parts stores. George Bradshaw, co-owner of Tri-Star Racing, was the owner of *two* auto parts stores when he became involved in racing. To make the story seem even more improbable, Bradshaw picked as his driver Bobby Hamilton, after Hamilton starred behind the wheel during a Winston Cup race that was filmed for the Tom Cruise movie *Days of Thunder*.

In another in a series of unusual events, Bradshaw got Country Time lemonade drink as a sponsor after the Country Time racing simulator was stolen, and Chuck Rider's Bahari Racing hired Tri-Star to build it a new one for a trade show.

Little of Tri-Star's history is commonplace, and unlikely as it may seem, in 1991 Bobby Hamilton in George Bradshaw's car won Rookie of the Year honors.

GEORGE BRADSHAW: "In 1987 a young driver named Derrike Cope and car owner Fred Stokes opened a race shop here in Hendersonville. They came into my auto parts store and bought paint and miscellaneous auto parts.

"Twenty years ago I owned a Late Model Sportsman, which ran on what is now the Busch Grand National circuit. We paid $800 for one of Cecil Gordon's old Chevrolets. At the time I was working in an auto parts store, worked eight to five-thirty, went home to eat, and then went to the race shop and helped fabricate the car until eleven at night. Back then you could run one engine for half a season, because most races were twenty-five lappers or maybe fifty. On a half-mile dirt track like Greenville Pickens you might only put twenty-five miles on the engine during a race, fifty at the most.

"Then I wanted to participate more as a driver, so I got out of Sportsmen and began racing motorcycles. I did that for three years, and I'm still carrying a trophy around on my leg.

"I raced a 250 Stiletto for $5 and $10 trophies. I was in my early twenties. Our daughter was born in October, and the following April I entered a race about six miles from here with a total purse of $1,000. I had had pretty good success, but in this race I fell and broke my leg and was on crutches for about thirteen months. I had a brace on my leg for a year and a half, and after that I realized I had obligations to meet, a family to raise, so I got out of racing, got into the auto parts business for myself, and got consumed in my work. I'm kind of a workaholic—whatever I'm involved in, I'm very competitive, want to be the best I can.

"My business pretty well started with zero. I had been auto parts manager in a Chevrolet dealership in Brevard, and then a cousin's husband came to Hendersonville and opened an auto parts store, and he didn't know anything about the business. I had been in it seven years, so I opened the business for them, spent six months getting it on its feet, and then I went up to Skyland near Asheville and purchased a second store—we were partners in both stores. I had mortgaged my house, so I started in the red.

"I opened that second store on December 1, 1971, and four days later my partner came to me and said, 'I have tax problems. I'm going to give you half of this store and take your half of this Skyland store.' The Skyland store was going to be much more profitable, but I thought, 'What can I do?' So I agreed. I came back and turned that first store around. Here's how I did it.

"I was selling auto parts. Other stores were selling the same auto parts, same quality, same price. There are no bargains. I had to make a profit, like the other stores, and I decided the way to do it was to offer services with the sale. I tried to give the customer more for his money—not cheaper parts, but rather better service than anyone else. If he was having a problem, I would help. I'd advise him and give him the right part so he wouldn't have to make two or three trips.

"I always told my employees, 'We are in a service business. Their car is broken-down. They're mad.' Very few people come in in a happy mood. Things always cost more than they anticipate. So we had two strikes against us. If we didn't treat them right and try to sympathize with them and give them their money's worth, they would go somewhere else.

"I came to Hendersonville, opened a store in '81 where there were already thirteen other auto parts stores, and right now I have one of the highest-volume stores in the state of North Carolina. We are the biggest All Pro accounts in the state.

"And every year until 1991, both stores have had sales increases, even in the down years. It's a misconception that when new car sales are down, people are fixing up old cars. It's just the opposite. Most people take care of a car and trade it in for a better one after two or three years.

"What I enjoy is the competition of selling. If you come in and you need a set of brakes for your car, I have the brakes and you have the money, so I'm competing with you. Same way when we go out on a racetrack. It was a challenge to sell him the part I had, and to build a good relationship to where he would want to come back.

"And skipping way ahead, it's the same way in racing. I try to do more for our sponsor. Just painting 'Country Time' on the side of our car is not going to do a whole lot for them. We entertain their customers and their people. If there is any way I can assist them in selling lemonade or helping entertain their customers, we do it, because without them, we'd be back to running six or seven races a year, or no races. When I go at something, I want to succeed at it.

"And when Fred came into my store, I could see what they were trying to do, and I enjoyed it, got the bug again. I helped them by becoming an associate sponsor, helped them work on it. It was a low-budget operation. They had great expectations, but it was tougher to break into Winston Cup racing than anticipated.

"In '87 Fred went along without a sponsor. You don't acquire a sponsor overnight—there are too many people out there looking. It's not an overnight success. Derrike didn't have a magic last name like Petty or Allison or Waltrip. You can be a son or grandson to a Petty or a brother to a Waltrip or Wallace and you have name recognition.

"Derrike had run on the Winston West circuit and won Rookie of the Year. He came up three points short of winning the Winston West championship. It was a natural progression for him to move South and go for the big bucks in racing.

"Fred was a successful businessman, and he invested quite a bit of his own money. In '87 and '88 I told him, 'If you can get into the sport and stay in it, it will be just as valuable as having an NFL or a baseball franchise.' After all, there are only thirty to forty teams out there. I'm no guru and don't profess to be, but I could see racing was a great way for Corporate America to get name recognition to sell their products.

"Despite my advice, Fred decided he wanted to close up shop, and I felt like this was something I wanted to get involved in, and Derrike stayed on and got involved with Dave Fuge and Mark Smith, and I continued as an associate sponsor—B&W Auto Supplies—and went to races with them. And when Derrike found Purolator with Jim Testa, I stayed on with them as an associate sponsor. I was just doing it to participate. I was selling auto parts to the locals. They weren't going to come from Alabama or Watkins Glen to buy parts from me. I did it because I enjoyed it.

"In '88 Derrike raced with Testa, and in '89 went three races when Testa, who was in the car business and had some health problems, shut down the operation. He called Purolator and said he was getting out of racing.

"Derrike had a sponsor and no car to drive, so he lined up with Bob Whitcomb, who had cars and no driver and no sponsor. Testa, meanwhile, had hired Dave Fuge and Mark Smith to work with him, so Dave, Mark, and I decided to buy out Testa's cars and equipment in a fire sale.

"I had saved up some money. When you go to work for yourself and you are working seven days a week, twelve to fourteen hours a day, it doesn't leave time to spend much money. I always believed in investing, and I invested a lot of money in Tri-Star Motorsports. I have not reaped any returns as yet. I felt like it would be five years before we broke even.

"We didn't have a sponsor, didn't have a driver. But we knew we had a good team. Dave had been in the car-building business in the state of Washington and had been crew chief and chassis consultant for Fred Stokes and Jim Testa. Mark Smith had worked for Mopar, Fisher Engineering. He built motors for David Hobbs and Willy T. Ribbs in Trans Am racing. Dave knew chassis and Mark knew engines, and we formed a partnership. And a lot of our people had worked for Fred Stokes when he gave up too early and had been with Jim Testa when he gave up too early, and with those same people in 1991 we won Rookie of the Year and did really well for the first year, competing against teams with more money and more experience.

"The first race our new team went to was Talladega in early May of 1989. We took a driver, Ron Esau, who didn't have that much experience. He had driven a lot on the West Coast. We knew we needed to make a good impression, so we decided to rent an engine from RAHMOC. You pay $10,000 to rent an engine. Well, we went out and made half a lap with the engine in practice before qualifying, and it blew up going down the backstretch before we completed a single lap!

"In most cases, if the engine blows up, it's yours and you pay, but they realized it was something they had done, which is very unusual in this sport, and so they refunded our money, and we had to qualify with one of our own engines. We hadn't done that much work on it, and we qualified thirty-somethingish.

"Esau ran 117 laps and crashed, tore up the race car. We won $2,000 that day, and it cost us $50,000 to run that race.

"When we got the car back to the shop, it didn't look like the damage was that bad. But we had to put a front clip on it, and you're looking at a $10,000 repair bill. We had rented an engine to try to attract a sponsor, and you're not going to attract a sponsor finishing thirty-eighth in a race.

"I was a little naive when I got into this sport. For any one race, there are thirty-nine losers and one winner, and if I don't win, I'm disgusted. I knew we had a good engine builder and chassis man, but I was a little naive as to what it really takes to go out there and compete against guys who had been doing it all their lives.

"In 1990 we changed our strategy. In '89, if a driver who was fairly capable came along and we had the money to run the race, we went into the rent-a-car business. We were the Budget Rent A Car of racing. We had the car and a skeleton crew, guys who worked night and day, but we went to some races with drivers we shouldn't have hired. We went on the premise it is better to be seen than not seen at all, but after '89 and the limited success we had, we looked at things a little differently. We decided we were only going to go if we had enough money to go, looked good, and had a good driver.

"Hut Stricklin had run second in '89 for Rookie of the Year, but after the season was over his car owner, Rod Osterlund, released him because he said he wasn't aggressive enough. I had gone to all the races, talked to people trying to attract a sponsor, and I watched Hut drive and was impressed with him. We talked to him about driving the Daytona 500 for us in '90. We came down with one car.

"We qualified second-round fastest and were sixteenth overall qualifying for that race. We went with our own engine and were in seventh or eighth place in one of the 125s. If we finished seventh, we were assured of getting into the 500 and starting in a good position.

"Hut was right there, steadily in seventh with one lap to go. Kenny Schrader and Mark Martin thought they were racing for the lead, but they were actually racing for second place, but Hut moved low to let them pass, slowed down, didn't want to take any unnecessary chances. He came out of turn four, heading for the finish, and Kenny spun out right in front of Hut, and there was no place for Hut to go, crashed into him and wiped out the car. It was totaled.

"We had only gone with one car. We had been assured of a starting spot in the 500, and here we were without a car. Kenny felt bad about it.

He made a mistake he shouldn't have made. Hut was disappointed, and we were too. Our success had been a surprise to a lot of people, not to ourselves.

"At the time the movie *Days of Thunder* was being shot, and Rick Hendrick was supplying cars for the movie. Rick Hendrick's car was the one that had taken us out, and he had some movie cars, and I approached Rick about them letting us use a backup car. They gave us a backup to a backup. They felt some responsibility and so they didn't charge us. Hut could have hit Darrell Waltrip's car, but he made an evasive move to keep from wiping out that car, and they appreciated that. This was a gesture on their part to compensate.

"This occurred on Thursday, and we had to start the race Sunday. We qualified thirty-fourth on speed, even though we didn't have a car to start.

"They gave us this old Lumina that was designed to be a road-course car, not designed for a speedway. It had no engine in it, no brakes, a hull of a car they were using in the crash scenes as part of the movie. They brought that car over, and everyone else said, 'There is no way.' Normally it takes a good four weeks in the shop to prepare a car for Daytona. Possibly you could do it in three weeks. We had to convert everything out of the crashed Pontiac into this Lumina—the motor, the suspension parts, put brake lines in it, fuel lines, put the fuel cell in it, make windows for it. And we accomplished all this in three days! On Saturday during the last practice, we got out and ran about three laps.

"The car was painted black primer. They won't let you run a primer car, so we borrowed paint from Richard Childress. We got a painter from Phil Barkdoll's team Saturday night after practice, and we got him to squirt a little paint in the primer and shot it clear, so it looked shiny black. We were number 18.

"We finished the race, came in thirty-third. It was a miracle to get the car on the racetrack.

"All along we were trying to secure a sponsor, and we came close. The Publix supermarkets car didn't make the field, and they were talking about giving us $25,000 for a one-race deal, but then we crashed.

"And after the race we had to take the Hendrick car apart and return it to him the way we got it, and that took a week because the enthusiasm for taking it apart was not nearly as great as it was in putting it together. We were very appreciative, though.

"We continued. We qualified at Atlanta and had a rocker arm break. Our search for a sponsor continued. We were pitching Hut for some sponsorships, but in 1990 before a race Davey Allison got hurt. Davey's first cousin is Hut's wife, Donnie Allison's daughter, Pam. Well, Davey passed out before the race at Rockingham, so Hut had to fill in and drive for him. Davey and some of the crew were involved in horseplay, and one of the crew members grabbed him by the nuts, and he passed out, and he went to the hospital and they couldn't find anything wrong, but NASCAR didn't want to take a chance, because they didn't know what had caused him to pass out.

"Bobby Allison then took Davey out of his car and put Hut in. We were still without a sponsor, and now we didn't have a good driver.

"I thought we were going to get Mello Yello as a sponsor. We put Brad Teague in the car. He was a capable driver. We went to Charlotte and qualified fourteenth, ran fairly decent in the Winston Open, the race for the nonwinners before the Open. We had run the race with a Mello Yello sponsorship, a one-race deal.

"The year before we had run Ernie Irvan in an ARCA race in Atlanta. Ernie was under contract with D. K. Ulrich and was looking for a better ride, so we got together to run that ARCA race. We qualified second, led 172 of 204 laps, dominated the race. We had talked Mello Yello into sponsoring us for that race, and the next morning we had an appointment with Brian Lanahan, who was branch manager for Mello Yello, Coca-Cola in Atlanta.

"We went in and were able to go in with a big presentation and a big trophy won the day before, only to find out they had gotten involved in the *Days of Thunder* movie deal and had committed money to that—the car Tom Cruise drove in the movie was a Mello Yello car. They were going to spend a million bucks and ended up spending $7 million. Anyway, they told me to get back in touch with them, and we'd talk about sponsorship in '91.

"In the meantime, when I called on them in '91, Brian Lanahan had moved on. They had a new branch manager, and I called him up for an appointment, and he didn't know who I was, didn't know Tri-Star Motorsports, and he was reluctant to even listen to our pitch. We lost out to a bigger name, Kyle Petty.

"Without a sponsor, we were reduced to running part-time and building some race cars. Then an odd event occurred that changed everything for us. The Country Time simulator, their show car, got stolen. A simulator doesn't have an engine in it. It has electronics, like a flight simulator. You get behind the wheel, shift gears, put on the brakes, and you watch yourself race on a 25-inch screen in front of you. If you go too fast, you spin out. It's a great marketing tool. They were making an appearance with it in Atlanta, and somebody got in the truck and trailer and drove it off.

"At the time Country Time was the sponsor for Bahari Racing, owned by Chuck Rider and Lowrance Harry. Chuck Rider owned All Pro Auto Sales, and I was in the auto parts business, and I was one of Chuck's big customers. He knew of our situation. Bahari was toward the end of the season and didn't have time to build another simulator, and so Chuck asked me if we would be interested in building one for him.

"The national sales meeting for Country Time was coming up in October. We had only a few weeks' time. Atari gave us the specs for the simulator.

"We signed the contract with the marketing firm for Country Time on a Thursday, and that night Hurricane Hugo hit! We were without power for eleven days and without a phone for seventeen days. We rented generators, and we completed the job two or three days ahead of schedule, and they were extremely proud, because it was much better than the previous simulator. Even though it was a show car and not a real race car, our guys take pride in everything they do, and it turned out to be an exceptionally good car.

"Four months later they found the stolen simulator. It was a shell. In 1990 Country Time and Maxwell House were cosponsors of the Bahari car, and so we took the old simulator and rebuilt it as a show car for General Foods and Maxwell House, so they could have two of them, and they are the only two in existence.

"When Bahari Racing and Country Time ended their relationship after 1990, and Country Time went looking for another race team, we were recommended because of the pride the guys had taken to build the simulator, that we could complete it on time under such adverse conditions. It spoke well for our determination, which was one of the traits they were looking for in a race team.

"At the same time we found a driver in Bobby Hamilton. We ran with Bobby in 1990 in the October race at Charlotte and qualified sixth, his first Winston Cup race. After drivers saw our performance, about fifteen drivers applied for the ride. We talked to Rick Mast, Chuck Bown, and to other drivers under contract I wouldn't want to name, in addition to Bobby, who I had seen drive for the first time in '89 when he qualified fifth in Phoenix driving one of the cars in the *Days of Thunder* movie.

"For that movie several locations were used. They put a camera in the movie cars in several Winston Cup races and filmed part of the action for the movie. Rick Hendrick's team prepared the movie cars, and Bobby was driving one of those cars, and in Phoenix he was actually leading the race, but they black-flagged him because it was embarrassing to have a movie car running up front. It was the next-to-last race of the season, and they got all the footage they needed, so he only got to drive part of the race.

"After that, I got to watching him drive Busch Grand National races, and he did real well. He didn't drive over his head. He wouldn't go storming into something and bounce off someone else. We had already experienced a driver who had smashed up our cars.

"Bobby's agent called us and asked for an interview, and we saw the determination he had. We saw his desire. You meet people and talk to them and read determination in their eyes. You can see that in talking to him. He had qualities we were looking for, so we ran him in the Charlotte race in '90, and he did real well. Ironically, in that first race he was involved in an accident early in the race. Dale Earnhardt crashed and some debris came up, and Bobby cut a tire. He was in the middle of turn one and two and ran over it and flattened his tire straighter than a wallet, and he wrecked up the car. But Bobby and Dave Fuge, who is a one-third owner and our crew chief, communicated well, and that's something you have to have.

"When we went to Country Time, we had several choices. Mike Chase, a Winston West driver, was one, but the driver we felt most comfortable with was Bobby. When I went to the first meeting with Country Time, they had fourteen teams on their list. We met at Michigan, they interviewed eight teams and narrowed it to four—us, Bud Moore and Morgan Shepherd, Alan Kulwicki, and Felix Sabates and Kyle Petty.

"After that meeting, they set up another meeting in New York with me and Bobby. He flew from Nashville, met me in New York, and we went up to the meeting in White Plains, New York, with Dick Stollard, who was the man who signed us to make the simulator.

"We went to a board meeting with one of the biggest corporations in America, General Foods, and they made us feel real comfortable. The people at Country Time were a real family-oriented group. There were marketing people with bells and whistles and a pony and dog show, and here were these two country boys setting down in a boardroom with the people from Country Time. They asked us direct questions and we answered them. We spoke from the heart, expressed determination we were going to win the Winston Cup championship, and I firmly believed that. I told them we would win Rookie of the Year. I told them the same thing I told Bobby, that we wanted them to be the only sponsor we ever had and that we wanted to have a long-term relationship.

"We were asking for $1.8 million. That's what it takes to run a season competitively, to do a good job. We didn't want to go out and ask for half that amount and run at the back of the pack. You get a stigma attached if you do. You're known as a back marker and you get a reputation as an also-ran. Tri-Star Motorsports is *not* going to be an also-ran.

"I'd have no enjoyment doing that. When we run back there, I'm not happy. Before you become competitive, you have to run back there, and I understand that, but . . .

"Country Time gave us less money than what we asked for, but they stepped it up in '92, and then we signed a three-year contract where we get an increase every year. And they have an option each year.

"We agreed to qualify for all twenty-nine races, and I told them I would refund one twenty-ninth of the sponsorship money for any race we didn't qualify. If we don't make that race, we didn't do our job. If we don't do our job, we don't want to get paid for it. I never want the hunger to be gone. So often you see free agents in baseball sign big contracts, and then the hunger is gone. I never want that.

"The deal is good for us and also for Country Time. Promoting a race team is the cheapest and the best form of advertising there is. Our sponsor uses racing to entertain customers. They come to Daytona and rent the Sheraton in Orlando, rent the Fun on Wheels park and bring in the influential buyers and the brokers who are their customers, and they go back home and place orders.

"Earlier we did a one-race deal with Diamond Ridge Reality. I had never heard of it. At Charlotte they didn't make the race, and we didn't have a sponsor and through Felix Sabates, who is friends with Gary Bechtold, we painted the car up in their colors. Diamond Ridge was a retirement facility in Charlotte, and Gary brought several of his key people in, and Caspar Weinberger was working for them as a consultant, brought a lot of people into the suites and condos at Charlotte and entertained them, and mostly he was rewarding the employees.

"When Country Time puts decals on that car, the job is not done. The car is just a tool. The way I look at it, that car is a 200-mile-an-hour billboard.

"I told Country Time what we would do for them, that we would win Rookie of the Year. We left the meeting feeling we could realistically finish in the top twenty.

"We went to Daytona, the first race, and in the 125-miler started in the tenth row, and finished tenth. Bobby drove a good, smart race. It was quite a feat, hard to duplicate. It was our first race with a major sponsor. It was the World Series, the Super Bowl, and we finished tenth!

"Our sponsor was elated. So were we. During the 1991 season we led the Rookie of the Year competition from the start. We started fourteenth at Talladega in May and went all the way to second place. We were the fastest car there. Dale Earnhardt was first, Darrell Waltrip third, and we had a rain delay during the race. We learned there are other factors in addition to putting out the fastest car.

"We lost radio communication with Bobby because there was a wire broken. He didn't pit when the leaders did. He didn't know, and so he lost the draft, and we wound up finishing twelfth, back in the pack. He learned something about drafting, and we learned some things as a team.

"It takes some time to learn to win. Even if you go out with the best car, you have to have the breaks go your way. The caution flags have to fall at the right times. A lot comes into play that you have to learn about. It's a tough sport.

"We had some other top ten finishes, and we won Rookie of the Year. We took a lot of pride in how we did. They based their whole advertising campaign for '92 on our winning it.

"We finished first among the rookie drivers seventeen times, Ted Musgrave won ten, and two other rookie drivers won the other two."

"The highlight was winning. The sponsor was putting some pressure on us. We won it by 17 points. Our average finish for the last ten races of the '91 season was 11.7 place. Earnhardt won the driving championship averaging in 8.9 place for the year. And that doesn't count a solid fifth-place finish we would have had if a $3 bolt that drove the oil pump hadn't broke with less than fifty laps to go in the race. The bolt broke, and that kicked the belt off, and the pulley came off, and there was no oil pressure, and it burned the bearings. We wound up finishing twenty-ninth.

"We completed the season having lost only one engine. We had *one* engine failure. We had one accident that was Bobby's making. We were at the first Pocono race, and he didn't feel comfortable with the track. Our car was out in left field, which happens every now and then, and he got in a situation where he was running too hard. Ted Musgrave got past him, and he passed Ted back, and he overdrove and crashed. We finished thirty-fifth. But what was so great, we came back to the second Pocono race and finished eleventh overall, two spots ahead of Ted.

"So we feel going into '92 we have a top-fifteen team. If you don't wreck and don't have engine problems, you're going to finish in the top ten most of the time.

"As Bobby and Mark and Dave and I gain more experience, this team has nowhere to go but up. We don't plan on the sophomore jinx. We will go to the races prepared.

"Bobby and I have meetings and set goals. One of his goals last year was to be accepted by the other drivers and not make rookie mistakes, like some of them do, to crash and take out some of the better cars, and I think over the year he has gained that respect. There are veteran drivers out there I call magnets. If there is an accident out there, they are going to be involved in it. It comes from being overaggressive and sometimes panicking. They drive right at the end of their hood.

"The successful drivers drive with their heads, not just with their feet, know when to drive aggressively, when to pace themselves and see two drivers ahead. If they see two cars beating and banging against each other and tempers are flaring, they have to know the personalities and be able to say, 'Somebody is going to get tired of this, and there is going to be an accident.' A lot of times I or Dave or Mark will tell Bobby, 'Be ready. There is an accident ready to happen.'

"We were involved in a wreck in Bobby's second race. He said later he should have known better. We tried to pass Joe Ruttman on the outside, and Joe's ego just didn't want to let the rookie pass him. Joe drove in too far and lost control, and his car went up toward the wall and wrecked Bobby. Part of the learning process is knowing who you can pass and when. You have to have the confidence the other driver isn't going to do something stupid.

"Most of the top drivers, the consistent drivers, wreck very seldom, and that comes from knowing where the edge is. Last year Harry Gant was a master at it.

"Ernie Irvan is one of the better drivers out there. He has the determination and winning attitude, but he doesn't have the experience yet, and he's gotten in trouble a time or two, caused some bad accidents, got a bad reputation. He had to go to Talladega and ask for forgiveness from all the drivers. It took a big guy to do that. At the drivers' meeting race director Dick Beaty said, 'It's a give-and-take situation, and sometimes you have to take it and not always give.'

"Dale Earnhardt is aggressive, but you see him crashing very seldom. He knows where that edge is. He can drive on the edge longer and more intensely than a lot of drivers will. He'll take an ill-handling car, a tenth-place car, and he'll stay fifth with it, where a lot of drivers couldn't. Other drivers seem to have a lapse, but he doesn't ever seem to have one.

"Darrell Waltrip has been good at knowing where the edge is, although he has been involved in some accidents not of his making. Early in his career Michael Waltrip, Darrell's brother, crashed quite a bit. One of the quotes I remember best is what Darrell told Michael: 'The only way you're going to win the race is to be there on the last lap.'

"Michael drives for Chuck Rider, a good friend. I've seen Michael mature, but he still hasn't won. Chuck had a choice between Derrike Cope and Michael Waltrip and chose Michael because of his last name. But Derrike has won the Daytona 500 and the Dover race, and Michael has yet to win a race—and that's not to say that Derrike is a better driver. The driver can only last so long on a father's or brother's name. You have to start winning, like Davey Allison. Kyle Petty stumbled along in this sport for ten years before Felix gave him some direction and he started winning. Kyle was just having a good time, and it was not a real job to him. But Felix gave him direction, and it matured Kyle, and I have the utmost respect for Kyle. I can remember after one race at North Wilkesboro, some of the drivers rolled up their windows on the way out so they wouldn't have to talk to the fans. It's a bear getting out of the infield. The fans crowd around the cars, and here Kyle was driving a Rolls-Royce, his wife Patty beside him, and he was reaching out his window signing autographs for everybody, doing the things his father had done, and he thoroughly enjoyed it. He was having as good a time as the fans were.

"I'll never forget what happened last year at Bristol. Bobby Hamilton was driving out of the track after the race, and little kids were coming up to him and he was signing autographs, and behind him drivers were blowing their horns, and they forced him to keep going.

"Afterward, he said, 'I just experienced the worst feeling I ever had in sports.' I couldn't figure out what it was. I said, 'What is it, Bobby?' He said, 'Not being able to sign those autographs for those kids.' He was afraid they might think he was stuck-up. He feels it's an honor when someone asks him for his autograph.

"I said, 'Just as long as you always have that attitude, you will make it.' Because without those fans buying the product and coming to the races, we wouldn't be here.

"Last year we spent more money than what Country Time gave us. We are doing what needs to be done to run and be competitive. We didn't use a penny of the Country Time money to build our shop. We used our own money to do that. If we had used their money for the shop, we wouldn't have had money for tires, and Bobby would not have finished as good.

"I don't expect to make money in this for the first three to five years. Country Time is a tremendous sponsor and works with us real well. Their business has doubled since 1988, and that's when they got involved in racing. There has to be some correlation between the success they are having and their sponsorship. Hopefully, as we grow, their sponsorship dollars will grow. We are real fortunate to have them.''

Kyle Petty (*l*) and Felix Sabates (*r*)

Felix Sabates

Only in America

It was the day before the race at the Michigan International Speedway, summer of 1985. The thermometer read 94 degrees.

Cale Yarborough had just finished his practice laps out on the track, and after he came into the garage and climbed out of the car, he put wet rags around the top of his neck and around his uniform.

Richard Petty's car was in the stall area right beside Yarborough's. Richard was stretched out on the ground, and he had a dozen or so rags soaked with water all over his face and uniform in an attempt to keep cool.

Into the garage walked two young drivers, Kyle Petty and Michael Waltrip. Kyle looked at his father and said, "King, you look like you're pretty hot." Kyle often called him King.

Richard said, "Doggone right it's hot. Wait till you get to be my age. The heat works a little bit different than for you kids prancing around here."

Kyle and Michael walked off laughing.

Richard looked at Cale and said, "I want to tell you one thing. That's my son. And Michael came and lived with me for about a year. I bought them a brand-new lawn mower that set out there, and the grass grew up around that lawn mower.

"I said to Kyle, 'Don't you think it's about time to go out and use that lawn mower to cut the grass?' And Kyle looked at Michael, who was standing with him, and Kyle said, 'I thought something was wrong with that lawn mower. It hadn't moved an inch, and we've given it three weeks now. I thought it would do something. We gave it a chance, and it hasn't done a thing.' "

Richard said to Cale, "I want to tell you, those two individuals there better be glad that they've got racing, because I don't know a single thing they can do other than that. I just hope they make it.''

For a long while there was a question whether Kyle Petty would "make it." He was part of a group of young racers, including Rick Wilson and Michael Waltrip, who enjoyed joyriding on Charlotte's streets on their motorcycles at high speeds. Those who knew better called them the Harley Group. Kyle was having a lot of fun in his life, but from 1979 through 1985 he failed to win a single Winston Cup race. He was criticized for not being hungry enough because he had grown up with a silver and Petty-blue spoon in his mouth.

Driving for the Wood Brothers, Kyle won a race at Richmond in '86 and another at Charlotte in '87, but after he was shut out in '88 observers continued to whisper that he wasn't serious enough about racing, that he preferred his guitar and the life of a country and western singer, though few felt he had the voice to make it professionally.

But then in 1989 Kyle was hired to drive for Felix Sabates, one of the new breed of self-made racing owners. Sabates got Petty to put away his guitar and concentrate on the business of winning races. In 1989 Petty won $117,000 in purses, and the next year he won a race at Rockingham, after which Sabates bought him a Rolls-Royce as a bonus. His winnings that year soared to $746,300.

As the race teams prepared for the '92 Daytona 500, experts recognized that the Mello Yello 42 Pontiac with Kyle Petty behind the wheel would be a contender, because of Kyle Petty's newfound maturity, and because Felix Sabates didn't get rich settling for anything less than success.

The team had but one question mark concerning '92. During the Winston 500 at Talladega in '91, Kyle Petty broke his left thigh bone in a horrific multicar crash, his first major accident. He missed part of the season, spending four months in therapy and training. His leg is healed, but the concern was whether Kyle Petty would continue to be the hard-charger he had been before the accident.

Felix Sabates's success is the story of America. Sabates fled Fidel Castro's Cuba in January 1959, wandering from Miami to Boston to Kansas City, then to Lexington, North Carolina, before moving permanently to Charlotte, where he worked as a dishwasher and parked cars in the airport for a rental car firm, making minimum wage.

Next he began selling electronic equipment for a Charlotte wholesaler. He was befriended by the owner, who admired his industriousness, and six years later his mentor permitted him to buy the company, lending him the money at a generous rate.

During an era when sales of electronics equipment boomed in America, Felix Sabates, through his hard work and foresight, became super-rich selling stereo systems, Nintendo and Atari video games, and computer products.

Sabates, one of the four original owners of the Charlotte Hornets basketball team, has always loved sports, and after he was approached to start a Busch Grand National team, Sabates was lured into the big leagues by his close friend, Rick Hendrick, who was selling off one of his teams. Sabates built a competitive race team that boasts Kyle Petty as his driver and Robin Pemberton as crew chief.

A multi-multi-millionaire, Sabates is as wealthy as any man in racing. He is in the same league as Hendrick, but for all his money, the SABCO Pontiac has won but two races, once each at Rockingham in 1990 and 1991, proving, as the old-timers contend, that money can buy speed but that money alone isn't enough to win consistently in Winston Cup racing.

Felix Sabates isn't fazed. He has faith in himself and his team, and why not, for it was his hard work and his ability to motivate his employees that reaped for him his large fortune in the first place.

FELIX SABATES: "I left Cuba when I was sixteen years old in 1959. My father was the head of a small conglomerate of different companies, a family-owned business, involved in jewelry and car dealerships, service stations, drugstores, cattle, and sugar.

"Fidel Castro took over Cuba in January of 1959, and the day he took over we knew we had a problem. Castro pretty much said he was going to wipe out everybody, and that's pretty much what he did. We were all afraid for our lives.

"It wasn't hard to leave Cuba. We went through a lot of gyrations, but it wasn't like I escaped in the middle of the night. I left through normal channels, through the United States Embassy, which was able to give me a visa to get out.

"I came by myself, landed in Miami, and from Miami I went to Boston to live with an uncle, and from there I went to Kansas City, Missouri, when my uncle moved, but I didn't get along with his wife, so I left. By that time the Catholic Church had relocated a lot of Cubans all over the United States. My mother and seven brothers and sisters were relocated to Lexington, North Carolina. My dad was still in Cuba. He couldn't get out yet. So I moved to Lexington, and in 1962 I worked for a furniture factory there, sanding legs and doing odd jobs, making about 80 cents an hour. They let me work overtime, so I was making about $65 a week. I was the only one in my family who was working, so I had to support them.

"In late 1963 I moved to Charlotte and went to work at the airport parking cars for National Car Rental. I washed cars, put gas in them. I got a big raise, pushing my salary to $1 an hour. That was a *big* raise.

"Then I went to work at City Chevrolet, working with Rick Hendrick selling cars. Rick didn't own it then. In 1967 I caught a break and was given the opportunity to come to work for Top Sales Company, a distributor of electronics equipment, housewares, and automotive products throughout the southeastern United States. Six years later, I bought the company.

"When I began at Top Sales, I was a salesman. The gentleman who owned the company, Walter Reich, was getting old, and he had two sons who had no interest at all in coming into the business, and he became like a second father to me. He was the one who gave me the opportunity to come into the business and buy it.

"He wanted less than a couple hundred thousand to buy it, which in those days might have been $10 million, but he gave me five years to pay him off, and I paid him back in three years.

"People try to say I made my money selling Nintendo games or Atari, but that is not true. Everyone wants to put a label on what you do. Our business grew within its roots, the sale of electronic equipment and computers. Nintendo and Atari were product lines we sold, but we never had one product that dominated more than 20 percent of our sales.

"If I follow any one business philosophy, it is to spread your risk. Don't put all your eggs in one basket. This is why Winston Cup racing sometimes is very dangerous, because you have everything in one car, one team, one driver. I'm thinking that perhaps the multiple-team philosophy that Rick Hendrick has is the way to do it.

"If I have a management philosophy, it's to give your people enough rope to hang themselves. I'm a hands-off manager. I don't tell people how to do their job. I tell them how I'd like for them to do it, and then they execute, and it works for me, because I've had the same people—including the president—for seventeen years, and I don't have many personnel changes. People don't leave, and we don't fire them, so it works for me personally. You must give people enough responsibility to do their jobs, and if you do, they will be fine.

"Prior to being in racing, I was one of the two original founders of the Charlotte Hornets basketball team. George Shinn and myself were first, and then Rick Hendrick, and Cy Behackle came in at the very end. We paid $32 million in 1987.

"George Shinn bought all of us out and now owns it himself. Recently I offered him $85 million for the team, and he turned me down. George wants to buy a baseball team, and someday if he ever gets a chance to buy one, maybe he will sell the Hornets back to us.

"Ted Condor is the man who got me involved in Winston Cup racing. Ted's an independent salesman, and he was renting an office from me upstairs, and one day he brought driver Bobby Hillin to my office and told me he wanted to start a Busch Grand National team.

"I thought it would be kind of fun, so I put up a couple thousand dollars, and we ran our first year and won a race. That year Teddy owned a third, Bobby a third, and I owned a third.

"That same year I had a one-race deal with Peak antifreeze to run a Winston Cup race in October at Charlotte. Car number 47. Peak was going to sponsor our Busch car the next year. I wasn't interested in running Winston Cup more than one race.

"Rob Moroso had a shop right across the street from ours. Rob, who was eighteen at the time, was walking by our driveway one day, and I saw him. I said, 'Robby, want to drive for us?' He said, 'Sure, how much do you want me to pay you?' I laughed. I said, 'No, we'll pay you.'

"We qualified sixteenth and finished sixteenth. We were happy. It was the start of Robby's Winston cup career.

"Before the next year Rick Hendrick called me one day and said, 'I have to sell one of my teams, because I have too many. Chevrolet is telling me I can't have four teams.'

"I met with Rick and Gary Nelson, and at the time Kyle Petty was looking for a ride. I knew Kyle from the Busch Grand National circuit, liked him, and so I bought the team from Rick Hendrick.

"When I got in with the Winston Cup, I had three goals in mind. I didn't want to make the same mistake a lot of car owners made, coming into the sport and blowing their brains out the first year financially, so I was looking for a driver I could take out and sell, to package as a driver and a spokesman. I talked to quite a few drivers, and I felt Kyle was the best spokesman out there by far. There is no one who even comes close to Kyle. That was one consideration.

"Number two, he had the Petty name. And number three, I felt that Kyle had never been given a chance to develop himself as a race car driver. Believe me, a lot of people questioned why I hired him.

"He had been picking the guitar and singing. But I felt he hadn't had anyone to work with him to give him the moral support he needed, like

I have given him. He was twenty-eight at the time, and I felt he was just coming into his own because of age, and I felt he had a great opportunity to better himself with me. So I took a chance on him. Everybody questioned me. Drivers came by and told me I was crazy. One car owner said, 'You're crazy. Kyle isn't serious about being a race car driver.' As I said, at the time he was picking his guitar.

"I sat down with Kyle and I said, 'You have two choices: You can either drive or pick the guitar. You can't do both.'

"He said, 'Picking the guitar is a hobby.'

"I said, 'Well, do it in the shower. Don't do it in front of a TV camera.' And he came to work for me with that understanding, and Kyle is at the point now where he is going to explode as a race car driver. He could be a dominant factor like Dale Earnhardt has been.

"I picked Gary Nelson to be the crew chief. Gary was part of the Hendrick R&D team. He is one of the most analytical persons I ever met, besides being one of the nicest. He's very innovative, good with people, and one of the reasons I bought the team from Rick Hendrick was because of Gary, his reputation and past record.

"This year Gary wanted a change in his career. He had the chance to become the head inspector for NASCAR.

"We talked about it, I felt it was a good opportunity for him, and I helped him get it.

"I must have had twenty phone calls from crew chiefs. A lot of them wanted to work for me; most all of them wanted to work with Kyle. I never met anyone who doesn't like Kyle. Our team has a good reputation.

"Robin Pemberton was the crew chief in the 6 car driven by Mark Martin. He wanted to come with us, and I chose him because the Mark Martin team has been very good for three years. Robin is very innovative, and I felt he'd be the one who would get along with me and the rest of the team the best.

"We're pointing toward the Daytona 500 in '92. I think we're going to win. We should have won it last year. We led the most laps of anybody, and with ten laps to go, Davey Allison and Dale Earnhardt got into a wreck in front of us. We had the best car that day. They got into a wreck, and we got into it, and Ernie Irvan ended up the winner.

"Any time we go to the racetrack I think we're going to win. You have to think that, to have that attitude. I don't go to the racetrack thinking we're going to finish second. I go thinking we're going to win, so I think we're going to win the Daytona 500. I think we're going to win *every* race we enter. I know it's not realistic, but that's my goal.''

LAP 28

Derrike Cope

The 1990 Daytona 500 Winner

In 1986 Bob Whitcomb sold his sand and gravel business for significant millions. A New Hampshire boy, Whitcomb owned Arthur Whitcomb Inc., which helped build Interstate 91 along the New Hampshire-Vermont border. The company owned twenty sand, gravel, and ready-mix concrete plants. It was a thriving business, and when he sold it, Bob Whitcomb needed an outlet for his energies. He decided he would start a Winston Cup team and go racing.

In 1988, Whitcomb hired Ken Bouchard as his driver. Financed solely by Whitcomb's money, Bouchard, from Fitchburg, Massachusetts, won Rookie of the Year honors. So far, so good.

The next year began disastrously. Bouchard finished a respectable sixteenth in the Daytona 500, but after he ran thirty-eighth at Rockingham, thirtieth at Atlanta, and twenty-second at Darlington, Bob Whitcomb made a discovery rookie owners make every year: Winston Cup racing is incredibly difficult to break into successfully and, even if you're running a limited schedule, it's a heavy drain on the bank account. Whitcomb was learning Junior Johnson's first commandment of racing: ''The best way to make a small fortune in racing is to start with a big one.''

After the Darlington disappointment, Bob Whitcomb called team members together and told them he was closing the doors. Without a sponsor, he could no longer afford to continue.

Two days later, he was sitting at his desk when the phone rang. It was the president of Purolator filters. The owner of the Purolator race team, Jim Testa, was ailing and was getting out of racing. Purolator was looking for a new team to sponsor. If Whitcomb would fire his driver and hire Derrike Cope, Whitcomb could have the sponsorship for the remainder of the '89 season.

393

Derrike Cope

That year Bob Whitcomb Racing finished in the top ten four times. Cope finished ninth at Michigan, sixth at the second Michigan race, eighth at Dover, and sixth at Charlotte in October—but then there were the disasters, like the one at Watkins Glen where the engine died after three laps. Whitcomb saw Cope had the ability to win races, but the question in his mind was whether his large fortune would continue to shrink so badly he would have to get out before he ever saw his first victory.

Going into the Daytona 500 of 1990, Bob Whitcomb was questioning his staying power. Purolator was giving him less than half of what he needed to run the full schedule. The rest of the money had to come out of his own pocket. If nothing significant happened in '90, he could not continue. After putting $5 million of his own money into the team, he decided that enough was enough: His team would have to do something spectacular in order to inspire Purolator to up its sponsorship dollars.

At the Daytona 500 in 1990, Derrike Cope trailed Dale Earnhardt going into the final lap. Earnhardt, the three-time driving champion, had never won a Daytona 500. But Earnhardt ran over debris on the track, his tire blew, and while Earnhardt's car careened out of control, Derrike Cope crossed the finish line first, shocking the racing world.

Proving the victory was no fluke—as his competitors whispered it was—Cope went on to win at Dover, and at the end of the year Bob Whitcomb signed a three-year deal with Purolator, giving him substantially more than $2 million a year and putting him on a par with the most competitive teams.

Winning the Daytona 500 was a dream come true for Cope. It provided Bob Whitcomb Racing with a purse of $188,150, it gave Purolator the impetus to greatly increase its support for the team, and it enabled Bob Whitcomb to remain in racing. Such can be the importance of winning the Daytona 500.

DERRIKE COPE: "I was born in San Diego and lived there until I was four, and then I moved to the Seattle-Tacoma area. My father was a top fuel drag racer, a professional from Southern California, and his brothers, my uncles, were also involved. When we moved to the Pacific Northwest, he retired from drag racing and opened an engine-rebuilding facility.

"I had played baseball since I was six years old, and that's what I wanted to do professionally. As I got to high school I became more emphatic that professional baseball was what I wanted to do, and racing took a backseat. I was a catcher. I was scouted by the Chicago Cubs organization. I went to Whitman College in Walla Walla, Washington, and during a game my cleat got stuck in the grass and I had a complete blowout of my right leg, and it ended all thoughts of my playing baseball. Rehabilitation would have been very long, and I had no mobility. The knee didn't become straight for three years.

"It was devastating. I had a very severe void in my life. Basically, playing baseball was all I did my entire life. I played, worked out, ran. When that happened, I went to work for my dad, and I didn't know what to do with myself. I didn't know where to turn, because when you play in front of crowds and then the cheering stops, it's a *very* large void to fill.

"I was very fortunate that my brother was involved with a Late Model Sportsman race car along with some of the guys in my dad's shop. I started helping him and got interested, and I got behind the wheel, and *that's* when I felt like that was what I was meant to do.

"My father bought us a '67 Chevelle, a very old stock car, something for us to cut our teeth on. My father wanted to see if we were willing to put that much effort into it. My brother and I traded off. One night he'd race; one night I raced. At the end of the year my father asked us what we wanted to do. My brother said he wanted to chase women and play slow-pitch softball. I said I wanted to drive a race car.

"My father had sponsored Jackie Cooper, a prominent West Coast late-model Sportsman driver. He was retiring. I made a deal with him that I could use the car, a Pontiac Ventura, and I would return it to him at the end of the year in as good a shape or better.

"The winter of 1979–80 I started working on the car with the help of Dave Fuge, who now is co-owner of the Country Time lemonade car. Dave was working for Bill Schmidt out of Southern California, and I would call him on the phone, and he would tell me how to put a front-end clip on this car. So with the help of Dave and Jay Disophina, we got the car ready to go racing.

"When I started, my father sat down and looked at racing, and he laid out each step that it would take to drive in Winston Cup racing. He asked me, 'We have to look at all the options. Do you want to go Indy racing? Do you want to drive Winston Cup?' I said, 'I like Winston Cup.'

"He said, 'I think that's where the future is. That's where the sponsors are going to be, where the longevity is. You need to be in Winston Cup.'

"He said, 'If you're going to be successful, there are a lot of things you're going to have to do, and one of them is to surround yourself with the best people possible, and to be successful, you're going to have to be an excellent spokesman outside the race car.' So I took speech classes at Fort Steilacoom Community College in Tacoma. And my father made me very accessible to the media. When they needed me to do radio spots, TV spots, or sign autographs, my father let me off work, and I became more comfortable at it. He's a very, very smart man. If it weren't for him, I would not have gotten to Winston Cup racing.

"By 1982 I was building my own motors, assembling, dynoing, doing cylinder head port work—everything. I have an excellent feel for a motor—that's my specialty—and I also did some chassis work, built my race cars myself, so I do have some chassis knowledge.

"People don't realize that the majority of the drivers have had to cut our teeth and work very, very hard, scratch and claw to get this far in the sport, that it takes time. You just don't get into one of these race cars and overnight be a success. You have to serve your apprenticeship and work very hard and become proficient in a lot of different areas.

"My father and I tried to surround ourselves with the best possible people. I was tutored very well. I didn't make a lot of the mistakes some racers go through, because of Dave Fuge's tutoring. He had been with Ron Eden, who was a very, very big name on the West Coast, very smooth, very smart. Dave tutored me, and I may have bypassed some of those mistakes.

"He would say, 'Try to get a feel. Try to sit back in the seat, relax, feel the race car, and understand what the race car is telling you.' He wanted me to relate to the race car, and then to relate back to David what I was feeling so he could change the car and make it go faster.

"I remember when I first got into a race car, it was all a new experience. I remember vividly going down the front straightaway at Yakima Speedway, thinking I was just hauling the mail, and Ron Eden, Don Dowdy, and Harry Jefferson passed me so fast. I thought, 'How will I ever be able to get to that point? Those guys are incredible.'

"But every time I got into the race car, I learned something. I was always asking questions. I would talk to Don Dowdy or Ron Eden, and they were always very receptive, and I would listen intently and I'd go back and tell David. I'd say, 'I want to try that to feel that.'

"For instance, when you're driving the car into a corner, you have to make sure you're always turning left. Well, lots of times the car is loose going into the corner, and it'll turn to the right. But as a young race car driver, you aren't able to tell that. When you go into the corner at high speed, you do something, but you don't actually know what you're doing, and Dave was trying to make me aware of what my hands were doing without looking at them—at those speeds you don't dare look down at them—to know whether I was turning to the right if it was loose or turning left.

"He taught me to fixate on my hands and to know what I was doing and still be able to drive the car and look way ahead. Because you have to look way beyond your hood. You have to look *where you want the car to go*, and at the same time know if you are turning left or right. A driver also has to know if a car has what we call yaw—going into the corner the tail end gets out from underneath you. If the car goes in the corner and wants to plow the front end into the wall, sometimes you can feel it tighten in the steering wheel. It's an indicator. You feel it all in your hands and in your butt. And that's where David would tell me, 'Be relaxed and calm in the race car so you can *feel* and absorb all the things the race car is telling you.'

"My first year in 1980 I won one race against some excellent race car drivers. I won Rookie of the Year. The next year I was offered a ride with George Jefferson, one of the only Ford owners on the West Coast at that time, and that first year we had a very unsuccessful year. He had some antiquated equipment, and everyone started saying I was a flash in the pan.

"At that point I didn't have a lot of experience to draw from. I was looking at myself, trying to stay receptive, thinking, 'Maybe I am doing something wrong.' But the Ford was a rear-steer car, and I had been used to a front-steer car. I had seen myself as the problem, but at the end of the year we decided we could not be successful with those cars, and with George's blessing, David opted to build a new car, a very innovative-styled car, and in 1982 I had my first big, successful year, and that was a turning point.

"It was a lean year for George in the logging business, and I helped finance it a little bit, but George later paid me back, and from that point through 1985 George funded the entire program.

"That 1982 season I sat on the pole in seven of the thirteen events, and I won seven times, won the track championship, and finished second in the overall Sportsman championship. The next year I won six races and won both the track championship and the overall Sportsman championship, and that year I drove a Winston West car, and in my first Winston West race, at Portland Speedway, I sat on the pole. We cut a tire and finished fifth.

"On the West Coast the late-model Sportsman cars were also Winston West cars. They were heavy, so all my driving came in the heavy cars suited to Winston West driving, and that was a big plus for me.

"The most successful Winston West drivers were also Late Model Sportsman drivers, like Don Dowdy, Ron Eden, Harry Jefferson.

"In 1984, when I ran my first full season in Winston West, we acquired one of the first major sponsors on the West Coast, the Southland Corporation, owner of 7-Eleven convenience stores. We were the only Ford on the entire West Coast, and we had some factory help. Rod Campbell from Campbell and Co., a firm that used to find major sponsors and do PR work for Ford, brought us to Detroit, and we spent five days with them, toured their facilities and Jack Roush's facilities, and they went to work to help us acquire a sponsor, and we carried the colors of Southland Corporation in 1984 to run the full season in Winston West.

"I won two races and halfway through the season locked up Rookie of the Year and went into the Winston Cup race at Riverside with a 10-point lead for the driving championship, only to have motor trouble at Phoenix and lose to Jim Robinson by four points. I came very close to being the first driver in the thirty-one-year history to win the rookie title *and* the driving championship.

"In 1985 we ran fast but broke a lot of motors. We were sponsored but were still underfinanced. Most Winston West owners are self-employed and run their race teams as a hobby. I was doing the motors myself, buying used parts from the East Coast racers. I was using one-race parts from Bill Elliott, and we got to where we were so down on funds we couldn't buy new pieces. My crew chief, Jackie Johnson, used to work for Bud Moore. He made the cars work very well. I drove them very, very hard, and we ended up breaking a lot of those pieces.

"We were running up front, leading races, but breaking at the end.

"The next year I met two wealthy, prominent Seattle businessmen, Warren Rizore and Steve Banchero, who wanted to go auto racing. They wanted to go East, and so the day after Christmas the three of us packed up and set up shop at Campobello, South Carolina, close to Spartanburg, because Jackie Johnson was close to Bud Moore, had friends in the area, and it was neat for him to have a team there in Campobello.

"We were late getting started. We didn't get a car done until April 1986. We went to Martinsville for the first race, and I qualified seventeenth, sat between Harry Gant and Neil Bonnett and finished ninth.

"The next race was at Talladega. The biggest track I had ever run was in Phoenix, one mile but very flat and no sensation of speed. Riverside had a long straightaway, but I had never been on anything bigger than a five-eighths-mile track. At Talladega, they were running 208 miles an hour.

"My first time there, I was out there testing. We were running 190-something miles an hour, but I was lifting my foot off the gas pedal going into the corners. I was talking to Ron Bouchard and I told him it was very hard for me not to lift and at the same time squeeze back on the throttle. At Talladega the banking turns the race car, and the air holds the car on the ground.

"Ron took my car out and ran around flat-footed and said the car was fine and would go around flat out, so that gave me confidence to go ahead and know I could do it. I didn't want to crash, because it was the only car we had. And once I knew the car would go under a flat foot, it was then a matter of him telling me, 'Take your left foot and stick it on top of your right foot, and keep her down.'

"So I went down the back straightaway and put my left foot on top of my right foot, and I said to myself, 'This time she's staying down,' and I drove through turns three and four flat-footed for the first time, and when I came to one and two I took my left foot and put it back on the floorboard, and I ran a 202. It was quite an experience.

"We didn't run that race. We were only testing, and the next place we went was the Charlotte Motor Speedway.

"When I first arrived, I sought out Richard Childress. He bought me lunch in the cafeteria in the infield, and he and Dale Earnhardt talked to me about the racetrack and how Dale drove the car in the corners, how they rolled out of the throttle and used a little bit of the brake and never got off the gas all the way, and then put it back down to keep the car tight going into the corners.

"Bill Elliott told me the same thing. Those things you learn by someone telling you. Earnhardt and Elliott, two fantastic drivers, gave me insight into something that worked for them, and I was able to master it and use it. I was serving an apprenticeship, and if you are humble and receptive and ask for help, those people will help you—to the point that you are fast and running well, and then you are on your own. But if you're new, they don't want to see you get in trouble, because they could be behind you when you get in trouble.

"We qualified at Charlotte, started thirty-fifth, but had a distributor problem and finished thirtieth.

"At that point my car owner, Warren Rizore, had visions that we should be winning races. We had finished ninth at Martinsville, and he thought we should go to Charlotte and win the race. He felt if we were spending a million dollars, we should be winning. When it didn't happen, he got disenchanted. He felt he was a little fish in a big pond, and we pulled our horns in. After the Darlington race in September, we pulled up stakes and I drove back across the United States.

"I was under a three-year contract, and so we ended up running the remainder of the season in the Winston West.

"I told Warren, 'I feel I belong in Winston Cup. If I found another situation to go back to Winston Cup racing, would you let me out of my contract?' He said he would.

"I went to work. It's not easy to find a million dollars. I didn't have fifty dollars.

"I am very diligent. I wanted to be in Winston Cup racing. I had had a taste of it, and I felt I belonged on the East Coast.

"There was to be an awards banquet in Las Vegas for the Winston West circuit, and I didn't want to go, but my father said, 'You ought to go. Go down and see the people and be seen and talk.' So I flew down there, and I ran into Fred Stokes, who had been running a Winston West car. He was sitting at the bar, and I sat down and started talking to him. He asked me about what had happened back East. He was interested in going East, and I told him I wanted to go back, and he asked if Warren would let me out of my contract to go back East. I said he would.

"We did some more talking, corresponded, and when Fred wanted to go, Warren was a man of his word and let me go. I went out and loaded the truck and the day after Christmas again I left Washington and drove Fred's equipment along the southern route toward our destination of Hendersonville, North Carolina. Fred had a crew chief who was friends with car builder Banjo Matthews, who lived in Hendersonville.

"We got settled and got ready to prepare a car for Daytona for the '87 season. We weren't that fast, but I ran a good qualifying race, finishing twelfth.

"My dream had always been to win the Daytona 500. That is what I always told everybody, that I was going to be a Winston Cup racer and win the Daytona 500. My adversaries on the Winston West circuit would say, 'You'll never do it.' They said that I would never amount to anything. At that point I was winning races, and there was a lot of animosity. I had been cheered coming up as I was getting faster, but when I got to the top and started winning a lot of races, the other guys no longer could beat me, and all of a sudden, they no longer were rooting for me. That's the way things are.

"I remember sitting in the car before the Daytona 500. I had the same type of feeling as before my first Winston Cup race at Riverside. There was an eagerness to get the race going, yet jitters, the anxiousness of actually being in the race for the very first time, of actually being a little bit scared.

"One of the fears was spinning out in front of Dale Earnhardt on national television. I didn't want to cause problems for somebody. That was my main concern, trying to serve your apprenticeship, to stay within your means, to stay out of trouble, keep your nose clean, learn. You serve that time, become a better race car driver, and if you don't cause problems for the veteran drivers, they are more receptive to helping you, and you are going to learn at a quicker rate. So I was very conscious about trying to stay out of trouble and learn from every lap I was out on the racetrack.

"I remember the atmosphere of that first Daytona 500. So much is happening around you, around the actual race. It has a way of putting a lump in your throat, raising the hair on the back of your neck without anything going on. The place has an incredible aura.

"The race began, and I was running conservatively, running very well, staying out of trouble. Something then hit the window, and I had a cracked windshield, and after a lengthy pit stop to change it, I went out and cut a rear left tire and spun out. The car slid around and pushed up the air dam, and I ended up dropping out after 124 laps when the engine overheated. Still, it was the greatest feeling, and I gained an enormous amount of experience.

"We were on a very limited budget in '87. Fred Stokes, Jim Fox, and Dave Fuge were working on the car. I was getting paid no money. I was living in a two-bedroom apartment above a garage on a mattress in a living room. We were running for Rookie of the Year, but we knew we didn't have a chance, because we could only afford to run twelve races. We felt we had to showcase our potential in those twelve races to the best of our ability, and to do that we bought engines from an engine builder on the West Coast.

"In '87 in June we sat on the outside pole at Michigan. Rusty Wallace had the pole. The last practice session I was running with Tim Richmond and Davey Allison, and we were very fast.

"We decided to get a clean-plug check. When you go for your final check, you shut the motor off clean. You push the clutch in and shut the motor off at the same time so it shows what the fire is on the spark plug.

"I shut the motor off, and the motor ran backwards for a second, and when it did that, it sheared the timing pin off on the camshaft. And we didn't catch it. We put the car on pit road, checked the tires, covered the car up, and went back to the motel. We didn't have a stall.

"It rained that morning, so we had a problem with the pilot bearing seizing on the input shaft of the transmission. We were going to pull out the transmission to make sure that we were right. After it stopped raining, we put everything together, and while I was at the drivers' meeting, they tried to start the motor, and it wouldn't start. When I came out of the meeting they told me the camshaft was broken. We had one more motor, but we didn't have the time to put it in. So we could not start the race.

"Everyone said we were cheating, that Derrike Cope, an outsider, an unknown, had sat on the outside pole because we were cheating, that we had been caught and now we couldn't start the race.

"We didn't have the money to go back to Michigan—we had wanted to go someplace closer to Hendersonville, but we said, 'We're going back to prove I can get up front again.'

"I went back there, and I qualified tenth, and Rusty qualified twentieth. In the very first laps, I went to fifth, ran up front, and then broke the motor. But we showed people we were for real, that we didn't cheat the time before, and that we were definitely someone to be reckoned with.

"Of the twelve races we ran, we qualified ninth at Charlotte, but in that race I passed Dale Earnhardt, but then I crashed because of my lack of experience being in a very fast race car and having Dale Earnhardt manipulate the air.

"I remember, Rusty Wallace and I passed Dale going into turn three and four. My car was loose. I was driving the race car very hard, maybe driving a little over my head, trying to show someone that Derrike Cope could drive a race car. I had the car up front, I was trying to showcase that, and maybe if I had been smarter I would have pulled back, dropped back four or five positions, settled into the first pit stop, and tightened the race car so I had something for four o'clock. I didn't do that. I kept going full out, passed Dale, and he pulled up on my rear bumper going into turn one, and he ducked right out from behind my car going into turn one to the outside and took the air off my spoiler, and the car turned sideways, and then he eased up alongside me, didn't give me any room—I had my car saved if he had given me some room to maneuver, but he didn't, and we touched, and we both spun, and we took out Kenny Schrader at the same time. I got bad-mouthed. But I took it and said, 'Yes, it's my fault. The car spun.' I knew *why* it had spun—because Dale had taken the air off the car. But I learned something from it. I took the heat, because I felt that was the best thing to do at the time.

"Dale Earnhardt can manipulate a race car as well as anyone. He manipulates the air, understands how to do it. There are so many variables in this sport that people don't have any idea about. I learned a very valuable lesson, sucked it up, took the grief, and went on.

"The lesson I learned was if your race car is not quite right, no matter who it is—Derrike Cope, Dale Earnhardt, Rusty Wallace, or Bill Elliott—you're not going to get it done by the driver alone. You are only as good as your equipment, and you must drive to the capabilities of the car and not beyond that. You drive as hard as you can, as safe as you can, and you wait. You have all day. You have until four o'clock in the afternoon. You have to be there at the end to have something left for them, so if it's not quite right, wait, come in, adjust it, go back when you have something more to go at them with.

"I also learned what the car is going to do as you go into the corner when somebody pulls off you. I felt the next time Dale was there, I wouldn't make the same mistake, that if I anticipated what he'd do, I could compensate and keep the car under control.

"Toward the end of the year we were out of money. We had been searching for a sponsor. I had made $10,000 working for my father on engines, and I had put it in my bank account so I could search for sponsors, and throughout the year that money had dwindled down to where I had about $1,600 left. All my Visa cards were maxed out. And Fred decided he could not spend any more of his money and was packing it in, going back to California.

"Fred had packed up, turned the power off on our building, and left, and I was in a motel room in Charlotte still trying to find a sponsor. Right about this time, I got a call from a gentleman named Ron Alrich, out of High Point, North Carolina. He is in an advertising firm, and he would pitch certain drivers who didn't have rides or were starting out, trying to find them sponsors so he could get a commission. And he had been using my name and pitching me in a proposal, and he told me that Purolator filters out of Tulsa, Oklahoma, wanted to talk to me, so he gave me the number, and I called them, and they wanted me to come to Tulsa to meet with them.

"And I found out later that Dave Currier, who was the one who put the Alka-Seltzer deal together for Jimmy Means, also brought up my name in a proposal.

"And the then president of Purolator, Carol Warner, had seen me race in the Streets of Tacoma race, where I sat on the pole and ended up second. My car was very beautiful, with 'GTE Sylvania' on it, and he remembered my name and how pretty the car was.

"He asked me to come to Tulsa, which cost me $600, so I was down to $1,000 in the bank. I had one suit to my name. I flew to Tulsa. I sat in the corporate boardroom with the vice president of marketing and president of the company, knowing I needed the money to secure a ride.

"I was not going home. I told myself, 'I will stay in Charlotte. I have motor-building experience. I can go to work for somebody building motors, but I *am not* driving back across the United States. I belong here. I'm staying here.'

"At Tulsa they wanted to know about me. We talked about the Winston West deal and about the East Coast situation. They said they had a small amount of money, that they wanted to get their feet wet, and they wanted to know if I had a race team.

"This was very unorthodox, because I didn't have a race team behind me. I told the Purolator people what I could do for them, told them I would work very hard outside the race car, that I felt I was very proficient as a spokesman and speaker, and I said I would give my personal services unlimited for the first year and would guarantee them that by the end of the year they would want to pay me.

"I spent the morning talking. I went to lunch and came back and they told me, 'Congratulations, you're the driver we're going to go with. Go back and find a race team.'

"They had $400,000 to spend, of which $25,000 would go to press kits and PR. I had $375,000 to try to run a full schedule, or as close to it as we could. I didn't have much money.

"A gentleman named Pat Patterson, who now runs *Motorsports* magazine, had a firm called the Charlotte Sports Group. Pat was trying to help me stay afloat, and he sat down with Jim Testa and discussed the possibility of our working together. Jim had some cars and motors, and he was looking for a major sponsor. He felt we could do a decent job. Purolator understood for that kind of money it was going to be a tight situation. Carol Warner was willing to work with us. And we were hoping we could get our feet wet and show them racing was a great venue for them to be in. Jim Testa and I were banking on an increase in dollars the following year.

"We struck a deal. I would drive the car for a minimal $30,000, but it didn't matter at all to me. I had been living on nothing. I had been eating a hamburger a day. I was in debt. And Jim Testa was giving me the opportunity to drive a race car.

"We got to work and prepared for the 1988 Daytona 500. Elmo Langley was the crew chief. We made the race, started in the twenty-second position and finished twenty-seventh, seventeen laps behind the winner, who was Bobby Allison.

"We ran the whole year on a *very* limited budget, ran twenty-six of the races, and qualified for every event we entered. It wasn't bad for a driver with no experience to draw from.

"I was pretty aggressive. I tore up some cars. I like to go fast. I like to win.

"I tried to tone down. The key was finishing. It was a good learning experience.

"One problem was Elmo and I didn't see eye to eye. I felt I had to fire

Elmo, and I had the power to do it, and that was a very difficult decision for me. He had been in racing a long time, but I felt we weren't doing everything we could do to get faster, that we were going through the motions, doing antiquated things. I felt we could try different things with the chassis, that Dave Fuge could do more than he could, that Fuge could take me to another level, help me progress faster.

"I respected Elmo. He was doing the best he could with the little money we had. I understood that. But it was something inside me—I expected and wanted more. I am not one to be stagnant, I always want to move forward, and I took the chance and fired him.

"Elmo and I didn't get along for a long time after that. Now we talk and get along fine. But at that time he didn't have any respect for me. He felt I was just a kid with no experience. It was a hard thing for Elmo to take, I'm sure. I felt bad about it. And after I fired him, the word got out that I wanted to run my own race team.

"I cared about the political part of the game, worried about it, but I felt if I could go out and be successful, if I could produce on the racetrack, that was more important than what people were saying behind my back. I felt producing would end the rumors, so I was hell-bent on getting that done, and the way to do it was to surround myself with people I could relate to and go in the direction I was comfortable with.

"I'm very intense, very focused, and sometimes I get irritated, but I expect a great deal out of whoever works for me. I expect a great deal out of myself. I want very badly to win, and I just won't settle for mediocrity.

"And so I fired Elmo and brought in Dave Fuge, and things progressed. We became more innovative and got better.

"We had qualified for every race and gave Purolator a great deal of exposure for its $375,000. We were hoping for more money. And Purolator *did* come back with more.

"The following year we returned and ran until the first Darlington race. Jim Testa was having health problems—he had had a heart attack—and it was a difficult time for his businesses, and Jim decided he needed to get out of racing.

"At that point Bob Whitcomb, my current car owner, did not have a sponsor. Kenny Bouchard had been his driver. Bob had sold his asphalt company in New Hampshire for some millions of dollars and got into racing, and the year before Kenny had won Rookie of the Year, but he just could not put a sponsorship deal together, and so Bob was looking to pull his horns in and lock the doors until he could come up with a better driver or a sponsor.

"At Darlington Jim told me, 'This is going to be our last race. I have to get out.'

"I said, 'You have an obligation to Purolator. You've used some of their money, and you have an obligation and will be in breach of contract if we don't do something. Why don't you go talk to Bob Whitcomb and see if he'll accept the remaining portion of your money and take on your obligation for Purolator for the remainder of the year.'

"I met with Bob Whitcomb, we talked, and Bob and I flew to Tulsa to talk with Carol Warner and Purolator. They felt very comfortable with Bob and his background and his financial stability, and it was a situation where Bob wanted the sponsor on the race car in hopes Purolator would come back the next year with *more* money.

"Everything worked out. I went to work for Bob Whitcomb, and now people began saying that Derrike Cope stole Kenny Bouchard's ride. You have to live down one thing to gain another. Bob Whitcomb told Kenny it was his last race, and it just worked out. Timing is everything, and everybody was comfortable with everyone else. And I was able to keep Purolator consoled.

"We hired Buddy Parrott as crew chief. We were a mediocre race team. Bob had bought some engines, and they just didn't have any power. We needed a good motor, and Buddy Parrott talked to Rick Hendrick about leasing us one of his R&D motors. The deal was we would not even look at it. They would send a guy over, put it in the car, we'd run it, we'd come back to the shop and pull the motor out, and we'd never look at it.

"We leased a Hendrick motor to run at Michigan in late June, and we ran exceptionally well. We ran up front and had a shot to win, running second behind Rusty Wallace. We ran out of gas and finished ninth.

"But that thrust us into the spotlight. We ran great the remainder of the year with the Hendrick motor. We had a great run at Phoenix and at Atlanta, were in position to win both races, and finished fourteenth and twelfth.

"Through Hendrick we got a deal with Chevrolet for the 1990 season. We began preparing ourselves for the 1990 season.

"With backing from Chevrolet, we had the use of their wind tunnel. Their engineer helped us with the body. We changed things. Buddy had been around racing a long time and helped make us better.

"Buddy also hired Keith Dorton, the brother of Randy, to make an engine for us. Keith felt he had a great motor, and he wanted us to test it at Daytona, so we put it in, and it ran very well, better than the

Hendrick motor, and so we opted to use the Keith Dorton motor at Daytona in 1990. We would use the Hendrick motor the rest of the year. Keith worked with us hand in hand, did an enormous amount of work, really was a committed person, he and his son, for our team going into the Daytona 500.

"In testing at Daytona, we were one of the faster cars. The problem was we had gremlins. They had us by the throat. The first time we went to qualify, the car went flat. Same thing in the second round.

"The guys put their heads together and found an ignition problem. It took them four or five days, but it felt like an eternity. We were pulling our hair out, because we were the fourth-fastest car in testing, and the press was saying, 'These guys cheated.' Meanwhile, we stayed focused and found the problem.

"We decided not to try to requalify for a third time. We stood on our time and went to the qualifying race. Thirty-five cars start each race. They take the top sixteen cars into the 500. If we crashed, we were out. We started *way* back. We tried to run a smooth, calculating, patient race, and we worked our way up to finish sixth.

"I drafted with Dale Earnhardt and was fast, and I caught Lake Speed to go into sixth place, and I told Buddy I could go to the front. I said, 'I can get more.' He said, 'Hold off. Just ride there, finish this thing, and get in the race and come back at them.'

"The car was a little bit loose, and I thought better of it, and so we stuck there and took sixth place to the finish. We would start twelfth in the Daytona 500.

"I'm not one to boast—I hate to eat crow. I don't want to have feathers outside my mouth, but I remember calling my brother Darren and my dad the night before the race on the phone, and Darren said, 'What do you think?' I said, 'Darren, this is not like me, but I think I can win the Daytona 500. The race car is fast. The motor is good.'

"He said, 'Go out and do it.'

"We went to the track the next day. I remember Dave Despain from *Motor Week Illustrated*. He asked me what I thought. I said, 'I feel really good. I think I have a race car that can run up front. We're looking for a top ten finish. I'm excited.'

"Before the race I walked from our trailer through the garage area. I was very calm. I wasn't thinking about much, really. Then the drivers went out one by one, forty elite drivers, and walking toward the cars waiting on pit road.

"I saw all these people staring at me. It raised the hackles on the back of my neck. I started to sweat a little bit, felt it incredible that all these people were looking at me, watching me! I walked out onto the grass with the flags painted on them to get introduced. I thought to myself, 'I am very fortunate. I'm appreciative and love these people.' And then I thought, 'I love what I do.'

"We started the race. We took off, passed a number of cars, and were running right up front. I remember Mark Martin was running right in front of me, and he was motioning to me to stay in line with him. He knew I was fast, and he wanted to lead the race. I said to myself, 'I can pass you,' and so I did.

"The key was, I was racing very conservatively. The race car *wanted* to be there, *wanted* to go on, so I just gave the car its head in a very conservative manner.

"Kenny Schrader had the fastest car on the racetrack. He had won the pole, and he passed me and pulled in behind Dale Earnhardt, who was leading.

"I motioned Mark to stay behind me, and he did, and we went on, and I pulled away from him until I reached third place behind Earnhardt and Schrader.

"I got on the radio and told Buddy, 'Kenny Schrader has the fastest car here. We are definitely a third-place race car.'

"I sat behind them, and then Kenny broke in lap 58, and for most of the day Dale Earnhardt led and I ran second.

"It was a very quiet day. I don't talk much on the radio, and Buddy doesn't either. He told me to be patient, be calm, to take care of the car and give the car its head, and that's what I was doing. The car was a little bit loose—in the turn the back end was swinging toward the wall, climbing the bank—and I kept telling him that.

"I was running high on the track, trying not to abuse the tires, and doing what I could do to get through traffic. We lost ground to Earnhardt, but not much. Buddy kept saying, 'All you want to do is stay on the lead lap. If you're on the lead lap, there will be yellows, we'll get all bunched up, and we'll be in position. That's all we have to do here.'

"I did what Buddy told me, didn't press the car, tried to stay patient, tried to stay calm, stay poised, and run the car to keep it on the lead lap.

"Earnhardt and I pitted for gas under the green. There was a caution with twelve laps to go when Rick Wilson lost a bell housing, and then the last caution came out with eight laps. It took a couple laps to get it all cleaned up.

"At that point you have the option to take on tires or fuel, or not. Most of the leaders did. Dale Earnhardt came in for new tires and gas, and so did other guys on the lead lap. Buddy Parrott opted to stay out on the track with used tires.

"When Dale went in, I was leading the race. I, Derrike Cope, was leading the Daytona 500. With five laps to go, I saw Dale Earnhardt coming. I was on the outside, and he pulled to the inside. I saw him, but he had help. He had Geoff Bodine, who was a lap down, pushing him, drafting behind him. Bodine was pushing to get the lap back, but I was able to hold off Bodine. I stayed on the high side, trying to keep the momentum up; I fought him off, and he had to pull back.

"I had enough steam to pull back on Earnhardt, and I caught his draft. Behind me were Terry Labonte and Bill Elliott, and the four of us took off!

"When the car is in the draft, with a car in front and cars behind you, the car is jumping around, getting buffeted by the wind. You feel there is a nail stuck down through the hood and the back of the car is moving around it. I remember I was *very* loose—a pit stop earlier Buddy had knocked the spoiler down to try to go faster, I was on used tires, and Terry Labonte's nose was up my rear end. When the car is loose, it climbs the racetrack.

"I was trying to hang on, to stay close to Earnhardt, and I noticed I was able to catch him. He'd pull away from me from the middle of the corner out, and by the time I got going in turn one again, my car would draft back up and I would be on his bumper. It was remarkable: I was on Dale Earnhardt's tail nearing the end of the Daytona 500! During the race he had pulled away because I had been lifting off the throttle, conserving the race car. Now I never lifted my foot off the floorboard. I was driving the wheels off that thing the last eight laps. I told myself I was not lifting my foot off that floor for any reason, and I planted both feet on the edge of the floorboard, and that's where they remained to the end of the race.

"I really felt I had a shot to win the Daytona 500. I had a plan. My race car kept going up the track because I was loose. Dale Earnhardt kept seeing that, and he kept moving up the racetrack with me. I felt that eventually he would go up to block the track, and on the last lap I was going to go to the bottom of the track.

"With two laps to go going down the back straightaway, Terry Labonte and Bill Elliott pulled out on me, trying to draft by me. They couldn't do it. They had to pull back in line. So I knew the two of them had nothing for me. At that point I knew I could concentrate on Dale Earnhardt. My mind went back to Dale.

"We came around for the last lap. I was still on his rear bumper going into turn one. Inches. Terry Labonte was right on my rear bumper. And going into turn one I remember thinking, 'I have a shot to win this thing.' And right at that moment Terry got me loose, and the car went way high, and I almost hit the wall coming off turn two.

"I came within an inch. I thought I might have scraped it; it was that close. When the car is that loose and light, it's like I'm bolted into the seat but I'm not in the seat. You feel like you are raising yourself out of the seat, and you're hanging on. I had never ridden a bronc before, but it must be the same feeling. You've got both hands on her, and boy, you are riding this thing. Anyone who says he isn't scared is lying.

"I lost two or three car lengths to Dale Earnhardt, and I remember coming off turn two thinking that if Labonte and Elliott would stick with me, I could pull back on him and maybe hang him out to dry, and I might have a chance.

"Going down the back straightaway close to turn three, I started pulling back on Earnhardt. I could see myself inching back on him, and I was excited, and all of a sudden Dale's right rear tire started to elongate and unravel. I remember thinking, 'It's going to blow. It's coming apart.'

"I stayed right behind him. Something flew back and hit my car, but I stayed behind Dale.

"I was going to the bottom of the racetrack no matter what. I didn't care. I knew I was loose, but somehow I was going to keep the car on the bottom of the racetrack. Dale was keeping the car straight, and pieces were flying off it, and he turned hard down into the corner, and as I started to turn, in front of me his car turned sideways. He corrected and tried to save the car. I kept going right where I was, never lifting the throttle. I drove to the bottom of the racetrack, and as soon as I got down alongside him, I just hoped he wouldn't hit me. I thought we were going to crash. Most of the time when a tire is coming apart and the driver goes to turn, the car turns sideways and you all crash. But evidently the inner liner of Dale's tire stayed up enough to give him some control, and he saved the car—it was a masterful job. I don't think anybody would have saved the race car other than Dale. He took it up the racetrack out of harm's way and didn't crash. He finished fifth.

"At the point I thought we were all going to crash I drove by him, and when I looked back in the mirror, I saw Labonte was a car length or so back, and I looked back and said to myself, 'Where is Elliott?' Elliott was a car length behind him. I said to myself, 'They can't beat me. If I don't lift and if I don't hit the wall coming round turn four, it's my race.'

"I was coming off four heading down the front straightaway. I looked back. They were trying to do something, but I said, 'Boys, it's all over.'

"I drove past the checkered flag and did a double take. At that point I was overcome. I had tears in my eyes.

"I slowed down and kept driving around the track. As I drove down the back straightaway, Bill Elliott came up alongside me and waved. Bill and I had become good friends. He had helped me quite a bit. Bill gave me the thumbs-up, and I returned it, and I mouthed, 'Do you believe that?' He just drove on by.

"I had the window net down, and I was waving to the fans, and all I could think about was what I was going to say on Victory Lane. I wanted to get out of that race car and stay poised and do my sponsors proud, to do what a true professional would do, and that was to be very proficient *outside* the race car. That was my main concern coming down toward pit road.

"As I drove pit road, I remember every crewman from every other team was out there, and the first one I remember seeing was Dave Fuge. I went by and slapped every one of those guys' hands. All I could see were people. I couldn't even see my own guys.

"On the radio I asked Buddy, 'Where are you guys?' He said, 'Keep coming.' When I got to them, they all jumped on the car, and we all drove to Victory Lane.

"I said it was a fantastic race, and I thanked Buddy Parrott and all the guys, they had made the right decisions, and I said I had a great race car to drive.

"I said, 'This Purolator filter Chevrolet Lumina did its job for us, and it was an outstanding effort. Dale Earnhardt had the fastest race car. Dale deserved to win, but we were very fortunate to have the opportunity to be in Victory Lane.'

"The Daytona 500 in 1990 was my first win in Winston Cup racing and at the same time the biggest thing that can happen to you in the sport of stock car racing. It was quite a lot to handle.

"I always felt I was capable of winning races. I had learned how to win. I felt that when my time came to be in a position to win a race, I would stay poised and make the right decisions. I prided myself on being smart, on being patient, and when push came to shove, I *did* do all the right things. And at the same time I thought about all those people who had helped me in the past—George Jefferson, Fred Stokes, Warren Rizore. George had told me, 'All I want to do is sit in front of the TV and watch you win the Daytona 500 and for me to be able to say, "I put you there." ' And George had that right. Warren had that right. Fred, my dad, my uncle, Dave Fuge—all those people had a claim to a piece of that Daytona 500.

"I had been a West Coast driver, and in Winston Cup all West Coast drivers are stepchildren. Nobody feels West Coast drivers can come East and compete, never mind win the Daytona 500. I felt I did something for Winston West, for all those people competing out there, to prove we all put our pants on the same way, and that's what I was thinking about.

"After my little speech at Victory Lane, they had me sit in the car and wait for CBS to come back on. Mike Joy did the interview. Then I went to the fence, and hundreds of media people with TV cameras from all over the United States were there, and you start at one end of the fence and do interview after interview after interview after interview, and you go all around this fence, and after this is done, you get in front of the car, and you put on dozens of different hats, picture after picture after picture, with lots of the different sponsors.

"A policeman took me, Bob Whitcomb, Buddy Parrott, and my girl-friend, who was with me at the time, to the press room in the tall glass building at the speedway. The press from all over the world was there, and they started asking questions. People were grasping for press kits, trying to find out about us. Everyone wanted to know, 'Derrike who?' They wanted to know where I was from. And they wanted to play up 'The Fluke.'

"We tried to handle it as best we could. I tried to stay humble. I said, 'Dale Earnhardt had a fast car and he ran all day.' But people didn't know I had lifted all through the race and conserved my race car. If I had run flat out and hung the car up, I could have run with Dale. I felt we were close. Kenny Schrader had us both covered, but he broke. And it's the Daytona 500, not the Daytona 499. I bit my tongue.

"I was tickled to have the opportunity. Nobody can take the Daytona 500 away from me. I felt we proved ourselves. I told the press, 'We ran up front. Look who was behind me—two Winston Cup champions: Terry Labonte and Bill Elliott—and another champ, Dale Earnhardt, was in front of me.'

"I said, 'If you want to give me second place, give me credibility for second place. That's a pretty incredible feat right there.'

"I said, 'We are happy with what we did. We showcased what we were capable of doing. We put on a great race. Buddy made the right car, and it all came together for us, and that's what racing is all about.'

"Afterward we went to the Unocal suite and you are toasted with champagne and you get to keep the glasses. I got to see the ring I was going to get.

"I got out of the press box at 7:30 to go back to Victory Lane to do 'CNN Live' at 7:45. My girlfriend, Jennifer, and I got back in the police car. When I got back to Victory Lane, I remember standing there getting ready to do the show. It was dusk. The sun was red in the sky. I thought, 'I must smell and look terrible.' I had champagne all over me.

"I finished the CNN interview. I didn't have my wallet. I thought, 'My God, my guys must all be gone.' Jennifer and I walked to the garage area, and they were still there. They were all heading for a party thrown for us. I changed clothes and went to the party and spoke, and I had to be back at the Speedway at 11:30 for a satellite feed to Tulsa for Purolator. That was my last interview, and then I got to go back to the motel.

"This is an amazing sport. It touches every emotion you have, and if there are others, it touches them too. It totally consumes you. I think about that all the time. That's why it's so tough to quit—I think about Richard Petty—there is nothing else to compete with this. I can't fathom what Richard is going through, because I can't consider the thought of quitting this sport. I know how much I love it. And I know how much Richard means to this sport. It hurts me to see that this will be his last year. He is a great ambassador for the sport. There will never be anyone like him. I try to emulate him as much as I can. Richard has given so much of himself, loves the sport so much, and for him to be getting out of the race car, that is going to be a very difficult task for him.

"I can still close my eyes right now and feel the sun on my face in the winner's circle. To this day. It's incredible. When we were all standing there, the sun was warming my face. I can remember all the things that went on, and I remember standing there and closing my eyes. Right now I can close my eyes and can feel the sun on my face. It's that much a part of me, that race is. I wish every driver could feel that feeling, because there is nothing like it. It took Darrell seventeen years to win the Daytona 500, and Dale still hasn't done it. I feel very fortunate to have it this early."

LAP 29

Larry McClure

The 1991 Daytona 500 Winner

Chemistry between owner, driver, and crew chief can seem almost mystical. A driver with potential can struggle along without victory, switch race teams, and then suddenly win, and often even the insiders aren't sure why. Perhaps the cars made by the new team are better. Perhaps not. Often, the real reason is that elusive quality of chemistry.

Ernie Irvan, a talented young driver with little success, joined the Morgan-McClure race team in 1990. Irvan was a hard-charger, a protégé and clone of Dale Earnhardt, but he was impatient, often reckless out on the track. When he was hired by co-owner and team manager Larry McClure to drive the Kodak Film Chevrolet, McClure did nothing to rid him of his aggressiveness. He told Irvan that he had hired him *because* he was that way.

McClure, who had been unsatisfied with the cautious driving style of Phil Parsons, told Irvan, "I'm aggressive. I want my driver to be the same way."

Driving for Morgan-McClure in 1991, Irvan pulled a surprise in the Daytona 500 when he sat on the outside pole and then won the race. With three laps to go, Dale Earnhardt and Davey Allison collided, ending any chance of their coming back to catch him.

It was a huge win for the Morgan-McClure racing team, the highlight of its season. After winning at Watkins Glen in August, Morgan-McClure and driver Ernie Irvan became a force to be reckoned with.

Irvan was also a force of mass destruction, becoming at times a one-man wrecking crew. If he wanted to pass, he passed, even when prudence might have told him to be more patient. Because of Irvan's hard-charging, out-of-my-way style, wrecks occurred.

The worst occurred at Talladega in early May 1991. A caution flag

Larry McClure

came out, and on the restart Irvan was up front. But in order to run fast at Talladega, you have to be lined up in front of or behind somebody. There were two lines of cars nose-to-tail. Irvan discovered he wasn't in either one of them. And because he didn't have anyone to draft with, very quickly he began to fall back. After only a few seconds, he had fallen to tenth.

Desperate, Irvan drifted up the track, hoping for an opening. With none there, he wished one to occur. It didn't work out that way. His right front fender hit Kyle Petty's left rear quarter panel. That turned Kyle's car in and sent it down to the bottom of the track, which put him in Ernie's path. After Ernie hit Kyle, he bounded over and caught the left rear quarter panel of Mark Martin's car and turned him in the opposite direction.

All this was happening at about 180 miles an hour. With Irvan, Kyle Petty, and Mark Martin spinning, the other cars behind them started bouncing off each other like orbs in a pinball machine. Martin's car kicked sideways and kept on coming around, actually got backwards, and was on its nose and about to fly when Wally Dallenbach, Jr., hit Martin's left front fender, the only part still on the ground, and banged the car back down. The car stayed on the ground. It was *that* close to disaster, because if the car had started to fly, when it landed the car would have been torn to pieces and Martin would have suffered serious injuries.

Eight cars were demolished. Only Kyle Petty, who suffered a broken leg, was seriously injured.

To everyone who saw the accident, it was obvious whose fault it was: Ernie Irvan's. After the race everyone expected him to say, "I screwed up," or "I was overanxious," but instead he blamed the accident on Kyle Petty, insisting that Petty had come up and hit him.

For about two months the press hounded the uncontrite Irvan about the Talladega wreck. In the meantime, the other drivers were upset, up in arms, because Irvan wouldn't admit he had caused the accident.

At Pocono in July, Irvan was running second behind Hut Stricklin. Stricklin said Irvan hit him from behind; Irvan said he merely took air off his spoiler. Either way, Hut spun out, and he took out Darrell Waltrip, Richard Petty, and other front-runners. Richard Petty, in one of his better efforts, was running third at the time.

The other drivers caucused. They decried Irvan's recklessness and told NASCAR something had to be done. NASCAR then requested an apology from Irvan. At the next race, which was back at Talladega, the site of his biggest transgression, Ernie Irvan stood before the other drivers and apologized for driving over his head. After that, the controversy sub-sided.

During that race, with forty laps to go, Buddy Baker hit him, spun him out, and wrecked him.

Going into 1992, the consensus was that Ernie Irvan had matured, that he seemed to have calmed down, that he still drove aggressively but not over his head. The reason, the other drivers said, was the public apology he'd had to make. In the stock car racing culture, accountability is very important.

Sometimes eating crow is the hardest thing to do. Sometimes it makes a man out of you. Would another Talladega occur again? For Ernie Irvan and the Morgan-McClure race team, that was the question everyone was asking.

LARRY MCCLURE: "My father worked in the coal mines for forty-six years. We had a small farm in southwest Virginia, and he worked 100 miles away, commuting each weekend back and forth to work. He also had a Packard franchise, and that's how the car business got in my blood, from him.

"He was president of a local union, and he was a partner in Mountain Motor Sales, and he would work one shift in the mines and one shift at the dealership. There were six boys and two girls in the family, and he had to work to support us all.

"As a kid, cars were important to me. That's what we talked about. We always had a new car because dad had the franchise, but I didn't have one.

"You are either competitive or not. I was competitive. As a kid, when I rode my bicycle, I wanted a faster bicycle, wanted to be more daring than the next guy. Then you graduate from bicycles to cars, and our interest became cars. I had an uncle who was a wild and crazy guy. He'd come by our house, pick me up, and we would go through the country roads with the running boards scraping the road on the turns, the sparks flying, and I really enjoyed that. Fast cars were in my blood.

"My brother and I started listening to the radio in the fifties. My first favorites were the Flock brothers. Then it was Richard Petty, when he started at Martinsville driving a convertible. I remember his first race. He ran pretty good, had a decent finish, and the announcer was exciting. We were laying across the bed listening to the race.

"When I was twelve years old I began working on my friends' cars, and all through high school I worked on them. I'd fix the carburetor, put dual exhausts on them, tune them up. That was real interesting to me.

"When I got out of high school, I worked for a used car dealer for a year, and then I went on to college in Richmond. It was called Richmond Professional University—it later merged with Virginia Commonwealth University. When I came back home, I wanted to get in the car business, so my father signed me a note for $500 and I opened a little service station.

"My brother Ed was working in Washington, D.C., at the time, and he was tired of working away from home. I told him that if he joined me, half of what I had would be his. As it turned out, it was half of not too much, but together we started a small used car business, and from 1965 through 1979 I was in the used car business.

"That year I bought my first car dealership. I had met my partner; his name is Tim Morgan. He was working for a Chevrolet-Cadillac dealer in the town of Norton, near the coal fields, and we became friends. I was a used car man, buying wholesale from that dealership. He was a young college graduate who was hired to sell those used cars. We cultivated a relationship. We liked each other, and when this dealership became available, we bought it.

"In 1983 we sponsored a local Winston Cup driver by the name of Travis Tiller in the Daytona 500. Travis had a complete car and engine. We gave him $2,500 just to put "Morgan-McClure" on the side of the car. We went to Daytona with him.

"He didn't qualify, but at that time they had a race for all the cars that didn't qualify for the 500, and in that race he ran pretty good. He was running third, and he finished fourth. I remember how much we enjoyed it. We were able to get into the garage area and see Richard Petty and Cale Yarborough, David Pearson, G. C. Spencer, Junior Johnson—all the heroes of automobile racing I had heard about on the radio but never had seen.

"Our dealership was very successful, and in 1983 G. C. Spencer came by and asked if we were interested in buying his race team. He had retired, and so we went to his home in Bluff City, Tennessee, and looked at his race car, spare parts, tow truck, trailer, some good equipment, and we bought it all for $20,000.

"In the beginning Tim and I were doing this for fun. We wanted to be part of racing. We hired G. C. Spencer to run the team and his driver, Connie Saylor, to drive the car, and we ran one race with Connie, tried to qualify for another race, and didn't make the race.

"We decided maybe we needed another driver—that's what we thought at the time. We weren't running as good as I thought we should, and looking back, I can see that he was a much better driver than I was a car owner. He probably wasn't the fault. We weren't any good.

"We said, 'We need another driver, and we need some new engines.' I bought two engines from Junior Johnson and hired Mark Martin, who didn't have a ride. Before that, Mark had driven for J. D. Stacy. We ran pretty decent.

"We went to Daytona for the Fourth of July race. A. J. Foyt qualified third at Daytona in a Chevrolet Monte Carlo, and during Saturday's practice he wrecked. He pulled himself out of the race, so we bought his car. We repaired it and entered it in the fall race at Talladega. We qualified eighth and finished tenth. My fourth race. I said, 'Man, I love this. This is easy.'

"We got more interested and spent more money. I began to understand that the driver wasn't the problem; getting Junior Johnson's engines wouldn't solve the problem. Inexperience on *my* part—*that* was the problem. I felt we could be successful if I could gain enough experience and knowledge to make good judgments.

"The leader has to lead. He can't let the tail wag the dog. We were spending all kinds of money, going through drivers, buying new cars . . . and nothing seemed to work. Meanwhile, I began learning about racing engines, how to adjust valves, how to set the timing, how to read spark plugs, how to take care of the engine, what a gear would do to it, how the front end settings worked, how to communicate with the driver, what tire stagger is—how all those things affect the performance of the race car. And I was aware enough to know I had to be able to do that before I could tell somebody else, 'Hey, we need to do this.' Or before I could hire a man smart enough to know how to do it.

"Early on I hired Tony Glover. He had been employed by Petty Enterprises. His father, Gene Glover, had been a Grand National driving champion. Tony's from Kingsport, and he wanted to move back to east Tennessee, about forty minutes from Abingdon. He wanted to take care of his ailing grandmother, who had raised him. He asked us for a job, and in 1984 we hired him, because we felt he would bring us the most experience for the buck. Tony was hired as crew chief. He was the second full-time person on the race team after G. C. Spencer.

"On the advice of G. C. Spencer, we felt that Mark Martin wasn't giving 100 percent, or else the combination just wasn't working, and we let him go. But looking back on it, all the drivers I had up through Rick Wilson were better than the race team. Regardless, I was making headway, gaining experience, learning how to run a race team.

"In 1984 we ran twenty races with Tommy Ellis. We finished in the top ten once. And we were able to get Folgers coffee involved. A good friend of G. C. Spencer's, a Nashville attorney named Gary Baker, called us and said he was one of the managers for country singer T. G. Sheppard, who was involved with Folgers. He said Folgers was interested in getting its feet wet and sponsoring us for eight races. He asked if we would fly to Cincinnati to meet with Folgers.

"Folgers gave us $300,000 for sixteen races. It wasn't bad. It started paying a little bit of our expenses and gave us a better feel for what was going on. Joe Ruttman drove for us in '85, and we had one top five finish and four top ten finishes. We won $81,000 in prize money.

"We had been spending *a lot* of money, but to me what was important was having a successful business and being able to race. What good would the money do in the bank if I couldn't enjoy it? And it was a lot more money than I had ever had before.

"Then the costs began to escalate. Tim and everyone at the dealership became concerned when the money was *really* starting to eat into our profits, so at that time Tim and my three brothers formed a corporation and bought stock in the race team. We felt it would help take care of the expenses. Over the next two or three years there was a lot of concern voiced that we should call it quits and sell our stuff and get out.

"I wouldn't let them. I decided we needed to do this, that we could make it a successful business.

"We didn't have a sponsor in '86. Folgers saw that racing was good for business, and they wanted to be with a race team that could win races. We showed we could run fast but we weren't consistent, and they were looking for something better. They were lured into Rick Hendrick's stable, which is okay.

"At the end of the '85 season Rick Wilson came to us and said he was interested in driving for us. So did Davey Allison. Rick said he thought he had Sea World as a sponsor, and as it turned out, he didn't have a sponsor.

"We shifted from Chevrolet to Oldsmobile, got a little factory participation from Oldsmobile, and in '86 we went to Daytona for the 500. He ran good, ran fast. Captain Cody's restaurant chain in Daytona sponsored us for a few races that year, and then we attracted Kodak for a select few races.

"Kodak had been lured into Winston Cup racing by some people in North Wilkesboro, North Carolina, who had sold them on having a race team when they didn't own anything. The guy borrowed cars and later bought cars from other race teams, entered seven or eight races, but didn't make any races. Kodak had spent most of its racing budget with those people, and to get their tails out of hot water, they had to do something. A corporation like Kodak is usually involved with winners, so they had to make a change, and they didn't have much money left.

"They had a problem. We had a problem. Kodak's representative told us, 'We have $100,000. We'd like to sponsor you for eight races.' I said I was interested.

"I went to Rochester. We had our Oldsmobile representative from the factory there. I brought Rick Wilson, and we talked about their problem and said we wanted to be their race team. We negotiated a $250,000 deal for eight races. It turned out even better than that.

"I actually did a pretty good selling job. I told them if they couldn't afford to spend that much money, they couldn't afford to be in racing. And we sold them on the fact that we could do the job for them.

"We started running better, qualifying better, as our whole race team was gaining experience. We were starting to mature. We had been involved in it for four years, and in 1987, with Rick Wilson driving, we almost won the Pepsi Firecracker 400 at Daytona. We had a wheel-to-wheel finish with Bill Elliott. It was disappointing, because all day long we had the fastest car. Once we almost lapped Bill Elliott but didn't, and when there was a caution flag, he was able to make up the distance and come on and win the race. Lack of experience beat us again.

"Kodak sponsored us in '87, '88, and '89, but each year we had to wait until the end of the year to really push them to make a decision. Their sponsorship money wasn't equal to the better teams, but we still had to compete with them.

"All during '89, we had run in the top ten in the Winston Cup points, and we felt Rick was going to be able to do a good job for us. He had gained experience. Tony gained experience. The cars were running good. We had just started our own engine program, and things looked like they were going to work out.

"And then at Watkins Glen in August of the 1989 season, Rick Wilson decided that the water looked better on the other side of the river—and that maybe he was better than the race team—and I found out he was going to leave. I asked him how much it would take for him to stay, and I could not give him that much. I couldn't afford him. At the end of the year he went to RAHMOC. When Rick left, so did Oldsmobile.

"There we were at the end of '89—no driver, no factory sponsorship, and the possibility Kodak would not renew, because our deal was just from year to year. It was the worst possible time for Rick to leave.

"Around that time I went to my people and said, 'Through all the years of our involvement in racing, I have listened to other people and let the tail wag the dog. I'm telling you that whether this thing is successful or not, it's going to be my responsibility. I want to try to be the leader and not let the buck pass anymore.'

"I dedicated myself and made a commitment to my race team that I was going to do everything I could do to see we were more successful. And I asked them for the same commitment.

"It was time for me to lead. Guys grow up, and you need to make a decision. I had to start making hard decisions. I had eighteen people working for me. And the bills go on.

"Before Rick departed, the word was out. At Darlington, Phil Parsons came to me and asked if I would be interested in him. Phil is a nice-looking young man who won a race at Talladega. We also looked at Ernie Irvan and Morgan Shepherd. Ernie was driving for a team, U.S. Racing, that had less money than we had. Ernie had run well in spurts. I talked to Kodak and told them I had talked to Phil, Ernie, and Morgan, and who would they be interested in? They wanted Phil, because he was a past winner. It was 'Ernie who?' Phil was also a good-looking blond man, an eloquent speaker, a good family man—had everything going for him.

"So we started the 1990 season with Phil Parsons. That lasted for three races.

"We went to Daytona with a brand-new car and were involved in a big accident. Phil and A. J. Foyt and two or three other cars were running real close, and we wrecked. One said it was the other one's fault, and the other said it was the other's. We were the first car out of the race. We came back home.

"We went to Richmond with two more new cars, wrecked one in practice, and then we wrecked one in the race. We went to Rockingham and didn't have a very good race.

"We liked Phil, supported him, but I just didn't feel I could give him what he needed to be successful. I thought he was a good driver. I had hired him, but the chemistry between us all wasn't working for what we needed to win.

"I decided that Phil had to go.

"I got together with Tony and with our engine builder Runt Pittman and talked with my brothers and told them we were leaning toward Ernie Irvan.

"The problem I now had was that I had told Kodak that Phil was the right man for the job, and it didn't turn out like that. After telling Phil I was making a change, I called Kodak. Now Kodak is this big corporation, and they had already invested in souvenirs, shirts and jackets and posters and mugs with Phil Parsons's picture on it. Changing drivers in the middle of the season becomes a *big deal.* I'm certain they had some unsure feelings, but Kodak from the start agreed to stay out of the day-to-day operations, and luckily, we had just changed from Rick Wilson to Phil Parsons and we only had a few souvenirs and there was not a lot of interest in them, and luckily, Kodak supported me. They said, 'If that's what you want to do, do it.'

"Ernie hadn't really done anything. He had led some races. He was young and aggressive. And we wanted somebody aggressive. Phil was laid-back. Hell, we wanted somebody who would go up there and take the lead. And we felt our car was capable of doing that.

"We didn't sign a contract; we just shook hands. When I hired him, I said, 'Ernie, first thing: I want you to drive the wheels off this car. That's why we're hiring you. If you wreck it, we'll fix it!'

"Well, he took me for my word. The first race at Atlanta in mid-March, we started thirty-third and finished third. We were tickled to death. After the race we signed him formally.

"I also decided to change automobile manufacturers in mid-season, from Olds to Chevrolet. That was a difficult decision, but we felt long-term racing was going to be a Ford-Chevrolet competition, that Ford and Chevrolet would be the two main players. We decided that over the long term the Bowtie Brigade would be beneficial to Morgan-McClure racing. So we switched. And along with that, we got an increase in sponsorship money from Kodak because Chevrolet was more aggressive in the marketplace than Oldsmobile, and all of a sudden Kodak and Chevrolet could do some marketing together.

"The race after Atlanta was Darlington. We qualified the fourth-fastest car, a real fast car. Ernie had gone from fourth to second and was trying to pass Geoff Bodine early in the race—real early, about the thirtieth lap. In Ernie's mind he was telling himself, 'My owner told me to drive the wheels off this car.' He went for the lead, side by side, and spun our car right in front of us down the racetrack backwards. He made a real pretty move, didn't hit anything, went on, and didn't lose a lap.

"During that spin, the tires went flat, the car dropped down, and we broke an oil line. We didn't know it at the time, and we went back out and ran another ten or fifteen laps, and still the car was running good, but a little smoke was starting to appear, so we had to come into the pit area. We lost nine or ten laps to make the repairs.

"Ernie went back out, the car was still as fast as it was, and he was a little bitter, mad at himself for being that aggressive, and he wanted to make up for it. He knew he had the car that could win the race.

"After we put a new set of tires on the car, I said, 'Ernie, go get your laps back.' So he ran side by side with Kenny Schrader for three or four laps and eventually wrecked—he caused a large wreck. A lot of cars were involved. Ernie took out ten or twelve of the front-running cars. So that got us in hot water at the very beginning. Later at Martinsville, Ernie was called down for aggressive driving. They accused him of being too reckless, of hitting too many cars.

"After the wreck at Darlington, the car could still drive a little bit. Ernie pulled off the track and came into the pits. He looked up at me and said, 'Well, you told me to drive the wheels off of it.' We laughed. I was having a *good* time. That was the first time Morgan-McClure Racing was ever in a winning situation. And Ernie, Larry McClure, and Tony Glover were growing up.

"In late August in 1990 at Bristol, Tennessee, just down the road from our race shop in Abingdon, Virginia, I negotiated a three-year contract with Eastman Kodak. It was a real good, first-class contract.

"It was an exciting race that night at Bristol. It was a night race covered nationally by ESPN, and Ernie carried the in-car camera that night as he drove our Kodak Film Chevy Lumina to victory over Rusty Wallace, Mark Martin, Terry Labonte, and Sterling Marlin.

"It was just like a fairy tale. Bristol had always been one of our favorite tracks and one of Ernie's favorite tracks. He had only been involved in Winston Cup racing for three years, but he had always run well at Bristol. It was Morgan-McClure's first Winston Cup victory.

"Chevrolet was very high on us. The fans loved Ernie Irvan's aggressive style. The demand for Kodak souvenirs increased. The extra excitement started to make their promotions work. And after we won at Bristol, it was like somebody had lifted fifty tons of concrete off my back. Along with that, our confidence level increased 500 percent. We felt like we could win *every* race.

"Our confidence was growing, growing, growing. The confidence of Runt Pittman and our engine room was growing, growing, growing. At the point we hired Ernie, we were thirty-third, and we went on and finished ninth in the Winston Cup points.

"We worked particularly hard on our restrictor plate engines. You want a balanced team, but four of the biggest races of the year happen to be at the largest racetracks, Daytona and Talladega. We know these races are important, and so we made an extra investment in the fall of 1990 to prepare for the 1991 season, and Daytona and Talladega in particular.

"When other people were enjoying Christmas and weekends and were home nights with their families, we were here at the shop getting ready for Daytona. We just *knew* we could win it. Dale Earnhardt had never won it. But we had confidence in Ernie that he could learn and win.

"We went to all the test sessions at Daytona. Through Chevrolet we were able to use their computer equipment that told us a great deal about our race car. George Gardner is our computer expert. He communicated what he learned to Tony and Ernie.

"We went to Daytona and qualified on the outside pole. Davey Allison beat us by one one-hundredth of a second.

"It was a high when we qualified second. We were automatically in the field for the 500, no matter what happened in the 125 qualifying race. We didn't win the pole, but we knew we were stout.

"Our next competition was the Busch Clash. You can only be part of it if you won a pole position in a race the year before. It's an invitational, just an extra race. It was a pretty good purse and gives your sponsor more press and airtime. And in our fraternity, if you can win the Busch Clash, you beat the rest.

"The Busch Clash is in two segments. At the end of the first segment, the field is inverted. We started the first segment and finished second, behind Earnhardt. At the end of the segment we were beating on his bumper, literally tapping him.

"For the second segment Ernie and Earnhardt went to the back of the pack. They dropped the green flag, and they took off. They went into the first corner, and Ernie dropped his left wheel off the apron and broke the rotor button, which retarded the timing so the car wasn't up to par.

"We knew something had happened, but we didn't know what. The race ended, and we were disappointed. That was a low time.

"We prepared for the qualifying race, the 125. Even if you have a pole position, you have to participate. Again we raced with Dale Earnhardt, and again we were beating on him. We finished second to Dale Earnhardt.

"He had won the Busch Clash *and* the qualifying race, but we were still real confident, because though we hadn't won, we were right there. In the back of our mind we knew not to wreck Dale Earnhardt and create a big accident, because everyone still was blaming us for the Darlington accident.

"After the qualifying race Richard Childress came up to me and said, 'Dale's mad.' I said, 'Oh, is he?' He said, 'Yeah. Ernie was beating on him.' I said, 'That wasn't the way I looked at it. Looked to me like Dale was blocking him.' I said, 'Dale's a big boy. He'll get over it.'

"Dale had always been successful, and here was Ernie Irvan beating on him all of a sudden. I guess he didn't like it that we were able to compete with him head-on. We were putting on the pressure.

"Ernie and I joked about Dale's complaints. But then Ernie went over and talked to Dale, told him he hadn't meant to hit him, that Kyle Petty was behind him and Ernie had let off the gas, so Kyle hit Ernie and Ernie hit Dale. I'm not sure that's exactly what happened, but that's what Ernie told Dale.

"We didn't want Dale mad at us. Because of Darlington we didn't feel we needed to have *anybody* mad at us. But we felt confident we could beat Dale Earnhardt, could beat anybody.

"We started the 1991 Daytona 500 on the outside pole. We told Ernie to take his time and be patient. He was. 'Get yourself a drafting partner.' At the time nobody wanted to be our dancing partner.

"During our first pit stop under a green flag, as Ernie went out of the pit, one of his wheels went up on the yellow line, which you're not supposed to do, and NASCAR penalized us, made us come back in. We lost two-thirds of a lap to the field.

"We found we could go a little farther on gasoline than most of the cars. We were running the fastest laps. We still didn't have a drafting partner, except when Ernie would come up on somebody and get a little draft and go on past. We were still faster by ourselves than cars drafting together.

"The race ran under green until late in the race, and we made up the two-thirds of a lap. Luckily for us, a caution flag came out with about twenty-five laps to go. We were running second to Darrell Waltrip. Darrell wasn't running very fast, but he was getting excellent fuel mileage, and with twenty-five laps to go, without a caution he would have won the race. His lead was so great we would not have been able to make up the difference.

"But Richard Petty crashed on the backstretch, closing up the field.

"We did not pit. We stayed on the racetrack. Dale was second. We were fifth in line. Davey Allison was a couple cars behind us. Kyle Petty also was still in the race.

"When the green flag came out, we yelled, 'Ernie, go get 'em.' And sure enough, he did.

"On the restart, Dale and Ernie hooked up together and passed the cars in front of us. Dale was in front, we were behind, and here came the 28 car flying past everyone into third.

"We had passed Dale on the track earlier, and we knew we could beat him. Davey Allison we weren't sure about, because he had qualified on the pole. But during the race we were better.

"We made one lap coming back up through the tri-oval, with Dale, Ernie, and Davey running one-two-three.

"There were ten laps to go. We wanted to be in front, and it was time for Ernie to make his move, because he might not have gotten another chance. Also, it had been hard to pass Dale during the Busch Clash and the 125. You've heard the saying that Dale Earnhardt can make his car very wide. We knew when the opportunity arose we had to take it.

"Going into turn one, Ernie just pulled over and whoosh, he passed Dale and kept on.

"With three laps to go, Davey and Dale wrecked. Davey was trying to get past Dale, and he was on the high side and Dale was on the low side, and Dale's car got loose and turned around, and Kyle Petty's car got tore up in that, and so Sterling Marlin, who hadn't been in the race all day, finished second.

"And *we* won the Great American Race, which was exciting to us, but to be honest, it wasn't nearly as exciting as winning Bristol.

"Winning the Daytona 500 means so much to a race team. You win the largest purse of the year. Doors are opened to all the motorsports magazines. You get more press. The more stories are written about you, the more valuable your people get and your race team gets, and the more value your sponsor gets.

"It got Ernie Irvan an invitation to the White House. He had dinner with President Bush. He really didn't want to go, but I explained to him, 'A lot of people go through life and never get that opportunity.' So he went, and he was glad. And then he went on the David Letterman show and handled himself very well.

"And now, when we go to renegotiate our contract, we can say, 'We won the Daytona 500.' That's like winning the World Series; you've won the championship race. And the most important thing is what it means to your heart, that you have beaten everybody.

"Now that we've had that taste and we know how to start our year out, we're going for back-to-back championships in 1992 at Daytona. There haven't been many of those. We have been the fastest GM car so far, and we feel like we can win it all again.

"In 1991 we were the fastest GM car in qualifying twenty-one times. We won at Daytona; won at Watkins Glen, a road course; won at Bristol, which is a high-bank short track, so we feel we're a well-rounded team. Throughout the year the biggest thing that hurt us and kept us from winning the Winston Cup championship was that we were involved in five or six accidents, and most of those were caused by not being patient enough and maybe being too aggressive, but the same thing that makes Ernie a great race car driver is the same thing that creates problems. At the same time we feel a lot of the pressure put on us by NASCAR and the racing community was created by people jealous of our success.

"Ernie was involved in an accident at Talladega last year in May. We asked if we could get up before our competitors, and said, 'Hey, maybe we've been too competitive.' That helped. People were talking back about us, and that helped turn it around. We had to be the guys who didn't make any mistakes then, because the way everyone was talking, Ernie was the only one making the mistakes. That period cost us the championship, because before Talladega we were ten points out of first place, and after that accident, it was one thing after another. The criticism came, and it broke our concentration.

"But that's over and past, and this year we feel we can go on and win the championship."

LAP 30

Qualifying

Earning a starting position in the Daytona 500 is a grueling ordeal. Race teams begin to fabricate their Daytona cars and build the engines for those cars as early as six months before the race. If the race team has the backing of either Ford or General Motors, the team takes its car to the factory's wind tunnel for more testing. Then in December and January, during what is euphemistically called the "off-season," the race team will come to the Daytona International Speedway for two four-day stretches to test the car to see whether it's everything the crew had hoped it would be.

It never is. No matter how well a car is running, it isn't good enough. Most races teams veil their progress in secrecy, so no matter how well a car is running, the question always remains: Is someone running better?

After testing, the race teams return to Charlotte, or to Hendersonville, North Carolina; Dawsonville, Georgia; Spartanburg, South Carolina; Stuart, Virginia, or wherever to do more work on the car, and then two weeks before the Great Race the cars once again are hauled to Daytona to endure still more practice to prepare for the time trials.

One week later, the trials begin as the drivers compete to see which two cars will begin in the first row at the start of the race and to determine who starts where in the preliminary 125-mile races.

(In the time trials, NASCAR's rules had mandated that each driver would be timed running one lap around the 2.5-mile track. But because of complaints from independents and less well-financed teams who couldn't afford special, expensive, taller-geared transmissions made especially for qualifying, in mid-December NASCAR ruled that each car would run two laps and it would accept the faster of the two laps.)

The two fastest cars then start up front in the 500, unless in the 125-race, which everyone must enter, the pole car crashes and cannot be fixed in time for the 500 race, in which case the car has to start at the rear of the pack with all those unfortunates who have to compete in backup cars.

The positions in the 500 are determined by the finishes in two 125-mile qualifying races. The top fifteen drivers (not including the pole sitters) are chosen in their order of finish in the two preliminary races. To fill out the field, the officials consider the trial times of the cars not already selected and then complete the 42-car field.

Depending on whether you see a glass half full or half empty, the ritual for getting into the Daytona 500 is either complicatedly simple or simply complicated. Because the cars run at speeds approaching 200 miles an hour, you can't be sure what's going to happen—even on practice days when the cars are just running around the track by themselves.

Bill Elliott, for instance, arrived at Daytona in January with a car that was faster than anyone's, but during a practice session, as he drove around the oval all by himself getting ready for the time trials, his oil system failed. The housing with the oil filter and oil pump sheared off, the engine dumped all its oil, the engine seized, oil spilled onto the track, and before Elliott could regain control, he had whapped the wall and totaled the car.

Then there was the Derrike Cope incident. Derrike sat in his Purolator Chevrolet, helmet on, the engine off, waiting for the track official to tell him he could go onto the track for his practice laps. He got the signal, started his engine, and roared down pit road and up onto the track—without looking at the traffic. Cope knew he wasn't the only car practicing at that time, but like so many of us who drive our highways, he had a mental lapse—he didn't once peek into his rearview mirror, so he didn't see the green and white Kodiak Chevrolet of Kenny Schrader come roaring down the straightaway in front of the grandstand at 188 miles an hour right toward him.

Schrader, surprised by the streak of metallic orange suddenly thrust into his path, was left with two choices: He could either go low onto the grass and risk a thrill-ride skid and a trip into the wall, or he could plow right into Cope.

Schrader thought to himself, "Buddy, you don't know what's about to hit you."

Cope's Lumina was totaled. Schrader's car also was a wreck. Back in the pit area a contrite Cope, a gentleman, admitted he had goofed up badly by not looking first.

Later that day Hendrick Motorsports general manager Jimmy Johnson called up Bob Whitcomb Racing's general manager Bob Tomlinson to bellyache about Cope's carelessness.

"I had to yell at someone," said Johnson, also a gentleman.

A few days later Tomlinson, who is a natural storyteller, was commenting on the incident. He said it reminded him of an old story, and he proceeded to tell a tale about a trucker who got into a bad wreck. Tomlinson recounted that the trucker was asked, "What did you do when you saw it coming?"

"I woke up LeRoy, who was sleeping behind the cab."

"Why did you do that?" the trucker was asked.

"Because," said the trucker, "Leroy loves to watch a good crash."

Their cars mangled, both Cope and Schrader would have to use a backup car for the time trials.

The time trials are not particularly interesting to watch, unless there is a crash, which is rare. As important as the time trials may be, watching the cars go around the track one at a time for an entire day can seem rather monotonous. You can amuse yourself by studying the line each driver takes around the track. You can bring your stopwatch and verify what the announcer and scoreboard tell you after each run. Or you can work on your tan.

Nevertheless, more than twenty thousand of the NASCAR faithful sat between turn four and the start-finish line to watch and cheer as the drivers challenged the track and the times were announced.

Before the trials themselves, everyone knows who the favorites are. While the cars test on the track during December and January, dozens of stopwatches click and pens record everyone's times on team clipboards.

The cars that had tested fastest were Ford Thunderbirds. Ten of the fastest eleven cars were Fords. Only the fifth-fastest car, Kyle Petty in his Mello Yello Pontiac, managed to horn in on the Ford monopoly.

Bill Elliott was first at 193.340 miles an hour, with his stablemate, Sterling Marlin, second at 193.092, making Junior Johnson's two cars the only ones to record speeds at the 193-mile-per-hour mark. Mark Martin, Morgan Shepherd, Kyle Petty, and Phil Parsons were in the 192-mile-an-hour range, and behind them were nine drivers, including Ernie Irvan, Davey Allison, and Ricky Rudd, at 191 miles per hour.

The General Motors cars dominated the 190–189-mile-an-hour range. Darrell Waltrip, Harry Gant, Rusty Wallace, Dale Earnhardt, Alan Kulwicki, Ken Schrader, and Michael Waltrip all were in the 190-mile-per-hour group, and Richard Petty, Dale Jarrett, Hut Stricklin, and Derrike Cope were clocked at 189 miles per hour.

The difference between the fastest car, Bill Elliott's Ford (46.55 seconds), and the thirtieth-fastest car, belonging to Cope (47.52 seconds), was but a second and three one-hundredths.

The time trials for the Busch Pole competition began January 9. One by one the cars spent the day vying for the $2,500 prize and the vaunted pole.

The first car on the track was the Hendrick Chevrolet driven by Ricky Rudd. There is no more beautiful car than Rudd's red, orange, yellow, and white Tide car, and after two laps, the scoreboard announced he had reached 189.89. As Michael Waltrip began his two-lap run, Rudd got out of his car on pit road by the photographers' crow's nest, answered a couple of softball questions over the public-address system, and posed in front of his car for a phalanx of press photographers.

As Rudd stood there, he kept switching hats—a red one for the Winston Cup series, a black one with a bow tie for Chevrolet, and several others for other associate sponsors. Once that was over with, Rudd headed for the garage. Each driver would repeat the ritual throughout the day.

There were few surprises. The day was sunny, and the track was hot, so the times were slowed by about a second per lap for each car. The two fastest cars in practice were still the two fastest cars in the time trials, only it was the Maxwell House car of Sterling Marlin that sat on the pole, with the Budweiser car of Bill Elliott on the outside. Junior Johnson didn't much care: The pole was his either way.

Entering his first Daytona 500, Dorsey Schroeder, a forty-year-old SCCA and IMSA champion but little known to Winston Cup racing, surprised everyone by running a 191.404 lap, which placed him on the outside pole for the second of the Gatorade 125-mile qualifying races. Schroeder's owner was Junie Donlavey, an old-timer with a knack for building fast cars. The other surprise was the poor showing of Kenny Schrader, the driver of the Hendrick Motorsports Kodiak Chevrolet. Schrader qualified in 186.621. He would start in twenty-first place in the first of the two qualifiers.

Afterward Schrader told reporters, "We're running good. The car feels good in the draft." No reporter was crass enough to suggest that because Schrader was running five miles per hour slower than Elliott or Sterling Marlin, he would be too slow to even get in their draft.

But then Schrader made up for his rose-colored statement by admitting, "As far as finding out what's been our problem, I can't say. We don't know. We've tried three different engines and tried everything we knew to try, but once we got in race mode, we were pretty good." Pretty good? Say what?

* * *

After the trials, the cars then practiced for several more days before the twins 125s, which were scheduled for the Thursday before the Big Race. Racing, you always have to keep in mind, is comparative, and every mechanic and driver always believes his car can go faster if you give him a little more time to work on it.

On Wednesday morning, one day before the qualifying races, there was a six-car accident during practice. Brett Bodine was running behind Jimmy Spencer and Kyle Petty, grouped closely, when Spencer began to lose control of his car. Bodine backed off to allow Spencer a chance to right himself. Ricky Rudd, who was behind Bodine, realized too late what was happening and plowed into the back of Bodine's car, sending Bodine's green Quaker State car spinning.

Plowing into the careening cars were Wally Dallenbach, Jr., driving his first Daytona 500, A. J. Foyt, and Bobby Hillin. Michael Waltrip drove to the bottom of the track. He thought he had cleared everyone, but then the spinning cars came back down the track, hit him on the right corner, and sent him flying up into the wall.

Kyle Petty and Jimmy Spencer, the guy who'd started the chain reaction, escaped damage. Jimmy Spencer, a wonderful character, once was asked to wear a toupee by his sponsor, who thought a well-coiffed Spencer would be more appealing to the public. At first Spencer agreed, then balked at the pretentiousness of it all. He shed the rug and finished the year au naturel.

The cars of Waltrip, Dallenbach, and Hillin were wrecked beyond salvageability. Under the rules, because they'd have to race in backup cars in the 125s, they would have to start at the back of the pack.

Dorsey Schroeder, whose lucky star kept rising, had been scheduled to be out on the track during the big crash, but he had remained on pit road when his starter malfunctioned.

Said Schroeder afterward, ''I hope I'm not using up all my luck too early, because the week's young yet.''

Davey Allison was involved in two incidents that day. In the first one Allison, who drove one of the faster cars during practice, was taking a leisurely ride around the track in third gear when he was struck from behind by rookie Stanley Smith. That's the thing about rookies, veteran drivers will tell you: They don't have experience, and as a result they are involved in a lot of accidents.

The veterans shudder when they hear that the Daytona 500 starting lineup is filled with rookies or inexperienced drivers. Many rookies are turned down by track officials and ordered to launch their careers on a smaller, slower track.

Neither Allison's nor Stanley Smith's car sustained much damage. Allison's car was scraped up and there were tire marks down the right side, making it necessary to repaint the car for the 125-mile race.

Said a compassionate Davey Allison, "Stanley just hit me. I'm not mad at him. It's inexperience, and he'll learn from this. That's the only way you learn."

Late in the day, with perhaps a dozen cars running at top speed, Davey was among a group of cars out on the track showing their stuff at top speed when he came around turn two and went to pass Sterling Marlin, the pole sitter. Apparently Marlin didn't see him, and as Marlin moved into his path, Davey had to dart low, losing control and sending his car rocketing into the wall.

Adding to the intensity of the moment, a member of Davey's PR staff, who carried a scanner and had only heard what had happened, since it was out of her sight, exclaimed, "Davey's been in a bad wreck." A pall of silence settled over the track as the ambulance, siren blaring, raced to the scene. Everyone was relieved to see that Davey had escaped with only bruises. His car, however, was totaled, and he, too, would start far back in his 125-mile preliminary race.

There were close to one hundred thousand racing fans packed into the Daytona International Speedway for the Twin Gatorade 125s, perhaps the largest assemblage ever for a "mere" day of qualifying for a race. I was amazed that so many people would show up. It was Thursday, the middle of the week, and all these people had taken a sick day or a vacation day or picked this week to go on vacation.

"This is nothing," I was told by veteran photographer Don Grassmann. "On Sunday you can add fifty thousand *more* fans to the size of this crowd." The additional fans are equal to all the people at an NFL football game on a given Sunday afternoon.

Early in the day a thick fog obscured visibility. Skies were overcast, but no one seemed concerned. The joke about the track is that it never rains the week of the Daytona 500: Bill France wouldn't allow it. Not since Freddie Lorenzen won in 1965, when rain stopped the race at 133 miles, and again in '66, when Richard Petty won as rain halted it after 495 miles, has a Daytona 500 been interrupted.

By 11:30, an hour before the first 125, the gray, billowing clouds receded to the deep background. Blue, clear skies shone over the speedway. Jackets and sweaters were shed. Somewhere, Bill France was smiling.

As the first qualifying race neared, the tension in the pits and the excitement in the grandstands was palpable. In addition to paying a purse of $35,000 each, the 125-mile qualifying races are considered the most fearsome of the season. They are like the League Championship Series in baseball. Ask any ballplayer, and he'll tell you that the World Series is a piece of cake compared to the LCS. After all, they will tell you, if you don't win the LCS you don't get into the World Series. Same thing with the 125 qualifying races. After all, once you're in the 500 or in the World Series, you've at least made the show. Not to get there, that's what hurts most.

Richard Petty once explained it in his own particular patois: "The deal is you have a bunch of cats trying to get into the Daytona 500. They take all sorts of chances they wouldn't otherwise. It's made it a dangerous situation for everybody."

In all, four drivers have been killed or died from injuries suffered in the qualifying races. Talmadge Prince, competing in his first Grand National race, was killed instantly in 1970. Veteran Friday Hassler died in 1972 when his car was T-boned in the backstretch. Rookie Ricky Knotts of Paw Paw, Michigan, died when his car hit the inside concrete wall in 1980.

His father, Richard, was the crew chief on the ill-fated Oldsmobile. "My son is dead, and I cannot believe it. All he wanted to be was a Grand National driver. He won't now. But he was never afraid . . . never scared."

And Bruce Jacobi, a part-time driver, lay in a coma for years after a violent wreck in one of the 1983 races. He died in 1987.

"It used to be," said Bob Tomlinson, the general manager of the Bob Whitcomb race team, "every Tom, Dick, and Harry who owned a race car would go to Daytona and race, and because of that, several drivers have been killed.

"I can remember one boy's father bought him a race car from one of the major teams. He had qualifying trouble, and they put him in one of the 125-mile qualifying races, and he got killed. Come to find out the next day the most experience he had had was in the rookie division of his local track. So he was stepping from a three-eighth-mile track into a two-and-a-half-mile speedway where you run over 200 miles an hour. I personally feel for his family, but I don't see how his father could have bought the car for him and let him take such a big step. You don't start with a Piper Cub and two weeks later fly a jumbo jet.

"Experience creates a good driver. The more track time, the more experience. That's why a lot of drivers in Winston Cup also drive in the Busch series, because they want even more track time. The good drivers *never* get enough seat time. They want to drive and drive forever."

A large man in brightly checkered shorts walked up to the security guard behind pit road and showed his identification. It was Kim Bokamper, a gigantic football player for the Miami Dolphins. The security guard politely informed him that he could not enter the pit area wearing shorts.

"Sorry, there are no exceptions," said the guard firmly. Bokamper, as big as a walk-in refrigerator, didn't argue. He turned and walked away.

"NASCAR," said the guard, "has a dress code for pit lane and the garage area during the running of a race. No shorts for men or women, no tank tops for women." The guard chuckled at his remembrance of the race in 1984 when NASCAR sprung the rules on an unsuspecting public.

"You should have seen the women scrambling to buy towels to wrap around them so they could get into the pits," said the guard.

Behind the pit wall, all the teams had equipment to service their cars. There were generators, tools, hoses, and rows of tires piled up by fours. There was constant activity, busywork most of it, but important busywork that was accompanied by nervousness. Hose couplings had to be greased, and all the tire-changing equipment was placed just so. No time could be wasted searching for the right piece of equipment. The diligence and concentration of the team members was evident.

Just as there are rookie drivers, so there are rookie fans. Not wanting to feel like a rube, I constantly asked questions about the Daytona experience—what I would need, what equipment to buy, what I should be attuned to.

In addition to buying a Robic multisport timer, which tells the month, the day of the month, the time of day, the time per lap, the miles-per-hour per lap, and the average time of all the laps, I also purchased for $400 a Uniden bearcat scanner and a headset to keep out the roar of the cars so that the eavesdropper can listen in on the drivers and their crew chiefs as they talk to each other during the race. Race fans can get the radio frequencies for each team from a club of such devotees.

As with every other aspect of racing, there is a right way to program the radios. Being a novice, I didn't have a clue, so when I saw two men sitting on a wooden crate behind pit lane obviously discussing their scanners, I decided to ask their advice on setting up the channels.

The men, who were executives with Jasper Engines, the sponsor of sophomore driver Ted Musgrave and car 55, explained that the proper procedure is to correlate the channel on the scanner with the number of the car. In other words, if you want to listen to Dale Earnhardt, who drives car 3, put his frequency on channel 3. Davey Allison should be on channel 28, Dave Marcis on channel 71. As there are forty-two entries, it takes a while to punch in all the numbers.

After the Jasper exec explained the system, he then set about punching in all the frequencies for me. I protested, but he offered that he was happy to do it. Imagine a stranger at a baseball game filling in the lineups for a novice? I couldn't. It was to be a day of wonderful experiences like that.

About fifteen minutes later I was standing behind Richard Petty's pit crew when I nonchalantly asked a race fan if you were allowed to watch the race itself from the pits. He took me literally and said no. I learned later that watching the race from right behind the team pit areas was fine, but not *in* the pit itself.

"Then where do *you* go to watch it?" I asked.

He pointed to a long row of VIP suites looming above me right behind pit lane. "The best place is up there," he said, "and I have an extra ticket; my wife couldn't go." Before I could say a word, he handed me the ticket.

Earlier I was chatting with a businessman from Long Island and his son, who drove race cars. He told me, "Daytona is the most civilized track of them all. If you want to see a different culture, see the pickup trucks and the rowdies, go to Talladega." He gave me his seat number, said he had extra space, and invited me to join him for the race. In racing, it seemed, there are no strangers; there are only race fans you haven't met yet.

Most sports have a modicum of pomp before the contest. For the stick and ball sports, it's usually "The Star-Spangled Banner."

Since stock car racing developed in the milieu of the Bible Belt, tracks like to mix a little religion with the standard patriotism. The opening remarks came from a member of the cloth.

In prayer, the minister intoned, "We thank thee for the excitement of the racing." He asked God to keep the drivers safe and ended, "Bless this day. Amen."

An ROTC color guard marched into the infield, and the hundred thousand spectators softly sang, "The Star Spangled Banner."

The fans were not privy to the command to start the engines for the first 125-miler, but after the engines started up, they could certainly hear the din of the twenty-nine engines roaring as one. Many spectators feel uncomfortable with the pounding in their ears. They wear earplugs or soundproof mufflers. I found the combination of the incessant roar, the acrid smell of the 108-octane fuel, and the lurking sense of imminent danger to be intoxicating. My mind wandered to stolid, unblinking George Washington sitting on his horse while British guns shot at him. "Ah, the sweet sound of bullets," George apparently exulted. He'd have made a great racer.

The red pace car, driven by former racer Elmo Langley, slowly exited pit road, dutifully followed by the competing cars riding in double file. Sterling Marlin, in his deep blue Maxwell House Ford, had the inside pole. Next to him was Mark Martin, driving his white, blue-and-red-trimmed Valvoline Ford. Phil Parsons, also in a Ford, was in the second row. Dale Earnhardt, in his black and silver Chevy Lumina, began right behind Martin. Spread behind them were cars driving by Richard Petty, his son Kyle, Dale Jarrett, Ernie Irvan, Alan Kulwicki, Rusty Wallace, Harry Gant, and Ken Schrader, all the way back in the twenty-first position.

After the cars roared away and out of sight of the first turn, it wasn't more than a couple minutes before they rounded the fourth turn and made another pass by pit road, this time to check their tachometers. A car doesn't have a speedometer or a gas gauge. The driver must figure out his speed by his rpms, or revolutions per minute. Entering and leaving pit road a driver has to keep the rpms under 3,200 or risk a penalty.

The cars disappeared from view, and after a short period of time returned for a second pass and another tach check. In November 1990, during the Atlanta Journal 500, Mike Rich, a crewman on the Harry Melling car driven by Bill Elliott, was changing the right rear tire on Elliott's car when he was killed by Ricky Rudd's Lumina as Rudd was racing into the pits for gas and tires.

Rich had talked his way into his first job with a pit pass he'd made himself, and had gotten the job on the Elliott car after a close friend was seriously injured in a pit road accident. Just before he was struck, Rich had exchanged high fives with gas catch-can teammate Mike Thomas, jumped over the wall, and begun changing tires. Rudd came toward him out of control and crushed Rich between his front bumper and Elliott's rear. That night, Mike Rich died.

For years the drivers knew that zooming down pit road at 100 miles an hour, slamming on the brakes, and stopping on a square of pavement just larger than the car itself would one day lead to disaster. That day in Atlanta the pit lane was too narrow. One car came into the pits a little sideways, another tried to fit where there was only room for one, and Mike Rich was struck and killed. So by slowing down the cars, NASCAR was taking measures to make sure pitting was no longer a game of Russian roulette for crew members.

The cars came around again, Langley's red pace car leading the field. The green flag waved in front of the speeding cars. Langley quickly drove off the asphalt out of their way, and the first of two races to determine the positioning of the Daytona 500 was under way.

By the second lap, pole sitter Sterling Marlin, in his blue Maxwell House car, had fallen back. Dale Earnhardt, in his sinister black and silver Chevy Lumina, took the lead, followed closely by Dale Jarrett in the lime-green and black Interstate Batteries Chevy 18. Mark Martin's navy and white Ford was inside Earnhardt, but because Martin had no one to draft, two laps later he lost position to both Kyle Petty and Sterling Marlin.

Alan Kulwicki, back in the pack, came on the scanner. "A little loose," was all he said, moments before his orange and white Hooters Ford turned sideways, out of shape, out of control, a 3,700-pound hunk of potential danger.

Kulwicki's car brought chaos. Turn four of lap four became the site of a mad ballet of careening vehicles. You couldn't hear the crunching over the roar of the engines, but you could see the smoke and knew cars were being wrecked and mangled.

When the mayhem was over, eight cars were damaged or destroyed. Kulwicki was wrecked, as was Hut Stricklin's Raybestos Chevy, A. J. Foyt's Copenhagen Olds, Richard Petty's STP Pontiac, Rick Wilson's Snickers Ford, Terry Labonte's Sunoco Chevy, and cars driven by Ben Hess and Dave Mader.

As the tow trucks cleared the debris, Terry Labonte was asked by a radio commentator, "What happened out there?" I expected Labonte to respond something like Jimmy Connors might have: "What do you think happened out there, you dummy? Get out of my face. Can't you see my car just got smashed to bits?"

But Labonte, like the other drivers, maintains NASCAR's standards of decorum. He held on to his inner emotions and without anger said, "Alan was out of control and got tangled up. Ask him what happened."

When Alan Kulwicki climbed out of his car, he was limping, and he was immediately put on a stretcher and driven to the infield infirmary, out of reach of all microphones. Rick Wilson, who had wrecked, attempted to explain what had happened out there.

"Alan turned sideways, and we came into it from behind. No one had anyplace to go," he said.

For Kulwicki, Labonte, Foyt, Wilson, Hess, and Mader, the day was over after just four laps. Richard Petty, mashed from behind by Hut Stricklin, was able to drive his crunched-up Pontiac to the pits, where his crew members tried valiantly to bang out some of the dents. Petty roared back out onto the track, but he didn't go two laps before heading for the garage.

Asked what happened, the always-courteous Petty explained, "Twelve [Stricklin] spun in front of me. He messed my front end up."

Petty would have to begin the final Daytona 500 of his illustrious career from the thirty-second position.

The race resumed. Junior Johnson's Maxwell House Ford, driven by Sterling Marlin, was in the lead. Behind Marlin in third place was Mark Martin. Challenging Marlin on the inside was runner-up Dale Earnhardt, but with no one to draft with, he was forced to drop back.

By lap 15, it was a five-car train leading the way. In the lead was Sterling Marlin, then Mark Martin, the surprising Dale Jarrett in Joe Gibbs's initial effort, Earnhardt, and Kyle Petty.

Earnhardt, fighting for supremacy, snuck behind Marlin, tapped him gently, ducked away, and sent Marlin's beautiful blue car spinning. Junior Johnson held his breath. His 22 car was assured the pole in the 500. If it hit the wall and was totaled and another car had to be substituted, he would lose his pole position.

The car hit—nothing. It came to a rest on the grassy part of the infield in one piece. Johnson ordered Marlin off the track. The rule was he had to start; there was no rule saying he had to finish. He would forfeit the prize money for the race, but there was no point risking the pole any further. For Sterling Marlin, that was it for the day.

In the stands the backers of the popular Sterling Marlin and other Ford rooters stood to protest the rogue Earnhardt, firm in their belief that Dale had deliberately wrecked one of their favorites. They rose as one and began to boo lustily, a cacophony heard even over the car engines. They sounded like a lynch mob.

In the pit area, Junior Johnson hustled over to the Earnhardt pit crew to protest Dale's rough driving. The normally calm Johnson's face had turned red. He was livid.

After the race Marlin told reporters, "It looked like I got a little push. That's pretty typical."

Earnhardt, in his own defense, charged that Marlin had slowed down, causing him to hit Marlin's car from behind. Marlin wasn't buying it.

"That's pretty much what he always says," he replied.

Earnhardt, meanwhile, continued on the track. This was war, and of all the warriors, Dale Earnhardt was the fiercest.

On the radio, Kirk Shelmerdine, Earnhardt's crew chief, asked his driver, "Dale, do you want some new tires?"

"No," was all he said.

The race droned on, with Mark Martin in the lead, followed by Earnhardt, Jarrett, Greg Sacks, Harry Gant, Ernie Irvan, Kyle Petty, Kenny Schrader, Phil Parsons, Rusty Wallace, Dave Marcis, Eddie Bierschwale, Wally Dallenbach, Phil Barkdoll, Kerry Teague, Brad Teague, rookie Mike Potter, Delma Cowart, Andy Belmont, and a sputtering, banged-up Hut Stricklin.

Trouble continued for some of the drivers. Dave Marcis called his crew on the radio to say he was having trouble with his gearbox. Then Wally Dallenbach dropped a valve and had to leave the race.

A NASCAR official announced on the radio that one of the cars on the track was spraying oil. Since he didn't know which car, he ordered a caution flag on lap 33 so the cars could parade down pit road and let the officials figure out who the leaker was. Gary Nelson, NASCAR's head cop, noticed that Eddie Bierschwale had a smudge on his bumper. Bierschwale, in his SplitFire Oldsmobile, was black-flagged and parked for the day.

Still under the yellow, Rusty Wallace, in his black and gold Miller Pontiac, asked over the radio whom he should draft with. His pit crew suggested Kyle Petty's Mello Yello Pontiac. The only problem was that Kyle was six cars behind him. As a red truck was dumping "oil dry" on the track, Wallace's pit crew was giving him instructions.

"When this thing starts again, RW, we'll have twenty laps to run."

"I'm ready."

"Close up."

It was green again. Wallace, passing Ernie Irvan, was up to eighth place.

On lap 33 of this 50-lap race, Mark Martin, driving for Jack Roush in his Valvoline Ford, still held the lead. Behind him was Dale Jarrett, driving for Joe Gibbs, and lying in wait, third, was Dale Earnhardt. Greg Sacks, in a Chevrolet festooned like a box of Kellogg's Corn Flakes, was fourth, and Handsome Harry Gant, in his Skoal Bandit, was fifth.

On lap 34, Earnhardt passed Jarrett. Gant, following behind Earnhardt, battled Jarrett for third.

A lap later, with just fifteen laps to go, owner Joe Gibbs learned firsthand about the vicissitudes of racing. Though Dale Jarrett was running fourth, he was driving faster than the ability of his car to stay under control at that speed, something that often happens with drivers for new teams or with drivers who want to prove to their owners that they can win even if the car isn't competitive. But a driver on the edge can only go so long without eventually losing concentration or just losing control. And so it was with Dale Jarrett.

Running fourth, he lost control and headed up the track—into an unsuspecting Kyle Petty. Both cars were damaged badly, and neither could return.

After he got out of his car, Jarrett, a gentleman, explained: "I got in a bad position. The car was loose. I messed up. It was a shame Kyle was in it."

When interviewed, Kyle Petty refused any comment. Clearly, he was angry. As he walked toward the pits, men with microphones approached him. His crew members yelled at the media, "Get out of his face. Let him walk away." And walk away he did.

Because of the crash Kyle Petty would have to start the 500 in the thirty-third spot, one behind his father. Jarrett would start in spot 35 in the 42-car race.

Ten laps remained in this first qualifier. Mark Martin had taken over the lead from Earnhardt, and he led a train of four cars, with Earnhardt, Greg Sacks, and Kenny Schrader behind him. On the inside in third place was Ernie Irvan, with Harry Gant behind him.

Schrader went high on the bank in an attempt to pass Sacks. He made it look easy, and then Harry Gant passed Sacks under him. Now only Martin and Earnhardt were ahead of Schrader, but that accomplishment was immediately forgotten as Dale Earnhardt, making a daring, brilliant move, wrested the lead from Mark Martin.

Schrader, Martin, and Earnhardt were three across, always a dangerous maneuver, but there is only one Dale Earnhardt, and he got by Martin as Martin was passing Schrader. Martin tucked in behind Earnhardt, and in single file Earnhardt, Martin, and Irvan raced together, picking up speed in their draft, leaving Ken Schrader, Greg Sacks, and the rest of the pack far behind.

With five laps to go, it was the threesome of Earnhardt, Martin, and Irvan—Goodwrench, Valvoline, and Kodak—lined up one after the other, with nobody else even close.

One lap remained. The order remained the same.

"Temperature?" Kirk Shelmerdine calmly asked Earnhardt.

"One-sixty on the water," replied Earnhardt evenly. No one was going to catch him, and he knew it.

The race wasn't yet over, but on the radio Shelmerdine was telling his crew, "Everyone help get our stuff out of the way of the 11 car." He was reminding his men to clear out for the crew occupying the space in the next race.

The checkered flag came down as the black and silver Goodwrench Chevrolet crossed the start-finish first. Mark Martin and Ernie Irvan following behind, unable to generate the speed to get past Earnhardt.

On Earnhardt's radio, no one said a thing, almost as though this were just another day at the office. The Goodwrench crew methodically put away the hoses and toolboxes and pulled in the racing banners. In the stands the resounding cheers and boos were divided. Dale Earnhardt had found another way to win a race. He took home a purse of $35,400.

I rose from my seat in the paddock club suites behind pit road, cheering, clapping, and smiling at the brazen manner in which Earnhardt had won another one. I couldn't help but admire the guy. He drove with arrogance, like the Robert Conrad character in the TV ad where Conrad dares anyone to knock the battery off his shoulder. He was a lot like Muhammad Ali during the days when The Champ would make predictions of what round he'd knock his opponent out and then do it. Earnhardt isn't garrulous like Ali, nor nearly as personable, but he has real star quality. He fills seats and causes talk and controversy, and there is no one else in the sport like him.

Next to me one of the race fans couldn't help but notice my exuberance. He said, "You're grinning like a Chevy fan, even if he did have to spin out a Ford to do it." The man, fiftyish, was smiling, but at the same time he was upset. Over the years Earnhardt had spun out many a Ford— and other Chevys too—and Earnhardt's spinout of the pole sitter, Sterling Marlin, earlier in the race had left the man angered. That anger was tempered only by his grudging admiration for the inhospitable hombre from Welcome, North Carolina.

I asked the man why he rooted for Fords.

"You could buy them cheap, and they'd run forever," he said. I had visions of him farming tobacco in the hills near Charlotte and in the evening racing his '40 flathead Ford.

"Are you from the Carolinas?" I asked.

"New York," he said.

With the first qualifying race at an end, one set of pit crews worked calmly and methodically to pack their gear, and then they headed for the garage area while a second set began unloading their supplies and paraphernalia.

As in the first race, Fords were expected to have the best chance of winning, but this time Earnhardt and his Lumina wouldn't be around to challenge them. Four Fords—driven by Bill Elliott, Dorsey Schroeder, Davey Allison, and Brett Bodine—had run fastest during the time trials. Their closest non-Ford competitor would be Ricky Rudd, starting in the fifth spot behind the wheel of his Tide Chevy Lumina for the Rick Hendrick team. Beside him was Chad Little, driving for the first time in Cale Yarborough's TropArtic Ford. Darrell Waltrip, his brother Michael, Derrike Cope, Morgan Shepherd, and Bobby Hamilton were some of the other name drivers in the race.

As before, the roar of the engines signaled the start of the second of the twin 125 races. As the cars sat along the pit wall, ready to go, crew members of quite a few of the cars stood behind their cars, pulling down hard on the rear spoilers, giving up a little horsepower in an attempt to try

Dale Earnhardt wins the first preliminary race at the 1992 Daytona 500.

to avoid the loss of control and the rending of metal that had marked the first race.

Once again pace car driver Elmo Langley led the cars away from the pits, and when the green flag dropped, Bill Elliott, in his dark red and white Budweiser Ford, and Ricky Rudd, in his colorful red, orange, yellow, and white Tide Chevy, took the early lead. It was going to be interesting to see whether Rudd could compete with the Fords. The experts were doubtful. Despite having to race a backup car because of his crash during practice, Bill Elliott appeared to have the fastest car. The big question was whether luck would be on his side.

Behind Elliott and Rudd was Dorsey Schroeder, the SCCA Trans Am champion in 1989 and the IMSA GTO winner in 1990. Dorsey could drive all right. What he lacked was Winston Cup experience. He had never run on a track as long as Daytona. Schroeder, driving a Whistler Ford owned by Junie Donlavey, had succeeded in running 191.449 miles an hour in the time trials. But running in traffic at those speeds was very different from running alone. In fourth place was Brett Bodine's Quaker State Ford, followed by the TropArtic Ford driven by Chad Little.

From the start, Ricky Rudd expressed concern. "I'm a little sluggish as I exit the corners," he told his pit crew. By the eighth lap Rudd still trailed closely behind Elliott, as the blood-red Budweiser car and the brilliantly painted Tide car maintained a substantial distance over the competition. Rudd asked his crew, "How many cars are behind me?" Four, came the reply. Rudd was right on Elliott's tail throughout the ninth lap.

"That's a good line going into turn three," his crew told him. "You're closing in on him." Behind Rudd was Brett Bodine and then Chad Little. Though back in thirteenth place, Darrell Waltrip was running at 190 miles an hour. Waltrip, once a hard-charger, had matured as a driver. Early in the race, Waltrip liked to pace himself and his car so he would be there at the end.

"Just hang with them, pardner," sang Jeff Hammond, his crew chief. "You're looking good." There were thirty-nine laps to go, plenty of time to move up. Even though Waltrip was thirteenth, he was still on the lead lap, which was all he cared about. One caution flag would wipe out any disadvantage.

In lap 14, Morgan Shepherd, driving the Wood Brothers Ford, pulled into third place behind Elliott and Rudd. Shepherd, who had the fourth-best qualifying run with a time of 192.143 in his white car with the red Citgo logo, joined the colorful procession at the front. All three cars looked strong, like they could run forever, but of course any failure would come from the inside and could announce itself at any time.

During lap 18, Davey Allison joined the front-runners in his Ford, and Ricky Rudd began to slip back. A lap later, with four Fords at the front, Rudd dropped to sixth, behind Derrike Cope in his orange and white Purolator Chevy. Cope had wrecked his primary car during practice, but his team had slaved over his backup car, and Derrike was in the hunt.

At the halfway point a train of Elliott, Davey Allison, and Morgan Shepherd was running away from the field.

A second group of five cars, led by Ricky Rudd and followed by Derrike Cope, Brett Bodine, Chad Little, and Michael Waltrip, trailed in another tight pack.

Behind them, a wide margin back, came Darrell Waltrip, Dorsey Schroeder, Dick Trickle, and Geoff Bodine.

Watching the Fords of Elliott, Allison, and Shepherd fly away from the field, Terry Labonte, who had crashed his Chevy on the fourth lap of the first race, enviously commented, "If you run a Ford and can't go 192 miles an hour, they ought to take it away from you."

By lap 30, Bill Elliott was on his own. His lead over Morgan Shepherd had grown to five car lengths. A caution flag thrown on lap 32 when car 97, driven by Mark Gibson, spun out enabled Shepherd to close the gap again.

Elliott tried to fool Shepherd and Allison by faking a move into the pits, then at the last moment staying on the track. Neither Shepherd nor Allison took the bait. They kept going too.

Ricky Rudd, in seventh place, had closed on the leaders because of the caution flag.

"You look good," Rudd was told. "You really look good." Rudd wanted to know whether he could finish the race without having to pit for fuel.

"Our fuel technician said we'll be okay on fuel," he was told.

With thirteen laps to go, the leaders were purring along in a colorful train: Budweiser deep red; Citgo red and white; Texaco black, yellow, and red; Tide yellow; TropArtic neon yellow; and Pennzoil yellow, followed by Darrell Waltrip's multicolored white, black, red, and silver Western Auto car and Geoff Bodine's red and white Motorcraft car.

With ten laps remaining, Bill Elliott was off by himself. He held a ten-car lead over Morgan Shepherd, whom Davey Allison sought to pass on the low side. Ricky Rudd followed on Allison's tail.

Allison didn't succeed, and as Darrell Waltrip moved up, Rudd dropped to fifth.

Rudd passed Darrell Waltrip back again, and with five laps to go, it was Elliott way in front, then Shepherd, Allison, Rudd, Darrell Waltrip, and brother Michael in sixth.

"Keep digging, Ricky. You're gaining on him," his crew exhorted. Darrell Waltrip, in fifth, was told by his crew, "You're in fifth, and Michael is sixth, but there's a big gap behind you, if he makes a move."

Morgan Shepherd, showing surprising speed, closed the gap on Bill Elliott, the leader, and with one lap to go, Elliott began weaving back and forth to keep Shepherd away.

Lacking someone to draft with, Shepherd had no way to catch him. At the end, Bill Elliott removed all drama and suspense. He had led forty-nine of the fifty laps, surrendering the lead for only one lap when he made a pit stop. It was a piece of cake for the taciturn racer from Dawsonville, Georgia, who won a purse of $35,200. Morgan Shepherd finished second, a comfortable distance behind.

Davey Allison finished third, Rudd fourth. Despite the admonition from his crew, Darrell Waltrip was passed by his younger brother on the final lap, so Michael finished fifth, and Darrell sixth.

As he crossed the finish line, Darrell, normally excitable, seemed at ease. There was nothing shabby about starting the 500 in the twelfth position.

"I'm real happy," Darrell told his crew.

"We'll get it fixed. We'll make it better," crew chief Jeff Hammond replied.

After the race Bill Elliott told reporters, "If we can keep things going, I feel real good about this Budweiser Ford. This car ought to be good for Sunday." Few thought otherwise.

Morgan Shepherd, asked why he wasn't able to pass Elliott at the end, commented, "You need someone to run with you to pass the leader by. Those three cars were looking out for each other." No one bothered to ask him which three cars he was talking about. I sure would have liked to know.

The field for the Daytona 500 was now set. It was back to work for all the crews. They had just three more days of grueling work to make their cars better and faster.

Bill Elliot wins the second preliminary race at the 1992 Daytona 500.

Starting Lineup for the 34th Annual Daytona 500 by STP
Daytona International Speedway—February 16, 1992

ROW	STR POS	CAR NO.	DRIVER	TEAM/CAR
1	1	22	Sterling Marlin	Maxwell House Ford
	2	11	Bill Elliott	Budweiser Ford
2	3	3	Dale Earnhardt	GM Goodwrench Chevrolet
	4	21	Morgan Shepherd	Citgo Ford
3	5	6	Mark Martin	Valvoline Ford
	6	28	Davey Allison	Havoline Ford
4	7	4	Ernie Irvan	Kodak Chevrolet
	8	5	Ricky Rudd	Tide Chevrolet
5	9	41	Greg Sacks	Kellogg's Chevrolet
	10	30	Michael Waltrip	Pennzoil Pontiac
6	11	33	Harry Gant	Skoal Bandit Oldsmobile
	12	17	Darrell Waltrip	Western Auto Chevrolet
7	13	1	Rick Mast	Skoal Classic Oldsmobile
	14	66	Chad Little	TropArtic Ford
8	15	25	Ken Schrader	Kodiak Chevrolet
	16	15	Geoff Bodine	Motorcraft Ford
9	17	2	Rusty Wallace	Miller Genuine Draft Pontiac
	18	26	Brett Bodine	Quaker State Ford
10	19	9	Phil Parsons	Melling Racing Ford
	20	10	Derrike Cope	Purolator Chevrolet
11	21	03	Kerry Teague	Team U.S.A. Oldsmobile
	22	68	Bobby Hamilton	Country Time Oldsmobile
12	23	71	Dave Marcis	Big Apple Market Chevrolet
	24	47	Buddy Baker	Close Racing Oldsmobile
13	25	73	Phil Barkdoll	X1R Oldsmobile
	26	31	Bobby Hillin	Team Ireland Chevrolet
14	27	0	Delma Cowart	Master's Economy Inn Ford
	28	75	Dick Trickle	Rahmoc Oldsmobile

ROW	STR POS	CAR NO.	DRIVER	TEAM/CAR
15	29	77	Mike Potter	Kenova Construction Chevrolet
	30	49	Stanley Smith	Ameritron Batteries Chevrolet
16	31	90	Dorsey Schroeder	Whistler Radar Ford
	32	43	Richard Petty	STP Pontiac
17	33	42	Kyle Petty	Mello Yello Pontiac
	34	94	Terry Labonte	Sunoco Chevrolet
18	35	18	Dale Jarrett	Interstate Batteries Chevrolet
	36	95	Bob Schacht	Shoney's Oldsmobile
19	37	16	Wally Dallenbach, Jr.	Keystone Ford
	38	8	Rick Wilson	Snickers Ford
20	39	14	A. J. Foyt	Copenhagen Oldsmobile
	40	55	Ted Musgrave	Jasper Engines Chevrolet
21	41	7	Alan Kulwicki	Hooters Ford
	42	12	Hut Stricklin	Raybestos Chevrolet

The Daytona 500

"Guys, crank 'em up and go," said Grand Marshal Richard Petty. Silence. The drivers, including Petty, had no intention of turning on their engines until pace car driver Elmo Langley set off down pit road for the wide expanse of the speedway track. In a race where gas mileage is critical, no one wanted to waste any gas idling before leaving pit road for the three warm-up laps, including two through the pits prior to the green flag.

As the cars began to move off pit road, Alan Kulwicki, who was starting all the way back in the forty-first position because of his wreck in the first 125, asked his crew, "Are we going through pit road?"

"Next time by, Alan." The rules regarding pit safety were still new to the drivers.

Kulwicki replied, "Three warm-up laps, fifty-one more before we pit. You didn't do anything to the carburetor, did you?" Drivers don't like surprises.

"No," answered crew chief Paul Andrews. "It's just the way you wanted it."

After the cars made their required passes down pit road to check the proper rpms for entering and leaving the pits, the green flag fell, and amid the road of engines and that of the huge throng of one hundred and fifty thousand spectators, the 34th Daytona 500 was under way.

As the flag dropped, most of the huge crowd held its collective breath, because these race fans, versed in the ways of the superspeedways, well knew that if there was going to be a massive pileup, starts and restarts were the most likely time. Forty-two cars were running in two long trains, nose-to-tail at speeds approaching 200 miles an hour down the straightaway, faster than some of the drivers wanted to go. All it would take to start the bumper-car carnage would be one car accelerating too slowly or getting out of shape to impede the roaring thunder behind or two cars meeting at the same spot and starting a chain reaction of out-of-control metal.

With two hundred laps and a little more than three hours of hard racing ahead of them, down the front straightaway and into turns one and two Sterling Marlin and Bill Elliott led the two long strings of cars. Dale Earnhardt, starting in the second row, impulsively made a move to pass low, only to lose the draft of the car in front of him and fall back from his third spot. Mark Martin, Morgan Shepherd, and Davey Allison whipped past the black and silver Goodwrench Chevy Lumina in a line, leaving Earnhardt with the task of having to chase five of the more-powerful Ford Thunderbirds.

On the seventh lap the first car fell out. It was car 95, an Oldsmobile Cutlass driven by rookie driver Bob Schacht, who had to leave the track with a busted fuel pump.

Around the track the colorful strings of cars roared, and on the eighth lap, Bill Elliott indicated early that it was mostly irrelevant that Sterling Marlin was his teammate in Junior Johnson's shop. Elliott drove past Marlin to take the lead in a pack of eleven race cars. Earnhardt, keeping in contention, sat fourth behind Davey Allison.

Budweiser red, Maxwell House blue, Havoline black and red, and Goodwrench black roared around the track single-file, followed by the yellow Pennzoil Pontiac driven by Michael Waltrip. Twenty more cars followed. Early, Richard Petty's STP Pontiac was far back. Fans were disappointed to see that The King's magic was still a thing of the past.

Meanwhile, the disconsolate pit crew of Brett Bodine quietly began packing their gear. The Quaker State Ford owned by Kenny Bernstein had a faulty distributor and was forced out of the race.

After fourteen laps, the lead car of Bill Elliott was averaging 188 miles per hour. Geoff Bodine, driving his red and white Motorcraft Ford, owned by Bud Moore, climbed into fourth behind Earnhardt. By lap 16, Bodine, Earnhardt's longtime nemesis, managed to wrest third place away from him.

Two laps later, as the cars crossed the start-finish line in front of the grandstand, Bill Elliott, Sterling Marlin, and Geoff Bodine opened a four-car lead over the rest of the pack, followed by a group of five cars—Davey Allison, Earnhardt, Morgan Shepherd, Mark Martin, and Michael Waltrip.

By lap 20, Earnhardt was back to eighth. The jockeying continued with a dangerous ferocity. Sterling Marlin and Bill Elliott were teammates, but no one believed either driver would go out of his way to help the other, unless he was looking for a drafting partner. Teammates in racing do not sacrifice one for the other. What makes them teammates is that the paycheck comes from the same bank account. In the case of Elliott and Marlin, the checkbook belonged to Junior Johnson.

On lap 23 Marlin took back the lead from teammate Bill Elliott, with Geoff Bodine third, Davey Allison fourth, Morgan Shepherd fifth, and Mark Martin sixth—Fords all.

One lap later Bodine overtook Elliott for second, and a lap after that Davey Allison took second, with Elliott third and Bodine fourth.

Allison, who everyone predicted would provide the strongest competition for the two Junior Johnson cars, called his crew two laps later. "I'm loose," was all he said. Allison had to hope for a caution flag so his crew could fix his car without their losing too much ground.

The race continued with Sterling Marlin in his Maxwell House Ford looking very strong. Marlin had had the best qualifying time, at 192.213, and only one other car, that of teammate Bill Elliott, had been in the 192s, at 192.090.

On lap 27 Marlin led Davey Allison and Bill Elliott, the three roaring around the speedway as one and opening a gap in front of a three-car pack made up of Geoff Bodine, Morgan Shepherd, and Mark Martin.

On lap 41, with Geoff Bodine and Morgan Shepherd running together in turn two, Bodine's Motorcraft Ford got out of shape and became airborne, knocking a dent into the side of Shepherd's Citgo Ford and causing Shepherd to graze the wall.

Shepherd told Leonard Wood over the radio, "Bodine liked to knock me out."

The nose of Bodine's car was bent, not enough to bring about a pit stop, but enough to keep the car from peak performance.

The banging wasn't enough to send Shepherd's car to the pits either, even though Shepherd's rear end was knocked out of alignment. Though the car continued to run well, not slowing perceptibly, it never handled as well as it had before the incident. Bodine and Shepherd drove on. It would be a long, satisfying day for both of them.

Dale Earnhardt, still on the lead lap, was running tenth, part of a four-car group that was twenty car lengths behind the leaders.

Marlin and Allison were nose-to-tail on lap 45, with Elliott three lengths behind, when Marlin's team decided to pit.

"Let's take four. It's too early to gamble now," said Maxwell House crew chief Mike Beam.

"Go, boys, go," said Sterling Marlin over the radio.

Davey Allison came onto pit road behind Marlin. Over in the pit of car 28, Davey Allison asked, "Did the 22 car change four tires?"

"Yeah," was the reply.

Allison's crew chief, Larry McReynolds, decided to change only two tires. McReynolds also took out some of the bite in the car, hoping it would handle better. Adjusting a car was one of McReynolds's strengths. Allison's car would run better than ever now.

With the leaders pitting, Rick Hendrick's car 25, the Kodiak Chevrolet driven by Kenny Schrader, took the lead.

In the pit, driver Phil Barkdoll crawled out of the 73 car, which had started the race in the twenty-fifth position. Jim Sauter took over for him as Barkdoll announced he was too out of shape to continue. After the race the fifty-seven-year-old Barkdoll told reporters, "I'm a bit overweight."

With more than one hundred miles on the books, there hadn't been a single caution flag. Only three times in the history of the Daytona 500 had the race gone the full distance without a caution flag—in 1959, 1961, and 1962, a long, long time ago. At these speeds a crash-free race was unlikely.

By lap 60, Larry McReynolds's magic was taking hold. Davey Allison retook the lead from Ken Schrader, who himself had to pit, and Allison led a three-car train with Sterling Marlin and Bill Elliott that left the rest of the pack far behind. In his Lumina, Dale Earnhardt told his crew over the radio, "The car is pushing real bad, pushing in the corners. We can't run behind the leaders."

Earnhardt was the one Chevy given a shot at beating the Fords. The Fords had the better engines, but the Chevys were supposed to handle better. If Earnhardt's crew couldn't improve the handling of his car, it was going to be a long day for the five-time champion who had never won a Daytona 500.

Bill Elliott, in his deep red Budweiser Ford, then took the lead, followed by teammate Marlin, the hard-charging Ernie Irvan, and Davey Allison. Behind Allison in fifth pace was the neon red and black Chevy with the silver number 17 driven by Darrell Waltrip, followed by Michael Waltrip, Dale Jarrett, Mark Martin, and Earnhardt, who seemed to be losing ground on the leaders.

During lap 72 it began to drizzle over the western part of the track. The rain came down lightly, but because rain brings a slickness to the asphalt that can lead to carnage on superspeedways, track officials kept close watch over track conditions. As the rain mottled the raceway, Bill Elliott purred along in the lead. A long train of cars kept up behind him.

Suddenly, without warning, a puff of smoke appeared behind the Chevrolet driven by Ricky Rudd. The colorful Tide car with the number 5 on its side had blown an engine. Rudd, who had been riding in thirteenth place, had to leave on lap 79, a crushing turn of events for Rudd, engine builder Waddell Wilson, GM Jimmy Johnson, and owner Rick Hendrick. (When asked what happened, Rudd explained, "The car lost all its water and finally let go.")

Of the forty-two cars that had started the race, thirty-nine were still on the track.

Two laps later, the caution flag appeared when rain continued to fall on turns one and two, but harder. All the cars in the lead lap headed for the pits. Dale Earnhardt's crew could be seen playing with the angle of the spoiler.

Three laps of driving under the yellow closed the field. Twelve cars were bunched up behind each other, with Elliott leading in his red Budweiser Ford and teammate Sterling Marlin in his equally beautiful blue Maxwell House Ford right behind. In third place was Ernie Irvan in the Kodak Chevrolet, and then Davey Allison, Morgan Shepherd, Darrell Waltrip, brother Michael, Dale Jarrett, Mark Martin, and a struggling Earnhardt.

The rain let up, ending the caution period, and for four laps the speeding armada of machines roared around the track. A restart at Daytona can be as dangerous as the start of the race; a long line of cars traveling at top speeds invites disaster.

The race continued to lap 91, almost the halfway point, when havoc and destruction began to reign. Ernie Irvan, who in 1990 had wiped out the field at both Talladega and Pocono, struck. With Bill Elliott and Sterling Marlin racing side by side for the lead, the strong-willed, gambling Ernie, who the fans call Swervin' Irvan, decided to pass the two side-by-side cars on the inside and go for the lead.

There are certain strategies that seem to court disaster. One is to attempt to pass three abreast at Daytona. If you look down at the Daytona speedway from above, you can see a band of black about twelve feet wide on the asphalt. Two car-wide grooves mesh into one continuous black band. This is the area that is safest to travel. To run higher than the band, or lower, is to invite mayhem. Some tracks are more forgiving. You can leave the groove at Talladega or Michigan and have a good shot at remaining unscathed. Not so at Darlington or Daytona.

Running three abreast at Daytona is like trying to squeeze three wide through the two-laned Lincoln Tunnel. There's room, but there isn't much more than about an inch of space between cars to maneuver safely. What Ernie Irvan did may have been very brave and daring. Given what followed, it also proved incredibly reckless and stupid.

If Irvan had succeeded in making the pass, he would have been hailed for his daring. But it was still early in the race, and with more patience, he well might have found a safer strategical opening to make his move later in the race.

Ernie had watched his mentor, Dale Earnhardt, successfully go three abreast in the 125-miler and take the lead, and he decided to mimic Earnhardt's earlier strategy.

In choosing to try to get out front by going three abreast, Irvan came in low under the two Junior Johnson Fords and held his foot to the floor. He led Sterling Marlin when he ducked back in front of him, but he failed by inches to clear Marlin's dark blue Thunderbird. At 188 miles an hour, failing by inches means havoc and mayhem.

The right rear of Irvan's yellow Kodak Chevrolet with the red numeral 4 rubbed up against the left side of Sterling Marlin's Ford. Marlin, pushed out of shape, began sliding up the bank and sideswiped Bill Elliott's car. Suddenly, amid dust and smoke, cars began flying, spinning, and whirling in every direction, and the Daytona 500 began to look like a demolition derby. This time fourteen cars—a third of the field— would be damaged or destroyed, including Irvan's.

Who survived and who didn't was a matter of luck. Out on the track, cars skidded haphazardly out of control. This is what all those owners, crew chiefs, and drivers had been talking about when they said that driving skill and a good car are never enough.

Whether a driver made it through the wreckage or not depended on where he was on the track at the time all the cars began careening. The two cars that had been tucked in directly behind the Irvan-Marlin-Elliott sandwich were the 28 Havoline Thunderbird driven by Davey Allison and the 21 Citgo Thunderbird driven by Morgan Shepherd. Both Allison and Shepherd went high on the track as the three-acrossers came together in the middle, and so the 28 and 21 cars got through safely. Michael Waltrip, in his yellow Pennzoil car, somehow snuck through the carnage too. Alan Kulwicki's orange Hooters car also somehow made it through.

Rusty Wallace, in his black Miller Lite Draft Pontiac, got banged around and caught on fire. Kenny Schrader's Kodiak bear got crunched. Schrader badly injured his ankle.

The backstretch filled with smoke and dust and the sound of crunching metal. Chad Little in Cale Yarborough's TropArtic car, Dale Jarrett in the Interstate Batteries car, and the unlucky Hut Stricklin in Bobby Allison's

Raybestos car were wrecked. The front end of Richard Petty's beautiful STP Pontiac was accordioned. He could still drive the car, but The King, driving his final Daytona 500, would no longer be in contention.

As the pileup was beginning, Darrell Waltrip's spotter called out over the radio, "We got a bad wreck developing on the back straightaway." Waltrip was aware of the potential danger, and as he sped through was sure he had avoided danger, but Sterling Marlin was hurtling on his way back down the track after hitting the wall, and Marlin crushed Darrell, spinning him. Down through the infield Waltrip flew. Fortunately, Waltrip was out of control going forward, not sideways, or he would have flipped going down the back straightaway.

Darrell Waltrip's Chevy was a mess of crumpled sheet metal. On his radio Morgan Shepherd noted that Darrell had crashed.

"Poor Darrell got into it again," Shepherd told Leonard Wood.

Mark Martin's blue and white Valvoline car was crumpled in front. Both Sterling Marlin and Bill Elliott, favorites to win the race just moments before, were wrecked badly. Elliott had a big dent in his front quarter panel.

The drivers of the damaged cars returned to the pits. In the race for the Winston Cup driving championship, it's important to get back onto the track and finish as high as possible, even if it means finishing twenty laps back. Pit crews worked feverishly to pull metal away from tires, to make their cars as aerodynamic as possible, using Band-Aids, bondo, chewing gum, and spit.

The cars driven by Ken Schrader, Chad Little, Dale Jarrett, and Sterling Marlin had to leave the race. Considering that Ricky Rudd had blown an engine earlier, the loss of Schrader's car was a cruel blow to the Hendrick Motorsports team. The other drivers involved in the crash—Dale Earnhardt, Richard Petty, Hut Stricklin, Bill Elliott, Ernie Irvan, Darrell Waltrip, and Rusty Wallace—sat in the pits as their crews urgently attempted to remold or remove body parts so the cars could get back onto the track.

The radio announcers stuck mikes in the faces of the victims and sought explanations. It was similar to the local TV newscaster who goes to a member of a family whose house has burned to the ground and whose dog has died in the fire and asks, "How do you feel?"

"What happened?" Mark Martin was asked.

"I don't know. Couldn't see. Smoke."

Said Bill Elliott, "I don't know what happened. First thing I know, I was turning left."

Darrell Waltrip was tight-lipped, but put a positive spin on the mishap.

"Cars 22 and 11 got hooked together. We can go back out in this Western Auto Chevrolet. We'll go back out." And he did, but his car, no longer sleek, could only limp along for the rest of the day.

Rusty Wallace publicly expressed anger at Ernie Irvan for causing the mayhem, but said it in a roundabout way.

When asked what had happened, Wallace replied, "Those three up front started banging around, and everything went flying. We were running so good. I was waiting for someone to screw up, and they did it."

Dale Jarrett was another victim of the crash who placed blame.

"It's a shame," he said, "to come from thirty-fifth up to the top ten and then have somebody up there not use their head very well and take you out of the first race of the year.

"I really don't know what happened. Apparently, some of them got to racing three wide. There's a time to race three wide and there's a time not to. The halfway point of the 500 isn't the time to be running that way."

Before the crash, it had looked like Junior Johnson's big day. He had had the two best-qualifying cars. Now Junior had a pile of blue-painted junk and a banged-up, red-painted jalopy with bad aerodynamics.

Sterling Marlin, now a spectator, explained what had happened: "We ran out of real estate. Bill was coming down and Ernie was coming down. I stood on the brakes, and it was 'Katie bar the door.' "

One man who did not blame Irvan was Junior Johnson, a man who all his life has drawn his own conclusions and acted on them. Junior wasn't 100 percent positive, but his hunch was that Sterling Marlin had caused the crash—that Marlin had had to put on his brakes to avoid hitting Bill Elliott, and that he would have hit Elliott even if Ernie Irvan hadn't been where he was.

Later, after viewing the videotape over and over and over, Junior Johnson became more certain than ever that Marlin, who had yet to win a Winston Cup race, was the one who had screwed up. If Marlin didn't win soon, all his poles and second places wouldn't mean a hill of motor oil to Johnson.

It took six slow laps under the yellow before the track was cleared of debris. When the green flag finally came out, the field had been narrowed considerably. Only four cars involved in the crash were out, but ten more were either in the pits still getting fixed up or were limping badly, never to contend.

Davey Allison's black Ford with the red and white Texaco star was in the lead, followed by Tri-Star's Oldsmobile Cutlass, driven by Bobby Hamilton. In third place was Michael Waltrip in his Bahari Racing Pontiac, with Derrike Cope's Chevy fourth and Dick Trickle's Oldsmobile fifth. Alan Kulwicki, who started the race in the very last row, had moved all the way up to sixth place.

As the race neared the halfway point, the enthusiasm of the crowd began to wane. The Daytona 500 is a *long* race, and the high speeds, noise, and pressure exhaust everyone. It isn't possible for a spectator to stay "up" for three hours. Moreover, the crash had brought great disappointment to much of the crowd, because so many of their favorite drivers—Ricky Rudd, Mark Martin, Sterling Marlin, Bill Elliott, Rusty Wallace, Hut Stricklin, Ernie Irvan, and Darrell Waltrip—had been eliminated from contention. Dale Earnhardt, the Black Hat whom everyone loved to hate, was still in the race, but his Lumina had suffered enough body damage to keep him from being at his competitive best. The fans understood that Earnhardt could drive a damaged car as good as or better than anyone else, but would he be able to catch Davey Allison, whose car was undamaged and very fast? Doubtful. There were a hundred laps to go to find out.

Davey Allison, because he led at the halfway point, picked up a check for $10,000 from Gillette. Behind him in second place was the surprising Bobby Hamilton in the Country Time Oldsmobile, with Bahari's Michael Waltrip third, Alan Kulwicki fourth, and Wally Dallenbach, Jr., fifth in the red and white Keystone Beer Ford owned by Jack Roush.

One lap later, Alan Kulwicki in his Hooters Ford sailed past Hamilton to sit just behind the leader.

A new challenger appeared. On the 105th lap, Morgan Shepherd, driving the Wood Brothers' Citgo Ford, motored into fourth place, just ahead of Dale Earnhardt, and just behind Allison, Hamilton, and Kulwicki. Shepherd had finished second in the latter of the twin 125s. His time at the trials was 189.609. His car was running smoothly. As Shepherd pulled in behind the leaders, Eddie Wood told him over the radio, "If we have any kind of luck, we can win it."

By lap 108 Shepherd was comfortably in second place behind Davey Allison, the two cars running all by themselves ahead of the field. Everyone else seemed to be struggling.

Alan Kulwicki, in third, was a lap down from the leaders. Behind him was Bobby Hamilton and driver-owner Stanley Smith. Dale Earnhardt and Geoff Bodine followed. Limping around the track were Richard Petty, Darrell Waltrip, and Ernie Irvan, who after the crash broke a shock on the right side, adding to his troubles.

Roaring through the competition and running far out in front were Davey Allison and Morgan Shepherd, two Fords sponsored by competing oil companies. On lap 119 Shepherd tried to pass and grab the lead. He went low. Allison stayed high. The powerful Robert Yates car held Shepherd off. Without a drafting partner, Allison now knew, Shepherd could not catch him.

In third place, forty car lengths back, was the surprising Dick Trickle. Driving for the team of Butch Mock and Bob Rahilly, Trickle was giving his Oldsmobile the ride of his life. The Rahmoc car was beginning the season without a sponsor, and maybe now someone with big bucks might take notice. The survival of the race team was hanging in the balance.

On the 120th lap, blue smoke began puffing from the back of Derrike Cope's Purolator Chevrolet. Cope slowed, and when he got to pit road turned for the garage area. He was through for the day, finishing a very disappointing thirty-fourth. Five laps later Bobby Hamilton busted a piston, and the Tri-Star Olds also was finished. Around this time Mark Martin's Valvoline Ford returned to the track, hoodless and thirty laps down.

On lap 144 rookie Kerry Teague and Rick Wilson, in his Snickers Ford owned by the Stavola Brothers, tangled. A caution came out as both cars headed for the pits. The leaders headed in for gas. When the green flag came out again, there were seven cars in the lead lap.

Davey Allison, the leader since the pileup on lap 91, was first, with Morgan Shepherd behind him, Michael Waltrip third, and Geoff Bodine fourth, followed by Dick Trickle, Alan Kulwicki, and Kyle Petty in his Mello Yello Pontiac.

With fifty-six laps to go, the question remained: Could Davey Allison finish the race without having to make another pit stop? If he could, he'd win it hands down.

Robert Yates, the owner of the Havoline car, said he thought his team could finish without having to stop. Down pit road, Leonard and Glen Wood, owners of Morgan Shepherd's car, were facing the same decision. What they did would depend on what Robert Yates did.

By lap 156 only four drivers—Allison, Shepherd, Michael Waltrip, and Dick Trickle—were in the lead lap. If Waltrip, in a Pontiac, could win the race, it would be the first Daytona win for a Pontiac since Cale Yarborough had done it in 1983. More important to Michael Waltrip, it would be his first win in Winston Cup competition. Running strongly, this was a very impressive performance for Bahari Racing.

Bill Ingle, Michael Waltrip's crew chief, said his stomach was all tied up in knots worrying about how to catch the Fords.

"Can you go all the way on the gas?" he was asked.

"Whether we can or not, we're going to," was his answer.

Paul Andrews, the crew chief for Alan Kulwicki's car, also was asked about the fuel. "We topped off on the yellow," he said. "I have no doubt we can go all the way."

Around and around they went, with Davey Allison leading Morgan Shepherd, Texaco against Citgo, Robert Yates Racing against the famed Wood Brothers. As the race went on, it was clear that Allison had the better-handling car. Morgan was complaining that his car was pushing. When Shepherd turned, the front of his car would drift up toward the wall. Allison, who had had some handling problems in the early part of the race, had no problems now.

On lap 165, Ernie Irvan, many laps down, cut a tire and spun out. This had not been a good day for Irvan. First the crash, then a bad shock absorber, and now a tire. The caution flag was brought out.

Irvan's hard driving had wreaked havoc on others on lap 91, and now his cut tire caused fortunes to turn once again. The question of whether Allison or Shepherd would run out of gas became moot. Under the caution, Allison headed his Ford for the pits, where it took on four new tires and a full tank of gas, and when he did, so did Shepherd, Michael Waltrip, and Alan Kulwicki, the others still in the hunt.

As Glen Wood was putting a can of gas in Morgan Shepherd's car, a tow truck was pulling Ernie Irvan off the track for more repairs. Ernie, one of the fans' favorite drivers, got a loud ovation.

Because Davey Allison took the time to change tires in addition to getting gas, Michael Waltrip beat him off pit road and onto the track and led the race after lap 168. Allison came out second, followed by Morgan Shepherd, Alan Kulwicki, and Geoff Bodine, who had run conservatively all race long, saving his Motorcraft Ford until he was now in serious contention.

Then Michael Waltrip had his day in the sun for three laps, leading from lap 168 through lap 170.

"Michael is so due to win a race," declared track commentator Eli Gold. The commentators then noted that his yellow Pennzoil Pontiac had baby-blue wheels. It turned out that the Bahari team had needed a set of stickers (tires that grip the road), and the Richard Petty STP racing team had obliged by selling Bahari a set. Hence the baby-blue wheels.

After three laps of Michael Waltrip holding the lead, Allison and Kulwicki, drafting together, came down low and buzzed right by him. It was to be the end of the day's magic for the yellow (and baby-blue) car 30. Morgan Shepherd's Citgo Ford and Geoff Bodine's Motorcraft Ford were on Waltrip's tail, poised to pass.

Kulwicki, always a hard-charger, informed his crew, "I'm going after his car now." Somebody in his crew should have said, "What's your hurry?" It was a serious tactical mistake. When Kulwicki pulled out to pass Davey Allison in an attempt to take the lead, he lost the draft and fell so far back that he was passed by Waltrip, Shepherd, and Geoff Bodine, in Bud Moore's Motorcraft Ford.

Asked one of the track commentators: "Is Bud Moore chewing his tongue?"

The reply: "He's up to about 8,500 rpms."

Lurking in the background, a lap behind, was Dale Earnhardt, in sixth place. Earnhardt's goal for the moment was to get back to the lead lap. Then, if there were a caution flag . . . Even when banged-up, Earnhardt could never be counted out.

The cars raced on in a blur. With twenty-one laps to go, Davey Allison, Michael Waltrip, and Morgan Shepherd—none of whom had ever won the Daytona 500—were running together nose-to-tail in a train, gaining speed and ground on everyone else.

In fourth and fifth, Geoff Bodine and Alan Kulwicki ran together in a duet, followed by Dick Trickle, Terry Labonte, and Ted Musgrave in car 55, then Dale Earnhardt and Kyle Petty.

With fifteen laps to go, the order of finish remained unchanged. It was Allison, then Michael Waltrip, then Morgan Shepherd.

Shepherd kept trying to get by the yellow Pontiac, but Waltrip was running too strong. Alan Kulwicki and Geoff Bodine were two seconds behind them, with Dale Earnhardt five seconds farther back.

With only three laps remaining, a puff of smoke emanated from the back of Michael Waltrip's car, signaling to everyone in the huge arena that he was finished for the day. Determined to the end, Waltrip refused to leave the track, chugging slowly around as competitors whizzed past. To have come so close . . . Waltrip's engine failure meant the difference between second place and eighteenth, the difference between $37,000 and $244,000.

On MRO radio, Bill Ingle, crew chief for Bahari, told the crowd, "We're not giving up. We'll be back." Grace under pressure.

Later Michael Waltrip would say, "The Daytona 500 is cruel. It is not a nice race, and it was cruel to us today. Every time we think we have a chance to win a race, something goes wrong."

Waltrip's blown engine was also a blow to Morgan Shepherd. With Waltrip finished, the race came down to Allison and himself. There was not another car within striking distance. Unless Shepherd broke, he was guaranteed second. But short of pulling a miracle, without a drafting partner that was where he was going to remain.

Morgan Shepherd kept trying to gain an opening to pass Davey Allison, but each time Shepherd made a move, Allison outran him. Davey Allison kept his left front tire on the inside line of the track. Shepherd was going to have to go inside if he was to pass him. It didn't seem possible.

Four seconds behind the two leaders, Alan Kulwicki and Geoff Bodine fought for third. The sponsorless Dick Trickle ran fifth, and Kyle Petty climbed to sixth.

One lap to go. Davey Allison stayed high on the track, and with Morgan Shepherd nose-to-tail, he dropped low to shake the draft.

With the finish line in view, Allison roared toward the stripe, two car lengths ahead of Shepherd. The flagman stood waving the black-and-white-checkered banner. Morgan Shepherd could gain no more ground. Davey Allison, loser to his dad Bobby in 1988, crossed the line first—three hours, seven minutes, and twelve seconds after the race had begun—as the hundred and fifty thousand fans rose to cheer the spectacle, and especially the young Allison.

Geoff Bodine whizzed past the line in third place. Alan Kulwicki, who had started in the very last row, proved he could run with the best and finished fourth. Dick Trickle was fifth, and Kyle Petty sixth. When Petty got out of his car, he almost fainted.

"I got bad air and couldn't breathe," he said. "When I got to driving a little crazy and passed Earnhardt on the outside, I couldn't breathe from there on out."

After Petty came Terry Labonte and Ted Musgrave. Dale Earnhardt, struggling valiantly all day with his banged-up Goodwrench Chevrolet, was ninth. After Phil Parsons and Buddy Baker came Harry Gant, with Rick Mast, Greg Sacks, and Wally Dallenbach, Jr., next. Richard Petty, driving in his final Daytona 500, was sixteenth. Jim Sauter, finishing the race for Phil Barkdoll, was seventeenth. Michael Waltrip finished eighteenth, then Dorsey Schroeder. Dave Marcis, still unsponsored, finished twentieth. His $26,210 purse would help, but not much.

Of the drivers in cars banged up during the lap 91 crash, Hut Stricklin limped home twenty-fourth, Darrell Waltrip twenty-sixth, Bill Elliott twenty-seventh, Ernie Irvan twenty-eighth, Mark Martin twenty-ninth, and Rusty Wallace thirty-first.

In the pit area, Morgan Shepherd said what everyone watching the race knew: "I needed help from behind to get by him."

Davey Allison, on his way to Victory Lane with crew chief Larry McReynolds and the rest of his pit crew, exulted. He had had a good car, and he had been lucky, the two ingredients that complete the formula—

along with a great driver—for winning NASCAR superspeedway races.
When asked about the big crash, Allison explained, ''I saw the thing
happen. I moved to the outside. Everything happened on the inside.''

In one reflexive move, Davey Allison had put himself in position to
win the jackpot of $244,050. For Davey Allison and the Texaco Havoline
Ford of Robert Yates Racing, it was a big, big day.

Davey Allison, who became the second son to join his father on the roll
of Daytona 500 winners—along with Lee Petty and his son Richard—
paid tribute to The King who had driven his last Daytona 500.

''Richard Petty won two hundred races,'' Davey said solemnly. ''I
don't think I'll get that far, since I've only got fourteen so far. But sitting
here, at the age of thirty, I'm happy that I've done just one of the things
he did.''

The afternoon sun was still shining across sunny Florida as the thousands of fans slowly exited the mile-long grandstands and headed for
nearby restaurants, bars, Souvenir Row, and their cars. Some continued
to sit in their seats, ruing that the day was over.

The vehicles that filled the infield and parked nose-to-tail all around the
huge speedway began revving up, their tired but exhilarated passengers
ready to make the slow trek back to wherever they had come from. None
were in a hurry. They well knew that because of the traffic snarl, for the
next two or three hours they would still be in Daytona or close by. No
matter. The three hours in the sun watching their heroes, breathing the
Unocal gas, eating the Gwaltney hot dogs and drinking the Budweiser
beer had left them emotionally spent. They had their souvenirs and their
memories. For this small city of fans, there is nothing quite like the
Daytona 500, and it would be a long year until the next one. For them,
the wait would be a lot harder than the long ride home.

Results of the 1992 Daytona 500

FIN	STP	DRIVER	CAR	LAPS	EARNINGS	STATUS
1	6	Davey Allison	Ford	200	$244,050	160.256 mph
2	4	Morgan Shepherd	Ford	200	$161,300	Running
3	16	Geoff Bodine	Ford	200	$116,250	Running
4	41	Alan Kulwicki	Ford	200	$ 87,500	Running
5	28	Dick Trickle	Olds	200	$ 78,800	Running
6	33	Kyle Petty	Pontiac	199	$ 67,700	Running
7	34	Terry Labonte	Chevy	199	$ 58,575	Running
8	40	Ted Musgrave	Chevy	199	$ 52,750	Running
9	3	Dale Earnhardt	Chevy	199	$ 87,000	Running
10	19	Phil Parsons	Ford	199	$ 49,150	Running
11	24	Buddy Baker	Olds	199	$ 38,375	Running
12	11	Harry Gant	Olds	199	$ 51,100	Running
13	13	Rick Mast	Olds	199	$ 40,355	Running
14	9	Greg Sacks	Chevy	199	$ 38,790	Running
15	37	Wally Dallenbach, Jr.	Ford	198	$ 29,700	Running
16	32	Richard Petty	Pontiac	198	$ 32,530	Running
17	25	Phil Barkdoll	Olds	198	$ 27,960	Running
18	10	Michael Waltrip	Pontiac	197	$ 37,150	Engine failed
19	31	Dorsey Schroeder	Ford	196	$ 25,720	Running
20	23	Dave Marcis	Chevy	195	$ 26,210	Running
21	39	A. J. Foyt	Olds	195	$ 23,055	Running
22	30	Stanley Smith	Chevy	195	$ 24,150	Running
23	38	Rick Wilson	Ford	195	$ 24,045	Running
24	42	Hut Stricklin	Chevy	188	$ 27,740	Running
25	27	Delma Cowart	Ford	188	$ 23,285	Running
26	12	Darrell Waltrip	Chevy	180	$ 33,580	Running
27	2	Bill Elliott	Ford	178	$ 60,225	Running
28	7	Ernie Irvan	Chevy	166	$ 43,370	Running
29	5	Mark Martin	Ford	162	$ 49,675	Running
30	29	Mike Potter	Chevy	151	$ 21,710	Fuel pump
31	17	Rusty Wallace	Pontiac	150	$ 30,455	Running
32	22	Bobby Hamilton	Olds	125	$ 27,350	Piston
33	21	Kerry Teague	Olds	122	$ 22,445	Crash
34	20	Derrike Cope	Chevy	120	$ 23,115	Radiator
35	1	Sterling Marlin	Ford	91	$ 34,435	Crash
36	35	Dale Jarrett	Chevy	91	$ 19,790	Crash
37	15	Ken Schrader	Chevy	91	$ 30,500	Crash

FIN	STP	DRIVER	CAR	LAPS	EARNINGS	STATUS
38	26	Bobby Hillin, Jr.	Chevy	91	$20,370	Crash
39	14	Chad Little	Ford	90	$22,760	Crash
40	8	Ricky Rudd	Chevy	79	$34,350	Engine failed
41	18	Brett Bodine	Ford	13	$25,150	Distributor
42	36	Bob Schacht	Olds	7	$18,250	Fuel pump

STP—starting position

Time of race: 3:07:12. Margin of victory: 2 car lengths. Caution flags: 4 for 22 laps. Lead changes: 15 among 7 drivers. Lap leaders: Marlin 1–5, Elliott 6–19, Marlin 20–47, Elliott 48, D. Waltrip 49, Schrader 50–55, Allison 56–83, Elliott 84–91, Allison 92, Shepherd 93–97, Allison 98–144, Shepherd 145, Allison 146–166, Shepherd 167, M. Waltrip 168–170, Allison 171–200.

Epilogue

One of the certainties of Winston Cup racing is change. Every year, drivers and crew members leave or are fired by their teams and sign on with the competition. Sponsors leave teams and anoint others. Owners come. Owners go. So it was in 1992.

Ed Carroll, the general manager of the fledgling Joe Gibbs team, wasn't even around for the Daytona 500. Chosen in part because of his Christian beliefs, Carroll never got along with owner Joe Gibbs's right hand man, Don Meredith, and he was fired two weeks before Christmas.

Joe Gibbs meanwhile learned how difficult it is to compete for the Winston Cup. Dale Jarrett and his Interstate Batteries team had but one top-five finish in '92.

The crew chief for the 17 car, Jeff Hammond, left his blood brother, Darrell Waltrip, in mid-season to work for Felix Sabates. Sabates, owner of Kyle Petty's Mello Yello ride, announced that in 1993 he would set up a second team driven by Kenny Wallace. Sabates asked Hammond if he was interested in being Wallace's crew chief and made him an offer. When Hammond told Waltrip about the offer, Waltrip refused to match it.

When I visited Kirk Shelmerdine, the crew chief for Richard Childress and Dale Earnhardt, before the '92 season, he seemed frustrated that the success of RCR had diverted too much of Dale's time from the task at hand. He wondered whether these distractions would severely hurt the team.

In '92, Earnhardt won just one race, and the team finished out of the top ten in the drivers' standings. It was the first time in NASCAR history a driving champion finished out of the top ten the following year. At the end of the season, Shelmerdine announced he was leaving racing entirely.

Andy Petree left Harry Gant to run Earnhardt's team in '93.

Bill Ingle, the crew chief for Bahari Racing, quit in the middle of the '92 season. Dissatisfied with the driving of Michael Waltrip, who has yet to win a Winston Cup race, Ingle went to Chuck Rider and told him that either Waltrip had to go or he would. When Rider told Ingle that he would stick with Waltrip, Ingle walked.

Dave Marcis continues despite his lack of money. Marcis never once took a backup car to a race in 1992, and he managed to finish every event. He didn't crash, not even once.

Cliff Champion was hired as a crew chief for Phil Parsons' Busch Grand National Race Team.

Junior Johnson soured on Sterling Marlin very early in the '92 season. After Junior blamed Marlin for the crash that finished both him and Bill Elliott at Daytona, rumors flew that Marlin would be gone as Junior's driver at the end of the year.

Midway through the season, it was announced that Marlin would sign with the Stavola Brothers in '93, replacing Dick Trickle. It was also announced that Maxwell House would start its own team, with owner Bill Davis and Bobby Labonte, a talented Busch circuit driver. And finally, Junior Johnson announced that Hut Stricklin, who had been fired from Bobby Allison's Raybestos team, would drive Junior's second car in '93 under the McDonald's banner.

After a mediocre year in '92, Bob Whitcomb closed down. Derrike Cope went to drive for Cale Yarborough. Bahari Racing and Michael Waltrip had a sub-par year. So did Tri Star and Bobby Hamilton. All will have to improve in '93 to keep their sponsors.

Richard Petty endured his endless Fan Appreciation tour as his fans bought Petty cars and Petty cards and Petty clocks and Petty belts and Petty knives and Petty Smith & Wesson's and Petty Pontiacs and Petty sunglasses and on and on and on. My office at home is filled with Petty memorabilia. I cherish every piece of it.

Petty, who is *the* most remarkable personality in sports, spent his final year accepting awards and signing autographs. It was a common sight in '92 to watch Petty walk from point A to point B with a crowd of hundreds of people handing him programs, photos, tickets, clothing, and just about anything else you can think of for his signature. Pen in hand, he signed everything thrust his way, smiling all the while. Surrounded by the faithful, he looked like Mahatma Gandhi in Petty-blue race colors.

In his final race at Atlanta in November 1992 Richard Petty survived a fiery crash and retired. Petty joked that as he sat in his burning car, the firefighters were approaching him for autographs. "I sent them back to get a fire extinguisher," Petty said.

After the race the always entertaining Petty told reporters, "I wanted to go out in a blaze of glory, but this wasn't what I had in mind."

Along with Petty, the number 43 will be retired, and in '93 Rick Wilson will drive for Petty Enterprises in car 44.

"After fifty-five years, I'm going to have to grow up," said Petty. "I can't play no more."

With the departure of The King came the initial appearance in Winston Cup competition of twenty-one-year-old Jeff Gordon, signed by Rick Hendrick and sponsored by Dupont. Many predict Gordon, a Busch series star, will be the next Winston Cup superstar.

In '92 Bud Moore and the Wood Brothers proved they can still compete and win. After Jake Elder replaced Jeff Hammond, Darrell Waltrip finished first three times and earned for himself almost $800,000. Darrell finished ninth in the point standings for the driver championship.

Terry Labonte was eighth, Ricky Rudd seventh, and Mark Martin sixth. Kyle Petty had his best season, winning two races and finishing fifth. Harry Gant finished fourth, demonstrating Andy Petree's excellence as a crew chief.

Finishing in third place was Davey Allison, who in '92 showed heart, soul, and guts and earned the admiration of a legion of new fans.

After winning the Daytona 500, Davey was a shoo-in for the driving championship until Pocono, when he flipped eleven times and just did escape death. He suffered multiple injuries, including a broken arm, in the crash, but somehow he didn't miss a single race.

Later in the year, his younger brother, Clifford, died in practice for a NASCAR Grand National race. And yet Davey kept racing, and he led in points up until the final race in Atlanta.

During that race, wildcard Ernie Irvan, who began the season by wiping out Bill Elliott and a slew of other cars in the big crash at Daytona, cut a tire and careened into Allison's car, causing Davey to wreck. Allison was relegated to finishing twenty-seventh in the Atlanta race, costing him the championship by sixty-three points.

The sport will never be the same after the retirement of Richard Petty, and it seemed almost fitting that the '92 racing championship would be decided by the two drivers who refuse more autographs than they sign, the too-often surly Bill Elliott and the snippy Alan Kulwicki. Elliott—who hires a PR staff to help him win the Most Popular Driver award, which he wins year after year despite his loathing of interaction with the public and the press—may despise the attention racing confers upon him, but he is a superb racer. So is Kulwicki, who proved Junior Johnson and all the other naysayers wrong by barely edging out Elliott for the driving championship in the final race at Atlanta.

Kulwicki won the championship because the man has ice water in his veins. The weight of the world was on his shoulders during the race in Atlanta, where he had to battle Elliott and owner Junior Johnson for the title along with the rap that an independent owner can't win anymore.

To win the driving championship, Kulwicki knew, he had to finish second to Elliott in Atlanta and at the same time lead more laps than Elliott. As Kulwicki and crew chief Paul Andrews made clear throughout the race, this was the strategy.

Kulwicki ran a perfect race. He kept out of trouble and followed the game plan. He stayed ahead of Elliott long enough to be assured of winning more laps than Elliott, giving Alan the five bonus points to put him over the top.

He then allowed Elliott to pass, and concentrated on conserving fuel and finishing second. When the checkered flag came down, he was safely in second as he gained the prestigious driving title and the million dollars that went with it.

Kulwicki thus became the first owner-driver to win the championship since Richard Petty did it in 1979. Said Kulwicki, "If you were to bet money back in '86 that I'd be where I am today, you'd be as rich as I am."

As Kulwicki crossed the finish line, two of his crew members tried to talk to him at once. He was a million dollars richer, was sitting on top of his profession, but to listen to him grumble to his crew members on the scanner, you never would have known it.

"You're both talking at once," Kulwicki barked. "I can't understand what you're saying." One of them shut up. Said the other, "You ran a great race, Alan."

"Thanks," he said without emotion. He may be moody and a little strange, but in 1992 the Ice Man, Alan Kulwicki, proved himself the best damned stock car racer in these here United States.

On the eve of the 1993 Daytona 500 by STP, talk had shifted from the Ford drivers to the Chevy men, despite Davey Allison's Daytona win in '92 and Alan Kulwicki's championship. It seems the aerodynamics of the '93 cars had put the Fords at a disadvantage, and everyone knew it.

Kyle Petty, finally out from under his father's long shadow, had the best trial lap (189.426 miles per hour) and took the pole position for the 500, with Dale Jarrett, driver of the second-year Interstate Batteries team, on the outside. The winners of the two Gatorade twin 125s were also Chevies, driven by Dale Earnhardt and rookie sensation Jeff Gordon. The talk proved that the experts know their stuff. In the '93 Daytona 500, Dale beat Dale, but the winner wasn't the Dale everyone was rooting for and against. Dale Earnhardt's car began acting up with just a few miles to go, but it was enough of a disadvantage to allow Dale Jarrett to pass him with two laps remaining, and Joe Gibbs became the first person ever to win a Super Bowl and a Daytona 500. Geoff Bodine and Morgan Shepherd, two underrated and overlooked drivers of great skill, came in third and fourth. The Kid, Jeff Gordon, the first-lap leader, came in fifth after challenging for the lead late in the day. Gordon, who is only twenty-one, surely will be someone to watch closely in the years ahead.

Life and racing have certain similarities. One characteristic common to both is you never know what's around the bend.

On April 2, 1993, Alan Kulwicki was flying to the Bristol race track in a private, two-engine plane owned by Hooters, his sponsor. As the plane was approaching the airport, it went down without warning. Four men, including Alan Kulwicki, were killed.

Three months later, the racing world was again jolted when Davey Allison, perhaps the most beloved driver in NASCAR, was killed in a helicopter crash.

It never should have happened. Davey had owned the helicopter for three weeks. He was flying with Red Farmer to a practice session at Talladega Speedway. Inexplicably, Davey decided to land in a fenced-in area in the infield. Witnesses say the tail section hit the fence, which caused the craft to spin violently and crash on its side—Davey's side. The thirty-two-year-old Allison had to be cut from the wreckage. Farmer, who suffered broken bones, survived.

The next day Davey died.

That Davey Allison could be dead was inconceivable. Millions of NASCAR fans mourned him as though he had been family.

It will be a long time before we who knew him get over it. Though the number 28 Havoline Ford is back on the track, it is difficult to accept that someone other than Davey is behind the wheel.

Davey Allison's win at Daytona in 1992 was his finest hour. I am proud that *American Zoom,* which profiles that race, memorializes Davey Allison, one of the finest, warmest athletes I have had the pleasure of knowing. Good-bye, Davey. We will never forget you.

*   *   *

At the end of 1993, NASCAR again crowned Dale Earnhardt its champion, the sixth crown for racing's Black Knight. Dale began the season coming in second in the Daytona 500 to the other Dale, Ned Jarrett's boy. With Andy Petree replacing Kirk Shelmerdine as crew chief, the Goodwrench Chevrolet won six races, finished in the top five 17 times, and failed to finish in only one race, giving Earnhardt an 80-point victory over Rusty Wallace and his Miller Genuine Draft Pontiac. Mark Martin finished third.

I personally was able to experience the thrill of being involved with a race car when Ron Slyder, the owner of White Rose Collectables, ran the American Zoom Chevrolet in a Busch race at Charlotte in October.

Slyder, who has built the sales of Matchbox race car miniatures into a multimillion-dollar business, sold this book to the racing memorabilia shops that sold his toy cars. In fact, to boost sales of the book, he made toy *American Zoom* race cars to go with the book. The little car was painted in a red, white, and blue motif with stars. On the hood it read: AMERICAN ZOOM in yellow and white. Since I have a large collection of Matchbox race cars, I was thrilled when I learned what he was doing. Now he was on the phone with an even bigger marketing idea.

"We're going to run a big car in the Busch race in Charlotte to look like the little one," he said. I couldn't believe it. This was an unexpected dream come true.

The qualifying for the race was scheduled for Thursday, October 7.

"You can be on the pit crew," Ron said. I wondered what they wanted me to do. After all, I don't even know how to change the oil in my own car.

The weekend in Charlotte was bright and beautiful. After picking up my credentials, I walked into the Busch garage area to find the race car. I was expecting to find a sizable crew of men working diligently to get the car ready. After wandering through the maze of huge trailers, I found it. It was painted just as Ron Slyder had said: red, white, and blue. It was beautiful.

Standing inside the front end was a recent friend, Cliff Champion. Cliff, chapter 20 in *American Zoom,* was the crew chief. Working with him to tighten the screws on the gas tank was Phil Parsons, the owner and driver of the car. They were alone. They *were* the crew. That was the whole team—Phil and Cliff.

I was discovering firsthand what it meant to run a car on a limited budget. Some teams had substantial money. Other teams, like ours, had to make do on limited funds.

Neither man seemed deterred, and why should he? The car had several top-ten finishes. Cliff had been a top crew chief, and as late as 1988 Phil had been among the top-ten in the Winston Cup driver standings.

Nevertheless, Phil had to compete against teams with big, big bucks that could afford sizable crews and all new parts. Phil didn't have that luxury.

After the first day of time trials, the car didn't qualify. The engine wasn't running right, and no one was sure why. Cliff and Phil would take the entire engine apart before the qualifying race the next afternoon.

Was it possible that the car wouldn't qualify? In racing, anything is possible.

If we didn't qualify, I asked Cliff, what would happen to Ron Slyder's sponsorship money? Wry looks.

"That's racing," I was told.

The next day Phil made the field just fine, finishing seventh in the qualifying race. After NASCAR inserted the four provisional race teams, we were placed at number 41 (out of 44) in the All Pro Auto Parts 300.

Our lowly placement notwithstanding, the next day I felt great pride in our American Zoom Chevrolet as I helped Phil and Cliff push it from the garage area onto the race track before the large crowd of spectators.

As I walked the hallowed pit area of the Charlotte Motor Speedway, I couldn't help reconfirming in my own mind just how interesting and wonderful this sport had turned out to be. The machines were what the fans saw on the track, but for me the sagas of the men behind the machines provided the drama of the sport.

Take our team. Phil had lost his Winston Cup ride. A couple weeks earlier team owner Larry Hedrick had hired Waddell Wilson to run the team, and Waddell had come in and fired Phil as driver, replacing him with Dick Trickle. There are feuds in racing, and apparently this was one of them. It wasn't the first time Waddell had fired Phil, who now had to make a strong showing in his Busch races to convince another Winston Cup team to hire him as driver.

I had heard the talk about how rude Phil Parsons could be to the fans and the fact that he had crashed too often during his career as a Winston Cup driver, but from our first meeting, he was friendly and warm, and I came to admire his great dedication and his driving skill. He was *my* driver. I rooted for him with all my heart and soul.

Phil, moreover, *needed* a good showing for the prize money. Racing, we all understand, is a *very* expensive endeavor.

Our crew chief, Cliff Champion, had single-handedly worked on the car nonstop from Thursday through the starting time on Saturday to prepare the motor and chassis as best he could for the race. Cliff had had a rough year. After our discussion, which became his chapter in the book, life became even more trying for him. For months working on the car was what he was holding onto to maintain his sanity.

Except for this part-time job working for Phil, Cliff had been out of work and had suffered through some terrible personal problems, but he had found inner peace through God, and his future in racing was looking up: Rick Hendrick Motorsports was talking to him about a job, and he was hopeful it would come through. A good showing in the race would benefit him as well.

Before the race Cliff Champion informed me that my job on the crew would be to make sure Phil was never thirsty. Each time he came in for a pit stop, I was to take a large cup of cold water—"Go easy on the ice"—put it at the end of a long pole and from behind the wall extend the pole out to Phil so he could take the cup of water if he so desired.

"Could I practice once or twice?" I asked Cliff.

"No time for that," he said. "You can handle it."

My friend Tom Cotter had told me that he had been given that job for one race.

"I dumped the water in the driver's lap," Cotter said. "It isn't as easy as it looks." Which, I was discovering, was pretty much true for every aspect of this sport.

The cars lined up for the start of the race. Driving some of the cars in this Busch race were some of the top Winston Cup drivers like Dale Earnhardt, Mark Martin, Ernie Irvan, Terry Labonte, and Michael Waltrip. Suddenly this didn't seem fair to me. I felt it was like letting major leaguers play in the triple A games in their spare time. I couldn't understand why no one else seemed bothered by this.

The cars left the pit area for the start of the race. They lined up, the pace car left the track, and the green flag dropped. After the pole cars rumbled past our pit, which was very close to turn 4, it was a while before the American Zoom Chevrolet appeared. The race was 200 laps. Anything could happen, I told myself.

After ten laps, we had moved up to 30th place, and after ten more laps, it was 24th, as some of the cars dropped out and others proved noncompetitive. Phil drove with skill and care, avoiding the fender-benders, moving past some of the more heralded performers, the future Winston Cuppers like Randy Lajoie, Joe Nemecheck, and Bobby Dotter.

By lap 120 the American Zoom Chevrolet was performing as if by a movie script. Phil had passed everyone but Michael Waltrip and Dale

Earnhardt, and he was making it look easy. We were running third, right behind the leaders. No one else was even close. Mark Martin, we realized, probably had the fastest car, but he had pitted when he shouldn't have, and he was placed at the back of the field. Before the day was over, Martin would work his way back to the front, and victory.

At this juncture, however, it was Waltrip, Earnhardt, and Phil Parsons, driving the American Zoom Chevrolet in third place.

In racing, you can't fake success. Our pit crew was sensational. Cliff Champion had his men changing tires and giving gas in no time flat. Phil even got his water when he wanted it. We were a winning combination. We were *good*.

I can't remember ever being that proud—even though my entire contribution had been the name on the car and my skill at delivering water to Phil. But I felt we were like the biblical David, against a field of mighty Goliaths, little American Zoom (most of the fans didn't even know what American Zoom meant) running with two industry giants, Pennzoil and GM Goodwrench.

The Performance Radio Network came over to ask me how I felt. To answer, I had to scream over the loud roar of the cars. I had watched enough races on TV to know what to say:

I shouted into Bill Hennessey's microphone: ''The American Zoom Chevrolet is running great. Our driver, Phil Parsons, is doing a great job, and our crew chief, Cliff Champion, has done a fine job preparing the car. I feel wonderful.''

I'm sorry I don't have a tape of the race. But I will never forget that feeling of pure exultation.

With only fifty laps to go, we were still third, but gaining on both Waltrip and Dale. I now know from personal experience how all owners and crew members of contenders must feel toward the end of a race: You dream of glory, but you expect disaster.

Our lap times were better than both Waltrip and Earnhardt. Only Mark Martin was running as good, but he was still a ways back. We'd worry about him later.

Ron Slyder, who had paid the entire freight for the car to run in the race, came over and we hugged. ''I'm satisfied right now,'' he said. I was glad. He was spending a lot of money to advertise my book.

My adrenaline was pumping. The drama was building. You can tell how well you're doing by the company you attract. Former racing champion Benny Parsons came over to our pit. Benny, who is sixteen years older than Phil, expressed his happiness for his little brother.

The TV crew also made its way over to see us. Phil had come from way in the back of the pack into contention. The American Zoom Chevrolet suddenly was the big story of the day. Would I stand by for an interview? Then on lap 152 Michael Waltrip and Dale Earnhardt flew by, but not Phil. It's hard to explain the feeling of disappointment. It's like a death, in a way. You expect to see your car fly by—it had been racing by like clockwork lap after lap—and then, all of a sudden, it's not there. Did it have a heart attack? A stroke? Something had killed my beloved car. What? The carburetor had broken. The American Zoom Chevrolet was done for the day. Just like that, it was over. The dream was over.

Benny Parsons shook his head. "I'm sorry," he said. "But that's racing."

The television crew walked away with their cameras.

"Come back," I wanted to yell. But I also knew we were no longer the story.

I would have thought that we would have at least gotten a mention in the Charlotte paper the next day. Nothing doing. Phil had gone from number 41 to third, but because of the bum carburetor he finished 22nd. It just wasn't good enough to make the papers.

In the trailer after the race, Phil, Cliff, Ron Slyder, and the crew sat quietly, discussing the might-have-beens. Phil was as calm and gracious after the race as he had been before. What temper? What crashes? Driving in a race in which he couldn't afford to crash, he had masterfully weaved his way through traffic right to the front.

"I hope you get another Winston Cup ride," I told him. "You certainly deserve it."

Phil nodded his head in reply. In 1988 he had finished eighth in the Winston Cup points standings. This was 1993, and his future was not looking rosy. What had gone wrong? I'm sure he wished he knew.

At the end of the day it was time to go. We all shook hands. We all felt terrible, for Phil especially, but for ourselves as well. We had been deprived of the glory, the recognition, the fame. All because of a faulty carburetor.

"That's racing." Benny Parsons had said it best.

And he was right, of course.

All wasn't lost, however. Two days later Cliff Champion was hired full-time by Rick Hendrick Motorsports. I was thrilled for Cliff. He was back in racing, the world he knew best and loved most.

But because of his new job, when Ron Slyder decided to run the American Zoom Chevrolet at Rockingham in the next Busch race, Cliff Champion couldn't work on the car, and Phil wasn't able to compete without Cliff's help.

We didn't qualify at Rockingham. Had we stood on our time, 25.89, we would have made it, but the next day we thought we'd run faster, not slower, and when it was announced we had run our lap in 26.34, we knew we were sunk.

Late in the day Phil was trying to convince the Busch racing officials to give us a provisional, to no avail. As the car sat in the pit area, rain began to fall.

Kenny, one of our crew members, and I contemplated whether to put the tarp over it. We suspected the American Zoom Chevrolet would never perform again. Phoenix was too far, and the field for Atlanta had already been set.

"Shall we put it on?" I asked.

"Let's just stare at it a few more minutes," he said.

I was feeling the same emotions.

The rain began to fall harder. Kenny and I knew we had to do the right thing. We got out the blue tarp and covered the car with sadness.

One final note: In racing, it's important that all the members of the crew get their deserved credit. Part of the reason *American Zoom* did as well as it did was the diligent fact-checking of Al Pierce and Greg Fielden. The book went to press before I had the chance to thank them and express my deepest gratitude. You men did a great job.

My thanks too to all those race fans who were so kind to buy *American Zoom* and make it the success it became. Racing fans are the greatest fans in the world. I hope to be able to meet as many of you as possible the next time around the track. See you then.

APPENDIX A

NASCAR Victories Lifetime
(through 1992)

Richard Petty	200	Tim Richmond	13
David Pearson	105	**Ricky Rudd**	**12**
Bobby Allison	85	Donnie Allison	10
Darrell Waltrip	**84**	Paul Goldsmith	9
Carl Yarborough	83	Cotton Owens	9
Lee Petty	54	**Terry Labonte**	**9**
Dale Earnhardt	**53**	**Mark Martin**	**7**
Ned Jarrett	50	Marshall Teague	7
Junior Johnson	50	Bob Welborn	7
Herb Thomas	48	Jim Reed	7
Buck Baker	46	**A. J. Foyt**	**7**
Tim Flock	40	Darel Dieringer	6
Bill Elliott	**38**	**Ernie Irvan**	**6**
Bobby Isaac	37	**Kyle Petty**	**6**
Fireball Roberts	33	Ralph Moody	5
Rex White	26	Tiny Lund	5
Fred Lorenzen	26	Dan Gurney	5
Jim Paschal	25	**Dave Marcis**	**5**
Joe Weatherly	24	Alan Kulwicki	5
Jack Smith	21	Pete Hamilton	4
Benny Parsons	21	Ken Schrader	4
Rusty Wallace	**21**	Bob Flock	4
Speedy Thompson	20	**Hershel McGriff**	**4**
Neil Bonnett	19	Lloyd Dane	4
Fonty Flock	19	Ed Pagan	4
Buddy Baker	**19**	Eddie Gray	4
Davey Allison	**18**	Glen Wood	4
Curtis Turner	**17**	Nelson Stacy	4
Marvin Panch	**17**	Billy Wade	4
Harry Gant	**14**	Charlie Glotzbach	4
Dick Hutcherson	14	Parnelli Jones	4
Lee Roy Yarbrough	14	Gwyn Staley	4
Geoff Bodine	**13**	Dick Linder	3
Dick Rathmann	13	Frank Mundy	3

BOLDFACE = active drivers

481

Bill Blair	3	Chuck Stevenson	1
Morgan Shepherd	**3**	Johnny Kieper	1
Derrike Cope	**2**	Royce Hagerty	1
Red Byron	2	Bill Amick	1
Gober Sosebee	2	Danny Graves	1
Danny Letner	2	Frank Schneider	1
Marvin Porter	2	Shorty Rollins	1
Billy Myers	2	Bill Rexford	1
Johnny Beauchamp	2	Jim Cook	1
Tom Pistone	2	Jim Roper	1
Bobby Jones	2	Jack White	1
Emanuel Zervakis	2	Joe Eubanks	1
Jim Pardue	2	Dick Brooks	1
Elmo Langley	2	Harold Kite	1
James Hylton	**2**	Mark Donohue	1
Joe Lee Johnson	2	Johnny Mantz	1
Al Keller	2	Leon Sales	1
Ray Elder	2	Lloyd Moore	1
Tommy Thompson	1	John Rostek	1
Dale Jarrett	**1**	Johnny Allen	1
Brett Bodine	**1**	Larry Frank	1
Greg Sacks	**1**	Johnny Rutherford	1
Bobby Hillin	**1**	Wendell Scott	1
Phil Parsons	**1**	Sam McQuagg	1
Lake Speed	**1**	Paul Lewis	1
Jody Ridley	**1**	Earl Balmer	1
John Soares, Sr.	1	Jim Hurtubise	1
Bob Burdick	1	Mario Andretti	1
Neil Cole	1	Richard Brickhouse	1
Marvin Burke	1	Earl Ross	1
Denny Weinberg	1	Lou Figaro	1
Bill Norton	1	Jim Florian	1
Buddy Shuman	1	Lennie Pond	1
Dick Passwater	11	Ron Bouchard	1
Art Watts	1		

APPENDIX B

1992 Winston Cup Points

Driver	Points	St.	Wins	Top 5	Top 10	Money
1. Alan Kulwicki	4078	29	2	11	17	$ 947,010
2. Bill Elliott	4068	29	5	14	17	1,256,105
3. Davey Allison	4015	29	5	15	17	1,621,730
4. Harry Gant	3955	29	2	10	15	804,455
5. Kyle Petty	3945	29	2	9	17	908,870
6. Mark Martin	3887	29	2	10	17	851,505
7. Ricky Rudd	3735	29	1	9	18	671,215
8. Terry Labonte	3674	29	0	4	16	504,070
9. Darrell Waltrip	3659	29	3	10	13	792,920
10. Sterling Marlin	3603	29	0	6	13	578,965
11. Ernie Irvan	3580	29	3	9	11	913,180
12. Dale Earnhardt	3574	29	1	6	15	863,885
13. Rusty Wallace	3556	29	1	5	12	608,975
14. Morgan Shepherd	3549	29	0	3	11	585,090
15. Brett Bodine	3491	29	0	2	13	450,530
16. Geoff Bodine	3437	29	2	7	11	673,515
17. Ken Schrader	3404	29	0	4	11	598,240
18. Ted Musgrave	3315	29	0	1	7	407,610
19. Dale Jarrett	3251	29	0	2	8	381,465
20. Dick Trickle	3097	29	0	3	9	393,645
21. Derrike Cope	3033	29	0	0	3	277,215
22. Rick Mast	2830	29	0	0	1	349,740
23. Michael Waltrip	2825	29	0	1	2	410,545
24. Wally Dallenbach, Jr.	2799	29	0	1	1	219,245
25. Bobby Hamilton	2787	29	0	0	2	366,065
26. Richard Petty	2731	29	0	0	0	348,120
27. Hut Stricklin	2689	28	0	0	4	336,215
28. Jimmy Hensley	2410	22	0	0	4	225,160
29. Dave Marcis	2348	29	0	0	0	217,295
30. Greg Sacks	1759	20	0	0	0	177,870
31. Chad Little	1669	19	0	0	1	145,805
32. Jimmy Means	1531	22	0	0	0	133,160
33. Jimmy Spencer	1284	12	0	3	3	183,585
34. Bobby Hillin	1135	13	0	0	0	102,160
35. Stanley Smith	959	14	0	0	0	89,650

Driver	Points	St.	Wins	Top 5	Top 10	Money
36. Mike Potter	806	11	0	0	0	74,710
37. Jim Sauter	729	9	0	0	0	56,045
38. Lake Speed	726	9	0	0	0	49,545
39. Jimmy Horton	660	9	0	0	0	50,125
40. Bob Schacht	611	9	0	0	0	58,815
41. Charlie Glotzbach	592	7	0	0	0	48,060
42. James Hylton	476	8	0	0	0	37,910
43. Andy Belmont	467	8	0	0	0	39,820
44. Jeff Purvis	453	6	0	0	0	45,545
45. Dave Mader III	436	5	0	0	0	69,635

APPENDIX C

Active Drivers' Winston Cup Career Record Through 1992
(in order of their finish in the point standings in 1992)

Driver	Starts	Poles	Wins	Top 5	Top 10	Winnings
Alan Kulwicki	202	24	5	25	72	$ 3,520,181
Bill Elliott	377	43	39	132	212	12,103,979
Davey Allison	175	14	18	60	84	5,876,691
Harry Gant	424	15	18	119	189	6,710,931
Kyle Petty	350	7	6	35	117	4,569,637
Mark Martin	202	18	7	61	98	4,701,659
Ricky Rudd	439	20	13	113	220	6,765,920
Terry Labonte	419	20	10	117	225	7,142,147
Darrell Waltrip	566	58	84	262	348	11,923,061
Sterling Marlin	248	7	0	34	82	3,272,129
Ernie Irvan	136	7	6	26	48	2,803,426
Dale Earnhardt	419	13	53	180	268	16,043,204
Rusty Wallace	270	12	21	73	131	7,446,707
Morgan Shepherd	322	7	3	45	119	3,795,123
Brett Bodine	160	3	1	12	39	2,045,608
Geoff Bodine	320	29	13	82	140	6,298,742
Ken Schrader	236	11	4	36	91	4,651,368
Ted Musgrave	62	0	0	1	7	625,710
Dale Jarrett	168	0	1	8	31	1,542,913
Dick Trickle	116	1	0	12	27	1,271,701
Derrike Cope	157	0	2	4	16	1,576,846
Rick Mast	93	0	0	1	6	943,927
Michael Waltrip	207	2	0	11	33	2,061,174
Wally Dallenbach	40	0	0	1	1	273,265
Bobby Hamilton	61	0	0	0	6	638,235
Richard Petty	1185	126	200	552	694	7,754,659
Hut Stricklin	101	0	0	4	17	978,472
Jimmy Hensley	51	1	0	17	13	225,160
Dave Marcis	620	14	5	83	193	3,742,712
Greg Sacks	160	1	1	3	16	1,134,357
Chad Little	82	0	0	0	2	483,925
Jimmy Means	437	0	0	0	17	1,787,575
Jimmy Spencer	84	0	0	4	14	808,045
Bobby Hillin, Jr.	240	0	1	8	42	2,333,501

Driver	Starts	Poles	Wins	Top 5	Top 10	Winnings
Stanley Smith	27	0	0	0	0	150,850
Mike Potter	58	0	0	0	0	74,710
Jim Sauter	70	0	0	0	4	56,045
Lake Speed	247	0	1	12	61	1,682,479
Jimmy Horton	31	0	0	0	0	50,125
Bob Schacht	19	0	0	0	0	58,815
Charlie Glotzbach	116	12	4	0	50	248,060
James Hylton	597	4	2	140	300	337,910
Andy Belmont	10	0	0	0	0	39,820
Jeff Purvis	17	0	0	0	0	45,545
Dave Mader III	10	0	0	0	0	69,635

GLOSSARY OF RACING TERMS

ARCA Automobile Racing Club of America. It's two levels below Winston Cup. Similar cars, shorter races, and the races don't pay as much.

Busch racing One step below Winston Cup racing. Some of the top Winston Cup racers also drive in the Busch races.

CART Championship Auto Racing Team. The Indy-type car drivers. A few years ago CART split from USAC, and though they have united, there are still two organizations.

Drafting The phenomenon discovered in 1959 with the first Daytona superspeedway race, when the drivers noticed that two cars running nose-to-tail together could go faster than any single car running by itself.

Grand National circuit This was what Winston Cup racing was called before R. J. Reynolds became involved in 1972. It was the top level of stock car racing.

IMSA International Motor Sports Association. Primarily foreign prototype racing cars. They race at Sebring and other closed-circuit road courses.

Loose The car is oversteering. The car wants to hit the wall with the back end.

Pushing The car is understeering. The car wants to hit the wall with the front end. When you want to go left, the car wants to go straight.

SCCA Sports Car Club of America. A private club that holds regional races and rallies around the United States. The races are held on closed-circuit road courses.

Sprint car There are two types of sprint cars. USAC open-wheel cars with an upright roll cage, and the World of Outlaws sprint cars, which are basically the same type cars plus a large wing mounted on top for stability.

Stock car The car on the track is stock showroom condition. That was the ideal back in the late forties when Bill France organized NASCAR. But in reality there is not a single stock part in any of the race cars. Today they merely *look* like the car in the showroom.

Stroker A racer who races in the middle of the pack, waiting for accidents to decimate leaders to enable him to finish higher than his car otherwise could take him.

Taking air off the spoiler Ordinarily the air travels across the hood and chassis of the car, and then across the spoiler, a device to hold the rear of the car on the track. Sometimes when a car follows directly behind, the air will travel across the hood and chassis and go directly across to the trailing car. The air thus misses the spoiler, making the car harder to handle.

USAC United States Auto Club. Many different classes, including Indy cars, sprint cars, Silver Crown cars, and midgets. No late-model racing at this time.

Wedge The amount of difference in the downward tire pressure on the rear end of a car. The wedge can be adjusted on either side. It is the wedge that determines whether the car is pushing, loose, or just right. The wedge is like sticking a piece of paper under a wobbly leg of a table.

Winston Cup The top NASCAR circuit, the major leagues of stock car racing.

INDEX

489

Peter Golenbock is one of America's most successful and distinguished sports authors. Born on July 19, 1946, he went on to graduate from Dartmouth College in 1967 and the New York University School of Law in 1970.

His first book, *Dynasty: The New York Yankees 1949–64*, was the bestselling definitive history of the Casey Stengel-Ralph Houk-Yogi Berra era of Yankee greatness. He has since put together a string of bestsellers with such provocative books as *The Bronx Zoo* with New York Yankee pitcher Sparky Lyle, *Number 1* with Billy Martin, *Balls* with Graig Nettles, and *Personal Fouls*, which examined the corrupt basketball program at North Carolina State University as it was run by coach Jim Valvano.

Golenbock's other books include *Guidry* with Yankee pitcher Ron Guidry, *Bums: An Oral History of the Brooklyn Dodgers*, and *Bats*, a diary of the 1985 baseball season with New York Mets manager Davey Johnson. His most recent projects were the critically acclaimed children's book *Teammates*, which describes the relationship between Jackie Robinson and Pee Wee Reese, *The Forever Boys*, chronicling the 1989–90 season with the St. Petersburg Pelicans of the Senior Professional Baseball League, and *Fenway*, an in-depth look at the colorful history of the Boston Red Sox.

Peter Golenbock lives in St. Petersburg, Florida.